AF352583

CONSTRUCTING THE FAMILY

Marriage and Work in Nineteenth-Century
English Law

Constructing the Family

Marriage and Work in Nineteenth-Century English Law

LUKE TAYLOR

UNIVERSITY OF TORONTO PRESS
Toronto Buffalo London

ISBN 978-1-4875-4652-6 (cloth)   ISBN 978-1-4875-4494-2 (EPUB)
ISBN 978-1-4875-4480-5 (PDF)

Library and Archives Canada Cataloguing in Publication

Title: Constructing the family : marriage and work in nineteenth-century
   English law / Luke Taylor.
Names: Taylor, Luke (Assistant professor of law), author.
Identifiers: Canadiana (print) 20220214948 | Canadiana (ebook)
   20220215138 | ISBN 9781487546526 (hardcover) |
   ISBN 9781487544942 (EPUB) | ISBN 9781487544805 (PDF)
Subjects: LCSH: Domestic relations – England – History – 19th century. |
   LCSH: Labor laws and legislation – England – History – 19th century.
Classification: LCC KD750 .T39 2023 | DDC 346.4201/5–dc23

We wish to acknowledge the land on which the University of Toronto
Press operates. This land is the traditional territory of the Wendat, the
Anishnaabeg, the Haudenosaunee, the Métis, and the Mississaugas of the
Credit First Nation.

This book has been published with the help of a grant from the Federation
for the Humanities and Social Sciences, through the Awards to Scholarly
Publications Program, using funds provided by the Social Sciences and
Humanities Research Council of Canada.

University of Toronto Press acknowledges the financial support of the
Government of Canada, the Canada Council for the Arts, and the Ontario
Arts Council, an agency of the Government of Ontario, for its publishing
activities.

Contents

Acknowledgments

This book draws upon research that I conducted as a graduate student at the University of Toronto Faculty of Law. I want to express my deep gratitude to Brenda Cossman and Kerry Rittich. Each of them provided me with the freedom to forge my own intellectual path, while also adroitly directing my research in crucial ways. Their incisive comments have fundamentally shaped this book in ways that I could not have imagined at the beginning of this process. This book simply would not exist without them. Thanks also to Joanne Conaghan, Angela Fernandez, and Carol Rogerson for invaluable feedback and advice.

Parts of this book were completed while I was a Boulton Fellow at the Faculty of Law, McGill University. I thank the faculty, in particular Dean Robert Leckey, for their support. Early versions of parts of this book also benefited from feedback from various participants at the 2017 Yale Law School Doctoral Scholars Conference; the 2018 meeting of the Canadian Law and Society Association; the 2018 "Law, Culture, Humanities" conference at Georgetown University Law Center; "The Sexual Contract: 30 Years On" conference held at Cardiff Law School in 2018; and the 2018 meeting of the Law and Society Association in Toronto.

I gratefully acknowledge the financial support provided by the Social Sciences and Humanities Research Council of Canada through a CGS Joseph Armand Bombardier Doctoral Scholarship, the Faculty of Law at the University of Toronto, and the Mark S. Bonham Centre for Sexual Diversity Studies at the University of Toronto.

Thanks to Daniel Quinlan at UTP for shepherding me through this process.

Finally, to Matheus Grasselli and Tina Taylor, for everything else that made this possible.

CONSTRUCTING THE FAMILY

Marriage and Work in Nineteenth-Century
English Law

Household Dissolution and the Construction of the Legal Family

The "family," in the sense in which the term is used today, emerged only after a long process of historical development. The many figures that populated the family in the seventeenth and eighteenth centuries gradually disappeared until the couple of husband and wife took centre of the stage, and the marriage contract became constitutive of domestic relations.[1]

In his 1755 *Dictionary of the English Language*, Samuel Johnson defined "family" as "those who live in the same house."[2] Soon after, William Blackstone in his *Commentaries on the Laws of England* declared: "The three great relations in private life are, 1. That of *master and servant*; ... 2. That of *husband and wife*; ... 3. That of *parent and child*."[3] The century following the publication of the *Commentaries* saw "[w]ork, in the form of wage labor, ... removed from the center of family life, to become the means by which family life was maintained. Society divided, and the family became the realm of private life."[4] By 1885, the primary English text on the Law of Domestic Relations had re-ordered Blackstone's relations and placed husband and wife at the head of the list, with marriage in its new guise as a form of legal status; the discussion of master and servant included only those workers who retained a connection to the household: domestic servants and apprentices.[5] Seventy years later, in

---

1 Carole Pateman, *The Sexual Contract* (Palo Alto: Stanford University Press, 1988) at 116.

2 Naomi Tadmor, *Family and Friends in Eighteenth-Century England: Household, Kinship, and Patronage* (Cambridge: Cambridge University Press, 2001) at 19.

3 William Blackstone, *Commentaries on the Laws of England*, 4 vols. (Oxford: Clarendon Press, 1765–9) book I at 410 [*Commentaries*].

4 Eli Zaretsky, *Capitalism, the Family, and Personal Life*, revised ed. (New York: Harper & Row, 1986) at 41.

5 William Pinder Eversley, *The Law of the Domestic Relations: Including Husband and Wife, Parent and Child, Guardian and Ward, Infants, and Master and Servant* (London: Stevens and Haynes, 1885).

the first significant English text on Family Law, Peter Bromley characterized the family "as a basic social unit which consists normally of a husband and wife and their children."[6] The emergence of the "little world of the married couple and their children, now taken for granted as constituting a proper 'family,'"[7] and the idea that "family" involves only (or at least primarily) relations characterized by blood and affect, not work and exchange, is thus a relatively recent legal-historical phenomenon. As Jane Collier, Michelle Rosaldo and Sylvia Yanagisako have noted, "[t]he Family as we know it is not a 'natural' group created by the claims of 'blood' but a sphere of human relationships *shaped by a state* that recognizes Families as units that hold property, provide for care and welfare, and attend particularly to the young."[8] And, as Janet Halley and Kerry Rittich point out, this process involved (and was partially constituted by) the emergence of Family *Law* as an exceptional domain of regulation.[9]

This book is concerned with the dissolution of the household and the construction of the family in English law and legal thought in the long nineteenth century.[10] It examines (intersecting) intellectual and institutional dimensions of this process, focussing on *shifting legal concepts* of work and family, and some of the specific *legal-institutional moves* (statutory, judicial, administrative) that contributed to the creation of the family's "categorical status in the social and legal order" and a distinct and exceptional body of rules – Family Law – for its governance.[11] It is concerned to show how a confluence of laws and ideas helped to shape the modern disaggregation of work and family, and adherence within

---

6 Peter M. Bromley, *Family Law* (London: Butterworths, 1957) at 1. Marriage, he wrote, was "the basis of the family," while the legal relationship between the head of a household and his servants and lodgers – including apprentices and domestics – was "essentially contractual," and hence non-familial: at 2–3.

7 Pateman, *supra* note 1 at 127.

8 Jane Collier, Michelle Z. Rosaldo, and Sylvia Yanagisako, "Is There a Family? New Anthropological Views" in Barrie Thorne with Marilyn Yalom, eds., *Rethinking the Family: Some Feminist Questions* (New York: Longman Press, 1982) 25 at 33 (emphasis added).

9 Janet Halley and Kerry Rittich, "Critical Directions in Comparative Family Law: Genealogies and Contemporary Studies of Family Law Exceptionalism" (2010) 58(4) *Am J Comp L* 753.

10 The bulk of the analysis falls within the conventional time-scale of 1789–1914. However, chapter 2 stretches from Blackstone's mid-eighteenth-century *Commentaries on the Laws of England, supra* note 3, through to mid-twentieth century texts on Family Law, while for the sake of context and completeness other chapters treat these temporal boundaries in a flexible manner.

11 Halley and Rittich, *supra* note 9 at 756.

Anglophone legal systems to regulatory models premised on divisions between realms of production and reproduction.[12]

In the context of eighteenth-century England, it is difficult to identify a representative household structure because, as Bridget Hill has pointed out, "households were never static."[13] Nevertheless, the integration of work and family amounted to a common basal feature.[14] In earlier centuries, "economy" meant "family economy" or "household economy";[15] it referred to the productive household, in which the distinction between work and family was blurred.[16] Family members worked for the benefit of the household in order to achieve a measure of autarky;[17] and workers also lived with the family and, to varying degrees, were considered part of it. In the largest, wealthiest households, dozens of servants performed myriad activities ranging from care of livestock to polishing the silver, while the work of those whom they served was perhaps more in the nature of administration than manual labour. Further down the wealth chain, the household of an artisan might have comprised his wife and children, live-in servants,

---

12 See, e.g., Joanne Conaghan, "Family, Work, and the Discipline of Labour Law" in Joanne Conaghan and Kerry Rittich, eds., *Labour Law, Work, and Family: Critical and Comparative Perspectives* (Oxford: Oxford University Press, 2005) 19 at 26. In this respect, the analysis presented in this work intersects with the much broader story of the development of modern, market-based capitalism.

13 Bridget Hill, *Women, Work, and Sexual Politics in Eighteenth-Century England* (Oxford: Basil Blackwell, 1989) at 26. The idea of the household can be traced back to the ancient Greek concept of the *oikos*. In Aristotelian terms: "The household is the institution in which we labor to provision ourselves in the things necessary for life; but it is also where we seek to emancipate ourselves, as far as we are able, from the drudgery that is our estate. The *oikos*, in its struggle for autarky, is the locus of our efforts to free ourselves from another, related, sort of limitation: the dependency on others which flows from poverty. The household, then, is the means by which we secure such freedom as is possible from the poverty of our condition and in which we avoid a freedom-robbing dependence on others. Autarky and leisure, two overlapping forms of freedom, are the principal goods of the household to which its productive activities are subordinated." William James Booth, *Households: On the Moral Architecture of the Economy* (Ithaca: Cornell University Press, 1993) at 8.

14 Helen Berry and Elizabeth Foyster, "Introduction" in Helen Berry and Elizabeth Foyster, eds., *The Family in Early Modern England* (Cambridge: Cambridge University Press, 2007) at 9.

15 See Hill, *supra* note 13 at 22–4; Louise A. Tilly and Joan W. Scott, *Women, Work & Family* (New York: Routledge, 1989); Berry and Foyster, *supra* note 14 at 9.

16 See K.D.M. Snell, *Annals of the Labouring Poor: Social Change and Agrarian England, 1660–1900* (Cambridge: Cambridge University Press, 1985) at 320–1.

17 Karl Polanyi, *The Great Transformation: The Political and Economic Origins of Our Time* (Boston: Beacon Press, 2001) at 55–6.

and one or more apprentices learning the trade and becoming, for the seven years' of (usually) his training, a member of the family.[18] The poorest households might have comprised only those whom we now designate as "family," but each member of this household was, if able, engaged in productive labour, tilling the field if they were fortunate enough to possess a strip of land, or foraging for food and fuel in common areas. The "household," then, refers to a diverse set of historical configurations; but it is also an idea – lexical and conceptual shorthand for the integration of work and family life.[19]

Heterogeneity in household structure was matched by historical variety in the forms and legal understanding of work. Prior to the eighteenth century, "work as an activity cannot be allowed to imply a single conceptualization of labor as a form of social action, such that *labor* can be understood as an expression of common-denominator social and legal characteristics reproduced across a diversity of relationships."[20] Daniel Defoe, in his *Plan of the English Commerce* (1728), spoke of the different forms and categories of work in terms that demonstrate its multifarious nature:[21]

Those concern'd in the meaner and first Employments, are called in common, Working Men or Labourers, and the *labouring Poor*; such as the meer Husbandmen, Miners, Diggers, Fishers, and in short, all the Drudges and

---

18 See, e.g., Snell, *supra* note 16 at 320–1.

19 I make no claim about the presence or absence of extended networks of family relations; the demographic analysis of Laslett and Wall suggests that stem families were unusual in England, but this is a separate issue. See Peter Laslett, "Mean Household Size in England since the Sixteenth Century" in Peter Laslett and Richard Wall, eds., *Household and Family in Past Time* (Cambridge: Cambridge University Press, 1972) 125; Richard Wall, "Mean Household Size in England from Printed Sources" in Laslett and Wall, *supra* note 19, 159. For a critique of Laslett and Wall see Wally Seccombe, *A Millennium of Family Change: Feudalism to Capitalism in Northwestern Europe* (London: Verso, 1992) at 236.

20 Christopher L. Tomlins, *Freedom Bound: Law, Labor, and Civic Identity in Colonizing English America, 1580–1865* (New York: Cambridge University Press 2010) at 357.

21 Daniel Defoe, *A Plan of the English Commerce Being a Compleat Prospect of the Trade of this Nation, as well the Home Trade as the Foreign* (1728) at 4–5. See also Holly Brewer, "The Transformation of Domestic Law" in Michael Grossberg and Christopher Tomlins, eds., *The Cambridge History of Law in America: Volume I, Early America (1580–1815)* (New York: Cambridge University Press, 2008) 288 at 315; Simon Deakin and Frank Wilkinson, *The Law of the Labour Market: Industrialization, Employment and Legal Evolution* (Oxford: Oxford University Press, 2005) at 45–6; Robert J. Steinfeld, *The Invention of Free Labor: The Employment Relation in English and American Law and Culture, 1350–1870* (Chapel Hill: University of North Carolina Press, 1991) at 20–1; Tomlins, *supra* note 20 at 356.

Labourers in the several Productions of Nature or of Art: *Next to them*, are those who, tho' laboring perhaps equally with the other, have yet some Art mingled with their Industry, and are to be particularly instructed and taught how to the perform their Part, and those are called Workmen or Handicrafts.

Superior to these, are the Guides or Masters in such Works or Employments, and these are call'd Artists, Mechanicks or Craftsmen; and in general, all are understood in this one Word Mechanicks; such are Clothiers, Weavers, &c. Handicrafts in Hardware, Brass, Iron, Steel, Copper, &c.

Superior to these are the Dealers who only buy and sell, either by wholesale or retale as above; these are the Factor, the Pedlar, and the Merchant.

To this list can be added those workers most intimately connected to the family: "*menial servants*; so called from being *intra moenia*, or domestics," in Blackstone's estimation;[22] and apprentices, whom Defoe presumably incorporated among those "to be particularly instructed and taught," but whose description does not quite capture the domestic nature of the relation.

Marriage was also a rather more plural institution prior to the eighteenth century. To the extent that generalization is possible,[23] it seems that the aristocracy tended towards an approach to marriage that foregrounded lineage and property; affection between spouses was not antithetical to these concerns,[24] but it does not appear to have been the driving force in most upper class marriages.[25] Concern with family name and wealth meant that wealthier couples tended to comport not only with the basic canonical requirements concerning exchanges of promises, but also, for prudential reasons, with the Church's preference for solemnization *in facie ecclesiae*.[26] Among the lower classes a more

---

22 Blackstone, *supra* note 3 at 413.

23 See Michael Anderson, *Approaches to the History of the Western Family 1500–1914* (Cambridge: Cambridge University Press, 1995) at 14, suggesting the impossibility of a single history of the Western family.

24 Berry and Foyster, *supra* note 14 at 11; Ralph A. Houlbrooke, *The English Family, 1450–1700* (Harlow: Longman Group, 1984) at 77: "Among the propertied classes, the language of passionate love can be found even in letters of the fifteenth century."

25 John R. Gillis, *For Better, For Worse: British Marriages, 1600 to the Present* (New York: Oxford University Press, 1985) at 12; Randolph Trumbach, *The Rise of the Egalitarian Family: Aristocratic Kinship and Domestic Relations in Eighteenth-Century England* (New York: Academic Press, 1978) at 291; John Eekelaar, "The End of an Era?" (2003) 28:1 *J Fam Hist* 108 at 110.

26 Rebecca Probert, *Marriage Law and Practice in the Long Eighteenth Century* (Cambridge: Cambridge University Press, 2009) chapter 2. See also Katherine O'Donovan, *Sexual Divisions in Law* (London: Weidenfeld and Nicolson, 1985) at 45: "Formal marriage

flexible approach seems to have been taken,[27] though the "importance of material considerations was generally appreciated by those who entered into marriage."[28] By the seventeenth century, peasant marriages were no longer subject to the control of landlords (one of the ways that patriarchy solidified in new forms as feudal and household structures broke down), but marriage remained tethered to the formation of households, meaning that it was often only when land became available through gift or inheritance that marriage became viable.[29] A similar situation confronted artisans, for whom marriage was realistic only upon the completion of training, when economic independence became possible; while the peripatetic lives of labourers and migrant wageworkers appears to have resulted in a more flexible approach to coupling.[30] For these sectors of the population, private or informal forms of marriage seem to have been legitimate options.[31] According to John Gillis, it was only among the early middle class – yeomans who had profited from enclosure, and merchants involved in commercial trade and production – that "[m]arriage came to be seen as a sanctified partnership, the relationship most conducive not only to productivity but to the fulfillment of all other spiritual and emotional needs."[32]

These heterogeneous work relations and modes of coupling were by no means devoid of power imbalances or patriarchal control; as William Booth has pointed out, the "rank-ordering of the household

---

suited the needs of the upper class for reasons of security of contract, legitimacy of heirs and protection of the rights of property-owners." See further chapter 5.

27 O'Donovan, *supra* note 26 at 46.

28 Houlbrooke, *supra* note 24 at 74.

29 Gillis, *supra* note 25 at 13.

30 *Ibid.* See also Stephen Parker, *Informal Marriage, Cohabitation and the Law, 1750–1989* (Houndmills, Basingstoke: Macmillan, 1990) at 4.

31 According to Gillis, the poor "removed to the alehouse or the village green, where they set out signs called 'bride stakes' or 'bride bushes' to announce their wedding feast": Gillis, *supra* note 25 at 98. The extent of private or informal marriage in England prior to and after the introduction of *Lord Hardwicke's Act 1753* (*An Act for the Better Preventing of Clandestine Marriage 1753*, 26 Geo II, c 33) is a matter of controversy among scholars. The most sustained criticism of the position taken by Gillis and Parker (among others) comes from Rebecca Probert, who regards the evidence relied upon by these authors as unreliable and falling far short of indicating that informal modes of marriage such "broomstick weddings" were common or commonly accepted. See Probert, *supra* note 26; Rebecca Probert, "Chinese Whispers and Welsh Weddings" (2005) 20 *Cont Change* 211. For a critique of Probert's own historical method see Craig Lind, "The Truth of Unmarried Cohabitation and the Significance of History" (2014) 77:4 *Mod L Rev* 641.

32 Gillis, *supra* note 25 at 14.

... determine[d] the source of command and ... the purposes to be served by the community."[33] However, the extent and form of patriarchal control varied. Men were certainly viewed as the dominant heads of their households, however large or small, but the integration of production and reproduction meant that women were not only involved in producing necessary items for household consumption (and possibly sale) but also that their work within the household was valued as productive.[34] Wives' bodily subjection was assumed (most notably in husbands' rights to chastise and force themselves sexually upon their wives[35]), and in law wives' personhood was subsumed within that of their husbands,[36] but their economic contributions meant that women were not confined to the private sphere in quite the same way as they became in the nineteenth century.[37] The measure of control exercised by masters over their servants also varied according to context. Workers who were closely attached to the household (domestic servants, servants in husbandry, apprentices) were liable to the most abject forms of subordination[38] (for apprentices this might vary according to their social position and the premium paid by their parents for instruction); labourers and artisans, however, were not – at least in legal terms – subject to the measure of control by masters that emerged in the eighteenth and nineteenth centuries.[39]

---

33 Booth, *supra* note 13 at 8.

34 Nancy Folbre, "The Unproductive Housewife: Her Evolution in Nineteenth-Century Economic Thought" (1991) 16:3 *Signs* 463; Berry and Foyster, *supra* note 14 at 9.

35 On the marital rape exemption see John Frederick Archbold, *A Summary of the Law Relative to Pleading and Evidence in Criminal Cases; with Precedents of Indictment, &c. and the Evidence Necessary to Support Them* (1822) at 259. The exemption was not overruled at common law until 1991: see *R v R* [1991] UKHL 12. On the right to chastise see Blackstone, *supra* note 3, book I at 432–3. See generally Pateman, *supra* note 1.

36 Blackstone, *supra* note 3, book I at 430–3.

37 Pateman, *supra* note 1 at 130; John Dewar and Stephen Parker, "English Family Law since World War II: From Status to Chaos" in Sanford N. Katz, John Eekelaar and Mavis Maclean, eds., *Cross Currents: Family Law and Policy in the United States and England* (Oxford: Oxford University Press, 2010) at 126 (referring to the nineteenth-century "legal edifice founded on patriarchal assumptions").

38 See, e.g., *Turner v Mason* [1845] 153 ER 411.

39 See Tomlins, *supra* note 20, chapter 8; Deakin and Wilkinson, *supra* note 21, chapter 2; Steinfeld, *supra* note 21; Douglas Hay, "England, 1562–1875: The Law and Its Uses" in Douglas Hay and Paul Craven, eds., *Masters, Servants, and Magistrates: Britain & the Empire, 1562–1955* (Chapel Hill: University of North Carolina Press, 2004) 59.

This book's focus on broad shifts over the *longue durée* is necessarily selective in scope; in other words, I do not claim to present in these pages a complete picture of legal change but rather a selection of conceptual and regulatory shifts that were, in my estimation, important for the development of English family law. Part of the point of this exercise is to expose what can initially appear as law's "reified logic or inevitability" by attending to the processes that generated present "assumptions, classifications and pedagogy."[40] As David Sugarman has argued: "It is as if the logic and categories of the law make the choices for us and as if we have little say in the matter. This profoundly unhistorical view of legal phenomena de-emphasizes that they are *human* constructs embodying political and moral choices. This dulling of our consciousness inhibits attempts to explore alternatives and even hinders an awareness of the values and assumptions of the common law frame of mind."[41] This approach "can be seen as breathing new life into a once flourishing scholarly project, long defunct or modified beyond recognition and drained of its original animating idea: historical jurisprudence" of the sort practiced by Friedrich Carl von Savigny and Henry Sumner Maine. This new form of historical jurisprudence "recovers the animating spirit of Old Historical Jurisprudence rather than its particular manifestation in Savigny's work"[42] (the digging up and dusting off of "shards of pure law from a particular, great, 'age' of (Roman) law"[43]).

Using the Blackstonian household (an integrated domain of work and family life) as a launching pad, the story told here follows two mutually reinforcing narratives. One movement involved the staged extrusion of productive work relations (in the narrow sense of work for pay) from the household, and their re-characterization as market-based activities exterior to the family and governed by a legal regime that blended

---

40 David Sugarman, "Legal Theory, the Common Law Mind and the Making of the Textbook Tradition" in William Twining, ed., *Legal Theory and Common Law* (Oxford: Basil Blackwell, 1986) 26 at 28. In this sense, the approach taken here to the legal-historical treatment of the family is broadly consistent with critically minded interventions in other areas of law, for example, Alan Norrie's seminal work, *Crime, Reason and History: A Critical Introduction to Criminal Law*, 2nd ed. (London: Butterworths, 2001).

41 *Ibid.*

42 Markus D. Dubber, "New Historical Jurisprudence: Legal History as Critical Analysis of Law" (2015) 2:1 *Crit Analysis L* 1 at 10.

43 Markus D. Dubber, "Legal History as Legal Scholarship: Doctrinalism, Interdisciplinarity, and Critical Analysis of Law" in Markus D. Dubber and Christopher Tomlins, eds., *The Oxford Handbook of Legal History* (Oxford: Oxford University Press, 2018) 99 at 114.

contract and coercion. Certain household-based forms of work, notably domestic service and apprenticeship, were treated in a different manner because of their ongoing connection to the family, but eventually they too were deemed non-familial (but also subject to differing schemes of regulation). The other movement involved a new legal emphasis on marriage as the core relation within the non-productive private family, which involved the conceptualization and treatment of marriage as a site of legitimate public concern and intervention.[44] That process relied in part on a set of scholarly, judicial and (to a lesser extent) legislative moves that distinguished marriage from contract on the basis of the English state's perceived interest in regulating conjugal practices. Thus, while the overarching concern in this book is the development of Family Law and the legal construction of the family, the analysis of the processes involved in this historical evolution is equally attentive to both marriage and work.

Noticeably and deliberately absent from this picture is the law of parent-child (and guardian-ward) relations. By no means is this omission intended as an erasure: parent-child relations unquestionably became the counterpart to husband-wife relations within the modern understanding of family and Family Law.[45] However, this process only

---

44 Halley and Rittich, *supra* note 9 at 756–7. The extent to which marriage dominated scholarly approaches to the law of the family in the late nineteenth century is abundantly clear in Eversley's 1885 *Law of Domestic Relations, supra* note 5, with approximately half its roughly 1100 pages devoted to husband and wife. In contrast, parent and child received just over 100 pages.

45 In the very broadest of brushstrokes, the regulation of parent-child relations in the nineteenth and early twentieth centuries may be said to have involved a relative diminution in the power of the father from a position of utter dominance to one of presumptive but rebuttable control. In essence, legislation made inroads upon the common law right of fathers to the custody of their children, and subjected "the absolute right of the father … to the discretionary power of the judge": Eversley, *supra* note 5 at 527. Correlatively, mothers, who were legally invisible in the mid-eighteenth century, began to enjoy limited rights to the custody of their children. Through measures such as the *Custody of Infants Act 1873*, 36 & 37 Vict, c 12, the *Guardianship of Infants Act 1886*, 49 & 50 Vict, c 27, and the *Custody of Infants Act 1891*, 55 Vict, c 13, the law began "to recognize in a fuller manner than formerly the rights of the mother, which under the old law were kept in the background": *ibid* at 525. Perhaps most importantly, children themselves became figures of legal attention in their own right. No longer was the concern simply with the transmission of name and estate; those matters remained relevant, but the interests of the child became paramount. Despite the common law presumption of parental control, "the moral welfare of the child [became] the dominant matter for the consideration of the court," and "the court arrogate[d] to itself the right to say that if in its opinion the parent, however free from misconduct, [was] placed in such a position that would

began in the late nineteenth century and consolidated in the twentieth century.[46] For this reason, I focus primarily on the intersection of marriage and work in the breakdown of the productive household, and how those relations contributed to the construction of an exceptional domain of family regulation. Children therefore appear in the section concerning apprenticeship,[47] and as figures of concern in debates around the Poor Laws and discussion of the nineteenth-century veneration of domesticity, but the focus is otherwise on relations between adults.

The claim that over the course of the eighteenth and nineteenth centuries the legal model of the household model broke apart, and a radical shift occurred in the *legal* conceptualization and treatment of work and family relations,[48] is grounded in recent scholarship on Family Law Exceptionalism (FLE). In Halley and Rittich's words, "family and family law are often treated as occupying a unique and autonomous domain – as exceptional," in ways both descriptive ("the law curriculum, for instance, implicitly claims that family law is an autonomous domain of legal regulation") and normative ("family law itself is saturated with claims that family law (or marriage, or 'the family') *should* be different because of the unique, special, crucial, affective, altruistic, social-ordering, and/or sacred nature of the relationships that it houses").[49] As they point out, this construction of the family and its law was the result of distinct historical processes of disaggregation and invention: the shift away from the "intergenerational authoritarian structure of premodern

---

warrant the court in superseding the natural rights of the parent, it [would] not restore the custody of the child to him." *Ibid* at 519–20. For a social analysis of the emergence of childhood and the figure of the child see Philippe Ariès, *Centuries of Childhood: A Social History of Family Life*, translated by Robert Baldick (New York: Vintage Books, 1962).

46 To a point where many modern writers argue "that the parent-child relationship now takes centre stage" in English Family Law: Sonia Harris-Short, Joanna Miles and Rob George, *Family Law: Text, Cases, and Materials*, 3rd ed. (Oxford: Oxford University Press, 2015) at 2. See also Gillian Douglas, "Marriage, Cohabitation, and Parenthood – from Contract to Status?" in Katz, Eekelaar and Maclean, *supra* note 37 at 212; Rebecca Probert and Maebh Harding, *Cretney and Probert's Family Law*, 10th ed. (London: Sweet & Maxwell, 2018) at 2; Dewar and Parker, *supra* note 37 at 131.

47 See chapter 4, part III.

48 For analysis of this process of household dissolution in the context of political thought see Booth, *supra* note 13 at 10, observing how, in the eighteenth and nineteenth centuries, "virtually all human relations, including economic ones, [were placed] on a contract-like footing," and the economy was "disembedded from the *oikos* and start[ed] to resemble … something like the market." For a socio-economic analysis see Seccombe, *supra* note 19 at 234–5.

49 Halley and Rittich, *supra* note 9 at 754.

patriarchy" to the family as a "nuclear affective unit" was constituted as much by the movement of "work for pay … out of the home, both in social life and in legal taxonomy," as it was by sentimental notions of the private family.[50] These moves were, furthermore, brought about by a constellation of intellectual and institutional forces across the legal spectrum: laws and legal ideas concerning marriage, divorce, and work were crucial; but so too were interventions in property, contract, tort and welfare.[51]

In accordance with critical legal history's emphasis on the value of doctrinally based analysis and "the constitutive role of law in social relationships,"[52] this book deliberately focusses on black-letter sources of law and legal knowledge – statutes, cases, parliamentary debates, and scholarly texts. This theoretical and methodological approach has, of course, itself been the subject of a rich vein of criticism. In particular, Robert Gordon's invitation to study "mandarin materials"[53] (for

---

50 *Ibid* at 756–8. It is worth noting that the Family Law Exceptionalism (FLE) heuristic does not deny that aspects of what is now considered the corpus of Family Law have always, to some extent, been exceptional domains of regulation within European (and other) legal systems. Most relevant for present purposes is the fact that marriage in England was administered by the ecclesiastical courts according to the canon law of the Roman Church until the Reformation, and thereafter (with some to-ing and fro-ing) according to the rites of the Church of England until 1753 when Lord Hardwicke's Act, 26 Geo. III, c 33, introduced civil rules governing marriage formation (though the Church's role in marriage ceremonies was mandated until 1836: 6 & 7 Will. IV, c 135): see chapter 5, part II(A). The point that FLE makes is that the cabining of legal rules governing the family from other areas of the law (most notably work) was a formative aspect of the nineteenth-century remaking of Anglo-American law; and remains a defining feature of present-day legal taxonomy and thought.

51 On background rules in law see Robert Hale, "Coercion and Distribution in a Supposedly Noncoercive State" (1923) 38 *Pol Science Quart* 470; Halley and Rittich, *supra* note 9 at 761.

52 Robert W. Gordon, "Critical Legal Histories" (1984) 36 *Stan L Rev* 57 at 106; see also at 116–22. For a discussion of Gordon's influence on social historians concerned with the role of law and legal discourse in shaping broader social patterns and relations (notably, Christopher Brooks) see David Sugarman, "Promoting Dialogue between History and Socio-Legal Studies: The Contribution of Christopher W. Brooks and the 'Legal Turn' in Early Modern English History" (2017) 44:S1 *J Law & Soc* S37 at S46–S47.

53 Gordon, *supra* note 52 at 120. Gordon posited that "mandarin ideology may represent an elaborated, purified, and formalized version of a consciousness whose primary producers are to be found all over the society": *ibid* at 121. See further Angela Fernandez and Markus D. Dubber, "Introduction: Putting the Legal Treatise in Its Place" in Angela Fernandez and Markus D. Dubber, eds., *Law Books in Action: Essays on the Anglo-American Legal Treatise* (Oxford: Hart, 2012) 1.

example, in the mode of Duncan Kennedy[54]) has been described as unduly narrow and premised on a tenuous causal linkage between elite and popular consciousness.[55] Certainly, if Gordon's claim (or Kennedy's) was that legal history can *only* be written through the analysis of doctrine located within elite texts, it would be worryingly exclusive. But as Gordon noted in a 2012 issue of *Law & Social Inquiry* dedicated to the impact of "Critical Legal Histories," "I was not trying to privilege the history of legal doctrine over other kinds of legal history, not identifying 'critical' history with the history of doctrine, and not even arguing that high-level doctrine determines or necessarily even influences the shape of law in every aspect of social life, although sometimes it surely does."[56] In other words, doctrinal analysis is *a* mode, not the only mode, of doing legal history. And it is in this same spirit that I offer the history in this book – as one piece of the broad narrative of English law and family life. I don't deny the value of functionalist histories of legal change,[57] or that official law has not always filtered down to, or even had much effect upon, actual social practices.[58] I do, however, insist that law and legal thought are distinctive regulatory and intellectual forces that are worthy of study in their own right and upon their own terms.[59]

---

54 See Duncan Kennedy, "The Structure of Blackstone's Commentaries" (1979) 28:2 *Buff L Rev* 205 [Kennedy, "Blackstone's Commentaries"]; Duncan Kennedy, *The Rise & Fall of Classical Legal Thought* (Washington DC: Beard Books, 2006) [Kennedy, *Rise & Fall*].

55 See, e.g., Stephen Diamond, "Not-So-Critical Legal Studies" (1985) 6 *Cardozo L Rev* 693 at 706–7; Christopher Tomlins, "What Is Left of the Law and Society Paradigm after Critique? Revisiting Gordon's 'Critical Legal Histories'" (2012) 37:1 *Law & Soc Inquiry* 155.

56 Robert W. Gordon, "'Critical Legal Histories Revisited': A Response" (2012) 37:1 *Law & Soc Inquiry* 200 at 20–5. As the final part of the quote makes clear, this is not to suggest that elite thought has *no* bearing on popular ideas. For example, Gordon has elsewhere observed that "the notion of a division between state and market is theorized by legal intellectuals and economists long before it became an element in popular consciousness": see David Sugarman, "Robert W. Gordon in Conversation with David Sugarman," *Law & History Review*, https://lawandhistoryreview.org/article/robert-w-gordon-in-conversation-with-david-sugarman/ (accessed 25 March 2021).

57 The paradigm example is the work of James Willard Hurst, for instance, his *Law and the Conditions of Freedom in the Nineteenth-Century United States* (Madison: University of Wisconsin Press, 1956).

58 See, e.g., Hendrik Hartog, "Pigs and Positivism" (1985) 7:4 *Wis L Rev* 899; Laura F. Edwards, *The People and Their Peace: Legal Culture and the Transformation of Inequality in the Post-Revolutionary South* (Chapel Hill: University of North Carolina Press, 2009).

59 See further the essays collected in Fernandez and Dubber, *supra* note 53.

Accordingly, I emphasize in this book the intellectual dimensions of legal change – "legal historiography as the rise and fall of paradigm structures of thought," in Gordon's words.[60] Institutional legal shifts in the form of legislative change and common law development were crucial elements in the nineteenth-century legal construction of the family,[61] but these movements relied on and were produced by particular modes of legal thought: "the way legal minds – lawyers, judges, scholars – thought about law itself."[62] Analysing "the history of our own modes of thought" allows us "to identify when our categories for organizing how we speak about law solidified into something like their present shape."[63] (When, for instance, did English legal thought begin to speak of the law of the family instead of the law of the household or the Law of Domestic Relations?[64]) It also permits us to see that "the power exerted by a legal regime consists less in the force that it can bring to bear against violators of its rules than in its capacity to persuade people that the world described in its images and categories is the only attainable world in which a sane person would want to live."[65] Specific statutory interventions or judicial decisions are therefore the products of a consciousness oriented towards the resolution of specific issues, and also "reproduce that consciousness by confirming it."[66]

Duncan Kennedy's analysis of Classical Legal Thought (CLT) is especially pertinent here.[67] In his reading, English and American scholars

---

60 Gordon, *supra* note 52 at 116.

61 As Holly Brewer has observed, "[t]he law's very success in normalizing family relations has obscured its own agency in shaping them": Brewer, *supra* note 21 at 288.

62 David Kennedy and William W. Fisher III, "Introduction" in David Kennedy and William W. Fisher III, eds., *The Canon of American Legal Thought* (Princeton: Princeton University Press, 2006) 1 at 1. Consciousness in this formulation is expressly elitist; it is concerned with the ways that judges, legislators, and scholars think and have thought about law. Attention to popular forms of legal consciousness (what ordinary people think about law/how they experience law) is a variation of this idea (see, e.g., Susan Silbey, "After Legal Consciousness" (2005) 1 *Ann Rev Law Soc Sci* 323), but it is not the primary focus here.

63 Gordon, *supra* note 52 at 99. On a more general historiographical level see R.G. Collingwood, *The Idea of History* (Connecticut: Martino Publishing, 2014) at 213 ff.

64 This question is the focus of chapter 2.

65 Gordon, *supra* note 52 at 109.

66 *Ibid* at 111.

67 Kennedy, *Rise & Fall*, *supra* note 54; Duncan Kennedy, "Three Globalizations of Law and Legal Thought" in David M. Trubek & Alvaro Santos, eds., *The New Law and Economic Development: A Critical Appraisal* (New York: Cambridge University Press, 2006) 19 at 27 [Kennedy, "Three Globalizations"]. Like Gordon, Kennedy's concern with doctrinal change and the ideological superstructure of law has been

and judges in the second half of the nineteenth century developed "a way of thinking about law as a system of spheres of autonomy for private and public actors, with the boundaries of spheres defined by legal reasoning understood as a scientific practice."[68] This manifested in a particular concern with ensuring that laws helped people to "realize their wills, restrained only as necessary to permit others to do the same."[69] Contract was the specifically legal device selected for this ideological commitment to possessive individualism;[70] CLT therefore developed the Law of Contract as an autonomous set of abstract principles, and established separate conceptual categories for relations thought to retain elements of "regulation, paternalism, community and informality" – most importantly, for present purposes, "a specialized law of persons, and … a new category of status, that grouped together and explained the peculiar character of rules incompatible with the new vision of the nature of 'real' contracts."[71]

While the concept of the household is used here as a launching pad, this book is not an origin story. Nor is the story of emergence that it presents – of the family and Family Law – the complete historical picture or "the final term of a historical development."[72] Rather, the excavation

---

subjected to some fairly biting criticism. Joan Williams has argued that critical legal history, and particularly Kennedy's work, sets up a monolithic form of liberalism "masking in context after context the fundamental contradiction between our need for and fear of others": Joan C. Williams, "Culture and Certainty: Legal History and the Reconstructive Project" (1990) 76 *Va L Rev* 713 at 719. While this may be a fair criticism of Kennedy's analysis of Blackstone's *Commentaries* (*supra* note 54; see also the criticism of that piece by Alan Watson in his own paper entitled "The Structure of Blackstone's Commentaries" (1988) 97:5 *Yale LJ* 795), Kennedy fairly quickly recanted from his insistence on viewing law as a series of attempts to mediate the fundamental contradiction between self and other: Peter Gabel and Duncan Kennedy, "Roll Over Beethoven" (1984) 36:1 *Stan L Rev* 1 at 14–16. Indeed, I view my own project within these pages as at least partially congruent with the type of doctrinal history that Williams endorses (at 720 note 40): "the history of legal ideology as expressed in legal doctrines."

68 Kennedy, "Three Globalizations," *supra* note 67 at 20–1.

69 *Ibid* at 26.

70 See C.B. Macpherson, *The Political Theory of Possessive Individualism: Hobbes to Locke* (Toronto: Oxford University Press, 2011).

71 Kennedy, *Rise & Fall, supra* note 54 at 185. See also Kennedy, "Three Globalizations," *supra* note 67 at 33: "[I]t was the 'will of the state' rather than that of the parties that fixed the relations of the parties. In this way, CLT sharply split family law from the law of obligations (contract, property, and tort), placing it on the side of morals and politics, rather than science and will."

72 Michel Foucault, "Nietzsche, Genealogy, History" in Paul Rabinow, ed., *The Foucault Reader* (New York: Pantheon Books, 1983) 77 at 83.

of law and legal thought in the following chapters is designed to highlight particular intellectual and institutional moves and processes that played an important role in the disaggregation of the legal household and the emergence of Family Law; and, in so doing, reveal the constructed,[73] contingent nature of the legal family and its specialized domain of Family Law. "It is," as Michel Foucault put it, "a matter of making things more fragile through this historical analysis, or rather showing both why and how things were able to establish themselves as such, and showing at the same time that they were established through a precise history."[74] Rather than "accept[ing] the family as a transhistorical, natural human form"[75] – "a concrete 'thing' that fulfills concrete 'needs'"[76] – this book emphasizes the serious institutional and intellectual legal work that was involved in creating the private, non-economic family. In other words, law did not simply play functional handmaiden to pre-existing social forces; law and legal thought were productive, constitutive factors in the development of the "separate spheres"[77] of family and work.[78] This recognition and its accompanying historical analysis is designed to cast light on the mutability of ideas and rules concerning the family, and provide a basis for further questions about the organization of material and affective (or productive and reproductive) realms,[79] with a view towards bringing together "the elements of the world that it sets in opposition."[80] It is thus history for the sake

73 In the sense of "created" not "fabricated." For an argument that Robert Gordon slips between these two meanings and hence assumes his own neutrality and superior insight when critiquing others' claims to rationality, see Stanley Fish, "Anti-Professionalism" (1986) 7:3 *Cardozo L Rev* 645 at 657–8.

74 Michel Foucault, *The Politics of Truth*, edited by Sylvère Lotringer, translated by Lysa Hochroth and Catherine Porter (Los Angeles: Semiotext(e), 2007) at 138–9.

75 Halley and Rittich, *supra* note 9 at 756.

76 Collier, Rosaldo, and Yanagisako, *supra* note 8 at 37.

77 See Leonore Davidoff and Catherine Hall, *Family Fortunes: Men and Women of the English Middle Class 1780–1850*, revised edn. (London: Routledge, 2002).

78 This approach can, as Collier, Rosaldo, and Yanagisako observed in a critique of anthropological practice that applies equally to legal scholarship, "lead to a more refined analysis of historical change in the American or Western family than has devolved upon us from our functionalist ancestors": Collier, Rosaldo, and Yanagisako, *supra* note 8 at 37.

79 See chapter 1, note 29 for an overview of various objections to the liberatory potential of critique, and my own response to those critiques.

80 Halley and Rittich, *supra* note 9 at 754. As Halley and Rittich note, family law was "invented" through an historical process of disarticulating work and family life. Once we recognize this history of construction, and the contingency of Family Law as a category, it becomes possible "[t]o deconstruct FLE … [and] to put the family and the market, family law and contract, back into contiguity." *Ibid* at 758. See also

of historical understanding, and history "to confront the present" and contribute to what Christopher Tomlins and John Comaroff have called "a critical knowledge of the here-and-now: the moment, it might be said, when the origins of the present 'jut manifestly and fearsomely into existence.'"[81]

In conformity with this book's concern with the intellectual and ideational dimensions of legal change, chapter 1 canvasses a set of fundamental (and fundamentally nineteenth-century) ideological binaries that operated in a mutually constitutive manner with the intellectual/institutional moves that constructed the nineteenth-century legal vision of the family: family/market, public/private, individualism/paternalism (framed in terms of contract/status), and male/female.[82] The chapter also introduces the idea that the transformation of the legal family formed part of a new approach to governance based around the idea of population management. It commences with Foucault's claim that in the eighteenth century, Western governance practices moved away from a concern with implementing theoretical models of sovereignty based upon the patriarchal family, to improvement of the condition of the population and a conception of the family as "a privileged instrument for the government of the population."[83] It then connects these ideas to eighteenth- and nineteenth-century shifts in English

---

Joanne Conaghan and Kerry Rittich, "Introduction: Interrogating the Work/Family Divide" in Conaghan and Rittich, *supra* note 12 at 6.

81 Christopher Tomlins and John Comaroff, "'Law As …': Theory and Practice in Legal History' (2011) 1:3 *UC Irvine L Rev* 1039 at 1044, quoting Walter Benjamin, "Critique of Violence" in Walter Benjamin, *Selected Writings, 1913–1928*, edited by Marcus Bullock and Michael W. Jennings (Cambridge, Mass: Belknap Press, 1996) at 236–42. See also Deakin and Wilkinson, *supra* note 21 at 33.

82 In my view, one of the better arguments marshalled against Critical Legal Studies (CLS) came from feminists who objected to its failure to take into account the material conditions of women's lives, and who charged it with being paradigmatically male in its basic assumption that humans live in a state of tension between self and community. See Robin West, "Jurisprudence and Gender" (1988) 55:1 *U Chicago L Rev* 1; Carrie Menkel-Meadow, "Feminist Legal Theory, Critical Legal Studies, and Legal Education or 'The Fem-Crits Go to Law School'" (1988) 38 *J Legal Educ* 61. My explicit focus in this book on gender and the ways that law and legal doctrine affected women is intended to avoid this general shortcoming in the CLS oeuvre.

83 Michel Foucault, *Security, Territory, Population. Lectures at the Collège de France, 1977–1978*, edited by Michel Senellart, translated by Graham Burchell (New York: Vintage, 2007) at 105 [Foucault, *STP*].

governance and political theory, notably the utilitarianism of Jeremy Bentham and Thomas Malthus.

Chapter 2 seeks to answer the question posed earlier on: When did English legal thought begin to speak of the law of the family instead of the law of the household or the Law of Domestic Relations? Taking inspiration from Halley's genealogical analysis of American Family Law,[84] it approaches this issue through the lens of legal doctrine, as set out in texts produced by legal scholars. As A.W.B. Simpson put it, "[d]octrinal legal history … is a special branch of the history of ideas, of their reception, evolution and interaction."[85] Focussing on "mandarin materials"[86] makes methodological sense in this context because they are "among the richest artifacts of a society's legal consciousness. Because they are the most rationalized and elaborated legal products, you'll find in them an exceptionally refined and concentrated version of legal consciousness."[87] From this theoretical and methodological premise, the chapter traces the emergence of Family Law as an autonomous legal domain within English scholarly legal thought. Mirroring the general lines of inquiry that underpin this work as a whole, the chapter shows how the invention of English Family Law (and the shift away from Blackstone's household model of "private œconomical relations") hinged on two primary shifts: the extrusion of productive work relations from the household; and an emphasis on the public importance of, and state involvement in, marriage, which manifested in a simultaneous elevation of the husband-wife relation within the nineteenth-century Law of Domestic Relations, and a more complex scholarly effort to distinguish the marital relation from the emerging Law of Contract by framing marriage as a form of status. The result of these intersecting processes was the early twentieth century emergence

---

84 Janet Halley, "What Is Family Law? A Genealogy. Part I" (2011) 23:1 *Yale JL & Human* 1; Janet Halley, "What Is Family Law? A Genealogy. Part II" (2011) 23:2 *Yale JL & Human* 189.

85 A.W.B. Simpson, *A History of the Common Law of Contract: The Rise of the Action of Assumpsit* (Oxford: Clarendon Press, 1987) at vii.

86 Gordon, *supra* note 52 at 120.

87 *Ibid.* As noted earlier (*supra* note 55), this claim has been the subject of serious criticism. My own response is that mandarin materials are one, not the only, entry point to studying the history of law. Moreover, understanding elite legal consciousness may (but sometimes won't) help us to better comprehend interactions between "high" and "low" legal thought. See further Susanna L. Blumenthal, "Of Mandarins, Legal Consciousness, and the Cultural Turn in US Legal History: Robert W. Gordon. 1984. Critical Legal Histories. *Stanford Law Review* 36: 57–125" (2012) 37:1 *Law & Soc Inquiry* 167.

of Family Law as a discrete, exceptional category devoid of work relations and focussed exclusively on the nuclear family. Reflecting Simpson's insight that studying legal-intellectual processes "contributes to an understanding of how a sophisticated legal system works and, at a more profound level, in what it consists,"[88] the analysis in chapter 2 also situates this relatively specific story of legal change within the broader context of nineteenth-century English legal thought and the question of whether English law, despite its historical obsession with procedure, was capable of systematic arrangement and explication – law "as" a formal scientific system.[89]

One of the insights of FLE is that analysis of the "core" rules of family law (marriage, divorce, parent-child relations) is inadequate for understanding the economic function of families; attention must also be paid to "other rules, lying in the background, that could, and often did, play an equally important distributive role."[90] This concern with background rules is also salient in the historical context.[91] As chapter 3 demonstrates, eighteenth and nineteenth-century legislation concerning property and poverty played a critical role in transitioning English society and economy, and legal conceptions thereof, away from household-based modes of production and towards the paradigmatic form of modern work: wage labour. Focussing on parliamentary enclosure and Poor Law reform, it shows how English lawmakers compromised poor families' abilities to engage in forms of subsistence production, disincentivized the hiring of live-in servants, and then augmented this institutional push in the direction of wage labour by abolishing the Speenhamland system of wage supplementation and adopting instead the utilitarian principle of less eligibility in reform of the Poor Law. The second part of the chapter shows that this shift towards forms of wage work performed outside of the domestic realm was accompanied and partly constituted by a series of statutory and common

---

88 Simpson, *supra* note 85 at vii.
89 See Catherine L. Fisk and Robert W. Gordon, "'Law As …': Theory and Method in Legal History" (2011) 1:3 *UC Irvine L Rev* 519; Tomlins and Comaroff, *supra* note 81.
90 Halley and Rittich, *supra* note 9 at 761.
91 This approach is indebted to American Legal Realism, which "taught us to see that a regime of free contract delegates to those who contract legal powers, subject to a host of important legal exceptions, to coerce performance according to the contract; and the establishment of private property gives the proprietor a set of legal powers, again subject to important legal limitation, to dictate to others the terms of access to his property": Gordon, *supra* note 52 at 104 (citing Wesley Newcomb Hohfeld, *Fundamental Legal Conceptions as Applied in Judicial Reasoning and Other Legal Essays*, edited by Walter Wheeler Cook (New Haven: Yale University Press, 1923); Morris R. Cohen, "Property and Sovereignty" (1927) 13 *Cornell L Rev* 8; Hale, *supra* note 51).

law moves that extended the subordination inherent in the old master and domestic servant relation to workers in general. In this respect, it shows that aspects of the patriarchal household model were preserved through the transformation of work into a putatively consent-based framework.[92]

Paradoxically, the extension of the domestic service model to wage workers in general was accompanied by a distinct absence of, and even a retreat from, regulation of domestic workers. Building on the discussion in chapter 2, which demonstrates how nineteenth-century scholars constructed a distinction between paradigmatically "domestic" forms of work – domestic service and apprenticeship – and other work relations, chapter 4 considers the legal treatment of domestic labour (encompassing paid service and unpaid domestic work) and apprenticeship – areas of particular importance for women and children. It begins with paid domestic work, demonstrating that the subordination of workers continued along similar lines to those adumbrated by Blackstone in the mid-eighteenth century,[93] albeit through a more (or less) clearly defined legal lacuna that continued to vest authority in the heads of households without statutory backing; in other words, the nexus between domestics and the families they served (and possibly, though to a decreasing extent, formed part of) constituted the basis for a legal distinction (still with us[94]) between paid work occurring within and outside of the home. The effects of this distinction fell disproportionately on women, as domestic service became thoroughly feminized over the course of the nineteenth century. Women were also channelled towards unpaid forms of domestic work, and away from paid work in the public sphere, by increasingly exclusionary laws and policies in the nineteenth and early twentieth centuries. These moves compounded and reinforced the ideology of separate spheres and women's presumed responsibility for care of the home and its family members, while veneration of market relations resulted in the characterization of this work as unproductive.[95] The heyday of laissez-faire was thus accompanied by a strengthening of male control over women that, alongside the extension of masters' control over waged workers, amounted to a legally influenced perfection of patriarchy.[96]

---

92 On preservation through transformation see Reva B. Siegel, "'The Rule of Love': Wife Beating as Prerogative and Privacy" (1996) 105:8 *Yale LJ* 2117.
93 Blackstone, *supra* note 3, book I at 416.
94 See chapter 7.
95 Folbre, *supra* note 34.
96 See Tomlins, *supra* note 20, chapter 8.

The second part of chapter 4 addresses apprenticeship, positing a transformation in the relation paralleling the broader disaggregation of the household along family/work lines. It traces a shift in the treatment of traditional apprenticeship (in which a youth voluntarily or through parental suasion joined a master's household in order to learn a particular trade, and the master and his wife assumed parental responsibilities for the apprentice) away from its familial origins, and towards an understanding of the relation premised on work and instruction only. In contrast, parish apprenticeship (in which pauper children were placed with families pursuant to the Poor Law[97]) shifted over time, and with some wavering, in the direction of home-based family care, eventually shedding its association with work and emerging in refashioned form as boarding out – the precursor to fostering, and an area of legal regulation traversing family and welfare law.

Alongside these shifts in the legal conceptualization and placement of work relations was an emphasis on the state's role in regulating family life, in particular, marriage, which was increasingly constructed as a relation of public importance. As Philomila Tsoukala has noted, "[h]istorically, the process of shifting the regulation of marriages from the local to the national level has often been a crucial step in … the process of nation-building";[98] in England, the shift was from local to national, but also (and more importantly) from church to state. Chapter 5 thus focusses on the legislative dimensions of the English state's assertion of power over marriage. It commences with *Lord Hardwicke's Act 1753*, which transferred the question of marital validity from ecclesiastical to civil law; further legislation passed in the nineteenth century then consolidated this "civilizing" move. Drawing on Foucault's insight that eighteenth- and nineteenth-century governmentality treated the family as an instrumental tool of society (as opposed to a model for sovereign governance),[99] the second part of the chapter considers how (background) legislative measures also constituted marriage as the basis for certain financial rights and obligations: the bastardy provisions in the *Poor Law Amendment Act 1834*[100] figured the "Malthusian couple"[101] as the state's

---

97 *An Act for the Relief of the Poor 1601*, 43 Eliz I, c 2. The Poor Law was an integral part of early modern English labour law, sitting alongside the *Statute of Artificers 1562*, 5 Eliz , c 4: Deakin and Wilkinson, *supra* note 21 at 110–11.

98 Philomila Tsoukala, "Marrying Family Law to the Nation" (2010) 58:4 *Am J Comp L* 873 at 873–4.

99 Foucault, *STP, supra* note 83 at 103–5. See further chapter 1(B) herein.

100 *An Act for the Amendment and better Administration of the Laws relating to the Poor in England and Wales 1834*, 4 & 5 Will IV, c 76.

101 Michel Foucault, *The History of Sexuality. Volume I, The Will to Knowledge*, translated by Robert Hurley (London: Penguin Books, 2008) at 105.

preferred relational model by imposing sole financial responsibility for illegitimate children on mothers; later in the century, eligibility for certain forms of financial compensation was made conditional upon the existence of one's own (or one's parents') marriage. The final part of the chapter addresses the mid-nineteenth-century introduction of judicial divorce,[102] and the subsequent extension of equitable protection of married women's property into the legislative domain.[103] It shows that alongside the liberalizing dimensions of these laws existed a deeply conservative and regulatory concern with "shaping and producing a certain form of homogeneous identity."[104] Divorce was presented as a means of stabilizing the institution of marriage, and hence the English state, by weeding out its defective initiates; while property reform was instituted along strict class lines that conferred a limited measure of financial protection on poorer women in order to temper their intemperate men and bring harmony to the family unit. The patriarchal dimensions of these laws are apparent in the higher standard for divorce claims by women, and the refusal to extend wealthier women's control over their property for fear of challenging the authority of their (temperate) husbands.

One of the ways that English legal thought in the nineteenth century emphasized the public importance of marriage was by categorizing it as a form of status, arising out of, but also distinct from, contract. Whereas chapter 2 investigates this process within scholarly legal thought, chapter 6 focusses on its manifestation in judicial thought and common law doctrine. In particular, it focusses on two areas of law that rose to prominence in the nineteenth century as a result of provisions in *Lord Hardwicke's Act*: the action for breach of promise to marry, which became the default remedy for jilted parties following the Act's prohibition on ecclesiastical orders for specific performance; and questions over the validity and dissolubility of marriages with a foreign (particularly a Scottish) connection. The latter became especially salient after the mid-eighteenth century because *Lord Hardwicke's Act*'s prohibition on clandestine marriages did *not* extend to marriages celebrated outside of England and Wales. In each these spheres, the analysis shows how judicial constructions of marriage shifted away from its canonical framing as a private exchange of promises, moving instead towards a view of

---

102 *An Act to amend the Law relating to Divorce and Matrimonial Causes in England 1857,* 20 & 21 Vict, c 85.

103 *Married Women's Property Act 1870,* 33 & 34 Vict, c 93; *Married Women's Property Act 1882,* 45 & 46 Vict, c 75.

104 Tsoukala, *supra* note 98 at 876.

marriage as an exceptional species of contract: one whose formation was regulated by the state; to which ordinary contractual principles did not always apply; and which in its essence was, at least in certain contexts, a form of status owing to the degree of state control over its existence. Concerning breach of promise, the chapter identifies how judges deviated from ordinary contractual principles by effectively restricting the action to women, lowering the standard of proof in questions over offer and acceptance, and permitting damages awards based on emotional harm. The conflicts analysis traces a shift away from judicial treatment of marriage as homologous with commercial contracts, towards a conception of marriage as a relation of deep interest to the English state – one that justified the extra-territorial application of certain aspects of English law to the marriages of its domiciliaries, and lent marriage the character of status. The chapter thus demonstrates the judicial use of contract (the master legal symbol of *private* law[105]) to construct *public* norms in the domain of marriage and domestic relations; and points to the exceptional character of contract when it touched upon the family.

The concluding chapter revisits the principal intellectual and institutional shifts canvassed in chapters 1–6. It also considers how this historical lens provides a platform for analysis of the contemporary moment. Drawing on the idea, generally associated with Critical Legal Studies, that "legal rules and concepts as they now are should not be treated as natural or inevitable, but as contingent and subject to change"[106] (what Karl Klare and Roberto Unger, among others, have called the "false necessity" of our institutional and imaginative context[107]), it seeks to highlight the modernity and mutability of the legal construction of the family and Family Law. Upon this basis, the conclusion also gestures towards potential avenues for dealing with some of the issues raised by the family's exceptional legal status in law and legal thought.

---

105 Hugh Collins, "Contract and Legal Theory" in Twining, *supra* note 40 at 136.

106 Brian H. Bix, *Jurisprudence: Theory and Context*, 7th ed. (London: Sweet & Maxwell, 2015) at 240.

107 Karl Klare, "Labor Law as Ideology: Toward a New Historiography of Collective Bargaining Law" (1981) 4:3 *Indus Rel LJ* 450 at 482: "The mission of all critical social thought is to free us from the illusion of the necessity of existing social arrangements. The more total the criticism, the greater the emancipation from the mental and political constraints of false necessity." Roberto Unger's "antinecessitarian" approach to social circumstance emphasizes the possibility of disrupting established structures, using "a style of social and historical analysis that does not treat the institutional and imaginative molds of social life as inevitable or as determined by an irresistible dynamic of change." Roberto Mangabeira Unger, *False Necessity: Anti-Necessitarian Social Theory in the Service of Radical Democracy. Part I of Politics: A Work in Constructive Social Theory* (Cambridge MA: Cambridge University Press, 1987) at 12.

Chapter One

Ideology and Population Management

Our understanding of the world around us is based on theory.[1]

The process of constructing a separation between family and work involved law in multiple modalities; law was, in E.P. Thompson's memorable words, "at every bloody level,"[2] but for different reasons and in different ways. This chapter surveys a range of ideas and motivations that were influential in the development and deployment of the intellectual and institutional moves that helped to constitute the modern legal family and Family Law. The discussion thus functions as a lexical and conceptual toolbox, reflecting and helping to unpack the glossolalia of law[3] and legal thought in the specific context[4] of (long) nineteenth-century England. It begins with a set of ideological binaries that operated in a mutually constitutive manner with the intellectual/institutional shifts and interventions addressed in subsequent chapters: family/market, public/private, status/contract, and, cutting across all three, male/female.[5] It then presents an additional or alternative lens

---

1 Katherine O'Donovan, "Family Law and Legal Theory" in William Twining, ed., *Legal Theory and Common Law* (Oxford: Basil Blackwell, 1986) 184 at 192.

2 E.P. Thompson, *The Poverty of Theory and Other Essays* (New York: Merlin Press, 1978) at 96.

3 See Christopher Tomlins, "Foreword: 'Law As …' III – *Glossolalia*: Toward a Minor (Historical) Jurisprudence" (2015) 5 *UC Irvine L Rev* 239.

4 According to Fisk and Gordon, "the enduring insight of the 'law and' framework, is the importance of *context* in the study of law": Catherine L. Fisk and Robert W. Gordon, "'Law As …': Theory and Method in Legal History" (2011) 1:3 *UC Irvine L Rev* 519 at 524.

5 In the sense of what it means (and meant) to be a woman and a man, and how ideas around family and work, and public and private, intersected with and were cathected to questions of gender. Because of this degree of imbrication (and, I presume, a greater measure of reader familiarity with traditional conceptions

for analysing certain of the legal processes discussed in this work: Michel Foucault's theory of population management, which identifies a shift in the eighteenth and nineteenth centuries away from governance based on the model of the patriarchal family, towards concern for the condition and practices of the population; and in which the family appeared as an instrument of, not a model for, governance.[6] It suggests that the efficacy of Foucault's claim is apparent in the works of the English Utilitarians, most notably Jeremy Bentham and Thomas Malthus, and is discernible in nineteenth-century English governance practices.

Two preliminary qualifications are in order. First, the point of combining these theoretical frameworks is to draw upon their strengths while acknowledging their potential weaknesses. The focus on ideology is, of course, congruent with the Critical Legal Studies (CLS) insight that law creates and legitimates ideology,[7] though it can hardly be said to have originated with the crits.[8] Nevertheless, I am mindful of the point made by critics of CLS that viewing law solely through the lens of ideology and legitimation, and particularly as a set of moves designed to mediate the supposedly fundamental contradiction between self and other,[9] can result in unduly narrow and dogmatic analysis,[10] and/or insufficient attention to questions of power (at least in non-state-centric forms).[11]

---

of gender), I do not independently address the male/female binary but instead consider its operation and reification across other ideological terrains.

6 See Michel Foucault, *Security, Territory, Population. Lectures at the Collège de France, 1977–1978*, edited by Michel Senellart, translated by Graham Burchell (New York: Vintage, 2007) at 105 [Foucault, *STP*].

7 See, e.g., Dennis Davis and Karl Klare, "Transformative Constitutionalism and the Common and Customary Law" (2010) 26:3 *SAJHR* 403 at 448; Robert W. Gordon, "Critical Legal Histories" (1984) 36 *Stan L R* 57 at 93–5, 101.

8 Gordon, *supra* note 7 at 93.

9 Exemplified in Duncan Kennedy, "The Structure of Blackstone's Commentaries" (1979) 28:2 *Buff L Rev* 205 [Kennedy, "Blackstone's Commentaries"]. But see Peter Gabel and Duncan Kennedy, "Roll Over Beethoven" (1984) 36:1 *Stan L Rev* 1 at 14–16.

10 See, e.g., Joan C Williams, "Culture and Certainty: Legal History and the Reconstructive Project" (1990) 76 *Va L Rev* 713; Phillip E Johnson, "Do You Sincerely Want to Be Radical?" (1984) 36 *Stan L Rev* 247. Concern over the crits' focus on ideology also resulted in some fairly crude allegations of overt (and covert) Marxism: see Robert W. Gordon and William Nelson, "An Exchange on Critical Legal Studies between Robert W. Gordon and William Nelson" (1988) 6:1 *Law & Hist Rev* 139; Paul D. Carrington, "Of Law and the River" (1984) 34:2 *J Legal Educ* 222.

11 See, e.g., Robin West, "Jurisprudence and Gender" (1988) 55:1 *U Chicago L Rev* 1; Carrie Menkel-Meadow, "Feminist Legal Theory, Critical Legal Studies, and Legal Education or 'The Fem-Crits Go to Law School'" (1988) 38 *J Legal Educ* 61; Kimberlé Crenshaw, "Race, Reform and Retrenchment: Transformation and Legitimation in Antidiscrimination Law" (1988) 101 *Harv L Rev* 1331.

I therefore view ideology as a useful, but by no means the only, way to approach legal history and change – hence supplementing the prism of ideology with the lens of Foucault. In my view, Foucault's theory of population management helps us to see that the legal construction of the family was achieved not only through the constitutive power of legal decisions and texts, but also through various state-centric and more diffuse modes of law – what he called discipline and governmentality.[12] In this sense, the CLS-ish focus on ideology, when combined with Foucault's insights into the variegated and diffuse nature and operation of power, allows us to examine and appreciate the constitutive role of law in shaping and legitimating broad social structures, to trace the ways that ideology and law work upon one another, and to appreciate how states have used law in fairly instrumentalist ways (going far beyond the simple use of command and interdiction) to govern and manage the population.

Second, these frameworks are intended to function as both substantive explanations of contemporaneous practices (why people did and thought what they did at the time), and as retrospective overlays – explanatory heuristics to better understand the connections between, and deeper meanings of, particular moves and processes (how we think about what people did and thought at a particular point in time). In this respect, and comporting with recent legal-historical theory, the specific legal ideas and enactments/decisions considered in subsequent chapters may be viewed "as" instances of ideology or population management;[13]

---

12 I acknowledge that Foucault's understanding of law is controversial. However, as discussed in further detail below (see text accompanying notes 170–8, *infra*), I believe those criticisms can be met. Some readers may also find the combination of ideological and Foucauldian analysis incongruous given Foucault's focus on discourse over ideology: see Michel Foucault, *Power/Knowledge. Selected Interviews and Other Writings 1972–1977*, edited by Colin Gordon, translated by Colin Gordon *et al* (New York: Vintage, 1980) at 118. It seems to me, however, that utilizing different theoretical frameworks permits analysis of ideas and events from multiple perspectives, and thus enables a richer analysis than is possible through a singular use of, for instance, critical or Foucauldian frameworks alone. Moreover, as Terry Eagleton has noted, the fact that ideology is generally connected to questions of power does not mean it is present in every instance of its discursive appearance. "It is," he says, "perfectly possible to agree with Nietzsche and Foucault that power is everywhere, while wanting for certain practical purposes to distinguish between more and less central instances of it." Terry Eagleton, *Ideology: An Introduction* (London: Verso, 1991) at 8. Words such as "family" and "market," and discussions that touch upon their meaning and operation, may, therefore, be ideological in one context and not in another – whether they are "is a function of the relation of [the] utterance to its social context." *Ibid* at 9.
13 "Law as ..." seeks to build upon and transcend the more typical mode of "law and" society/economics/politics that developed in the mid-twentieth century with the

equally, one may prefer to say that law and legal thought shaped, and were shaped by, ideological affinities and practices of governance.

I. Ideology

"Ideology" as used here refers to systems of thought (or structures of consciousness[14]) "conditioned by social circumstances and shared by groups of individuals, including the individuals engaged in ideological analysis."[15] Put differently, we might say that a particular ideology constitutes a set of beliefs or ideas that structure and condition thought and action.[16] This framing draws on sociological conceptions of ideology

---

work of James Willard Hurst: see, e.g., James Willard Hurst, *Law and the Conditions of Freedom in the Nineteenth-Century United States* (Madison: University of Wisconsin Press, 1956). It rejects the basic predicate of "law and," characterized by Fisk and Gordon as "causally functional and empirical accounts of law": *supra* note 4 at 521. Eschewing programmatic formulas, "law as ..." offers legal history "the potency of metaphors of appearance," and the possibility of multiple analytical frameworks: Christopher Tomlins, "Law 'And,' Law 'In,' Law 'As': The Definition, Rejection and Recuperation of the Socio-legal Enterprise" (2013) 29:2 *Law in Context* 137 at 156.

14 Frances Olsen, "The Family and the Market: A Study of Ideology and Legal Reform" (1983) 96:7 *Harv L Rev* 1497 at 1498.

15 John B. Thompson, *Ideology and Modern Culture: Critical Social Theory in the Era of Mass Communication* (Cambridge: Polity, 1990) at 48–9 (discussing Karl Mannheim's general formulation of ideology: see Karl Mannheim, *Ideology and Utopia. Collected Works of Karl Mannheim: Volume 1* (Oxford: Routledge, 1997)).

16 While this section is unlikely to meet Lewis Kornhauser's complaint that early CLS work failed to offer "well-developed, competing theories" concerning ideology to those developed by the Frankfurt School and Jurgen Habermas (see Lewis A. Kornhauser, "The Great Image of Authority" (1984) 36 *Stan L Rev* 349 at 372), I hope that by being as clear as I can be about the ways in which I am (and am not) using the term "ideology," I will at least avoid the charge of vagueness levelled by Kornhauser at the early crits. More substantively, I reject the intrinsic association between ideology and false consciousness that Kornhauser detects (at 372–5) in CLS work: see further *infra* note 20. I also think that there are problems with Kornhauser's understanding of the idea that law is constitutive of consciousness. The claim that "legal ideology affects all individuals, legal and nonlegal alike" does not mean that "[t]he primary task of Critical legal theory, then, is to reveal to people their true interests"; rather, it is to appreciate that legal rules are derived from particular world views and by the very fact of their existence help to reproduce those world views: see Gordon, *supra* note 7 at 111. The point of critical scholarship, then, is to reveal some of those underlying forces, not to dictate where people's "true interests" lie. Kornhauser's further charge that CLS scholars failed to identify "how legal ideology can affect the consciousness of the ordinary person" (at 380) is perhaps true on a micro-level, but to my mind also misses the point, which is that exposing the latent ideological dimensions of law is designed to reveal how law "helps create the conceptual universe shared by all parties": Gordon, *supra* note 7 at 118. It is not, therefore, necessary to "elaborate the process by which the

without seeking to deny the term's association with and development by Marxist thinkers:[17] ideology in this usage is concerned with "the function of ideas within social life,"[18] and the ways that "social practices in the relations of production"[19] (and, crucially, reproduction) shape consciousness.[20] From a legal-historical perspective, paying attention to the ideological dimensions of law and legal change ("by 'decoding' its doctrinal literature") helps to "uncover the constellation of assumptions, values and sensibilities about law, politics and justice" evinced in particular texts (scholarly, statutory, judicial, political), and "to reveal their latent patterns and structures of thought."[21] Law as ideology thus focusses on the intellectual dimensions of legal change – what Duncan

---

ideology embedded in contract or tort opinions reaches … individuals" (at 383). Individual understandings of the implications and ideological dimensions of legal pronouncements obviously differ, as does the extent to which a particular ruling or statute can be said to reflect and perpetuate a certain ideology; the point, though, is that law is such a pervasive social force that it structures the very ways in which people perceive the world, even if they are not able to articulate those associations in those terms.

17 It is perhaps debatable whether a distinction between sociological and Marxist conceptions of ideology is useful or indeed possible. Terry Eagleton distinguishes between two mainstream approaches to ideology: the epistemological ("much preoccupied with ideas of true and false cognition, with ideology as illusion, distortion and mystification") in which Marx is a central figure, and the sociological ("concerned more with the function of ideas within social life than with their reality or unreality"): Eagleton, *supra* note 12 at 3. Hugh Collins, however, points to a much broader epistemological approach to ideology within Marxist thought – one that rejects the "crude materialism" of false consciousness; in this respect, he argues that Marx "introduced a modern style of sociological explanation of the origins of knowledge and consciousness by arguing that ideas were constructed through practical activities and social interaction": Hugh Collins, *Marxism and Law* (Oxford: Clarendon Press, 1982) at 37–8. I use both terms in order to acknowledge these different approaches, without making any claim about the extent to which Marxist analysis is or is not sociological, and vice versa.

18 Eagleton, *supra* note 12 at 3.

19 Collins, *supra* note 17 at 43.

20 I do not mean to suggest that ideology acts in a totalizing manner upon passive recipients who are incapable of reflecting on the interaction between ideas and material reality. In other words, false consciousness *might* be a result of ideological influences, but the relationship between ideology and consciousness is much more nuanced than the reductive materialist position that "present dominant conceptions of the world" are *necessarily* false: Collins, *supra* note 17 at 35–6; Eagleton, *supra* note 12 at 3; Gordon, *supra* note 7 at 93 (noting that adherents to this view consider law as simply a tool of the ruling class, used to coerce, cheat, and disorganize the working class, for instance, through prohibition on worker combinations and employer-friendly provisions in labour laws).

21 Karl Klare, "Labor Law as Ideology: Toward a New Historiography of Collective Bargaining Law" (1981) 4 *Indus Rel LJ* 450 at 451 [Klare, "Ideology"].

Kennedy calls "legal consciousness"[22] – in order to uncover the operative assumptions or allegiances that undergird or which are embedded within particular legal structures and developments; put differently, how law "fits into a complex of discursive practices that together structure how people perceive."[23] Legitimation is an important dimension of this approach to (law as) ideology.[24] As Terry Eagleton has noted, the term ideology "seem[s] to make reference not only to belief systems, but to questions of *power*"; in particular, "*legitimating* the power of a dominant social class or group."[25] In the legal context, variations of this idea can range from straight instrumentalism ("law is a means for organizing the ruling class and for coercing, cheating, and disorganizing the working class") to more diffuse forms of influence (the discursive structure of law acts "to reproduce or to try to change people's social reality").[26] The ideological dimensions of a law or set of laws are not, therefore, necessarily produced by a conscious process (though of course this is possible); rather, "laws enacted according to the dictates of a dominant ideology will appear to the members of that society as rules designed to preserve the natural social and economic order."[27] Following Karl Klare, paying attention to the ideological dimensions of law and legal thought in history thus unmasks the ways that they "make the historically contingent appear necessary."[28] In this respect, a focus on legal consciousness and ideology advances the critical project of exposing the mutability of extant legal structures and the potential for legal, political and social transformation.[29]

---

22 Duncan Kennedy, *The Rise & Fall of Classical Legal Thought* (Washington, DC: Beard Books, 2006), chapter 1 [Kennedy, *Rise & Fall*].
23 Gordon, *supra* note 7 at 95.
24 See David Sugarman, "Law, Economy and the State in England, 1750–1914: Some Major Issues" in David Sugarman, ed., *Legality, Ideology and The State* (London: Academic Press, 1983) 213 at 233 ff [Sugarman, "Law, Economy"]; Klare, "Ideology," *supra* note 21 at 451–2.
25 Eagleton, *supra* note 12 at 5.
26 Gordon, *supra* note 7 at 93–5.
27 Collins, *supra* note 17 at 43. For a variation of this idea see Kennedy, "Blackstone's Commentaries," *supra* note 9 (suggesting that Blackstone sought to provide a legal legitimation of the social-political status quo).
28 Karl Klare, "The Public/Private Distinction in Labor Law" (1982) 130:6 *U Penn L Rev* 1358 at 1358 [Klare, "Public/Private"].
29 The idea that exposing contingency and paths not taken can "give content to … suppressed alternative visions" (Robert W. Gordon, "Unfreezing Legal Reality: Critical Approaches to Law" (1987) 15 *Fla St U L Rev* 195 at 200) has also been the subject of strenuous criticism. Stephen Diamond has argued that "there is something academic about the notion that people are liberated by knowledge"

A. *Family/Market*

Perhaps the most pervasive ideological dimension of the productive household's disaggregation in the eighteenth and nineteenth centuries was the distinction (still with us[30]) between family and market – "the idea that the market structures our productive lives and the family

---

(Stephen Diamond, "Not-So-Critical Legal Studies" (1985) 6 *Cardozo L Rev* 693 at 703), while Neil Duxbury has characterized the idea as "extremely vague and highly speculative": Neil Duxbury, *Patterns of American Jurisprudence* (Oxford: Oxford University Press, 1995) at 482. See also Johnson, *supra* note 10 at 281–9 (arguing at 281 that "Critical legal writing has practically nothing to suggest in the way of a positive political program"); Richard Michael Fischl, "The Question That Killed Critical Legal Studies" (1992) 17:4 *Law & Soc Inquiry* 779 (listing at 781–2 a series of attacks made on Mark Kelman's *A Guide to Critical Legal Studies* (Cambridge, MA: Harvard University Press, 1987) centring on its absence of positive prescriptions). A variation of this critique made by William Nelson suggested that critical legal history (CLH) is inferior to traditional legal history (presumably of the functionalist rather than the formalist variety) because CLH eschews analysis of preferable competing doctrines in favour of contingency and thus undermines, or at the very least fails to contribute to, respect for the rule of law: see Gordon and Nelson, *supra* note 10 at 165–7. At its nadir, this type of argument suggested that some crits are essentially legal nihilists with no place in professional education: see Carrington, *supra* note 10; Peter W. Martin *et al*, "'Of Law and the River,' and of Nihilism and Academic Freedom" (1985) 35:1 *J Legal Educ* 1 at 10–12.

As Fischl has pointed out, though, these sorts of criticisms presuppose a normative attitude to law that critical scholars simply reject in their effort to better understand "where we *already* are and to recognize what we *already* do," rather than what needs to be done to change the law: Fischl, *supra* note 29 at 783 (emphasis in original). Moreover, as Gordon observed in his exchange with Nelson, "it's a very odd complaint to bring against historians, especially critical ones, that they don't have concrete programmatic suggestions for the reformation of society; they might reasonably think that supplying such proposals wasn't their function; that simply helping us to understand our situation might be a useful foundation for an intelligent politics": Gordon and Nelson, *supra* note 10 at 175. Like Gordon, I maintain that, in his words "one of the functions of a legal historian is trying to break some of the false bonds that tie us to the past, to relieve us of the pressures of false necessity and false legitimation": David Sugarman, "Robert W. Gordon in Conversation with David Sugarman," *Law & History Review*, https://lawandhistoryreview.org/article/robert-w-gordon-in-conversation-with-david -sugarman/ (accessed 25 March 2021). Accordingly, I think it is perfectly legitimate to show, as I do in this book, that the family as we now think of it is, in important ways, a legal (and social) *construct* – one that is not immune to further change – *without* engaging in prescriptive or normative analysis of what those changes should be.

30 Janet Halley and Kerry Rittich, "Critical Directions in Comparative Family Law: Genealogies and Contemporary Studies of Family Law Exceptionalism" (2010) 58:4 *Am J Comp L* 753.

structures our affective lives."[31] The different spheres created by the separation of the household had different logics attributed to them: "while the market was the locus of self-interest, governed by the logic of utility maximisation, the family and the household became identified as the repository of moral values such as altruism and sharing."[32] The ideologies of market and family were thus mutually constitutive. "The family and home were seen as safe repositories for the virtues and emotions that people believed were being banished from the world of commerce and industry."[33] Yet the glorification of the home was accompanied by its devaluation.[34] Constructed in terms of the feminine, the home was simultaneously desired and denigrated.[35] The market, meanwhile, was presented as a neutral entity, masking (somewhat) its deeply patriarchal status as the domain of *men's* productive endeavours – a public space constructed in opposition to the private, feminine domain of the family.[36]

"The market," as it is now conceived, is a distinctly modern concept, arising out of eighteenth and nineteenth century economic thought. In ancient and medieval times, "market" and "economy" were not homologous; the latter referred to the *oikos* or household[37] – an integrated

---

31 Olsen, *supra* note 14 at 1498. See also Ruth Gavison, "Feminism and the Public/ Private Distinction" (1992) 45:1 *Stan L Rev* 1 at 21–2.

32 Kerry Rittich, "Making Natural Markets: Flexibility as Labour Market Truth" (2014) 65:3 *N Ir Leg Q* 323 at 325.

33 Olsen, *supra* note 14 at 1499.

34 *Ibid*. See also Nancy Folbre, "The Unproductive Housewife: Her Evolution in Nineteenth-Century Economic Thought" (1991) 16:3 *Signs* 463.

35 Olsen, *supra* note 14 at 1499–1500 referring to Nancy F. Cott, *The Bonds of Womanhood: "Woman's Sphere" in New England, 1780–1835* (New Haven: Yale University Press, 1977) at 62.

36 As chapter 4 shows, women's domestic labour therefore came to be treated as outside the ambit of "work," which denoted (male) wage labour. The exceptions that were made to laissez-faire economic policies in the nineteenth century reflected and reinforced these associations. Protective labour laws, in particular, focussed exclusively on women and children, who, it was thought (in some respects not unreasonably), needed protection from the self-interest of the market. While those laws only applied to certain industries, and by no means ended women's participation in factory labour, they helped to constitute a world view in which women were cast as homemakers rather than active participants in the masculine world of paid work. Thus, in a variation of the protective laws, some employers later in the century implemented policies that directly excluded married women from employment on the basis of an ideological distinction between market (male) and family (female).

37 Karl Polanyi, *The Great Transformation: The Political and Economic Origins of Our Time* (Boston: Beacon Press, 2001) at 55–6; Janet Halley, "What Is Family Law? A Genealogy. Part I" (2011) 23:1 *Yale JL & Human* 1 at 8.

sphere where boundaries between production, subsistence and care were not always clear.[38] As late as the mid-eighteenth century, Jean-Jacques Rousseau spoke of "economy" in terms of "the wise government of the house for the common good of the whole family"; and the central problem of political economy remained the question, "how to introduce this wise government of the family, *mutatis mutandis*, ... within the general management of the state"?[39] The shift to economy as market, however, inverted the idea that markets were simply "accessories of economic life";[40] in the new self-regulating model, all production came to be viewed in terms of its market potential, and all income derived from the operation of the market.

In the classical (eighteenth and nineteenth century) version derived from the work of Adam Smith,[41] David Ricardo,[42] and John Stuart Mill,[43] the market was figured as "free and autonomous";[44] it reflected the "laws" of supply and demand, and arose (and functioned) independently of the state.[45] Possessive individualism was a governing principle,[46] and domination and subordination arising through the operation of market forces were seen as by-products beyond the scope of legitimate state intervention.[47] Non-intervention was treated as the default position because of the market's simultaneous fragility (adopting a version of the butterfly effect) and strength (all but the most radical interventions would inevitably fail).[48] Market ideology was thus treated as synonymous with laissez-faire; in the legal sphere, this translated into the idea that enforcement of rights and interests was permissible only insofar "as the courts merely facilitate[d] free market transactions

---

38 This is not to suggest an accompanying degree of overlap in gender roles.

39 Foucault, *STP*, *supra* note 6 at 95, citing Jean-Jacques Rousseau, "Discours sur l'économie politique" (1755) in *Oeuvres completes*, vol 3 (1964) at 241. See further section B below.

40 Polanyi, *supra* note 37 at 71.

41 See Adam Smith, *An Inquiry into the Nature and Causes of the Wealth of Nations*, vol 1 (London, 1776) at 459–65.

42 See David Ricardo, *On the Principles of Political Economy and Taxation* (London: Murray, 1817).

43 See John Stuart Mill, *Principles of Political Economy With Some of Their Applications to Social Philosophy* (London: W. Parker, 1848).

44 Olsen, *supra* note 14 at 1502.

45 See John Stuart Mill, *On Liberty*, edited by Gertrude Himmelfarb (London: Penguin Books, 1974) at 164.

46 C.B. Macpherson, *The Political Theory of Possessive Individualism: Hobbes to Locke* (Toronto: Oxford University Press, 2011) at 3, 264–5.

47 Olsen, *supra* note 14 at 1502.

48 *Ibid* at 1503.

without jeopardizing or compromising state neutrality."[49] In reality, the supposed correlation between markets and laissez-faire was not intrinsic – when the operation of the market was threatened, legal regulation going beyond basic enforcement of contract, tort, and property law[50] was by no means anathema to nineteenth-century lawmakers.[51]

Foucault situated the rise of markets and market ideology within what he called "liberal governmentality,"[52] which emerged in the mid-eighteenth century out of a concern not with "the rights of man against the sovereign or despot," or states' concerns with their "power, wealth and position vis-à-vis other states."[53] Rather, it was recognized that the market "must be left to function with the least possible interventions precisely so that it can both formulate its truth and propose it to governmental practice as rule and norm."[54] The market was thus constituted as a site of truth, and governmentality was concerned with the appropriate *limits* of state action, "the recognition and embrace of a self-limiting rationality that emanates from the properties or truths of the entities that are to be governed."[55] The market, being one such entity, thus claimed the right to set the parameters of its own (frugal) governance.[56] Foucault's point "is that the market ... became a new limit on the state even as it began to saturate and construe the state with its distinctive form of reason ... liberalism was born with a market governmentality."[57] Within this new logic, "the market appeared as something that obeyed

---

49 *Ibid.*

50 *Ibid.*

51 Polanyi, *supra* note 37 at 146. In theory, the free market for labour permitted workers to associate for the purpose of lobbying employers for better wages and conditions. As nineteenth century Anti-Combination Laws show, though, in conflicts between laissez-faire and the market, the latter usually won. See further Sugarman, "Law, Economy," *supra* note 24 at 242, noting that, "the evidence is clear that *laissez-faire* and state intervention were not polar opposites but rather, different sides of the same coin: both co-existed in nineteenth century England." For a specific example in the context of nineteenth-century cotton production see Sven Beckert, *Empire of Cotton: A Global History* (New York: Vintage Books, 2015) at 79.

52 Michel Foucault, *The Birth of Biopolitics. Lectures at the Collège de France, 1978–1979*, edited by Michel Senellart, translated by Graham Burchell (New York: Palgrave Macmillan, 2008) at 78 [Foucault, *Biopolitics*].

53 Rittich, *supra* note 32 at 330.

54 Foucault, *Biopolitics*, *supra* note 52 at 30.

55 Rittich, *supra* note 32 at 330.

56 Foucault, *Biopolitics*, *supra* note 52 at 28, 32; Rittich, *supra* note 32 at 330.

57 Wendy Brown, *Undoing the Demos* (New York: Zone Books, 2015) at 58. See also Foucault, *Biopolitics*, *supra* note 52 at 293.

and had to obey 'natural,' that is to say, spontaneous mechanisms" – interference "would only impair and distort."[58]

A central feature of late eighteenth- and nineteenth-century market ideology was its totalizing nature; markets existed not only for the sale of goods "but also for labor, land, and money" (resulting in wages, rent, and interest).[59] The problem, as Polanyi pointed out, is that labour, land, and money are "fictitious commodities" because they are not produced for sale.[60] With respect to labour, the hierarchical relation of master and servant gave way (it was said) to a market-based relation between supposed equals, the wage labourer standing "as a civil equal with his employer in the public realm of the capitalist market."[61] That is, at least in theory, the worker sold his labour (power) in the market using the legal mechanism of contract. Taken to its logical conclusion, this freedom to contract permitted the worker to enter into agreements that in reality ceded control over his person to the employer – the worker could "exemplify his freedom by entering into a civil slave contract."[62] Economic theory maintained that what was being sold on the market was not the worker himself, but merely the worker's labour power – "the commodity that can be subject to contract."[63]

Within political thought, the idea of labour's severability from the individual can be traced back to John Locke's theory of government. In the *Second Treatise*, Locke claimed that the ability to alienate and sell one's labour derived from the fact "every man has a *property* in his own *person*." Thus, "[t]he *labour* of his body, and the *work* of his hands, we may say, are properly his."[64] In Locke's view, whatever a man "removes

---

58 Foucault, *Biopolitics, supra* note 52 at 31. The result of this spontaneity is the "natural" or "true" price – an equilibrium created by the intersection of supply and demand, "which reveals something like a truth": *ibid* at 31–2.

59 Polanyi, *supra* note 37 at 72.

60 Adam Smith argued that labour "was the first price, the original purchase money that was paid for all things … its value, to those who possess it and who want to exchange it for some new productions, is precisely equal to the quantity of labour which it can enable them to purchase or command." Labour is therefore "the real measure of the exchangeable value of all commodities." Smith, *supra* note 41 at 36.

61 Carole Pateman, *The Sexual Contract* (Palo Alto: Stanford University Press, 1988) at 117.

62 *Ibid*.

63 *Ibid* at 151. Thus, as chapter 3 discusses, the illusion of a free market for labour in the nineteenth century was maintained despite the existence of laws that expressly drew on master-servant style subordination by providing for imprisonment of workers (not employers) who breached the terms of their contracts.

64 John Locke, *Second Treatise of Government*, edited by C.B. Macpherson (Indianapolis: Hackett, 1980) at §27.

out of the state that nature hath provided, and left it in, he hath mixed his *labour* with, and joined to it something that is his own, and thereby makes it his *property*."[65] Thus, man's ability to engage in labour gives rise to private property rights – the worker has property in his own person and is therefore free to sell that property to a purchaser (master), who thereafter owns the products of that worker's labour power.[66] Locke's ideas also influenced subsequent configurations of land and money in terms of market relations,[67] and provided an intellectual rationale for the extension of private property rights, the appropriation of land, and its subjection to market forces – ideas that were crucial to the moves discussed in chapter 3.

The ideology of the family emerged in parallel with the creation of market economies and market ideology.[68] As agricultural reform and industrialization broke apart the productive household, what remained – the family – became idealized in terms of domesticity, marriage, and feminine care.[69] As production and workers moved out of the household,[70] "the bourgeoisie ... formulated a very different ideal of the family – that of an enclave protected from industrial society."[71] In Michael Anderson's words: "An increasing individualism was associated with increasing differentiation of the conjugal family as a discrete and private social unit and with a growing emphasis on individual autonomy and rights. At the same time the role of familial interest

---

65 *Ibid*.

66 Locke refers to the fact that "the turfs my servant has cut ... become my *property*, without the assignation or consent of any body. The *labour* that was mine, removing them out of the common state they were in, hath *fixed* my *property* in them." *Ibid* at §28. According to Macpherson, these passages show that Locke assumed that labour was "naturally a commodity and that the wage relationship which gives me the right to appropriate the produce of another's labour was a part of the natural order." Macpherson, *supra* note 46 at 220.

67 Macpherson, *supra* note 46 at 209.

68 Eli Zaretsky, *Capitalism, the Family, and Personal Life*, revised ed. (New York: Harper & Row, 1986) at 17.

69 This is not to say that the everyday experience of people necessarily reflected these ideals. As Susan Moller Okin has argued, though, "whatever the actual facts of family life amongst the upper strata in the eighteenth century, there seems little doubt that idealized conceptions and expectations of family life were indeed changing in the direction of the companionate marriage": Susan Moller Okin, *Justice, Gender, and the Family* (New York: Basic Books, 1989) at 73–4. In her view, the establishment of the sentimental family acted "as a *reinforcement* for the patriarchal relations between men and women that had been temporarily threatened by seventeenth-century individualism": *ibid* at 74 (emphasis in original).

70 See chapters 2, 3, and 4.

71 Zaretsky, *supra* note 68 at 33.

declined and an increasing emphasis was placed on emotion as the prime basis of family relationships."[72] A central feature of this affective conception of the family was a shift away from a transactional, economically oriented approach to marriage, towards a view of the relation as based on love and mutual companionship.[73] Lawrence Stone has famously argued that the ideal of companionate marriage arose among the English middle and upper classes in the eighteenth century, citing the claims of European visitors to England that some three-quarters of English upper- and middle class marriages were based in sentiment (La Rochefoucauld, 1784), and the "well-known fact that 'so many love-marriages' are made in England" (Sophie von La Roche, 1786).[74] According to Leonore Davidoff and Catherine Hall, this construction of marriage and the family was intimately connected to its function as the oppositional counterpart to the market. In their words: "A society based on market forces necessitated relationships beyond the grasp of the cash nexus, a site for moral order – located where else but in an idealised femininity and childhood, within the sacred bounds of family and home?"[75] Max Weber made a similar point in the course of his analysis of the generative connections between Puritanism and capitalist society. He observed that "the Puritan outlook … favoured the development of a rational bourgeois economic life; it was the most important, and above all the only consistent influence in the development of that life. It stood at the cradle of modern economic man." And, he noted, part of

---

72 Michael Anderson, *Approaches to the History of the Western Family 1500–1914* (Cambridge: Cambridge University Press, 1995) at 30.

73 Wally Seccombe, *A Millennium of Family Change: Feudalism to Capitalism in Northwestern Europe* (London: Verso, 1992) at 235. See also Olsen, *supra* note 14 at 1521. Running in tandem with the emphasis on marriage was a concern for the care and wellbeing of infants within the family – a responsibility that fell almost exclusively on women.

74 Lawrence Stone, *The Family, Sex and Marriage in England, 1500–1800*, abridged ed. (Harmondsworth: Penguin Books, 1979) at 219–20. For criticism of Stone's analysis see Anderson *supra* note 72 at 36, 75. For a more recent assessment and critique see the essays collected in Helen Berry and Elizabeth Foyster, eds., *The Family in Early Modern England* (Cambridge: Cambridge University Press, 2007). Randolph Trumbach has advanced a similar argument to Stone in relation to the aristocracy, suggesting that the generation of 1720–50 was the first "in which romantic marriage became truly prestigious, and people who made such marriages began to take for granted that a husband and a wife took most pleasure, first of all, in each other's company and then in the care of their children": Randolph Trumbach, *The Rise of the Egalitarian Family: Aristocratic Kinship and Domestic Relations in Eighteenth-Century England* (New York: Academic Press, 1978) at 291.

75 Leonore Davidoff and Catherine Hall, *Family Fortunes: Men and Women of the English Middle Class 1780–1850*, revised ed. (London: Routledge, 2002) at xxx.

this bourgeois life involved "set[ting] the clean and solid comfort of the middle-class home as an ideal."[76] The family was thus constructed as the private sanctuary into which men could retreat from their labour in the public sphere.[77]

By the middle of the nineteenth century, there were "few aspects of their society the Victorians regarded with greater reverence than the home and family life within it"; it was "axiomatic that the home was the foundation and the family the cornerstone of their civilization and that within the family were first learned the moral, religious, ethical and social precepts of good citizenship."[78] C.J. Bunyon's 1875 text *Domestic Law* is an example of this attitude. In it, he declared, "[t]he end of civil society is happiness, and the sum of the duties of every moral being the perfection of his own nature. These primary objects, according to our English notions, are best sought in the Family." At the centre of this English family stood the married couple, among whom "[m]utual

---

76 Max Weber, *The Protestant Ethic and the Spirit of Capitalism*, translated by Talcott Parsons (New York: Dover Publications, 2003) at 109, 171, 174.

77 See John Stuart Mill, *The Subjection of Women*, 3rd ed. (London: Longman, Green, Reader, and Dyer, 1870) at 175–6 [Mill, *Subjection*]. I acknowledge that this sort of 'separate spheres' analysis is not without its critics. Amanda Vickery, for instance, has made the valid point that reducing the roles and lives of men and women in the eighteenth and nineteenth centuries to simple associations between work and family or public and private can obscure the complex ways that people negotiated their own particular circumstances, as well as regional, class-based, and temporal distinctions: Amanda Vickery, "Golden Age to Separate Spheres? A Review of the Categories and Chronology of English Women's History" (1993) 36:2 *Hist J* 383. I think that Vickery is undoubtedly correct that sexual divisions of labour have existed throughout history, and that many women resisted the domestic ideal (and that some men refused the ideal of the public, commercial man). Nevertheless, the weight of the evidence still seems to me to support a broad separate spheres analysis, particularly on the level of ideology, where it appears almost unquestionable that a strong association existed between women and the domestic realm, and men with the domain of work and the market. Indeed, in my reading, the sexual division intensified in the long nineteenth century through the emergence of a more clearly demarcated division between home and work (or family/market).

78 Anthony Wohl, "Introduction" in Anthony Wohl, ed., *The Victorian Family: Structure and Stresses* (New York: St Martin's Press, 1978) 1 at 1–2. See also the statement from Lord Shaftesbury at 1–2: "There can be no security to society, no honour, no prosperity, no dignity at home, no nobleness of attitude towards foreign nations, unless the strength of the people rests upon the purity and firmness of the domestic system." Wohl cites C. Potter, "The First Point of the New Charter, Improved Dwellings for the People" (1871) XVIII *Contemporary Review* 547 at 555–6. No date is given for Lord Shaftesbury's declaration; it is simply noted that it was made "recently."

affection, or love, to use the dear old word, stands first, and marriage is naught without it."[79]

The keeper of this exalted family was, in Lord Tennyson's words, "the maiden, crown'd with marriage."[80] In a more utilitarian register, Bentham in his *Theory of Legislation* declared: "woman is better fitted for the family, and man for matters out of doors. The domestic economy is best placed in the hands of the women; the principal management of affairs in those of the men."[81] Marriage statistics indicate the extent to which this idea about a woman's role was adopted: the 1871 census shows that almost 90 per cent of women in England aged between 45 and 49 were or had been married.[82] This relegation (or elevation as it was seen at the time[83]) to the domestic realm also carried a strongly prescriptive set of behavioural ideas centring on virtue, delicacy and submission;[84] "the more dependent and child-like they became, women were told, the more they would be cherished."[85] In this respect, the construction of the family as a feminine domain, and the corresponding emphasis on marriage as the key to and cornerstone of family life, functioned as a means for consolidating male dominance over women.

B. Public/Private

The dichotomy between public and private is contextually specific and varies along descriptive and normative lines.[86] Historically, it can be

---

79 C.J. Bunyon, *A Profitable Book Upon Domestic Law* (London: Longmans, Green, and Co, 1875) at 59.

80 Alfred Lord Tennyson, "Vastness" in *The Works of Alfred Lord Tennyson* (London: Macmillan & Co, 1895) at 850–1; see Walter E. Houghton, *The Victorian Frame of Mind, 1830–1870* (New Haven: Yale University Press, 1985) at 341.

81 Jeremy Bentham, *Theory of Legislation*, translated from the French of Etienne Dumont by R. Hildreth, vol 1 (Boston: Weeks, Jordan, & Company, 1840) at 56 [Bentham, *Theory of Legislation*].

82 Mary Lyndon Shanley, *Feminism, Marriage, and the Law in Victorian England, 1850–1895* (Princeton, NJ: Princeton University Press, 1989) at 9 citing Jane Lewis, *Women in England 1870–1950* (Bloomington: Indiana University Press, 1984) at 3.

83 See Mill, *Subjection, supra* note 77 at 76: "we are perpetually told that women are *better* than men, this being said by people who are totally opposed to treating them as if they were as good: so that the saying about women's natural goodness has become a piece of tiresome cant, intended to put a complementary face on an injury."

84 Saskia Lettmaier, *Broken Engagements: The Action for Breach of Promise of Marriage and the Feminine Ideal, 1800–1940* (Oxford: Oxford University Press, 2010) at 56.

85 *Ibid* at 62.

86 Gavison, *supra* note 31.

traced (at least) to the Greek distinction between the *polis* (the public, masculine realm of diplomacy and statecraft) and the *oikos* (the private realm of the household, ruled by the patriarch; a site of production and reproduction).[87] However, as the household split along family/market lines in the eighteenth and nineteenth centuries, a more complex set of meanings and ascriptions arose. In classical liberal thought, the state remained quintessentially public,[88] while the family was "regarded ... as unproblematically private and as a barely visible appendage to civil society. Enveloped by the values of *Gemeinschaft* [community], the family was thought not to be the proper subject of state regulation."[89] The variable in this framework was the market. As Frances Olsen has noted, the market came to be viewed as public when compared to the private family, and private when read as part of civil society and contrasted with the (public) state.[90] In the liberal cartography of public and private, then, the major division is that between state (public) and civil society (private). Civil society, in turn, is broken into market (public) and family (private).[91] These distinctions are also gendered,[92] most obviously in the association between masculinity, work, and the (public) market; and femininity, domestic labour (incorporating care), and the (private) family.[93]

---

87 Margaret Thornton, "The Cartography of Public and Private" in Margaret Thornton, ed., *Public and Private: Feminist Legal Debates* (New York: Oxford University Press, 1995) 1 at 3; Graham Burchell, "Peculiar Interests: Civil Society and Governing 'The System of Natural Liberty'" in Graham Burchell, Colin Gordon and Peter Miller, *The Foucault Effect: Studies in Governmentality* (Chicago: University of Chicago Press, 1991) 119 at 120.

88 Burchell, *supra* note 87 at 121.

89 Thornton, *supra* note 87 at 4–5.

90 Olsen, *supra* note 14 at 1501. As Morton Horwitz has pointed out, "in reaction to the claims of monarchs and, later, parliaments to the unrestrained power to make law, there developed a countervailing effort to stake out distinctively private spheres free from the encroaching power of the state." Morton Horwitz, "The History of the Public/Private Distinction" (1982) 130:6 *U Penn L Rev* 1423 at 1423.

91 Thus, as Duncan Kennedy puts it, "[c]lassical legal thought should be associated not just with precedent and principle, but also with a particular ordering of substantive principles around the public-private distinction, iterated and reiterated at every level of doctrine." Duncan Kennedy, "From the Will Theory to the Principle of Private Autonomy: Lon Fuller's Consideration and Form" (2000) 100:1 *Colum L Rev* 94 at 107.

92 Simone de Beauvoir, *The Second Sex*, translated by Constance Borde and Sheila Malovany-Chevallier (New York: Vintage Books, 2011) at 67: "for man she [the woman] is a sexual partner, a reproducer, an erotic object, an Other through whom he seeks himself."

93 This was by no means an Anglophone phenomenon: *ibid* at 129.

The ascription of public/private status to particular arenas is normative as well as lexical – it carries ideological weight. According to Margaret Thornton, the Western intellectual tradition has tended towards an Aristotelian prioritization of the public realm – the site in which men attend to affairs of state. Carole Pateman has made a similar argument. In her reading, "[t]he story of the social contract is treated as an account of the creation of the public sphere of civil freedom. The other, private, sphere is not seen as politically relevant."[94] A similar ideological prioritization of the public sphere is evident in the market (public) / family (private) dichotomy – "while men sentimentalized the family and exalted domesticity, they continued to behave in the marketplace as if they believed that 'profane,' worldly goals represented the greatest good."[95] On the other hand, classical liberalism valorized the (private) market not only vis-à-vis the family but also as against the (public) state, while the ideology of the family treated it as a private "haven" from its public opposites: the avaricious market[96] and the overbearing state.[97]

In legal thought, the public/private distinction tracked and also inverted the forms noted above, with implications for the formal arrangement of law and its substantive content. According to Morton Horwitz, "[t]he emergence of the market as a central legitimating institution brought the public/private distinction into the core of legal discourse during the nineteenth century." [98] The basic architectural division was the state/civil society distinction, with "Public Law" encompassing constitutional, administrative, criminal laws, and "Private Law" covering the rest, most notably property, contract, tort, and family laws. In this respect there was a correspondence between legal and socio-political conceptions of public/private. However, while the division *within* civil society (market/family) also carried over into "Private Law," the ascription of public and private to those domains actually flipped. The "public" domain of the market was, in legal thought, the quintessential private realm of contract, whereas the "private" realm of the family[99] also had a public aspect owing to the interference of the state in its operation. As Kennedy has pointed out, this division hinged

---

94 Pateman, *supra* note 61 at 3.

95 Olsen, *supra* note 14 at 1500.

96 *Ibid* at 1504. See further Christopher Lasch, *Haven in a Heartless World: The Family Besieged* (New York: Basic Books, 1979).

97 Olsen, *supra* note 14 at 1506 (citations omitted).

98 Horwitz, *supra* note 90 at 1424.

99 The classic judicial framing of the family's private nature is found in *Balfour v Balfour* [1919] 2 KB 571.

on the idea of "will," where "the will [was] either the will of the parties or the will of the state."[100] The former was "true" private law, centred on contract (the ideology of private individuals meeting in the market); the latter housed areas such as tort (since the obligation arose through the will of the state) and laws concerning status (in the legal sense of non-modifiable state-imposed regulation[101]), including family laws.[102] In ideological terms, Classical Legal Thought of the late nineteenth century prioritized "core" private law and construed all relations that were not attributable to the will of autonomous individuals as part of the "periphery." In this respect, it adhered to the broader socio-political priority given to the (public) market over the (private) family. Again, though, the ideology operated in different ways at different times. Just as the family was socially constructed as an affective oasis from the market, in law it was treated as both "a domain into which the King's writ does not seek to run,"[103] and a site of significant public interest. In this sense, Klare may have been correct when he declared, "[t]here is no 'public/private distinction.'" However, as he went on to acknowledge, "[w]hat does exist is a series of ways of thinking about public and private that are constantly undergoing revision, reformulation, and refinement."[104] Particularly in matters of history, recognizing the ideological significance of these categories remains important,[105] even as we call into question their application.

C. Status/Contract[106]

In Roman law "status" denoted "the entire position of an individual regarded as a legal person"; that is, "the person who had status was the normal citizen, the *civis* who had full liberty, citizenship and family rights."[107] In medieval English law and legal thought, status was inti-

---

100 Kennedy, *Rise & Fall, supra* note 22 at xiii.

101 See section A(iii) below.

102 Kennedy, *Rise & Fall, supra* note 22 at xiii, 123.

103 *Balfour v Balfour* [1919] 2 KB 571 at 579 (Atkin LJ).

104 Klare, "Public/Private," *supra* note 28 at 1361.

105 Gavison, *supra* note 31 at 44.

106 From an ideological perspective it would perhaps be more accurate to frame the status/contract distinction in terms of external (state or familial) constraint versus individual autonomy, with status and contract as the legal manifestations of those ideologies. However, since I want to maintain the focus on the specifically legal aspects of this broader division, I use status/contract instead of the broader and perhaps more felicitous distinction.

107 R.H. Graveson, *Status in the Common Law* (London: Athlone, 1953) at 4–5.

mately related to land. A man's "status as a legal person depended on his legal estate and tenure in English land."[108] As feudalism died out, however, the ideas of status and estate became disengaged, "the former being limited to personal legal condition, and the latter more or less exclusively applied to an interest in land."[109] Status therefore came to be associated with personal incapacity by reason of ascribed characteristics.[110] Within the household, the *paterfamilias* held full legal capacity, while those beneath him had their capacity limited by law owing to their status as wife, child or servant.[111]

In the seventeenth century, as contractual ideas around social and political obligation began to emerge, patriarchal theory gave voice to long-held but largely unarticulated ideas of duty and subservience.[112] Most famously, Robert Filmer propounded "divine right absolutism on the ground that the political order of Stuart England had evolved from the family; magistrates were therefore entitled to the same filial obedience that children owed to their fathers."[113] Locke directly challenged Filmer and patriarchalism.[114] Instead of natural duty, he asserted, "[t]he *freedom* then of man, and liberty of acting in accordance to his own will, is *grounded* on his having *reason*, which is able to instruct him in that law he is to govern himself by."[115] From individual reason it was a short step to a theory of obligation based on individual consent:[116] "the *beginning of politic society* depends upon the consent of the individuals, to join into and make one society."[117] Under the sway of such ideas, England moved

---

108 *Ibid* at 7. See also Frederick Pollock and Frederic William Maitland, *The History of English Law Before the Time of Edward I* (Cambridge: Cambridge University Press, 1895), Vol 2 at 78: "It is of course characteristic of this age that a man's estate – his general position in the legal scheme – should be determined by his relation to land."

109 Graveson, *supra* note 107 at 10–11.

110 Pateman, *supra* note 61 at 10.

111 See, e.g., John Dud and Robert Cleaver, *A Godly Forme of Household Government, for the Ordering of Private Families* (1598); Gordon J. Schochet, *Patriarchalism in Political Thought: The Authoritarian Family and Political Speculation and Attitudes Especially in Seventeenth-Century England* (Oxford: Blackwell, 1975) at 4.

112 Schochet, *supra* note 111 at 55.

113 *Ibid* at 1.

114 Of course, Locke did not single-handedly bring patriarchalism to an end – "the identification of all status relationships with one another and specifically the social and the familial with the political" was a world view that was already beginning to collapse by the time Locke wrote the *Two Treatises*: ibid at 274.

115 Locke, *supra* note 64 at §63. For a critique of social contract theory see Bentham, *Theory of Legislation, supra* note 81 at 93–5.

116 Schochet, *supra* note 111 at 8–9.

117 Locke, *supra* note 64 at 56, §106.

away from traditional notions of ascribed status,[118] becoming what Alan Fox has called "a contract society," in which "the individual, liberated from ... traditional shackles and their fixed unchanging duties, is given the freedom to shape his own destiny and choose his own obligations through the bargaining processes of the market."[119] For the household, the implications of individual consent as the basis of obligation were profound: "The contractarian (liberal) household is set on radically new foundations, expressed variously as equality, consent, and autonomy. The household economy is thus morally relocated from one embedded in a hierarchical community, under the master's command and oriented principally toward his purposes, to one in which persons are self-owners (or Kantian autonomous agents), pursuers of their own abilities, and individuals over whom control can be exercised, or exchanges effected only through their consent."[120] Contractual ideology was also intimately related to the emergence of market ideology and foreshadowed the sense in which contract is now generally understood – as a "purposive, economic-exchange relationship."[121] As Eric Hobsbawm has observed, the pursuit of self-interest made it "advantageous or unavoidable to enter into certain relations with other individuals, and this complex of useful arrangements – which were often expressed in the frankly commercial terminology of 'contract' – constituted society."[122] Political and legal notions of contract therefore intersected with classical (eighteenth and nineteenth century) economic thought, and helped to constitute one another. In Patrick Atiyah's words, "[t]he model of contract theory which implicitly underlay the classical law of contract ... was the model

---

118 In sociological literature "achieved status" is open to individual achievement and not dependent on birth, while "ascribed status" is "assigned to individuals without reference to their innate differences or abilities": Irving S. Foladare, "A Clarification of 'Ascribed Status' and 'Achieved Status'" (1969) 10:1 *Soc Quart* 53 at 53 referring to and quoting from Ralph Linton, *The Study of Man: An Introduction* (New York: Appleton-Century-Crofts, 1936) at 115–31.

119 Alan Fox, *Beyond Contract: Work, Power and Trust Relations* (London: Faber, 1974) at 210.

120 William James Booth, *Households: On the Moral Architecture of the Economy* (Ithaca: Cornell University Press, 1993) at 10. See also Stone, *supra* note 74 at 165 on the waning influence of patriarchy in households in the eighteenth century.

121 Fox, *supra* note 119 at 154.

122 Eric J. Hobsbawm, *The Age of Revolution: Europe 1789–1848* (London: Weidenfeld and Nicolson, 1962) at 278–9 quoted in Fox, *supra* note 119 at 164. See also Patrick S. Atiyah, *The Rise and Fall of Freedom of Contract* (Oxford: Clarendon Press, 1985) at 70: "Political society becomes a calculated device for the protection of ... property and for the maintenance of an orderly relation of exchange."

of the market."[123] Legal contracts therefore "exemplif[ied] the freedom that individuals exercise when they make the original pact."[124]

In England, the idea that legal relationships were, as a general matter, created by (and depended on) the free choice of individuals began to solidify from around 1800.[125] This notion was part of a more general effort to rationalize the common law,[126] and started a process whereby contract came to be reconceived as an abstract body of principles based on individual agreement – what is often called the "Will Theory" of contract:[127] the idea "that the whole root of contract was to be found in the will of the parties."[128] The will-based model, which drew on works by the civilian jurists Robert-Joseph Pothier[129] and Friedrich Carl von Savigny,[130] emphasized the centrality of agreement between contracting

---

123 Atiyah, *supra* note 122 at 402.

124 Pateman, *supra* note 61 at 7. See also Collins, *supra* note 17 at 136. In reality, though, as chapter 3 explains, foregrounding intention and individual consent did not remove subordination from English law.

125 David J. Ibbetson, *A Historical Introduction to the Law of Obligations* (Oxford: Oxford University Press, 2001) at 220.

126 Atiyah, *supra* note 122 at 352; Ibbetson, *supra* note 125 at 220. It was also related to the gradual demise of the forms of action (it remained necessary to identify a form of action in a summons until 1852: Warren Swain, *The Law of Contract, 1670–1870* (Cambridge: Cambridge University Press, 2015) at 18–19 citing (1852) 15 & 16 Vict, c 76, s 3) and the move away from jury trial in civil matters. According to Baker, "there was very little law of contract at all before the last century [i.e., the nineteenth century] because there was no machinery for producing it and most of the questions were left to juries as questions of fact." J.H. Baker, "Review of The Rise and Fall of Freedom of Contract. By P.S. Atiyah" (1980) 43:4 *Mod L Rev* 467 at 469.

127 Atiyah, *supra* note 122 at 41, 399–405. See also Duncan Kennedy, "Three Globalizations of Law and Legal Thought" in David M. Trubek & Alvaro Santos, eds., *The New Law and Economic Development: A Critical Appraisal* (New York: Cambridge University Press, 2006) 19 at 26 [Kennedy, "Three Globalizations"]; Kennedy, *Rise & Fall, supra* note 22, chapter 4.

128 Ibbetson, *supra* note 125 at 216.

129 Pothier's *Traite des obligations* was first published in 1761, but was not translated into English until 1802: see Robert Joseph Pothier, *Treatise on Obligations, considered in a Moral and Legal View, translated from the French of Pothier*, 2 vols (Newberg NC: Martin & Ogden, 1802). In particular, Pothier emphasized the importance not only of offer but also of acceptance. His definition of a contract is as follows: "An agreement by which two parties reciprocally promise and engage, or one of them singly promises and engages to the other to give some particular thing, or to do or abstain from doing some particular act." *Treatise on Obligations*, art I, s I. In contrast, a promise not yet accepted by the person to whom it is made is a mere pollicitation: art I, s II.

130 See Friedrich Carl von Savigny, *System of the Modern Roman Law*, translated by William Holloway (Madras: J. Higginbotham, 1867). See further Ibbetson, *supra* note 125 at 220–1.

parties; in particular, Pothier stressed the importance of not only offer but also acceptance in forming contractual relations. Thus, as David Ibbetson puts it, "[l]ogically central to the Will Theory was the idea that contractual liability depended on the voluntary, intentional, act of the parties" – leading in turn to the elevation of the requirement of intention to create legal relations.[131] The process of elevating contract to the core of the private law universe – largely completed in England by the 1870s[132] – also relied on a process of distinguishing contract from what it was not; in particular, jurists were concerned to draw a line between contract and what contract was understood to have supplanted: status. Thus, in perhaps the most famous aphorism in legal history, Henry Sumner Maine declared "that the movement of the progressive societies has hitherto been a movement *from Status to Contract*."[133] Maine was concerned to distinguish modern ideas of individual freedom from the type of patriarchal domination seen in Roman family law, governed as it was by the *patria potestas*.[134] Whereas Maine was concerned with status

---

131 Ibbetson, *supra* note 125 at 232–3.

132 In his 1876 treatise, *Principles of Contract at Law and in Equity: Being a Treatise of the General Principles Concerning the Validity of Agreements, With a Special View to the Comparison of Law and Equity, and With References to the Indian Contract Act, and Occasionally to Roman, American, and Continental Law* (London: Stevens, 1876), Frederick Pollock brought intention to create legal relations into the English "doctrinal heartland" – and in doing so acknowledged his debt to Savigny. See Ibbetson, *supra* note 125 at 23. Specifically, Pollock wrote that it is necessary that "the parties *concur in expressing a common intention*": Pollock, *supra* note 132 at 3 (emphasis in original). A few years later, another titan of English jurisprudence, John Salmond, opened an article entitled "The History of Contract" with the following statement: "The modern law of contract consists of a general theory, forming the bond of union between numerous, and otherwise unconnected, classes of contracts." John Salmond, "The History of Contract" (1887) 3 *Law Q Rev* 166 at 166. For judges, freedom of contract was, by this time, "a starting-point, a part of the natural background, and it was 'interference' which had to be justified": Atiyah, *supra* note 122 at 386. Thus, in the 1875 case of *Printing and Numerical Supply Co v Sampson* (1875) LR 19 Eq at 465, Jessel M.R. emphasized the necessity that men "have the utmost liberty of contracting, and that their contracts when entered into freely and voluntarily shall be held sacred ... you are not lightly to interfere with this freedom of contract."

133 Henry Sumner Maine, *Ancient Law* (New York: Dorset Press, 1986) at 141 (emphasis in original). See further Roscoe Pound, *Interpretations of Legal History* (New York: Macmillan, 1923) at 54.

134 In this respect, Maine's statement was accurate, particularly since he expressly limited himself temporally ("the movement ... has *hitherto* been") and excised personal conditions arising by agreement ("avoid applying the term [status] to such conditions as are the immediate or remote result of agreement") from the scope of

in its older sense of hierarchic and hereditary personal conditions,[135] other nineteenth-century jurists and thinkers[136] attempted to distinguish contract from another, more modern form of status that rested on distinctions between state/civil society and public/private.[137] As Kennedy points out, this process involved "subtracting" specific branches of law from the contractual core:

> The adoption of the will theory was manifested in (a) the dismantling of contracts by the spinning off of Quasi-Contract and Tort; (b) the rise in jurisprudence of an ordering of private law based on two distinctions: rights against the world versus rights against individuals; and rights arising from private agreement vs. those created by the state; (c) the emergence of the concept of status to deal with legal relationships organized in a way inconsistent with this scheme; (d) the reordering of the residuum of pure contract in terms of the will of the parties and the will of the sovereign; and (e) the organization of the brand new field of tort law into intentional torts, negligence and absolute liability.[138]

The key point is that "the rise in jurisprudence of an ordering of private law" was based in part on "rights arising from private agreement vs. those created by the state," and "the concept of status [emerged] to deal with legal relationships organized in a way inconsistent with this scheme." Status in this understanding "grouped together and explained the peculiar character of rules incompatible with the new vision of the nature of 'real' contracts."[139] That is, the sets of non-modifiable terms that accompanied entry into particular legal relations (such as marriage[140]) rendered those relations forms of achieved (rather than

---

his consideration. Indeed, such a definition continued to make sense in England until the demise of feudalism, which broke the linkage between land and status in English law: Graveson, *supra* note 107 at 40–1.

135 Manfred Rehbinder, "Status, Contract, and the Welfare State" (1971) 23:5 *Stan L Rev* 941 at 949.

136 In *The Subjection of Women*, John Stuart Mill spoke of the "peculiar character of the modern world," in which "human beings are no longer born to their place in life": Mill, *Subjection, supra* note 77 at 29.

137 A relation that was private in the sense that it involved members of civil society was also "public" if the relation arose because of state intervention; it therefore could not be considered properly private, that is, contractual. See the discussion of public-private in section A(ii) above.

138 Kennedy, *Rise and Fall, supra* note 22 at 171.

139 *Ibid* at 185.

140 See chapter 2.

ascribed[141]) status, standing outside of and in opposition to the (putatively) autonomous private ordering symbolized by contract.

This new conception of status involved a "shift from status as a derivative of paternal arbitrariness to status as a derivative of sovereign rather than individual will."[142] It amounted to a *public* form of status imposed by the state in recognition of the social importance of a particular position or relation. In R.H. Graveson's words, it was, "a special condition of a continuous and institutional nature, differing from the legal position of the normal person, which is conferred by law and not purely by the act of the parties, whenever a person occupies a position of which the creation, continuance or relinquishment and the incidents are a matter of sufficient social or public concern."[143]

II. Population Management

In *Security, Territory, Population*, lectures delivered at the Collège de France in 1977–78, Michel Foucault set forth a genealogy of modern governance practices in which he suggested that, "starting from the eighteenth century, modern Western societies took on board the fundamental biological fact that human beings are a species."[144] Hitherto, population was "conceived of as a set of elements and forces contributing to the state's greater wealth, strength and glory, or as the sum of useful individuals to be put to work in accordance with the regulatory decrees of the sovereign's rational will."[145] Within this older framework, "the art of government" was concerned with the following question: "[H]ow to introduce economy – that is to say, the proper way of managing individuals, goods, and wealth, like the management of a family by

---

141 See *supra* note 118.

142 Kennedy, *Rise and Fall, supra* note 22 at 205.

143 Graveson, *supra* note 107 at 2. As to what this special condition involves,
    Wolfgang Friedmann has suggested that its core comprises two aspects: "first, the
    aggregate of a person's capacities and incapacities, as determined by that person's
    membership of a class or group in society; second, the sum of legal conditions
    imposed by the operation of law, as distinct from rights and duties acquired by the
    voluntary act of a person." Wolfgang Friedmann, "Some Reflections on Status and
    Freedom" in Ralph A. Newman, ed., *Essays in Jurisprudence in Honor of Roscoe Pound*
    (Indianapolis: Bobbs-Merrill, 1962) 222 at 222.

144 Foucault, *STP, supra* note 6 at 1. See also Michel Foucault, *Society Must Be Defended.
    Lectures at the Collège de France, 1975–1976*, edited by Mauro Bertani and Alessandro
    Fontana, translated by David Macey (New York: Picador, 2003) at 35–6, 245
    [Foucault, *SMBD*].

145 Burchell, *supra* note 87 at 126.

a father who knows how to direct his wife, his children, and his servants, who knows how to make his family's fortune prosper, and how to arrange suitable alliances for it – how to introduce this meticulous attention, this type of relationship between father and the family, into the management of the state?"[146] The management of the household was therefore taken as a model for the management of the state – in much the same way that Filmer formulated his patriarchal model of the state in seventeenth-century England by reference to the power of the father over his family. The rise of contract theory within political thought (most notably the works of Thomas Hobbes, Locke, and Rousseau) provided a new kind of framework, though "it always remained at the level of the formulation of general principles of public law."[147] The model of governance was, therefore, "caught between an excessively large, abstract, and rigid framework of sovereignty on the one hand, and, on the other, a model of the family that was too narrow, weak, and insubstantial."[148]

According to Foucault, linking the art of government to "the problem of population" unblocked the impasse created by these differing conceptions of governance.[149] The "reality of phenomena specific to population" made it possible to "eliminate the model of the family and to re-focus the notion of economy on something else."[150] As we have seen above, that "something else" was the market, which became its own "level of reality and … field of intervention for government."[151] In Graham Burchell's words, "[b]oth the family and economic processes [were] disengaged from the essential connections they [had] with each other within the model of oeconomy."[152] This shift by no means erased the family from political sight; instead, "the family now appears as an element within the population and as a fundamental relay in its government":[153]

> In other words, prior to the emergence of the problematic of population, the art of government could only be conceived on the basis of the model of the family, in terms of economy understood as management of the family.

---

146 Foucault, *STP, supra* note 6 at 95.
147 *Ibid* at 103.
148 *Ibid*.
149 *Ibid* at 103–4.
150 *Ibid* at 104.
151 *Ibid* at 95. See section A(i) above.
152 Burchell, *supra* note 87 at 126–7.
153 Foucault, *STP, supra* note 6 at 104.

When, however, the population appears as absolutely irreducible to the family, the result is that the latter falls to a lower level than the population; it appears as an element within the population. It is therefore no longer a model; it is a segment whose privilege is simply that when one wants to obtain something from the population concerning sexual behavior, demography, the birth rate, or consumption, then *one has to utilize the family. The family will change from being a model to being an instrument; it will become a privileged instrument for the government of the population* rather than a chimerical model for good government ... What enables population to unblock the art of government is that it eliminates the model of the family.[154]

The practice of government therefore shifted from a concern with implementing theoretical models of sovereignty based on the patriarchal family to improvement of the condition of the population – "to increase its wealth, its longevity, and its health."[155] The "problem of sovereignty" remained within this new political matrix, but it was reformulated into the question of "what juridical form, what institutional form, and what legal basis could be given to the sovereignty typical of a state."[156] Statehood and nation-building were thus deeply embedded within this new art of government,[157] which acted "directly on the population itself through campaigns, or, indirectly, by, for example, techniques that, without people being aware of it, stimulate[d] the birth rate, or direct[ed] the flows of population to this or that region or activity."[158] Population thus became "the object that government will have to take into account in its observations and knowledge, in order to govern effectively in a rationally reflected manner."[159]

Foucault's work on sexuality sheds light on the manner in which this mode of governance attended to the family. Alongside "the hysterical woman, the masturbating child, ... and the perverse adult" was "the Malthusian couple,"[160] whose fertility was subject to "a political socialization achieved through the 'responsibilization' of couples with regard to the social body as a whole."[161] Within this matrix, "what is

---

154 *Ibid* at 104–5 (emphasis added).

155 Foucault, *STP, supra* note 6 at 105–6.

156 *Ibid* at 106.

157 *Ibid* at 107: "So sovereignty is absolutely not eliminated by the emergence of a new art of government that has crossed the threshold of political science. The problem of sovereignty is not eliminated; on the contrary, it is made more acute than ever."

158 *Ibid* at 105.

159 *Ibid* at 106.

160 Michel Foucault, *The History of Sexuality. Volume I, The Will to Knowledge*, translated by Robert Hurley (London: Penguin Books, 2008) at 105 [Foucault, *HoS*].

161 *Ibid* at 105.

pertinent is the link between partners and definite statutes"; the family thus "conveys the law and the juridical dimension in the deployment of sexuality."[162] In other words, regulation of the family was part of a broader strategy of managing the sexual practices of the population, making it possible "for the deployment of sexuality ... to develop along its two primary dimensions: the husband-wife axis and the parents-children axis."[163] In this respect, regulation of the "family cell" was intimately connected to the wellbeing of the modern state, comprised (in theory) of sexually responsible married couples.[164]

The field in which this newly instrumentalized family unit operated was the economy, which shifted away from its medieval familial denotation and came to "be re-focused on a level of reality that we now describe as the economic."[165] Burchell describes how this shift involved market-based ideology of the type described above:

> The principle of *laissez-faire*, then, is premised on a type of objectification of population and wealth which constitutes an epistemological precondition for the possible specification of new, practicable techniques of management ...
>
> ... It is a government which depends upon the conduct of *individuals* who are parts of a population and subjects of particular, personal interests. That is to say, the individual subject of interest is at once the object or target of government and, so to speak, its "partner."
>
> This individual living being, the subject of particular interests, represents a new figure of social and political subjectivity, the prototype of "economic man," who will become the correlate and instrument of a new art of government.[166]

Governmentality, as Foucault called it, and its new governmental technique, is thus premised on interaction between macro-level state interventions and micro-level individual responses within the field of economy.

Unsurprisingly, Foucault discerned a correlative shift in the way that law came to be conceptualized and deployed within this new art of population management. In essence, he perceived a shift away from the "juridico-legal" model (revolving around sovereign power and criminal

---

162 *Ibid* at 106, 108.

163 *Ibid* at 108.

164 This was not a simple repression of sexuality; rather, the role of the family was "to anchor sexuality and provide it with a permanent support": *ibid* at 108.

165 Foucault, *STP, supra* note 6 at 104.

166 Burchell, *supra* note 87 at 127.

laws[167]) towards mechanisms of security;[168] the question was no longer "a matter of imposing a law on men, but of the disposition of things, that is to say, of employing tactics rather than laws, or, … as far as possible employing laws as tactics; arranging things so that this or that end may be achieved through a certain number of means."[169] Statements of this sort have led some scholars such as Alan Hunt, Gary Wickham and Boaventura de Sousa Santos to assert that Foucault's own understanding of law is essentially "juridical."[170] Recourse to his theories would, on this view, potentially involve falling into the same trap that critics of CLS charge it with, namely, focussing on "high law" to the exclusion of regulatory interventions and micro-instances of power. As Victor Tadros has pointed out, though, Foucault's conception of governmentality does not exclude law; rather, it envisions law as a much more diffuse practice than the blunt edge of criminal prohibitions – laws as tactics.[171] Indeed, Foucault is quite clear that governmentality involves "an increasingly huge set of legislative measures, decrees, regulations, and circulars that permit the deployment of these mechanisms of security."[172] Law in Foucault's scheme thus partly retained its juridical form,[173] but alongside direct applications of force by sovereigns (which clearly continued in the domain of criminal law and the application of criminal sanctions to civil infractions[174]) there were "a series of adjacent, detective, medical, and psychological techniques … which fall within the domain of surveillance, diagnosis, and the possible transformation of individuals."[175] In other words, "regulatory controls"[176] and discursive norms began to

---

167   The juridical model "consists in laying down a law and fixing a punishment for the person who breaks it, which is the system of the legal code with a binary division between the permitted and the prohibited": Foucault, *STP, supra* note 6 at 5.

168   Thus, "'governmentality' … has the population as its target, political economy as its major form of knowledge, and apparatuses of security as its essential technical instrument": *ibid* at 109.

169   *Ibid*.

170   Victor Tadros, "Between Governance and Discipline: The Law and Michel Foucault" (1998) 8:1 *Oxford J Leg Stud* 75, critiquing Alan Hunt and Gary Wickham, *Foucault and Law: Towards a Sociology of Law as Governance* (London: Pluto Press, 1994), and Boaventura de Sousa Santos, *Toward a New Common Sense: Law, Science and Politics in Paradigmatic Transition* (London: Routledge, 1995).

171   Tadros, *supra* note 170 at 92.

172   Foucault, *STP, supra* note 6 at 7.

173   Indeed, "getting these systems of security to work involves a real inflation of the juridico-legal code": *ibid* at 7.

174   For example, the imposition of criminal penalties on workers for breach of contract in eighteenth-century English legislation: see chapter 3.

175   Foucault, *STP, supra* note 6 at 5. See also Foucault, *SMBD, supra* note 144 at 38.

176   Foucault, *HoS, supra* note 160 at 139.

gain in importance "at the expense of the juridical system of the law."[177] Law, in Foucault's account of eighteenth and nineteenth century practices, thus "takes its place amongst a more general technical apparatus of governmental control which intervenes into the lives of individuals and groups in response to knowledge collected about those lives."[178] The theory of population management is therefore a useful complement to analysis of ideology precisely because Foucault's understanding of law is *not* limited to prohibitory enactments and decisions but also encompasses regulatory manoeuvres to direct and manage the population into self-discipline and particular sets of behavioural norms – which may reflect or reinforce particular ideological impulses.

Piecing these elements together, the relationship between family, economy, state, and law may be summarized as follows: prior to the eighteenth century, the patriarchal family (in its productive household form) constituted a model for government, with the relationship between a master and his household subordinates seen as paradigmatic for the relations between monarch and subjects. However, as social contract theory and individualism took hold, the household (as idea and entity) began to break down and no longer stood as the primary model for governance. Freed from the patriarchal family, states instead focussed their attentions on the living, breathing, copulating[179] reality of populations. The economy, in its new, market-based form, became the favoured terrain for population-oriented interventions, and the family (in its increasingly narrow meaning) was reconceived as a crucial relay point in this matrix. In this latter respect, it is important to bear in mind that what occurred was not a diminution in the importance of the family to states, but rather a reconfiguration of the relationship between family and state – a move from model to instrument. This shift is perfectly consistent with ideological veneration of "the family"; arguably, it even depended upon it because "when one wants to obtain something from the population concerning sexual behaviour, demography, the birth rate, or consumption, then one has to utilize the family."[180] The family was therefore in service to the state, *and vice versa*, because the state's wellbeing depended in part on the strength of its constituent family cells.

In the English context, the nineteenth century administrative or regulatory revolution in government points to the efficacy of Foucault's claim

---

177 *Ibid* at 144.
178 Tadros, *supra* note 170 at 93.
179 On the importance of sexuality as a site of strategic importance in the nineteenth century see Foucault, *SMBD, supra* note 144 at 251–2.
180 Foucault, *STP, supra* note 6 at 105.

about the emergence of population-centred approaches to governance.[181] According to Oliver MacDonagh, this transformation "destroyed belief in the possibility that society did or should consist, essentially or for the most part, of a mere accumulation of contractual relationships between persons, albeit enforced so far as need be by the sovereign power."[182] In its place emerged a conception and practice of government that stressed its role in the alleviation of social ills. This new model generally commenced with the public identification of an intolerable issue affecting some segment of the population.[183] Next came a series of (often ineffective) legislative measures, followed by the appointment of executive officers and administrators to ensure that the good intentions embodied in law were actually realized. The first hand experience of these officers generated further calls for specific legislation and "an equivalent demand for centralization" in order to more clearly define the powers and duties of government officials. Eventually, these administrators "began to undertake more systematic and truly statistical and experimental investigations," calling upon knowledge from different fields "to find answers to intractable difficulties in composing and enforcing particular preventive measures." Once the root cause of a problem "had been clearly proved, the corresponding regulations passed effortlessly into law."[184] Thus: "[U]nperceived, the ripples of government circled ever wider. In the course of these latest pressures towards autonomy and delegated legislation, towards fluidity and experimentation in regulations, towards a division and a specialization of administrative labour, and towards a dynamic role for government within society, a new sort of state was being born."[185] Two of the intellectual polestars for this population-centred approach to governance in England were Bentham and Malthus. According to Bentham: "The public good ought to be the object of the legislator; general utility ought to be the foundation of his reasonings. To know the true good of the community is what constitutes the science of legislation; the art consists in finding the

---

181 As Foucault declared, "Utilitarianism is a technology of government": Foucault, *Biopolitics, supra* note 52 at 41.

182 Oliver MacDonagh, "The Nineteenth-Century Revolution in Government: A Reappraisal" (1958) 1 *Hist J* 52 at 57.

183 *Ibid* at 58. See also David Thomson, *England in the Nineteenth Century, 1815–1914* (Harmondsworth, Middlesex: Penguin Books, 1950) at 69.

184 MacDonagh, *supra* note 182 at 61.

185 *Ibid*. See also Thomson, *supra* note 183 at 73, referring to "a new kind of State in Britain: … in which the ordinary citizen was subjected to a much greater degree of administrative interference, direction, and control from the centre."

means to realize that good."[186] There is a discernible correspondence between this passage and Foucault's claim that in the eighteenth and nineteenth centuries, the end of government became "not just to govern, but to improve the condition of the population."[187] For Bentham, the "interest of a community" corresponds to that which "tends to augment the total sum of the happiness of the individuals that compose it."[188] He therefore criticized governments which, "entirely occupied with wealth and commerce, look[] upon society as a workshop, regard[] men only as productive machines, and care[] little how much it torments them, provided it makes them rich."[139] The end of government, in his view, was *not* a mercantilist increase in wealth and troops; rather, it was the wellbeing of the population. A measure of government was, therefore, "conformable to or dictated by the principle of utility, when in like manner the tendency which it has to augment the happiness of the community is greater than any which it has to diminish it."[190]

The Utilitarian concern with population is most pronounced in the work of Malthus.[191] According to Stephen Leslie, "the Malthusian theory

---

186 Bentham, *Theory of Legislation, supra* note 81 at 13. Utility, for Bentham, meant "the property or tendency of a thing to prevent some evil or to procure some good"; accordingly, "[t]hat which is comformable to the utility, or the interest of an individual, is what tends to augment the total sum of his happiness": *ibid* at 14.

187 Foucault, *STP, supra* note 6 at 105. Like Foucault, Bentham is often read as a criminalist in his understanding of the function and operation of law. Certainly, Bentham's basic conception of law focussed on legislation and penal sanction. In his *Theory of Legislation* Bentham declared, "[l]egislation can have no direct influence upon the conduct of men, except by punishments": Bentham, *Theory of Legislation, supra* note 81 at 80. See further Michael Quinn, "Jeremy Bentham, Choice Architect: Law, Indirect Legislation, and the Context of Choice" (2017) 43:1 *Hist Eur Ideas* 11 at 12. However, paralleling Foucault, Bentham also made space in his scheme of governance for indirect legislation, which, in his view, involved "the conquering of an Evil at a less expence [*sic*] of Punishment than could be done in the direct way." "Indirect Legislation," Bentham Papers in the Library of University College, London, lxxxvii at 42, quoted in *ibid* at 14. Punishment remained part of the calculus, but Bentham also allowed for interventions that operated less by direct interdiction than through secondary phenomena. See Angela Marciniak, "'Prevention of Evil, Production of Good': Jeremy Bentham's Indirect Legislation and Its Contribution to a New Theory of Prevention" (2017) 43:1 *Hist Eur Ideas* 83 at 92.

188 Bentham, *Theory of Legislation, supra* note 81 at 14–15. See also Jeremy Bentham, *An Introduction to the Principles of Morals and Legislation* (Oxford: Clarendon Press, 1876) at 2 [Bentham, *Morals and Legislation*].

189 Bentham, *Theory of Legislation, supra* note 81 at 28.

190 Bentham, *Morals and Legislation, supra* note 188 at 3.

191 Stephen Leslie, *The English Utilitarians* (London: Duckworth & Co, 1900), vol 2 at 138.

of population was the most essential article" of the Utilitarian faith.[192] In essence, Malthus identified a disjunction between the geometrical increase of population and the arithmetical increase in the means of subsistence;[193] in other words, population tends to increase at a faster rate than the food supply.[194] Absent (moral or regulatory) intervention, he argued, a workable proportion between population and subsistence was maintained through "misery and vice"; that is, natural and man-made disasters periodically reduce the population to levels that can be supported by the available means of production. To ameliorate the chances of devastating forms of population decrease, Malthus directed attention to the need for governmental and individual measures to control population growth and hence improve the condition of the population. Institutional reform and moral restraint thus went hand-in-hand. On the former front, "two measures would obviously be necessary; private property must be instituted in order to stimulate prudence; and marriage must be instituted to make men responsible for the increase of the population."[195] Property rights were the necessary precondition for a spirit of independence and the avoidance of over-reliance on charity,[196] while marriage amounted to an institutional framework for the proper reproduction of the population. In turn, these laws respecting property and marriage would, Malthus said, encourage moral restraint by inculcating a desire among the population to improve their own condition. Law and morality were, therefore, the means proposed by Malthus to avoid a state of hopeless poverty and depression, and instead improve the condition of the population.

---

192 *Ibid.*

193 In this respect, Malthus' reliance on statistics, however inaccurate, may be viewed as an instance of 'the science of government' that Foucault speaks of in his discussion of population management: see Foucault, *STP, supra* note 6 at 104.

194 Leslie, *supra* note 191 at 148. Malthus by no means viewed population increase as an intrinsic evil – "when it follows in its natural order [it] is both a great positive good in itself, and absolutely necessary" for an increase in wealth: *ibid* at 165 quoting The Rev Thomas R Malthus, *An Essay on the Principle of Population; or, A View of its Past and Present Effects on Human Happiness; with an inquiry into our prospects respecting the future removal or mitigation of the evils which its occasions*, 6th ed. (London: John Murray, 1826), vol 2 at 241.

195 Leslie, *supra* note 191 at 151.

196 *Ibid* at 177.

Chapter Two

The Invention of Family Law in English Scholarly Legal Thought

Family law did not always exist; rather, it was invented.[1]

I. Introduction

Nineteen fifty-seven was a momentous year for English Family Law. The centenary of the *Matrimonial Causes Act 1857*,[2] it also saw the emergence (after a lengthy gestational period) of the field of family law as an academic and conceptual category with the publication of Peter Bromley's treatise *Family Law*, and R.H. Graveson and F.R. Crane's edited collection of essays, *A Century of Family Law*.[3] In a review of the latter work published in 1959, the German legal scholar Wolfram

---

1 Janet Halley and Kerry Rittich, "Critical Directions in Comparative Family Law: Genealogies and Contemporary Studies of Family Law Exceptionalism" (2010) 58:4 *Am J Comp L* 753 at 755.

2 *An Act to amend the Law relating to Divorce and Matrimonial Causes in England 1857*, 20 & 21 Vict, c 85. The preceding year had also seen the publication of the *Royal Commission on Marriage and Divorce Report 1951–1955* (London: HM Stationary Office, 1956).

3 Peter M. Bromley, *Family Law* (London: Butterworths, 1957); R.H. Graveson and F.R. Crane, *A Century of Family Law, 1857–1957* (London: Sweet & Maxwell, 1957). As discussed in Part VIII, these works were not the first to use the term "Family Law" to describe the field of law governing relations between husbands and wives, and parents and children. The *Digest of English Civil Law* (Edward Jenks, ed., *A Digest of English Civil Law*, 5 vols (London: Butterworth & Co, 1905–17) [Jenks, *Digest*]) included a book entitled *Family Law*. In 1953 Jack Hamawi published a text also entitled *Family Law* (London: Stevens, 1953). Hamawi's work was not, however, especially well received, and subsequent scholars have tended to mark the emergence of the field by reference to Bromley's, and Graveson and Crane's, respective works. As parts IV and VI also note, the term "family law" is, if not a direct legal transplant from German legal thought (notably the work of Friedrich Carl von Savigny), at the very least a product of its influence.

Müller-Freienfels noted that, "a few years ago there existed in England no topic of legal instruction called 'family law.' Reference was commonly made only to 'domestic relations.'"[4] *A Century of Family Law* was, unsurprisingly, concerned with the history of the law concerning family relations in the century from 1857 to 1957; it did not, however, deal with the development of the field of Family Law as an autonomous legal-intellectual domain – an omission suggested by the work's arguably anachronistic title.[5] A similar elision is evident in Bromley's *Family Law*, which commenced with a consideration of "The Nature and Scope of Family Law," but did not address the intellectual dimensions of the shift from Domestic Relations to Family Law, and the crucial role played by legal scholars in the disaggregation of the legal family from its progenitor: the household.[6] These observations are not intended as criticism. As works effectively establishing the field, it would have been premature – and arguably hubristic – for the authors and editors to include consideration of the lineaments of this barely completed process of taxonomic change.

Yet the elision has largely continued. In the most recent (2015) edition of Bromley's text, by Gillian Douglas and Nigel Lowe, there is no discussion of the historical significance of the original work, or the moves that facilitated its emergence.[7] In the 2015 edition of Frances Burton's *Family Law*, the opening paragraph declares that, "it is essential to understand the context in which this area of law now operates, [and] the origins from which it has come."[8] Noting that "Family law as a separate discipline, and especially as an academic subject of study, is of fairly recent invention: credit for this usually goes to the late Professor Peter Bromley," the text then goes on to consider the "historical, cultural and conceptual timeline" – but only from 1957.[9] "Naturally," Burton acknowledges, "there was a corpus of family law before that date," but the dimensions of its

---

4 Wolfram Müller-Freienfels, "Book Reviews: Graveson, R.H. – Crane, F.R. (eds.) *A Century of Family Law 1857–1957*. London: Sweet & Maxwell Ltd., 1957. P. xviii, 459" (1959) 8:1 *Am J Comp L* 92 at 92.

5 *Cf.* Rebecca Probert, "Family Law – A Modern Concept?" [2004] *Family Law* 901.

6 Halley and Rittich, *supra* note 1.

7 Nigel Lowe and Gillian Douglas, *Bromley's Family Law*, 11th ed. (Oxford: Oxford University Press, 2015). The same can be said of earlier editions of the work. This is not to suggest that historical discussion is entirely absent from the 2011 edition, but as the authors expressly declare, "this book … is concerned with family policy and regulation as it is currently elaborated in the law," at 3.

8 Frances Burton, *Family Law*, 2nd ed. (London: Taylor & Francis, 2015) at 2.

9 *Ibid.*

historical development (including the fact that this corpus of law was not generally known as "family law" until the mid-twentieth century), or at least its intellectual dimensions, are left untouched.[10] Similarly, Rebecca Probert and Maebh Harding in the most recent edition of *Cretney and Probert's Family Law* note that "[t]he scope of 'family law' as a subject is in part dictated by convenience and the need to identify a coherent body of law that fits into the confines of the standard university course," and refer to Lord Evershed's functionalist description of the field in *A Century of Family Law* as simply "a convenient means of reference to so much of our law … as directly affects that essential unit of the English social structure, the family."[11] Convenience and pedagogy are certainly part of the story, but a distinctly intellectual concern with taxonomy and legal boundaries also played an important role.

The notable exception to this general lack of attention to the intellectual dimensions of Family Law's emergence is in fact an article written by Müller-Freienfels, nearly 50 years after his review of *A Century of Family Law*, entitled "The Emergence of *Droit de Famille* and *Familienrecht* in Continental Europe and the Introduction of Family Law in England."[12] The paper is a brilliant exercise in comparative legal history, providing important detail on the emergence of Family Law in England in the twentieth century, and linking those elements to earlier developments in civilian thought. However, like the texts mentioned above, it largely ignores the nineteenth century and the efforts of English jurists in that period to fashion a freestanding law of the family. In response to Müller-Freienfels, Rebecca Probert penned a short piece pointing out the importance of the *Matrimonial Causes Act 1857*, and the existence of nineteenth-century texts that foreshadowed the emergence of Family

---

10 *Ibid.*

11 Rebecca Probert and Maebh Harding, *Cretney and Probert's Family Law*, 10th ed. (London: Sweet & Maxwell, 2018) at 4 quoting from Graveson and Crane, *supra* note 3 at vii-viii. In a similar vein, see Sonia Harris-Short, Joanna Miles and Rob George, *Family Law: Text, Cases, and Materials*, 3rd ed. (Oxford: Oxford University Press, 2015); and Mary Welstead and Susan Edwards, *Family Law*, 4th ed. (Oxford: Oxford University Press, 2013). See also John Dewar and Stephen Parker, "English Family Law since World War II: From Status to Chaos" in Sanford N. Katz, John Eekelaar and Mavis Maclean, eds., *Cross Currents: Family Law and Policy in the United States and England* (Oxford: Oxford University Press, 2010) 123.

12 Wolfram Müller-Freienfels, "The Emergence of *Droit de Famille* and *Familienrecht* in Continental Europe and the Introduction of Family Law in England" (2003) 28:1 *J Fam Hist* 31.

Law as a discrete field.[13] It is a useful starting point, but there is a great deal more that can and in my view ought to be said about the intellectual and textual development of the field.

Again, no criticism is intended by these observations. Müller-Freienfels was expressly concerned with the *introduction* of Family Law in England, not its historical evolution. Douglas and Lowe follow the arrangement of Bromley's original text, opening the work, as he did, with a discussion of "The Nature and Scope of Family Law" (though updating Bromley's hetero-normative description of the family with a more neutral reference to "a basic social unit constituted by at least two people").[14] They, and the authors of the other leading texts mentioned above are, I suspect, more than justified in excluding what is admittedly a relatively niche concern with intellectual and taxonomical developments from works oriented towards students and those who want to understand the law in its present form. Nevertheless, this has left something of a lacuna within the literature on the development of Family Law in England.

This chapter seeks to fill in some of these gaps,[15] and in the process to expose the profoundly constructed and contingent nature of Family Law as a modern legal category, making "its historicity and its varying ideological investments discernable and available for resistance."[16] Heeding the call in recent scholarship on FLE to "study[] its emergence as well as global diffusion,"[17] and drawing on a critical tradition that emphasizes the importance of intellectual legal history and the constitutive role of scholarly texts in developing law and legal consciousness,[18]

---

13 Probert, *supra* note 5. See also Dewar and Parker, *supra* n 11 at 124–5.

14 Lowe and Douglas, *supra* note 7 at 2.

15 See David Sugarman, "Legal Theory, the Common Law Mind and the Making of the Textbook Tradition" in William Twining, ed., *Legal Theory and Common Law* (Oxford: Basil Blackwell 1986) 26 at 28 (noting "the lack of an adequate intellectual history of modern legal education and thought in England").

16 Janet Halley, "What Is Family Law? A Genealogy. Part I" (2011) 23:1 *Yale JL & Human* 1 at 95; Halley and Rittich, *supra* note 1 at 754–5. On a broader level this stance shares characteristics of Unger's "antinecessitarian" approach to social circumstances: Roberto Mangabeira Unger, *False Necessity: Anti-Necessitarian Social Theory in the Service of Radical Democracy. Part I of Politics: A Work in Constructive Social Theory* (Cambridge, MA: Cambridge University Press, 1987) at 12. See also Karl E. Klare, "Labor Law as Ideology: Toward a New Historiography of Collective Bargaining Law" (1981) 4 *Indus Rel LJ* 450.

17 Halley and Rittich, *supra* note 1 at 754.

18 See Robert W. Gordon, "Critical Legal Histories" (1984) 36 *Stan L Rev* 57; Susanna L. Blumenthal, "Of Mandarins, Legal Consciousness, and the Cultural Turn in US Legal History: Robert W. Gordon. 1984. Critical Legal Histories. *Stanford Law Review*

the chapter traces the emergence of Family Law[19] as an autonomous legal domain within English scholarly[20] legal thought.[21] It thus contributes to existing work on the development of laws concerning the family by foregrounding "internal juridical modes of thought and conceptualization";[22] a move that is designed to complement sociological and functionalist accounts, and enrich understanding of the field's multiple histories.

The chapter provides a genealogy of conceptual and taxonomical change spanning a nearly 200-year period via close readings of a range of primarily English, but also American and German subject-specific

---

36: 57–125" (2012) 37:1 *Law & Soc Inquiry* 167; Angela Fernandez and Markus D. Dubber, "Introduction: Putting the Legal Treatise in Its Place" in Angela Fernandez and Markus D. Dubber, eds., *Law Books in Action: Essays on the Anglo-American Legal Treatise* (Oxford: Hart, 2012) 1 at 5.

19 This process of emergence tracked, reflected, and helped to shape broader cultural visions of the private, non-economic family made up of a married couple and their children. This chapter, however, is only concerned with the specifically legal dimensions of this process. On broader changes in conceptions of and attitudes towards the family see, e.g., Leonore Davidoff and Catherine Hall, *Family Fortunes: Men and Women of the English Middle Class 1780–1850*, revised ed. (London: Routledge, 2002); John R. Gillis, *For Better, For Worse: British Marriages, 1600 to the Present* (New York: Oxford University Press, 1985) [Gillis, *For Better, For Worse*]; Carole Pateman, *The Sexual Contract* (Palo Alto: Stanford University Press, 1988); Wally Seccombe, *A Millennium of Family Change: Feudalism to Capitalism in Northwestern Europe* (London: Verso, 1992).

20 Judges and legislators were, of course, critical players in the development of the laws governing work and family. Mention is made here of certain key cases and statutory developments (on cases see the discussion of *Duntze v Levett* in part III and *Brook v Brook* (*infra* note 258); on legislation see Part V) but the overriding focus is scholarly texts, partly for reasons of scope, but more substantively because I want to show how scholars effected change in the architecture of law.

21 Kennedy and Fisher define legal thought as "the way legal minds – lawyers, judges, scholars – thought about law itself": David Kennedy and William W. Fisher III, "Introduction" in David Kennedy and William W. Fisher III, eds., *The Canon of American Legal Thought* (Princeton: Princeton University Press, 2006) 1. Duncan Kennedy uses the term "legal consciousness," which refers to "the particular form of consciousness that characterizes the legal profession as a social group, at a particular moment" – it is "the body of ideas through which lawyers experience legal issues": Duncan Kennedy, *The Rise & Fall of Classical Legal Thought* (Washington, DC: Beard Books, 2006) at 3 [Kennedy, *Rise & Fall*].

22 Simon Deakin and Frank Wilkinson, *The Law of the Labour Market: Industrialization, Employment and Legal Evolution* (Oxford: Oxford University Press, 2005) at 28.

treatises,[23] works of analytical and historical jurisprudence,[24] and institutional texts.[25] Beginning with William Blackstone's household model of "private œconomical relations,"[26] which grouped together the laws of master and servant, husband and wife, and parent and child, the chapter suggests that the invention of English Family Law hinged on two inter-related shifts in legal thought.[27] The basic outlines of these shifts are encapsulated in Figure 2.1.

---

23 The term "treatise" as it is used here corresponds with T.F.T. Plucknett's discussion of the modern English textbook: "It begins with a definition of the subject matter, and proceeds by logical and systematic stages to cover the whole field. The result is to present the law in a strictly deductive framework, with the implication that in the beginning there were principles, and that in the end those principles were found to cover a large multitude of cases deducible from them." T.F.T. Plucknett, *Early English Legal Literature* (Cambridge: Cambridge University Press, 1958) 19, quoted in A.W.B. Simpson, "The Rise and Fall of the Legal Treatise: Legal Principles and the Forms of Legal Literature" (1981) 48:3 *U Chicago L Rev* 632 at 633.

24 Most notably, in the analytical vein, John Austin's *Lectures on Jurisprudence or The Philosophy of Positive Law*, 4th ed., edited by Robert Campbell (London: John Murray, 1873) [Austin, *Lectures*]; and, in the historical vein, Friedrich Carl von Savigny's *System of the Modern Roman Law*, translated by William Holloway (Madras: J. Higginbotham, 1867) [Savigny, *System*].

25 Such as Blackstone's *Commentaries on the Laws of England* (Oxford: Clarendon Press 1765–9) [Blackstone, *Commentaries*], which continued in the vein of Roman legal science, most notably, the *Institutes* of Gaius: Simpson, *supra* note 23 at 632 note 2, 633–4.

26 Blackstone, *Commentaries*, *supra* note 25, book I at 410.

27 The nineteenth century also saw the beginnings of a move towards centralizing parent-child relations within the sphere of what eventually became Family Law, but it was not until the twentieth century and the emergence of the field out of the ashes of Domestic Relations that parent-child relations came to occupy anything like their present, arguably dominant position: see, e.g., Gillian Douglas, "Marriage, Cohabitation, and Parenthood – from Contract to Status?" in Katz, Eekelaar and Maclean, *supra* note 11 at 211, 212; Harris-Short, Miles and George, *supra* note 11 at 2; Probert and Harding, *supra* note 11 at 2; Dewar and Parker, *supra* note 11 at 131. Accordingly, this chapter focusses almost exclusively on the shifts pertaining to marriage and work, leaving to one side the evolution of parent-child relations. For a very brief overview of changes in the law of parent-child relations see chapter 1, note 22. For discussion of parent-child relations prior to the eighteenth century see Holly Brewer, "The Transformation of Domestic Law" in Michael Grossberg and Christopher Tomlins, eds., *The Cambridge History of Law in America: Volume I, Early America (1580–1815)* (New York: Cambridge University Press, 2008) at 288. For an incisive examination of changes in the law of child custody in nineteenth-century England and their relationship to the development of Family Law see Danaya C. Wright, "The Crisis of Child Custody: A History of the Birth of Family Law in England" (2002) 11:2 *Colum J Gender & L* 175.

Figure 2.1. From the law of the household to Family Law

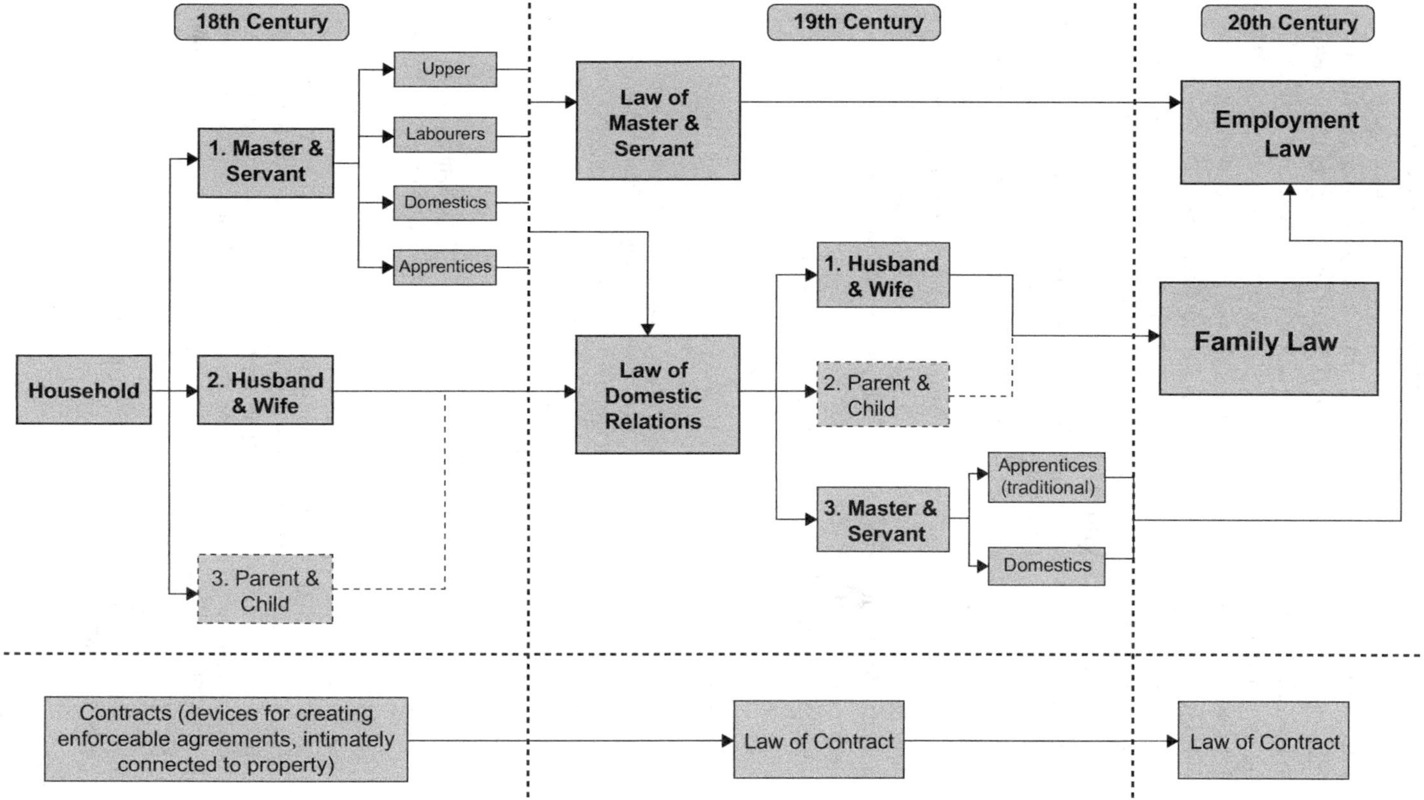

One movement involved the staged extrusion of productive work relations (in the narrow sense of work for pay) from the household. This process involved re-characterizing most forms of work as market-based activities exterior to the family, and locating those relations within an increasingly freestanding Law of Master and Servant, which became the general legal template for the regulation of wage labour in the eighteenth and nineteenth centuries through an interplay of legislation, case-law and scholarly texts.[28] Certain household-based forms of work, notably domestic service and apprenticeship, remained nested within the legal household – or the Law of Domestic Relations, as it became known, until the twentieth century when they too were shifted into the domain of work.[29] The final step in this process was the re-characterization of the Law of Master and Servant as the Law of Employment – a move that responded to the late nineteenth-century removal of criminal penalties for workers' breach of contract,[30] and which resulted in some scholars making a further (questionable[31]) move towards characterizing Employment Law as a specialized branch of the Law of Contract.[32] (To be clear, this chapter deliberately refrains from theorizing the process by which the modern contract of employment emerged.[33] At times I refer to the nature of work relations in particular texts or periods of time, but this

---

28 Robert J. Steinfeld, *The Invention of Free Labor: The Employment Relation in English and American Law and Culture, 1350–1870* (Chapel Hill: University of North Carolina Press, 1991) [Steinfeld, *Free Labor*]; Christopher L. Tomlins, *Freedom Bound: Law, Labor, and Civic Identity in Colonizing English America, 1580–1865* (New York: Cambridge University Press 2010).

29 Which is not to say that those relations were treated equally in law: domestic service, for instance, remained outside of most legal regulation owing to its *situs* in the home.

30 See chapter 3.

31 The continued existence of nineteenth-century common law obligations of loyalty that in practice subordinated workers' interests to those of their employers necessarily undermined the idea that relations between employers and employees, as they were coming to be known, were contractual in ways analogous to commercial contracts. In this respect, the move can be seen as ideological rather than empirical: treatise writers *wanted* employment relations to fit within the paradigm of contractual freedom, but in legal reality they simply didn't because of the lingering influence of nineteenth-century master and servant law. In this respect, the development of the contract of employment, hedged as it was on all sides by rights and obligations that parties could not, or only with extreme difficulty, contract out of, resembles in important ways the development of the marriage contract traced in this chapter.

32 Jenks, *Digest, supra* note 3.

33 See further Deakin and Wilkinson, *supra* note 22 at 28; Steinfeld, *Free Labor, supra* note 28; Tomlins, *supra* note 28.

is done with a view to locating those relations in the broader context of the story being told here: the emergence of Family Law.)

Running in parallel with these shifts in the legal conceptualization and placement of work relations was an emphasis on the public importance of, and state involvement in, marriage; and a corresponding elevation of the husband-wife relation to the forefront of Domestic Relations, and eventually Family Law. This movement occurred in part through a structural repositioning of the husband-wife relation at the front of the various Domestic Relations. It also involved a more complex effort by scholars to distinguish the emerging Law of Contract (which was only consolidated into an abstract form modelled on commercial relations and an ideological commitment to the market-based realization of individual wills in the second half of the nineteenth century[34]) from household-based relations that were seen as not "properly" contractual because of superadded elements that individuals could not "will" their way out of using contract.[35] In particular, scholars (and judges) began to question whether marriage was, as Blackstone put it, "a civil contract,"[36] or whether the non-modifiable terms accompanying marriage, which derived from the social and political significance of marriage as a tool for the management of the population,[37] lent it the character of (achieved rather than ascribed) status.[38] Over the course of the nineteenth century, this view of marriage as status gained ground, and the essence of marriage, at least in legal terms, came to be seen as the

---

34 See, e.g., Hugh Collins, "Contract and Legal Theory" in Twining, *supra* note 15 at 137.

35 See Kennedy, *Rise & Fall*, *supra* note 21 at 185–206. Treatise writers were not denying that household relations could and did involve the exercise of individual will; the marriage relation, for instance, remained grounded in the consent of the parties. What they were saying was that the imposition of a suite of rights and obligations by the state lent relations such as marriage a public character that distinguished them from the private and putatively *wholly* intention-based relations of commercial parties. That construction of commercial relations was, however, more ideological than empirical since true "freedom of contract," if it ever existed, did so for only a very brief period in the late nineteenth century. See Patrick S. Atiyah, *The Rise and Fall of Freedom of Contract* (Oxford: Clarendon Press, 1979) at 231–6.

36 Blackstone, *Commentaries*, *supra* note 25, book I at 421.

37 Michel Foucault, *Security, Territory, Population. Lectures at the Collège de France, 1977–1978*, edited by Michel Senellart, translated by Graham Burchell (New York: Vintage, 2007) at 103–5.

38 This modern form of status, which looks to the degree of intervention by the state in a particular relation, differs from the hierarchical and patriarchal form associated with heritable conditions such as slavery. See generally R.H. Graveson, *Status in the Common Law* (London: Athlone, 1953). See further chapter 1, note 118; and *Salvesen (or Von Lorang) v Administrator of Austrian Property* [1927] AC 641.

degree of state involvement in its formation, subsistence, and eventually its dissolution.[39] At the same time, though, scholars never dispensed entirely with the idea that contract was the formal legal device by which the status of marriage was created (or achieved).[40] In other words, the creation of marriage, or at least its initial underlying exchange of promises, remained contractual, but the degree of state regulation of actually existing marriages lent those relations the legal character of status. The same can be said of the much more famously posited legal move from status to contract:[41] the Law of Contract arose in the nineteenth century based on an ideological commitment to the realization of individual wills,[42] but in reality freedom of contract (especially in the case of work) was, even at the very apex of laissez-faire thinking, subject to varying degrees of governmental regulation.[43]

In constructing the genealogy of legal thought that follows, I have drawn significant insights from Janet Halley's emphasis on the movement within nineteenth-century American legal thought *away* from a conception of marriage as contract and *towards* a status-based understanding of the relation.[44] However, this chapter also differs from Halley's work by paying greater attention to the extrusion of work relations from the productive household, and the processes by which the Law of Master and Servant, and eventually Employment Law, emerged as fields distinct from Domestic Relations and Family Law. I am also more concerned than Halley with the purely scholarly dimensions of

---

39 In *social* terms one of the primary functions of marriage in the nineteenth century came to be seen, broadly speaking, as companionate relations between husbands and wives: Michael Anderson, *Approaches to the History of the Western Family 1500–1914* (Cambridge: Cambridge University Press, 1995) at 30; Frances Olsen, "The Family and the Market: A Study of Ideology and Legal Reform" (1983) 96:7 *Harv L Rev* 1497 at 1521; Seccombe, *supra* note 19 at 235.

40 This hybridity bears some resemblance to the more recent idea of "contract-status," which "denotes the idea that contracts in modern society are more often than not created by way of formal agreement only to subsequently be governed by 'status'-like or relational elements": Katharina Isabel Schmidt, "Henry Maine's 'Modern Law': From Status to Contract and Back Again?" (2017) 65:1 *Am J Comp L* 145 at 179.

41 Henry Sumner Maine, *Ancient Law* (New York: Dorset Press, 1986) at 141: "the movement of the progressive societies has hitherto been a movement *from Status to Contract*" (emphasis in original).

42 Hugh Collins has pointed out that "the classical requirement of consent or agreement for the creation of contractual obligations provides a justification for the obligation, which appears compatible with respect for individual liberty, and, at the same time, the need for consent preserves that liberty from unwanted imposed obligations": Collins, *supra* note 34 at 136. See also Atiyah, *supra* note 35 at 235–6.

43 See generally Atiyah, *supra* note 35, chapters 16 and 21.

44 Halley, *supra* note 16.

this process; for this reason, I avoid almost entirely discussion of cases, concentrating instead on scholarly legal texts. I also propose a slightly different reading of the move from contract to status within the law of marriage – one that is perhaps simply explained by the different jurisdictional focus. In essence, where Halley discerns a relatively clear movement from contract to status in nineteenth-century American marriage law, I see a slightly more textured transition at work in England – one in which status certainly became the operative legal category governing marriage,[45] but in which contract remained the legal-conceptual basis through which the relation arose.

As Halley's work in other contexts demonstrates, oscillations between status and contract are not merely of antiquarian interest but continue to inform and frame debates around new modes of relationship recognition, most noticeably the status-based arguments deployed by proponents of same-sex marriage.[46] Halley is by no means alone in deploying the language of status and contract to explain and consider the boundaries of modern family (and commercial[47]) law. The continued valence of these terms as shorthand descriptors denoting, for instance, the tension between regulation and paternalism, and individual freedom, is also apparent in modern English discussions of Family Law. Douglas and Lowe, for instance, observe that while the definition and alteration of status was historically the law's main role owing to medieval and early modern concerns with property, more recent times have seen a shift in favour of granting people "greater freedom ... to shape and agree the legal consequences of their personal relationships."[48] While this remains "an important trend ... the extension of marriage to same sex couples ... the automatic acquisition of parental responsibility by unmarried fathers so long as they are named on the child's birth certificate and the fact that extra-marital cohabitation already attracts certain legal consequences suggests that relationship status is still an important source of legal rights."[49] Other scholars such as Jonathan Herring have suggested that "family law is moving away from placing weight on status and is instead focussing more on the intent of the parties"[50] – a sentiment echoed by

---

45 Kennedy, *Rise & Fall, supra* note 21 at 185.

46 Janet Halley, "Behind the Law of Marriage (I): From Status/Contract to the Marriage System" (2010) 6 *Unbound* 1 at 4–12.

47 See, e.g., Schmidt, *supra* note 40.

48 Douglas and Lowe, *supra* note 7 at 3.

49 *Ibid.* See also John Eekelaar, "The End of an Era?" (2003) 28:1 *J Fam Hist* 108.

50 Jonathan Herring, "Introduction" in Jonathan Herring, ed., *Family Law: Issues, Debates,* Policy (Milton Park: Willan, 2001) 1 at 4–5; see also Gillian Douglas,

Joanna Miles in the wake of the UK Supreme Court's decision in *Radmacher v Granatino*,[51] in which she characterized the judgment in distinctly Maine-like[52] language as "an important staging post in the evolution of English law's attitude to marital agreements and the movement of English marriage law along the spectrum 'from status to contract.'"[53] Jens Martin Scherpe and Brian Sloan have advanced a slightly different reading of English marriage law in the wake of *Radmacher*; drawing on Baroness Hale's dissent in that case, in which she noted that "the parties are not free to determine all its legal consequences for themselves [and] [t]hey contract into the package which the law of the land lays down," they insist that "both aspects of marriage are indeed reflected in English Law."[54]

In view of the ongoing currency of status and contract within modern discussions of English (and Canadian, American, and global[55]) family law, it seems both useful and, from an historical perspective, necessary to pay particular attention to the ways in which scholars deployed these terms in the process of constructing the field of Family Law. In this latter

---

"Marriage, Cohabitation, and Parenthood – from Contract to Status" in Katz, Eekelaar and McLean, *supra* note 11, 211 at 231.

51   [2010] UKSC 42; [2011] 1 AC 534 [*Radmacher*] (upholding the validity of an ante-nuptial agreement in calculating maintenance).

52   Maine, *supra* note 41.

53   Joanna Miles, "Marriage and Divorce in the Supreme Court and the Law Commission: For Love or Money?" (2011) 74:3 *Mod L Rev* 430 (referring to Stephen Cretney, "From Status to Contract" in Francis Rose, ed., *Consensus Ad Idem: Essays in the Law of Contract in Honour of Guenter Treitel* (London: Sweet & Maxwell, 1996)).

54   Jens Martin Scherpe and Brian Sloan, "Contractualisation of Family Law in England & Wales: Autonomy vs Judicial Discretion" in Frederik Swennen, *Contractualisation of Family Law – Global Perspectives* (Cham: Springer, 2015) 165 at 178–9 (citing *Radmacher* [2010] UKSC 42; [2011] 1 AC 534 at [132]) [Swennen, *Contractualisation*]. See also Swennen's chapter in the same volume, which identified trends across the 27 countries surveyed in the volume, and adopts the language of status and contract to theorize the move towards private ordering in European family law: Frederik Swennen, "Private Ordering in Family Law: A Global Perspective" in Swennen, *supra* note 54, 1 [Swennen, "Private Ordering"].

55   See, e.g., Swennen, "Private Ordering," *supra* note 54; Robert Leckey, "Shifting Scrutiny: Private Ordering in Family Matters in Common-Law Canada" in Swennen, *Contractualisation, supra* note 54; Elizabeth S. Scott and Robert E. Scott, "From Contract to Status: Collaboration and the Evolution of Novel Family Relationships" (2015) 115:2 *Colum L Rev* 293; Brian Bix, "Private Ordering and Family Law" (2010) 23:2 *J Am Academy Mat L* 249; Emily Stolzenberg, "The New Family Freedom" (2018) 59:6 *Boston College L Rev* 1984; Jill Elaine Hasday, "The Canon of Family Law" (2004) 57:3 *Stan L Rev* 825; Mary Ann Glendon, *The Transformation of Family Law: State, Law, and Family in the United States and Western Europe* (Chicago: University of Chicago Press, 1989).

respect, the chapter supplements and complicates Henry Maine's thesis concerning "the movement of the progressive societies ... *from Status to Contract*"[56] by showing how a new, specifically legal form of status centred upon state-imposed, non-modifiable conditions attaching to consensual relations[57] (a form that Maine was aware of but which he deliberately excluded from his posited movement[58]) arose and largely (but not entirely) supplanted contract as the ordering legal principle in family relations – at least until the mid-twentieth century, when this chapter concludes. It also shows that the notion of individual will *was* used as an ordering principle in certain areas of nineteenth-century English law and legal thought (a movement towards contract), *but* that this move (like Maine's dictum) was as much ideological as empirical given the degree of regulation that attended most contract-making[59] – especially, in the present context, contracts for work and service.

The critical emphasis on legal thought and scholarly texts[60] in this chapter also connects the relatively narrow doctrinal story presented here with much broader questions in eighteenth and nineteenth century legal thought concerning the nature of law and the structure of the English legal system.[61] In particular, many jurists in this period were concerned with the question of whether English law, despite its historical obsession with procedure,[62] was capable of systematic arrangement

---

56 Maine, *supra* note 41.

57 See Graveson, *supra* note 38.

58 Maine's aphorism was limited to Status in the sense of "personal conditions" deriving from "the powers and privileges anciently residing in the Family"; he "avoid[ed] applying the term to such conditions as are the immediate or remote result of agreement." In other words, Maine was only suggesting a movement away from traditional, patriarchal (ascribed) status towards relations based on "the free agreement of Individuals"; modern, legal (achieved) status he left to one side. Maine, *supra* note 41 at 140–1.

59 Atiyah, *supra* note 35, chapters 16 and 21.

60 See Gordon, *supra* note 18; Blumenthal, *supra* note 18. On legal history as "a mode of *critical analysis of law*" see Markus D. Dubber, "New Historical Jurisprudence: Legal History as Critical Analysis of Law" (2015) 2:1 *Critical Analysis of Law* 1 at 2 (emphasis in original).

61 For example, it was during the nineteenth century that the Law Society of England and Wales "established itself as the predominant voice of the solicitors' profession, the arbiter of admission to the profession and proper conduct, the defender and extender of the profession's monopolies, and an influence of major significance on legislation and legal practice": David Sugarman, "Bourgeois Collectivism, Professional Power and the Boundaries of the State: The Private and Public Life of the Law Society, 1825 to 1914" (1996) 3 *Int'l J Legal Prof* 81.

62 See, e.g., J.H. Baker, *An Introduction to English Legal History*, 3rd ed. (London: Butterworths, 1990) at 63–83. On an institutional level, the clearest indication of

and explication – law "as" a formal scientific system.[63] For all the criticism that may be levelled at Blackstone for the confused structure of his *Commentaries on the Laws of England*,[64] it was the most significant (but by no means the first[65]) attempt to treat the mess of English common law in a scientific manner akin to that seen in Roman law.[66] The subsequent process of disaggregating Blackstone's "private œconomical relations" (the law of the household) into separate domains was part of this larger narrative of English jurisprudential and taxonomical development.[67] As A.V. Dicey argued in his inaugural lecture at Oxford University, there was a need (in his view, to be fulfilled by law professors) to "set forth the law as a coherent whole – to analyse and define legal conceptions – to reduce the mass of legal rules to an orderly series of principles and to aid, stimulate and guide the reform or renovation of legal literature."[68]

---

this move was the procedural fusion of law and equity under the *Supreme Court of Judicature Act 1873*, 36 & 37 Vict, c 56, which abolished the longstanding need to plead legal and equitable causes of action in separate courts.

63 See Catherine L. Fisk and Robert W. Gordon, "'Law As …': Theory and Method in Legal History" (2011) 1:3 *UC Irvine L Rev* 519; Christopher Tomlins and John Comaroff, "'Law As …': Theory and Practice in Legal History" (2011) 1:3 *UC Irvine L Rev* 1039.

64 See, e.g., Duncan Kennedy, "The Structure of Blackstone's Commentaries" (1979) 28:2 Buff L Rev 205 [Kennedy, "Structure"]. Kennedy's other argument – that the *Commentaries* amount to Blackstone's attempt "to legitimate the status quo" (*ibid* at 211) – somewhat resembles aspects of Bentham's philippic against the *Commentaries* in his 1776 *Fragment on Government*. See Jeremy Bentham, *The Collected Works of Jeremy Bentham: A Comment on the Commentaries and A Fragment on Government*, edited by J.H. Burns and H.L.A. Hart (Oxford: Oxford University Press, 1977) at 391–501.

65 The structure of the *Commentaries* clearly indicates the influence of Matthew Hale's *The Analysis of the Law: Being a Scheme, or Abstract, of the Several Titles and Partitions of the Law of England, Digested into Method* (1713), which in turn derived its own divisions in the law from Roman law. See John W. Cairns, "Blackstone, an English Institutist: Legal Literature and the Rise of the Nation State" (1984) 4:3 *Oxford J Leg Stud* 318; Alan Watson, "The Structure of Blackstone's Commentaries" (1988) 97:5 *Yale LJ* 795 at 810–11; Simpson, *supra* note 23 at 640–1.

66 See Daniel J. Boorstin, *The Mysterious Science of the Law* (Cambridge MA: Harvard University Press 1941) at 19–20.

67 For example, Lindsay Farmer convincingly argues that it was only in the nineteenth century that criminal law coalesced into its modern form. Specific crimes obviously existed in earlier times, but "there was no separate understanding of the idea of criminal law as a unified and purposive body of rules – of criminal law as an institution": Lindsay Farmer, *Making the Modern Criminal Law: Criminalization and Civil Order* (Oxford: Oxford University Press, 2016) at 64. For analysis of the development of the English Law of Contract in its broader political and economic context see Atiyah, *supra* note 35.

68 A.V. Dicey, *Can English Law Be Taught At The Universities?* (London, 1883) at 18. This trend within legal thought was part of a broader emphasis within English

The result of this process was more than simply a formal rearrangement of legal categories; it was a shift in the very nature of English law.[69]

II. Blackstone, Legal Science, and the Productive Household

Blackstone's *Commentaries* were published in four volumes between 1765 and 1769, based on lectures he delivered as inaugural Vinerian Professor of English Law at Oxford University.[70] Though generally well received upon publication, the *Commentaries* were much derided among the legal cognoscenti in the wake of Bentham's attack in his *Fragment on Government*.[71] The twentieth century saw a reassessment of Blackstone's achievement, and recognition among many scholars that the *Commentaries* were a crucial step in the shift away from a legal system based around forms of action to one concerned with substantive principles.[72] One explanation for these opposing views is that Blackstone attempted, not altogether successfully, "to reconcile two potentially hostile ways of thinking about law in one framework";[73] in essence, he "wanted to create a theoretically coherent view of English law using a Roman structure."[74]

In the early eighteenth century, legal thought in England remained grounded in the ancient common law – a system based on inductive reasoning and an apparent inner logic, and operating in a responsive manner to issues brought before the courts through the procedurally oriented system of writs and actions.[75] This system stood in contrast to the

---

intellectual life on scientific advancement, most notably the publication in Charles Darwin's *On the Origin of Species* (1859).

69 See Deakin and Wilkinson, *supra* note 22 at 26.

70 See generally Cairns, *supra* note 65; Michael Lobban, "Blackstone and the Science of Law" (1987) 30:2 *Hist J* 311; Simpson, *supra* note 23.

71 Cairns, *supra* note 65 at 318 (noting further attacks in the nineteenth century from John Austin, William James, and Henry Sumner Maine). Later in the nineteenth century, Dicey, in a more measured tone, said that "Blackstone affords us rather an example for encouragement than a model for imitation": Dicey, *supra* note 68 at 30. See further Richard A. Posner, "Blackstone and Bentham" (1976) 19:3 *JL & Econ* 569.

72 See especially S.F.C. Milsom, *The Nature of Blackstone's Achievement* (London, 1981). See also Cairns, *supra* note 65; Lobban, *supra* note 70.

73 Lobban, *supra* note 70 at 312.

74 *Ibid* at 312. See further Blackstone, *Commentaries*, *supra* note 25, book I at 35.

75 Lobban, *supra* note 70 at 313. According to David Lemmings, this meant that barristers were the eighteenth century's "professors of the law," despite a decline in litigation rates when compared to the sixteenth and seventeenth centuries: *David Lemmings, Professors of the Law: Barristers and English Legal Culture in the Eighteenth Century* (New York: Oxford University Press, 2000). The dramatic increase in litigation during those centuries, and the role of lawyers sitting below the elite bar, is canvassed by Christopher W. Brooks in *Pettyfoggers and Vipers of the Commonwealth:*

civilian approach to law as science, a corpus of rules reducible "to a set of self-contained principles set in a mutually supportive system, where one could look at various parts of the system and see a functioning whole."[76] Blackstone attempted to bridge the gap between these two approaches, and according to Michael Lobban, he was the first English writer "to use the Roman structure on its own terms."[77] In his *Analysis of the Laws of England*, which predated the *Commentaries*, Blackstone declared his desire "to mark out a Plan of the laws of ENGLAND, so comprehensive, as that every Title might be reduced under some one of it's [*sic*.] general Heads, which the student might afterwards pursue to any Degree of Minuteness."[78] In the *Commentaries*, Blackstone connected "[t]he science thus committed to his charge, to be cultivated, methodized, and explained in a course of academical lectures" to the "most remarkably deficient" state of legal knowledge among "the gentlemen of England."[79] This deficiency was, in his view, not merely an intellectual stain on English culture, but also undermined the existence of "that science, which is to be the guardian of his natural rights and the rule of civil conduct."[80]

In simplified diagrammatic form, the pertinent aspects of Blackstone's taxonomy of English law look something like the diagram in Figure 2.2. As S.F.C. Milsom noted in his Selden Lecture on "The Nature of Blackstone's Achievement," Blackstone's determination to provide a view of the law from an exterior perspective led him to "reject the arrangement which generations of patchwork treatment ... imposed upon the law," and instead "organize his materials around the relationships of life."[81] Thus, in book I of the *Commentaries*, "Of the Rights of Persons," one finds a distinction between "public relations of magistrates and people," and "private œconomical relations." As chapter XIV of book I proceeds to explain, "[t]he three great relations in private life are, 1. That of *master and servant*; ... 2. That of *husband and wife*; ... 3. That of *parent and child* ...."[82]

The "Lower Branch" of the Legal Profession in Early Modern England (Cambridge: Cambridge University Press, 1986).

76 *Ibid* at 315. For statements concerning his determination to approach law in a scientific manner see William Blackstone, *An Analysis of the Laws of England*, 3rd ed. (Oxford, 1758) at iv [Blackstone, *Analysis*], cited in Lobban, *supra* note 70 at 321. See also Blackstone, *Commentaries*, *supra* note 25, book I at 4.

77 Lobban, *supra* note 70 at 321.

78 Blackstone, *Analysis*, *supra* note 76 at iv, cited in Lobban, *supra* note 70 at 321.

79 Blackstone, *Commentaries*, *supra* note 25, book I at 4.

80 *Ibid*.

81 Milsom, *supra* note 72 at 3.

82 Blackstone, *Commentaries*, *supra* note 25, book I at 410. Blackstone also included Guardian and Ward, and Corporations, within same category. See *supra* note 27 on the rationale for not including those relations in the analysis herein.

Figure 2.2. Blackstone's taxonomy of law

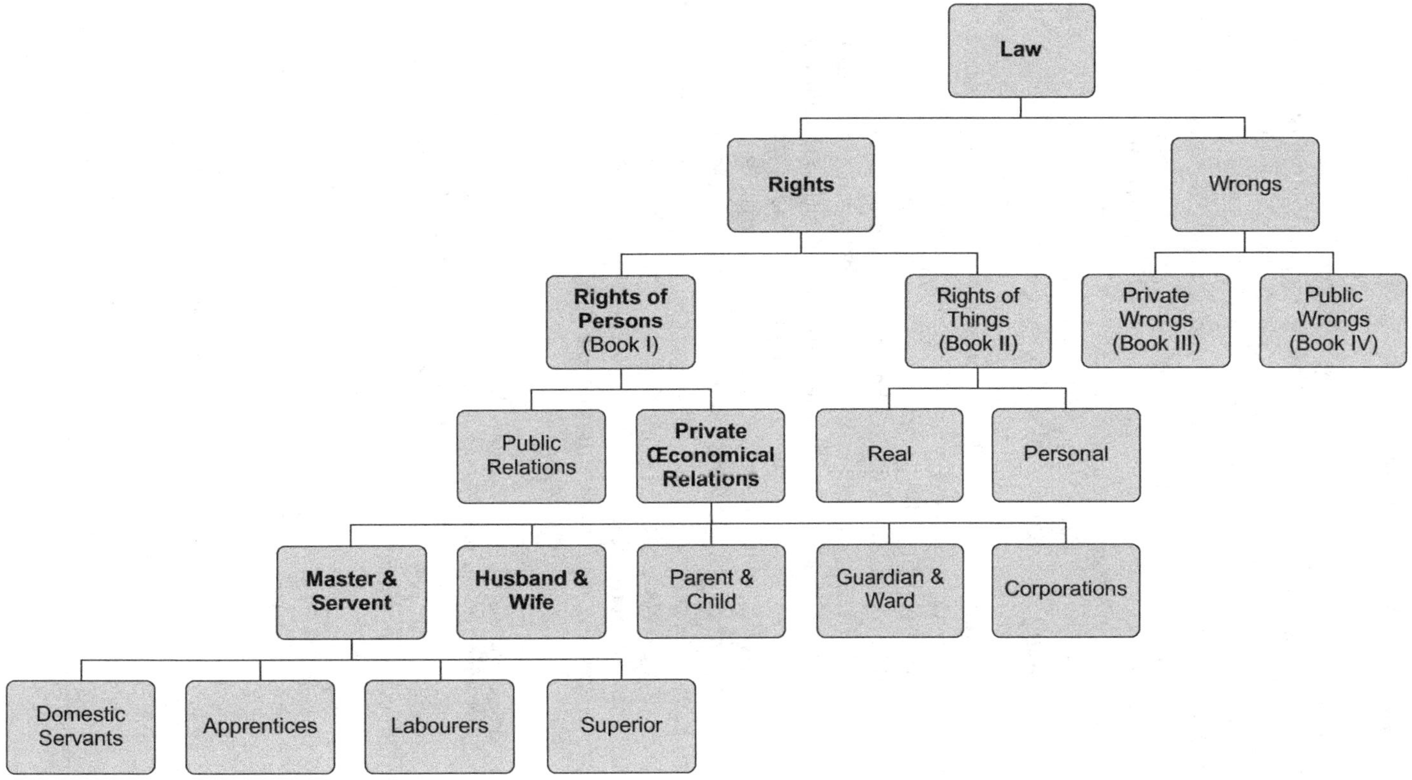

A. The "Private Œconomical Relations"

Blackstone's arrangement of private relations is clearly indebted to Matthew Hale's *The Analysis of the Law of England*,[83] but their collocation also had a strong social basis in the productive household. In the mid-eighteenth century, the term "œconomical" meant, "of or relating to household management, or to the ordering of private affairs; domestic."[84] Thus, in Blackstone's legal scheme, the law of master and servant – governing work relations including domestic service, apprenticeship *and* early forms of wage labour performed by labourers and journeymen – formed part of the same overarching category of legal relations housing those existing between husband and wife, and parent and child. As Otto Kahn-Freund observed in his discussion of Blackstone's treatment of master-servant relations, "[i]n bygone centuries" it was "quite natural" that "the law of master and servant should have appeared in the context of domestic relations" because of the high proportion of "farmers, artisans, and householders employing domestics, and the servants of those persons." [85] In other words, the distinction between family and market, and the corresponding treatment of those domains as private and public (but governed according to their inverse – state (public) regulation for the private family realm, and contractual (private) ordering for the public realm of the market) remained, legally speaking, nascent. On a broader political level, Blackstone's adherence to the household model of "private œconomical relations" can be viewed as a partial exercise in legitimation of the status quo[86] – of the family as a patriarchal, hierarchical, as well as productive, unit of society.

---

83 Hale, *supra* note 65. While there are differences between their schemes, notably Blackstone's treatment of Wrongs as encompassing Remedies, and his distinction within that category between Public and Private, there is striking similarity in the progression of each jurist from Rights of Persons through to (Private) Oeconomical Relations, comprising (in different orders), husband and wife, parent and child, and master and servant. See Watson, *supra* note 65.

84 Halley, *supra* note 16 at 8, quoting Economic Definition B.1.a, *Oxford English Dictionary Online*.

85 Otto Kahn-Freund, "Blackstone's Neglected Child: The Contract of Employment" (1977) 93 *Law Q Rev* 508 at 508–9. Note, though, that in Kahn-Freund's view Blackstone's household-based treatment of work relations reflected an older historical model and was inaccurate by the mid-eighteenth century.

86 "Partial" because his description of these relations, and his broader emphasis on rights, also signals the influence of classical liberal thought. On this dimension of Blackstone's thought, and the legitimating, apologetic aspects of the *Commentaries* see Kennedy, "Structure," *supra* note 64. On the normative dimensions of legal treatises see Fernandez and Dubber, *supra* note 18 at 5.

By the time of the *Commentaries'* publication it seems that this model of the productive household was in a state of decline (the extent is a matter of debate among legal historians[87]) as England moved towards a wage-based system of work,[88] and a more insular approach to domestic life;[89] on a philosophical level, classical patriarchy in the form espoused by Robert Filmer was also collapsing under the weight of Lockean notions of consent and contract.[90] These tensions are reflected in Blackstone's treatment of the "private œconomical relations." As John Cairns has pointed out, Blackstone's approach to the law of persons was based on a society "in which the system of rule – king, nobility, church, commoners – was intimately part of the general societal system affecting not only government but family and other relations between persons."[91] That model, as Michel Foucault observed in *Security, Territory, Population*, began to break apart in the eighteenth century, and the family moved from being a model for government to its modern position as a tool to be used by government.[92] In these respects, the *Commentaries*

---

87 See Kahn-Freund, *supra* note 85 at 508–9 (arguing that by the mid-eighteenth century Blackstone's vision of social ordering was outdated); Cairns, *supra* note 65 at 345–7 (defending Blackstone's treatment of labour relations and household structure); Deakin and Wilkinson, *supra* note 22 at 50–1 (suggesting that Cairns's defence of Blackstone "rests on what is arguably a misperception of the nature of household employment in the period prior to industrialization"). See further John Rule, *The Experience of Labour in Eighteenth-Century Industry* (London: Croom Helm, 1981) at 30 (noting that by the eighteenth century "only a minority of the workers was employed in large-scale production units of any kind" and "factory employment can hardly be at the centre of the concern of the historian of the adult male worker even by the 1790s"); Seccombe, *supra* note 19 at 173 (arguing that until the mid-eighteenth century, "wage income constituted a fairly small fraction of effective demand in the marketplace," but that around the time of the *Commentaries* the move towards wage labour began in earnest).

88 Deakin and Wilkinson, *supra* note 22, chapter 2.

89 Louise A. Tilly and Joan W. Scott, *Women, Work & Family* (New York: Routledge, 1989) chapter 6; Davidoff and Hall, *supra* note 19, chapters 3, 7.

90 See generally Gordon Schochet, *Patriarchalism in Political Thought: The Authoritarian Family and Political Speculation and Attitudes Especially in Seventeenth-Century England* (Oxford: Blackwell, 1975).

91 Cairns, *supra* note 65 at 346. In this respect, as Cairns notes, the *Commentaries* probably performed a legitimating function along the lines of that claimed by Kennedy, "Structure," *supra* note 64, but it must be borne in mind that situating these relations within the law of persons was by no means unusual, and Blackstone was clearly influenced by earlier writers as much (if not more) than by ideology: Cairns, *supra* note 65 at 351.

92 Foucault, *supra* note 37 at 103–5.

point to a world on the cusp of (or already in the process of) dramatic social and legal change.[93]

B. *Master and Servant*

Blackstone divided servants into four classes: domestic or menial servants; apprentices; labourers hired by the day or the week; and those "in a superior, a ministerial, capacity; such as *stewards, factors,* and *bailiffs.*"[94] This division appears to have been based upon the distinctions between groups of workers in the *Statute of Artificers 1562,*[95] which made certain classes of people "not lawfully retained according to the true meaning of this Statute ... [able to] be compelled to be retained to serve in Husbandry by the year, with any person that keepeth Husbandry";[96] and provided for punishment of servants (including artificers and labourers) who refused to perform their duties or who departed from service without notice.[97] Thus, while Blackstone referred to the "contract" between servants and their masters, the law of master and servant was, in Kahn-Freund's words, "largely – in theory, though to a rapidly decreasing extent in practice – the law of the *status* of those liable to be directed to work at wages fixed without their concurrence and liable to be punished for not accepting work on demand."[98] The existence of contract was acknowledged[99] – just as it was in the Elizabethan statute – but it is not possible "to point to juridical recognition of a contract of service or employment" at this juncture, owing to the highly regulated nature of work in the eighteenth century.[100] One of

---

93 Deakin and Wilkinson, *supra* note 22 at 50–1.

94 Blackstone, *Commentaries, supra* note 25, book I at 413–15 (emphasis in original).

95 5 Eliz, c 4. See Deakin and Wilkinson, *supra* note 22 at 45.

96 5 Eliz, c 4, s 5 (spelling modernized).

97 5 Eliz, c 4, ss 6, 10.

98 Kahn-Freund, *supra* note 85 at 513 (emphasis added).

99 Though contract had a very different meaning at this point in time. In essence, contract here must be understood in a manner consonant with the eighteenth-century emphasis on property, and with classical liberalism's acceptance of subordination under contract: the contract between domestic servant and master could be made "for any larger or smaller term" than the standard annual hiring (i.e., a contract for life was possible), and various classes of person were "compellable by two justices to go out to service." See Blackstone, *Commentaries, supra* note 25, book I at 413.

100 Deakin and Wilkinson, *supra* note 22 at 51. In this period, domestic servants, living-in journeymen, and apprentices – whether their entry into service was voluntary or compelled – were considered to be quite literally full-time workers. See L.D. Schwarz, "Custom, Wages and Workload in England During Industrialization" (2007) 197 *Past & Present* 143 at 156–9. Legal handbooks of the period do not discuss

the crucial shifts within scholarly legal thought over the next century and half was a move towards disarticulating work relations from the household and resituating them within the increasingly freestanding Law of Master and Servant (a move that the *Commentaries* actually portend through the placement of different work relations under the banner of Master and Servant[101]). That body of law developed primarily out of a series of eighteenth- and nineteenth-century statutes that expanded criminal penalties for breach of contract by workers, and common law decisions that effectively transformed the deeply subordinating relation between master and *domestic servant* into the general paradigm for wage labour. While criminalization of disobedient workers ended in 1875, common law obligations of loyalty and obedience remained extant, thus fundamentally dispensing with the possibility of a simple transition from status to contract in the employment domain.[102] (In fact, nineteenth-century work contracts resembled status-infused marriage contracts in significant ways.)

C. Husband and Wife

On the topic of marriage, Blackstone was equally insistent that it, too, was a species of contract. Indeed, he declared that English law viewed marriage "in no other light than as a civil contract."[103] "[T]aking it in this civil light," he continued, "the law treats it as it does all other contracts; allowing it to be good and valid in all cases, where the parties at the time of making it were, in the first place, *willing* to contract; secondly, *able* to contract; and, lastly, actually *did* contract, in the proper forms and solemnities required by law."[104] In other words, a valid marriage contract required consent, capacity,[105] and

---

    hours of work because it was understood that such workers were *always* on-call, and amenable to punishment for transgression of their duties: *ibid* at 158 referring to Richard Burn, *The Justice of the Peace, and Parish Officer* (1755 and 1793 editions).

101 This move was not simply the continuation of centuries-old practices but instead "confirmed the emergence of 'master and servant' as a generic legal category applicable to all relations of employment": Tomlins, *supra* note 28 at 350.

102 *Employers and Workmen Act 1875*, 38 & 39 Vict I, c 90. See further Deakin and Wilkinson, *supra* note 22, chapter 2; Steinfeld, *Free Labor, supra* note 28; Douglas Hay, "England, 1562–1875: The Law and Its Uses" in Douglas Hay and Paul Craven, eds., *Masters, Servants, and Magistrates: Britain & the Empire, 1562–1955* (Chapel Hill: University of North Carolina Press, 2004).

103 Blackstone, *Commentaries, supra* note 25, book I at 421.

104 *Ibid*.

105 Capacity to contract marriage referred to the legal and ecclesiastical impediments that would render a marriage void or voidable. Legal impediments included "prior marriage, or having another husband or wife living"; want of age, such that

adherence to form[106] – a position that largely comported with longstanding ecclesiastical law. Canon lawyers had emphasized consent since at least the twelfth century, and according to George Howard, "[t]he theory of the classic canon law, formulated by Gratian [in the twelfth century] … had far-reaching consequences in [English] matrimonial jurisprudence. Marriage became a simple consensual contract."[107] Hitherto, consummation had also been treated as necessary to create an indissoluble bond.[108] Thereafter, though, the distinction arose between present consent (*verba de praesenti*) and future consent (*verba de futuro*). Inspired by the marriage between Joseph and the Virgin Mary, "this theory held that present consent alone created a perfect marriage and an indissoluble bond. Consent, not coitus, makes a marriage valid. Future consent, on the other hand, created an indissoluble union only when followed by sexual relations."[109] It was therefore canonically possible for a valid marriage to occur by the mere exchange of words between the parties (*per verba de praesenti*), though canon law directed (but did not make mandatory) that solemnization should take place in the presence of clergy.[110]

By the time Blackstone wrote, however, *Lord Hardwicke's Act 1753*[111] had modified the ecclesiastical position on consent and imposed formal

---

marriages involving boys under age fourteen and girls under age twelve were "inchoate and imperfect" and able to be declared void by the child upon coming of age; want of consent of parents or guardians; and want of reason. Canonical disabilities included pre-contract, consanguinity, affinity, "and some particular corporal infirmities"; a marriage affected by such incapacity was voidable, and hence until such time valid at common law. *Ibid* at 422–7.

106 See further Halley, *supra* note 16 at 11.

107 George Elliott Howard, *A History of Matrimonial Institutions Chiefly in England and the United States with an Introductory Analysis of the Literature and the Theories of Primitive Marriage and the Family* (Chicago: University of Chicago Press, 1904) at 336 (citation omitted).

108 R.H. Helmholtz, *Marriage Litigation in Medieval England* (Cambridge: Cambridge University Press 1974) at 26.

109 *Ibid*. See also John Witte Jr., *From Sacrament to Contract: Marriage, Religion, and Law in the Western Tradition*, 2nd ed. (Louisville, KY: Westminster John Knox Press, 2012) at 94, 111; Howard, *supra* note 107 at 336–7.

110 Difficulties of proof meant that in practice it was necessary to comport with this direction. However, until the mid-eighteenth century, it was permissible for parties to purchase a licence to marry, or publish banns, in any parish, making possible the evasion of family who might object to an unsuitable match.

111 *An Act for the Better Preventing of Clandestine Marriage 1753* (UK), 26 Geo II, c 33. The Act was designed to preclude clandestine marriages hitherto made with the connivance of willing church officers (so-called "Fleet marriages") by requiring that banns be published in both parties' parishes of residence, or a licence procured in a parish where at least one party had been resident for a minimum of four weeks.

requirements for marriage – thus explaining the description of marriage as a *civil* contract.[112] This element of state control over the marriage relation became crucially important in subsequent legal thought because it inaugurated an idea of marriage as both a relation of significant public interest and an instrumental tool for the governance of the population.[113] Whereas for Blackstone state intervention modified the contractual essence of marriage only insofar as it rendered the contract "civil," nineteenth-century scholars developed the view that the state-imposed non-modifiable aspects of marriage altered the nature of marriage in more fundamental ways, transforming the initial contract into a form of status.

Blackstone's description of marriage as a "contract" treated by "the law … as it does all other contracts" is less easily explained than his "civil" designation, particularly given that there simply was no free-standing Law of Contract in the mid-eighteenth century.[114] In fact, the most sustained discussion of contract in the *Commentaries* is found in chapter 30 of book II, "Of Title by Gift, Grant, and Contract," which in turn forms part of a series of chapters concerned with "Property in Things Personal."[115] This connection between contract and property is hardly surprising in light of English law's general preoccupation with protection of private property.[116] But if contract and property remained conceptually imbricated at this point, what did this mean for the contract of marriage? One possibility is that Blackstone was analogizing marriage to a transfer of personal property. Stephen Cretney has observed that, "[f]or Blackstone, marriage was accurately classified among the

---

The concern in Parliament was primarily with preventing minor children from wealthy families entering into disadvantageous unions. See generally Rebecca Probert, *Marriage Law and Practice in the Long Eighteenth Century* (Cambridge: Cambridge University Press, 2009) chapter 6.

112 Halley, *supra* note 16 at 10.

113 See chapter 5. Marriage remained in part a religious rite, but one "capable of being deployed by the British state for the extension of its administrative power": Lisa O'Connell, "'By Ordinance of Nature': Marriage, Religion and the Modern English State" (2011) 28:2 *Parergon* 149 at 154.

114 James Gordley, *The Philosophical Origins of Modern Contract Doctrine* (Oxford: Clarendon Press, 2011) at 134.

115 Blackstone, *Commentaries, supra* note 25, book II at 440.

116 Atiyah, *supra* note 35 at 90. As Pollock and Maitland observe, "[e]ven in the schemes of Hale and Blackstone it [contract] appears as a mere supplement to the law of property." Frederick Pollock and Frederic William Maitland, *The History of English Law Before the Time of Edward I* (Cambridge: Cambridge University Press, 1895), vol. II at 182.

methods of acquiring property";[117] and from a social perspective this framing makes a certain amount of sense – in earlier times the transfer of personal property is precisely what marriage often involved.[118] As Kennedy has observed, Blackstone's scheme "suggested that the two main concerns of legal actors are the control of other members of a society with fixed social roles, and the control of physical objects that represent power, particularly land."[119]

This being said, it seems equally likely that framing marriage in terms of contract was related to the aforementioned canonical emphasis on consent, particularly in post-Reformation Protestant England.[120] As Henry Swinburne declared in his late seventeenth-century *Treatise of Spousals*, "solemnities are not of the Substance of Spousals, or of Matrimony, but consent only; … So that it may be justly inferred, that the only want of Solemnity doth not hurt the Contract."[121] Alternatively, or perhaps in concert with older religious conceptions, Blackstone may

---

117 Stephen Cretney, "The Family and the Law – Status or Contract?" (2005) 15:4 *CFLQ* 403 at 403.

118 By the mid-eighteenth century, feudal interests in land had largely given way to social and legal relations characterized by exchange (however illusory the equality of bargaining power may have been), but marriage maintained its function as a legal means of furthering the commercial and social interests of families. According to Gillis, "[b]ecause banks and stock markets were still poorly developed, inheritances, loans from kin, and *marriage portions* constituted a leading source of the capital that financed the world's first industrial revolutions": John R. Gillis, *A World of Their Own Making: Myth, Ritual, and the Quest for Family Values* (Cambridge MA: Harvard University Press, 1996) at 64 (emphasis added). While the ideal of companionate marriage was coming into vogue by the time of the *Commentaries*, Gillis argues that it was "subscribed to by only a very small number of people and … was not fully accepted, even among the new middle classes, until the Victorian period." Gillis, *For Better, For Worse, supra* note 19 at 14. For much of the population, including those fortunate enough to include companionship in their selection criteria, marriage in the mid-eighteenth century remained decidedly instrumental; it was a means of "sheer survival for the masses, production and reproduction for the peasantry, and familial advancement for the higher social groups": Anderson, *supra* note 39 at 38. See also Davidoff and Hall, *supra* note 19 at 221.

119 Kennedy, *Rise & Fall, supra* note 21 at 121. This association between contract and property is also evident in Thomas Wood's *An Institute of the Laws of England; or, The Laws of England in their Natural Order, according to Common Use* (London, 1720): Michael Lobban, "Mapping the Common Law: Some Lessons from History" (2014) 1 *NZLR* 21 at 27.

120 See Howard, *supra* note 107 at 376–7.

121 *Ibid* at 379 quoting Henry Swinburne, *A Treatise of Spousals, or Matrimonial Contracts: Wherein All the Questions relating to that Subject are ingeniously Debated and Resolved* (London, 1686) 194–6. According to Howard, Swinburne's text was actually written a century prior to its publication: Howard, *supra* note 107 at 378, n.1.

have been influenced by the connection between consent, contract, autonomy and modernity in the works of classical seventeenth-century liberal theorists.[122]

A further possibility is that Blackstone simply slipped into the historically typical English concern with form – evident in Locke's political theory and the legal system's concern up to that point with forms of action – in defining the legal nature of marriage by reference to the requirements for entry into the relation, more than the rights and obligations attached to marriage, of which coverture is perhaps the most glaring example. As Blackstone noted in his discussion of the effects of marriage, "the husband and wife are one person in law; that is, the very being or legal existence of the woman is suspended during the marriage, or at least incorporated and consolidated into that of the husband";[123] and one of the results of this coverture was that "a husband on marriage became for most purposes the almost absolute master of his wife's property,"[124] irrespective of any contract between husband and wife.[125] In this respect, while it may appear that a contractual analysis of marriage in the mid-eighteenth century (and earlier) is substantively problematic because of the rights and obligations that attached to marriage, it is equally clear that as a matter of legal thought – which is, after all, the primary concern in this chapter – the consequences of marriage did not, for Blackstone or earlier legal thinkers,[126] translate into a conception of marriage as anything more than a personal contract (setting aside questions over its possibly sacramental nature[127]).

---

122 The *Commentaries* are full of references to John Locke. In this respect, the tension between marriage-as-contract and the existence of coverture might be explained by the fact that classical liberal theory did not view the existence of subordination in a particular relation as antithetical to individual freedom so long as the agreement/contract was consensual: Pateman, *supra* note 19, chapters 3, 5. Recognizing the formalistic way in which contract was conceptualized in the mid-eighteenth century, then, might suggest that it was perfectly thinkable and indeed quite reasonable for Blackstone to characterize marriage as a contract in spite of its non-modifiable results.

123 Blackstone, *Commentaries, supra* note 25, book I at 430.

124 A.V. Dicey, *Lectures on the Relation Between Law and Public Opinion in England During the Nineteenth Century* (London: Macmillan, 1905) at 371.

125 Wealthier families, however, protected wives' interests through equitable marriage settlements. See generally Lee Holcombe, *Wives and Property: Reform of the Married Women's Property Law in Nineteenth-Century England* (Toronto: University of Toronto Press, 1983).

126 See Howard, *supra* note 107 at 336, 379.

127 See *ibid* at 393.

D. Blackstone and Nineteenth-Century Legal Thought

Where does the preceding analysis leave us in terms of a basis for further analysis? Blackstone's "private œconomical relations" indicate that the legal conception of the family in mid-eighteenth-century England was in essence (if perhaps not in social fact) based on a household model in which distinctions between family and work, public and private, and contract and status, were hazy. Work remained tethered to the household, and at least some workers were considered part of the family; the relations between masters and servants were treated as contractual insofar as they were based in consent, yet the ongoing element of state compulsion and subordination also lent many work relations the character of status. Marriage – the second of the household relations – was presented by Blackstone as a contract, apparently for reasons of (liberal and religious) ideology, a concern with form, and because of the historically instrumental nature of English marriage. Yet here, too, the picture is more complicated. *Lord Hardwicke's Act* had rendered marriage a civil contract, subject to state intervention; and whatever Locke said about consent and subordination,[128] marriage carried a suite of state-imposed non-modifiable conditions, most notably coverture, that gestured in the direction of status, even if legal thinkers of the time maintained that its essence lay in contract.

On a broader level, the *Commentaries* stand as the most significant attempt, at least up to that point, by an English jurist to reconcile common law and Roman law; and they portend the nineteenth century trend in English legal thought towards systematization and formal clarity.[129] In part because Blackstone did not succeed in his attempt to harmonize English and Roman law, valiant an effort though it was, subsequent jurists tended to focus on producing more specialized works that set out the basic principles and formal structure of a particular area; other, more philosophically minded thinkers eschewed the mess of actually existing English law altogether, in favour of conceptual maps of the law.[130] As subsequent sections show, this treatise tradition[131] combined with English analytical jurisprudence and German historical jurispru-

---

128 John Locke, *Second Treatise of Government*, edited by C.B. Macpherson (Indianapolis: Hackett, 1980) §§ 27, 28, 44, 81, 82. See further C.B. Macpherson, *The Political Theory of Possessive Individualism: Hobbes to Locke* (Toronto: Oxford University Press, 2011) at 214–20; Pateman, *supra* note 19 at 116–17.

129 Simpson, *supra* note 23 at 655, 664–6.

130 Lobban, *supra* note 70 at 334.

131 See generally Simpson, *supra* note 23 at 664–6.

dence to produce a different approach to the legal family, one in which productive work relations were shifted outside of the household, the relation between husband and wife was elevated to principal position in the Law of Domestic Relations, and the essence of marriage came to be viewed in terms of its ongoing existence as mediated by the state (status), more than its initial basis in consent (contract).

III. Household and Marriage in the Early Nineteenth Century

The first significant move towards establishing Blackstone's "private œconomical relations" as a field in its own right came from across the Atlantic in 1816:[132] Tapping Reeve's *The Law of Baron and Femme*,[133] the object of which was "to exhibit the Common Law of England" according to "the *principles* which govern each subject."[134] "By this means," Reeve declared, "a desirable *uniformity* in the law will be observed; and its *symmetry* will be preserved from being marred."[135] Adopting a structure that would become popular in subsequent works on Domestic Relations, Reeve re-ordered Blackstone's relations by placing husband and wife ("baron and femme," in his case) at the head of the list, and relegating master and servant to the bottom. In Halley's words, "Reeve introduces into Anglo-American law, perhaps for the first time, a legal classification that can meaningfully be tied, genealogically, to modern family law."[136]

---

132 Legal texts from the late eighteenth century did not depart in any significant way from Blackstone's scheme. Arthur Browne's 1798 work, *A Compendious View of the Civil Law*, was self-described as "a short work, in the method and order adopted by Mr. Justice Blackstone, in his Commentaries on the Laws of England," and was designed to induce common lawyers "to take at least a cursory and general view" of Roman law and its modern descendants. Like the *Commentaries*, book I deals with "The Rights of Persons." Chapters I-VI correspond to the "private œconomical relations" but place husband and wife at the top of the order (and replace "Parent and Child" with "Father and Son"). The "relation between husband and wife" is simply described as "the contract of marriage." Arthur Browne, *A Compendious View of the Civil Law, and of The Law of the Admiralty, Being the Substance of a Course of Lectures Read in the University of Dublin, Vol I* (Butterworth, 1798) at iii, 2.

133 Tapping Reeve, *The Law of Baron and Femme; of Parent and Child; of Guardian and Ward; of Master and Servant; and of the Powers of Courts of Chancery, with an Essay on the Terms, Heir, Heirs, and Heirs of the Body* (New Haven: Oliver Steele, 1816).

134 *Ibid*, Preface (emphasis added). Despite being American, Reeve's focus on English law makes the text a legitimate and useful resource in tracing nineteenth-century English legal thought, particularly given the degree of cross-pollination between English and American legal scholarship at this point in time.

135 *Ibid* (emphasis added).

136 Halley, *supra* note 16 at 9.

On the nature of the master-servant relation and the character of marriage, however, Reeve was rather less inclined to amendment. Like Blackstone, his treatment of master and servant encompassed "apprentices, menial servants, day labourers, [and] agents of any kind," though Reeve also listed (but did not discuss) slaves. Echoing the transactional approach to marriage evident in the *Commentaries*, chapter I of *The Law of Baron and Femme* is entitled "The Right which the Husband acquires to the PERSONAL PROPERTY of the Wife in POSSESSION, and to her CHOSES IN ACTION." Its opening line notes that "[t]he husband, by marriage, acquires an absolute title to all the personal property of the wife, which she had in possession at the time of the marriage; such as money, goods or chattels personal of any kind."[137] The contractual nature of the actual marriage was simply assumed – what required a measure of explanation was the property-related implications of the contract. As the quote above shows, Reeve largely followed Blackstone – and the general position of the common law – on that front. He differed, however, on the underlying rationale for a husband's rights over a wife's property. In his view, the unity of person doctrine was an error: "The law does not view the husband and wife as one person; for a deed or devise of land to a wife, vests in her, and not in the husband. As to real property, then, they are two distinct persons."[138] What this suggests is that in the early nineteenth century it was conceivable that marriage might continue down a contractual path by emphasizing individual autonomy more than state interest. There was (relatively) solid authority in the form of Blackstone's pronouncements on the topic, and Reeve indirectly gestured towards the possibility of a future move away from coverture by challenging the single legal personhood of the married couple.[139] As we will see, however, from this point on scholars tended to emphasize the public, state-influenced dimensions of marriage more than its contractual features, though elements of the old approach remained.

An example of this hybridity is William Burge's 1838 *Commentaries on Colonial and Foreign Law Generally, and in their Conflict With Each*

---

137 Reeve, *supra* note 129 at 1.

138 *Ibid* at 89. This did not mean that coverture ceased to operate; it was simply the underlying coexistence of husband and wife that Reeve rejected.

139 This is not to suggest that Reeve was an open or even closeted feminist. Part of his motivation in fact seems to have been a desire for married women to be permitted to make wills devising property to their husbands. See Angela Fernandez, "Tapping Reeve, Coverture and America's First Legal Treatise" in Fernandez and Dubber, *supra* note 18.

Other, and With the Law of England. Chapter V is entitled "Contract of Marriage," but its immediate subtitle is "The Status of Marriage, or the Relation of Husband and Wife." Echoing Blackstone, Burge introduced his discussion of consent and capacity with the statement, "Marriage, which in its origin is a contract of natural law, has become, in civil society, a civil contract, regulated by law, and endowed with civil consequences"; its validity, moreover, depends on criteria shared by "every other civil contract."[140] In conflicts cases, however, Burge noted that marriage was treated as a status "conferred by the laws of the domicile, which are described as personal, universal laws, and to which resort must be had in the adjudication of rights derived from, or dependent on, those qualities or capacities."[141] (Nevertheless, the question as to whether a marriage valid in the place of celebration should be treated as valid in the place of domicile, even if the place of domicile would have prevented its celebration, was still answered in a firmly contractual manner; that is to say, "Yes" – *lex loci celebrationis* prevailed.[142] The shift away from that particular approach to marital validity within the common law of conflicts occurred later in the nineteenth century.[143])

In 1841, one of the first works devoted to *marriage* – not husband and wife, and not including master and servant – appeared: Leonard Shelford's *Practical Treatise of The Law of Marriage and Divorce*.[144] According to Halley, the change in locution from "husband and wife" to "marriage" was more than cosmetic; its emphasis on the element of state involvement shifted marriage from the private and re-inscribed it as "public and communal, not private and individual; and it is therefore governed by public law, not private law."[145] Shelford expressed a similar view:

---

140 William Burge, *Commentaries on Colonial and Foreign Laws: Generally, and in their Conflict with Each Other, and with the Law of England* (London: Saunders and Benning 1838) at 136.

141 *Ibid* at 57.

142 *Ibid* at 187. See *Scrimshire v Scrimshire* (1752) 2 Hag Con 395 at 417. Deference to *lex loci contractus* was the approach taken in commercial cases in this period. See *Robinson v Bland* (1760) 2 Burr 1077; *Male v Roberts* (1800) 3 esp. 163.

143 See *Brook v Brook* (1861) 9 HLC 193, discussed *infra* note 258.

144 The full title is the absurdly cumbersome, *A Practical Treatise of The Law of Marriage and Divorce, and Registration; as altered by the recent statutes; containing also the mode of proceedings on divorces in the Ecclesiastical Courts and in Parliament; the right to the custody of children; voluntary separation between husband and wife; the husband's liability to wife's debts; and the conflict between the laws of England and Scotland respecting divorce and legitimacy* (London: S Sweet, 1841).

145 Halley, *supra* note 16 at 42.

> Marriage is the most solemn engagement which one human being can contract with another. It is a contract formed with a view not only to the benefit of the parties themselves, but to the benefit of third parties; to the benefit of their common offspring, *and to the moral order of civil society*. The importance of this contract is sufficiently obvious, since *it is the basis of civilized society* and of sound morals, and *the source of the domestic affections*, and of the delicate ties and relations subsisting between parents and children and other degrees of kindred.[146]

We see here the beginnings of a new conceptualization of marriage as a relation of public importance, and its elevation to prime position within the domestic relations. Shelford also gestured towards the unusual nature of the marriage contract by noting that while it "originates in the will of the parties, ... after being contracted, the duration of the union is totally *independent of the will of the parties* ... in this *the marriage contract is distinguished from every other species of contract*."[147] This was a significant departure from Blackstone's assertion that English law considered marriage "in no other light than as a civil contract" and "treats as it does all other contracts." In Shelford's formulation, marriage begins as a will-based contract, but it is subsequently transformed into an exceptional species of contract because of its ongoing non-will based dimensions.

Further on in his discussion of marriage, Shelford included a section entitled "Peculiarities of Marriage Contract."[148] Here, he took the next step and referred to marriage as a form of status owing to the attached set of rights and obligations arising out of "municipal regulation, over which the parties have no control, by any declaration of their will."[149] Upon closer analysis, however, it is clear that the text in this section is in fact an almost direct (and inadequately attributed) quote[150] from a Scottish text from 1817: James Fergusson's *Reports of Some Recent*

---

146 Shelford, *supra* note 140 at 3 (emphasis added).

147 *Ibid* at 3 (emphasis added). This indissolubility appears to be based on a blend of religious and civil injunctions: "In entering into the marriage state it is expressly declared, that the parties shall be joined together till death shall separate them": *ibid*.

148 *Ibid* at 16.

149 *Ibid*.

150 Shelford's first words, "Marriage is a contract of a peculiar nature" remove the Latin from the original version, which reads "marriage is a contract *sui generis*." The rest of the text in the section is a word-for-word quote. While Shelford includes a footnote acknowledging the source as Fergusson's *Reports*, *infra* note 146, he does not include quotation marks indicating the extent of his debt to the original. *Ibid* at 16–17.

Decisions by the Consistorial Court of Scotland in Actions of Divorce, Concluding for the Dissolution of Marriages Celebrated Under the English Law. Given the absence of any indication that Shelford disagreed with the text in Fergusson's *Reports*, or included it simply for the sake of comparison, it seems reasonable to infer that he endorsed its content (and hence the idea of marriage as a form of status), though we should keep in mind that the words are not Shelford's but rather remarks made by Lord Robertson in the case of *Duntze (or Levett) v Levett*,[151] as reported by Fergusson. In essence, the case concerned a wife's application to the Scottish courts for dissolution of her English marriage, based on her husband's adultery in Scotland. To guard against the incursion into Scotland of "benighted, feudal English marriage rules"[152] preventing divorce, Lord Robertson characterized marriage in the following terms:

> [M]arriage is a contract *sui generis*, and differing, in some respects, from all other contracts, so that the rules of law, which are applicable in expounding and enforcing other contracts, may not apply to this. The contract of marriage is the most important of all human transactions. It is the very basis of the whole fabric of civilized society. The *status* of marriage is *juris gentium*, and the foundation of it, like that of all other contracts, rests on the consent of the parties. But it differs from other contracts in this, that the rights, obligations, or duties, arising from it, are not left entirely to be regulated by the agreements of the parties, but are, to a certain extent, matters of municipal regulation, *over which the parties have no control, by any declaration of their will* …
>
> … And *such laws must be considered as forming a most essential part of the public law of the country.*[153]

---

151 The case is reported in James Fergusson, *Reports of Some Recent Decisions by the Consistorial Court of Scotland in Actions of Divorce, Concluding for the Dissolution of Marriages Celebrated Under the English Law* (Edinburgh: Archibald Constable and Company, 1817) at 70 ff. In what follows I draw upon Halley's discussion of the case: Halley, *supra* note 16 at 22–3 [*Duntze*].

152 Halley, *supra* note 16 at 23.

153 *Ibid* at 23–4 quoting Joseph Story, *Commentaries on the Conflict of Laws, Foreign and Domestic, in Regard to Contracts, Rights, and Remedies, and Especially in Regard to Marriages, Divorces, Wills, Successions and Judgments* (Boston: Hilliard, Gray and Company, 1834) §§109–11 at 101–2 (quoting Fergusson, *supra* note 147 at 397–9 app. note G) (last emphasis added). English courts eventually adopted a similar approach to marriage conflicts that asserted the English state's interest in regulating the validity of marriages of its subjects. See *Brook v Brook* (1861) 9 HLC 193.

Lord Robertson and Shelford both distinguish marriage from ordinary commercial contracts by reference to "will."[154] This is important – the idea that marriage rules operate *irrespective of individual will* (setting aside consent to entry) portends one of the key ideas that informed Classical Legal Thought from around 1850: the identification of contract as a will-based legal device forming the core of Private Law, and the corresponding treatment of relations governed (in whole or in part) by state ascription in terms of status.[155] In part because the duration of marriage and its associated rights and obligations were, as Lord Robertson put it, "matters of municipal regulation, over which the parties have no control, by any declaration of their will," hence making marriage "a most essential part of the public law of the country" (features that were in turn related to the ideological significance of marriage within the private family and the mobilization of marriage as a tool for managing the population[156]), the marital relation came to be identified as a form of status. Not status in the sense used by Maine, but rather in the modern legal sense of "a special condition of a continuous and institutional nature ... conferred by law and not purely by the act of the parties, whenever a person occupies a position of which the creation, continuance or relinquishment and the incidents are a matter of sufficient social or public concern."[157] This designation in turn rendered marriage exterior to the Law of Contract. In this respect, social and legal conceptions of public and private intersected and also flipped: in social discourse the family and marriage were paradigmatically private when placed against the public realm of the market;[158] but in legal terms the importance of the family and the degree of state intervention in its relations gave it the public character of status, while legal relations in the market were viewed through the lens of contract, itself constructed as the very heart of private law.

---

154 See also J.J.S. Wharton, *An Exposition of the Laws Relating to the Women of England; showing their Rights, Remedies, and Responsibilities, in every position of life* (London: Longman, Brown and Green, 1853) at 193–4, noting that while marriage "is treated by our law as a civil but indissoluble contract," it "differs from other contracts in this, that the rights, obligations, or duties arising from it, are not left entirely to be regulated by the agreement of parties, but are, to a certain extent, matters of municipal regulation, over which the parties have no control, by any declaration of their will."

155 Kennedy, *Rise & Fall, supra* note 21 at 185–206.

156 See, e.g., the discussion of the *Fatal Accidents Act 1846,* 9 & 10 Vict I, c 93, in chapter 5, part III.

157 Graveson, *supra* note 38 at 2.

158 Olsen, *supra* note 39 at 1499–506.

IV. The Influence of Jurisprudence

A. *The Analyst: John Austin*

The distinction between legal relations based on individual will (contract) and relations giving rise to non-modifiable rights and duties, capacities and incapacities (status), was one of the ideas espoused in what was unquestionably the most revolutionary work of mid-nineteenth century English jurisprudence: John Austin's *Lectures on Jurisprudence*.[159] Austin rejected Blackstone's emphasis on personal relations as the foundation blocks of the legal system in favour of an approach that prioritized abstract (contractual) relations over personal (status) relations.[160] For this reason, Kennedy has called the *Lectures* "the manifesto of CLT for the common law world."[161] In a broader context, Austin's attempt to present a systematic vision of English law was a reaction against the ongoing influence of the old forms of action on English legal thought and practice[162] – part of a broad intellectual trend towards developing a "scientific jurisprudence."[163] According to Michael Hoeflich, "[f]or Austin it was scientific to derive a 'taxonomy' of law, a systematic structure in which principles and rules could replace *genera* and species."[164]

Austin's "first great distinction of Law" was between the Law of Things and the Law of Persons. In his scheme, the Law of Persons is concerned with "certain *rights* and *duties*, with certain *capacities* and *incapacities* to take rights and incur duties, by which *persons*, as subjects of law, are variously determined to certain *classes*."[165] Those rights, duties, capacities, or incapacities "constitute a *condition* or *status* which

---

159 Though written in 1831–2, the *Lectures* in their entirety were not published until 1863: H.L.A. Hart, "Introduction" in John Austin, *The Province of Jurisprudence Determined* and *The Uses of the Study of Jurisprudence* (Indianapolis: Hackett, 1998) at viii [Austin, *Study of Jurisprudence*].

160 In particular, Austin was dismissive of what he perceived as Blackstone's insufficiently analytical approach: see Cairns, *supra* note 65 at 318.

161 Duncan Kennedy, "Three Globalizations of Law and Legal Thought" in David M. Trubek & Alvaro Santos, eds., *The New Law and Economic Development: A Critical Appraisal* (New York: Cambridge University Press, 2006) 19 at 27.

162 Michael H. Hoeflich, "John Austin and Joseph Story: Two Nineteenth Century Perspectives on the Utility of the Civil Law for the Common Lawyer" (1985) 29:1 *Am J Leg Hist* 37 at 43 [Hoeflich, "Austin and Story"].

163 *Ibid* at 45, noting also that this scientific movement "developed earlier in England and on the Continent" than in the United States.

164 *Ibid*. See also Austin, *Study of Jurisprudence*, *supra* note 159 at 367.

165 Austin, *Lectures*, *supra* note 24 at 706.

the person occupies."[166] The Law of Persons, therefore, "might be styled the 'Law of Status.'" In contrast, the "department of law which is opposed to the Law of Persons is commonly named the *Law of Things*,"[167] which "relates to rights and duties, but to rights and duties considered generally and in the abstract; exclusively of the rights and duties which are the constituent elements of conditions of *status*."[168] The law relating to contracts fell squarely within this (core) Law of Things, specifically, within primary rights *in personam*.[169] Austin described the relation between these areas as follows: "The Law of Things is *the* law; the *corpus juris*, minus the law of *status* or conditions."[170] In Kennedy's terms, abstraction (Things = Law) and subtraction (Law = Things – Status).[171]

Status for Austin was not something inherent to persons[172] but instead consisted of "sets of rights and duties ... detached for convenience from the body of the legal system."[173] As examples Austin gave "the rights and duties capacities and incapacities of husband and wife, parent and child, guardian and ward, master and slave."[174] Within Austin's scheme, then, the bulk of the household relations, and specifically marriage,[175] were shifted into the peripheral arena of status because the obligations inherent to these relations give rise to particular legal conditions.[176] Unlike early treatise writers, then, Austin seems to have been untroubled by the overlap between consent and contract in the formation of marriage, focussing instead on the ongoing legal dimensions of the relation. Treatise writers in the late nineteenth century followed this aspect of his approach.

---

166 *Ibid*.

167 *Ibid* at 707–8.

168 *Ibid* at 709.

169 In lecture XIV, "Act and Forbearance: Jus in Rem – Jus in Personam," under the margin note "Examples of rights *in personam*," we find "1ˢᵗ. A right arising out of a *contract*." The text says the following: "All Rights arising from *Contracts* belong to this last-mentioned class ... Rights, which, properly speaking, arise from *Contracts*, avail against the parties who bind themselves by contract, and also against the parties who are said to *represent* their persons." *Ibid* at 384.

170 *Ibid* at 709.

171 Kennedy, *Rise & Fall, supra* note 21 at 191.

172 An idea he dismissed contemptuously as "merely a case of the once current jargon about occult qualities": Austin, *Lectures, supra* note 24 at 720.

173 *Ibid* at 710.

174 *Ibid* at 711.

175 *Ibid* at 971, table II Notes, referring to "[t]he correlating conditions or *status* of husband and wife" (emphasis in original).

176 *Ibid* at 975.

While Austin referred to master and *slave* in the passage above, he also appeared to consider the relation of master and servant in terms of status:[177] "If you hire another *as your servant*, two *conditions* (those of master and servant) are created by the contract."[178] This is to be contrasted with a situation in which a person is hired "to do some single service (as to go on a given errand), [wherein] the conditions of master and servant are not created by the contract."[179] Elsewhere, he said that a servant could be sued "for breach of an obligation (*quasi ex contractu*) implied in the *status* of servant,"[180] and "the right of the master to the slave; the right of the master to the servant," are "matter for the Law of Persons and the Law of *Status*."[181]

Austin's approach stands in marked contrast to Blackstone's basic division between Rights and Wrongs.[182] His self-proclaimed rationale for his arrangement was functional – detaching the Law of Status from the Law (of Things) "tends to give clearness and compactness to the exposition of the bulk of the law."[183] This utilitarian explanation, however, somewhat conceals the more substantive rejection of social role as an operative basis for legal classification:[184] whereas for Blackstone the Law of Persons was a central component of the whole system because the law was designed around social relations, it was for Austin a peripheral category concerned with deviations from the norm – where the norm amounted to the Law of Things, including contract. Austin is opaque as to the deeper justification for his distinction between Persons and Things. As Kennedy has noted: "The division between the abstract core and the 'exceptional' periphery is almost never discussed. When it is, it seems enough to justify it on the basis of 'convenience.' Yet it has the most profound consequence for the substantive content of legal rules."[185]

---

177 See further John Macdonnell, *The Law of Master and Servant* (London: Stevens and Sons, 1883) 35 note (a).

178 Austin, *Lectures, supra* note 24 at 976, table II Notes (emphasis in original).

179 *Ibid*.

180 *Ibid* at 970 (emphasis in original).

181 *Ibid* at 815 (emphasis in original).

182 Austin also rejected the usual Roman tripartite scheme of things, persons, and *actions*, which he believed "had to be subsumed under the first two as arising necessarily and directly therefrom": Hoeflich, "Austin and Story," *supra* note 158 at 49.

183 Austin, *Lectures, supra* note 24 at 746. On this basis, Graveson criticized Austin for neglecting the social aspect of status: Graveson, *supra* note 38 at 60.

184 Kennedy, *Rise & Fall, supra* note 21 at 187–90.

185 *Ibid* at 190.

In essence, by relegating status to the periphery, Austin also shifted attention away from those legal relations "that most clearly embody the ideals of regulation, paternalism, community and informality."[186] Austin's emphasis on the abstract Law of Things was thus "part of a reforming that made it possible to shift *analytic* effort" onto the development of a liberal legal order centred upon relations between (putatively) autonomous individuals, realized in legal form via the device of contract.[187] Nevertheless, Austin also held on to the idea of the household as a unifying legal category,[188] in which the relation of master and servant appeared alongside what would eventually become family relations: husband and wife, and parent and child.

B. *The Historicist: Friedrich Carl von Savigny*

In his discussion of the distinction between Things and Persons, Austin expressly drew upon the work of the Prussian jurist Friedrich Carl von Savigny, excerpting the following passage from Savigny's 1814 *Vom Beruf* pamphlet: "I have remarked that the ideas of *jus in rem* et *jus in personam* (or *dominium et obligation*) are, in the Roman Law, all-pervading ... And the same remark will apply to the idea of *status*: for on the idea of *status* the distinction between the Law of Persons and the Law of Things is founded."[189] Savigny was an important influence on Austin,[190] though the Englishman was sceptical of the historical aspects of Savigny's

---

186 *Ibid.*

187 *Ibid* (emphasis in original). Whether or not Austin intended it, there was also a gendered dimension to this split that mapped neatly onto the consolidating distinction between male (work, market, contract) and female (housework, family, status) domains.

188 Possibly because of Austin's belief that jurisprudence ought to be devoted to giving order to the law as it is, rather than setting forth the law as it ought to be: Sugarman, *supra* note 15 at 35.

189 Austin, *Lectures, supra* note 24 at 719 quoting Friedrich Carl von Savigny, *Vom Beruf unserer Zeit fur Rechtsgeschichte und Getzgebung* (1814) at 98. According to Hoeflich, this was Savigny's "most influential early work ... and was translated into English by Abraham Hayward and published in London in 1831. Two years earlier the first volume of his *History of Roman Law in the Middle Ages* was translated by Cathcart and published in Edinburgh": Michael H. Hoeflich, "Savigny and His Anglo-American Disciples" (1989) 37 *Am J Comp L* 17 at 19 [Hoeflich, "Savigny"].

190 On a more general level, Sugarman has noted that "the real and substantial achievements that were effected by English scholars in Roman law, legal science and legal history are almost inconceivable without the impressive legal and historical scholarship of Germany": Sugarman, *supra* note 15 at 45.

jurisprudence.[191] In essence, Savigny argued that "the true origin of legal norms is in the *Volksgeist* or spirit of the particular people they govern, worked out through the unconscious long-term development of customs, then rationalized by national 'legal science.'"[192] Savigny analogized this latter component – the part that Austin agreed with – to geometry: "In every triangle … there are certain data, from the relations of which all the rest are necessarily deducible.… In like manner, every part of our law has points by which the rest may be given: these may be termed the leading axioms. To distinguish these, and deduce from the internal connection, and the precise degree of affinity which subsist between all juridical notions and rules, is amongst the most difficult of the problems of jurisprudence. Indeed, it is peculiarly this which gives our labours the scientific character."[193] In the English context, this systematizing feature of Savigny's thought is most apparent in the work of jurists from the second half of the nineteenth century, such as Frederick Pollock and Thomas Erskine Holland, who created and disseminated[194] the field of CLT. (In contrast, the historical component of Savigny's approach almost certainly influenced the greatest exponent of historical jurisprudence in England, Sir Henry Sumner Maine.[195]) Savigny's most notable work in this respect, *System of the Modern Roman Law*, was published in German between 1840–49 (after Austin wrote his *Lectures* but paving the way for their eventual enthusiastic reception in the 1860s[196]); the first volume was published in English in 1867.[197] In the

---

191 Austin therefore preferred the conceptual jurisprudence of the Pandectists, though he sympathized with the second stage of Savigny's approach, which involved systematizing the law discovered through historical analysis: Hoeflich, "Savigny," *supra* note 189 at 27.

192 Duncan Kennedy, "Savigny's Family/Patrimony Distinction and Its Place in the Global Genealogy of Classical Legal Thought" (2010) 58:4 *Am J Comp L* 811 at 811–12 [Kennedy, "Savigny"]. See further Savigny, *System, supra* note 24, Preface.

193 Friedrich Carl von Savigny, *Of The Vocation of Our Age for Legislation and Jurisprudence*, translated by Abraham Hayward (London: Littlewood and Company, 1831) at 38–9 quoted in Sugarman, *supra* note 15 at 31. On the connection between Savigny, law and geometry see Michael H Hoeflich, "Law & Geometry: Legal Science from Leibniz to Langdell" (1986) 30 *Am J Leg Hist* 95 [Hoeflich, "Law & Geometry"].

194 As Sugarman put it, "the university law school would constitute an important 'breeder of values' as the Inns of Court had been before them": Sugarman, *supra* note 15 at 31.

195 Hoeflich, "Savigny," *supra* note 189 at 25.

196 Hart, *supra* note 159 at xvii.

197 Savigny, *System, supra* note 24. See the review of this (and other works) in *The Edinburgh Review*, 1 October 1869.

System, Savigny established a legal taxonomy that, in basic form, looks like the diagram in Figure 2.3.[198]

Unlike Austin, Savigny's basic division was between Public Law and Private Law,[199] a binary that became fundamental to CLT (and which continues to structure legal thought in the present). Public Law comprised what we might now call constitutional and administrative law (States Law), criminal law, and the law of procedure. Private Law incorporated Potentialities – essentially, property, contract, and quasi-contract (or unjust enrichment as it became) – and Family Law.[200]

Within Private Law, Savigny drew a sharp distinction between Potentialities Law and Family Law.[201] The former, in his view, involved "the partial mastery over the acts of others by which that, which conceiving in its entirety we describe as commerce, is conditioned and formed."[202] In Kennedy's words, "potentialities law governs the relations between independent individuals exercising their wills vis-à-vis one another."[203] This market-based aspect of obligations law stands in "pervading contrast to family-law," which "consists[s] in a natural-moral relation." It is a mistake, according to Savigny, to classify family relations as Obligations

---

198   This diagram is taken from Kennedy, "Savigny," *supra* note 192 at 824. See further Müller-Freienfels, *supra* note 12 at 37–8.

199   Austin located the distinction between public and private within the Law of Persons: "Taken with its strict and definite meaning, public law ought not (I think) to be *opposed* to all the rest of the law, but ought to be inserted in the Law of Persons, as one of the limbs or members of that supplemental department." Austin, *Lectures, supra* note 24 at 771. In Austin's view, "the term public law is confined to that portion of the law which is concerned with political *conditions*: that is to say, with the powers rights duties capacities and incapacities, which are peculiar to political superiors, supreme and subordinate": *ibid* at 770–1.

200   Despite this difference, as Halley has noted, both Savigny and Austin "sought a general law, abstracting in part by subtracting from it law that was irretrievably particular": Halley, *supra* note 16 at 64. Their particular schemes differed, but both jurists shared an underlying commitment to legal taxonomy based on the general and the particular.

201   See further Müller-Freienfels, *supra* note 12 at 37–8.

202   Savigny introduced his discussion of the jural relations by declaring, "[t]he law serves morality, not by performing its bidding but by securing the free development of its power indwelling in each individual will." Enabling the exercise of free will is itself a moral act, to which the law should direct its attention. Rules of law, therefore, "consist[] in the assignment to the individual will of a province in which it is to rule independently of every foreign will." Thus, when Savigny wrote of "jural relations," he meant "a province of the independent mastery of the individual will." An obligation is therefore a type of jural relation. Savigny, *System, supra* note 24 at 270–1.

203   Kennedy, "Savigny," *supra* note 192 at 814.

Figure 2.3. Savigny's taxonomy of law

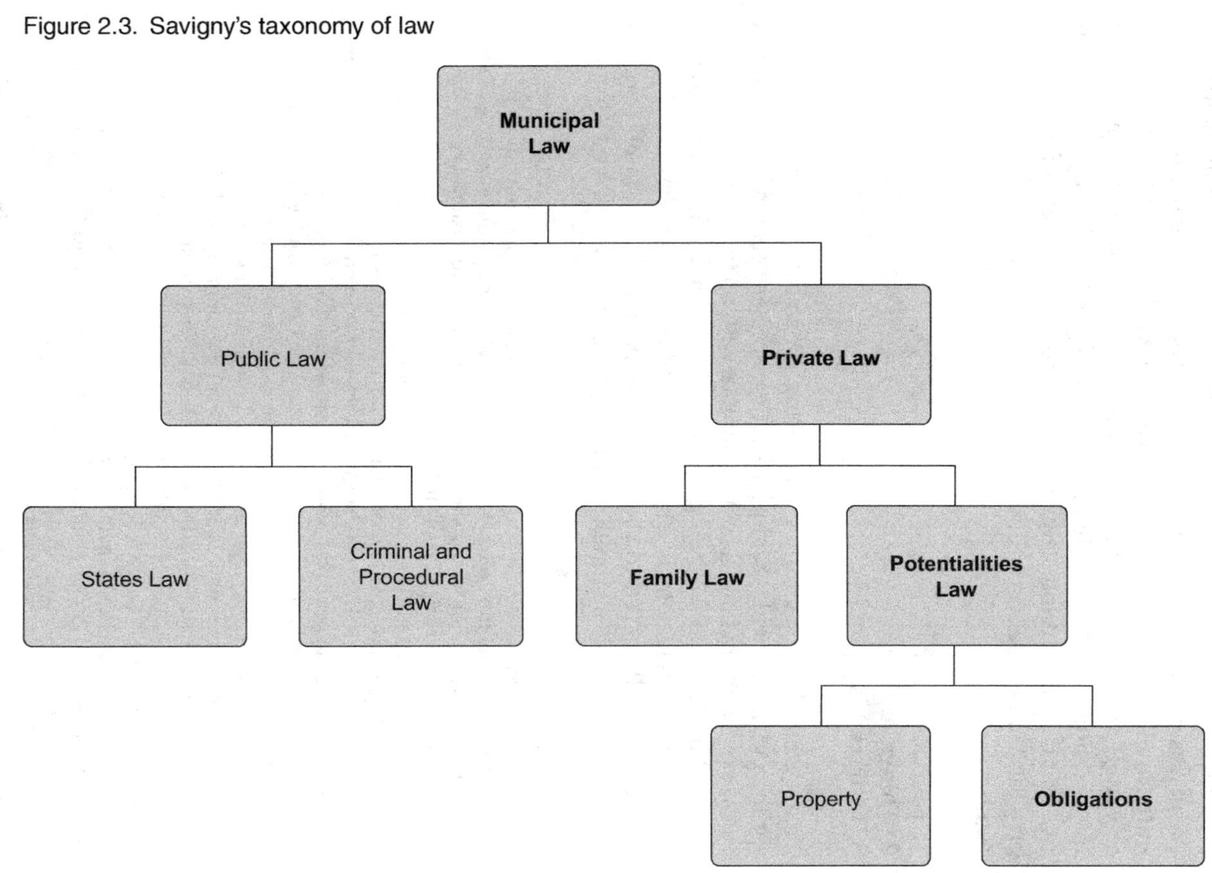

because of the "peculiar, completely distinctive, nature of the family."
In his words, "[t]he obligation is a rule of a transitory nature, the family
relation is destined for an enduring existence.… In families are embraced
the germs of the state and the completely formed state has families, not
individuals immediately for its constituent parts."[204] Accordingly, Savigny said, the family "belongs only in part to the province of law, while
the potentiality falls wholly and exclusively within it." By "potentiality," Savigny meant the Law of Obligations and the Law of Real Property (or Things). Accordingly, he set out three main classes of (private)
rights:

1. Families'-right.
2. Things'-right.
3. Obligations'-right.[205]

This system, by "establishing co-existing provinces of absolute mastery
for the individual will, provides a single, necessary content for the actual
rules of property and obligations"; Families Law, on the other hand, is only
partially based on individual will – as a natural, and cultural, relation (in
addition to a jural one), the content of Families Law is determined by the
Volksgeist (i.e., the spirit of each particular people).[206] The family, and its
law, is thus figured as morally saturated, while the market, and its law, is

---

204 Savigny, *System, supra* note 24 at 279. Savigny's veneration of family life and
   custom bears a resemblance to Hegel's rejection of marriage-as-contract. See G.W.F.
   Hegel, *Philosophy of Right*, translated by T.M. Knox (Oxford: Oxford University
   Press, 1969) at 58–9 [75], 112–14 [163]–[4], 262 [103]. This initial similarity, however,
   masks deeper differences between their theories, particularly on the role of
   positivity, which Savigny grounded in historicity, whereas Hegel took a more
   capacious approach. Direct influence between the two men also seems unlikely in
   view of their quite public dislike of one another. See Christoph Kletzer, "Custom
   and Positivity: An Examination of the Philosophic Ground of the Hegel-Savigny
   Controversy" in Amanda Perreau-Saussine and James B. Murphy, eds., *The Nature
   of Customary Law* (Cambridge: Cambridge University Press, 2007) at 125.
205 Savigny, *System, supra* note 24 at 280. "Now for the summary of all these
   completing relations – MARRIAGE, PATERNAL POWER, RELATIONSHIP –
   we call the FAMILY, and the institutions of law referring to it the LAW OF THE
   FAMILY." *Ibid* at 277–8. While Savigny developed his System by reference to
   Roman legal categories, he admitted that the description "Family Law" was not
   itself derived from Roman sources. Instead, he drew on the earlier work of Gustav
   Hugo (*Manual of Today's Roman Law* (1798), first published as *Institutionen des
   heutigen Romishchen Rechts* (1789)), to which he was introduced through Arnold
   Heise's *Outline of a System of the General Civil Law for Pandectist Lectures* (*Grundriss
   eines Systems des Gemeinen Civilrechts zum Behuf von Pandekten-Corlensungen* (1807)):
   Müller-Freienfels, *supra* note 12 at 37–8.
206 Kennedy, "Savigny," *supra* note 192 at 817.

presented as morally neutral.[207] The "true contents" or "proper nature" of jural relations pertaining to the family "consists in the place which the individual obtains in these relations, in his being not merely man in general but specially husband, father, son." Accordingly, Savigny argued that "family relations therefore belong especially to the *jus publicum* i.e. to the absolute law," and "each family relation of a man is called especially a *status* of that man, that is to say, his place or his existence to other men determined."[208] In this respect, Savigny's system foreshadows subsequent distinctions in English legal thought concerning the boundaries of public and private: Families Law is housed within Private Law because it is based on relations between individuals (hence the enduring translation of consent to marry into the legal form of contract), but since the law governing those relations comes from outside positive law, it also carries what we now tend to describe as a public dimension; in the English case, though, the reason was the degree of state involvement in familial relations (hence lending them the character of status) rather than the customary origins of those rules.

With respect to work, Savigny drew a critical distinction between what he called "hired service" and other forms of labour. The former, in his view, involved a moral element, and hence fell within "artificially extended family-law." Other forms of work, however, fell squarely within the law of obligations.

> From the stand-point of the Roman law, this [the law of hired servitude] admits of being conceived merely as a contract (*operae locatae*) and this contracted treatment was sufficient for the Romans, since by reason of the excessive number of the class of slaves the need of free domestic servants was almost wholly imperceptible. It is otherwise with us who have no slaves; whence that relation has become of very important and extended necessity. Now we are not satisfied with the narrow treatment of it like any other contract for labour and thus in the Prussian land-recht, *the law of hired service has been perfectly correctly received not under contracts but into the law of persons.*[209]

In essence, domestic or hired service carried with it a relational component that made its classification alongside other forms of work, which

---

207 Thus, despite family law and obligations both being part of the more general category of rights "[a]gainst individuals determined" (as opposed to rights against all – a taxonomic split analogous to the distinction between rights *in rem* and rights *in personam*), they are in fact distinct, "for in obligations it is a partial subjecting of the one to the will of the other; in the family it is a natural-moral, at the same time legal, relation of life which is to be continuously brought forth": Savigny, *System, supra* note 24 at 316.

208 *Ibid* at 284 note (e) (emphasis in original).

209 *Ibid* at 298–9 (emphasis added).

were in the nature of Obligations, inappropriate. This division is made clear in Savigny's subsequent analysis of the difficulty in determining "the boundaries between things'-law and obligations." "So far as the settlement of boundaries is concerned," he says, "certain extreme points doubtless present themselves in which the special nature of one or the other division is wholly unmistakeable: thus rigid property with unlimited vindication on the one side, the *contract of hired service and mandate on the other*."[210] So, within Savigny's system, domestic service appears to fall within "artificially extended family-law," while other labour relations are properly housed within the law of obligations. This distinction is absolutely critical. It portends the very process by which the English Law of Master and Servant split apart from the household by way of an initial distinction in the Law of Domestic Relations between work performed by persons residing in the home, and work performed outside of the home. As we will see most clearly in the work of William Pinder Eversley (1885),[211] work relations that retained a physical connection to the household/home, notably domestic service and apprenticeship, continued to be treated as part of Domestic Relations. This liminal phase, in which the legal household had been downsized and reordered but not yet transformed into the home with its exclusively familial relations, lasted until the early twentieth century, at which point domestic service and apprenticeship joined other forms of work in the taxonomical successor to the Law of Master and Servant: Employment Law.[212]

V. The Influence of Statutory Developments

Before turning to the heyday of CLT in England and the emergence of Family Law, it is worth pausing to consider the interplay between scholarly works and two significant nineteenth-century statutory developments in the realms of family and work: the introduction of judicial

---

210 *Ibid* at 303 (emphasis added).

211 William Pinder Eversley, *The Law of the Domestic Relations, Including Husband and Wife: Parent and Child: Guardian and Ward: Infants: and Master and Servant* (London: Stevens and Haynes 1885). See part VII below.

212 Which is not to suggest that all forms of paid work were regulated in the same manner. Domestic service remained (and remains to this day) subject to lower levels of regulation than other forms of wage labour. See Einat Albin, "From 'Domestic Servant' to 'Domestic Worker'" in Judy Fudge, Shae McCrystal and Kamala Sankaran, eds., *Challenging the Legal Boundaries of Work Regulation* (Oxford: Hart, 2012) at 231; Einat Albin and Jeremias Prassl, "Fragmenting Work, Fragmented Regulation: The Contract of Employment as a Driver of Social Exclusion" in Mark Freedland *et al*, eds., *The Contract of Employment* (Oxford: Oxford University Press, 2016) 209 at 226–8.

divorce and the abolition of ecclesiastical jurisdiction over divorce and matrimonial causes by the *Matrimonial Causes Act 1857*;[213] and the retreat from criminalization of contract breach in the *Master and Servant Act 1867*,[214] and the *Employers and Workmen Act 1875*.[215] These statutory developments, each of which concerned the legally permitted circumstances for exiting relations characterized by subordination, are considered in detail in subsequent chapters;[216] the concern here is simply with legal writers' responses to these shifts; specifically, how the new divorce regime affected scholars' conceptions of marriage, and what effects the work-related statutes had on the field of master and servant law.

A. Divorce and the Legal Character of Marriage

The years 1858 to 1860 saw works on divorce by John Fraser Macqueen,[217] William Brandt,[218] M.C. Merttins Swabey,[219] Robert A. Pritchard, and W.T. Pritchard,[220] and Richard Tidswell and Ralph Littler.[221] The next

---

213 20 & 21 Vict I, c 85. In these respects the Act continued the project begun by *Lord Hardwicke's Act*: bringing marriage and its incidents, including dissolution, under state control.

214 30 & 31 Vict I, c 141.

215 38 & 39 Vict I, c 90.

216 On the *Matrimonial Causes Act 1857* see Mary Lyndon Shanley, *Feminism, Marriage, and the Law in Victorian England* (Princeton NJ: Princeton University Press, 1985); Lawrence Stone, *Road to Divorce: England 1530–1987* (Oxford: Oxford University Press, 1990); Danaya Wright, "'Well Behaved Women Don't Make History': Rethinking English Family, Law, and History" (2004) 19:2 *Wis Women's LJ* 211. On the history of criminalization of contract breach in master-servant relations and the changes introduced by the 1867 and 1875 Acts see Deakin and Wilkinson, *supra* note 22, chapter 2; Hay, *supra* note 102; Steinfeld, *supra* note 28.

217 John Fraser Macqueen, *A Practical Treatise on Divorce and Matrimonial Jurisdiction under the Act of 1857 and new orders* (London: W. Maxwell, 1858). (Note that this is an abbreviated form of the full title, which lists all of the sub-headings dividing the book's contents.)

218 William Brandt, *A Treatise on the Law, Practice and Procedure of Divorce and Matrimonial Causes under the Act 20 & 21 Vict. c. 85; containing The Act, also the rules, orders and forms issued thereunder; together with precedents* (London: Butterworths, 1858).

219 M.C. Merttins Swabey, *The Act to Amend the Law Relating to Divorce and Matrimonial Causes in England, the Divorce Act Amendment Act (1858), and the Legitimacy Declaration Act, 1858* (London: Shaw, 1859).

220 Robert A. Pritchard and W.T. Pritchard, *A Hand-Book on the Law of Marriage and Divorce* (London: V. & R. Stevens and G.S. Norton, 1859). (Again, this is an abbreviated form of the absurdly long-winded full title.)

221 Richard Thomas Tidswell and Ralph Daniel Makinson Littler, *The Practice and Evidence in Cases of Divorce and other Matrimonial Causes: Together with the Acts, Rules, Forms, &c.* (London: W. Benning, 1860).

two decades saw further works on divorce by George Browne,[222] William Ernst Browning[223] and, most significantly, William John Dixon.[224] These early works on divorce were by and large practitioners' manuals concerned with presenting the procedural and substantive requirements for an action in the new Divorce Court.[225] It is not surprising, then, that they generally avoided theorizing the implications of divorce for English marriage law and its place within the broader legal landscape. However, those authors who did address the nature of marriage clearly did not perceive in the *Matrimonial Causes Act 1857* – or in the possibility of judicial divorce – any particular shift towards, or reinforcement of, a contract-based approach to marriage (in the sense that the extremely limited ability to dissolve a marriage *might* amount to a shift in the direction of will-based private ordering). Macqueen in his 1858 work observed that "marriage, however it is entered into, is more than a civil contract," though his rationale for this characterization was that it "is divine in its essence."[226] Dixon was much more explicit: marriage is "something more than a *contract*, either religious or civil – [it is] an institution."[227] In essence, these authors did not perceive the

---

222 George Browne, *A Treatise on the Principles and Practices of the Court for Divorce and Matrimonial Causes: With The Statutes, Rules, Fees and Forms Relating Thereto*, 2nd ed. (London: H. Sweet, 1868) (the first edition appears to be unavailable – not even the Bodleian Library at Oxford University possesses a copy).

223 William Ernst Browning, *An Exposition of the Laws of Marriage and Divorce, as administered in the Court for Divorce and Matrimonial Causes, with the method of procedure in each kind of suit; illustrated by copious notes of cases* (London: W. Ridgway, 1872).

224 William John Dixon, *Law, Practice and Procedure in Divorce and other Matrimonial Causes* (London: Reeves and Turner, 1883) (renamed *Law and Practice in Divorce and other Matrimonial Causes* in the second (Reeves and Turner 1891) and subsequent editions).

225 Conversely, works of the later nineteenth century that dealt with marriage, or the law of husband and wife, tended to shy away from detailed consideration of divorce. William Eversley, for instance, in his 1885 work, *The Law of the Domestic Relations*, included less than three pages on divorce and judicial separation in a work spanning more than 1100 pages (nearly half of which was devoted to Husband and Wife): Eversley, *supra* note 211 at 480–3. By the twentieth century the law of divorce came to be viewed as properly situated alongside the law of marriage. Edward Jenks' *Husband & Wife in the Law* (London: J.M. Dent & Co, 1909) [Jenks, *Husband & Wife*] devoted almost as much space to "Dissolution of Marriage Tie" as it did to "Liabilities Arising From Marriage" and "Special Privileges and Disabilities of Married Women," combined.

226 Macqueen, *supra* note 217 at v.

227 Dixon, *supra* note 224 at 5 referring to *Sottomayor v De Barros (No 1)* [1877] 3 PD 1 and *Hyde v Hyde and Woodmansee* (1866) 1 P&D 130.

expanded[228] possibility of extricating oneself from marriage (in certain prescribed circumstances, and along distinctly pro-male lines[229]) as lending the marital relation any additional contractual dimensions.[230]

B. Decriminalization and the Legal Character of Work

The 1860s and 1870s also saw the emergence of texts devoted specifically to the Law of Master and Servant as a discrete category, set apart from the relation of husband and wife, and parent and child – a development that responded to changes effected to the law of work by the *Master and Servant Act 1867* and the *Employers and Workmen Act 1875*.[231] James Edward Davis's 1875 text, *The Labour Laws*,[232] signals how this extrusion of productive relations occurred in a piecemeal manner. In the opening pages of the work, Davis makes the following important observation concerning the scope of his analysis:

> The relation of master and servant, arising out of the form of contract known to the law under the name of hiring and service, embraces many varieties of service. We have, in the first place, the broad distinction between domestic servants and every other class of servants. Next to these come servants employed in trade and business, such as clerks, shopmen, and the like. With the foregoing classes of servants the legislature has never thought it necessary to interfere. The respective rights and obligations of master and servant, as arising from the contract between them, have been left to be determined by the common law of the land, and any differences between them to be dealt with by the ordinary tribunals. *The contract of hiring and service, so far as it relates to servants of these two classes, is only incidentally referred to in these pages. Passing by these classes of servants,* we come to the numerous class who serve by placing at the service of their employers their labour, whether

---

228 Divorce by private Act of Parliament was possible before 1857, but it was a complicated and expensive process which, as a practical matter, was open only to the wealthy and the well-connected.

229 See Shanley, *supra* note 216; Wright, *supra* note 216.

230 It is difficult to see how such an argument could have been made given the institutionalized nature of the regime established under the Act, which made access to divorce dependent on the permission of the state (through newly constituted courts) and only in certain very limited circumstances.

231 The first of these texts appears to be Alexander Macdonald's quaintly named *Handybook of the Law Relative to Masters, Workmen, Servants, and Apprentices, in all Trades and Occupations* (London: W. Mackenzie, 1868).

232 James Edward Davis, *The Labour Laws* (London: Butterworths, 1875).

rude or skilled, according to the branch of productive industry or manufacture to which they belong.[233]

Davis's rationale for excluding domestic servants and "servants
employed in trade and business" – the lack of attention to these forms
of work in the Acts of 1867 and 1875 – reflects one of the more interesting features of late eighteenth and nineteenth-century English master-
servant law. In essence, at the same time as the master and *domestic*
servant relation was becoming the model for legal relations between
masters and servants in general,[234] domestic servants were situated
outside of the scope of laws regulating work.[235] This exclusionary position carried over into the 1867 and 1875 laws, and helped to structure
a legal consciousness in which domestic service (and apprenticeship[236])
remained tethered to the household.

---

233 *Ibid* at 2–3 (emphasis added). See also JE Davis, *Labour and Labour Laws*, 9th ed.
     (private reprint from *Encyclopaedia Britannica*, 1883) at 3: "Purely domestic service
     and the service of shopmen and clerks, as well as the work of contractors for the
     service of others, who do not work with their own hands, is excluded from specific
     notice here."
234 Tomlins, *supra* note 28, chapter 8.
235 While it was long assumed that the *Statute of Artificers 1562*, 5 Eliz, c 4, which re-
     codified "a great number of Acts and Statutes concerning the retaining, departing,
     wages and orders of Apprentices, Servants and Labourers, as well in Husbandry
     as in diverse other Arts, Mysteries and occupations" (Preamble, spelling and
     punctuation modernized) applied to domestics, it was decided by Lord Kenyon
     in 1796 that this was not so: *The King v Inhabitants of Hulcott* (1796) 6 Term 583,
     101 ER 716. Subsequent efforts to enact regulation of domestic servants faltered
     over the prospect of domestics suing their masters in court and airing the family's
     dirty laundry in public. See Hay, *supra* note 102 at 90; Anonymous, *Reflections on
     the relative situations of master and servant, historically and politically considered; the
     irregularities of servants; the employment of foreigners; and the general inconveniences
     resulting from the want of proper regulations* (London: W. Miller, 1800) at 24–5. See
     further the discussion of paid domestic labour in chapter 4, part II.
236 The major statutory intervention for apprenticeship actually occurred in 1814,
     with the repeal of the apprenticeship provisions in the *Statute of Artificers 1562*
     by the *Apprentices Act 1814*, 54 Geo III, c 96. The effect of that law was to render
     unnecessary the hitherto compulsory seven years' apprenticeship required to
     practice certain trades. The statute therefore helped to consolidate the more general
     social and legal move towards treating apprenticeship as a relation based on
     work and training *outside of the master's home* rather than the essentially familial
     relation it had been for centuries: see K.D.M. Snell, *Annals of the Labouring Poor:
     Social Change and Agrarian England, 1660–1900* (Cambridge: Cambridge University
     Press, 1985) at 228–69. Nevertheless, it is apparent that within legal thought the
     vestiges of this older conception of apprenticeship remained persuasive: like the
     legal household, the apprenticeship relation in the late nineteenth century was in
     a liminal state (at least in scholarly thought) – moving towards the freestanding

Higher status workers (Blackstone's "fourth species of servants, if they may be so called, being rather in a superior, a ministerial, capacity ... *stewards, factors,* and *bailiffs*"[237]) were also historically exempt from the statutory master-servant regime that governed labourers, artisans and journeymen.[238] Indeed, Deakin and Wilkinson have argued that it was in relation to these sorts of higher-status workers and their nineteenth-century analogues "that the modern contract of employment, based on true reciprocity of obligation and the placing of limits on the employer's powers of direction, first developed."[239] It was only after 1875, when criminal penalties for breach of work contracts were by and large removed from English statute law,[240] that this contractual model began to extend to other groups of workers.[241]

These distinctions between classes of worker become particularly important when considering texts from the late nineteenth century. As we will see, subsequent writers disarticulated the category of master-servant law from the household in a staged process that hinged on the nexus, or lack thereof, between work and the household (or home, as it was coming to be known);[242] that is, forms of

---

law of master and servant, but also tied in important ways to what remained of the household. For example, William Holdsworth in *The Law of Master and Servant: Including that of Trades Unions and Combinations* (London: Routledge, 1876) at 176–7 treated apprenticeship in generally contractual terms, but also noted that live-in apprenticeship was by no means obsolete – and where such a relation did exist, obligations beyond those found in ordinary wage labour contracts still existed.

237 Blackstone, *Commentaries, supra* note 25, book I at 415 (emphasis in original).

238 Between 1720 and 1792, when the household model of work and family life was breaking apart and wage labour was becoming the dominant form of employment in England, ten statutes extended the class of workers against whom orders for imprisonment could be made, added misbehaviour to the list of possible grounds for imprisonment, and increased potential prison sentences (and, in some cases, provided for whipping). See Hay, *supra* note 102 at 82. See further the discussion in chapter 3, part III.

239 Deakin and Wilkinson, *supra* note 22 at 74.

240 The *Employers and Workmen Act 1875*, 38 & 39 Vict I, c 90, did not entirely do away with criminal sanctions; what it did do, though, was make the process leading to incarceration cumbersome – employers were required to obtain an initial damages award, followed by an order to pay by instalments where possible, and the failure of a defendant subject to an order to make payment: s 9. Thus, as Steinfeld notes, the cessation of imprisonment for breach of labour contracts was more of a de facto development than a strictly legal one. Robert Steinfeld, *Coercion, Contract, and Free Labor in the Nineteenth Century* (Cambridge: Cambridge University Press, 2001) at 217–8.

241 Deakin and Wilkinson, *supra* note 22 at 74.

242 See also Charles E. Baker, *The Law of Master and Servant* (London: F Warne, 1881) discussing both domestic and non-domestic workers under the heading "master and servant," though noting "domestic servants are not as other servants: they are

non-household work were grouped together under the broadly con-tractual Law of Master and Servant, while household-based forms of work (domestic service and apprenticeship) became part of a much narrower category of Master and Servant within the Law of Domes-tic Relations – a category that, in a reversal of what we saw above in Davis' *The Labour Laws*, excluded most forms of wage-based con-tractual labour.

VI. Classical Legal Thought in England: Abstracting Contract and Subtracting Marriage

In the same year that the English translation of Savigny's *System* was published (1867),[243] a series of works by English (and American[244]) scholars "created the Classical field," in which the Law of Contract stood at the core of the legal universe, through a systematic process of subtraction ("these authors of the 1870's … purged quasi-contract, status and tort from the subject") and abstraction ("asserting and then trying to show that there had been an essence hidden at the core of the pre-Classical hodgepodge").[245]

---

of a class different from workmen, or even outdoor servants": at 7. *Cf.* Holdsworth, *supra* note 232 at 2 (adopting a more capacious definition that grouped domestics alongside "all persons between whom any contract exists for the render of service").

243 There is some evidence that Savigny's earlier works, and even the *System* itself, had an influence on English legal thought in the middle part of the nineteenth century. It seems likely that the foremost exponent of the historicist approach to law in England, Henry Sumner Maine, was influenced by Savigny, though the dearth of bibliographic references in *Ancient Law* and other works makes it difficult to pinpoint the precise nature and scope of this influence. See Hoeflich, "Savigny," *supra* note 189 at 25. The clearest example of Savigny's influence in England in the mid-nineteenth century appears to be a series of lectures published by the English barrister George Long, first reader in jurisprudence and civil law at the Middle Temple, in 1848. In the lectures, published as *Two Discourses Delivered in the Middle Temple Hall, with an Outline of the Course* (London: T. & J.W. Johnson, 1848) Long frankly noted (at 4) that, "[a]ny person who is acquainted with the work of Savigny, '*System des Heutigen Rumischen Rechts*,' to which I have often referred, will see how much I am indebted to it."

244 Most notably texts by Christopher Columbus Langdell and Oliver Wendell Holmes: Kennedy, *Rise & Fall, supra* note 21 at 207.

245 *Ibid.* This move towards abstraction is abundantly clear in the first of these English works, Martin Leake's *The Elements of the Law of Contracts* (London: Stevens, 1867).

A. Consolidating Contract by Distinguishing Marriage: Pollock and Anson

The work of Frederick Pollock "signalled the beginning of a change from one juristic era to another" – a move away from what Thomas Holland called "chaos with a full index" to a systematic, principles-based approach to law, legal thought, and legal education.[246] In his *Principles of Contract at Law and in Equity* (1876),[247] Pollock admitted to "follow[ing] almost literally" Savigny's analysis of contract in the *System of the Modern Roman Law*.[248] Accordingly, Pollock claimed that the glue that turned a merely consensual agreement into a legally enforceable contract was intention,[249] or will: a meeting of the minds and an intention to create legal relations, in modern parlance. As Neil Duxbury has noted, this conceptual analysis was itself fairly unremarkable in light of civilian works, but in the context of English legal thought "it has a fair amount of historical significance" as a marker of the will theory's emerging role in common law approaches to contract and other areas of law[250] – especially those that did not fit within this framework.

---

246 Neil Duxbury, *Frederick Pollock and the English Juristic Tradition* (Oxford: Oxford University Press, 2004) at 280 citing Thomas Erskine Holland, "The Classification of the Statutes" (1869) in Thomas Erskine Holland, *Essays Upon the Form of the Law* (London: Butterworths, 1870) at 171. Pollock did, however, remain a fervent believer in the common law and what he called its scientific method. See "The Science of Case Law" in Frederick Pollock, *Essays in Jurisprudence and Ethics* (London: Macmillan, 1882) chapter IX [Pollock, *Essays in Jurisprudence*].

247 Frederick Pollock, *Principles of Contract at Law and in Equity: Being a Treatise of the General Principles Concerning the Validity of Agreements, With a Special View to the Comparison of Law and Equity, and With References to the Indian Contract Act, and Occasionally to Roman, American, and Continental Law* (London: Stevens, 1876) [Pollock, *Principles of Contract*]. This text, and Pollock's subsequent treatise on torts (Frederick Pollock, *A Treatise on the Principles of Obligations Arising from Civil Wrongs in the Common Law* (London: Blackstone, 1887)) were said by William Holdsworth to have been "the first books in which the principles of these branches of law were treated in a manner which was both scientific and literary": Duxbury, *supra* note 246 at 188 quoting William Holdsworth, *Some Makers of English Law: The Tagore Lectures. 1857–56* (Cambridge: Cambridge University Press, 1938) at 285.

248 This influence is apparent in Pollock's definition of a contract as "an agreement which produces an obligation," expressed in the form of a promise: Pollock, *Principles of Contract, supra* note 247 at 5.

249 *Ibid* at 1–2.

250 Duxbury, *supra* note 246 at 192. It should be noted, though, that Pollock progressively backed away from the will theory in successive editions of *Principles of Contract*: *ibid* at 194.

Pollock's abstract approach to the nature of contract was matched by his insistence on "subtracting" non-core elements from his discussion.[251] In particular, Pollock gestured towards the difficulty posed by marriage for Classical contracts scholars. In the course of discussing fraud on marital rights[252] Pollock suggested that the right of a husband to rescind a contract to marry if the relevant fraud by the intended wife was discovered before the marriage took place, "might well be put on a broader ground than appears in the cases." He reasoned that "[t]he contract to marry gives rise to a new status between the parties, to which mutual duties are incident beyond the simple performance of the contract by marriage at the time expressed or contemplated."[253] One such duty was the obligation of good faith; accordingly, conduct of the type under consideration could be treated as evincing "a want of confidence which the other party is entitled to treat as incompatible with the marriage contract."[254]

Pollock's distinction between ordinary contracts and the status-laden marriage contract is made even clearer in his subsequent discussion of the virtual impossibility of avoiding a completed marriage on the ground of fraud. In this respect, "marriage is an exception to the general rule."[255] However, this distinction was explicable because "marriage, though including a contract, is so much more than a contract that the exception is hardly a real one."[256] In other words, marriage retained a contractual element at the level of form(ation), but in its essence it was so far from the market-based core of contract rules that it could scarcely be considered a contract. This rationale was a marked shift from the treatment given to the topic in Chitty's

---

251 For instance, Pollock devoted just one paragraph of chapter I, "Agreement, Proposal, and Acceptance," to quasi-contracts, and suggested that the 1872 *Indian Contract Act* "provides for matters of this kind more simply in form and more comprehensively in substance than our present law, by a *separate chapter* entitled 'Of Certain Relations resembling those created by Contract' (ss 68–72, esp. s 73)." Pollock, *Principles of Contract, supra* note 247 at 29 (emphasis added).

252 Specifically, a woman's conveyance of property to her own separate use prior to marriage but after making representations to her intended husband regarding the property.

253 Pollock, *Principles of Contract, supra* note 247 at 232.

254 *Ibid.*

255 *Ibid* at 475. One might wonder why fraud shouldn't more readily unravel a status-based relationship. Perhaps paradoxically, the reason, at least according to Pollock, was that the public importance of marriage meant that only fraud arising to the level of deception about the identity of the spouse was sufficient to impugn its validity: *ibid.*

256 *Ibid.*

1826 edition of Blackstone's *Commentaries*. There, in a footnote to the statement that parties "must contract themselves in due form of law, to make it a good civil marriage," Chitty added, "[e]rror about the family or fortune of the individual, though produced by disingenuous representation, will not at all affect the validity of a marriage."[257] The change from Chitty to Pollock is not in the remedy provided by the law – the marriage remained as valid in 1876 as it was in 1826. The shift is rather in the way that marriage and contract were conceptualized. For Chitty, pre-marital misrepresentation was simply an insufficient ground to impugn the marriage. For Pollock, it was an exception to what could by then be called general rules of the Law of Contract based on the view that marriage was "so much more than a contract" – it had become a status.[258]

This trend is also evident in the first edition of William Anson's *Principles of the Law of Contract*.[259] Anson raised the awkward relationship between marriage and contract in the context of defining Contract. Like Pollock, Anson drew on Savigny in defining a Contract as "that form of Agreement which directly contemplates and results in an Obligation."[260] The critical point for the characterization of marriage comes in Anson's discussion of Agreement. He says:

Under the definition of Agreement at which we have arrived would fall –

...

(2) Agreements which effect a change of status immediately upon the expression of the consent of the parties, such as Marriage, which, when consent is expressed before a competent authority, alters at once the legal relations of the parties in many ways.

...

---

257 Joseph Chitty, *Commentaries on the Laws of England: By the Late Sir W. Blackstone* (London: W. Walker, 1826) book I at 438, note 24.

258 See also James Schouler, *A Treatise on the Law of the Domestic Relations Embracing Husband and Wife, Parent and Child, Guardian and Ward, Infancy, and Master and Servant* (Boston: Little, Brown & Co, 1870) at 23: "we are then to consider marriage, not as a contract in the ordinary acceptation of the term; but as a contract *sui generis*, if indeed it be a contract at all."

259 William Anson, *Principles of the Law of Contract* (Oxford: Clarendon Press, 1879). Abstraction is also a feature of Anson's text. See in particular his discussion of quasi-contract in the Preface. See further Kennedy, *Rise & Fall, supra* note 21 at 205.

260 Anson, *supra* note 259 at 1. An Agreement, in turn, "is the expression by two or more persons of a common intention to affect the legal relations of those persons" (at 3); while Obligation "gives to one man a control over the actions of another, definite in character, and capable of being reduced to a pecuniary value": at 5–6.

> It would seem then that Agreements the effect of which is immediate in creating rights *in rem*, or in effecting a change of status, are not such as we ordinarily term Contracts.[261]

This exclusion-by-definition is a stark example of how CLT in England constructed a distinction between the Law of Contract and the status of marriage. Scholars would continue to refer to the "marriage contract" to denote the element of consent that underpinned entry into the relation, but from this point on it became increasingly apparent that the totality or essence of the marital relation involved much more than this initial expression of consent because of the immediate and ongoing ascription of rights and duties by the state, irrespective of individual will.[262]

B. Translating CLT into Taxonomy: Holland

From a jurisprudential perspective, the most important English work of the late nineteenth century was Thomas Holland's *The Elements of Jurisprudence*.[263] It was, in Holland's own words, "an attempt to set forth and explain those comparatively few and simple ideas which underlie the infinite variety of legal rules."[264] General principles of this sort were necessary "scientific equipment" to enable "the student ... to cut a path for himself through the tangled growth of enactment and precedent, and so

---

261 *Ibid* at 3.

262 See *supra* note 35 on the coexistence of individual will concerning entry into marriage and its subsequent non-modifiable elements. From a different angle, the distinction between the initial contract to marry and the status to which it gives rise parallels in important ways the development in this same period of the distinction between the formal and essential validity of marriage in the common law of conflicts. Whereas the validity of a foreign marriage was traditionally ascertained by reference to the law of the place of celebration (*lex loci celebrationis*), in 1861 the House of Lords decided that the interest of the English state in the regulation of its subjects' marriages meant that the validity of a marriage solemnized abroad rested on *lex loci celebrationis* only in respect of the formal aspects of solemnization; the essential validity of the marriage (in essence, the capacity of the parties to marry according to law) remained a question governed by English law. Thus, in the case in which this doctrine was laid down, *Brook v Brook* (1861) 9 HLC 193, a marriage between English subjects celebrated in Denmark was held to be void under English law because it contravened the legislative prohibition on a man marrying his deceased wife's sister (*An Act to render certain Marriages valid and, to alter the Law with respect to certain voidable Marriages*, 5 & 6 Will VI, c 54 (1835)).

263 Thomas Erskine Holland, *The Elements of Jurisprudence* (Oxford: Clarendon Press, 1880).

264 *Ibid* at 1.

to codify for his own purposes."[265] Accordingly, Holland characterized jurisprudence as a "formal legal science," not a material one; "that is to say, that it deals rather with the various relations which are regulated by legal rules than with the rules themselves which regulate those relations."[266] Upon his death in 1926, Holland's colleague J.L. Brierly wrote in an obituary published in the *Law Quarterly Review*, that "[s]ubstantially Holland's doctrine was that of Austin, but he made it less vulnerable by discarding many of Austin's crudities and inconsistencies."[267] Despite this narrowness and removal of crudities, Holland's scheme remained relatively complex; for ease, it is represented in Figure 2.4 in diagrammatic form. It will be apparent that distinctions between public/private, status/contract, and family/contract play an important structural role.

Like Savigny, Holland's primary division was "the ancient and fundamental"[268] one between Public and Private Law.[269] Within Private Law, however, Holland's approach displays the influence of Austin: the basic division is between Things and Persons, with the former treated as the general law applying to persons of full capacity, while the Law of Persons is concerned with persons of abnormal capacity, or status, in Holland's usage.[270] For this reason, the Law of Persons is "distinct from and much smaller than the residue of the Law, which is generally called the Law of Things."[271] Pollock, in his assessment of Holland's scheme, largely agreed with this structure, and declared "the importance of the

---

265 *Ibid*.

266 *Ibid* at 5.

267 J.L. Brierly, "Sir Thomas Erskine Holland" (1926) 42 *Law Q Rev* at 475, quoted in Sugarman, *supra* note 15 at 44. Sixty years on, and in a rather less charitable tone, Sugarman wrote that Holland "applied classical legal scholarship's enthusiasm for systematization, conceptualization and exposition in a manner that was dogmatic, narrow and pedantic": Sugarman, *supra* note 15 at 44.

268 Pollock, *Essays in Jurisprudence, supra* note 246 at 13: "It is satisfactory to find that Professor Holland retains the ancient and fundamental division of Private and Public Law."

269 Holland criticized Austin's scheme in this respect, in large part because "when so secondary a function is assigned to the division of the Law into Public and Private, it is impossible to find a satisfactory position in the Corpus Iuris for the law of Crime." Holland, *supra* note 263 at 82.

270 Thus, the distinction between the Law of Persons and the Law of Things turns "[u]pon the normal or abnormal status of the persons concerned," because "there are some rights in which the status of the persons concerned has to be specially taken into consideration, while in others this is not the case": *ibid* at 83. The Law of Persons deals with rights that are subject to fewer variations than rights concerning Things because "the possible varieties in juristic personality are far fewer than those in the juristic character of objects or acts": *ibid* at 87.

271 *Ibid* at 87.

Figure 2.4. Holland's taxonomy of law

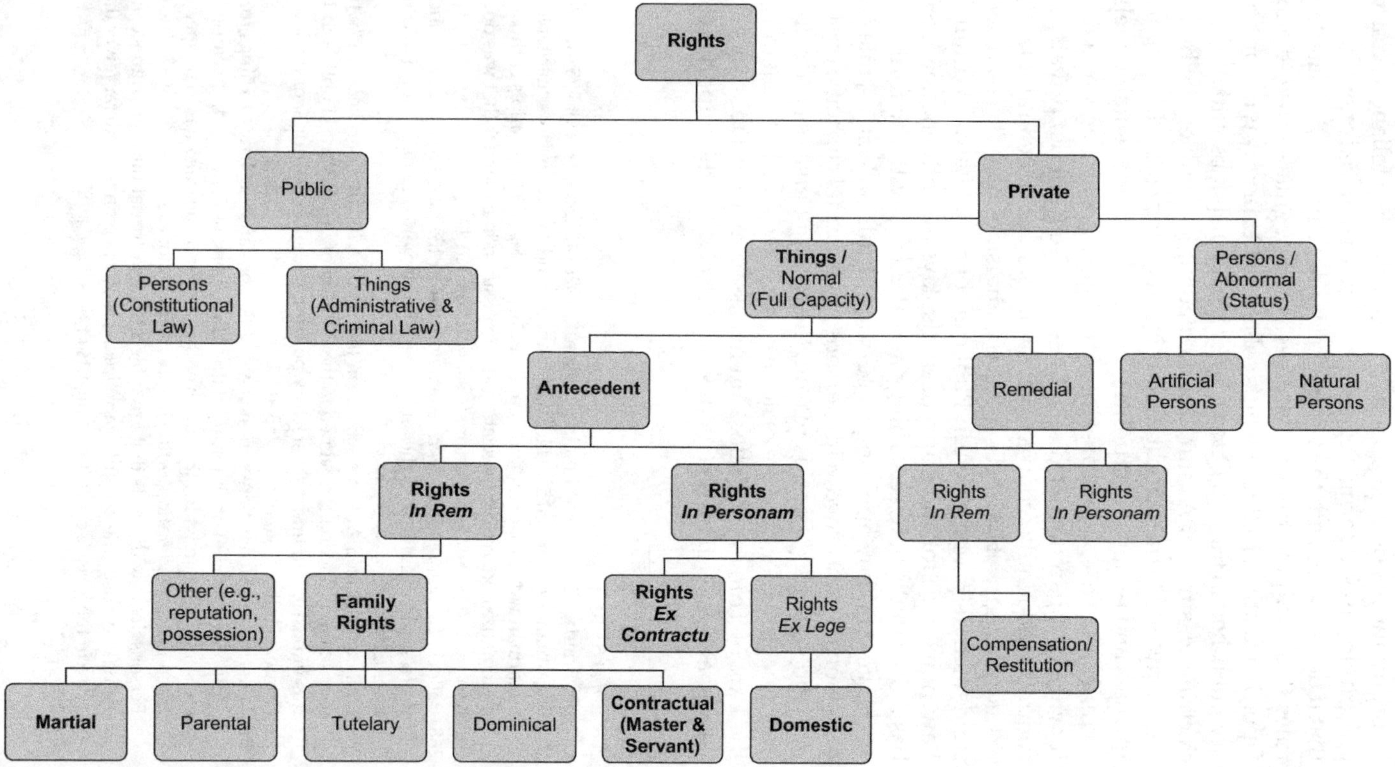

law of Persons as compared with the law of Things is ever on the wane in modern systems."[272] In Holland's own words, his scheme involved "abstracting the law of Persons from the rest of the law";[273] it is "supplementary and secondary to … the residue of the law, commonly called the law of Things."[274] (This is much the same process of abstracting and subtracting that Kennedy argues was fundamental to CLT; Holland inverted the terms but still ultimately divided the Law of Persons from the core Law of Things.)

Whereas Austin proceeded to situate the status of husband and wife within the Law of Persons, Holland took a rather more complicated approach. In essence, only "peculiarities" arising from artificiality (not being human), or a form of disability "on account of age, sex, mental incapacity, crime, alienage, or public station,"[275] situated a person within the Law of Status.[276] Family relations, therefore, along with contractual relations, are housed within the category of Antecedent Rights in the Law of Things (meaning rights that exist without any wrongful act or omission[277]). Within that category we find a further division into rights *in rem* versus rights *in personam*.

Turning first to rights *in personam*, Holland observes that they "either arise or do not arise out of a contract,"[278] a contract being a species of Obligation that involves (and here Holland quotes Savigny) "the union of several in an accordant expression of will, with the object of creating an obligation between them."[279] This class of rights is "by far the most important" of the *in personam* rights.[280] In other words, Contract is at the core of Private Law. The secondary class of rights *ex lege* contains, among others, "Domestic" rights, which comprise husband and wife, parent and child, and guardian and ward. *Not master and servant*. Instead, one finds discussion of "professional or domestic services" in a later section concerned with "Contracts for Service."[281] In this respect, Holland went a step further than Savigny – and foreshadowed developments in

---

272 Pollock, *Essays in Jurisprudence, supra* note 246 at 14.
273 Holland, *supra* note 263 at 89.
274 *Ibid.*
275 *Ibid* at 90.
276 *Ibid.*
277 *Ibid* at 93.
278 *Ibid* at 164.
279 *Ibid* at 173.
280 *Ibid* at 172.
281 *Ibid* at 192.

English legal thought in the twentieth century[282] – by placing domestic, as well as professional, forms of service in the contractual sphere.

However, Holland also complicated this neat contractual treatment of the service relation in his discussion of antecedent rights *in rem*, in which one finds "Family Rights," comprising the following: marital; parental; tutelary; dominical; and contractual. It is the last category with which we are presently concerned. There, Holland says:

> A master has a right, as against the world, to the services of his servant, and can sue any one who entices him away from the performance of his duties, or so injures him as to render him less capable of performing them: and this principle has been declared to apply not only to domestic service, but also to any kind of employment.[283]

No other type of contractual relation is discussed apart from employment. However, Holland also observes that "[r]ights to the society and control of one's family," which "result, directly or indirectly, from the institution of marriage,"[284] comprise only the first four of the rights listed: marital, parental, tutelary, and dominical. After discussing dominical rights (master and *slave*), Holland refers to "[c]ertain rights *arising out of contract* [which] strikingly resemble the two classes of family rights last considered,"[285] i.e., tutelary and dominical rights. It seems, then, that Holland did not really view the law of master and servant as a family right in the strict sense, especially since he emphasized that master and servant was a contractual relation; rather, he included it within the category of Family Rights because of its ongoing similarities (in terms of subordination and control[286]) to the core family relations of husband and wife, and parent and child.

Concerning marriage, Holland makes the following crucial statement in the section on Domestic rights *in personam* relating to husband and wife:

> It may appear questionable whether the rights of husband and wife can be reckoned among those which arise by operation of law rather than out of contract. It is however submitted that this is the true view. The matri-

---

282 See below part VIII(B).

283 Holland, *supra* note 263 at 117 (citation omitted).

284 *Ibid* at 112–3. Of course, "*one's* family" must be understood as referring to "*his* family," i.e., the *husband's* family.

285 *Ibid* at 117 (emphasis added).

286 *Ibid* at 134.

monial status is indeed entered upon, in modern times, in pursuance of an agreement between the parties, accompanied by certain religious or civil formalities; *but its personal incidents are wholly attached to it by uniform rules of law, in no sense depending on the agreement of the parties*, either at the time of the marriage or subsequently. The effect of the contract, coupled with the other acts required by law, in producing a status, to which rights of definite kinds are incident, closely resembles that of a sale of property … The necessarily resulting rights of the person newly invested with the status … are the creatures not of the will of the parties but of fixed rules of law.[287]

While Holland's conception of status generally hewed towards capacity/incapacity,[288] the passage above suggests that marriage also creates a sta-

---

287 *Ibid* at 165 (emphasis added). In a note to this passage, Holland refers to "the remarks of Hegel, Phil. Des Rechts, § 75, on the treatment by Kant, Rechtslehre, Werke, vii, p.76, of marriage as an obligatory contract": *ibid* at 165 note 2. This rather perfunctory reference points to an important disagreement concerning the nature of marriage between two of the foremost Western philosophers in the eighteenth and nineteenth centuries. In essence, Kant propounded a view of marriage-as-contract based on sexual ethics. In his view, "[t]he marriage contract establishes legitimate access to sexual property in the person." Kant asserted that marriage "is founded upon the natural Reciprocity or intercommunity (commercium) of the Sexes." This natural intercommunity (sex) "proceeds either according to the mere animal Nature … or according to Law," and it is only the latter that amounts to marriage. *Contra* Locke, Kant denied that "producing and educating children" is the purpose of marriage (though it "may be regarded as always the End of Nature" in implanting heterosexual desire). Instead, Kant argued that the point of marriage is "enjoyment in the reciprocal use of the sexual endowments … yet the Contract of Marriage is not on that account a matter of arbitrary will, but is a Contract necessary in its nature by the Law of Humanity." See Immanuel Kant, *The Philosophy Of Law: An Exposition of the Fundamental Principles of Jurisprudence as The Science of Right*, translated by W Hastie (Edinburgh: T. & T. Clark, 1887) at 109–13.

    In stark contrast to Kant, Hegel argued that, "[t]o subsume marriage under the concept of contract is … quite impossible; this subsumption – though shameful is the only word for it – is propounded in Kant's Philosophy of Law." Instead, Hegel said that marriage is an "ethical relationship." It can be said to begin in contract because it relies on "the free consent of the persons," but in truth "it is precisely a contract to transcend the standpoint of contract, the standpoint from which persons are regarded in their individuality as self-subsistent units." In other words, "marriage transcends the standpoint from which man and wife are deemed to have property in each other, especially in one another's sexual faculties." The point of marriage is for the parties "to renounce their natural and individual personality to the unity of one with the other"; marriage therefore "results from the free surrender by both sexes of their personality." Hegel, *supra* note 204 at 58–9 [75], 112–14 [163]–[4], 262 [103].

288 Kennedy, *Rise & Fall*, *supra* note 21 at 194.

tus and, from a taxonomic point of view, is not to be classified as contractual (though the agreement to enter into the relation is still referred to as a contract because breach enabled a claim for damages[289]). Moreover, the reason that marriage is status is not simply to achieve a "commodious arrangement," à la Austin, but because of the imposition of rights and duties *by the state*. That is, marriage had a distinctive public element, despite its placement within Private Law.[290]

Holland's scheme stands as a critical marker of trends in late nineteenth century English legal thought. His taxonomy of law shows how jurists set up a basic distinction between core (private law, specifically contract) and periphery (public law, state intervention, particularly status, and family relations); how the relation of master and servant was coming to be seen as fitting more within the contractual core than the domestic periphery; and how marriage was increasingly seen in terms of status (public) not contract (private). At the same time, Holland's scheme reflects the lingering influence of the idea of the productive household and contractual approaches to marriage, though he managed to deal with those aspects in such a way that they complicated more than undermined his broader framework.

VII. The Emergence of English Domestic Relations Law

The analysis thus far has been deliberately confined to "high mandarin" legal texts. At this point, however, it is worth briefly expanding the textual field to consider a work that "does not aspire to the dignity of a treatise, but seeks to convey information on some points of common domestic interest," in particular for the benefit of women: *A Profitable Book Upon Domestic Law*, by C.J. Bunyon (1875).[291] In the context of the

---

289 Holland, *supra* note 263 at 190.

290 Pollock expressly approved of this aspect of Holland's treatment of marriage. In the course of discussing what he called "rights annexed by law" (his preferred term for what Holland called rights *ex lege*), Pollock observed that the term "comprises the rights of husband and wife (because, though the existence of the state of marriage depends on the will of the parties, its incidents do not)": Pollock, *Essays in Jurisprudence, supra* note 246 at 17.

291 C.J. Bunyon, *A Profitable Book Upon Domestic Law* (London: Longmans, Green, & Co, 1875) at 13–14. Bunyon explained his desire for the book to be read by women by referring to the likely flood of legislation "in favour of women's rights" in the wake of the *Married Women's Property Act 1870*, 33 & 34 Vict I, c 93, and women's exclusion from legal practice, meaning "that the least that can be expected from the sex is that they should make themselves acquainted with the labours of their advocates" at 14.

present genealogy, the book itself is a profitable source on a number of fronts, and despite its middlebrow positioning, portends certain key features of subsequent and rather more highbrow texts on Domestic Relations and Family Law. In particular, Bunyon presents a vision of "The Family" (chapter 8) as the source of happiness in civil society, and comprised of the married couple and their children. Chapter 9, "The Household," discusses relations between masters and servants, but limits the discussion to *domestic* servants and appears to envisage a distinction between the Family and Household staff. (In a rather Panglossian manner, Bunyon emphasizes that "our right to their services arises from their own voluntary contracts, which they have the power to determine ... His will is free, and there is no necessary degradation even in personal service."[292])

With respect to marriage, Bunyon characterizes it as "a contract, and in the mutual consent its essence consists,"[293] yet he also emphasizes the "great ... interest ... [of] the State" in the marriage relation, which entitles it "to step in and require the observance of such solemnities of ceremony and registration as may conduce" to the "sanctity of family life."[294] In chapter 4, entitled "The Married State and the Rights of Property Therein," Bunyon "consider[s] what marriage really is." His answer: "It is an institution, and has been styled the parent, and not the child of society. It does indeed, as all other contracts do, give rise to mutual rights and liabilities, but beyond that it confers a status, namely, the position of husband and wife."[295]

The ideas put forward by Bunyon were more fully fleshed out in legal terms a decade later in the first English legal treatise to deal exclusively and comprehensively with the law of the domestic sphere: William Pinder Eversley's *The Law of the Domestic Relations: Including Husband and Wife, Parent and Child, Guardian and Ward, Infants, and Master and Servant* (1885).[296] While Eversley's subject groupings call to mind Blackstone's arrangement, he consciously replaced "private œconomical" with "domestic," and, like Tapping Reeve some 70 years earlier,[297] moved master and servant to the bottom of the list. Eversley appears to have been influenced by the American jurist James Schouler, whose own *Treatise on the Law of Domestic Relations* was first

---

292 *Ibid* at 183.
293 *Ibid* at 46.
294 *Ibid* at 47.
295 *Ibid* at 66.
296 Eversley, *supra* note 211.
297 Reeve, *supra* note 133.

published in 1870,[298] as well the Scottish jurist Lord Patrick Fraser, whose *Treatise on the Law of Scotland, as Applicable to the Personal and Domestic Relations, Comprising Husband and Wife, Parent and Child, Guardian and Ward, Master and Servant, and Master and Apprentice*[299] had appeared in 1846 and was regularly cited in United Kingdom courts in the 1860s–80s.[300] Influences aside, the change in locution registers an understanding of the domestic realm as separate from the market; as Halley notes, by the time Schouler wrote, the term "œconomical" or "economic" had "completely ceased to refer to the household and was primarily a term for monetary, financial, and commercial relations."[301] In this new, non-economic understanding of the household/home, the primacy of the relation of husband and wife in the family was a social fact, and marriage was the principal Domestic Relation in law. Eversley commenced his treatise with the following statement (which bears more than a passing resemblance to Bunyon's analysis of the Family):

> Whatever may have been the most early form of human society, it is now generally accepted that the Family is the parent of social and political life as it has existed from remote historic times down to the present period. The fundamental conception of the term family is the union of man and woman, the weaker protected by the strong, but ministering to his wants; and from this union spring other lives, which are bound together by their common origin and affection."[302] Eversley went on to characterize marriage, as "more than a contract, it is a *status*, the conditions of which are regulated for and not by those enter it.[303]

In support of this statement, Eversley pointed to Joseph Story's *Conflict of Laws*.[304] That work, in turn, relied upon Fergusson's *Reports*, specifically,

---

298 Schouler, *supra* note 258.

299 Patrick Fraser, *A Treatise on the Law of Scotland, as Applicable to the Personal and Domestic Relations, Comprising Husband and Wife, Parent and Child, Guardian and Ward, Master and Servant, and Master and Apprentice* (Edinburgh: T. & T. Clark, 1846). Eversley expressly drew on Fraser's work in the opening pages of *The Law of the Domestic Relations*.

300 I have adopted Halley's method of date-specific Westlaw case searches to gauge acceptance of the term "domestic relations," though I have expanded it to search also for references to Fraser's treatise. A search on Westlaw of United Kingdom cases in 1846–1885 turned up 18 decisions in which Fraser's *Personal and Domestic Relations* was mentioned. A further 30 cases used the term "domestic relations" in the same period. See Halley, *supra* note 16 at 75–6, note 262.

301 *Ibid* at 75.

302 Eversley, *supra* note 211 at 1.

303 *Ibid* at 2 (emphasis in original).

304 Story, *supra* note 153.

the report of Lord Robertson's judgment in *Duntze*, discussed above.[305] In a footnote referring the reader to Fergusson's *Reports*, Eversley made the following critical statement apropos *Duntze*: "This judgment was delivered in a Scotch case, but is equally descriptive of English marriages."[306] From this point, Eversley went on to declare that "the effect of marriage is not confined to that of ordinary contracts, for a new status is created between the contracting parties, which affects not only themselves but the society at large in which they have taken up their matrimonial abode. In other words, marriage in its widest sense is an Institution."[307] Again, contract remained present at the stage of formation, but from the point of solemnization onwards it was a form of status.

Despite Eversley's comments about the nature of the Family, and his placement of marriage at the heart of the Domestic Relations, the Law of Master and Servant remained present in his work. Eversley attempted to patch over this awkwardness by arguing that while Matthew Hale and Blackstone classed the relationship as "œconomical," it was actually "thoroughly domestic."[308] To make good on this claim, though, Eversley excised *non-household labour* from his scheme and dealt only with "the more limited relations of domestic servants and their hirers."[309] Introducing the section on master and servant, he said:

> The scope of this portion of the law of Domestic Relations will be *confined to domestic and menial servants*, and will embrace but a small portion of the law that is ordinarily treated of under the head of Master and Servant. Indeed, strictly speaking, the very term domestic or family relations would exclude all those persons who could not satisfy its requirements. That wide branch of the law which deals with *the relations of those who are popularly known as "Employers and Employed" will not be discussed* in the succeeding chapters.[310]

In other words, domestic service remained a Domestic Relation, but (almost all) the rest of the Law of Master and Servant was exterior to the Law of Domestic Relations. In a successive chapter, Eversley also characterized the relation between master and apprentice as

---

305 Fergusson, *supra* note 151. Like Shelford, Story extracted entire paragraphs from Fergusson's *Reports*, but the American was more forthcoming about his debt to the Scot. See *supra* note 150.

306 Eversley, *supra* note 211 at 6 note (a).

307 *Ibid* at 6.

308 *Ibid* at 908. See also Müller-Freienfels, *supra* note 12 at 44.

309 Eversley, *supra* note 211 at 909.

310 *Ibid* at 909 (emphasis added).

"essentially a domestic relation," and hence within the scope of his discussion of Master and Servant. However, Eversley also recognized that the relation of master and apprentice was "*[f]ormerly ...* more akin to that of parent and child than at the present day" because "[i]n many trades the master *used to* receive the apprentice into his house, supplying him with food and lodging, and treating him as one of his own household, and had more control over him than over an ordinary domestic servant."[311]

In Eversley's scheme, then, the only work relations that remained sufficiently domestic to warrant consideration in the context of the Law of Domestic Relations were domestic service and apprenticeship; the rest of the Law of the Master and Servant was not appropriately categorized within Domestic Relations.[312] The more "economic" of the private relations (in the modern, market-oriented sense of the word "economic") had, by this time, moved out of the household, into the market, leaving behind the other *familial* relations. In this regard, Eversley's text serves as a clear indication of the way that Blackstone's "private œconomical relations" shifted into what eventually became the Law of Domestic Relations by way of a piecemeal migration of the Law of Master and Servant out of the household and its (imperfect) identification with contract.[313] The next step involved shifting domestic service and apprenticeship back into contiguity with other work relations, but outside of the sphere of the household/home.

---

311 *Ibid* at 931 (emphasis added). See also Holdsworth, *supra* note 236.

312 A similar distinction between forms of work is evident in Macdonnell's *The Law of Master and Servant* from 1883. In a chapter entitled "Definitions of Master and Servant," Macdonnell says: "Originally the term [servant] indicated a sort of status. A servant was generally a member of his master's household. He was in a sense under his master's *potestas*. He is mentioned in the same context as the wife or son or daughter of the house ... [That] degree of intimacy ... is not now implied ... Mere casual temporary employment for a particular purpose will not suffice to make a person a servant within the meaning of some statutes. In the case of others this is enough." And then, in a footnote following the last excerpted sentence, Macdonnell adds: "It is often used as a synonym for domestic servant." Macdonnell's point seems to be that, by the late nineteenth century, the master-servant relation was generally no longer a household relation, the term "servant" having been expanded in scope over the course of the eighteenth and much of the nineteenth centuries to apply to most forms of work. At the same time, he seems to suggest that in certain contexts, "servant" was actually returning to its older, narrower, *domestic* meaning, while other forms of work were "employment" – precisely the distinction drawn by Eversley. See Macdonnell, *supra* note 177 at 37 and, on the same page, note (f) citing *Yewens v Noakes* (1832) 1 Mood CC 370.

313 Halley and Rittich, *supra* note 1 at 756–7.

VIII. The Emergence of Family Law

*A. Cementing the Family/Work and Status/Contract Distinctions:
Salmond*

The trends discussed in preceding sections – extrusion of (most) work
relations from the domestic realm, abstraction of contractual principles into the Law of Contract and subtraction of marriage therefrom,
and re-characterization of the essence of marriage as a form of status –
continued into the twentieth century. John Salmond's *Jurisprudence*,[314]
which first appeared in 1902, is perhaps the clearest example. Salmond
was a classical law don whose work continued in the systematic vein
established by Pollock, Anson, and Holland.[315] His concern was with
what he called "theoretical jurisprudence," or "the science of the first
principles of the civil law."[316]

Given Salmond's admiration of civilian legal arrangements (in chapter 1 of the work, entitled "The Science of Jurisprudence," Salmond
makes "[s]pecial mention … of the unfinished *System of Modern Roman
Law* by Savigny"[317]), it is unsurprising that he divided Substantive Civil
Law – the area with which we are concerned here – into Property, Obligations and Status, a division that bears more than a resemblance to
Savigny's treatment of Private Law (albeit in Salmond's scheme family
relations form a sub-set of Status, rather than a category on the same
level as Potentialities). With respect to Obligations, Salmond said, "its
most important branch … is the Law of Contract, which is itself divis-
ible into two portions – a general part dealing with the abstract principles of contractual obligation, and a special part concerned with the
particular kinds of contracts, such as sale, partnership, and suretyship."
The second branch of Obligations is tort.[318] Schematically, Salmond's
taxonomy looks like the diagram in Figure 2.5.[319]

---

314 John Salmond, *Jurisprudence*, 4th ed. (London: Stevens and Haynes, 1913) [Salmond,
　　Jurisprudence 1913].
315 See generally A.W.B. Simpson, "The Salmond Lecture" (2007) 38 *VUWLR* 669.
316 Salmond, *Jurisprudence* 1913, *supra* note 314 at 4.
317 *Ibid* at 7–8.
318 John Salmond, *Jurisprudence* (London: Stevens and Haynes, 1902) at 489 [Salmond,
　　Jurisprudence 1902]. This distinction between tort and contract was a shift beyond
　　Savigny's scheme and those of the earlier nineteenth century, in which tort
　　generally did not appear as a discrete category: Kennedy, "Savigny," *supra* note 192
　　at 813.
319 Salmond himself provided a map of the divisions in the law: see Salmond,
　　Jurisprudence 1902, *supra* note 318 at 492. My diagram is a slightly simplified version

Figure 2.5. Salmond's taxonomy of law

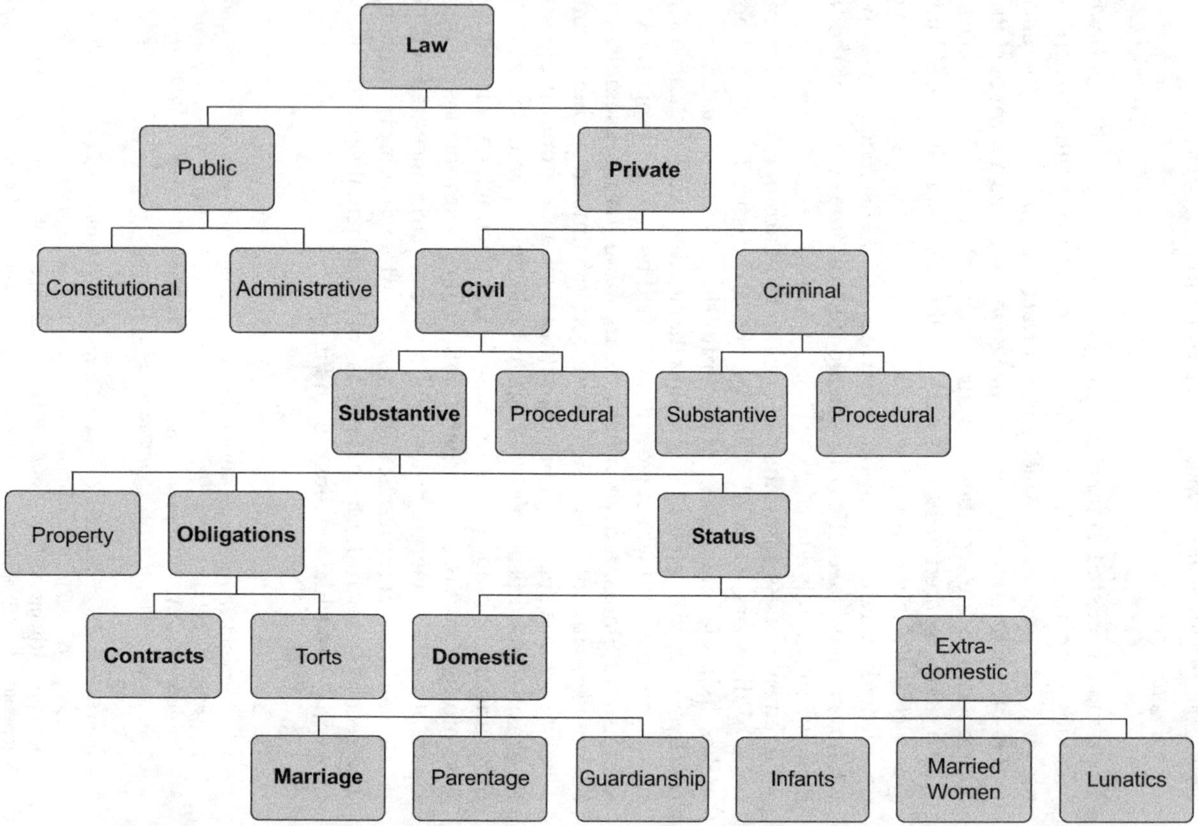

As a distinctly conceptual work, *Jurisprudence* provides little in the way of specifics regarding the master-servant relation. It appears, however, that Salmond envisaged work relations as falling within the sphere of contract: "The position of a slave is a matter of status, the position of a free servant is a matter of contract."[320] Salmond also refers to "rights vested in one person to the services of another: the rights, for example, which are created by a contract between master and servant, physician and patient, or employer and workman." In these instances, "the object of the right is the skill, knowledge, strength, time, and so forth, of the person bound." In a classically liberal register, Salmond then declared:

> A man may be the subject-matter of rights as well as the subject of them. His mind and body constitute an instrument which is capable of certain uses, just as a horse or a steam-engine is. In a law which recognises slavery, the man may be bought and sold, just as the horse or steam-engine can. But in our own law this is not so, and the only right that can be acquired over a human being is a temporal and limited right to the use of him, created by voluntary agreement with him – not a permanent and general right of ownership over him.[321]

In other words, relations between masters and servants, or employers and workmen, are contractual because they are based in mutual consent and the temporary alienation of labour power.[322] Salmond also does not appear to draw any distinction between forms of work – at least for the purposes of legal classification. While this may simply be a product of his perfunctory treatment of work relations, it can also be read as a signal pointing towards subsequent, clearer consolidations of work relations under a single banner.

In contrast with contract, status, according to Salmond, "is the sum of one's personal duties, liabilities, and disabilities, as well as of one's personal rights."[323] Thus, the status of a wife means "all the personal benefits and burden of which marriage is the legal source and title in a woman."[324] Proprietary rights, therefore, are outside of status.[325]

---

    of Salmond's, omitting, in particular, the "Introductory" areas of law that he situated alongside public and private.

320 Salmond, *Jurisprudence* 1913, *supra* note 314 at 211.

321 *Ibid* at 189–90.

322 See Locke, *supra* note 128, §§ 27–8.

323 Salmond, *Jurisprudence* 1913, *supra* note 314 at 210.

324 *Ibid*.

325 *Ibid* at note (6b).

Salmond also noted the usage adopted by some writers "to signify a man's personal legal condition, so far only as it is imposed upon him by the law without his own consent"; in his view, "[m]arriage creates a status in this sense, for although it is entered into by way of consent, it cannot be dissolved in that way, and the legal condition created by it is determined by the law, and cannot be modified by the agreement of the parties."[326]

Structurally, Salmond distinguished between "the Law of Domestic Status and the Law of Extra-domestic Status." The first category houses "the law of family relations" and comprises the laws of marriage, parentage, and guardianship. Extra-domestic Status "deals, for example, with the personal status of minors ... of married women (in relation to others than their husbands and children), of lunatics, aliens, convicts, slaves, and any other classes of persons whose personal condition is sufficiently characteristic to call for separate consideration." There is no mention of work relations in the discussion of Status. The reverse is not quite the case: Salmond does actually mention the "contract to marry, or ... the contract of marriage" (which is possibly his way of distinguishing between betrothal and completed marriage) in a section on The Nature of Obligations.[327] However, his purpose in doing so is actually to distinguish rights arising from relations such as marriage from choses in action – "[a] technical synonym for obligation," according to Salmond, because a "non-proprietary right *in personam*, such as that which arises from a contract to marry, or from the contract of marriage, is no more a chose in action in English law than it is an *obligatio* in Roman law."[328] That is, marriage is not properly part of the Law of Obligations; rather, it belongs within the Law of Status.

On a broad level, Salmond's taxonomy creates a clear distinction between the Family and its (personal) laws, and the market-based, proprietary laws of Contract. In this respect, despite some fairly significant differences in other matters of structure, Salmond and Holland were *ad idem*: each viewed contract as a species of Obligations[329] situated at the heart of private law, and treated work relations as a particular species of contract; marriage, on the other hand, was a form of status because

---

326 *Ibid* at 211.
327 *Ibid* at 423.
328 *Ibid*.
329 Although for Salmond, "[t]he coincidence ... is not logically complete: a promise of marriage, for example, being a contract which falls within the law of status, and not within the law of obligations": *ibid* at 428.

of the degree of public intervention in its regulation, and therefore sat outside of the Law of Obligations.

B. *Family Law and Employment Law Emerge and Diverge*

Textual confirmation of the transformation of Domestic Relations into Family Law, and the emergence of Employment Law as the successor to the Law of Master and Servant, came in the five-volume *Digest of English Civil Law* published between 1905 and 1917.[330] Book IV, by W.M. Geldart,[331] is entitled "Family Law" – and this is, as far I have been able to discern, the first time that the term appears as a classificatory tool in English legal texts dealing with contemporary law.[332] "Family Law" contains only two sections: "Marriage"; and "Relations of Children, Parents, and Guardians." The Law of Master and Servant is gone. Instead, those relations appear in book II, "Obligations," in a part written by R.W. Lee called "Obligations arising from Particular Contracts."[333] Section V of that Part is entitled "Employment."[334] The long process of disaggregating the legal household figured in Blackstone's "private œconomical relations" was almost complete: as shown in Figure 2.6, work and family were figured in the *Digest* as entirely distinct legal fields. Bearing testament to the influence of CLT, Employment was subsumed within the contractual realm of Obligations, while marriage was constituted in distinctly Savignian terms as the primary relation within the new field of Family Law.

---

330 Jenks, *Digest, supra* note 3.

331 W.M. Geldart, 'Family Law' in *ibid*, vol 4 (1916).

332 In their 1895 opus on medieval English legal history, Pollock and Maitland, *supra* note 120, employed the term "Family Law" to describe laws concerning "Marriage," "Husband and Wife" (essentially the property dimensions of marriage), and "Infancy and Guardianship": volume II, book II, chapter 7. Chapter 5 of the same work is entitled "Contract" but unsurprisingly does not deal with agreements concerning work; to the extent that such law existed in the period considered by the authors, it is found instead in volume I, book II, chapter 2, entitled "The Sorts and Conditions of Men," under the section "The Unfree," dealing with serfs. The usage of the term "Family Law" may be the result of the authors' familiarity with German and German legal thought, and in this respect the work may constitute another avenue through which German legal thought influenced English legal thought in the nineteenth century. However, given its medieval focus, I do not think the work can be considered centrally important in the reshaping of late nineteenth- and early twentieth-century English law, despite its canonical status within the discipline of legal history.

333 R.W. Lee, 'Obligations' in Jenks, *Digest, supra* note 3, vol 2 (1906) at 161.

334 *Ibid* at 207.

Given that we are dealing with a digest rather than a treatise, it is not especially surprising to find that Geldart avoided theorizing the nature of marriage. As such, it is difficult to tell whether he followed the general trend towards conceiving of the marriage relation as a form of (contract giving rise to) status. However, in the Preface written by Jenks (who had himself authored a work entitled *Husband and Wife in the Law* in 1909[335]), it is said that "the rules of English Civil Law which deal directly with family relationship are few in number, and of these a considerable part might, in strictness, be classed rather under Public than Private Law."[336] As we have seen, the public dimensions of marriage – especially the automatic imposition of a set of non-modifiable terms upon the parties to the relation – were crucial in the move towards a status-based conception of marriage. Accordingly, and in conjunction with the absence of any discussion of marriage in book II, "Obligations," the *Digest* overall tends to suggest a view of marriage as, at the very least, distinctly different from ordinary commercial contracts.

In contrast, work relations were expressly situated within the contractual domain, albeit as a particular species of contract. While this classification is open to question,[337] the important point for present purposes is that Lee's category of Employment reunited the laws of "Work and Labour" with "Master and Servant" and "Master and Apprentice,"[338]

---

335 Jenks, *Husband & Wife, supra* note 225. In this work, Jenks states that since the passage of *Lord Hardwicke's Act*, "the contract to marry, or 'engagement,' has been an ordinary secular contract": at 5. However, "[a]s the mere consequence of the marriage of two persons, certain rights are acquired by each, *without any special agreement*": at 35 (emphasis added). Further on, in a section entitled "Special Privileges and Disabilities of Married Women," Jenks notes the "considerable number of anomalous rules of law affecting the position of a married woman," and characterizes those rules as "survivals of the old status ideas, which are being rapidly replaced by the doctrine of free contract." Jenks therefore appears to envisage a general (and much simplified) legal move from status to contract in the mode of Henry Maine, *supra* note 41, but also suggests that in the realm of marriage, "old status ideas" remain operative. In this latter respect, he appears to use "status" in its older sense of hierarchic and hereditary personal conditions, rather than the more modern sense favoured by other legal writers.

336 "Nevertheless, the rules affecting marriage and its consequences are … important from the standpoint of the private citizen." Jenks, *Digest, supra* note 3, vol 1 (1905) at xvii.

337 See Deakin and Wilkinson, *supra* note 22 at 42–3; Adrian Merritt, "The Historical Role of the Law in the Regulation of Employment – Abstentionist or Interventionist?" (1982) 1 *Aust JL Soc* 56.

338 By this point, the traditional (as opposed to parish) master-apprentice relation was treated as generally contractual along the lines of the employer-employee relation; maintenance requirements existed only in specific – and by then

Figure 2.6. Structure of the *Digest of English Civil Law*

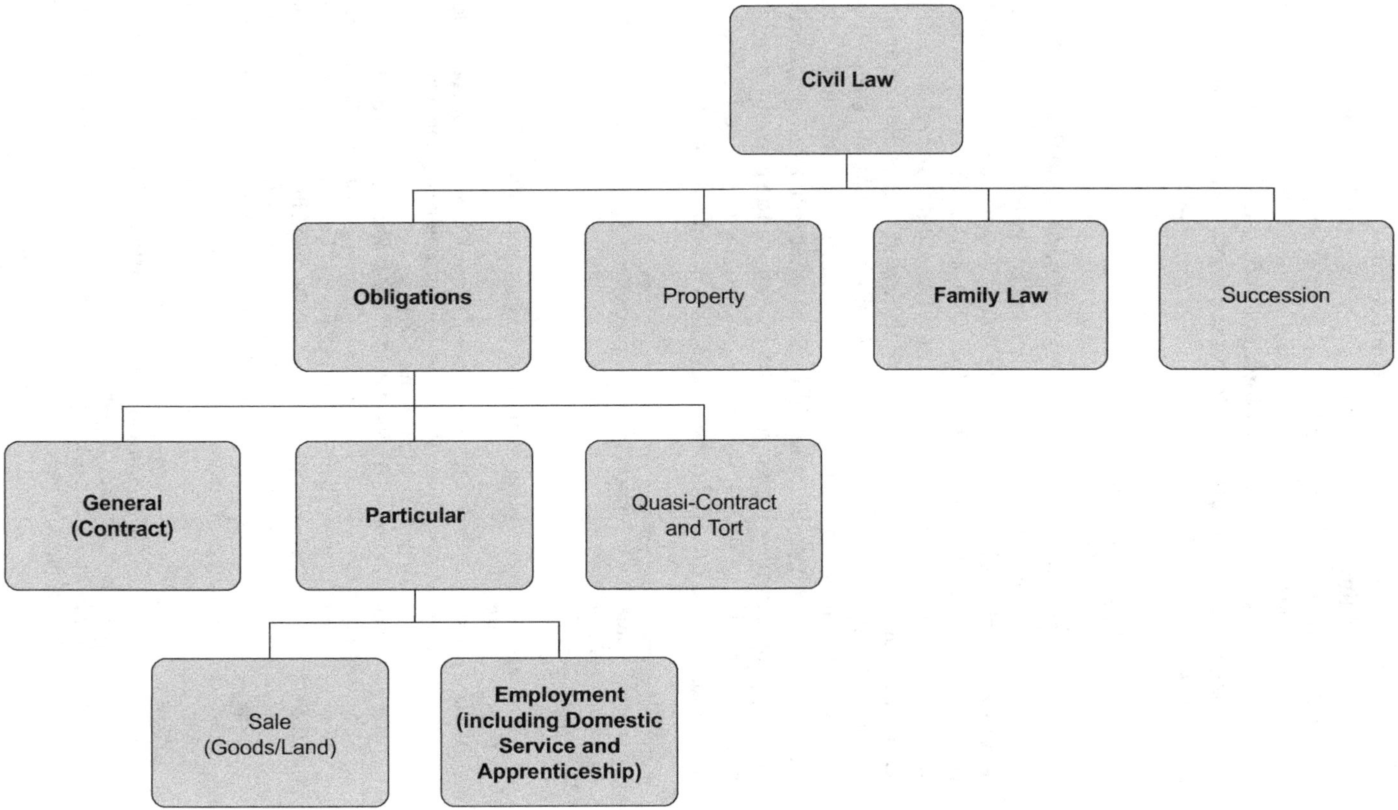

Civil Law

Obligations

Property

Family Law

Succession

General (Contract)

Particular

Quasi-Contract and Tort

Sale (Goods/Land)

Employment (including Domestic Service and Apprenticeship)

and thus eschewed the late nineteenth-century bifurcation of work relations according to the physical nexus (or lack thereof) with the household/home (most obviously seen in Eversley's *The Law of the Domestic Relations*). At the same time, the influence of nearly 200 years of generalized master-servant law is evident in the suite of non-modifiable terms that, by this time, attached to contracts of work and labour,[339] and contracts of service.[340]

C. *Family Law in the Textbook Tradition*

Despite the structural shifts evident in the *Digest of English Civil Law*, it took another 40 years for English legal thought to take the next step and generate a work exclusively focussed on the new field of Family Law.[341] (It also took until the early 1950s for an English university to offer a course on matters of family law. Müller-Freienfels credits the London School of Economics with this move,[342] though it seems that Peter Bromley was offering a course of lectures on Family Law at the University of Manchester in this same period.[343]) In 1957 both Peter Bromley's *Family Law*, and Graveson and Crane's *A Century of Family Law*, appeared.[344] I focus here on Bromley's text in conformity with the general concern in this chapter with treatises, and in view of what seems to be a general consensus among family law scholars that Bromley's text was the first

---

unusual – situations of household-based apprenticeship. See Lee, *supra* note 333, book II at 216–17.

339 *Ibid* at 222–3.

340 *Ibid* at 209–11.

341 See Michael Freeman, "Family Values and Family Justice" (1997) 50 *Current Leg Probs* 315 at 318.

342 Müller-Freienfels, *supra* note 12 at 44. King's College, University College London, and Cambridge soon followed. The course was not taught at Oxford until 1964 when Otto Kahn-Freund joined the faculty: *ibid*.

  One of the most important works of the 1970s also emerged from the LSE: Olive M. Stone's *Family Law: An Account of the Law of Domestic Relations in England and Wales in the Last Quarter of the Twentieth Century, with Some Comparisons* (London: Macmillan, 1977). Reflecting the gender bias of the times, though, Stone failed to obtain a professorship at the LSE despite nearly 30 years of service to the school.

343 Bromley, *supra* note 3, Preface: "I have written this book having in mind the present needs of my own students at Manchester, where I have for some years been delivering a course of lectures on this subject to third year undergraduates in the Faculty of Law of the University."

344 Bromley, *supra* note 3; Graveson and Crane, *supra* note 3. In the same year, Oliver McGregor published *Divorce in England: A Centenary Study* (London: Heinemann, 1957). While important, the book's focus is much too narrow to make it a rival to Bromley's field-defining work.

to unify the field.[345] In this respect, *Family Law* is not only instructive taxonomically and in terms of what it says about the nature of marriage; it is also an example of the continuation of the nineteenth-century scientific approach to law and legal classification evident in the textbook tradition of the early to mid-twentieth century.[346]

From a structural perspective, Bromley immediately demarcated his field, commencing in chapter I with a discussion of "The Scope of Family Law."[347] There, he stated, "[f]or our purpose we may regard the family as a basic social unit which consists normally of a husband and wife and their children."[348] Legal writers had made similar statements in the nineteenth century, but Bromley went a step further by characterizing "the legal relationship between the head of a household and his servants and lodgers [as] *essentially contractual and as such ... outside the scope of this book.*"[349] The inclusion by Bunyon and Eversley of domestic service and apprenticeship within domestic relations law was thus consciously avoided. Instead, the primary relationships in the new and considerably narrowed legal family of the twentieth century were "that of husband and wife *inter se*, and that of parent and child."[350] Normally, he said, "marriage is the basis of the family" and therefore constitutes the core of Family Law.[351]

On the nature of marriage, Bromley observed that it can be considered contractual in formal terms, but "it is, of course, quite unlike any commercial contract, and consequently it is *sui generis* in many respects,"[352] in particular because "marriage creates a status that limits the parties' power to make their own terms and also may affect their legal rights and duties with respect to other persons."[353] By status, Bromley meant "the condition of belonging to a particular class of persons to whom

---

345 Freeman, *supra* note 341 at 318; Müller-Freienfels, *supra* note 12 at 44; Burton, *supra* note 8 at 2; "Professor Peter Bromley," *The Times*, 28 March 2013 at 66 ("Peter Bromley was one of those rare scholars who single-handedly created a new legal discipline. He did so with the publication in 1957 of his magnum opus, *Family Law*."); Nigel Lowe, "Obituary: Professor Peter Mann Bromley," *Family Law*, 3 April 2013.

346 See Sugarman, *supra* note 15.

347 Bromley, *supra* note 3 at 1.

348 *Ibid*.

349 *Ibid* (emphasis added).

350 *Ibid*. Bromley continues by stating that "we must examine two other concepts: adoption ... and guardianship": *ibid*.

351 *Ibid* at 2. For an overview of developments in England post-Bromley see Müller-Freienfels, *supra* note 12 at 41–7.

352 Bromley, *supra* note 3 at 2.

353 *Ibid* 2–3.

the law assigns certain peculiar legal capacities or incapacities."[354] In essence, then, marriage was defined less by initial consent and more by the fact that "the spouses' mutual rights and duties are very largely fixed by law and not by agreement."[355] In other words, marriage still involved a little bit of contract, but its essence was a lot more status.

Bromley's approach to his subject was the culmination of a two-century process of change in English legal thought and taxonomy: Blackstone placed master and servant in front of husband and wife in the "private œconomical relations" of the household, and he treated marriage as nothing more than an ordinary contract; Eversley retained the master and servant category but only dealt with those work relationships that continued to exist within the home, and he placed husband and wife at the head of the list in its new guise as the status of marriage. Bromley followed this latter aspect but structurally he went one step further; following the division seen in the *Digest of English Civil Law*, he removed master and servant altogether because of its contractual nature, and situated *marriage* (in all its public and private importance) at the heart of the new field of Family Law.

This process of boundary-setting reified the emerging norm of the "traditional" nuclear family through a strictly legalistic focus on core principles affecting members of the marital family. In this sense, Bromley was continuing in the manner of classical treatise writers from the nineteenth-century by attempting to divest his subject of extraneous considerations (including certain persons and relationships), and by focussing in on the core legal principles said to govern the legal dimensions of family life. From this perspective, *Family Law* was the first of its kind in the field of what had hitherto been Domestic Relations; but it was also part of the longer trend, partially traced in this chapter, towards establishing discrete fields of private law that orbited the holy of holies: contract. And like treatises from the classical period, and others in the emerging field-defining textbook tradition of the twentieth century (such as Courtney Kenny's *Outlines of Criminal Law*[356] and P.H. Winfield's *Text-Book of the Law of Tort*[357]), *Family Law* exhibited a belief in the possibility of a principled exegesis of law through an almost exclusive focus on case law and, to a lesser extent, legislation.[358] As one slightly

---

354 *Ibid* 3.
355 *Ibid* quoting C.K. Allen, "Status and Capacity" (1930) 46 *Law Q Rev* 277 at 288.
356 Courtney Kenny, *Outlines of Criminal Law* (Cambridge: Cambridge University Press, 1902).
357 P.H. Winfield, *Text-Book of the Law of Tort* (London: Sweet & Maxwell, 1937).
358 Freeman, *supra* note 341 at 318.

exasperated reviewer of the second (1962) edition wrote: "True it is that your book is designed for English students who, like students everywhere, are primarily interested in passing exams. But could you not smuggle in some of the findings of the social sciences to pinpoint those areas where our law is defective?"[359]

As David Sugarman has pointed out, this formal approach had a practical as well as an ideological dimension. In view of the limited number of "institutions, students and therefore teachers teaching law" in England prior to the 1960s, jurists felt compelled to produce "textbooks that conceived of the law as unitary and principled and which verged on the 'dogmatic.'"[360] In this respect, "[t]he medium was the message. And the message was essentially about simplicity, and also through simplicity a celebration of the law as general principles, leading cases, judges and lawyers."[361]

IX. Conclusion

This chapter has traced the contribution made by legal scholars to the development of Family Law as a discrete and exceptional category within English law and legal thought. Commencing with Blackstone's eighteenth-century model of "private œconomical relations," it traced two primary movements. First, the disarticulation of productive work relations from the legal household in a staged process that turned on the nexus (or lack thereof) between work and the domestic sphere. In the nineteenth century, this approach led to the division of work relations across legal categories, with domestically located forms of work (service and apprenticeship) becoming housed in the category of Domestic Relations, while the Law of Master and Servant became the general home and template for wage labour. In the twentieth century, under the continuing sway of contractual ideology, the Law of Master and Servant morphed into Employment Law, and home-based forms of work were shifted therein.

The second, parallel movement involved the elevation of the marriage relation to the front of the list of Domestic Relations, and a general trend towards separating entry into marriage, which continued to be conceptualized in terms of consent and contract, from the ongoing essence of marriage, defined by the state's imposition of non-modifiable terms

---

359 Bernard Green, "*Family Law*. By P.M. Bromley. London. Butterworths. Second edition. 1962. Pp. xxv, 516." (1963) 15:1 *U Toronto LJ* 249.

360 Sugarman, *supra* note 15 at 50–1.

361 *Ibid.*

based on the public importance of the marital relation. That process was part of a broader effort to systematize English law and develop an abstract Law of Contract, which, because of its alignment with the ideology of individual will, was thought to require the subtraction of household-based relations with their accompanying sets of non-modifiable, state-imposed rights and obligations.

The emergence of the field of Family Law (and to a more limited extent, Employment Law) can thus be seen to have relied upon intersecting conceptual movements towards and away from both contract and status. Maine's aphorism does contain an important kernel of truth in the development of nineteenth century English legal thought, in particular its scientific tendencies and ideological valorization of contract; however, a movement from contract to status also took place in the domain of family relations. (And it must be remembered that neither movement was ever perfected.) The result of these mutually constitutive processes for the legal conception of the family is apparent in Bromley's mid-twentieth century text, *Family Law*, which expressly excluded all work relations, and pointedly situated the status of marriage at the heart of the field.

Chapter Three

Law and the Disarticulation of Work from Family Life

As in precapitalist society, throughout most of capitalist history the family has been the basic unit of economic production – not the wage-earning father but the household as a whole. While there was an intense division of labor within the family, based upon age, sex, and family position, there was scarcely a division between the family and the world of commodity production, at least not until the nineteenth century.[1]

I. Introduction

Over the course of the eighteenth and nineteenth centuries, the English family came to be defined in part by what it no longer was: an economically productive unit. This legal (and social) framing of the family's borderlines was, on one level, always mythical[2] – housework and care work continued to occur within the family and were productive endeavours whether or not they resulted in direct financial remuneration or legal recognition as such. On another level, though, the emergence of a conception of the family as a non-productive unit was a reality grounded in distinct historical processes through which relations that we now characterize as employment were physically and conceptually shifted out of the household. The preceding chapter showed how this process occurred on an intellectual level within scholarly legal thought, resulting in the disaggregation of the Blackstonian legal household

---

1 Eli Zaretsky, *Capitalism, the Family, and Personal Life,* revised ed. (New York: Harper & Row, 1986) at 13.

2 Janet Halley and Kerry Rittich, "Critical Directions in Comparative Family Law: Genealogies and Contemporary Studies of Family Law Exceptionalism" (2010) 58:4 *Am J Comp L* 753 at 754.

into the nineteenth-century categories of the Law of Domestic Relations and the Law of Master and Servant, and their eventual further re-characterization as Family Law and Employment Law. This chapter addresses some of the institutional legal factors (principally statute and common law) that developed and consolidated legal conceptions of, and social practices around, work, and its nexus (or lack thereof) with the family; in particular, the shift away from live-in service and autarkic modes of production towards intensified reliance on (partially) contractual forms of wage labour performed outside of residential spaces and in exchange for cash remuneration.[3]

Part II addresses what might be termed legal background conditions for the transition to modern conceptions and practices of work: parliamentary enclosure and relief of the poor.[4] In a direct sense, these eighteenth and nineteenth century programs were concerned with property law and indigence. On an operative level, however, enclosure laws and poor laws were crucial to the development of modern legal understandings of, and social practices around, wage labour and its disarticulation from the family.[5] Enclosure laws' consolidation of agricultural interests among wealthy landowners and the removal of common rights to land from the poor resulted, at least in certain parts of England, in a dramatic decline in household-based labour and intensified reliance on forms of wage labour for economic survival. These laws thus contributed to a social shift away from subsistence production and live-in service (most notably service in husbandry), towards short-term contractual forms of labour, which tended over time to eschew integration of work and family life.[6] Enclosure laws also point to the development in this period

---

3 According to David Levine, a "generous" estimate of the number of wage-dependent proletarians in the early sixteenth century is 600,000 in a population of 2,400,000. By the middle of the nineteenth century, "we find that four out of five members of the labor force were either 'employees' or domestic servants": David Levine, "Production, Reproduction, and the Proletarian Family in England, 1500–1851" in David Levine, ed., *Proletarianization and Family History* (Orlando: Academic Press, 1984) at 87, 88.

4 On background rules in law see Robert Hale, "Coercion and Distribution in a Supposedly Noncoercive State" (1923) 38 *Pol Science Quart* 470.

5 In this respect, part II also functions as a methodological reminder of the constructed nature of legal categories, the dangers of anachronism in historical approaches to intersecting modes of legal regulation, and the importance of paying attention to areas falling outside of the generally understood core of a particular legal domain. See further Halley and Rittich, *supra* note 2.

6 This was a staged process rather than a sudden complete shift. In the early years of industrialization cotton spinning and weaving continued to occur along family-based lines (the "putting-out" system), albeit subject to the demands of those providing

of a legal framing of work as a practice organized along strict spatial and temporal lines: outside of the home, and in accordance with the directions of masters.[7] (In this respect, the analysis also lends a measure of support to David Lemmings' claim that the eighteenth century in England saw a shift from consent to command in matters of governance and administration.[8]) In a corresponding manner, nineteenth century changes to the old Poor Law system drastically curtailed outdoor relief to the poor and instituted the workhouse system of indoor relief. This policy shift amounted to a sharp institutional push in the direction of wage labour, and signals the emergence of a legal understanding of personal support premised on the performance of work outside the home, backed up by private forms of support within the family, with state relief as a final (and designedly unpleasant) option.[9]

Part III considers how the transition away from a household model of the family towards disaggregated realms of (public) work and (private) family life, and specifically an economy based on wage (rather than household) labour, was partially constituted by legal developments that extended the patriarchal model of domestic service to workers in general. It shows how the move towards a legal understanding of work based on consent and contract occurred in conjunction with, and in reliance upon, the development of a statutory regime of master-servant law that criminalized breach of contract on the part of workers; and that this punitive code was augmented at common law by a series of

---

the raw materials. See Sven Beckert, *Empire of Cotton: A Global History* (New York: Vintage Books, 2015) at 39–40; John Rule, *The Experience of Labour in Eighteenth-Century Industry* (London: Croom Helm, 1981) at 37.

7 As chapter 4 shows in greater detail, this disaggregation of work and family also had significant gender implications as responsibility for these separate domains split along male/female lines.

8 David Lemmings, *Law and Government in England during the Long Eighteenth Century: From Consent to Command* (Basingstoke: Palgrave Macmillan, 2015). This argument chimes with Christopher Brooks' finding that litigation rates in England dropped sharply in the eighteenth century – a reflection, he suggested, of a reduced degree of civic participation and the elitism of eighteenth-century legal culture. Christopher W. Brooks, *Lawyers, Litigation and English Society since 1450* (London: Hambledon Press, 1998).

9 In this respect, the discussion shows that the early modern imbrication of laws governing work and poverty continued well into the nineteenth-century. As Deakin and Wilkinson have observed, "[t]he incomplete separation of wages and poor relief for much of this period was reflected in the tendency for the poor law to be simultaneously a law governing the work relationship and a body of regulation determining access to non-waged income." Simon Deakin and Frank Wilkinson, *The Law of the Labour Market: Industrialization, Employment and Legal Evolution* (Oxford: Oxford University Press, 2005) at 2–3.

decisions that expanded the legal meaning of "servant." It thus demonstrates how one of the key shifts that contributed to the conceptual and practical dissolution of the productive household – the move towards market-based forms of work that were disarticulated from family life – actually relied upon, and in certain respects extended,[10] the very same legal subordination that was fundamental to the much older (familial) authority enjoyed by masters over their servants.[11]

II. Property, Poverty, and Wage Labour

A. Property: Enclosure, Households and Work

> Most simply, it [enclosure] meant the extinction of common rights which people held over the farm lands and commons of the parish, the abolition of the scattered holdings in the open fields and a re-allocation of holdings in compact blocks, accompanied usually by the physical separation of the newly created fields and closes by the erection of fences, hedges or stone walls. Thereafter, the lands so enclosed were held "in severalty," that is, they were reserved for the sole use of the individual owners or tenants.[12]

The enclosure of England began in the fifteenth and sixteenth centuries. This "revolution of the rich against the poor,"[13] as Karl Polanyi called it, occurred ostensibly by agreement between large landowners.[14]

---

10 The demise of feudal obligations essentially perfected a master's patriarchal control over his servants, since no lord further up the feudal pyramid could make claims in respect of the servants of his vassals. See Christopher L. Tomlins, *Freedom Bound: Law, Labor, and Civic Identity in Colonizing English America, 1580–1865* (New York: Cambridge University Press 2010) at 71–2, 361–2.

11 It may thus be seen as an instance of what Reva Siegel has called "preservation through transformation": Reva B. Siegel, "'The Rule of Love': Wife Beating as Prerogative and Privacy" (1996) 105:8 *Yale LJ* 2117.

12 G.E. Mingay, *Parliamentary Enclosure in England: An Introduction to Its Causes, Incidence, and Impact, 1750–1850* (London: Longman, 1997) at 7. See also M. Dorothy George, *England in Transition: Life and Work in the Eighteenth Century* (Harmondsworth: Penguin Books, 1953) at 78–9.

13 Karl Polanyi, *The Great Transformation: The Political and Economic Origins of Our Time* (Boston: Beacon Press, 2001) at 37. However, Polanyi also argues that the Tudors and early Stuarts wisely limited the pace of reform, which otherwise "might have been ruinous, and have turned the process itself into a degenerative instead of a constructive agent": at 39 See also J.L. Hammond and Barbara Hammond, *The Village Labourer, 1760–1832: A Study of the Government of England Before the Reform Bill* (London: Longman, 1995) at 35; George, *supra* note 12 at 78–9.

14 Enclosure by agreement occurred through common consent of the owners of land. Enclosure could also occur "piecemeal," whereby "owners agreed among

Enclosure pursuant to private Acts of Parliament, however, became the primary mode of enclosing lands in the eighteenth century;[15] and it seems that in overall terms the bulk of enclosures were carried out with parliamentary approval.[16] Accordingly, and for reasons of temporal scope, this section is only concerned with parliamentary enclosure. More specifically, it shows that this "institutional or political intervention"[17] in the structure of English society helped to generate a legal and social model of work predicated on its exteriority to the household. It traces the connections between enclosure laws, loss of common rights, and the erosion of forms of subsistence once available to semi-proletarian families;[18] reduced demand for live-in servants; and the consequent increased dependence of poor families on short-term waged work.[19] This transformation in social practice was

---

themselves to take small pieces of land, ranging in size from 1 acre, to 5, 10 or 20 acres or more, out of the open fields or commons for their own exclusive use." Mingay suggests that the total area affected by these forms was "considerable," though reliable estimates are not possible. Mingay, *supra* note 12 at 11–12.

15 The reason seems to be that, during the eighteenth century, Parliament became willing to entertain bills for enclosure in which there was less than complete assent on the part of affected parties. Chancery, on the other hand, generally refused to enforce an enclosure award against dissenters. See Robert Tennyson, "From Unanimity to Proportionality: Assent Standards and the Parliamentary Enclosure Movement" (2013) 31:1 *L & Hist Rev* 199 at 209–10. For much of the century a four-fifths majority was required; this was later reduced to three-quarters by an Act passed in 1773: 3 Geo III, c 81, s 1. See K.D.M. Snell, *Annals of the Labouring Poor: Social Change and Agrarian England, 1660–1900* (Cambridge: Cambridge University Press, 1985) at 188–9.

16 J.M. Neeson, *Commoners: Common Right, Enclosure and Social Change in England, 1700–1820* (Cambridge: Cambridge University Press, 1993) at 329–30; Hammond and Hammond, *supra* note 13 at 26. J.R. Wordie argues that the bulk of enclosures occurred in the seventeenth century: "The Chronology of English Enclosure, 1500–1914" (1983) 36:2 *Econ Hist Rev* 483. His view does not appear to be shared by other historians: see, e.g., John Chapman, 'The Chronology of English Enclosure' (1984) 37:4 *Econ Hist Rev* 557.

17 Neeson, *supra* note 16 at 329–30; E.P. Thompson, *The Making of the English Working Class* (London: Penguin, 2013) at 217.

18 Jane Humphries, "Enclosures, Common Rights, and Women: The Proletarianization of Families in the Late Eighteenth and Early Nineteenth Centuries" (1990) 50:1 *J Econ Hist* 17 at 18. See also Robert J. Steinfeld, *The Invention of Free Labor: The Employment Relation in English and American Law and Culture, 1350–1870* (Chapel Hill: University of North Carolina Press, 1991) at 34: "Access to the common was crucial to the way of life that permitted many among the laboring poor to work for wages only on a casual basis." [Steinfeld, *Free Labor*] See further Deborah Valenze, *The First Industrial Woman* (New York: Oxford University Press, 1995) at 45: "the pattern of employment established by enclosure was the key to the fate of women in nineteenth century agriculture."

19 This was no accident of history. As Hickel notes in his analysis of global poverty and its historical creation, "[b]udding capitalists cannot get very far unless there are people willing to work for them in exchange for wages. We take this for granted

imposed by (property) law, but it also helped to consolidate the emerging legal understanding of work relations as situated outside of the household and oppositional to what remained after their exit: the private family.

I. COMMON RIGHTS

In legal terms, "right of common" was an incorporeal hereditament.[20] In his *Commentaries on the Laws of England*, Blackstone defined "common of pasture" as "a right of feeding one's beasts on another's land; for in those waste grounds, which are usually called commons, the property of the soil is generally in the lord of the manor; as in common fields it is in the particular tenants."[21] This "most universal right … was originally permitted, not only for the encouragement of agriculture, but for the necessity of thing. For, when lords of manors granted out parcels of land to tenants, for services either done or to be done, these tenants could not plough or manure the land without beasts; these beasts could not be sustained without pasture; and pasture could not be had but in the lord's wastes, and on the unenclosed fallow grounds of themselves and the other tenants."[22] Blackstone's legal description captures something of the social interdependence involved in the provision of common rights, but it does not quite reveal the importance of common rights to the rural poor.[23] According to Mingay:

> The common or commons (there might be more than one in the parish) consisted of areas of open land set aside for grazing during the summer months when the arable or crop lands in the fields were shut up to keep stock from damaging the growing corn. In addition to the

---

today, but there was a time, not long ago, when it wasn't quite so easy. Up through the Middle Ages, the vast majority of people in Europe – at least outside the city states – wouldn't have *wanted* to work for wages. People didn't need to earn wages in order to live." Jason Hickel, *The Divide: Global Inequality from Conquest to Free Markets* (New York: W.W. Norton & Co, 2018) at 74.

20 William Blackstone, *Commentaries on the Laws of England* (Oxford: Clarendon Press, 1765–9), book II, Table of Contents and 32.

21 *Ibid* at 32.

22 *Ibid* at 33. Blackstone included discussion of infringement of rights to commons under the broad category "Disturbances" in book IV at 237 ff (for example, "where any act is done, by which the right of another to his common is incommoded or diminished … [such as] where one who hath no right of common, puts his cattle into the land"). Blackstone also recognized the right to glean: book III at 212–13.

23 "[T]he commons," according to the Hammonds, "were the patrimony of the poor." Hammond and Hammond, *supra* note 13 at 103.

farmers, numbers of cottagers and others might have the right to graze a cow or horse on the commons, find pannage (acorns and beech-mast) there for pigs, cut brushwood or furze for fuel, and gather berries and herbs in season. Contemporaries also spoke of the "waste," a term which included small areas of stony or rocky ground together with more extensive stretches of heathlands, moors and bogs, as well as barren mountains and steep hillsides.[24]

For commoners of all sorts, the ability to maintain livestock on common areas was the most economically valuable common right,[25] though it was by no means universally enjoyed.[26] Cows, in particular, could form the basis of subsistence existence. According to Humphries, "with a decent cow producing six quarts of milk per day worth around a penny a quart in 1800, the revenue from sales of milk or butter, or from suckling calves, amounted to 3s 6d per week or £9 2 s per year" – amounts that "remain significant compared with laborer's wages."[27] There were also important by-products from cow keeping, such as skim milk left over from making butter (useful in particular for supplementing the diets of children[28] or as pig feed[29]), and manure for fields (to be used or sold).

---

24 Mingay, *supra* note 12 at 8.

25 "Even if their common rights provided only a summer keep, with several neighboring open field parishes it was possible to buy hay to feed the cows in winter." Humphries, *supra* note 18 at 25. See also Snell, *supra* note 15 at 174.

26 Mingay argues that few commons are likely to have provided cottagers with "really good pasture" for their cows: Mingay, *supra* note 12 at 135. Again, though, it seems that the extent of rights was regionally specific. Needwood Forest, for instance, supported cows belonging to numerous poor families. The *Staffordshire Advertiser* reported on a meeting chaired by Lord Vernon on the subject of enclosing the forest, stating, "it would be of material disadvantage in depriving them of keeping cows, by which their families are in great measure supported and kept from the Parishes": *Staffordshire Advertiser*, 11 October 1800 in Neeson, *supra* note 16 at 72, note 58. And, at Chipping Norton in Oxfordshire, prior to enclosure in 1769, every householding parishioner had the right to graze two horses or one cow on the 500-acre common: *ibid* at 73.

27 Humphries, *supra* note 18 at 24. See also Neeson, *supra* note 16 at 310–11; Mingay, *supra* note 12 at 135.

28 Milk helped to make potatoes and oatmeal into sufficiently nutritious meals to sustain families: Snell, *supra* note 15 at 178 referring to David Davies, *The Case of Labourers in Husbandry Stated and Considered, in Three Parts* (London, 1795) at 35–7.

29 Late eighteenth-century figures suggest that "[p]igs kept on skim milk [were] worth 18d per week," or roughly £2 to net annual profit: Humphries, *supra* note 18 at 26, table 1 (figures for Brownlow and Crutchley).

Access to pasture was not the only important common right.[30] Customary rights to "shrubs, woods, undergrowth, stone quarries and gravel pits" – commons of turbary, digging, and estovers in contemporaneous legal parlance[31] – were important sources of fuel[32] for cooking and wood for housing; foraging produced dietary supplements in the form of berries, nuts and wild herbs;[33] and gleaning could also result in crucial bushels of wheat for the family's diet.[34] In *Change in the Village*, George Sturt observed:

> By the peasant system ... people derived the necessaries of life from the materials and soil of their own countryside. Now, so long as they had the common, the inhabitants of the valley were in a large degree able to conform to this system, the common being, as it were, a supplement to the cottage gardens, and furnishing means of extending the scope of the ... home industries. It encouraged the poorest labourer to practise, for instance, all those time-honoured crafts which Cobbett ... had advocated as the one hope for labourers. The cow-keeping, the bread-making, the fattening of pigs and curing of bacon ... it was the common which made all this possible.[35]

The common, and the labour of women. As Humphries has pointed out, women were often the principal members of the household involved in subsistence-based production.[36] "Self-employment was an *economic*

---

30 Wally Seccombe, *A Millennium of Family Change: Feudalism to Capitalism in Northwestern Europe* (London: Verso, 1992) at 176; Bridget Hill, *Women, Work, and Sexual Politics in Eighteenth-Century England* (Oxford: Basil Blackwell, 1989) at 36–7 [Hill, *Women, Work*].

31 Blackstone, *supra* note 20, book II at 34. The right to fish in another's waters was known as "common of piscary": *ibid*.

32 Fuel was recognized as particularly important for poor families' budgets: Humphries, *supra* note 18 at 32 citing Pamela Horn, *Labouring Life in the Victorian Countryside* (Dublin: Gill and Macmillan, 1976).

33 Humphries, *supra* note 18 at 32 citing Alan Everitt, "Farm Labourers" in Joan Thirsk, ed., *The Agrarian History of England and Wales* (Cambridge: Cambridge University Press, 1967–85) at 396–465.

34 Humphries, *supra* note 18 at 35. According to the Hammonds, "[f]rom time immemorial the labourer had sent his wife and children into the fields to glean or leaze after the harvest.... To such a family gleaning rights represented the equivalent of some six or seven weeks' wages." Hammond and Hammond, *supra* note 13 at 107. See also Neeson, *supra* note 16 at 313.

35 Published under the pseudonym George Bourne, *Change in the Village* (New York: G.H. Doran, 1912) at 77–111, excerpted in Snell, *supra* note 15 at 166–7.

36 Humphries, *supra* note 18 at 40. See also Neeson, *supra* note 16 at 50; Hill, *Women, Work, supra* note 30 at 24–46; Mingay, *supra* note 12 at 139.

option"[37] for women – at least to some degree. Many women worked for wages prior to enclosure, but often only in a part-time capacity "while working for themselves on the commons and open fields as a feature of a more family-based economy";[38] as Ivy Pinchbeck argued in *Women Workers and the Industrial Revolution*, "the commons gave his [a labourer's] wife an opportunity of contributing to the family maintenance."[39]

Determining the numbers of commoners affected by enclosure is difficult. In some areas it seems that, "[c]ommoners with rights of pasture attached to land they worked or to cottages they occupied were perhaps half of the county population on the eve of enclosure," though this figure probably represents an upper limit.[40] To this group must be added landless commoners, who made use of commons and wastes on a customary basis.[41]

II. THE FORM AND EFFECTS OF ENCLOSURES

Parliamentary enclosure fundamentally altered this state of production and undercut the associated connection between work and family life by removing working families' abilities to support themselves in ways other than (or in addition to) waged work. Childcare responsibilities and the consolidating ideology of the private family[42] overseen by wives/mothers meant that married women increasingly remained within the home,[43] performing work that, owing to its unwaged nature, came to be constructed in legal and economic thought as unproductive,[44] while men engaged in paid (and hence productive) forms of labour outside of the home.

---

37 Humphries, *supra* note 18 at 32.

38 Snell, *supra* note 15 at 158.

39 Ivy Pinchbeck, *Women Workers in the Industrial Revolution, 1750–1850*, 3rd ed. (London: Virago, 1981) at 22.

40 Neeson, *supra* note 16 at 64, 224 (referring to Northamptonshire, a part of the Midlands, which were disproportionately affected by enclosure).

41 *Ibid* at 56. Determining their numbers is virtually impossible, though, given the absence of official records concerning the extent of their enjoyment, and subsequent loss, of common rights. *Ibid* at 64–71. Protests, both physical and literary, give a sense of the outrage felt by landless commoners and their supporters. *Ibid* at 290–1.

42 See chapter 1, part II(A)(i).

43 See Joanne Conaghan, "Time to Dream? Flexibility, Families, and the Regulation of Working Time" in Judy Fudge and Rosemary Owens, eds., *Precarious Work, Women, and the New Economy* (Oxford: Hart Publishing, 2006) 101 at 107–8, referring to E.P. Thompson, "Time, Work-Discipline, and Industrial Capitalism" (1967) 38 *Past and Present* 56, and noting the problems caused by timed work for women with caring responsibilities.

44 See further chapter 4.

The effects of the estimated 5,265 private enclosure Acts passed by the English Parliament in the eighteenth and nineteenth centuries[45] were felt most keenly in the Midlands, where some counties experienced enclosure of more than 50 per cent of their total area.[46] Elsewhere, though, significant areas were enclosed prior to parliamentary enclosures.[47] Thus, Turner estimates that parliamentary enclosures affected 6,794,429 acres in England, or 20.9 per cent of the land area.[48] Chapman, using a different method, gives a slightly higher figure of 24 per cent of the land area of both England and Wales.[49] Mingay concludes that, "parliamentary enclosure affected a very significant proportion of the country's agricultural land, about a quarter, or probably more."[50] (Obviously, then, the argument being made here is not that enclosure alone generated the transition to wage labour – it was *one* important factor among others.[51])

When an enclosure bill received parliamentary approval[52] (and they generally did[53]), "the Commissioners named in the Bill would descend

---

45 Mingay, *supra* note 12 at 14 referring to Michael Turner, *English Parliamentary Enclosure: Its Historical Geography and Economic History* (Folkestone: Archon Books, 1980) at 179, 181.

46 Mingay *supra* note 12 at 16; see also George, *supra* note 12 at 80.

47 Eric Hobsbawm and George Rudé argued in *Captain Swing* (London: Lawrence and Wishart, 1969) that common rights were vestigial by the eighteenth century and that the English peasantry had disappeared long before the main phase of enclosure: see Neeson, *supra* note 16 at 301.

48 Mingay, *supra* note 12 at 15; Neeson, *supra* note 16 at 329.

49 John Chapman, "The Extent and Nature of Parliamentary Enclosure" (1987) 35:1 *Agr Hist Rev* 25.

50 Mingay, *supra* note 12 at 15. This figure increases considerably (by around 7 per cent) when private Act enclosures that dealt only with commons and wastelands (as opposed to those dealing with arable open fields and associated commons) are taken into account: *ibid* at 19. This form of enclosure grew in significance over time, as open fields were progressively enclosed: *ibid* at 23.

51 Shifts in the nature of production, in particular the move towards industrial manufacturing, also played a transformative role in shaping work practices. See Beckert, *supra* note 6 at xii.

52 The process of parliamentary enclosure began with a petition in Parliament from a local person or persons, setting out the case for enclosing certain lands. Once leave was granted for a Bill to be introduced, it was read in the manner of public Bills and referred to a parliamentary committee (often comprising Members who were interested in the result) for consideration, alongside any petitions lodged against the proposed enclosure. For discussion of formalities see Hammond and Hammond, *supra* note 13 at 43–52, 73. See also Mingay, *supra* note 12 at 60; Snell, *supra* note 15 at 188–9.

53 According to Mingay, parliamentary scrutiny of Bills resulted "in a surprisingly high proportion of Bills being withdrawn – 22 per cent between 1750 and 1815 in

on the district and distribute the land."[54] Distribution of common rights was conducted by reference to existing legal interests; houses occupying part of the arable and meadowland of a village had rights to "portion of the herbage of the common pastures," but recently built dwellings and houses without land carried no such rights (which is not to say that the occupants of those houses were not permitted to use common areas).[55] According to Mingay: "Enclosure Commissioners were bound to give due compensation to the *legal owners* of the houses and lands to which common rights were attached: this meant, of course, that they could not offer compensation to those persons who were merely the *tenants* of such houses and lands, who often actually exercised the rights to use the common."[56] As one enclosure Act stated, "all other Common Rights in and upon the said Meadows and Pastures shall thenceafter be extinguished."[57] Formally, it was open to small proprietors and cottagers to plead their case to the Commissioners; in reality, it seems likely that many such persons did not possess the requisite knowledge or resources to bring claims in the proper form.[58]

The social impact of this legal framework was disastrous for small farmers and cottagers.[59] Interests granted to those who could prove

---

Northamptonshire": Mingay, *supra* note 12 at 68. This still leaves an approval rate of nearly 80 per cent.

54 Hammond and Hammond, *supra* note 13 at 43. The Commissioners possessed "a summary, and in most cases uncontrollable jurisdiction": *ibid* at 58, quoting *Report of the Select Committee on the Expense and Mode of Obtaining Enclosure* (1800).

55 Mingay, *supra* note 12 at 126–7.

56 *Ibid.*

57 39 & 40 Geo III, c 86, s 28. See the discussion of this Act, *supra* note 15.

58 Challenging the authority of Lords of the Manor and other large landholders in the parish must also have presented a formidable obstacle: Hammond and Hammond, *supra* note 13 at 63. As Christopher Hill has rather sarcastically noted: "All he had to do was to learn to read, hire an expensive lawyer, spend a few weeks in London and be prepared to face the wrath of the powerful men in his village." Christopher Hill, *Reformation to Industrial Revolution* (Harmondsworth: Pelican Books, 1969) at 270 [Hill, *Reformation*]. This being said, Peter King has argued that enclosure did *not* lead to a corresponding increase in convictions for theft: "If the nineteenth-century newspapers are any guide, the gleaners were probably let off with a strong reprimand." Peter King, *Crime and Law in England, 1750–1840* (Cambridge: Cambridge University Press, 2006) at 316.

59 According to the Hammonds, "enclosure was fatal to three classes: the small farmer, the cottager, and the squatter. To all of these classes their common rights were worth more than anything they received in return." Hammond and Hammond, *supra* note 13 at 97. This generally destructive image of enclosure is not a view shared by all historians. J.D. Chambers and G.E. Mingay contend that in an overall sense enclosure benefited the rural poor by providing them with new opportunities for

legal rights of common were often less valuable than former common rights owing to the small size of allotments and the inability to properly graze livestock. Furthermore, the land over which rights were granted pursuant to an enclosure Act still needed to be enclosed, which was often prohibitively expensive.[60] Commoners with allotments were, therefore, often left with little option but to sell and join the ranks of landless labourers.[61] Those who received no replacement rights were simply left without the ability to maintain their animals or forage for food and fuel.[62]

The change was momentous … To a greater or less extent, *most of them were already wage-earners, though not regularly* … the majority … had been obliged to sell their labour itself, when they required money. Wage-earning, therefore, was no new thing in the village; only, *the need to earn*

---

work: J.D. Chambers, "Enclosure and Labour Supply in the Industrial Revolution" (1953) 5:3 *Econ Hist Rev* 319 (though Chambers does state that "landless or semi-landless workers, together with the small tenants who disappeared through consolidation, represent the real victims of enclosure": at 326); J.D. Chambers and GE Mingay, *The Agricultural Revolution, 1750–1880* (London: Batsford, 1966). In contrast, Snell's work on post-enclosure unemployment patterns pushes against a reparative reading of enclosure. In his view, Chambers "exaggerated the benefits of any increase or new found regularity of 'employment' after enclosure": Snell, *supra* note 15 at 210. In his estimation, "the tendency towards a more acute distribution of unemployment in the early nineteenth century must have been partly an effect of enclosure": *ibid* at 147–9. For present purposes it is unnecessary to take a position on the qualitative question of whether the shift to wage labour benefited the rural poor. The crucial point – upon which both sides agree – is that the loss of common rights occasioned by parliamentary enclosure was an important causal factor in the breakdown of the productive household and the shift towards a system of work based around wage labour.

60 Snell, *supra* note 15 at 190–1; Hammond and Hammond, *supra* note 13 at 101; Deakin and Wilkinson, *supra* note 9 at 124.

61 Hammond and Hammond, *supra* note 13 at 97–9; Deakin and Wilkinson, *supra* note 9 at 125.

62 One villager in Bedfordshire declared to Arthur Young, "I kept four cows before the parish was enclosed and now I don't keep so much as a goose, and you ask me what I lose by it!" Snell, *supra* note 15 at 174 citing T. Batchelor, *General View of the Agriculture of the County of Bedfordshire* (1808) at 235. Arthur Young's 1801 "Inquiry into the Propriety of Applying Wastes to the Better Maintenance and Support of the Poor" suggested that the loss experienced by villagers was not only economic: "ownership of a little property, be it only a single cow, gave a man a feeling of independence in which he could take pride, a pride sufficient to keep him from looking to the parish for support from the poor rates": Arthur Young, "Inquiry into the Propriety of Applying Wastes to the Better Maintenance and Support of the Poor" (1801) XXXVI *Ann Ag* at 502, 581, in Mingay, *supra* note 12 at 136.

became more insistent, when so many more things had to be bought with the wages ... Unemployment, hitherto not much worse than a regrettable inconvenience became a calamity. Every hour's work acquired a market value ... so that a man was tempted to neglect his own gardening if he could sell his labour in somebody else's garden. Thus undermined, *the peasant outlook gave way, perforce, to that of the modern labourer,* and the old attachment to the countryside was weakened.[63]

In essence, by eliminating contributions derived from common rights, especially the contributions made by women,[64] "enclosure increased families' dependence on wages and wage earners, pressures which can only be understood in the context of the importance of family participation in securing an eighteenth-century livelihood."[65] This was a shift in property relations with inter-generational consequences, as families "lost the capacity to transmit productive property from one generation to the next through inheritance,"[66] thereby rendering those future generations reliant on wage labour for survival.

Enclosure also affected work patterns by consolidating the power of farmers over land, which appears to have been an important factor in the eighteenth and nineteenth century move away from reliance on servants in husbandry, towards the hiring of short-term labourers.[67] Traditionally, farm servants lived with the family. On larger farms they might be separately housed, but "generally on small farms they shared the same table and slept in the same rooms as the members of the family."[68] According to Ann Kussmaul, this pattern changed with enclosure: "Progressive farmers with large enclosed holdings hired (or [were told they] should hire) day-labourers; only small, inefficient farmers hired (or should hire) servants. The range of occupations bet-

---

63 George Sturt, *Change in the Village* (1912) at 77–111, excerpted in Snell, *supra* note 15 at 167 (emphasis added). See also Beckert, *supra* note 6 at 77.

64 Snell, *supra* note 15 at 157–8; Hammond and Hammond, *supra* note 13 at 107; Hill, *Women, Work, supra* note 30 at 24–68.

65 Humphries, *supra* note 18 at 19.

66 Seccombe, *supra* note 30 at 233.

67 Of course, this shift in farming practice and household structure was linked to loss of common rights. Farmers whose landholdings increased as a result of enclosure became the employers of "many new day-labourers, only recently freed from the incumbrance that smallholdings and commons had thrown between them and constant wage-employment": Ann Kussmaul, *Servants in Husbandry in Early Modern England* (Cambridge: Cambridge University Press, 1981) at 121. See also Deakin and Wilkinson, *supra* note 9 at 125.

68 Hill, *Women, Work, supra* note 30 at 75.

ter suited to the short contracts of labourers was greater on a large improved arable farm; large numbers of workers could not easily be lodged in the farmhouse and stable; the rising cost of the provisions fed to hearty young ploughmen and dairymaids was a growing burden on the household's accounts."[69] In contrast, "[w]here farms remained small and wastes unenclosed, farmers retained their need for servants, and servants their hope for adult independence from constant wage-labour in agriculture."[70] This measure of independence was itself a motive to hire servants, "so as to ensure supply of labour throughout the year"; many open-field crafts and trades (such as brickmaking, weaving, and basket making) "also involved demands for labour which favoured the hiring of farm-servants."[71] By the time of the 1834 Poor Law Commission, however, it seems that the household-based model of farm service had largely broken down. The Commission reported that because of "the improved condition of the farmers during the high price of agricultural produce, their families were unwilling to associate with labourers."[72] Servants in husbandry had become "labourers"[73] – that is, waged workers exterior to the household.[74]

III. IDEOLOGY, PATRIARCHY, AND THE LEGAL NATURE OF WORK

Part of the motivation undergirding enclosure was simple greed.[75] This acquisitive urge was, however, intimately related to deeper ideological currents, most notably veneration of market relations, private property rights,[76] and a perceived need to organize the population along

---

69 Kussmaul, *supra* note 67 at 120–1. The law of settlement also played a role, as farmers attempted to avoid the possibility of incurring fines from the parish by refusing to hire servants on an annual basis. Thus, Hill observes that, "[s]ervice was ... becoming indistinguishable from weekly hired labour": Hill, *Women, Work, supra* note 30 at 81.

70 Kussmaul, *supra* note 67 at 121.

71 Snell, *supra* note 15 at 216.

72 Kussmaul, *supra* note 67 at 128.

73 Hill, *Women, Work, supra* note 30 at 79. See also Carole Pateman, *The Sexual Contract* (Palo Alto: Stanford University Press, 1988) at 117.

74 Though many women who lost their productive role in agriculture as a result of enclosure also joined the ranks of indoor domestic servants: Kussmaul, *supra* note 67 at 15; Hill, *Women, Work, supra* note 30 at 52.

75 Hammond and Hammond, *supra* note 13 at 35.

76 In essence, Lockean notions of private property provided the institutional and intellectual framework for the removal of common rights and the consolidation of interests in land. This move, which was "'perfectly proper' in terms of capitalist-property relations involved ... a rupture of the traditional integument of village custom and of right": Thompson, *supra* note 17 at 238. For a contemporaneous

productive lines, which, it was thought, required the disarticulation of work and family life and the channelling of workers into wage-based labour. Thus, as Hill has written, "[t]he stimulus to agricultural revolution had come from the desire of landowners and capitalist farmers to make profits by producing for the market."[77] This desire (which had global repercussions[78]) was allied to an aristocratic (and judicial[79]) perception of the rural population as "a public encumbrance" that needed to be managed into paid work.[80] The framework for this management was supplied by market ideology in the form of classical economic liberalism: "When we remember that the enterprise of the age was under the spell of the most seductive economic teaching of the time, and that the old peasant society, wearing as it did the look of confusion and weakness, had to fear not only the simplifying appetites of the land-

---

critique of Lockean ideology in the domain of property see William Ogilvie, *An Essay on the Right of Property in Land, With Respect to its Foundation in the Law of Nature, and the Rights of the People!* (1780) (calling the right of private property in land "a most oppressive privilege").

77 Hill, *Reformation, supra* note 58 at 269.

78 For example, in the late nineteenth century a massive redistribution of land, analogous to English enclosures, took place in Egypt in order to produce cotton for the voracious English market: Beckert, *supra* note 6 at 297–8.

79 In the 1788 case of *Steel v Houghton*, 1 HBL 52, an action on the case for trespass, the Court of Common Pleas declared that gleaning was illegal at common law. In their plea of justification, the defendants averred that they, "being parishioners and inhabitants of the said parish of Timworth, legally settled therein, and being poor and necessitous, and indigent persons, after the crop growing in the year aforesaid, in and upon the said close, in which, &c had been reaped, cut down, taken and carried away by the said plaintiff from and off the said close, in which ... the said Mary (the defendant) entered into the said close, in which, &c to glean and gather the straw containing ears of barley, remaining and being dispersed and scattered abroad in the said close": at [51]. Lord Loughborough, "a pupil and friend of Adam Smith" (Neeson, *supra* note 16 at 25–6), rejected the defendant's justification on the ground that "[t]here can be no right of this sort enjoyed in common, except where there is no cultivation, or where that right is supported by joint labour; but here neither of those criteria will apply." He went on to declare that "[t]he consequences that would arise from this custom being established as a right, would be injurious to the poor themselves." In essence, Loughborough argued that gleaning amounted to "a charge on industry" that lessened the profits of farmers, which in turn reduced their contributions to poor rates, leaving the poor "liable to starve in the spring." That denying the exercise of this right in autumn might also lead to starvation was, for him, an insufficient justification for upholding the defendant's ancient privilege. For a discussion of the origins of this case and its broader social significance see King, *supra* note 58 at 281–307.

80 In Hickel's words, enclosure was "a national programme designed to 'sweep' human beings off the elite's newly privatized landholdings": Hickel, *supra* note 19 at 76.

lords, but the simplifying philosophy, in England of an Adam Smith, in France of the Physiocrats, we can realise that a ruling class has seldom found so plausible an atmosphere for the free play of its interests and ideas."[81] Within Parliament and the aristocracy, then, the view was generally taken that "it would be more economical for the labourer to spend on his ordinary employment the time he devoted to cutting fuel and turf, and to buy firing *out of his wages.*"[82] The reports issued by the Board of Agriculture spoke in favourable terms of making labourers "work every day in the year"; and by depriving the rural poor of economic independence through the abolition of common rights, the "subordination of the lower ranks of society ... would be thereby considerably secured."[83] According to Neeson, "many pamphleteers and most reporters to the Board of Agriculture *did* recommend the creation of complete wage dependence. They said that the discipline was valuable. They argued that the sanction of real or threatened unemployment would benefit farmers presently dependent on the whims of partly self-sufficient commoners."[84] As John Clark of Herefordshire wrote, "[t]he farmers in this county are often at a loss for labourers: the inclosure of the wastes would increase the number of hands for labour, by removing the *means* of subsisting in idleness."[85] A shift to wage dependency was also equated with moral improvement.[86] The commons were said to be "hurtful to society by holding forth a temptation to idleness, that fell parent to vice and immorality";[87] commoners were denounced as a "sordid race" needing correction and discipline.[88] These statements and the very form in which enclosure Acts were passed signal not only bias towards free market ideology but also a legal-political conception of work as a practice distinct from the household and familial relations, and based instead on putatively consensual commercial relations and the reciprocal exchange of labour power and wages.

---

81 Hammond and Hammond, *supra* note 13 at 40. See also Hill, *Reformation, supra* note 58 at 268.

82 Hammond and Hammond, *supra* note 13 at 106 (emphasis added).

83 Hill, *Reformation, supra* note 58 at 270.

84 Neeson, *supra* note 16 at 28. See also Thompson, *supra* note 17 at 243–4.

85 Neeson, *supra* note 16 at 28 quoting John D. Clark, *General View of the Agriculture of the County of Hereford* (London: Colin Macrae, 1794) at 29.

86 Snell, *supra* note 15 at 170.

87 *Ibid* at 171–2 quoting John D. Clark, "On commons in Brecknock" (1794) XXII *Ann Ag* 633. This notion of moral improvement was a persistent theme in the evidence given to the 1844 Select Committee on Enclosures.

88 Neeson, *supra* note 16 at 32.

The enforced reliance on waged work that enclosures helped to generate also resulted in new forms of patriarchal dominance. By removing cottagers' claims over land, enclosure consolidated the power of the nobility over the lives of the working poor, while the demise of feudal structures of obligation also meant that one lord's workers were no longer subject to the authority of a higher authority in the feudal chain of command: within his domain, the landed master was thus constituted as patriarch.[89] In turn, the new reliance of households on forms of wage labour tended to result in the relegation of women to the domestic sphere, rendering them reliant on the productive efforts of men.[90] On this smaller scale, the male waged worker was also thus constituted as patriarch, however humble his condition in life.[91]

B. Poverty: The Discipline of Work

Nineteenth-century laws concerning the relief of poverty were a further crucial means through which the English state constituted wage labour outside of the home as the presumptive means of economic survival for the English poor. In particular, the overhaul of the *Poor Relief Act 1601*[92] by the *Poor Law Amendment Act 1834*[93] and subsequent interventions over the course of the nineteenth century dramatically curtailed the provision of outdoor relief (payments made to the poor by the parish in cash or in kind) and directed that the standard of living in parish-run workhouses was to be set at a sufficiently low level that it would function as an inducement to all but the physically incapacitated to seek paid work. As Deakin and Wilkinson point out, "the history of the English poor law closely tracks the emergence of an industrial economy in which waged employment gradually became the principal means of support, directly or indirectly, for the vast majority of the population."[94] Failing that, the law sought to privatize responsibility for the unwaged poor by imposing support obligations on immediate family members. In these intersecting ways, the Poor Law helped to shape a legal under-

---

89 See Tomlins, *supra* note 10 at 361; Holly Brewer, "The Transformation of Domestic Law" in Michael Grossberg and Christopher Tomlins, eds., *The Cambridge History of Law in America: Volume I, Early America (1580–1815)* (New York: Cambridge University Press, 2008) 288 at 292–3.

90 Hill, *Women, Work, supra* note 30 at 48.

91 Tomlins, *supra* note 10 at 381.

92 *An Act for the Relief of the Poor 1601*, 43 Eliz I, c 2 [*Poor Act 1601*].

93 *An Act for the Amendment and better Administration of the Laws relating to the Poor in England and Wales 1834*, 4 & 5 Will IV, c 76 [*Poor Act 1834*].

94 Deakin and Wilkinson, *supra* note 9 at 110.

standing of work as essentially synonymous with wage labour performed outside of the sphere of family; and a corresponding idea of the family as a private unit constituted by marriage and birth alone.

I. THE OLD POOR LAW AND SPEENHAMLAND

The greater unity of work and family life prior to the eighteenth century was matched by the imbrication of work and measures to alleviate poverty: the *Statute of Artificers 1562* made certain classes of people "not lawfully retained … [able to] be compelled to be retained to serve in Husbandry by the year, with any person that keepeth Husbandry";[95] while the *Poor Act 1601* (first enacted in 1597 and subsequently re-enacted in much the same form) reiterated the duty to work by imposing on parish overseers an obligation to set to work "all such persons, married or unmarried, having no means to maintain them, and [who] use no ordinary and daily trade of life to get their living," providing only for "the necessary relief of the lame, impotent, old, blind, and such other among them."[96] The law thus established a duty to work and constituted labour as the vehicle through which the physically capable poor were to obtain the means for survival. In practice, though, the cost of setting the merely poor (as opposed to the physically incapable) to work meant that those persons "not lawfully retained" obtained outdoor relief along similar lines to the impotent. In both cases, eligibility for parish relief was contingent upon "settlement" – essentially a localized form of community citizenship gained through birth or service for twelve consecutive months. Laws concerning labour and poverty were thus mutually reinforcing, and "gave expression to a dense network of reciprocal obligations which linked together wage labour, the family, and the wider social order."[97]

In the eighteenth century, rapid population growth and a consequent oversupply of labour was compounded by the mobilization of land via enclosure, and improved agricultural methods that rendered farmers less reliant on live-in workers. These factors resulted in a socially destabilizing dearth of sufficient work and inadequate wages for those who were (forcibly or voluntarily) engaged in wage labour; and by the end of the century, the degree of social immiseration called for further intervention into the existing system of labour and poor laws. Accordingly, in May 1795, at the Pelican Inn in Speenhamland, the justices of Berkshire decided that, "subsidies in aid of wages should be granted

---

95 5 Eliz c 4, s 5 (spelling modernized).
96 *Poor Act 1601*, 43 Eliz I, c 2, s 1.
97 Deakin and Wilkinson, *supra* note 9 at 110.

in accordance with a scale dependent upon the price of bread, so that a minimum income should be assured to the poor *irrespective of their earnings*."[98] In essence, "whenever the wages of any class of labourers ... [fell] below the amount appointed by the scale, the difference [was] made up as a matter of course by the parish."[99] This practice was never enacted in a national statutory form, but it became a standard measure used by most parishes to determine the appropriate level of wage relief for workers whose wages were inadequate to support themselves and their families.[100] According to Polanyi, the Speenhamland system established "the right to live";[101] it also effectively blocked the emergence of a national labour market at a time when, as a result of enclosure and emerging forms of industrial manufacturing, large numbers of the labouring poor were entirely dependent on wages for survival (outdoor relief being contingent upon settlement, which could not always be proven or obtained through service).

The *Poor Act 1834* tore away the protections offered by Speenhamland (not without some justification[102]) and, depending on one's perspective, either enabled workers to sell their labour for a market-determined price free from the distortion of wage supplementation, or subjected them to the exploitative tendencies of employers, largely without the benefit of outdoor relief. The legal duty to work instituted by the *Statute of Artificers* and the *Poor Act 1601* was replaced by a disciplinary system that

---

98 Polanyi, *supra* note 13 at 82. See also Deakin and Wilkinson, *supra* note 9 at 125–9.

99 *Poor Law Commissioners' Report of 1834. Copy of the Report Made in 1834 by the Commissioners for Inquiring into the Administration and Practical Operation of the Poor Laws* (London: HM Stationary Office, 1905) at 26 [1834 Poor Law Report].

100 *Ibid* at 21. For example, in the County of Cambridge, the incomes of single men were standardized according to the price of four quartern loaves of bread per week; single women's wages were indexed to three quartern loaves: *ibid*.

101 Polanyi, *supra* note 15 at 82. The 1834 Poor Law Report includes evidence to the following effect: "The *bread money* is hardly looked upon by the labourers in the light of parish relief. They consider it as much their right as the wages they receive from their employers, and in their own minds, make a wide distinction between 'taking their *bread money*' and 'going on the parish'": 1834 Poor Law Report, *supra* note 99 at 28.

102 During the operation of the Speenhamland system, the poet John Clare wrote that "[t]he haughty demand by the master to his labourer was work for the little I chuse to alow you & go to the parish for the rest": John Clare, *Selected Poems*, edited by J.W. & A. Tibble (London: Dent, 1979) at 140 excerpted in Snell, *supra* note 15 at 67–8. The 1834 Poor Law Report claimed that "[e]ven the least contact with parochial assistance seems to be degrading": *supra* note 99 at 93. Evidence included in the Report included statements such as: "The change that is made in the character and habits of the poor by once receiving parochial relief, is quite remarkable; they are demoralized ever afterwards." *Ibid*.

incentivized waged work by removing (outdoor) wage relief and rendering indoor relief (via the workhouse system) a distinctly unpleasant last resort. The legal regulation of work and welfare remained deeply enmeshed, but the manner of its administration had shifted towards a market-based, individualist model that emphasized personal responsibility for economic survival; and a legal idea of work as a consent-based endeavour more than a duty owed to the community. At the same time, the law was just as coercive in the nineteenth century as it had been in the seventeenth century – it was just a little less direct about it, relying on the absence of wage relief as the legal means through which the population was managed into self-supporting labour; and in the absence thereof casting the private, non-productive family, rather than the parish or state, as the principal safety net for those unable to engage in waged work.

II. THE IDEOLOGY OF WAGE DEPENDENCE

The precursor to the *Poor Act 1834* was the Poor Law Commissioners' Report of 1834. To discourage reliance on the parish and channel people into wage-based forms of private support (of oneself and family members), the Report recommended not only the abolition of Speenhamland-style wage relief, but also the extension of the workhouse system of indoor relief and the introduction of a principle of "less eligibility," whereby the conditions within workhouses were to be maintained at a lower standard than that which could (at least in theory) be obtained by wage labour.[103] The idea, in the words of one Mr. Baker from the parish of Uley, Gloucestershire, was: "To provide for those who are able to work, *the necessaries of life,* but *nothing more,* to keep them closely to work, and in all respects under such restrictions, that though no man who was *really in want* would hesitate a moment to comply with them, yet that he would submit to them no longer than he could help; that he would rather do his utmost *to find work,* by which he could support himself than accept parish pay."[104] While wages had dropped to perilously low levels under Speenhamland, it was believed (again, not without *some* justification) that the removal of this "interference" in the market for

---

103 1834 Poor Law Report, *supra* note 99 at 227–8. The Report did not recommend the abolition of indoor relief entirely, but, echoing Bentham, it said that such relief should be confined to the indigent, not the merely poverty stricken, which it defined as "the state of one, who, in order to obtain a mere subsistence, is forced to have recourse to labour." See further Deakin and Wilkinson, *supra* note 9 at 133.

104 1834 Poor Law Report, *supra* note 99 at 230.

labour would lead to a correction in the level of wages,[105] making it possible for workers to support themselves and their families.[106] This new principle "was one of institutional support for the 'breadwinner wage,'" which, as chapter 4 explores in greater detail, became a key feature of the late nineteenth- and early twentieth century gendered division of work and family life. It was also an assertion of the primacy of private ordering – as the 1834 Poor Law Report declared, "external 'interference' in the contract between employer and employed should be removed."[107]

The ideological framework for the recommendations in the 1834 Poor Law Report was a blend of classical economic theory, Benthamite utilitarianism,[108] and Malthusian concerns over population increase.[109] In essence, the view was taken that the population needed to be managed[110] into a degree of self-sufficiency (without the land or rights to land that had hitherto enabled a measure of autarky[111]) through employment

---

105 According to Deakin and Wilkinson, "[i]t was widely believed that Speenhamland had become an unnatural distortion in the workings of the market": *supra* note 9 at 130. This view was linked to the population theories of Thomas Malthus, who argued that attempts to alleviate poverty through wage relief would be countered by an increase in population that would, in turn, absorb any surplus: *ibid* at 131 citing Thomas Malthus, *An Essay on the Principle of Population, as it Affects the Future Improvement of Society. With Remarks on the Speculation of Mr. Godwin, M. Condorcet, and Other Writers* (London, 1798) at 33.

106 1834 Poor Law Report, *supra* note 99 at 237–9. For example, evidence included in the Report claimed that, "the labourer becomes more steady and diligent; next, the more efficient labour makes the return to the farmers [*sic*] capital larger, and the consequent increase of the fund for the employment of labour enables and induces the capitalist to give better wages."

107 *Ibid* at 134.

108 Reflecting one of the ideas underpinning the Old Poor Law, Bentham held that poverty was simply the natural state of those persons who laboured for wages; only the indigent – those who were physically unable to work, or earn a subsistence wage – should be reliant on state relief. Accordingly, he argued that removing wage subsidies from able-bodied workers was the means by which to manage the population into self-sustaining, wage-based productivity. Jeremy Bentham, "Essay II. Fundamental Positions in Regard to the Making Provision for the Indigent Poor" (1796), in M. Quinn, ed., *The Collected Works of Jeremy Bentham: Writings on the Poor Laws, Volume I* (Oxford: Oxford University Press, 2001) 8, referred to in Deakin and Wilkinson, *supra* note 9 at 132. See also Anna Clark, "The New Poor Law and the Breadwinner Wage: Contrasting Assumptions" (2000) 34:2 *J Soc Hist* 261 at 264.

109 In essence, Malthus argued that "poverty resulted from population growth, driven by a lack of moral restraint or 'character' on the part of the poor, pressing on the food supply": Deakin and Wilkinson, *supra* note 9 at 131.

110 See chapter 1, part II(B).

111 See *supra*, section II(A).

and the receipt of wages. The liberalization of the labour market was, in this sense, designed to curtail parish and community responsibility towards the working population. As Antonella Picchio has observed, "[t]he labourer and the laboring population as a whole were to be made totally dependent on wages. The social insecurity inherent in wages thus was strengthened as the basic force for disciplining work, both outside and inside the family."[112] Adam Smith's invisible hand would, it was thought, result in an equilibrium wage level that workers would be forced to accept; they, in turn, would adjust their standards of living to whatever those wages afforded. Unemployment, therefore, was addressed as a moral question concerning workers' willingness to work. In E.P. Thompson's estimation, "the Act of 1834, and its subsequent administration by men like Chadwick and Kay, was perhaps the most sustained attempt to impose an ideological dogma, in defiance of the evidence of human need, in English history."[113] It was a "policy of psychological deterrence: 'labour, discipline and restraint,'"[114] based on the logic of the market. According to Polanyi: "The mechanism of the market was asserting itself and clamoring for its completion: human labor had to be made a commodity. Reactionary paternalism had in vain tried to resist this necessity. Out of the horrors of Speenhamland men rushed blindly for the shelter of a utopian market economy."[115] In reality, as the architects of the *Poor Act 1834* perceived, restricting state relief to the indigent was politically impossible; but removing wage subsidies was also not sufficient to ensure sweeping attitudinal shifts among the poor towards work and self-sufficiency. The solution they came up with was to make the alternative to wage labour sufficiently unattractive to ensure that only the indigent and desperate would view state relief as a viable option – the less eligibility principle, designed to ensure, as Bentham put it, that "the conditions of individuals, maintained without property of their own, by the labour of others," should not be "more eligible than that of persons maintained by their own labour."[116] In this respect, the *Poor Act 1834* was "accorded the task of bringing into being

---

112 Antonella Picchio, *Social Reproduction: The Political Economy of the Labour Market* (Cambridge: Cambridge University Press, 1992) at 62.

113 Thompson, *supra* note 17 at 295.

114 *Ibid*. See also Karel Williams, *From Pauperism to Poverty* (Abingdon: Routledge, 2017) at 58: "[T]he strategy of the 1834 *Report* was to use a blind, repressive discipline so as to reduce able-bodied male pauperism."

115 Polanyi, *supra* note 13 at 107.

116 Bentham, *supra* note 108 at 39.

what the political economists had simply assumed to exist: a functioning labour market."[117]

III. IMPLEMENTATION

Reflecting these ideas, and pointing to an emerging legal conception of work as essentially synonymous with waged labour and the principal means of economic support within English society, s 52 of the *Poor Act 1834* declared that "giving relief to persons or their families who, at the time of applying for or receiving such relief, were wholly or partially in the employment of individuals" was "productive of evil." Complementing existing criminal law provisions which made it an offence punishable by one month's hard labour to become chargeable to the parish where a person was "able wholly or in part to maintain himself, or his or her family, by work or other means, and wilfully refusing or neglecting to do so,"[118] the newly appointed Poor Law Commissioners were empowered to make regulations establishing the extent to which able-bodied persons and their families would be permitted to seek relief.[119] A decade later, the Outdoor Relief Prohibitory Order of 21 December 1844 made outdoor relief presumptively unlawful in those parishes and unions in which a workhouse had been established. Article 1 of the Order provided: "Every able-bodied person, male or female, requiring relief … shall be relieved wholly in the workhouse of the union, together with such of the family of every such able-bodied person as may be resident with him or her, and may not be in employment, and together with the wife of every such able-bodied male person, if he be a married man, and if she be resident with him."[120] Two additional Orders issued in 1842 and 1852 recognized that an outright prohibition on outdoor relief was impractical in urban and manufacturing areas,[121] and accordingly

---

117 Deakin and Wilkinson, *supra* note 9 at 134.

118 *Vagrancy Act 1824*, 5 Geo IV, c 83. This provision amended an earlier law that had criminalized the refusal to work only "for the usual and common wages given to other labourers in the like work": 17 Geo II, c 5 (1744). The 1824 Act therefore effectively required people to work for whatever wages were being offered, under the threat of criminal sanction.

119 *Poor Act 1834*, 4 & 5 Will IV, c 76, s 52.

120 Outdoor Relief Prohibitory Order, 21 December 1844, art 1(1), in Deakin and Wilkinson, *supra* note 9 at 136.

121 In rural areas it seems that outdoor relief continued throughout the country until the later decades of the nineteenth century when further directions were issued by the Local Government Board to curtail outdoor relief through sickness payments. Deakin and Wilkinson, *supra* note 9 at 137, note that in 1878 the Local Government Board "issued a memorandum recommending the adoption by unions of the

made such relief conditional on work tests. The general principle was that "no relief shall be given to any able-bodied male person while he is employed for wages or other hire or remuneration by any person," but where relief was necessary it was not to be given "free"; rather, recipients were "set to work by the guardians, and ... kept employed under their direction" for as long as relief was provided. The Poor Law Commissioners openly acknowledged that the underlying idea was "to supply a test of the reality of destitution on the part of the applicant, and thereby to afford him an inducement to seek for independent employment."[122] Workhouses augmented these restrictions on outdoor relief. Under the less eligibility principle, workhouses were deliberately constituted as places of "repressive discipline."[123] An Order issued in 1847 declared that inmates were to be put to work without the payment of wages,[124] and subsequent directions stipulated that this organization of work was to be conducted in such a way that no competition was created between workhouse and outdoor labour.[125]

Channelling the poor into wage labour was the central plank of the 1834 reforms, but the law also sought to privatize responsibility for family members – family in this context referring to the private, kinship model that was becoming dominant in English society. The 1834 Poor Law Report presented this move as one designed to revive family life, which had, it said, fallen prey to avarice and lassitude: "[I]n all ranks of society the great sources of happiness and virtue are the domestic affections, and this is particularly the case among those who have so few resources as the laboring classes. Now, pauperism seems to be an engine for the purpose of disconnecting each member of a family from all the others; of reducing all to the state of domesticated animals, fed, lodged and provided for by the parish, without mutual dependence or

---

regulations drawn up by the Manchester Board of Guardians; these forbade the payment of outdoor relief to the able-bodied except on the ground of sickness, set a six-week limit even then on the payment of outdoor relief to any able-bodied person, and an eight-week limit in all other cases" (referring to *Memorandum Relating to the Administration of Out-relief*, February 1878, in *Seventh Report of the Local Government Board, 1877–78*, Appendix at 217).

122 *Minute of the Poor Law Commissioners respecting the means of enforcing an out-door labour test*, 31 October 1842, in *Ninth Annual Report of the Poor Law Commissioners, 1843*, 381, in Deakin and Wilkinson, *supra* note 9 at 138.

123 Deakin and Wilkinson, *supra* note 9 at 141.

124 *Ibid* referring to General Consolidated Order, 24 July 1847, art 112.

125 *Ibid* at 142 referring to *Circular Letter of the Local Government Board to Unions and Parishes of the Metropolis*, 31 October 1888.

mutual interest."[126] Parish relief was thus presented as antithetical to family life. The solution, according to the Report, was a combination of wage labour (conducted by men) and unpaid forms of work within the home (conducted by women). The idea – entirely consistent with the emerging distinction between family and market – seems to have been that extra-familial forms of work would in fact strengthen ties within the family by re-imposing responsibility for welfare on families,[127] supported by the diligence and hard work of kin.[128]

Imposing support obligations on family members was by no means new: the *Poor Act 1601* had imposed a duty on the parents, grandparents and children of "every poor, old, blind, lame and impotent person, or other poor person not able to work" to relieve such persons, if they had the means to do so.[129] In reality, though, the settlement-based system of parish relief meant that family members often lived in different areas and were able to call on the parish for relief.[130] Reforms in the nineteenth century, however, shifted the law "to a position under which the obligation of family members came before that of the state."[131] The *Poor Relief Act 1819*[132] and subsequent laws empowered the Poor Law Guardians to seek maintenance orders against parents in respect of their children and their own parents who had become a charge on the parish;[133] while the *Poor Law Amendment Act 1844* further privatized responsibility for family members by making it an offence, punishable by up to three months' imprisonment, for a male able-bodied worker to desert his wife or children, or for a mother to abandon her children to parish relief.[134] Courts also denied relief when family members had the means to provide support.[135]

---

126 1834 Poor Law Report, *supra* note 99 at 95–6.

127 However, as chapter 5 explains, the *Poor Act 1834* also imposed sole financial responsibility for illegitimate children on mothers.

128 Thus, the Report claimed that those in receipt of wage relief "appear not to have the slightest scruple in asking to be paid for the performance of those domestic duties which the most brutal savages are in general willing to render gratuitously to their own kindred": 1834 Poor Law Report, *supra* note 99 at 97.

129 Deakin and Wilkinson, *supra* note 9 at 144.

130 *Ibid.*

131 *Ibid.*

132 59 Geo III, c 12.

133 *Ibid.*

134 *Poor Law Amendment Act 1844*, 7 & 8 Vict I, c 101, amending *Vagrancy Act 1824*, 5 Geo IV, c 83.

135 Deakin and Wilkinson, *supra* note 9 at 144 referring to *Coventry Corp v Surrey CC* [1935] AC 199, 205, referring to *Bazeley v Forder* (1868) LR 3 QB 559, 565.

In this respect, the poor law helped to constitute a legal understanding of family in the narrow terms with which we are now familiar: obligations existed simply as between parents and children (reciprocally, if the child was of age[136]), and spouses. Provisions regulating the administration of workhouses also sought to induce people to provide support to family members outside of the workhouses by compromising family life therein – only married couples infirm through old age or other cause were permitted (at the discretion of the guardians) to live in shared accommodation; other couples were separated into male and female areas, and children were separated from their parents. It was "the antithesis of the domestic ideal: families were fragmented, women worked, and men did not provide for their families."[137] The family was thus constituted as both punishment and reward in the English state's efforts to limit its financial responsibility for the poor and channel the population into wage labour.

Restrictions on relief grew tighter as the nineteenth century progressed.[138] According to Karel Williams, "a line of exclusion was drawn against able-bodied men after 1850; in accordance with official strategy, unemployment-related relief was virtually abolished by the middle of the century."[139] The concern was particularly with *men*.[140] While the 1844 Order concerning outdoor relief applied to able-bodied *persons*, it also included an exception for widows with dependent children. The 1852

---

136 According to Snell, "[i]t became customary after 1834 to place orders on sons or daughters, making them remit part of the cost of relief to the elderly – 1s. to 2s. a week": Snell, *supra* note 15 at 366.

137 M. Levine-Clark, "Engendering Relief: Women, Ablebodiedness and the New Poor Law in Victorian England" (2000) 11 *J Women's Hist* 107 at 122.

138 Deakin and Wilkinson, *supra* note 9 at 137.

139 Williams, *supra* note 114 at 59.

140 Regulatory Orders made under the *Poor Act 1834* also targeted indoor relief. The 1840 *Report of the Poor Law Commissioners to the Most Noble the Marquis of Normanby, Her Majesty's Principal Secretary of State for the Home Department, on the Continuance of the Poor Law Commission on the Continuance of the Poor Law Commission, and on Some Further Amendment of the Laws Relating to the Relief of the Poor* (London: HM Stationary Office, 1840) reinforced the principle of less eligibility, stating (at 28): "The only expedient, therefore, for accomplishing the end in view, which humanity permits, is to subject the pauper inmate of a public establishment to such a system of labour discipline and restraint as shall be sufficient to outweigh, in his estimation, the advantages which he derives from the bodily comforts he enjoys." Thus, the General Consolidated Order of 24 July 1847 provided for the employment of pauper inmates "according to their capacity and ability; and no pauper shall receive any compensation for his labour." General Consolidated Order, art 112. See Deakin and Wilkinson, *supra* note 9 at 141.

Outdoor Relief Regulation Order specifically excluded able-bodied *male* persons from outdoor relief[141] – and the available statistics on unemployment-related poor relief indicate that the number of men supported through outdoor relief dropped dramatically after 1850. Prior to 1834, "the poor law was massively involved in the outdoor relief of the unemployed and under-employed … 100,000 able-bodied men drew relief through the year 1802–03."[142] However, "from 1852 to 1912 inclusive, the day counts show 5,000 or fewer men 'in want of work' relieved outdoors in thirty-eight of the forty-one years for which statistics are available."

These figures strongly suggest that nineteenth-century legal interventions into the poor law made state-based forms of relief for the general population simultaneously less thinkable and less practically available.[143] Along with other factors such as agricultural and industrial development, the *Poor Act 1834* and related Orders (backed by the criminal law) constituted wage labour outside of the home as the presumptive means by which men (and those women who worked) obtained the necessary means to support themselves and their families. These legal interventions also cast the private family, rather than the parish, as the first port of call when wages alone were insufficient for survival. Nineteenth-century English poor laws were thus a crucial element of the broader legal process of (re)constructing work within the framework of wage labour performed outside of the domestic realm; and the simultaneous (re)construction of the family as a private unit constituted in law through the relations between husbands and wives, and parents and children.

III. Wage Labour, Contract, and the Subordination of Workers

The mid-sixteenth century saw the consolidation and extension of labour laws passed some 200 years earlier that had sought to manage

---

141 Williams, *supra* note 114 at 64–5.

142 *Ibid* at 71. As Williams notes, it is possible that large numbers of men were being relieved in different ways, for example, via indoor relief in workhouses. The absence of statistics for the number of persons in workhouses prior to 1891 makes it difficult to determine this question. However, Williams argues that this very absence may be seen as indicative of a relatively small number of such men, particularly after 1870, when the English state's mania for statistical analysis of the population took off: *ibid* at 72.

143 As a matter of legal consciousness, it seems likely that this process occurred on both elite and ordinary levels: state intervention became anathema within the classical political economy of the period, with apparent trickle-down effects as policies were implemented that drastically curtailed the availability of state relief.

the poor into productive labour.[144] Like the earlier laws, the *Statute of Artificers 1562*[145] was a response to labour scarcity caused by disease and civil unrest.[146] In essence, it made certain classes of people "liable to be directed to work at wages fixed without their concurrence,"[147] subjected workers to imprisonment for refusing work or for breach of contract, and confirmed existing rules concerning the required duration of apprenticeships.[148] In these respects, the *Statute* "gave labor regulation national-level expression."[149] Yet as Christopher Tomlins and others have pointed out, the actual operation and execution of the statute's provisions were distinctly localized: parliamentary control over wage rating was abandoned in favour of a "system of local regulation under the supervision of JPs";[150] orders for apprehension and imprisonment of workers (or payment of wages by masters) were subject to the authority of local JPs;[151] and craft companies retained significant control over every aspect of relations between masters and apprentices aside from duration, while regulation of apprenticeship in husbandry was minimal.[152]

There was an additional stratum of authority implicit in this localized model: that of masters. The *Statute of Artificers* quite clearly revolved

---

144 23 Edw III, c 1–8 (1349); 25 Edw III, Stat I, c I (1351) (*Ordinance* and *Statute of Labourers*, respectively). These laws, passed in the wake of the Black Death and catastrophic population decline (which enabled surviving workers to demand increased wages), imposed a suite of interlocking provisions designed to manage the poor into work: the obligation to work for masters who demanded their services; criminal sanctions to enforce this duty; minimum hiring periods of one year for certain agricultural labourers; and maximum wage rates. Enforcement of these laws was made the responsibility of justices of the peace – members of the "knightly classes with state authority." See Tomlins, *supra* note 10 at 234–5; Robert Steinfeld, *Coercion, Contract, and Free Labor in the Nineteenth Century* (Cambridge: Cambridge University Press, 2001) at 23, 40 [Steinfeld, *Coercion*].

145 5 Eliz, c 4.

146 Tomlins, *supra* note 10 at 237; Deakin and Wilkinson, *supra* note 9 at 47.

147 Otto Kahn-Freund, "Blackstone's Neglected Child: The Contract of Employment" (1977) 93 *Law Q Rev* 508 at 513 (emphasis added).

148 The *Statute of Artificers* did, however, reduce property requirements applying to parents of apprentices: Deakin and Wilkinson, *supra* note 9 at 48.

149 Tomlins, *supra* note 10 at 237.

150 *Ibid* at 239.

151 5 Eliz, c 4, ss 6, 10, 28, 39.

152 The *Statute* thus "embedded local labor markets 'within the rules and institutions of public law,' but the actual products of the national legal sphere were given all their practical effect and meaning by local officials responding to local contexts." Tomlins, *supra* note 10 at 244 quoting Margaret A. Somers, "Citizenship and the Place of the Public Sphere: Law, Community, and Political Culture in the Transition to Democracy" (1993) 58:5 *Am Soc Rev* 587 at 600.

around a patriarchal, household-based system of work and authority. It was the masters of households who were empowered to order designated persons to work irrespective of consent;[153] masters who were permitted to seek criminal sanctions against those persons who refused to enter service or continue under the terms of notionally consensual contracts governing work relations;[154] and masters who continued to exercise (familial) authority over apprentices and other live-in workers.[155] This Part of the chapter shows that the process of disarticulating work from the household and re-constituting it, at least ideologically, as a relation based on consent (expressed in the legal form of contract) actually relied upon the legal extension of this patriarchal model of worker subordination into the rapidly expanding domain of wage labour.[156] In other words, the eighteenth and nineteenth century legal construction of the family as a non-productive unit involved not only the disarticulation of work from the household, but also the application of medieval/early modern conceptions of (household-based) worker subordination to the new model of (contract-based) work.[157]

A. The Philosophical Basis of Coercion under Contract

Contract is the specifically modern means of creating relationships of subordination, but, because civil subordination originates in contract, it is presented as freedom.[158]

The relationship between master and servant in the sixteenth century was but "one form of the relationship heads of households bore to dependent members of their households"; that is, "like wives and children, resident servants were understood to be subject to a kind

---

153 Section 3 made designated persons "compellable to serve as yearly Servants in the several Arts in which they were brought up," while s 5 declared "All Persons between the ages of 12 and 60, not being otherwise employed, &c. … compellable to be yearly Servants in Husbandry."

154 5 Eliz, c 4, ss 6, 10, 28.

155 For example, section 14 of the Act imposed a penalty of imprisonment for one year on servants who assaulted their masters. No such equivalent penalty was imposed on masters who assaulted their servants.

156 See Tomlins, *supra* note 10 at 357; Beckert, *supra* note 6 at xvi.

157 On a broader level, "[t]he emergence of industrial capitalism in fact built upon such older hierarchies and relations of power and used them as a tool to revolutionize society more broadly": Beckert, *supra* note 6 at 188.

158 Pateman, *supra* note 73 at 118.

of jurisdiction that a head of household exercised over all household members."[159] Thus, in *A Godly Forme of Household Government, for the Ordering of Private Families* (1598), John Dud and Robert Cleaver declared: "The householder is called *Pater Familias*, that is, a father of a familie, because he should have a fatherly care over his servants, as if they were his children."[160] This "fatherly care" was deeply coercive: as the *Statute of Artificers* declared, the head of a household was entitled to require persons to enter into his service and seek their imprisonment for refusal or subsequent recalcitrance. Masters were also permitted to "correct," that is, physically chastise, their servants and apprentices (and wives and children).[161]

Over the course of the seventeenth and eighteenth centuries, this patriarchal model of household governance – and the related conjunction of familial and political obligation in political theory[162] – began to break apart under the weight of liberal ideas of consent and contract (in both legal and political senses). Coercion never disappeared, though; instead, it was re-packaged within the language of consent – servants *agreed* to become subject to the control of their masters. As Locke put it:

---

159 Steinfeld, *Free Labor, supra* note 18 at 55–6.

160 Gordon J. Schochet, *Patriarchalism in Political Thought: The Authoritarian Family and Political Speculation and Attitudes Especially in Seventeenth-Century England* (Oxford: Blackwell, 1975) at 67.

161 Brewer, *supra* note 89 at 306–7.

162 According to Schochet, *supra* note 160 at 54, the family was "an established and frequently employed category in political philosophy prior to the seventeenth century," but it was not until this time that "familial obligation was used as a direct justification of political obligation" (at 19). It was in fact the nascent stirrings of consent-based justifications for personal and political obligations (and arguably a new emphasis on the family in the wake of the Reformation) that catalysed patriarchal thinking into a fully-fledged theory of governance: the head of the household governed his dependents, and in this respect his authority was homologous with other polities, such that the political order was understood as "identical with the rule of a father or patriarch over his family": *ibid* at 7. In the English context, the clearest example of this symbiotic relationship between family and government is Robert Filmer's *Patriarcha* (1680), which presented patriarchal rule within the household as an explicit *justification* for political authority. John Locke famously attacked Filmer's patriarchal theory of political obligation. In the *Second Treatise* he rejected the equation of political and filial duty, declaring, "the power of a *magistrate* over a subject may be distinguished from that of a *father* over his children, a *master* over his servant": John Locke, *Second Treatise of Government*, edited by C.B. Macpherson (Indianapolis: Hackett, 1980) §2 (emphasis in original). Obligations, he said, were derived from freedom – "liberty of acting in accordance to his own will" (*ibid* at §63) – which in turn was a product of reason. Consent therefore formed the basis of obligations between individuals.

> *Master* and *servant* are names as old as history, but given to those of far different condition; for a freeman makes himself a servant to another, by selling him, for a certain time, the service he undertakes to do, in exchange for wages he is to receive: and though this commonly puts him into the family of his master, and under the ordinary discipline thereof; yet it gives the master but a temporary power over him, and no greater than what is contained in the *contract* between them.[163]

The servant (in theory) "enters the household as a free, equal, and independent person."[164] Labour was thus re-figured as an *individual* property right[165] that one could consensually agree to alienate;[166] it became "detached from the background of the hierarchical community, individualized in the idea of the juridical person as a self-owner, provided with a type of dignity, and made a central and equal part of the human condition."[167] In Robert Steinfeld's estimation: "[T]he rights to performance that masters had long enjoyed were reconceived as the product of a transaction in which one perfectly free individual sold the property he held in his own energies to another individual for a term or for a particular purpose. Thereafter, that property was the employer's, not the worker's, for the term or purpose stipulated."[168] Echoing this world view, Blackstone stated in book III of the *Commentaries* that the basis of an action by a master against a person who injured his servant was "the property which the master has by his contract acquired in the labour of the servant."[169] Servants, of course, had no such interest in their masters.[170]

This conception of the rights between masters and servants rested on a distinction between labour and what Karl Marx called labour power. The latter term refers to the idea that labour is a severable commodity; that, as C.B. Macpherson put it, "a man's energy and skill are his own,

---

163 Locke, *supra* note 162 at §85.

164 William James Booth, *Households: On the Moral Architecture of the Economy* (Ithaca: Cornell University Press, 1993) at 105.

165 In C.B. Macpherson's view, it is this aspect of liberal thought that gave rise to what he calls "possessive individualism": C.B. Macpherson, *The Political Theory of Possessive Individualism: Hobbes to Locke* (Toronto: Oxford University Press, 2011) at 3.

166 See Booth, *supra* note 164 at 161–2; Alan Fox, *Beyond Contract: Work, Power and Trust Relations* (London: Faber, 1974) at 167.

167 Booth, *supra* note 164 at 162.

168 Steinfeld, *Free Labor, supra* note 18 at 6.

169 Blackstone, *supra* note 20, book III at 142.

170 Brewer, *supra* note 89 at 321–2: "Servants initially consent to labor and then are bound, unless the master releases them. Blackstone cemented hierarchy into the setting of consent by interpolating an element left over from the medieval common law: the idea of people as property."

yet are regarded not as integral parts of his personality but as alienable possessions, the use and disposal of which he is free to hand over to others for a price."[171] The "master symbol" of this possessive individualist approach to labour was (and arguably still is) contract.[172] In Alan Fox's words, "[v]oluntary agreement forged through bargaining over specific terms, the essence of economic exchange, was seen as the mechanism which articulated atomistic, self-regarding individuals into the collaborative aggregates and linked processes necessary for civil society."[173] As Carole Pateman has argued, though, the notion of labour power is a fiction because the "employment contract, necessarily, gives the employer political right to compel the worker to use his capacities in a given manner, or the right to the worker's obedience." It is in fact "a contract in which, since he cannot be separated from his capacities, he sells command over the use of his body and himself."[174] Subordination was thus intrinsic to liberalism's consent-based framework,[175] but because it originated in contract, it was presented as freedom:

> The property that masters had enjoyed for centuries in the labor of their servants now began to be reimagined as the product of a voluntary transaction struck between two separate and autonomous individuals, one of whom traded away to the other the property in his own labor for wages or other compensation. Thereafter, as a result of this voluntary transaction between two autonomous individuals, the hirer of labor had the legal right to control, use, and enjoy the other's personal energies for the term or purposes specified in the agreement. Far from being inconsistent with unfree labor, the logic of early modern possessive individualism actually gave unfree labor new life.[176]

Indeed, the ascendance of contractual ideology was part of a broader process of change that enabled the perfection of patriarchal authority within the household, not its erasure. As Tomlins has pointed out, the

---

171 Macpherson, *supra* note 165 at 48.
172 Fox, *supra* note 166 at 181.
173 *Ibid*.
174 Pateman, *supra* note 73 at 151. More than other contract theorists, Hegel appreciated the falsity of the labour power notion: "By alienating the whole of my time, as crystalized in my work, and everything I produced, I would be making into another's property the substance of my being ... my personality." *Ibid* at 147.
175 For example, Locke was quite clear that the head of a family was a master, "with subordinate relations of *wife, children, servants,* and *slaves,* united under the domestic rule of a family": Locke, *supra* note 162 at §86.
176 Steinfeld, *Free Labor, supra* note 18 at 80.

breakdown of the feudal system of obligation had the effect of limiting the extent to which lords could command the services of their vassals (and their vassals' servants);[177] agreements between particular masters and servants were, therefore, no longer subject to supervening forces, effectively completing the authority enjoyed by the master.[178] Essentially, while consent was figured as the basis for (contractual) obligations between masters and servants, the law governing those relations remained imbued with the type of coercion and paternalism that was characteristic of the medieval/early modern household model.[179] The needs of masters in the early industrial period "were met by infusing the employment contract with the traditional law of master and servant, thereby granting them a legal basis for the prerogative they demanded. What resulted was a form of contract almost as far removed from the pure doctrinal form as the status relationship which had preceded it."[180] In other words, the type of subjection that in the sixteenth and seventeenth centuries characterized the relation between masters and *household* servants became, over the course of the eighteenth and nineteenth centuries, the default model for a much broader range of work relations.[181] As Tapping Reeve put it in his early nineteenth century treatise on domestic relations, "a master is one who, *by law*, has a right to a personal authority over another; and such person, over whom such authority may be rightfully exercised, is a servant."[182]

B. Punishment and Performance

Reflecting and consolidating this understanding of work, the early eighteenth century saw the enactment of the first of a series of statutes that extended legal compulsion in the labour sphere beyond the

---

177 The *Ordinance* and *Statute of Labourers* relied upon the authority of the "knightly classes" for enforcement, but their powers were a product of state authority: Tomlins, *supra* note 10 at 235. In this respect, the law both used and destabilized the medieval feudal system.

178 Tomlins, *supra* note 10 at 361–2, 371–2.

179 For analysis of the application of these ideas in the American context see Beckert, *supra* note 6 at 284–5; Amy Dru Stanley, "Beggars Can't Be Choosers: Compulsion and Contract in Postbellum America" (1992) 78:4 *J Am Hist* 1274.

180 Fox, *supra* note 166 at 184. Deakin and Wilkinson generally agree with Fox on this issue, but also caution that "the element of subordination introduced by the master and servant laws was more innovative and less traditional" than Fox perhaps implies: *supra* note 9 at 62.

181 Tomlins, *supra* note 10 at 350. See also Brewer, *supra* note 89 at 295, 315.

182 Steinfeld, *Free Labor*, *supra* note 18 at 16 (emphasis added).

provisions of the *Statute of Artificers 1562* (which made workers who departed from their masters prior to completing work subject to one month's imprisonment).[183] Commencing in 1720, these laws expanded the class of workers against whom orders for imprisonment could be made, added misbehaviour to the list of possible grounds for imprisonment, and increased potential prison sentences (and, in some cases, provided for whipping).[184] Masters were not subject to criminal punishment for their own breaches of contract but instead were subject to civil wage recovery claims by defined groups of servants/employees. The *Master and Servant Act 1823*[185] consolidated these various overlapping laws into a single punitive statute that made absconding from work and refusing to enter into work under a contract of hiring punishable by up to three months' imprisonment.[186] The courts aided this legislative process by expanding the scope of "service" to encompass a broad range of waged workers, not just domestic and menial servants,[187] and by adopting distinctly pro-master positions in cases concerning dismissal. The combined result of these moves was a regime "based on the *personal subordination* of the worker to the employer ... a model incorporating an open-ended duty of obedience."[188] It was not until the passage of the *Employers and Workmen Act 1875* that criminal sanctions were replaced with civil remedies for breach of contract (by workers only),[189] at which point a model of work based on reciprocity of obligation began to be extended beyond higher-level workers.[190] The duty of obedience, however, remained in the form of an implied contract term – a legacy of the eighteenth and nineteenth century master-servant regime.[191]

For masters, the appeal of criminal sanctions for breach of contract was not so much actual imprisonment of workers, but rather the

---

183 5 Eliz, c 4, s 13.

184 Douglas Hay, "England, 1562–1875: The Law and Its Uses" in Douglas Hay and Paul Craven, eds., *Masters, Servants, and Magistrates: Britain & the Empire, 1562–1955* (Chapel Hill: University of North Carolina Press, 2004) 59 at 82.

185 *An Act to enlarge the Powers of Justices in determining Complaints between Masters and Servants, and between Masters, Apprentices, Artificers and others, 1823*, 4 Geo IV, c 34 [*Master and Servant Act 1823*].

186 Deakin and Wilkinson, *supra* note 9 at 63.

187 See William Holdsworth, *The Law of Master and Servant: Including that of Trades Unions and Combinations* (London: Routledge, 1876) at 2.

188 Deakin and Wilkinson, *supra* note 9 at 61.

189 *Employers and Workmen Act 1875*, 38 & 39 Vict I, c 90. The *Master and Servant Act 1867*, 30 & 31 Vict I, c 141, largely did away with imprisonment except in cases of "aggravated misconduct": see sections 9, 11 and 14.

190 Deakin and Wilkinson, *supra* note 9 at 74.

191 *Ibid* at 61–2, 74.

leverage created by its threat.[192] The ultimate point was to secure performance by workers.[193] From the standpoint of masters, this approach made sense given the general move away from household-based forms of labour, in which a master exercised direct control over his servants, towards a more diffuse and spatially segregated model based on contractual ties. Damages were of course an option for breach of contract,[194] but this remedy was of little utility against low-paid workers. What was needed, it was thought, was the additional element of state-backed coercion in the form of imprisonment – a public supplement to private agreements.[195] The conceptual justification for this unequal system came from the legal core of liberalism: private property and contract. In essence, the worker's property in his own person enabled him to consensually sell his labour power upon such terms and conditions as he wished. This agreement, reflected in the contract between the parties, conferred upon the purchaser (the master) a property interest in the servant's alienated labour power akin to that previously enjoyed only in respect of domestic servants (and, with some differences, apprentices); and that interest could be enforced using the coercive mechanisms offered by the criminal law. The ideology of classical liberalism and contract was thus deployed in law as a way to manage the working population into submission to both the market and patriarchy.[196]

---

192 Hay, *supra* note 184 at 60–1.

193 *Ibid* at 61. There is, therefore, a historical tradition within English law of specific performance for personal services – it just operated indirectly via the medium of the criminal law. See Steinfeld, *Coercion, supra* note 144 at 53 ff. Indeed, the *Master and Servant Act 1867*, 30 & 31 Vict I, c 141, s 9, conferred jurisdiction to *order* specific performance. As the 1874 Royal Commission into master-servant law observed, the "mode in which courts having jurisdiction to order specific performance enforce their authority is by imprisonment." By 1899, though, one English treatise writer stated "the Court does not grant specific performance of contracts for personal service, such, for instance, as contracts of hiring and service": William Donaldson Rawlins, *The Specific Performance of Contracts: An Expansion of an Article in the Encyclopaedia of the Laws of England* (London: Sweet & Maxwell, 1899) at 52.

194 See Blackstone, *supra* note 20, book III at 116, speaking of "pecuniary satisfaction in damages; as in case of assault, breach of contract, &c." Procedurally, such a claim would have been brought as an action in special assumpsit: David J. Ibbetson, *A Historical Introduction to the Law of Obligations* (Oxford: Oxford University Press, 2001) at 148.

195 This approach foreshadowed that which was later seen in the *Poor Act 1834*, 4 & 5 Will IV, c 76, which instituted the system of less eligibility into indoor relief schemes as a means of "encouraging" people into the labour market.

196 "[S]ubduing labor without enslaving it," as Beckert has described the approach to cotton workers: Beckert, *supra* note 6 at 71.

I. THE EIGHTEENTH CENTURY

The first addition to the *Statute of Artificers* was *An Act for Regulating the Journeymen Taylors within the Weekly Bills of Mortality*, passed in 1720 in response to "masters' complaint[s] that 7,000 London journeymen had combined to raise wages and reduce hours."[197] It provided:[198]

> any Person actually retained or imployed as a Journeyman Taylor, or Servant, in the Art of Mystery of a Taylor … [who] depart from his Service before the End of the Term or Time for which he is or shall be hired or retained, or until the Work, for which he was hired or retained, shall be finished, or not being retained or imployed, shall refuse to enter into Work or Imployment (after request made for that Purpose by any Master Taylor, for the Wages and Hours limited, or to be limited and appointed, as aforesaid) unless it be for some reasonable or sufficient Cause, to be allowed by Two Justices of the Peace within the Limits aforesaid; Then in every such case every Person, so offending, being thereof lawfully convicted, as aforesaid, shall be sent to the House of Correction, there to be kept to Hard Labour for any time not exceeding Two Months.

This limited intervention was insufficient to satisfy Daniel Defoe, who, in *The Great Law of Subordination Consider'd*[199] decried the fact (as he saw it) "that tho' Masters have the Name of Government indeed, the Servants really govern throughout this Nation, and especially that Part of them who we hire for daily Labour"; and suggested that "we shall soon have a very severe Law upon that Subject."[200] Legal change was perhaps not quite as speedy as Defoe would have liked, but his "very severe Law" eventually emerged in 1747 in the form of a more comprehensive master and servant statute that provided for the "better adjusting and more easy Recovery of the Wages of certain Servants; and for the better

---

197 Hay, *supra* note 184 at 83.

198 *An Act for Regulating the Journeymen Taylors within the Weekly Bills of Mortality*, 7 Geo I, c 13 (emphasis added). Similar industry-specific anti-combination laws were passed with respect to shoemakers (1722), weavers and framework knitters (1725), and glove and shoemakers (1740). In 1749 a more general anti-combination law was passed covering trades in cotton, iron, leather, hat-making, and dyeing and pressing. See Deakin and Wilkinson, *supra* note 9 at 59.

199 Daniel Defoe, *The Great Law of Subordination Consider'd; or, the Insolence and Unsufferable Behaviour of Servants in England duly enquir'd into* (London, 1724). (Note that this is an abridged form of the exceptionally long title.)

200 See Tomlins, *supra* note 10 at 335; see also the discussion at 347–8.

Regulation of such Servants, and of certain Apprentices."[201] It applied to "any such Servant, Artificer, Handicraftsman, Miner, Collier, Keelman, Pitman, Glassman, Potter, or Labourer," in respect of "any Misdemeanor, Miscarriage or Ill-behaviour, in such his or her Service or Employment."[202] The punishment was "Commitment to the House of Correction ... [with] hard Labour for a reasonable Time, not exceeding one Calendar Month, or otherwise by abating some Part of his or her Wages, or by discharg[e]."[203]

The significance of the 1747 Act is two-fold: for the first time it brought together a variety of forms of work and collectively housed them under the umbrella of master-servant relations (though the Act pointedly excluded domestic servants from its scope[204]) – a distinct shift from the more heterogeneous approach to forms of work seen in the seventeenth century;[205] and it extended the encompassing nature of masters' powers over their workers along lines that hitherto applied only in respect of domestic servants. Under the *Statute of Artificers*, imprisonment was available in cases of departure or failure to complete work;[206] it was not available on the grounds of quality of work or behaviour. The 1747 Act, however, made it possible for masters to seek imprisonment of workers – particularly those persons who, in Defoe's words, "we hire for daily Labour" – based on their "Misdemeanor, Miscarriage or Ill-behaviour." The 1766 *Act for better regulating Apprentices, and Persons working under Contract*[207] extended the 1747 Act by making it an offence to quit before the end of the agreed term,[208] and increased the maximum penalty for a contravention of the terms of an agreement to three months' imprisonment.

---

201 *An Act for the better adjusting and more easy Recovery of the Wages of certain Servants; and for the better Regulation of such Servants, and of certain Apprentices 1747*, 20 Geo III, c 19.

202 20 Geo III, c 19, s 2.

203 20 Geo III, c 19, s 2.

204 The Act clarified that the servants to which it applied were servants in husbandry. On the differential treatment of domestic service relations see chapter 4.

205 Tomlins, *supra* note 10 at 357. See also Daniel Defoe, *A Plan of the English Commerce Being a Compleat Prospect of the Trade of this Nation, as well the Home Trade as the Foreign* (London, 1728) at 4–5.

206 5 Eliz, c 4, s 13. Servants who departed from their master's service without giving one quarter's warning could also be imprisoned until undertaking to complete their service: s 9.

207 6 Geo III, c 25.

208 6 Geo III, c 25, s 4.

In this context, Blackstone's approach to work relations in the *Commentaries* (1765–9) takes on a particular salience.[209] His decision to group various classes of workers (domestics, apprentices, labourers, and those "in a superior, a ministerial, capacity"[210]) under the banner of Master and Servant was not simply the continuation of centuries-old practices but instead "confirmed the emergence of 'master and servant' as a generic legal category applicable to all relations of employment."[211] The shift is particularly apparent when one considers the treatment of work in what was perhaps the most influential legal text of the seventeenth century: Michael Dalton's *Countrey Justice*. Chapter 31 of that work is simply entitled "Labourers," and commences with the statement, "Every Justice of Peace, upon request, may cause all such Artificers and other persons as be meet to labour, (by his discretion) to worke by the day in Hay-time, and Harvest-time."[212] Master and Servant was not, at that point, the overarching organizational framework that it became in the *Commentaries*.

This emerging understanding of service as the governing model for work relations more generally received a significant boost from the courts soon after the publication of the *Commentaries*. In *Hart v Aldridge*,[213] the King's Bench decided that for the purposes of the *Statute of Artificers* the term "servant" applied not only to servants in husbandry and domestic servants, but also to persons working for a set time or performing piecework.[214] In other words, artificers and labourers were treated as servants. The case was an action for trespass on the case brought by one master (Hart) against another (Aldridge) "for enticing away several

---

209 See further chapter 2.

210 Blackstone, *supra* note 20, book I at 410.

211 Tomlins, *supra* note 10 at 350. See also Deakin and Wilkinson, *supra* note 9 at 50; Steinfeld, *Free Labor, supra* note 18 at 21–2; Brewer, *supra* note 89 at 295. Of course, Blackstone was not the first to take this step. Matthew Hale classified work relations under the banner "Of the Relation of Master and Servant," but provided such inadequate discussion as to render his treatment otherwise virtually useless. More substantive was Richard Burn's 1755 text, *The Justice of the Peace, and Parish Officer*, in which one finds the category of "Servants," and the statement that "[u]nder this title are also comprehended labourers, journeymen, artificers, and other workmen": Richard Burn, *The Justice of the Peace, and Parish Officer* (London, 1755) vol 2 at 350.

212 Michael Dalton, *The Countrey Justice, Containing the Practice of the Justices of the Peace out of their Sessions: Gathered for the better help of such Justices of Peace as have not been much conversant in the studie of the Lawes of this Realme*, 5th ed. (printed by the assignes of John Mori, 1635) at 78.

213 1 Cowp 55 (1774).

214 Hay, *supra* note 184 at 88.

of the plaintiff's servants who used to work for him in the capacity of journeymen shoemakers." The journeymen were hired on a piece-work basis and were alleged to have each left a pair of shoes unfinished. Hart's solicitor argued: "[A] journeyman is as much a servant as any other person who works for hire or wages; that neither in reason nor at common law is there any distinction between a servant in one capacity or another, and that the injury of seduction is in all cases the same, though the recompense in damages may be different." For Aldridge, it was argued that, "the term 'journeyman' does not import that they belong to any particular master"; the question, therefore, was the extent to which a non-resident worker "belongs" to his or her master. The Court upheld the plaintiff's claim. Lord Mansfield declared, "[a] journeyman is a servant by the day; and it makes no difference whether the work is done by the day or by the piece"; he accordingly characterized the action thus: "That the defendant has enticed a man away who stood in the relation of servant to the plaintiff." The rationale for this expansion of the legal approach to governance of work relations was made by clear by Aston J, who declared that "very bad consequence[s] in trade" might result if pieceworkers such as journeymen were able to abandon their work without penalty. That is, a servile relationship characterized by control – precisely the model that characterized relations between masters and domestic servants – was considered necessary and justifiable, even in the case of day workers, in order to protect the economic interests of masters.

Some twenty years later, the King's Bench declared that domestic servants were *not* subject to the *Statute of Artificers*.[215] That decision took from domestics the summary wage remedies enjoyed by other workers, but it also deprived their masters of recourse to the magistrates (though not of their common law right to correct troublesome servants).[216] Thus, the following year, "a master dealing with a recalcitrant coachman had to convince the court that the servant also performed odd services on his hobby farm,"[217] which brought the servant within the scope of provisions in the *Statute of Artificers* and the 1747 Act concerning servants in husbandry. In other words, at the same time that law and legal thought was consolidating the law of work into a general framework

---

215 *The King v Inhabitants of Hulcott* (1796) 6 Term 583, 101 ER 716. See the discussion in chapter 4, part II(A).

216 Hay, *supra* note 184 at 89.

217 *Ibid* citing Public Records Office (London), KB 1/29 pt 1, Mich 37 Geo III no 1, affidavits in application for a rule nisi against Edward Read esq. for wrongful committal of Thomas Brown for conspiracy.

based around the subjection inherent in the old master and (domestic) servant relation, that very same relation was undergoing a parallel process of change, albeit one characterized by the law's partial *retreat* from regulation based upon deference to the ongoing *familial* nature of the master-domestic servant relation – an aspect that was thought not to apply to other work relations, hence the need for additional legal forms of control.

This process of increasing the power of masters over their non-domestic workers continued in statutory form in the later parts of the eighteenth century. The 1777 Act "for the more effectual preventing of Frauds and Abuses"[218] in the various clothing manufactures provided for conviction for embezzlement of materials based upon the oath of one person that the accused "hath or have purloined or embezzled," "although no Proof shall be given to whom such Materials belong."[219] The Act also provided that "if any Person, being hired, retained, or employed, to prepare or work up any Materials, whether mixed or unmixed, for any Master or Masters, shall wilfully neglect or refuse the Performance thereof for eight Days successively," or take in materials from another Master before a prior job was completed, "or permit himself or herself to be employed or retained in any other Occupation or Employment whatsoever, sooner than eight Days before the Completion of the Work first taken," that person "shall be sent to the House of Correction, or other public Prison, there to be kept to hard Labour for any Time not exceeding three Months, nor less than one Month."[220] For

---

218 *An Act for amending and rendering more effectual the several Laws now in being, for the more effectual preventing of Frauds and Abuses by Persons employed in the Manufacture of Hats, and in the Woollen, Linen, Fustian, Cotton, Iron, Leather, Fur, Hemp, Flax, Mohair, and Silk Manufactures; and also for making Provisions to prevent Frauds by Journeymen Dyers*, 17 Geo III, c 56. Similar Acts were also passed in 1740 (13 George II, c 8), 1749 (22 George II, c 27) and 1792 (32 George III, c 44).

219 17 Geo III, c 56, s 6. The penalty was the same as that for "Persons convicted of buying or receiving any such Materials" – namely, a fine of between £20 and £40, which, if unpaid, was converted into a sentence of imprisonment of between three and six months: s 3. In the words of Alexander Macdonald, "[m]ore arbitrary powers could hardly have been given to any judge than these": Alexander Macdonald, *Handybook of the Law Relative to Masters, Workmen, Servants, and Apprentices, in all Trades and Occupations* (London: W Mackenzie, 1868) at 101. In 1843, 17 Geo III, c 56 was replaced by 6 & 7 Vict, c 40, which enacted that if any person was convicted of pawning or embezzling any of the materials or tools referred to in the Act, by the oath of the owner of the materials or any other credible witness, before two or more justices of the peace, he shall forfeit the full value of the materials and be liable to a penalty not exceeding ten pounds. See Macdonald, *ibid* at 158.

220 17 Geo III, c 56, s 8.

masters, there could be little economic utility in having piece-workers sent to prison for three months; the point was to secure performance and instantiate a relationship of servility by threatening imprisonment of persons who were tardy or who accepted work from more than one master at a time.

By the end of the eighteenth century, then, the integrated household model of work and family life was breaking apart, but legal subordination of workers had been transplanted and extended across a variety of work types, and the patriarchal authority of masters was undergoing transformation and renewal into the contractual – and equally subordinating – authority of employers.

II. THE NINETEENTH CENTURY

In 1806, the King's Bench in *Lowther v Earl of Radnor & Anor*[221] followed the example set in *Hart v Aldridge* by finding that pieceworkers were servants; this time, though, the Court dealt with the statutory master-servant regime, specifically, the 1747 Act. The case was ostensibly about wage recovery – specifically, the scope of the phrase "Servants in Husbandry ... and *other Labourers*" in the 1747 Act. The defendants were Justices of the Peace who had made an order against the plaintiff concerning wages said to be owed by him to one James Sopp, a labourer who had dug and steaned[222] a well for Lowther on the basis that he would be paid two shillings per foot. The question was whether Sopp was a labourer for the purposes of the Act, and hence whether the defendants' order was valid. Lord Ellenborough found for the defendants on the basis that "other Labourers" meant "other labourers in any trade or business."[223] Insofar as wage recovery was concerned, this ruling might be considered a victory for labourers because it brought them within the scope of the 1747 Act. However, the ruling also made servants in husbandry *and wage labourers generally* subject to the "Misdemeanour, Miscarriage or Ill-behaviour" part of the statute. This was a significant expansion of the regime constituted by the *Statute of Artificers*,[224] which had permitted imprisonment only for failure to complete work, not the quality of work or the manner of its performance – and only for one month, not the three months allowed by the 1747 Act.

---

221 (1806) 8 East 113.

222 Construction of part of the lining and wall of the well.

223 (1806) 8 East 113, 123–4.

224 That Lord Ellenborough's motivation, at least in part, was to achieve this end is suggested by his repeated references in the judgment to the Act's object being "the better regulation of servants," as well as "the payment of wages to them."

Lord Ellenborough took a similar approach some eight years later in *The King v Inhabitants of Barton-upon-Irwell*.[225] The parish of Barton-upon-Irwell claimed that the pauper Edwards had not gained a valid settlement through service because he was imprisoned for misbehaviour towards his master, two months in to an annual hiring. The master in fact sought and obtained Edwards' early discharge, and Edwards remained in his service for another 17 months. The Court found against the parish on the basis that imprisonment did not determine the contract. In essence, the duty of service owed by a servant was held to be sufficiently strong "that perhaps his labour might have been required of him by the master even while he was in prison,"[226] since "during the whole time he was subject to his master."[227] The commitment to prison "did not free the servant from his contract" because this would have amounted to a boon for workers (prison was presumably not a sufficient punishment in itself) and, more worryingly, would have conferred a measure of decisional freedom on servants.[228] The ruling thus strengthened the ability of masters to secure performance by reliance on the criminal law without any concern that such recourse determined the contract. A master could have a worker committed and then, with the worker suitably chastened, he could have him released after a brief period to return to service. Any further refusal would simply lead to a repeat of the process.

Soon after *Barton-upon-Irwell*, the Court in *Spain v Arnott*[229] affirmed that masters could summarily dismiss workers for minor acts of insubordination. The case concerned the validity of a master's dismissal of his servant (in husbandry) and subsequent refusal to pay wages for the period worked.[230] The worker in this case was accustomed to having

---

225 (1814) 2 M&S 329.

226 (1814) 2 M&S 329 at 332 (Ellenborough CJ).

227 (1814) 2 M&S 329 at 332 (Le Blanc J).

228 (1814) 2 M&S 329 at 333 (Bayley J). In a later case under the 1766 statute, *In re William Baker* (1857) 2 H & N 219, the Court was split as to whether a conviction and time spent in prison dissolved a contract. Two members of the Court (Watson B. and Bramwell B.) found that such a contract remained operational, meaning that a worker (in this case a potter) could be re-convicted if he refused to return to his master after time in prison. In contrast, Pollock C.B. rejected this construction on the basis that such a man "might spend the whole year, except a few days, in gaol." Martin B. found himself unable to express a concluded opinion on this point. For a fuller discussion of this case see Hay, *supra* note 184 at 59–60. See further *infra* note 248.

229 (1816–19) 2 Stark 256.

230 At this time wages under yearly hirings were paid annually, and not at all in the case of a servant's breach.

his dinner at 2pm; when Arnott ordered him to attend the horses at this time, he refused to do so until he had eaten. Arnott "told him to go about his business, and the plaintiff went accordingly."[231] In the Chief Justice's view, the master was perfectly entitled to act as he did because "it would be exceedingly inconvenient if the servant were to be permitted to set himself up to control his master in his domestic regulations ... the question really comes to this, whether the master or the servant is to have the superior authority."[232] By affirming the master's right to dismiss an annual servant, without wages, on grounds as trifling as the time of dinner, the Court affirmed the almost total subjection of servants – a much expanded class in light of the judgments in preceding cases – and the case "became the leading authority for the servant's subordination, and for the entire contract doctrine in employment cases."[233] The coexistence of coercion and contract, and the extension of the subordination inherent in the older household-based model of (domestic) service to a vast range of work relations conducted outside of the home, was clear.[234]

Nevertheless, with the repeal of the wage-setting and apprenticeship clauses of the *Statute of Artificers* in 1813–1814,[235] "state regulation of the labor market is thought to have been largely eliminated, leaving the terms of labor to be set primarily through bargaining between employers and workers under the common law of contract."[236] The reality, as George White's 1823 review of master and servant laws[237] makes clear, is that an "oppressive and unequal Code" was in force in the early nineteenth century. "The law," said White, "is now totally in favour of the master, and the end of it is, that the master is grinding down the workman, till he looks upon work as a secondary employment,"

---

231 (1816–19) 2 Stark 256 at 256–7.

232 *Ibid* at 257.

233 Hay, *supra* note 184 at 114.

234 According to Hay, *ibid* at 109, "high-court judges heard more cases about labor contracts, and they did so in a period, from 1800 to 1850, when 'freedom of contract,' notably a will theory of contract, was reaching its apogee and permeating the courts' reasoning in many areas of law. Its consequences for the common law of master and servant were many."

235 *Wages, etc. of Artificers, etc., Act 1813*, 53 Geo III, c 40; *Apprentices Act 1814*, 54 Geo III, c 96.

236 Steinfeld, *Coercion, supra* note 144 at 41.

237 George White, *A Few Remarks on the State of the Laws, at Present in Existence, for Regulating Masters and Work-People, Intended as A Guide for the Consideration of the House, in Their Discussions on the Bill for Repealing Several Acts Relating to Combinations of Workmen, and for More Effectually Protecting Trade, and for Settling Disputes Between Masters and Servants* (London, 1823).

preferring instead thievery.[238] White drew particular attention to the injustice caused by masters' reliance on the terms of written contracts, which were too often contrary to oral agreements, and which servants often did not understand. In such cases, White wrote, a servant (which by this time referred to most workers) "now finds that he is obliged, under a heavy penalty, to keep his master's secrets, to work all night if his master chuses to employ him, – that his master can make him work to the letter of the contract."[239] As White discerned, this coexistence of contract and subordination was intellectually rooted in the "doctrine[s] of *modern* political enconomists [*sic*.], who seem to think, that provided a man agrees to any contract, he cannot be oppressed or injured. They do not, or will not, see the immense difference between masters and servants, and contracts for purchase in markets, contracts for renting land, houses."[240]

While White warned his readers that "*slavery [was] at hand immediately*" under this system because a man "has only got to sell, or hire himself, for life, and then, by his own agreement, he may become the property of his master,"[241] the *Master and Servant Act 1823*[242] consolidated and extended the powers conferred by earlier Acts. Section 3 provided:

> That if any Servant in Husbandry or any Artificer, Calico Printer, Handicraftsman, Miner, Collier, Keelman, Pitman, Glassman, Potter, Labourer or other Person, shall contract with any Person or Persons whomsoever, to serve him, her or them for any Time or Times whatsoever, or in any other manner, and shall not enter into or commence his or her Service according to his or her Contract (such Contract being in Writing, and signed by the Contracting Parties), or having entered into such Service shall absent himself from his or her Service before the Term of his or her Contract, whether such Contract shall be in Writing or not in Writing, shall be completed, or neglect to fulfil the same, or be guilty of any other Misconduct or Misdemeanor in the Execution thereof, or otherwise respecting the same, then and in every such Case it shall and may be lawful for any Justice of the Peace … to commit every such Person to the House of Correction, there to remain and be held to hard Labour for a reasonable Time, not exceeding

---

238 *Ibid* at v.
239 *Ibid* at 93.
240 *Ibid* at 105–6.
241 *Ibid* at 108 (emphasis in original).
242 4 Geo IV, c 34.

Three Months, and to abate a proportionable Part of his or her Wages, for and during such Period as he or she shall be so confined ...

That is to say, absconding from work and refusing to enter into work under a contract of hiring were made offences punishable by up to three months' imprisonment. The provision was the culmination of a century-long process of tightening and "uniformalizing" the legal culture of work, resulting in "the creation of a ubiquitous legal structure for an increasingly uniform economy, grounded on the criminalization of employment breach wherever it might occur."[243]

House of correction registers show the impact of these statutes on the lives of workers.[244] The prison sentences in early eighteenth-century London (60 per cent of them for less than two weeks) contrast sharply with the evidence a century later, from several counties: in Staffordshire less than 7 per cent of sentences of workers were this short. The increase in statutory penalties during the eighteenth century was reflected in early nineteenth-century average and modal sentences of about a month, ranging from a week to three months depending on the offense. It was possible to pass such sentences because of the greatly increased capacity of county prisons and houses of correction (which earlier were often decayed and tiny lockups) in the period 1790 to 1850.[245]

Hay's analysis of four sample years from early nineteenth-century records in Staffordshire revealed "more than 1,000 convictions of servants for breach of contract. In the same four years, the total number of theft convictions in the county was 169. In other words, there were six times as many workers punished for master and servant offenses as there were thieves punished by the 'ordinary' criminal law."[246]

---

243 Tomlins, *supra* note 10 at 350.

244 Precise national statistics are impossible to obtain before 1858, when the central state began collecting annual statistics of master and servant cases: Hay, *supra* note 184 at 101.

245 Indeed, there is evidence that the increasing numbers of servants who were sentenced to incarceration under the Master and Servant Acts was one factor in the expansion of the English prison system in the nineteenth century. For example, "[t]he planners of Bedford's new prison, opened in 1820, listed their targets: poachers came first, followed by 'servants in husbandry and other labourers for misbehaviour in their employment.'" In Gloucestershire and Staffordshire between 1790 and 1820, some 26 per cent and 39 per cent of prisoners, respectively, were imprisoned for breach of contract. Hay, *supra* note 184 at 95 quoting Bedfordshire Record Office, Q/S rolls 1820/69. Hay based these figures on analysis of "over 5,000 inmates recorded for Gloucestershire and Staffordshire houses of correction in the three decades after 1790."

246 *Ibid* at 108.

This pattern continued well into the middle of the century,[247] though opposition was mounting.[248] According to Alexander Macdonald's 1868 *Handybook of the Law Relative to Masters, Workmen, Servants, and Apprentices, all Trades and Occupations*, public opinion in the mid-1860s "had come to be decidedly unfavourable to a statute [the 1823 Act] which placed the British workman charged with the mere violation of an ordinary right, exactly in the position of the ruffian who committed a penal wrong."[249] After an aborted inquiry in 1865, a committee of the House of Commons chaired by Lord Elcho was convened in 1866. In clipped language, the Committee's Report noted: "Primary object of the present movement to remove the existing inequality, and to put the employer and the employed before the law in the same condition."[250] Further on, it stated:

> CRIMINAL OFFENCE (BREACH OF CONTRACT). – Inequality under the Act 4 Geo. IV. c.34, inasmuch as a breach of contract on the part of a workman renders him liable to a criminal prosecution, whilst a breach of contract on the part of the master renders him liable only to a civil action for damages.[251]

The Committee thus recommended that "punishment should be by fine," but "failing payment by distress or imprisonment."[252] Imprisonment was also recommended in "aggravated cases of breach of contract, causing injury to person or property."[253]

---

247 *Ibid* at 95–6; see also 108–09. However, unions in the 1840s did have some success contesting master and servant laws, in particular, stymying an 1844 attempt to extend existing penal laws to new groups of workers: *ibid* at 115.

248 The peculiar circumstance of judgments from two different courts on the same set of facts (not involving an appeal) points to divergent attitudes amongst the judiciary in the mid-nineteenth century towards the subjection of servants and the role of the criminal law in master-servant relations. See *Ex parte Baker* (1857) 7 El & Bl 687 (finding that a potter's contract continued throughout and after his imprisonment for leaving his employer's service, and that he was therefore liable to further imprisonment for refusing to return to service); *In re William Baker* (1857) 2 H & N 219 (noting in dicta that an employer could not repeatedly seek to have an employee imprisoned for breach of contract). According to Hay, the latter case provided "ammunition for the unions in presentations to parliamentary committees in the 1860s": Hay, *supra* note 184 at 60.

249 Macdonald, *supra* note 219 at 183.

250 *Ibid* at 184.

251 *Ibid* at 184–5.

252 *Ibid* 191 referring to Recommendation 4.

253 *Ibid* 191 referring to Recommendation 6.

The ensuing legislation, the *Master and Servant Act 1867*,[254] somewhat improved the position of servants, at least in cases of simple contract breach. Imprisonment was still available, but it was no longer the primary punishment. Instead it became "auxiliary to the jurisdiction, as the consequence of disobedience to the order of the court"; hard labour was also removed.[255] In essence, where the 1823 Act provided that if a worker "shall not have fulfilled such Contract, or hath been guilty of any other Misconduct or Misdemeanour as aforesaid, it shall and may be lawful for such Justice to commit every such Person to the House of Correction,"[256] the 1867 Act provided for abatement of wages, "Fulfilment of the Contract of Service, with a Direction to the Party complained against, to find forthwith good and sufficient Security," or annulment of the contract with apportionment of wages or a fine of up to twenty pounds.[257] The second option, "Fulfilment of the Contract of Service," indicates that while the means of achieving performance had changed, the goal was the same – instead of ordering imprisonment justices were directly empowered to make orders for the specific performance of a labour contract. The criminal law remained, however, as a sort of additional incentive. The Act stated:

> [I]f the Order shall direct the Fulfilment of the Contract, and direct the Party complained against to find good and sufficient Security as aforesaid, and the Party complained against neglect or refuse to comply with such Order, a Justice, Magistrate, or Sheriff may, if he shall think fit, by Warrant under his Hand, commit such Party to the Common Gaol or House of Correction within his Jurisdiction, there to be confined and kept until he shall so find Security, but nevertheless so that the Term of Imprisonment, whether under One or several successive Committals, shall not exceed in the whole the Period of Three Months.[258]

On its face, the provision applied to both servants and masters. Unsurprisingly, though, servants' complaints "generally resolve[d] themselves into claims for wages or damages, so that, as the law now stands, the employer will have all the benefit of the order for security of fulfill-

---

254 30 & 31 Vict I, c 141.
255 J.E. Davis, *Labour and Labour Laws*, 9th ed. (private reprint from *Encyclopaedia Britannica*, 1883) at 26.
256 4 Geo IV, c 34, s 3.
257 30 & 31 Vict I, c 141, s 9.
258 30 & 31 Vict I, c 141, s 9.

ment of his servant's obligation, while the latter can never compel his master."[259]

The effect of the Act is revealed by subsequent imprisonment and prosecution rates: the former certainly fell after 1867, but overall prosecution rates actually rose, with the greatest number of prosecutions between 1871 and 1875.[260] At least part of the reason seems to be the substitution of fines for imprisonment pursuant to the 1867 Act, although "[t]he number of fined workers greatly exceeded the decline in the numbers of those imprisoned."[261] "In the last four years of penal sanctions (1872–75) for breach of contract, the ratio of master and servant prosecutions to all theft prosecutions varied between 25 and 32 per cent. In the courts that heard both summary property and master and servant cases, the national ratio of accused workers to accused thieves varied between 31 and 41 per cent in those four years."[262] The remedial advantage enjoyed by masters was the subject of a Royal Commission convened in the wake of Disraeli's election in 1874. The Commissioners agreed that simple breach of contract "should be divested of all character of criminality." However, they also made abundantly clear the true rationale for penal sanctions: "[The] mode in which courts having jurisdiction to order specific performance enforce their authority is by imprisonment. There is therefore nothing exceptional in the application of this remedy in case of disobedience here." The "unique circumstances surrounding labour contracts" were held to justify the anomalous availability of criminal sanctions to enforce specific performance.[263] Accordingly, the *Employers and Workmen Act 1875*[264] did not entirely do away with criminal sanctions; what it did do, though, was make the process leading to incarceration cumbersome – employers were required to obtain an initial damages award, followed by an order to pay by instalments where possible, and the failure of a defendant subject to an order to make payment.[265] Thus, as Steinfeld notes, the cessation of imprisonment for breach of labour contracts was more of a

---

259 Macdonald, *supra* note 219 at 197.
260 Hay, *supra* note 184 at 108–9.
261 *Ibid* at 108.
262 *Ibid*.
263 Steinfeld, *Coercion*, *supra* note 144 at 211.
264 38 & 39 Vict I, c 90. The Act did not apply to "domestic servants, clerks, tutors, governesses, or other persons of the same kind who would not, in the ordinary acceptation of the term, be reckoned among 'the working classes'": Holdsworth, *supra* note 187 at 140.
265 38 & 39 Vict I, c 90, s 9.

de facto development than a strictly legal one.[266] Nevertheless, the law had effectively moved away from criminalizing breach of contract.[267] In 1876, William Holdsworth declared in *The Law of Master and Servant*, "proceedings in regard to disputes between employers and workmen are … to be regarded and treated in future as civil, and not criminal, in their character."[268]

In certain respects, this move formed part of the more general tendency within late nineteenth century law and legal thought towards treating different species of agreements "as different forms of the same thing: abstract, generalized contract."[269] While contract theory remained in principle compatible with subordination, the element of coercive state involvement in labour agreements stood in contrast to other sorts of (commercial) contracts that were not backed up by criminal law. According to Steinfeld: "As the tradition of understanding master and servant agreements as a distinct species of contract faded, it became more difficult to justify the unique remedies provided for the breach of these agreements. In the unitary universe of contract, those remedies began to seem more and more anomalous."[270] At the same time, however, employment agreements remained an awkward fit within the general framework of contract owing to the continued application of pro-master decisions from the courts, and associated common law obligations of loyalty and obedience on the part of employees as a general class – the legacy of a century and a half of legal consolidation of work relations under the general framework of the master and (domestic) servant relation, and the correlative extension of masters' domestic authority into the non-familial realm of consent-based work.[271]

---

266 Steinfeld, *Coercion, supra* note 144 at 217–18.

267 This is not to imply that with the emergence of the modern contract of employment, contract-based coercion ceased: see Pateman, *supra* note 73 at 148.

268 Holdsworth, *supra* note 187 at 145–6.

269 Steinfeld, *Coercion, supra* note 144 at 162. See further chapter 2.

270 *Ibid* at 163.

271 See Deakin and Wilkinson, *supra* note 9 at 61, 103. As Holdsworth declared in his 1876 treatise, *The Law of Master and Servant, supra* note 187 at 2, the term "master and servant" included "all persons between whom any contract exists for the render of service, or the fulfillment of duties on the one hand, and the payment of stipulated hire, wages, salary, or reward on the other, during a determinate or stated period or term, or until the expiration of a fixed notice to be given by either party. The manager of a railway, the head clerk in a large mercantile establishment, the tutor or governess in a gentleman's family, are in point of law as much servants as the domestics in a household." See also John Macdonnell, *The Law of Master and Servant* (London: Stevens and Sons, 1883) at 34: "A servant is one who for consideration agrees to work subject to the orders of another."

IV. Conclusion

This chapter has shown how a series of intersecting legal interventions in the eighteenth and nineteenth centuries helped to constitute the legal understanding and social practice of work as an activity cathected to the market, and distinct from the private family. Property law in the form of enclosure Acts was one dimension of this process, removing from poor families the ability to engage in autarkic modes of production, and helping to shift English agricultural practices away from live-in forms of service. The social dislocation caused by enclosure and industrialization was met with reforms to the Poor Law that sought to incentivize wage labour performed outside of the home by curtailing outdoor relief and enacting the principle of less eligibility in the provision of indoor relief. This institutionally driven disarticulation of work from the family was augmented by a series of statutory and common law measures that extended the patriarchal authority formerly enjoyed by masters over their domestic servants to a broad range of workers (newly constituted in law as servants), in particular by treating breach of contract on the part of workers as a criminal offense potentially leading to imprisonment.

The story presented in this chapter thus complicates the idea that the transition away from household-based understandings and forms of work and family, towards modern, wage-based conceptions and practices of work that were disarticulated from the private domestic unit, involved a neat linear progression in which one form of obligation (patriarchy and ascribed status) was supplanted by another (consent-based contractual ordering). There was ultimately an alteration in the legal understanding and social practice of work – from the status-based regime of the *Statute of Artificers* to a (heavily regulated) regime of contractual ordering – but this was a textured and gradual transition in which the legal idea of employment as a contract between juridical equals did not emerge until the late nineteenth century,[272] and arguably remains in a state of formation.[273]

---

272 Deakin and Wilkinson, *supra* note 9 at 41–2.

273 *Ibid*. See also Adrian Merritt, "The Historical Role of the Law in the Regulation of Employment – Abstentionist or Interventionist?" (1982) 1 *Aust JL Soc* 56.

Chapter Four

Women and Youth, Work and Family

Neither in England nor its colonies, however, did this emerging social world of covenants and contracts, of free labor exercised and its exercise enforced, encompass the full extent of the world of work. This world of labor sat atop another, defined by distinct structures of socio-legal relations – the world of the household, of production but also of reproduction.[1]

I. Introduction

A defining feature of the productive household was its integration of work and family life: workers, including apprentices, lived with and, to varying degrees, formed part of the family; and family members worked for the benefit of the household. As Bridget Hill put it, "within this unit work was directed towards the subsistence and maintenance of its members."[2] This work took many forms, including cultivation of crops and care of animals, the production of basic and artisanal goods for sale in the market, education of youths, preparation of foodstuffs, collection of fuel, and cleaning. In the eighteenth century all of these tasks, including what is now generally understood as "housework," were recognized as labour – productive contributions to the functioning of the household.[3] Over the course of the nineteenth century this approach to work that was attached in some way to the household shifted. The previous chapter addressed some of the legal factors that

---

1 Christopher L. Tomlins, *Freedom Bound: Law, Labor, and Civic Identity in Colonizing English America, 1580–1865* (New York: Cambridge University Press, 2010) at 358.

2 Bridget Hill, *Women, Work, and Sexual Politics in Eighteenth-Century England* (Oxford: Basil Blackwell, 1989) at 24.

3 Nancy Folbre, "The Unproductive Housewife: Her Evolution in Nineteenth-Century Economic Thought" (1991) 16:3 *Signs* 463 at 464.

helped to create a structural shift in English labour practices – ostensibly, a state-backed and directed move away from autarkic modes of production towards complete or predominant reliance by families on wage labour performed outside of the home; and underwritten by a suite of laws that imposed upon workers new variations of the old authority of the patriarchal master. This chapter considers how this broad trend towards exteriorized wage labour affected specific forms of work involving women and youth: paid and unpaid domestic labour, and traditional and parish apprenticeship.

Paid domestic work, which became a distinctly feminine occupation in the nineteenth century, came to be treated as a distinct species of work situated outside of the general paradigm of wage labour[4] because of its location in the familial realm of the home. While the master-domestic servant relation became the general model for labour in the nineteenth century, domestic workers were, in an ironic twist, largely excluded from the master-servant regime and situated instead on the periphery of law's regulation of work in a liminal space that traversed (and challenged the distinction between) family and market. Accordingly, as seen in chapter 2, legal scholars continued to situate domestic servants alongside other familial relations long after other, non-resident workers, had been shifted into the market-based sphere of employment. In the twentieth century domestic service began to be conceptualized alongside other forms of work, but its affiliation with the family-based sphere of the home remained a significant obstacle – the legacy of which is still with us in the form of different employment standards for domestic workers.[5]

Women who performed domestic work for their own families were never treated in law as workers (and remain outside of the bounds of modern labour law[6]), but as wage labour came to be conceptualized as a masculine domain, women's unpaid work in the home was rendered culturally mandatory while also being devalued and re-characterized as unproductive, creating what Nancy Folbre memorably called "the

---

4 See chapter 3.
5 Einat Albin, "From 'Domestic Servant' to 'Domestic Worker'" in Judy Fudge, Shae McCrystal and Kamala Sankaran, eds., *Challenging the Legal Boundaries of Work Regulation* (Oxford: Hart, 2012) 231; Einat Albin and Jeremias Prassl, "Fragmenting Work, Fragmented Regulation: The Contract of Employment as a Driver of Social Exclusion" in Mark Freedland *et al*, eds., *The Contract of Employment* (Oxford: Oxford University Press, 2016) 209 at 226–8.
6 Joanne Conaghan, "The Discipline of Labour Law" in Joanne Conaghan and Kerry Rittich, eds., *Labour Law, Work, and Family: Critical and Comparative Perspectives* (Oxford: Oxford University Press, 2005) 19 at 34: "labour law is not primarily or even predominantly about the world of work. It is about *paid* work and, indeed, about particular forms of paid work." [Conaghan, "Discipline of Labour Law"]

unproductive housewife."[7] Legal and policy-based interventions helped to constitute this situation by excluding married women from participation in market-based forms of work (through protective labour laws and marriage bars), rendering their participation in paid work less thinkable (partly a result of family wage ideology and industrial demands for male breadwinner wages – demands that were enabled by repeal of anti-combination laws), and devaluing work that occurred within the home (for example, the late nineteenth-century shift in the English census towards characterizing housework as unproductive). As a result of these intersecting processes, "married women's economic dependence on men's wages reinforced male privilege and power within the household."[8]

Major shifts also occurred in the legal and cultural treatment of what was once the paradigmatic familial work relation: master and apprentice. Prior to the eighteenth century, apprentices were considered members of the family and a master assumed parental as well as educational responsibilities for his apprentice. In the eighteenth and nineteenth centuries, however, traditional apprenticeship was gradually stripped of its familial components and re-imagined within the emerging framework of contract-based wage labour (albeit with a residual peculiarity in the form of the master's duty to teach). In stark contrast – one that points to the nineteenth-century family/market split – parish apprenticeship, in which a poor youth was placed with a family (a form of state-directed private welfare), eventually came to be divested of its labour components and re-cast within the framework of family-based care. In terms of the taxonomy discussed in chapter 2, then, traditional apprenticeship eventually docked in the law of employment, while parish apprenticeship became part of the law of welfare and family.

II. Women, Work, and the Domestic Sphere

A. Paid Domestic Labour

The legislative and judicial extension of the master and *domestic* servant model to most forms of paid work in the eighteenth and nineteenth centuries was coterminous with the gradual excision of domestic service

---

7 Folbre, *supra* note 3. See also Carole Pateman, *The Sexual Contract* (Palo Alto: Stanford University Press, 1988) at 136: "The labour of a (house)wife is aptly termed domestic servitude, or, more politely, domestic service. Housework is not 'work.' Work takes place in the men's world of capitalism and workplaces. The meaning of 'work' depends on the (repressed) connection between the private and civil spheres."

8 Sandra Fredman and Judy Fudge, "The Contract of Employment and Gendered Work" in Freedland *et al*, *supra* note 5, 231 at 235.

from this general legal template governing English work relations.[9]
The subordination of domestic workers continued, but more through a
lacuna created by the law rather than the direct statutory and common
law obligations and penalties imposed on workers operating outside of
the home.[10] In essence, the ongoing nexus between domestic workers
and the household – as it morphed into the private domain of the family
(home) – was treated as the basis for a legal distinction between paid
work occurring within and outside of the home. This split is clearly
apparent in legal texts from the late nineteenth century, which continued to treat domestic service as part of the Law of Domestic Relations
(subsidiary to husband-wife and parent-child), and pointedly excluded
domestic service from the Law of Master and Servant.[11] Eventually,
as the split between family (law) and work (law) hardened, domestic
service was shifted into the latter category,[12] but it remained an awkward fit due to the ongoing legal treatment of paid domestic labour as
somehow different to forms of work performed outside of the home/
family context. This longstanding (and ongoing) differential treatment
of domestic labour disproportionately affected (and continues to affect)
women, for whom domestic service became a primary (and potentially
the only available) form of work over the course of the eighteenth and
nineteenth centuries. The intersecting treatment of domestic labour as
exceptional vis-à-vis other forms of paid work, and the construction

---

9 In the mid-eighteenth century, the term "servant" referred to persons hired on an
   annual basis who lived within the master's household. The term thus extended
   to both domestic servants and servants in husbandry. See William Blackstone,
   Commentaries on the Laws of England, 4 vols (Oxford: Clarendon Press, 1765–9) book I
   at 413. Over the course of the nineteenth century, however, these forms of work came
   to be viewed as distinct, partially due to the general decline in farm service, and
   also due to increasingly strict legal distinctions between domestic service and other
   forms of work. See Ann Kussmaul, *Servants in Husbandry in Early Modern England*
   (Cambridge: Cambridge University Press, 1981) at 4. In what follows, I am generally
   concerned with the legal treatment of domestic servants, not servants in husbandry,
   but in earlier periods it is often impossible to draw clear legal boundaries between
   these forms of service.
10 Leonore Davidoff, "Domestic Service and the Working-Class Life Cycle" (1973) 26
   Soc Stud Lab Hist 10 at 10 [Davidoff, "Domestic Service"]; Simon Deakin and Frank
   Wilkinson, *The Law of the Labour Market: Industrialization, Employment and Legal
   Evolution* (Oxford: Oxford University Press, 2005) at 79.
11 See, e.g., William Pinder Eversley, *The Law of the Domestic Relations: Including
   Husband and Wife, Parent and Child, Guardian and Ward, Infants, and Master and Servant*
   (London: Stevens and Haynes 1885); John Macdonnell, *The Law of Master and Servant*
   (London: Stevens and Sons, 1883).
12 See, e.g., Edward Jenks, ed., *A Digest of English Civil Law*, 5 vols (London:
   Butterworth & Co, 1905–17).

of service as a female occupation, carried over into the twentieth century and became particularly apparent in the aftermath of the First and Second World Wars – with implications that continue to be felt in the present.[13]

I. THE EXCEPTIONAL LEGAL TREATMENT OF DOMESTIC SERVICE

The proximity between domestic servants and the families they served (and, according to early modern legal and social thought, formed part of) has long formed the basis of a distinction between domestics and other workers. As William Blackstone made clear in his mid-eighteenth century *Commentaries on the Laws of England*, domestic servants were so called because they resided "*intra moenia*, as part of the family,"[14] unlike labourers, "who are only hired by the day or the week, and who do not live *intra moenia*."[15] Labourers may have been considered part of the broader household, at least for the purposes of legal classification, but the relation between a master and his domestic servant involved a different degree of intimacy (and subordination). As late as 1785, the anonymous author of *Laws Concerning Master and Servants* said that "Master and Servant are Relatives," though the relation arose through "Agreement and retainer."[16] (At this point in time, the term "servant" still referred to domestic servants or servants in husbandry; the term was becoming, but had not yet fully morphed into, a general term for workers.[17]) This unique relation gave rise to a set of quite specific rights and obligations between masters and servants. Echoing the power of a father over his child, a master was permitted to "correct his apprentice or servant for negligence or other misbehaviour" – correction in this context meaning physical chastisement. However, the relation also gave rise to an obligation on the part of a master to "maintain" his servant, which generally meant the provision of basic lodgings, food, and possibly medical care.[18] Domestics were also distinguished from other

---

13 See Albin, *supra* note 5; Albin and Prassl, *supra* note 5.

14 Blackstone, *supra* note 9, book I at 414. Strictly, Blackstone is specifying here that labourers do not live *intra moenia*, and hence are not part of the family. By inference, his use of *intra moenia* to describe the situation of domestics therefore suggests that they were considered part of the family.

15 *Ibid.*

16 Carolyn Steedman, *Labours Lost: Domestic Service and the Making of Modern England* (New York: Cambridge University Press, 2009) at 18 [Steedman, *Labours Lost*].

17 See *supra* note 9.

18 The obligation to provide medical assistance was contingent on the master having accepted (or being found to have accepted) this degree of responsibility: Macdonnell, *supra* note 11 at 148.

workers in terms of legal recourse against their masters. Blackstone noted that menial servants were entitled to wages "according to their agreement," but they were not permitted to take their masters before the magistrates for non-payment of those wages; "it being impossible," he said, "for any magistrate to be a judge of the employment of menial servants, or of course to assess their wages." Labourers and servants in husbandry, on the other hand, were (at least in theory) able to bring wage claims before magistrates.

Domestic servants were also treated differently from other workers within eighteenth century economic thought and labour theory. In *The Wealth of Nations*, Adam Smith claimed that labour is of two sorts: "labour which adds to the value of the subject upon which it is bestowed"; and labour "which has no such effect": "The former, as it produces a value, may be called productive; the latter unproductive labour. Thus the labour of a manufacturer adds generally to the value of the materials which he works upon, that of his own maintenance, and of his master's profit. The labour of a menial servant, on the contrary, adds to the value of nothing."[19] Smith thus categorized labour according to whether it was productive or unproductive – a division that shaped (and continues to shape) Anglophone approaches to labour in the nineteenth and twentieth centuries, particularly the treatment of work performed in the home. For Smith, domestic services were unproductive "because they did not contribute to the accumulation of physical wealth. Domestic servants … merely enhanced their employers' standard of living."[20]

In legal terms, this differentiation of domestic and non-domestic forms of work solidified in the late eighteenth and nineteenth centuries in new and surprising ways. Essentially, at the same time as the domestic service model was extended to encompass the majority of work relations (a process described in the previous chapter), domestic service was, through a similar interaction between statute and common law,

---

19 Adam Smith, *An Inquiry into the Nature and Causes of the Wealth of Nations*, vol 1 (London, 1776) at 88.

20 Folbre, *supra* note 3 at 469. A century later, Karl Marx (of all people) echoed this aspect of Smith's reasoning: "[T]ypes of work that are consumed as services and not as products separable from the worker and not capable of existing as commodities independently from him … are of microscopic importance when compared with the mass of capitalist production. They may be entirely neglected, therefore." Karl Marx, *Capital*, vol I at 1044 quoted in Steedman, *Labours Lost*, *supra* note 16 at 42–3. By the late nineteenth century, though, economists generally treated paid forms of service as productive; a concession that did not, however, extend to the unpaid domestic work of wives, as section B of this chapter demonstrates.

pointedly excluded from this general body of law owing to its continuing affiliation with the home/family. Thus, the series of statutes passed in the eighteenth century that criminalized breach of contract on the part of a broad range of workers did not apply to domestic servants.[21]

However, in 1777, Lord Mansfield significantly extended the powers enjoyed by masters over their domestics (and thus provides us with an example of the oscillations between the legislative and judicial branches that has characterized the historical evolution of the law of work in England[22]). The case, *R v Inhabitants of Brampton*,[23] concerned the position of an unmarried pregnant servant. Lord Mansfield held that her master was legally permitted to dismiss her without even applying to a magistrate. It would have been *"contra bonos mores,"* he said, to keep the servant in the house, "and in a family where there are young persons both scandalous and dangerous." According to Thomas Walter Williams in his 1812 text, *The Whole Law Relative to the Duty and Office of a Justice of the Peace*, the case showed how "a master may of his own authority, and without the intervention of a magistrate, dismiss [a] servant for moral turpitude; even though it be not such for which the servant may be prosecuted at common law."[24] The reason summary dismissal was permitted was the servant's position within the household and her potential proximity to a master's wife and daughters; the familial nature of domestic service and the risk of moral contagion essentially justified the conferral of hitherto unknown (or at least non-legally recognized) powers on masters with respect to their domestic servants.[25]

Building on the view expressed by Lord Mansfield, in 1795 the author of a text entitled *The Laws Respecting Masters and Servants*,[26] James Barry Bird, suggested that the *Statute of Artificers 1562*[27] might provide a

---

21 Deakin and Wilkinson, *supra* note 10 at 79. See further chapter 3.

22 See generally Deakin and Wilkinson, *supra* note 10, ch 2.

23 *R v Inhabitants of Brampton* (1777) Cald 11.

24 Thomas Walter Williams, *The Whole Law Relative to the Duty and Office of a Justice of the Peace* (1812) vol 3 at 902–3 quoted in Steedman, *Labours Lost, supra* note 16 at 119, note 51.

25 Thirty years later, Lord Ellenborough adjudged a similar extension of masters' powers over servants in husbandry – and by extension non-household workers, in the wake of other decisions that had equated the obligations of servants, labourers, and pieceworkers. See *The King v Inhabitants of Barton-upon-Irwell* (1814) 2 M&S 329, discussed in chapter 3.

26 James Barry Bird, *The Laws Respecting Masters and Servants, Articled Clerks, Apprentices, Manufacturers, Labourers, and Journeymen* (London, 1795) (title abridged) [Bird 1795].

27 5 Eliz, c 4.

more general authority over domestic servants.[28] He wrote that while the *Statute* "related more particularly to artificers and servants of husbandry, ... it is imagined that that it may be well construed to give justices a general jurisdiction over servants of every description, and such jurisdiction is in fact exercised by them."[29] Bird's view was rejected the following year.[30] In *The King v Inhabitants of Hulcott*,[31] Lord Kenyon held that the *Statute of Artificers* did not apply to domestic servants (or other occupations not expressly mentioned). The effect of this decision was to solidify the emerging distinction between domestic servants and servants in husbandry (to which class the *Statute* expressly applied), and to situate the law of master and *domestic* servant outside of the Law of Master and Servant (itself derived from the older, domestically oriented understanding of service) that was, by this time, coming to govern most forms of wage labour.[32]

This excision of domestic service from the general law of master and servant led the anonymous author of a work entitled *Reflections on the relative situations of master and servant, historically and politically considered*, published in 1800, to declare: "It is a wonderful thing, but I believe my observation is just, that our stupendous pile of statutes does not contain one article of regulation for servants, as servants, except some antiquated statutes before the reformation, which are inapplicable to the present state of society. Many have been deceived, in imagining from the title in various law books, that the wise provisions made for *servants* in reign of Queen Elizabeth, would apply to our present domestic

---

28 According to Douglas Hay, "England, 1562–1875: The Law and Its Uses" in Douglas Hay and Paul Craven, eds., *Masters, Servants, and Magistrates: Britain & the Empire, 1562–1955* (Chapel Hill: University of North Carolina Press, 2004) 59 at 88, "[d]omestic servants in London, early in the century, had been presumed to be subject to penal sanctions, either under the Statute of Artificers or the vagrancy statute ... or perhaps on a rather general sense of what was required." Blackstone had also suggested that domestic servants could not be dismissed without a quarter's warning except upon a master's showing reasonable cause to a magistrate in the same manner as other servants under the Statute of Artificers: *ibid* referring to William Blackstone, *Commentaries on the Laws of England*, 4 vols, 12th ed. (London, 1793) book 4 at 425–6.

29 Bird 1795, *supra* note 26 at 2, note (b).

30 However, the passage remains in the third edition, published in 1799: James Barry Bird, *The Laws Respecting Masters and Servants, Articled Clerks, Apprentices, Manufacturers, Labourers, and Journeymen*, 3rd ed. (London, 1799) at 3 note (a) (title abridged) [Bird 1799].

31 (1796) 6 Term 583, 101 ER 716 [*Hulcott*].

32 As Conaghan has noted, "law is directly implicated in the construction of differences between workers": Conaghan, "Discipline of Labour Law," *supra* note 6 at 39.

attendants. But, in truth, they regard servants in husbandry only."[33] The author continued by calling for the extension of criminal penalties to domestic servants engaging in "embezzlement, quarrelling, swearing, domestic irregularities, insolence, drunkenness, or disobedience." By this measure, "heads of families would rest in secure peace and comfort; good servants would live happier, by having crimes repressed in bad ones; and the general mass of society would be benefited, because there is most happiness, where there is least vice, irregularity, and disorder."

While a bill seeking to regulate domestic service was in fact before Parliament at the time of the anonymous author's philippic, it was not passed. According to Douglas Hay, "[t]he fear was that such legislation would give domestic servants too much power, because they would have the right, like workers in other trades, to go to the justices for wage orders and to complain of mistreatment."[34] There was also a concern, perhaps even more pressing, that meddlesome "gentlemen in the country, acting in the commission of the peace, and many of them, perhaps, persons of inferior consequence," might make "themselves troublesome in the family concerns of their neighbours."[35] Masters wanted the ability to punish recalcitrant domestics, but their existence within the increasingly private realm of the home also meant there was a limit as what those same masters would permit in terms of oversight. In other words, the familial nature of the service in domestic service distinguished it from other forms of work.[36]

This distinction between forms of service continued with the passage of the *Master and Servant Act 1823*.[37] On the one hand, the Act confirmed

---

33 Anonymous, *Reflections on the relative situations of master and servant, historically and politically considered; the irregularities of servants; the employment of foreigners; and the general inconveniences resulting from the want of proper regulations* (London, 1800) 24–5. In tones recalling the outrage of Daniel Defoe in *The Great Law of Subordination Consider'd; or, the Insolence and Unsufferable Behaviour of Servants in England duly enquir'd into* (London, 1724) (title abridged), the author decries "these times of heedlessness and indifference," in which "it is the common cry of every one, that 'Servants are very bad;' just as they would say, 'The weather is very cold:' every one admits and shares the evil, but no one endeavours to remove it." Those with "levelling principles … foolishly imagin[e], that any irregularity, or any encroachment of the lower upon the higher orders, is favourable to liberty," when, according to the author, "[s]ervants are like schoolboys" and only "coercion and fear" will rouse the indolent and vicious among them.

34 Hay, *supra* note 28 at 90.

35 Anonymous, *supra* note 33 at 25.

36 See Albin, *supra* note 5 at 238.

37 *An Act to enlarge the Powers of Justices in determining Complaints between Masters and Servants, and between Masters, Apprentices, Artificers and others, 1823*, 4 Geo IV, c 34 [*Master and Servant Act 1823*].

the emergence of Master and Servant as a general category applicable to a broad array of work relations. Yet at the same time the Act pointedly excluded domestic servants from its ambit by permitting Justices of the Peace to make orders concerning the payment of wages due to "any Servants in Husbandry, Artificers, Labourers or other Person named in the said Acts," which were 20 Geo II, c 19 and 31 Geo II, c 11, neither of which applied to domestic servants.[38] The Act also provided that "any Servant in Husbandry or any Artificer, Calico Printer, Handicraftsman, Miner, Collier, Keelman, Pitman, Glassman, Potter, Labourer or other Person" who entered into a contract to serve another person was liable to imprisonment for up to three months if he or she "shall not enter into or commence his or her Service according to this or her Contract ... or having entered into such Service shall absent himself or herself from his or her Service before the Term of his or her Contract."[39] In these respects, the Act effectively mirrored Lord Kenyon's decision in *Hulcott*: domestic servants were unable to seek wage orders from magistrates but they were also protected from imprisonment for breach of contract.[40]

This approach continued into the second half of the nineteenth century. In 1875, the English Parliament introduced the *Employers and Workmen Act*.[41] The linguistic shift away from "masters and servants" in the *Master and Servant Act* was not simply cosmetic; the *Employers and Workmen Act* effectively did away with imprisonment for breaches of employment contract. Domestic servants, however, were once again excluded: "[t]he expression 'workman' does not include a domestic or menial servant."[42] And this time, the exclusion did not carry the benefit (relative to other workers) of immunity from imprisonment because that option was no longer practically available to employers of non-domestic workers; instead, it simply meant exclusion from the scheme of rights and remedies available to workers covered by the *Employers*

---

38 4 Geo IV, c 34, s 5.

39 4 Geo IV, c 34, s 3.

40 Soon after the passage of the *Master and Servant Act 1823*, domestic service was brought into a measure of alignment with other forms of work in one important respect: the abolition of settlement through service via the *Poor Law Amendment Act 1834*, 4 & 5 Will IV, c 76, s 64. This change meant that servants, like other workers, were not entitled to obtain settlement in a parish through their (365 consecutive days of) labour. See further K.D.M. Snell, *Annals of the Labouring Poor: Social Change and Agrarian England, 1660–1900* (Cambridge: Cambridge University Press, 1985) at 72–3, 97 [Snell, *Annals*]; Deakin and Wilkinson, *supra* note 10 at 117–18.

41 38 & 39 Vict I, c 90 [*Employers and Workmen Act*].

42 *Employers and Workmen Act*, s 10.

and Workmen Act.[43] This process of exclusion continued in the *Employers' Liability Act 1880*;[44] as the court in *Pearce v Lansdowne* subsequently declared, the reason for domestic servants' exclusion was that they were "persons whose personal relations in the household or retinue of their masters made it inconvenient that the disputes between them and their masters should be settled before magistrates."[45]

II. THE FEMINIZATION OF DOMESTIC SERVICE

This pattern of legal exclusion disproportionately affected women, whose participation in domestic service dramatically increased over the nineteenth century.[46] As Leonore Davidoff has noted:

> Family protection was so vital because no regulation in domestic service was ever considered, much less implemented. No authority would interfere in a relationship within a private home. Yet because of ... middle class ideology ... *all* girls left without family status were automatically expected to go into domestic service, it was the natural place for an unmarried girl or woman to be. [47]

Determining precise figures for the numbers of domestic servants in eighteenth and nineteenth century England is notoriously difficult, partly because householders themselves determined how to classify their subor-

---

43 Unsurprisingly, then, in his 1885 text, *The Law of Domestic Relations*, William Pinder Eversley included discussion of the law relating to domestic service (and apprenticeship) under the category of Master and Servant, but pointedly excised other, non-household-based forms of work owing to their contractual nature. Domestic service, it seemed, remained sufficiently familial for inclusion in a work on domestic relations – and sufficiently distinct from other forms of work "ordinarily treated of under the head of Master and Servant" that it made sense to simply exclude "[t]hat wide branch of the law which deals with the relations of those who are popularly known as 'Employers and Employed.'" Eversley, *supra* note 11 at 909.
44 43 & 44 Vict c 42.
45 [1893] 69 LT 316 discussed in Albin, *supra* note 5 at 239.
46 Hill, *supra* note 2 at 125.
47 Davidoff, "Domestic Service," *supra* note 10 at 11 (emphasis in original). This is not to suggest uniformity in the experiences of domestic servants or indeed the types of work they necessarily performed. "At one extreme there was found the better known form of service in a great house within a graduated hierarchy of servants, which could lead to a measure of autonomy, a high standard of living and a good deal over authority over others. At the other, and numerically more important extreme, was the less visible, less well known 'slavery' in the lower-middle class suburban or artisan household or lodging house." See Leonore Davidoff, "Mastered for Life: Servant and Wife in Victorian and Edwardian England" (1974) 7:4 *J Soc Hist* 406 at 410 [Davidoff, "Mastered"].

Table 4.1. Charles Booth, Appendix A(1), England and Wales – Occupations of the
           People, 1841–81 at 366 (Domestic Service)

	1841	1851	1861	1871	1881
Males					
under 15	82.1*	6.3	8.0	8.2	6.2
over 15	132.9**	92.0	82.0	94.4	94.7
Total	215.0	98.3	90.0	102.6	100.9
Females					
under 15	774.5***	61.4	86.7	111.1	98.9
over 15		722.9	894.8	1124.5	1170.4
Total	**774.5**	**784.3**	**981.5**	**1235.6**	**1269.3**
All	989.5	882.6	1071.5	1338.2	1370.2

* This figure is for males 20 and under – separate figures for males under 15 are not
given for 1841.
** This figure is for males over 20 (for the reason given above).
*** Only a cumulative figure for females of all ages is given for 1841.

dinates, and the census categories changed between different decades.[48]
Charles Booth's study of nineteenth-century census returns indicates that
between 1851 and 1871, "the proportion of women industrially employed
declined, while those in education and domestic service rose" – the number of male domestic servants decreased over the same period.[49] He provides the figures for indoor domestic service shown in Table 4.1.[50]

These figures clearly indicate a strong upward trend after 1851,
though Booth's methodology is distinctly questionable, particularly his

---

48 Edward Higgs, "Domestic Servants and Households in Victorian England" (1983)
   8:2 *Soc Hist* 201 at 202 (noting that the 1891 figure for domestic service was "inflated
   by a perverse decision to include with domestics all those female relatives returned
   in the census as employed in 'helping at home,' 'performing housework,' and so
   on") [Higgs, "Domestic Servants"]. See also Edward Higgs, "The Tabulation of
   Occupations in the Nineteenth-Century Census, with Special Reference to Domestic
   Servants" (1982) 28 *Loc Pop Stud* 58 [Higgs, "Tabulation"]; Guy Routh, *Occupations
   of the People of Great Britain, 1801–1981; with a Compendium of a Paper "Occupations of
   the People of the United Kingdom, 1801–81 by Charles Booth"* (Basingstoke: Macmillan,
   1987); Clara E. Collet, "The Collection and Utilisation of Official Statistics bearing on
   the Extent and Effects of the Industrial Employment of Women" (1898) 61:2 *J Royal
   Stat Soc* 219 at 219–20.

49 Charles Booth, "Occupations of the People of the United Kingdom" in Routh, *supra*
   note 48 at 8–9.

50 A different set of figures, demonstrating a broadly similar trend although indicating
   a decline from 1871 to 1881, is given by Collet, *supra* note 48 at 244–45.

treatment of women's work.[51] More recently, Ebery and Preston have used Booth's figures but attempted to more accurately control for the problems in the methods of the census and Booth himself. Their analysis suggests that "the apogee of the servant population in the census was in 1871."[52] What is quite clear is that domestic service became thoroughly feminized over the course of the nineteenth century.[53]

A confluence of factors seems to have generated this gender-based shift. In her late nineteenth-century analysis of census records, Clara Collet suggested that, "diminishing facilities for earning money at home" created "between 1851 and 1871 ... an unusual supply of domestic servants."[54] This reading makes a lot of sense.[55] We have already

---

51 See further Part B(ii), *infra*.

52 M. Ebery and B. Preston, *Domestic Service in Late Victorian and Edwardian England, 1871–1914* (Reading: University of Reading, 1976) in Higgs, "Domestic Servants," *supra* note 48 at 202. This view contradicts "the prevailing belief that the First World War represented a watershed in servant employment": Higgs, "Domestic Servants," *supra* note 48 at 202. Note that in a separate paper Higgs presented his own reworking of Booth's figures, in which he reduced the domestic service class by 48 per cent. However, this was based on trends in only two districts, and Higgs expressly stated that the "figures are really an invitation to others to make more refined calculations and probably represent hypothetical upper bounds": Edward Higgs, "Women, Occupations and Work in the Nineteenth Century Censuses" (1987) 23 *Hist Workshop J* 59 at 75–6. For a contrary view of the trajectory of workers employed in domestic service in the nineteenth century see Leonard Schwarz, "English Servants and Their Employers during the Eighteenth and Nineteenth Centuries" (1999) 52:2 *Econ Hist Rev* 236.

53 Hill, *supra* note 2 at 128. See also Katrina Honeyman, *Women, Gender and Industrialisation in England, 1700–1870* (Basingstoke: Macmillan, 2000) at 76: "Although the extent of domestic service has almost certainly been exaggerated, there is little doubt that as it became feminised through the eighteenth and nineteenth centuries, the number of servants, or those classified as such, grew." [Honeyman, *Women, Gender*] See also Eric J. Hobsbawm, *Industry and Empire: From 1750 to the Present Day*, revised ed. (London: Penguin Books, 1999) at 96, noting that in the period 1840–1895, "[t]hough the proportion of women working in manufacturing rose quite markedly, domestic service remained by far the largest single 'industry' employing them."

54 Collet, *supra* note 48 at 224. Jane Humphries has suggested a supply-side argument for the rise in female domestics: control of female sexuality and the perceived possibilities for indiscretion afforded by employment outside of the home. Jane Humphries, "'... The Most Free from Objection' ... The Sexual Division of Labor and Women's Work in Nineteenth-Century England" (1987) 47:4 *J Econ Hist* 929 at 937: "As work was increasingly separated from traditional safeguards against improvident marriage or bastardy, working people, as well as their social superiors, became increasingly anxious."

55 See Davidoff, "Domestic Service," *supra* note 10 at 10: "By and large girls were recruited to service because there was no alternative occupation in the area;

seen that parliamentary enclosures in the eighteenth and nineteenth centuries had a particular impact on women's abilities to engage in household-based subsistence production.[56] In addition, the shift towards factory-based production in the nineteenth century decimated home-based forms of textile production.[57] In the eighteenth century, the putting-out system gave rise to a vibrant (if precarious) system of family-based spinning and weaving,[58] until the invention of the water frame in 1773, the cotton industry – which formed part of England's industrial backbone – "was carried on entirely on domestic lines."[59] The "cotton worker's cottage was indeed a miniature factory, in which the father superintended the weaving, and the mother was responsible for all the preparatory processes and the training and setting to work of the children."[60] Over time, however, the water frame, the spinning jenny and the mule combined to make production in mills significantly more efficient than home-based production.[61] Thus, by 1830, "cleaning, carding, roving and spinning had been taken from the cottage into the factory, and spinning, for so many centuries a woman's industry, was now performed by a class of skilled work*men* on complicated machinery."[62] Ivy Pinchbeck's analysis of male workers' responses to this shift provides an indication of the extent to which opportunities for women had been curtailed:

> Many of the journeymen, particularly among the weavers, objected strongly to the growth of a system which deprived them of the assistance of their wives and children, and it was afterwards one of the bitterest

---

secondarily, working-class parents might also feel that service provided some security (and control) for teen-age girls."

56 See chapter 3, part II(A).

57 Sven Beckert, *Empire of Cotton: A Global History* (New York: Vintage Books, 2015) at 68.

58 As Daniel Defoe described it, "[a]mong the manufacturers' houses are likewise scattered an infinite number of cottages or small dwellings in which dwell the workmen which are employed, the women and children of whom are always busy carding, spinning etc so that no hands are ... unemployed": John Rule, *The Experience of Labour in Eighteenth-Century Industry* (London: Croom Helm, 1981) at 37.

59 Ivy Pinchbeck, *Women Workers in the Industrial Revolution, 1750–1850*, 3rd ed. (London: Virago, 1981) at 112–13.

60 *Ibid* at 113. John Rule has noted that "[t]he clothiers of the West Riding were very much a family economy both in their manufacturing and in their farming activities, with the wife adding domestic chores to assisting at the loom and feeding the livestock": Rule, *supra* note 58 at 16.

61 On the growth of industrialized cotton manufacturing in England, and especially in Lancashire, see Beckert, *supra* note 57 at 73.

62 Pinchbeck, *supra* note 59 at 117 (emphasis added).

complaints against the factory system that by it *women* and children *were deprived of employment which they could carry on in the home*. This objection was based upon the connection between the actual manual assistance given by women and children, which had been so necessary in some forms of domestic labour, and its financial value in contributing to the family wage.

For many married women, the consequence of this removal of opportunities to engage in home-based production was to tie them even more closely to the (non-productive) realm of the family and the work involved in administering the home (this is discussed in greater detail in section B below). For unmarried women whose families were unable to support them, domestic service became one of the only viable options for economic survival.[63]

It seems that tax law also played a role in the feminization of domestic service. In 1777 the English Parliament introduced a tax that applied specifically to male domestic servants. It was essentially a tax on luxury, designed to raise revenue for the war being conducted with the American Colonies.[64] In his 1884 *History of Taxation and Taxes in England*, Stephen Dowell said of the tax:

> The charge was a guinea for each servant kept; and care was taken to limit the tax to such servants as are acknowledged to bear a direct relation to the luxuries of life, that is, domestic servants, those employed in the stable, gardeners (if not mere day labourers), park-keepers, gamekeepers, and huntsmen and whippers-in – as contradistinguished from servants employed for the purposes of husbandry, manufacture, and any trade or calling by which the master gained a livelihood or profit.[65]

---

63 Changes in social attitudes towards service and work within the home also appear to have contributed to the feminization of domestic service. In particular, there appears to have been "a close relationship between the changing nature of 'housework' and the increased demand for female domestics"; that is, the work created by middle class wives' ideas of domestic comfort was more suited to female domestics. Putting it more bluntly, the drafters of the 1871 Census Report claimed that "[w]ives and daughters at home do now less domestic work than their predecessors, hence the excessive demand for female servants and the consequent rise of wages": Hill, *supra* note 2 at 127.

64 See Stephen Dowell, *A History of Taxation and Taxes in England From the Earliest Times to the Year 1885*, 2nd ed. (London: Longmans, 1888) vol 3 at 215–16.

65 *Ibid* at 216.

The connection to Adam Smith's conception of service as unproductive labour is clear.[66] Indeed, Dowell claimed that Lord North copied the tax "from the Dutch tax, to which Adam Smith had directed attention."[67] The tax was applied to female domestics in 1786 but this was quickly abandoned in 1792,[68] presumably because hiring women to perform domestic tasks was not considered "luxurious" but necessary. The tax on male servants thus effectively constituted domestic labour as presumptively female work: if such unproductive tasks had to be performed, the law seemed to say, they should be completed by women, and if not, then employers should pay for the privilege of wasting male labour power on unproductive domestic service tasks.

III. EXCLUSION AND FEMINIZATION IN THE TWENTIETH CENTURY

In the early years of the twentieth century, limited steps were taken to bring domestic service within the broader framework of employment, but these moves were at best partial. The *Workmen's Compensation Act 1906*,[69] which made employers liable to compensate workers for injuries received during the course of their employment (and workers' dependents in the event of death), did extend to domestic servants.[70] So did the much more generally important *National Insurance Act 1911*,[71] though it only applied to domestic servants who received wages.[72] In 1920, however, domestic servants were entirely removed from the scheme under the terms of the *Unemployment Insurance Act*;[73] that exclusion continued

---

66 Carolyn Steedman, *Master and Servant: Love and Labour in the English Industrial Age* (Cambridge: Cambridge University Press, 2007) at 75: "The liveried and bewigged manservant was an index of conspicuous consumption, just as was the hair powder increasingly purchased for valets rather than for their masters." [Steedman, *Master and Servant*]

67 Dowell, *supra* note 64 at 216.

68 Steedman, *Labours Lost, supra* note 16 at 57.

69 6 Edward VII, c 58.

70 See J.D. Casswell, *The Law of Domestic Servants*, 2nd ed. (London: Jordan & Sons, 1914) at 44–45. See also "The Workmen's Compensation Act, 1906," *The Lancet* (12 January 1907) at 113: "The Act therefore includes ordinary workmen of all kinds regularly employed, clerks, secretaries, medical assistants and dispensers, curates, lay readers, and nurses, and last, but not least, all domestic servants." See further *Aldridge v Merry* [1913] IR 308 (finding that a domestic servant could recover for injuries sustained as a result of plaster falling from the ceiling of the bedroom she occupied).

71 1 & 2 Geo V, c 55.

72 *National Insurance Act 1911*, 1 & 2 Geo V, c 55, Sched I, Part 2 (f).

73 *Unemployment Insurance Act 1920*, 10 & 11 Geo V, c 30, Sched I, Part 2 (b).

in the 1935 version of the Act.[74] Both Acts included an exception in cases where the person was "employed in any trade or business carried on for the purposes of gain"; that is, a person was deemed worthy of unemployment protection if he or she contributed to "gainful" enterprise. The implication, of course, was that domestic service was still unproductive in the eyes of the law.[75]

Unsurprisingly, this legal (and cultural-economic) framing of domestic service did not act as an encouragement to women to embark on a career in the field; and after the First World War, during which women were actively engaged in keeping the English economy running, it became apparent that service had come to be viewed as a distinctly unattractive option.[76] Accordingly, in 1919, the Ministry of Reconstruction issued the *Report of the Women's Advisory Committee on the Domestic Service Problem*,[77] which highlighted, and recommended the amelioration of, the basic division between domestic service and other forms of work. The Report's basic finding was that "domestic service should take its place as a skilled occupation, and that the conditions of employment should be made comparable to those which exist in other industrial and commercial occupations."[78] Training schools should be established, it said, and "training for domestic service should be regarded as on the same plane as that for a trade."[79] While the Report's authors were reluctant

---

74 *Unemployment Insurance Act 1935*, 25 & 26 Geo V, c 8, Sched I, Part 2 (2).

75 The judiciary occasionally pushed back against this treatment of domestic workers. For example, in *George v Davis* [1911] 2 KB 445, the Court treated the relation between the servant and her master as akin to other employment agreements. The servant in this case left her service without providing the requisite notice. The Court held that she had *not* forfeited her right to wages: "[T]he wages were payable monthly. At the expiration of the first one month's wages had accrued to her, and she had then a vested right to be paid those wages, and could have sued for them. If she subsequently committed a breach of contract by leaving without giving proper notice she would not forfeit the wages which had already accrued due to her, though her master might have a cross-claim against her for the damages for breach of contract." See Deakin and Wilkinson, *supra* note 10 at 81.

76 See Davidoff, "Mastered," *supra* note 47 at 417, noting that the "400,000 who left service during World War I were only the most striking case of what was a continuing pattern." See also Selina Todd, "Domestic Service and Class Relations in Britain 1900–1950" (2009) 203 *Past & Present* 181 at 184.

77 Ministry of Reconstruction, Women's Advisory Committee, *Report of the Women's Advisory Committee on the Domestic Service Problem together with Reports by Sub-Committees on Training, Machinery of Distribution, Organisation and Conditions* (London: HM Stationary Office, 1919).

78 *Ibid* at 7.

79 *Ibid* at 12.

to suggest legal limits for working hours of live-in domestic servants, they noted "that without substantial reduction of the length of the working day it will be impossible to make the occupation attractive."[80] For day workers living outside of the residence, a limit of not more than 48 hours per week was suggested.[81] It was also recommended that governing bodies should be established to monitor and regulate working conditions: "We think it desirable that domestic workers should unite, and we recommend that employers and all who co-operate in schemes of organisation, training, etc., should recognise Trade Unions."[82] In the interests of post-war nation building, then, the Report recommended that the government treat domestic service as a form of employment akin to other forms of work, irrespective of the fact that it involved labour performed in the home. In what can now be recognized as a portent of attitudes among legislators throughout the twentieth century, and up to the present moment, the governments of Lloyd George and successive Prime Ministers ignored the Report.[83]

Thus, the 1945 *Report on Post-War Organisation of Private Domestic Employment*[84] observed that, "the conditions under which domestic service was carried on almost to the threshold of the first World War were not only unregulated but *purely personal* … [involving] poor pay and few personal nights."[85] In the interwar period, domestic work "remained without organisation or any general improvement beyond the higher wages which the shrinkage of the supply enabled the worker to impose on the employer."[86] The 1945 Report also confirmed that domestic service remained an almost exclusively female occupation; it was "the oldest, the largest and the most unorganised form of *women's* employment,"[87] and "an entirely honourable and self-respecting occupation *for any woman*," providing "excellent training for the girl who

---

80 *Ibid* at 27.

81 *Ibid.*

82 *Ibid* at 26.

83 The reason is suggested in a further report issued in 1923, in which it was stated that wages and working conditions of domestic servants "are and must remain questions … of the personal relationship between employer and staff": Ministry of Labour, *Report of the Committee Appointed to Enquire into the Present Conditions as to the Supply of Female Domestic Servants* (London: HM Stationary Office, 1923) at 13.

84 Ministry of Labour and National Service, *Report on Post-War Organisation of Private Domestic Employment* (London: HM Stationary Office, 1945) [1945 Report].

85 *Ibid* at 5 (emphasis added).

86 *Ibid* at 6.

87 *Ibid* at 3 (emphasis added).

marries and has a home of her own."[88] In general terms the Report echoed the recommendations made in 1919 concerning the need for training, certification and the treatment of domestic work alongside other forms of employment. Once again, though, these recommendations failed to generate reform. While the Labour Government adopted the proposal to establish a National Institute of Homeworkers, funding issues meant that it never actually emerged.[89]

In other ways, the 1945 Report actually endorsed the idea that domestic work was situated at the lower end of a perceived employment hierarchy. "An educated woman," it said, "fitted by training and experience to make a *real contribution* to the national life must, if married, provide primarily for the needs of her household, her husband and her children. If no help is forthcoming in carrying out these tasks, inevitably she must discharge them herself." "Women as a body" were hence called upon to "come together and make an organised effort to help each other in domestic matters," lest "women's work outside the home ... suffer."[90] What this really meant was that working-class women should accept their lot in life and assist their middle class "sisters" to manage their homes.[91] This class-based dimension of the 1945 Report highlights both an historical truth about the composition of domestic workers as a group, and points forward in time to the reality that ongoing differential treatment of domestic work is rooted in both gender and class (and increasingly race).

B. Unpaid Domestic Labour

The construction of domestic labour as female, unproductive, and distinct from labour conducted outside of the home applied with particular force to unpaid domestic work.[92] In the eighteenth and nineteenth centuries, women, especially married women, were increasingly expected to refrain from engaging with the public, masculine realm of the market in favour of a domestically oriented existence.[93] For upper- and middle

---

88 *Ibid* at 3–4.
89 Judy Giles, "Help for Housewives: Domestic Service and the Reconstruction of Domesticity in Britain, 1940–50" (2001) 10:2 *Women Hist Rev* 299 at 312.
90 1945 Report, *supra* note 84 at 8.
91 See Fredman and Fudge, *supra* note 8 at 234.
92 For a Marxist perspective on this gender-based split see Eli Zaretsky, *Capitalism, the Family, and Personal Life*, revised ed. (New York: Harper & Row, 1986) at 14.
93 Wally Seccombe has suggested that "the rate of married women's extra-domestic employment throughout the nineteenth century in Britain (and North America) probably never rose above 10 per cent, except in a few textile districts": Wally

class women, this generally meant delegating household tasks to paid servants (and, depending on wealth and personal inclination, performing certain tasks themselves); working-class women tended to shoulder the burden of running the family home without paid help (and possibly supplemented family income through charring or factory labour). Intersecting cultural, economic and legal forces generated this structure and conception of unpaid domestic work.[94] Preceding sections have pointed to the importance of ideological distinctions (family/market, public/private, male/female) in the association of domesticity (and domestic labour) and femininity;[95] as well as the role played by agricultural and industrial reform in reducing married women's abilities to contribute to household production in ways that were compatible with their presumed responsibilities for care of family members.[96] The focus here is on some of the ways that nineteenth-century legislation and employer practices advanced the association between housework and housewifery by excluding wives from participation in forms of wage labour outside of the home;[97] the corresponding development of family wage

---

Seccombe, "Patriarchy Stabilized: The Construction of the Male Breadwinner Wage Norm in Nineteenth-Century England" (1986) 11:1 *Soc Hist* 53 at 69 [Seccombe, "Patriarchy"].

94 See further Louise A. Tilly and Joan W. Scott, *Women, Work & Family* (New York: Routledge, 1989); Leonore Davidoff and Catherine Hall, *Family Fortunes: Men and Women of the English Middle Class 1780–1850*, revised ed. (London: Routledge, 2002); Heid Hartmann, "Capitalism, Patriarchy, and Job Segregation by Sex" (1976) 1:3 *Signs* at 137; Pateman, *supra* note 7.

95 See chapter 1, part II(A).

96 See chapter 3, part II(A) on parliamentary enclosures, and part II(A) of this chapter on the erosion of family-based textile production in the nineteenth century.
On women's responsibilities for childcare, and the difficulties associated with combining paid work and care work, see Tilly and Scott, *supra* note 94 at 124; Jane Humphries, "The Sexual Division of Labor and Social Control: An Interpretation" (1991) 23:3–4 *Rev Rad Pol Econ* 269 at 281.

97 While Sonya Rose has pointed out that few working class men were able to support their families without some form of assistance from wives and children (Sonya O. Rose, *Limited Livelihoods: Gender and Class in Nineteenth-Century England* (New York: Routledge, 1992), chapter 4), Sara Horrell and Jane Humphries, suggest that "[i]nsofar as there was a heyday for the democratic sourcing of family incomes it appears to have been in the years after the Napoleonic wars and before 1835." Moreover, while "few families were entirely dependent on husbands and fathers, for many families male earnings were of crucial importance." Their analysis reveals a downward trend in women's employment from the mid-nineteenth century, "reflect[ing] the decline of outwork as well as emerging male-breadwinner ideologies and protective labour legislation": Sara Horrell and Jane Humphries, "Women's Labour Force Participation and the Transition to the Male-Breadwinner Family, 1790–1865" (1995) 48:1 *J Econ Hist* 89 at 105, 112.

ideology and the background role played by the repeal of combination laws in trade union agitation for the payment of wages that would permit women to remain (and hence perform unpaid work) within the domestic realm; and consolidation of the idea that unpaid domestic work was unproductive through late nineteenth century changes to the English census, and ongoing legal devaluation of women's contributions in the home.

I. CHANNELLING HOUSEWIVES

English law never treated domestic work performed by wives as "work" within the master-servant framework; labour of this sort was always instead the corollary of the status of wife[98] – a situation constituted in no small part by the common law of coverture which denied the separate legal personality of wives and thus (at least in legal terms) made wages earned by wives the property of their husbands,[99] and entry by wives into certain forms of paid work, notably domestic service, contingent upon the permission of husbands.[100] In the eighteenth and nineteenth centuries, as household-based forms of production fell into desuetude, economic necessity (and the ongoing influence of older and more positive attitudes towards women's work) resulted in a partial movement of women's work outside of the domestic space. However, this trend, particularly the participation of wives in paid employment outside of the home, was at odds with nineteenth-century family/market ideology that coded these domains in gender terms. Out of this tension came a series of legislative interventions that curtailed and complicated women's (especially wives') participation in certain forms of

---

98 See Pateman, *supra* note 7 at 116: "To become a wife entails becoming a housewife; that is, a wife is someone who works for her husband in the marital home." See also at 117, discussing the treatment of wives and servants in James Schouler, *A Treatise on the Law of the Domestic Relations Embracing Husband and Wife, Parent and Child, Guardian and Ward, Infancy, and Master and Servant* (Boston: Little, Brown & Co, 1870), and noting that the text "seems to leave no doubt that a wife was the 'servant' of her husband. Yet she is not classified as such." See also Fredman and Fudge, *supra* note 8 at 233: "housework and child-care were governed by the contract of marriage."

99 Late nineteenth-century statutory amendment of coverture via the *Married Women's Property Acts* granted some wives a limited measure of economic autonomy, albeit in terms that reflected and consolidated patriarchal control. See further chapter 5, part IV(B).

100 This being said, wives in the pre-industrial era were not generally quite as economically dependent on their husbands as wives in the nineteenth-century owing to the greater opportunities for subsistence-based production attached to the household: Pateman, *supra* note 7 at 130.

paid work outside of the home; and a corresponding call from unions and working-class organizations for the payment of (family) wages to men that would permit their wives to devote themselves to unpaid domestic work. Collectively, these moves emphasized the (legal and ideological) nexus between women, family, and the domestic sphere; and thus reproduced in new ways the older notion of wives as domestic workers,[101] or "the chief menial[s] of the household."[102] (This process in turn permitted men to engage in paid forms of work outside of the home, and to "commit their time exclusively, predictably and over the long term, to the benefit of their employers."[103])

Direct legal exclusion of women from certain forms of paid work began in the 1840s, following an inquiry into the employment of children in coal and iron stone mines. In 1842, the Children's Employment Commission reported not only on children's work, but also on the presence of women working underground.[104] According to Humphries, "[d]espite alleged surprise at the extent of this phenomenon, women's and girls' employment underground was not unusual," particularly in South Wales and eastern Scotland.[105] This fact alarmed the authors of the report not so much out of concern for the physical safety of the women involved, but because of the moral issue of close physical proximity between men and women in the dark environment of mines.[106] The government responded to the report by passing the first sex-specific protective legislation:[107] the *Mines and Collieries Act 1842*.[108]

---

101 This particular extension of patriarchal authority was but one of the ways that law in the eighteenth and nineteenth centuries helped to consolidate the position of masters and husbands within and outside of the home. See the discussion of subordination in the wage labour relationship (chapter 3); the ways that statutory amendment of marriage law and coverture relied upon the maintenance of male authority (chapter 5); and the judicial reinforcement of women's presumed reliance on men in cases concerning breach of promise to marry (chapter 6).

102 Thorstein Veblen, *The Theory of the Leisure Class: An Economic Study of Institutions* (New York: Modern Library, 1934) at 182, quoted in Pateman, *supra* note 7 at 125.

103 Joanne Conaghan, "Time to Dream? Flexibility, Families, and the Regulation of Working Time" in Judy Fudge and Rosemary Owens, eds., *Precarious Work, Women, and the New Economy* (Oxford: Hart Publishing, 2006) 101 at 108–9 [Conaghan, "Time to Dream?"].

104 Children's Employment Commission, *First Report of the Commissioners. Mines* (London: HM Stationary Office, 1842).

105 Jane Humphries, "Protective Legislation, the Capitalist State, and Working Class Men: The Case of the 1842 Mines Regulation Act" (1981) 7 *Feminist Rev* 1 at 5–7 [Humphries, "Protective Legislation"].

106 *Ibid* at 25.

107 *Ibid* at 28.

108 5 & 6 Vict c 99.

The Act commenced by stating, "it is unfit that Women and Girls should be employed in any Mine or Colliery," and proceeded to declare that "after the passing of this Act it shall not be lawful for any Owner of any Mine or Colliery whatsoever to employ any Female Person within any Mine or Colliery."[109] It is unclear what effect this particular Act had on the work practices of women in mining districts;[110] what is clear, though, is that legislators were imposing a particular conception of work and family life (largely premised on female virtue) on a specific community of workers. (In contrast to subsequent limitations on women's abilities to participate in certain forms of work, it seems that male miners were not in favour of the amendments due to the long-standing family-based organization of mining work.[111]) The Act may not have directly resulted in an upswing in the number of women who confined themselves to domestic work (since women already working in the mines were exempt[112] and others may have looked for alternate forms of work), but it was the opening move in a legal process of constructing particular forms of paid work as masculine, with the corollary implication that men were the economic providers for their families[113] and "what being a woman (wife) means is to provide certain services for and at the command of a man (husband)."[114]

The next piece of legislation, the *Factories Act 1844*,[115] did not categorically exclude women; rather, it cast them as minors, decreeing that women were "to be employed as young Persons" (i.e., persons between 14 and 18 years). Accordingly, "no Female above the age of Eighteen Years shall be employed in any Factory save for the same Time and in the same Manner as young Persons may be employed in Factories."[116] Accordingly, women were covered by provisions concerning the number of hours that could be worked in a single period, meal

---

109 5 & 6 Vict c 99, s 1.

110 While "[m]arried women's participation does appear to have declined during industrialization for families whose head worked in mining" (see Horrell and Humphries, *supra* note 97 at 100), it is not clear that this trend was directly related to the 1842 Act.

111 Humphries, "Protective Legislation," *supra* note 105 at 28.

112 5 & 6 Vict c 99, s 1 excluded from the scope of the prohibition "such [women] as were at or before the passing of this Act employed within such Mine or Colliery."

113 See Horrell and Humphries, *supra* note 97 at 105.

114 Pateman, *supra* note 7 at 128.

115 *An Act to amend the Laws relating to Labour in Factories 1844*, 7 & 8 Vict c 15. Earlier protective legislation concerning factories, *An Act to regulate the Labour of Children and young Persons in the Mills and Factories of the United Kingdom 1833*, 3 & 4 Will c 103, applied only to children.

116 7 & 8 Vict c 15, s 32.

times, holidays, and weekend work. The Act also confined the cleaning of machines whilst in motion to adult men.[117] Another Act passed three years later introduced a ten-hour day for women in textile industries.[118] Further Acts were introduced throughout the century, but there was little significant change to the conditions for female factory workers from the position established in the middle of the century: "in 1901 the working day in textile factories was still ten hours, with the maximum working week marginally reduced to fifty-five and half hours from the earlier fifty-eight…. Attempts to extend protection beyond textiles met with only limited success."[119]

Once again, it is difficult to point to any direct causal relationship between the *Factory Acts* and married women's participation (or lack thereof) in the paid labour market.[120] What these Acts did, though, was give legal form to a distinct ideology that treated women's paid labour outside of the home as productive of domestic and national discord. In this respect, even if the Acts did not directly lead women to reject factory work on the basis of domestic responsibilities (an option that was economically impossible for many working-class families), they reflected and helped to develop a legal and social world view that problematized and rendered less thinkable women's participation in paid work.[121] Within the context of ongoing legal and economic of subordination of wives within the marital relation, the implication of this legislative narrowing of women's economic vistas was clear: a wife's principal occupation was, or ought to be, (unpaid) maintenance of the family domain.[122]

Evidence drawn from parliamentary debates suggests that this was precisely the point; that is, the deeper foundation for the *Factory*

---

117 7 & 8 Vict c 15, s 20. As Sandra Fredman points out, provisions of this sort show "the clear and urgent need for protection this sort for all workers. What is striking, therefore, is not so much the inclusion of women, as the exclusion of men." Sandra Fredman, *Women and the Law* (Oxford: Clarendon Press, 1997) at 72.

118 *An Act to limit the Hours of Labour of young Persons and Females in Factories 1847*, 10 & 11 Vict c 29. In 1867 the law was extended to workshops: *Factory Acts Extension Act 1867*, 30 & 31 Vict c 103.

119 Fredman, *supra* note 117 at 72.

120 *Ibid* at 73.

121 On law as a tool for the creation of particular world views and modes of consciousness see Robert W. Gordon, "Critical Legal Histories" (1984) 36 *Stan L Rev* 57 at 109–10.

122 Thus, early in the twentieth century the British suffragist Cicely Hamilton penned *Marriage as a Trade* (London: Chapman and Hall, 1910), in which she put forward a conception of marriage itself as occupational in the sense that women received economic support from their husbands in exchange for the work they performed in the home. See Pateman, *supra* note 7 at 132.

Acts' (limited) protection of women was a concern with establishing "the proper and symbolic functioning of the separate spheres."[123] Lord Ashley, in his March 1844 speech to the House of Commons on the Ten Hours Bill, presented evidence from 17 of "the most eminent surgeons and physicians" in England concerning the physical inferiority of women and the deleterious effects of prolonged factory labour on women's ability to bear children.[124] He continued by asking where, in the conditions of extant factory life, "are the possibilities of domestic life? how can its *obligations* be fulfilled? Regard the woman as wife or mother, how can she accomplish any portion of her calling?"[125] As if this obligation was not sufficient, Ashley then placed responsibility for national wellbeing on wives' performing their domestic duties, asking, "if she cannot do that which Providence has assigned her, what must be the effect on the whole surface of society?"[126] As evidence of the disorder created by women's employment, Ashley presented the shocking fact that, "out of thirteen married females taken at one mill, only one knew how to make her husband a shirt, and only four knew how to mend one"![127] Women's work in textile mills thus "disturbs the order of nature, and the rights of laboring men, by ejecting the males from the workshops, and filling their places by females, who are thus withdrawn from their domestic duties,"[128] thereby "introducing into families disorder, insubordination, and conflict,"[129] and "annihilat[ing] ... domestic economy."[130]

In contrast to the antipathy of male miners towards the 1842 Act, there is also evidence that male factory workers supported and agitated in

---

123 Philippa Levine, "Consistent Contradictions: Prostitution and Protective Labour Legislation in Nineteenth-Century England" (1994) 19:1 *Soc Hist* 17 at 19. See also Conaghan, "Time to Dream?," *supra* note 103 at 111.

124 UK, HC Deb, 15 March 1844, vol 73, col 1089 (Lord Ashley). As Barrett and McIntosh put it: "What was most forcibly articulated in bourgeois philanthropy was the degeneration of the family caused by the conditions in which mothers undertook wage labour, the way in which working wives neglected the home and so drove their husbands to the alehouse, the moral impropriety of men and women and young people all working together in the same place, the moral danger of the influx of independent single girls to the factory towns." Michèle Barrett and Mary McIntosh, "The 'Family Wage': Some Problems for Socialists and Feminists" (1980) 4:2 *Capital & Class* 51 at 54.

125 UK, HC Deb, 15 March 1844, vol 73, col 1092 (Lord Ashley).

126 UK, HC Deb, 15 March 1844, vol 73, cols 1092–3 (Lord Ashley).

127 UK, HC Deb, 15 March 1844, vol 73, col 1093 (Lord Ashley).

128 UK, HC Deb, 15 March 1844, vol 73, col 1099 (Lord Ashley).

129 UK, HC Deb, 15 March 1844, vol 73, col 1096 (Lord Ashley).

130 UK, HC Deb, 15 March 1844, vol 73, col 1099 (Lord Ashley).

favour of the restriction of women's employment in factories.[131] In 1841, the Short-Time Committee of the West Riding of Yorkshire presented a series of demands to Sir Robert Peel and Lord Ashley, including "[t]he gradual withdrawal of all females from the factories."[132] When Peel objected that such a policy would exclude widows with children, the Committee responded that "[h]ome, its cares, and its employments, is woman's true sphere." For women to work outside the home was "an inversion of the order of nature and of providence – a return to the state of barbarism, in which the woman does the work, while the man looks idly on."[133] The *Ten Hours' Advocate* expressed a similar sentiment in 1846. "[M]arried females," it declared, "would be much better occupied in performing the domestic duties of the household, than following the never-tiring motion of machinery."[134]

This attitude among workers[135] gathered pace in the later decades of the century, and manifested in calls for male wages sufficient to enable

---

131 The reasons for this departure from working-class norms are contested and, as Valverde has noted, "not reducible to single meaning": Mariana Valverde, "'Giving the Female a Domestic Turn': The Social, Legal and Moral Regulation of Women's Work in British Cotton Mills, 1820–1850" (1988) 21:4 *J Soc Hist* 619 at 619. One interpretation, most forcefully propounded by Hartmann, is that "male workers viewed the employment of women as a threat to their jobs": Hartmann, *supra* note 94 at 155. There is an obvious logic to this reading: as collective family labour dissolved under the weight of the market, gender solidarity was replaced with a competitive capitalist ethos. The exclusion of women from mule spinning in the early nineteenth century, while customary rather than legal, lends support to this reading. However, it seems that trade union and worker agitation for regulation of women's work was also part of a strategy to reduce working hours across the board, and it was only when initial laws concerning children failed to engender more comprehensive reforms that workers adopted the strategy of limiting women's hours. See Beatrice Webb, *The Case for the Factory Acts*, 2nd ed. (London: G. Richards, 1902) at 197–8; B.L. Hutchins and A. Harrison, *A History of Factory Legislation* (London: P.S. King, 1903) at 65, 109. On this latter basis, Barrett and McIntosh would seem to be correct when they assert that "organisations of the working class colluded with pressure from the bourgeoisie to structure the working population along the lines of gender" (Barrett and McIntosh, *supra* note 124 at 54), but the motivation (which is not to be confused with the result) was perhaps less the entrenchment of gender division than a desire to limit the hours of all workers.

132 Hutchins and Harrison, *supra* note 131 at 65.

133 Pinchbeck, *supra* note 59 at 200, note 3. See also Valverde, *supra* note 131 at 628; Hartmann, *supra* note 94 at 155.

134 *Ten Hours' Advocate*, 24 October 1846, in Hartmann, *supra* note 94 at 155.

135 While it appears that a majority of male workers supported some form of limitation on women's participation in factory work (see *supra* note 131), the evidence regarding women's support is more mixed. Some women were certainly in favour of a gender-based distinction between work and family, but it appears

a man to support himself, his wife and his children.[136] It was an idea that went to the heart of English national wellbeing, and it comported with (and was derived in part from) prevailing attitudes towards the family and the market: only a sufficient wage for male workers would permit women and children to remain in the domestic realm and create "a serene refuge for their men-folk";[137] while men's wages could only rise to the necessary level by intervening in the labour market[138] and curtailing the employment of women and children.[139] By the early twentieth century, "this conception had become a pervasive and fervently held proletarian ideal."[140]

The push for a family wage largely came from trade unions, which adopted it "as a fundamental assumption ... in conscious opposition both to the Doctrine of Vested Interests and to that of Supply and Demand."[141] Rather than a privilege or reward, the family wage was

---

that the extent of this support varied across industries and regions. See further Jane Humphries, "Class Struggle and the Persistence of the Working-Class Family" (1977) 1:3 *Cambridge J Econ* 241; Harold Benenson, "The 'Family Wage' and Working Women's Consciousness in Britain, 1880–1914" (1991) 19:1 *Politics & Society* 71.

136 Barrett and McIntosh, *supra* note 124 at 51. Adam Smith accepted that a man's wage "must at least be sufficient to maintain him. They must even upon most occasions be somewhat more; otherwise it would be impossible to bring up a family, and the race of such workmen could not last beyond the first generation." However, Smith was by no means advocating a family wage to enable the wife of a workingman to remain at home; as he subsequently stated, "in order to bring up a family, the labor of the husband *and wife* together must, even in the lowest species of common labor, be able to earn something more than what is precisely necessary for their own maintenance." Smith, *supra* note 19, Vol 1 at 83 (emphasis added).

137 Fredman, *supra* note 117 at 105.

138 Intervention of this sort was perfectly consistent with market ideology: see chapter 1, part II(A).

139 Seccombe, "Patriarchy," *supra* note 93 at 55.

140 *Ibid* at 54. Seccombe traces the roots of family wage ideology in the working classes to the skilled artisan trades, which, from the late eighteenth century, began to exclude women from apprenticeships, thereby restricting the trades to men. As these trades were "proletarianized and their members left their households and small workshops to go to work in capitalist industries, they were the *only* wage workers could *afford* to forego the income of their wives and young children. The material conditions for the flourishing of an exclusive male breadwinner ideology were first realized here." *Ibid* at 65 (emphasis in original).

141 Sidney and Beatrice Webb, *Industrial Democracy* (London, 1898) at 588. Seccombe has noted that in 1875, the leader of the Trades Union Congress, Henry Broadhurst, declared that the goal of the labour movement had to be a situation in which wives and daughters remained "in their proper sphere at home": Seccombe, "Patriarchy," *supra* note 93 at 55.

reconceived as a right;[142] one that would "provide men with a more complete persona, by incorporating elements of both family responsibility and worker identity."[143] Thus, by the 1890s "the wives of skilled men did not usually work, for the ability to keep a wife had become a measure of working class male respectability."[144] Of course, the reality is that male employment fundamentally relied upon and presupposed women's performance of unpaid domestic labour; as Pateman put it, "the construction of the 'worker' presupposes that he is a man who has a woman, a (house)wife, to take care of his daily needs."[145] The family wage also compounded the problem of low wages for women who did continue to work outside of the home because it was, by design, payable only to men; the presumption (and preference) that women were not economically responsible for their families thus justified the payment of comparatively lower wages to women, thereby disincentivizing their engagement in paid work, and reinforcing the economic necessity of male support.[146]

In a direct sense, the law in England did little to foster the family wage.[147] Following the early nineteenth-century repeal of the wage-

---

142   Anna Clark, "The New Poor Law and the Breadwinner Wage: Contrasting Assumptions" (2000) 34:2 *J Soc Hist* 261.

143   Honeyman, *Women, Gender, supra* note 53 at 105.

144   Jane Lewis, *Women in England 1870–1950* (Bloomington: Indiana University Press, 1984) at 49.

145   Pateman, *supra* note 7 at 131. See also Conaghan, "Discipline of Labour Law," *supra* note 6 at 28–9; Kerry Rittich, "Feminization and Contingency: Regulating the Stakes for Work for Women" in Joanne Conaghan, Richard Michael Fischl and Karl Klare, eds., *Labour Law in an Era of Globalization: Transformative Practices and Possibilities* (Oxford: Oxford University Press, 2002) 117.

146   See further Pateman, *supra* note 7 at 138; Fredman, *supra* note 117 at 107–9.

147   In contrast, the family wage was expressly incorporated into law in Australia in the 1907 judgment of the Commonwealth Court of Conciliation and Arbitration in *Ex parte HV McKay* (1907) 2 CAR 1 (the Harvester judgment). In the course of defining a "fair and reasonable" rate of remuneration for factory workers (in order to determine an issue raised under the *Excise Tariff Act 1906* (Cth)), President Higgins declared, "I cannot think that an employer and a workman contract on an equal footing, or make a 'fair' agreement as to wages, when the workman submits to work for a low wage to avoid starvation or pauperism (or something like it) for himself *and his family*." He therefore took evidence concerning cost of living from "working men's wives"; and average figures for "rent, groceries, bread, meat, milk, fuel, vegetables, and fruit" were determined by reference the "average of the list of nine *housekeeping women*." In this way, President Higgins established the principle in Australian law that a "fair and reasonable" wage is one that supports not only a (male) worker, but also his wife and children. Working women, it was assumed, did not have to support a family.

setting provisions in the *Statute of Artificers*,[148] the closest England came to direct intervention regarding wage levels was the establishment of trade boards under the *Trade Boards Act 1909*,[149] which empowered wages councils to set rates in selected industrial sectors.[150] Legal amendments in the nineteenth century were crucial, however, in providing the background conditions enabling agitation for the family wage. In particular, the de-criminalization of combinations enabled worker mobilization and aggressive advocacy for improved wages and conditions of employment[151] – including advocacy for a family wage. For example, in 1893 the Miners' Federation of Great Britain adopted a particularly hard line position against attempts to institute a 25-per cent reduction in wages.[152] In early 1892, the Vice-President of the Federation

148 *Wages, etc. of Artificers, etc., Act 1813*, 53 Geo III, c 40.

149 9 Edw VII, c 22.

150 See Sheila C. Blackburn, "Curse or Cure? Why Was the Enactment of Britain's 1909 Trade Boards Act So Controversial?" (2009) 47:2 *Brit J Indust Rel* 214. Around the same time, welfare reforms, notably the establishment of labour exchanges, national insurance, and child-focussed policies such as the free school lunch, effectively consolidated the male breadwinner ideal through (somewhat) respectable forms of state assistance: Susan Pedersen, *Family, Dependence, and the Origins of the Welfare State: Britain and France, 1914–1945* (Cambridge: Cambridge University Press, 1993) at 49–58.

151 The *Trade Union Act* 1871, 34 & 35 Vict c 31, modified the common law by providing that "the purposes of any trade union shall not, by reason merely that they are in restraint of trade, be deemed to be unlawful, so as to render any member of such trade union liable to criminal prosecution for conspiracy or otherwise": s 2. The effect of this provision was to remove "restraint of trade" as an element of criminality. However, it did not de-criminalize combinations of workers for the purpose of "leav[ing] any service as to which they were under a binding contract, or to persuade other workers, under contract, unlawfully to absent themselves from their service": William Holdsworth, *The Law of Master and Servant: Including that of Trades Unions and Combinations* (London: Routledge, 1876) at 157. To that end, the *Conspiracy and Protection of Property Act 1875*, 38 & 39 Vict c 86, s 3, enacted the following provision: "An agreement or combination by two or more persons to do or procure to be done any act in contemplation or furtherance of a trade dispute between employers and workmen shall not be indictable as a conspiracy if such act committed by one person would not be punishable as a crime." The effect of this provision was that "[c]ombinations or conspiracies to commit or induce others to commit a breach of the contract between employers and employed are therefore not now generally punishable": Holdsworth, *supra* note 151 at 157.

152 The miners' position was soon put to the test when, in 1893, coal owners instituted a lockout of some 300,000 workers. The miners refused to acquiesce to the proposed reduction in wages and a 16-week standoff ensued, culminating in an agreement by the employers to re-open the mines, and by miners to re-commence work, at the previous rate. Soon after, the Chairman of the Federation addressed its Fifth Annual Conference and proclaimed, "we had made up our minds that having

had stated that the miners "held it as a matter of life and death … that any condition of trade ought to warrant the working man living."[153] In contrast to the more limited definition of a living wage that now exists, it appears that for workers in the late nineteenth century, a living wage meant "Shelter, Food, and Raiment both for ourselves, our wives, and our children."[154]

Around the same time that workers' organizations began to advocate for the family wage, employers began to institute policies of outright discrimination against married women.[155] The Post Office introduced England's first formal marriage bar in 1876.[156] By the time of the outbreak of the First World War, "marriage bars had become commonplace in occupations such as the civil service and banking and, to some extent, in teaching."[157] Edith Morley, in her 1914 book *Women Workers in Seven Professions*, referred to "the economically unsound, unjust and racially dangerous tendency in many salaried professions to enforce upon women resignation on marriage."[158] Marriage bars also operated in industrial sectors: the biscuit manufacturer Huntley and Palmer, for instance, had a policy of automatic dismissal for women who married.[159] While marriage bars tended to be lifted during the war, they were reinstated on an even greater scale in the interwar period. The *Sex Disqualification (Removal) Act 1919*[160] partially addressed the matter by making it unlawful to disqualify a person from entry into a civil

---

fought for and obtained a living wage, we were not going to allow the middleman, the coal-owner, or the commercial agent to bring the wages down to the point they were at prior to 1888." See R. Page Arnot, *The Miners: A History of the Miners' Federation of Great Britain 1889–1910* (London: Allen & Unwin, 1949) chapter 8.

153 Webb and Webb, *supra* note 141 at 589 quoting Speech of Sam Woods, MP, at the Annual Conference of the Miners' Federation of Great Britain, Hanley, January 1892, 9–10.

154 This is the definition given to the term by the United Silk Throwers of England in 1872: see Webb and Webb, *supra* note 141 at 587 quoting Preface to the Rules of the United Silk Throwers' Trade and Friendly Society, "commenced 24th October 1868" (Derby, 1872).

155 Of course, discrimination against women practicing certain professions was not new; women had long been precluded from entering certain professions such as medicine and law by training requirements that they were unable to meet: Fredman, *supra* note 117 at 111.

156 Kate Murphy, "A Marriage Bar of Convenience? The BBC and Married Women's Work 1923–39" (2014) 25:4 *Twentieth Cent Brit Hist* 533 at 538.

157 *Ibid*.

158 Edith Julia Morley, *Women Workers in Seven Professions: A Survey of Their Economic Conditions and Prospects* (London: Routledge, 1914) quoted in *ibid* at 538.

159 Lewis, *supra* note 144 at 186.

160 9 & 10 Geo 5, c 71.

profession on the basis of sex, but it also included a wide exception that permitted exclusion of married women within the civil and foreign service.[161] Thus, Treasury regulations issued in 1921 required women to resign from the civil service on marriage.[162] In 1927 a bill was introduced "to prevent the refusal to employ women in the public service by reason only of their being married,"[163] but it failed to pass. Five years later, the hitherto relatively progressive British Broadcasting Corporation (BBC) introduced a marriage bar, though "exceptional" women were allowed to remain employed upon marriage.[164] Between 1934 and 1937, the BBC operated a Marriage Tribunal to distinguish between married workers who would "remain in the ranks of women workers permanently" and those "whose mind is not here but their homes."[165] The Tribunal heard 29 cases and dismissed 13 women.[166] The effect of such rules, however, cannot be measured by the number of women forcibly dismissed from their positions since "it was custom, not enforcement, which led most women to leave paid employment when they married."[167] Marriage bars were essentially the culmination of a long process of managing women out of paid employment and into unpaid domestic labour – part of a generalized implementation of gender-based distinctions between family and work that "induced, if not compelled, such women to invest deeply in their roles as housewives and mothers. Hence, labour market regulations were mechanisms for the discipline, domestication, and maternalization of women."[168]

II. THE DEVALUATION OF HOUSEWORK

In one sense, the nineteenth-century legal and cultural emphasis on women's unpaid domestic labour involved a valorization of women's

---

161 Fredman, *supra* note 117 at 80–81. The courts also took a restrictive approach to the *Sex Disqualification (Removal) Act*, 9 & 10 Geo 5, c 71, finding that the exclusion of married women teachers was reasonable because of the inconvenience caused by their "periodic temporary absences," and that the Act did not prohibit public employers from specifying a particular marital status for a job: *Price v Rhondda UDC* [1923] 1 Ch 372 at 379, in Fredman, *supra* note 117 at 81–2.

162 *Ibid* at 81.

163 Married Women (Employment) Bill 1927, HC Deb, 11 February 1927, vol 202, col 440. See Lewis, *supra* note 144 at 102.

164 Murphy, *supra* note 156 at 536.

165 *Ibid*.

166 *Ibid* at 536–7.

167 *Ibid* at 539.

168 Rittich, *supra* note 145 at 131. Even when marriage bars were lifted in the 1940s and 1950s, women were still "channelled into jobs and occupations that were separate and distinct from men": Fredman and Fudge, *supra* note 8 at 235.

roles within the family. As John Ruskin put it, "wherever a true wife comes, this home is always around her," for it is "woman's true place and power."[169] This moral elevation of wives and domesticity was, however, "accompanied by the economic devaluation of the work performed" in the home.[170] This double move augmented the distinction between work and family life by assigning distinctly different normative and economic values to these domains; its particular gender-based configuration also enabled the maintenance and extension of male dominance over women in the new world of industrialized labour. A particularly clear demonstration of the devaluation of women's domestic work is found in changes instituted to the English census in the late nineteenth century.[171] The censuses themselves performed ideological work – they were not simply passive modes of data collection.[172] Paraphrasing Michel Foucault,[173] the census categories over time helped to eliminate the category of the household, and focussed the notion of economy on to the realm of work, specifically, work conducted by men.[174] In doing so, the census reinforced the idea that women's work in the home was unproductive.[175]

Decennial censuses began in Britain in 1801. The first census attempted to collect information on the occupations of each individual within a

---

169 John Ruskin, "Of Queen's Gardens" in John Ruskin, *Sesame and Lilies and The Political Economy of Art* (London: Collins, 1890) at 119.

170 Folbre, *supra* note 3 at 465.

171 See Catherine Hakim, "Census Reports as Documentary Evidence: The Census Commentaries 1801–1951" (1980) 28:3 *Soc Rev* 551. For analysis of the figures in the various censuses related to women's labour force participation, and consideration of the use and limitations of these figures, see Edward Higgs, "Women, Occupations and Work in the Nineteenth Century Censuses" (1987) 23 *Hist Workshop J* 59 [Higgs, "Women, Occupations and Work"]; Edward Higgs and Amanda Wilkinson, "Women, Occupations and Work in the Victorian Censuses Revisited" (2016) 81 *Hist Workshop J* 17.

172 As Nancy Folbre has written, "Census data consist of ordered sets of numbers. They appear objective and value-free, but their meaning grows out of socially constructed concepts that are laden with cultural and political values." Folbre, *supra* note 3 at 463.

173 On statistics as the "science of the state" see Michel Foucault, *Security, Territory, Population. Lectures at the Collège de France, 1977–1978*, edited by Michel Senellart, translated by Graham Burchell (New York: Vintage, 2007) at 101.

174 See further chapter 1, part II(B).

175 Folbre, *supra* note 3 at 465. In this respect, census categories built on Adam Smith's claim that services were unproductive, but also reflected a late nineteenth-century narrowing of Smith's claim by limiting its application to non-market (that is, unpaid) services. *Ibid* at 470. See also Pateman, *supra* note 7 at 127; Conaghan, "Discipline of Labour Law," *supra* note 6 at 29.

household. Householders, however, approached the issue from divergent perspectives – some classed women, children, and servants alongside men, while others omitted them entirely.[176] The censuses of 1811, 1821 and 1831 thus adopted a family-based (i.e., household) approach, with economic activity rates of 81 per cent, 81 per cent and 71 per cent, respectively.[177] The 1841 census marked a significant shift in practice. It was the first to use self-completion forms and record the names of individuals; and it attempted to record the occupations of individuals, rather than families' economic activity.[178] However, the instructions given to householders confined "labour" to particular categories; it advised that the "profession &c of Wives, or of sons or daughters living with and assisting their parents but not apprenticed or receiving wages, need not be inserted."[179] Thus, not only was a wife's "purely" domestic work excluded from consideration, but her economically measurable contributions (sale of domestically made products at market, for instance) were also ignored. Unsurprisingly, the results of the census showed a significant discrepancy between male and female economic activity.[180]

The 1851 census reversed course, and householders were instructed to record "the occupations of women who are regularly employed from home, or at home, *in any but domestic duties.*"[181] Thus, wives of innkeepers, butchers, and the like were recorded as "innkeeper's wife" or "butcher's wife."[182] Women engaged in unpaid domestic duties were included within the Fifth Class of Occupations which, according to the Census Report, "comprises large numbers of the population that have hitherto been held to have no occupation; but it requires no argument to prove that the wife the mother, the mistress of an English Family – fills offices and discharges duties of no ordinary importance." The Report went on to note "that in districts where women are much employed from home the children and parents perish in great numbers." In essence, the 1851 Report affirmed that a woman's place was in the home, caring for her family, but that role was sufficiently important to be considered "work," if only in a residual manner. This view is even

---

176 Hakim, *supra* note 171 at 554.

177 *Ibid* at 559.

178 *Ibid* at 551–2.

179 Higgs, "Women, Occupations and Work," *supra* note 171 at 63.

180 Hakim, *supra* note 165 at 555.

181 Higgs, "Women, Occupations and Work," *supra* note 171 at 63 (emphasis in original).

182 *Ibid* at 70.

clearer in the 1861 Census Report, which proclaimed "the occupation of wife and mother and housewife [to be] the most important in the country." Thus, under the category "Domestic Class," there were those who conducted paid (Order 5) and unpaid (Order 4) work.[183] When unpaid domestic work is counted, the economic activity rates for men and women were close to 100 per cent (1851–71); when such work is excluded, the rate for women falls to approximately 42 per cent.[184]

The crucial change came in 1881, when the census excluded unpaid domestic work from the definition of economic activity.[185] The Domestic Class therefore only included servants who received wages. "Wives and other women engaged in domestic duties were explicitly placed in the 'Unoccupied Class,' which apparently replaced the earlier 'Indefinite and Non-productive' category."[186] The Report attempted to explain this erasure of women's unpaid domestic work by noting "that a very large number of wives and daughters assist their husbands or fathers in business, and also that the most important of all female occupations, and that which employs the largest number, is altogether omitted from the reckoning, namely, the rearing of children and the management of domestic life."[187] Domestic work thus occupied an unusual space in the state's efforts to manage and quantify the population: it was at once unproductive and the "most important of all female occupations."

The point of this simultaneous elevation and devaluation of women's work in the home was, in large part,[188] the extension and perfection of patriarchy: women's work was valuable because it served men (and their

---

183 Hakim, *supra* note 165 at 556.

184 *Ibid* at 557.

185 Higgs has suggested that this change of course was possibly related to "pressure to reconstruct the occupational census in a form more acceptable to economists and social scientists": Higgs, "Women, Occupations and Work," *supra* note 171 at 71. See further Folbre, *supra* note 3 at 472. The absurdity of this classification was made abundantly clear by the Cambridge economist Arthur Pigou, who observed that if he hired a housekeeper or cook, national income and employment increased. Conversely, if he married the same woman, national income and employment decreased even if she continued to perform precisely the same work. See Guy Standing, *A Precariat Charter: From Denizens to Citizens* (London: Bloomsbury, 2014) at 11.

186 Folbre, *supra* note 3 at 472. The 1891 Census removed the "Unoccupied Class" altogether, and restricted the "Domestic Class" to those employed in domestic service: *ibid* at 473.

187 Census of England and Wales, 1881, 43 & 44 Vict c 37, *Vol IV, General Report* (London, 1883) at 29.

188 The valorization of women's domestic functions was also related to nineteenth-century concerns over the proper raising of children, though arguably that focus also ultimately sought to extend male sex rights through the inculcation of rigid gender roles.

children), but it was not so valuable that it merited economic independence from men (which would, in turn, have affected men's abilities to function as workers).[189] As Christopher Tomlins has argued, the liberal re-ordering of the world in this period "was founded upon a recomposition of patriarchal sex right … that was in its turn dependent not upon the dismantling of 'natural subjection' in the household, but its reassertion."[190] In a manner paralleling the process described in chapter 3, in which waged workers were made reliant upon, and subjected to the wills of, their masters (who were in turn divested of feudal obligations to overlords), wives were not only stripped of their productive functions and (limited) economic independence, leaving them wholly dependent on their husbands for economic survival; the work that was then assigned to them was deemed to be less valuable than that performed by men in the public sphere of the market. The old commonality between the powers of masters and husbands thus lived on in the new world of wage labour and private family life, with a flow of authority that, in the realm of work, travelled from the master to the servant. Within their separate homes, however, both masters and servants as men exercised authority over wives as women, whose principal function had become preparation of the home for the patriarch (whether master or servant) and his children.

The legal treatment of wives' domestic labour in late nineteenth-century English law supports this reading. While the *Married Women's Property Acts* conferred a (limited) measure of financial autonomy on married women by permitting them to hold certain forms of property separately from their husbands, most notably wages earned from work performed outside of the family, the reforms gave wives no direct interest in matrimonial property as a result of unpaid work performed in the home.[191] Accordingly, for the purposes of property distribution following marital breakdown, housework was treated as unproductive.[192] While maintenance orders conferred a measure of support for separated women, this

---

189 Friedrich Engels observed that within modern family structures, "[h]ousehold management lost its public character. It no longer concerned society. It became a *private service*; the wife became the head servant, excluded from all participation in social production." Friedrich Engels, *The Origin of the Family, Private Property, and the State* (London: Penguin, 2010) at 104–5. His solution to this state of affairs was the abolition of "the monogamous family as the economic unit of society"; with "the transfer of the means of production into common ownership, the single family ceases to be the economic unit of society": *ibid* at 105, 107.

190 Tomlins, *supra* note 1 at 381.

191 See chapter 5, part IV(B).

192 See further Otto Kahn-Freund, "Matrimonial Property – Some Recent Developments" (1959) 22:3 *Mod L Rev* 241 at 248.

structure simply reinforced the idea of female dependency, rather than conferring any sort of enforceable property interest based on equally valued contributions to the running of the family unit. In contrast, the common law of negligence treated women's work in the home as valuable when it suited the interests of men: the action for loss of services, historically available only to husbands in respect of losses (servitude and sex, or *servitium et consortium* as it was pleaded) occasioned to them by injuries to their wives,[193] remained open to men (only) well into the twentieth century.[194] Women's domestic labour was thus treated as legally and economically valuable only when its absence affected men.

III. Youth, Work, and the Paths of Apprenticeship

Apprenticeship was historically one of, if not *the*, most "familial" of work relations. In its traditional form, a youth joined his (or less commonly her) master's household while learning a particular trade or craft; the master and his wife assumed parental responsibilities for the apprentice, and the family of origin was effectively replaced – at least for the term stipulated in the indenture. Keith Snell, in discussing the idea of the family in eighteenth century England, refers to the 1777 settlement examination of one Ann Bedford, deserted by her publican husband:

> She had five children – four were own, and the other, an apprentice aged fifteen, had been 'bound to her husband two years since, being also part of her family.' She also had a girl aged sixteen with her, the daughter by another marriage of her husband's, who was not included among her five children. The apprentice was removed with the family to the husband's settlement at Eveshott, and he was considered an integral part of the family – perhaps more so than Ann Smith's stepdaughter.[195]

It was around this time, however, that the treatment of apprenticeship in such familial terms began to fall into desuetude.[196] By the early

---

193 See *Brockbank v The Whitehaven Junction Railway Company* (1862) 7 H&N 834. See generally Margaret Thornton, "Loss of Consortium: Inequality Before the Law" (1984) 10:2 *Syd L Rev* at 260.

194 In 1952 the House of Lords held that the action was not open to wives in respect of the loss of services provided by a husband: *Best v Fox* [1952] AC 716. Other statutory remedies were made available to wives in the nineteenth century: see chapter 5.

195 Snell, *Annals, supra* note 40 at 320–1, citing Bedfordshire CRO, DDP 1/13/4/2.

196 There is significant disagreement among historians over the timing of the decline. For an overview of different positions see *ibid* at 229–30.

nineteenth century, apprenticeship was generally viewed as a reciprocal contractual agreement to teach and learn a particular trade, not as "a
period of further socialisation and familial discipline."[197]

Alongside traditional apprenticeship was parish apprenticeship, instituted at the beginning of the seventeenth century under the Poor Laws,
which imposed on householders the *obligation* to house and teach indigent children. This relation also transformed under the modern separation of family and work, but in different and rather more protracted
ways. Initially, there was a move towards factory apprenticeship – in
essence, work without family; state institutional care of pauper children
then became the norm. In the later nineteenth century, a movement arose
which emphasized the benefits of family-based care of pauper children
and orphans through poor law schools and, in particular, the boarding-
out system. The benefits for children of remaining with families of origin,
even when such families were poor, also began to be recognized in law.

From the perspective of legal form and structure, the transformation of apprenticeship law exemplifies the legal household's dissolution along family/work lines: the more respectable and comparatively
individualist form of (traditional) apprenticeship, involving training in
particular crafts and occupations by agreement (though with the possibility of compulsion), became over time a species of the law of work
(while the obligations of the apprentice's caregivers came to be found
in the law of the family).[198] In contrast, the decline of household-based
apprenticeship meant that increasing numbers of poor children were
boarded out to families for the primary purpose of ensuring their care
and protection; work and training were subsidiary concerns. In this
way, parish apprenticeship moved over time from early modern labour
regulation[199] and the nineteenth-century law of master and servant to
what became family and/or welfare law.[200]

A. Early Modern Apprenticeship Law

Apprentices, according to Blackstone, were "ANOTHER species of
servants" falling within the broader master-servant relation[201] that, by

---

197 *Ibid* at 253–4.

198 Tomlins, *supra* note 1 at 306.

199 Which comprised the *Statute of Artificers 1562*, 5 Eliz c 4, and the *Poor Relief Act
1601*, 43 Eliz I, c 2.

200 See, e.g., Frances Burton, *Family Law*, 2nd ed. (Milton Park, Oxon: Routledge, 2015)
chapters 20 and 22.

201 Blackstone, *supra* note 9, book I at 414. Matthew Hale, in *The Analysis of the Law:
Being a Scheme, or Abstract, of the Several Titles and Partitions of the Law of England,*

the mid-eighteenth century, had largely consolidated into an umbrella concept for work relations generally.[202] Apprentices were, Blackstone said,

> usually bound for a term of years, by deed indented or indentures, *to serve their masters, and be maintained and instructed by them*: for which purpose our statute law has made minors capable of binding themselves. *This is usually done to persons of trade, in order to learn their art and mystery*; and sometimes very large sums are given with them, as a premium for such their instruction: but it may be done to husbandmen, nay to gentlemen, and others. And *children of poor persons may be apprenticed out by the overseers*, with consent of two justices, till twenty-four years of age, to such persons as are thought fitting; who are also compellable to take them.[203]

There is a clear distinction in this passage between traditional apprenticeship "to persons of trade, in order to learn their art and mystery," and parish apprenticeship of "children of poor persons ... apprenticed out by the overseers." The primary difference between these forms was the mode of entry: the traditional form involved placement by agreement, wherein a child's parents or guardians placed a child with a master and paid a premium for the privilege[204] (in certain prescribed circumstances a master could also request a person under 21 become his apprentice); the parish variety involved compulsory placement of a pauper child with a master (a lower premium was paid by the parish[205]). Either way, however, the nature of the relationship was, at least in theory,[206] the same: apprentices were, as Blackstone put it, "to serve

---

Digested into Method (1713), did not refer to apprentices in his section on Master and Servant, but this is perhaps unsurprising given the extreme brevity of his treatment of the subject. Richard Burn, in his popular manual, *The Justice of the Peace, and Parish Officer* (1755), included a lengthy section on apprenticeship, but he did not attempt to place the relation in a broader legal context; rather, he confined himself to recounting the nature of extant statutory requirements and common law decisions.

202 See chapter 3, part III.

203 Blackstone, *supra* note 9, book I at 414.

204 Collyer's *Parents' Directory* of 1761 suggests a premium of between £5–£15: J. Collyer, *The Parents' and Guardians' Directory* (1761). On the basis of settlement examinations from Suffolk, Snell suggests a mean premium paid by the family of origin of about £13: Snell, *Annals*, *supra* note 40 at 233.

205 Snell estimates a premium of around £4 or £5: Snell, *Annals*, *supra* note 40 at 233.

206 In reality, apprentices who were voluntarily taken on, particularly where large sums of money were exchanged, may have experienced better treatment and instruction than those children whose placement was a product of compulsion.

their masters, and be maintained and instructed by them." Apprentices lodged with their masters, who were responsible for providing food and clothing, and, most importantly, instructing the apprentice in the arts and mysteries of the trade in return for the apprentice's faithful and industrious service.[207] The educational focus of apprenticeship meant that wages were not generally paid to apprentices;[208] equally, though, failure by a master to provide proper training and instruction was a ground for terminating the relation.[209]

Apprenticeship was a thoroughly domestic relationship,[210] perhaps "best ... described as paternalistic: the master acting as a surrogate father."[211] An advice booklet from 1761 entitled *The Parents; and Guardians' Directory in the Choice of a Profession or Trade*, said, "A boy, on his being put apprentice, ought to consider that his parents, or his friends, have for his advantage devolved their authority on his master; whom he should regard as the deputy of those who gave him being, and to whom he is under the highest obligation."[212] Thus, it was permissible for a master to moderately chastise (i.e., beat) his apprentice, since the apprentice was a member of the family.[213] At the same time, apprenticeship was governed by private agreement in the form of an indenture, which had to be signed (or marked) by the apprentice, and which set out the nature of the parties' obligations to each other.[214] In London

---

207 William Walker Knox, *British Apprenticeship, 1800–1914* (PhD Dissertation, University of Edinburgh, 1980) [unpublished] at 11. Wages were not required.

208 Blackstone, *supra* note 9, book I at 416.

209 Joseph Chitty, *A Practical Treatise on the Law Relative to Apprentices and Journeymen, and Exercising Trades* (London, 1812) at 74.

210 Although, according to Dunlop and Denman, from about 1680 onwards, "it was not uncommon" for items such as food, drink, lodging or washing to be omitted from the contract: O. Jocelyn Dunlop and Richard D. Denman, *English Apprenticeship & Child Labour: A History* (London: T. Fisher Unwin, 1912) at 195.

211 Knox, *supra* note 207 at 11. See also Dunlop and Denman: "The essential features of that system [of apprenticeship] were the contract of service and instruction for a definite term of years, usually seven; the active supervision by the local community of the operations of that contract; the withdrawal of the youth from his own home and the influence of his parents throughout the term of training, during which the master stood to him *in loco parentis*." Dunlop and Denman, *supra* note 210 at 20.

212 Collyer, *supra* note 204 at 303. See also George Howell, "Trades Unions, Apprentices, and Technical Education" (1877) 30 *Contemporary Review* 833 at 835.

213 Blackstone, *supra* note 9, book 1 at 416. See also Tapping Reeve, *The Law of Baron and Femme; of Parent and Child; of Guardian and Ward; of Master and Servant; and of the Powers of Courts of Chancery, with an Essay on the Terms, Heir, Heirs, and Heirs of the Body* (New Haven: Oliver Steele, 1816) at 374.

214 Bird 1799, *supra* note 30 at 27. Section 43 of the *Statute of Artificers 1562*, 5 Eliz c 4, provided that persons under the age of 21 "shall be bounden to serve for the years

and certain other places, indentures were dutiable instruments and the avoidance of payment by the master (within one year) enabled an apprentice to avoid the indenture.[215] This hybridity, in which a master was contractually appointed as both quasi-parent and teacher, but in which the youth was also subject to strict contractual obligations of duty and service, exemplifies (perhaps more than any other master-servant relation[216]) the integration of work and family in the early modern household. As Snell put it: "[Apprenticeship] was then so overladen with social and other assumptions and expectations, so tied to administrative, moral and political considerations, that *any 'economic' analysis which treated it as a distinct and separate activity would have been felt incongruous*. Work, training, socialization, finance and exchange, local political eligibility and involvement, family life and such concerns were all mutually integrated."[217] While apprenticeship has a history stretching much further back in time than the Elizabethan era,[218] it was in that period that its formal regulation by the state commenced through the *Statute of Artificers 1562*.[219] This is not surprising given the demographics of the period.[220] More than half the population in the mid-sixteenth century was aged 24 or younger.[221] As Blackstone later put it, "appren-

---

in their several Indentures contained, as amply and largely to every intent as if the same Apprentice were of full Age at the time of the making of such Indentures" (spelling modernized).

215 *Ibid* at 28.

216 Apprenticeship and domestic service were always treated as the most "familial" of the master-servant relations, but in the adoption of parental status apprenticeship went further down this path than domestic service. For example, while masters were required to provide food and lodging for apprentices and domestics, only apprentices were entitled to medical treatment at the expense of his or her master (though an obligation to provide domestic servants with such care might be inferred from the conduct of the parties): Macdonnell, *supra* note 11 at 147–48.

217 K.D.M. Snell, "The apprenticeship system in British history: the fragmentation of a cultural institution" (1996) 25:4 *Hist Educ* 303 at 305 (emphasis added) [Snell, "Apprenticeship"].

218 Dunlop and Denman, *supra* note 210 at 15.

219 5 Eliz c 4. Regulation of employment had been around since the mid-fourteenth century with the *Ordinance* (1349) (23 Edward III, c 1–8) and *Statute of Labourers* (1351) (25 Edward III, Stat I, c I) which were passed in the wake of the Black Death to counter workers' attempts to increase wages in the face of labour scarcity. Those laws did not, however, deal with apprenticeship.

220 "No century has been so conscious of the poor as the sixteenth." Henry Kamen, *European Society, 1500–1700* (London: Hutchinson, 1984) at 167, quoted in Wally Seccombe, *A Millennium of Family Change: Feudalism to Capitalism in Northwestern Europe* (London: Verso, 1992) at 151 [Seccombe, *Family Change*].

221 Joan Lane, *Apprenticeship in England, 1600–1914* (London: UCL Press, 1996) at 243.

ticeships are useful to the commonwealth, by employing of youth, and learning them to be early industrious."[222] There was also a protectionist agenda undergirding the *Statute*'s apprenticeship provisions. "At the common law," wrote Bird in his 1795 work on master and servant law, "every person was at liberty to follow whatever trade or profession he chose, without any previous tuition or apprenticeship."[223] This situation, however, was "found very mischievous and detrimental to the public by frequently inducing people to exercise trades in which they had little or no experience or skill";[224] accordingly, the Statute proclaimed the following: "[I]t shall not be lawful to any Person or Persons, other than such as now do lawfully use or exercise any Art, Mystery or Manual occupation, to set up, occupy, use or exercise any Craft, Mystery or Occupation, now used or occupied within the Realm of England or Wales ; except he shall have been brought up therein seven Years at the least as an Apprentice, in Manner and Form abovesaid."[225] The Statute did not merely restrict the practice of certain trades to persons "brought up therein seven Years at the least as Apprentice" but also set strict rules about who could become, and who could take on, apprentices in particular fields.[226] In this respect, it "elaborated upon

---

222 Blackstone, *supra* note 9, book I at 415. According to Tomlins, *supra* note 1 at 306, "the institution of apprenticeship was, from its earliest days as a state-enacted programme (and long before 1563 too), a matter of moral, familial, social and political control, as well as a means of market and labour-force supervision, used as such by civic governments."

223 Bird 1795, *supra* note 26 at 17.

224 *Ibid*. See also Eversley, *supra* note 11 at 932: "Apprenticeship was devised less for the advancement of handicrafts than as a convenient and powerful weapon for upholding trade monopolies."

225 5 Eliz, c 4, s 31.

226 The heads of households "having and using Half a Plough-land at the least in Tillage" were permitted to take as apprentices persons between the ages of 10 and 18 "to serve in Husbandry, until his Age of one and twenty Years at the least, or until the Age of twenty-four Years, as the Parties can agree": 5 Eliz c 4, s 25. Householders over the age of 24 in corporate towns, using and exercising "any such Mystery, Art or Manual Occupation" were permitted to "have and retain the Son of any Freeman, not occupying Husbandry, nor being a Labourer" to serve as an apprentice "for seven Years at the least," with the term of expiry to occur after the apprentice reached the age of 24: s 26. (The age for completion was lowered to 21 in 1778: 18 Geo III, c 47.) Class divisions were built into and replicated by the proviso that various species of merchant could only take as apprentices their sons, or the sons of parents with specific monetary interests in land. In cities and corporate towns the parents of apprentices were required to have interests in land worth at least 40 shillings per annum: s 27. In market towns parents needed interests in land worth at least three pounds per annum: s 29. Section 32 provided

practices (control of entry to trades, limitation of numbers, the delegitimation of untrained rivals, discipline) long since used inside the craft companies to regulate craft apprenticeship and the craft itself for their own purposes."[227] Compulsion was built into the Statute by its provision that "any Housholder, having and using Half a Plough-land at the least in Tillage" was able to require any person under the age of 21 to become an apprentice "in Husbandry, or in any other Kind of Art, Mystery or Science." Upon refusal by a putative apprentice, a householder could make complaint to Justices of the Peace, and if "the said Person [were found] meet and convenient to serve as an Apprentice," he or she could be committed to ward until they agreed to serve.[228] The *Poor Relief Act 1601*[229] built on this provision, establishing the system of parish apprenticeship.[230] It provided:[231] "That it shall be lawful for the said Churchwardens and Overseers, or the greater Part of them, by the Assent of any two Justices of the Peace aforesaid, to bind any such Children as aforesaid to be Apprentices, where they shall see convenient, till such Man-child shall come to the Age of four and twenty Years, and such Woman-child to the Age of one and twenty Years, or the Time of her Marriage." The "Children as aforesaid" were those "whose Parents shall not ... be thought able to keep and maintain" them.[232] An Act of 1696 went a step further, compelling householders to receive parish children as apprentices at the pleasure of the authorities, or incur a

---

that woolen cloth weavers, except those in cities, could not take apprentices other than the children of persons having freehold of three pounds per annum.

227 Tomlins, *supra* note 1 at 241. Particular tradesman, however, were permitted to take as their apprentices children whose parents had no interests in land: 5 Eliz c 4, s 30.

228 5 Eliz, c 4, ss 35 and 36.

229 *An Act for the Relief of the Poor*, 43 Eliz I, c 2 (1601).

230 In 1662, *An Act for the better Relief of the Poor in this Kingdom*, 14 Cha II, c 12, built upon the *Statute of Artificers 1562*, 5 Eliz, c 4, and *An Act for the Relief of the Poor 1601*, 43 Eliz, c 2, by providing that apprentices, among others, could be removed from a parish if they had resided there for less than 40 days. What this meant in practice was that a valid apprenticeship, that is, one properly recorded in an indenture, conferred upon an apprentice a settlement in his master's parish after 40 days' residence therein. Settlement was a crucial form of community membership in this period. In essence, it conferred on the settled residents of a parish the right to seek poor relief, which was administered at the parish level. For this reason, parish officers often sought to bind poor children to masters in parishes other than their own in order to avoid the possibility of the child gaining a settlement in the parish and becoming eligible for poor relief. See Snell, *Annals*, *supra* note 40 at 308.

231 43 Eliz, c 2, s 5.

232 43 Eliz, c 2, s 1.

fine of ten pounds.[233] Unsurprisingly, many paupers were apprenticed to "excessively unpleasant occupations, such as chimney-sweeping, horn comb-making or cat-gut dressing, and to trades that were, before steam power, highly labour-intensive, especially textiles."[234] The more fortunate children were apprenticed through charity organizations, which tended to provide a basic education, ensuring that children "were both literate and used to discipline"; often these children were orphans whose fathers had been masters of particular trades and thus "a decent apprenticeship was the means of restoring the prosperity they had lost by their fathers' death."[235]

Despite their position within the household (and hence subjection to the personal authority of masters), apprentices were not immune from the statutory master-servant regime that began to tighten masters' control over workers in the eighteenth century.[236] Portending (and presumably in some instances influencing) the subsequent reformulation of (traditional) apprenticeship as a work relation, a law passed in 1747 empowered masters to bring suit against apprentices "concerning any Misdemeanour, Miscarriage, or Ill-behaviour, in such his or her Service," with the possibility of punishment "by Commitment to the House of Correction, there to remain and be corrected; and held to hard Labour for a reasonable Time not exceeding one Calendar Month."[237] Concern

---

233 *An Act for supplying some Defects in the Laws for the Relief of the Poor in this Kingdom 1696*, 8 & 9 Will III, c 30, s 5.

234 Lane, *supra* note 221 at 78. While an Act passed in 1816 required a certificate of a master's humanity and trustworthiness, "the scarcity of these documents in record collections suggests that either they were rarely given or that they were destroyed as of little value": *ibid* at 77. Note, however, Honeyman's more recent revisionist history of pauper apprenticeship, in which she suggests that the reality is a rather more complex story than one of simple exploitation: see Katrina Honeyman, *Child Workers in England, 1780–1820: Parish Apprentices and the Making of the Early Industrial Labour Force* (Aldershot: Ashgate, 2007) chapter 4 [Honeyman, *Child Workers*].

235 Lane, *supra* note 221 at 78.

236 Dunlop and Denman in fact suggest that 1720, the year of the first of the punitive eighteenth-century master-servant statutes (see chapter 3, part III), "perhaps best dates the time at which the definite collapse" of the old apprenticeship system began: *supra* note 210 at 224. The breakdown commenced in the woolen industry and, by 1780, "it had spread into all departments of the trade": *ibid* at 227. From around 1790, "a short training of two or three years had been in vogue": *ibid* at 242–3 citing *Report on Woollen Trade* (1806), Minutes of Evidence at 10, 71, 171, 184.

237 *Act for the better adjusting and more easy Recovery of the Wages of certain Servants; and for the better Regulation of such Servants, and of certain Apprentices 1747*, 20 Geo II, c 19, s 4. The same Act also provided that apprentices – whether parish or traditional –

over apprentices' behaviour was not new;[238] imprisonment, however, was.[239] The trend continued with an Act passed in 1766[240] that was oriented towards absconding apprentices. It required an apprentice "to serve his said Master for so long a Time as he shall have so absented himself from such Service"; the punishment for refusal under this law was *three* months' imprisonment. Like other master-servant statutes that applied to labourers, servants in husbandry, and artisans (but not domestic servants),[241] the goal was ultimately to secure performance by making an absconding apprentice liable to serve out not only his or her term but also time *in absentia*. And, *like ordinary workers*, apprentices who refused were subject to sanctions drawn from the criminal law.[242]

B. Household to Employment: The Transformation of Traditional Apprenticeship

In his 1812 *Practical Treatise on the Law Relative to Apprentices and Journeymen, and to Exercising Trades*, Joseph Chitty claimed with Benthamite zeal that the "greatest quantity of happiness" would result from "increase[ing] the effective demand for labour"; that, in turn, required limiting "every *direct interference* of the legislature with its subjects, by *prohibiting* or *restraining* any particular branch at the expense of another."[243] Accordingly, he said (echoing the economic liberalism of

----

could make complaint concerning their treatment by masters, with the possibility of discharge by order of two or more Justices of the Peace.

238 Numerous manuals in the late seventeenth century were devoted to apprentices' proper behaviour: Lane, *supra* note 221 at 164.

239 Under the *Statute of Artificers 1562*, 5 Eliz, c 4, s 35, apprentices found to be in "default" had been subject to whatever correction and punishment the justices, mayor or other head officer felt appropriate. It does not appear, however, that the *Statute* envisaged imprisonment of apprentices – other sections dealing with punishment of servants and pieceworkers for departing service and failing to perform work specifically mention imprisonment (see ss 9 and 13), whereas the provision concerning apprentices refers only to "correction and punishment" – precisely the type of language used in relation to a father's powers over his children. This being said, persons refusing to become apprentices could be imprisoned until they complied with an eligible householder's request: s 35.

240 *An Act for better regulating Apprentices, and Persons working under Contract 1766*, 6 Geo III, c 25. A further Act passed in 1792, which applied only to parish apprentices, extended the length of incarceration for parish apprentices to three months in cases of insubordination. 32 Geo III, c 57.

241 See *supra* part II(A); chapter 3, part III.

242 In practice, it seems that refractory apprentices had their indentures cancelled by justices, forfeiting whatever premium had been paid: Lane, *supra* note 221 at 173–5.

243 Chitty, *supra* note 209 at 1–2.

Adam Smith[244]), emphasis should be placed on enabling the exercise of individual will,[245] in particular, enabling a person trained in one particular trade to change his occupation to suit changing economic circumstances;[246] in other words, freedom of trade and contract. Chitty was far from alone in his view of the "injurious consequences" of labour restrictions.[247] Only two years after his treatise was published, the era of Elizabethan apprenticeship formally ended. The *Apprentices Act 1814*[248] repealed the provision in the *Statute of Artificers* that restricted entry into particular trades to those trained in their arts and mysteries.[249] It also provided that it was henceforth "lawful for any Person to take or retain or become an Apprentice, though not according to the Provisions of the said Act."[250] By these measures, centuries-old restrictions upon the practice of certain trades were dismantled, and the "freedom" of individuals to engage in wage labour with or without training was affirmed.

In this respect, the Act gave legal backing to a general shift away from the integrated model of work and family that characterized apprenticeship in the early modern era. By 1814, seven-year apprenticeships were out of favour among masters and potential recruits. A number of factors were at play, including masters' desires to avoid conferring settlements on apprentices;[251] structural shifts in the nature of work;[252] and concerns

---

244 See chapter 1, part II(A).

245 Chitty, *supra* note 209 at 3.

246 *Ibid* at 18.

247 *Ibid* at 1. Similar sentiments had been expressed earlier on by Lord Mansfield in *Raynard v Chase*, 1 Burr 2 at 6, where he opined that the *Statute of Artificers* constituted a "restraint of natural right … it is contrary to the general right given by the common law of this kingdom."

248 54 Geo III, c 96.

249 For an overview of the requirements for entry into various trades in the late nineteenth century see Howell, *supra* note 212 at 839 ff. According to Snell, the repeal was "bitterly resisted," though it can also be seen as recognizing changes that had already taken place in practice: Snell, *Annals, supra* note 40 at 228, 314.

250 54 Geo III, c 96, s 2.

251 Indentures thus specified a term shorter than seven years, which fell afoul of the *Statute of Artificers*, and thus avoided rights to settlement: Snell, *supra* note 40 at 314. He argues that this practice led to a permanent disengagement of apprenticeship from its broader social purposes.

252 Employers in the eighteenth century increasingly focussed on obtaining cheap, rather than skilled, labour, which was sometimes all that was necessary in the emerging world of factory production. See Howell, *supra* note 212 at 837. Note, though, that the role of factory-based production in the early Industrial Revolution should not be overestimated: Hobsbawm, *supra* note 53. Young people were also less willing to bind themselves for years since "the growth of employment

over class and exposure of one's (legal/biological) children to the lower orders.[253] Unsurprisingly then, apprenticeship after the *Apprentices Act 1814* was increasingly "outdoor"[254] – "clubbing out" apprenticeships, as Snell has called them.[255] In this scenario, "the apprentice remained in parental care, and it was the parents, and not the master, who were expected to outlay for clothing and food."[256] The mutual obligations of service and instruction remained in place, but the domestic, familial nature of the relationship between master and apprentice was removed. Instead, apprentices looked to their own families of origin for care and maintenance.[257] By 1843, the *Second Report of the Commissioners on Trades and Manufacturers* stated, "[i]n the city ... the great majority are out-door apprentices, notwithstanding there is a regulation by which the master is required to find 'sufficient meat, drink, apparel, lodging, and all other necessaries;' these stipulations being usually avoided by a bond of indemnity."[258] A lengthy article by George Howell appearing in the *Contemporary Review* in 1877 noted, "in the end the ancient universal rule of apprenticeship was more and more relaxed, until it is now very nearly abolished in all the more important trades of the country."[259] "Under

---

opportunities furnished a mass alternative to rural domestic service and parentally arranged apprenticeship as preludes to marriage"; it appears that youth also viewed (with some reason) such training as no guarantee of stable future employment. See Seccombe, *Family Change, supra* note 220 at 221; Snell, *Annals, supra* note 40 at 314. Thus, even when an apprenticeship was undertaken, by 1814 it tended to be for a lesser period than the traditional seven years: *ibid* at 236.

253 According to Knox, "[t]o maintain the integrity of the family and to ensure a certain degree of social and economic status for his daughters, the small master adopted a stance of social exclusiveness viz-a-viz his journeymen and apprentices": Knox, *supra* note 207 at 17–18. For the aspiring bourgeoisie of the nineteenth century, it was simply too risky to allow poorer children, especially boys, into their homes. *Ibid* at 20. See also Seccombe, *Family Change, supra* note 220 at 204.

254 This is not to say that the old system of apprenticeship, with its attendant legal requirements, simply dissolved; it remained entirely possible to enter into a household-based, seven-year apprenticeship – the problem was simply finding masters or apprentices who were willing to submit to this increasingly archaic form under the weight of the legal, social, and economic forces weighed against it.

255 Snell, *Annals, supra* note 40 at 257–8.

256 *Ibid* at 257; Knox, *supra* note 207 at 11.

257 Snell, *Annals, supra* note 40 at 257–9.

258 Children's Employment Commission, *Second Report of the Commissioners. Trades and Manufactures* (1843) at 26 [189]. Knox observes, though, that "the indoor system proved more obdurate than the 1843 Commissioners imagined," pointing to the existence of the older system in the Sheffield metal trades into the 1860s: Knox, *supra* note 207 at 13.

259 Howell, *supra* note 212 at 836.

these circumstances the conditions of apprenticeship were completely changed, not suddenly, but gradually, until the apprentice became merely the boy-worker, with less wages but more solemn engagements than a journeyman. The master to whom he was bound no longer taught him his trade; he was, so to speak, pitchforked into the workshop to pick up his trade as best he could, or to learn it from the many journeymen who were there employed."[260] In essence, the apprentice was no longer seen as part of his master's family, but instead as a worker or servant entitled to a measure of instruction.[261] In Snell's words, "[t]he apprenticeship system changed under these conditions to a more short-term and strictly contractual means to train skilled workers."[262] Indeed, it became increasingly common for outdoor apprentices to receive wages[263] – something that was almost unheard of in earlier centuries.[264] Moreover, by the later nineteenth century the educational component of apprenticeship was increasingly seen as a state responsibility, rather than something to be arranged by private individuals. Thus, the *Elementary Education Act 1870*,[265] which introduced compulsory education, effectively replaced, at least for younger children, apprenticeship and service as forms of preparation for adult occupations.[266]

In this context, it is somewhat surprising to find that the law which is generally credited with inaugurating a less punitive (which is not to say less coercive) regime of employment regulation, the *Employers and Workmen Act 1875*,[267] continued to provide masters with a means by which to seek imprisonment of recalcitrant apprentices.[268] Like domes-

---

260 *Ibid* at 835.

261 Snell, "Apprenticeship system," *supra* note 217 at 316.

262 Snell, *Annals, supra* note 40 at 256.

263 Holdsworth, *supra* note 151 at 176.

264 See Blackstone, *supra* note 9, book I at 416: "By service all servants and labourers, *except apprentices*, become entitled to wages." See further Snell, *Annals, supra* note 40 at 258.

265 33 & 34 Vict c 75. The Act empowered school boards to make regulations "[r] equiring the parents of children of such age, not less than five years nor more than thirteen years ... to attend school": s 74(1).

266 Seccombe, *Family Change, supra* note 220 at 235.

267 38 & 39 Vict, c 90.

268 The Act effectively abolished imprisonment for an employee's breach of contract by empowering magistrates to make orders only for security in lieu of damages, contingent upon performance of the contract, with a stipulated sum payable in the event of further non-performance: s 3(3). The provision concerning apprentices, however, was not premised on security but rather amounted to the simple power to "make an order directing the apprentice to perform his duties under the apprenticeship": s 6(1). If, after the expiration of at least one month, a court was of

tic servants, it seems that by this point it was accepted that apprentices were no longer legally part of the family; nor, however, was their transition to the domain of waged employment complete.[269] This ambiguity is apparent in legal treatises of the late nineteenth century. In his 1876 work, *The Law of Master and Servant*, William Holdsworth treated the apprenticeship relation as a contract-based form of employment, albeit one in which familial obligations might continue to exist "where the apprentice is to reside in his master's house." The following decade, however, William Eversley included apprentices alongside domestic servants in the category of "Master and Servant," but in his scheme that category did *not* include "relations of those who are popularly known as 'Employers and Employed.'"[270] In his view, apprenticeship remained a more familial form of work than other types of employment.

By the early twentieth century, however, it seems clear that as a matter of legal form and taxonomy, traditional apprenticeship had shifted outside of the family and into the sphere of work. The clearest example is Edward Jenks's *Digest of English Civil Law*.[271] The discussion of Employment in the *Digest* situated apprenticeship (but only traditional apprenticeship – the parish variation was expressly excluded[272]) alongside domestic service and "Work and Labour" agreements.[273] No mention of apprenticeship is made in the chapter on Family Law. By this point, as Snell put it, "[t]he apprenticeship system [had] changed ... to a more short-term and strictly contractual means to train skilled workers."[274] The master "became less the trained family craftsman, directing family-based production in which wife, children, and apprentice(s) played a part, and more the employer."[275] The apprentice, in turn, "was no longer seen as a member of the family, but as a boy-worker, taught (increasingly

---

opinion that "the apprentice has failed to comply therewith," it could "order him to be imprisoned for a period not exceeding fourteen days": s 6(2). Note that this only applied to apprentices for whom no premium was paid, or a premium of less than £25, or parish apprentices: s 12.

269 Thus, masters' obligations to provide sustenance and necessary medical attention for apprentices were also reinforced in the second half of the nineteenth century, first in the *Poor Law (Apprentices, etc) Act 1851*, 14 & 15 Vict, c 11, then by section 26 of the *Offences Against the Person Act 1861*, 24 & 25 Vict, c 100, and subsequently by section 6 of the *Conspiracy and Protection of Property Act 1875*, 38 & 39 Vict, c 86. See Macdonnell, *supra* note 11 at 148–9.

270 Eversley, *supra* note 11 at 909.

271 Jenks, *supra* note 12.

272 R.W. Lee, "Obligations" in Jenks, *supra* note 12, vol 2 (1906) at 220.

273 See chapter 2 for more detailed discussion.

274 Snell, *Annals, supra* note 40 at 256.

275 *Ibid* at 259.

reluctantly) by other journeymen employed."[276] Thus, a decade after book II of the *Digest* appeared, Frank Tillyard in his 1916 text, *Industrial Law*, introduced the topic of apprenticeship by stating: "The Common Law recognises a special form of the contract of service in the case of persons under 21 years of age which is known as apprenticeship. This differs from the ordinary contract of service in that the master undertakes to teach the apprentice."[277] It was still a "special form" of contract of service, but traditional apprenticeship had clearly become part of the general law through which, by this time, much of the domain of waged work was both constituted and governed.

C. Household to Family: The Transformation of Parish Apprenticeship

Parish apprentices were generally those "children of poor persons ... apprenticed out by the overseers ... to such persons as thought fitting."[278] Broadly speaking, it was the element of state compulsion to enter into apprenticeship that distinguished parish from traditional apprenticeship.[279] Aside from this difference in the mode of entry, the law did little to discriminate between apprentices – as members of the master's household, each was to be treated as a member of the family; correlatively, they were subject to "correct[ion] ... for negligence or other misbehaviour."[280] The 1747 Act "for the better Regulation ... of certain Apprentices" enabled masters to bring suit against parish and traditional apprentices "concerning any Misdemeanour, Miscarriage, or Ill-behaviour, in such his or her Service"; it also permitted both species of apprentice to make complaint "concerning any Misusage, Refusal of necessary Provision, Cruelty or other Ill-treatment" by a master.[281] However, this formal equality (or perhaps indifference) appears not to have carried over into the actual experiences of parish apprentices. Thomas Andrews, in his 1738 pamphlet, *An enquiry into the causes of the encrease and miseries of the poor of England*, claimed: "[A] most unhappy Practice prevails in most Places, to apprentice *poor Children*, no Matter to what *Master*, provided he lives *out of the Parish*, if the Child serves

---

276 *Ibid.*
277 Frank Tillyard, *Industrial Law* (London: A. & C. Black, 1916) at 30.
278 Blackstone, *supra* note 9, book I at 414.
279 While s 35 of the *Statute of Artificers 1562*, 5 Eliz, c 4, enabled certain householders to compel persons thought "meet and convenient" to serve as apprentices, this process did not involve direction by the overseers on the basis of poverty.
280 Blackstone, *supra* note 9, book I at 416.
281 *Statute of Artificers 1562*, 5 Eliz, c 4, s 3.

the first *forty Days*, we are rid of him for ever. The *Master* may be a Tiger in Cruelty, he may *Beat, Abuse, Strip-naked, Starve*, or do what he will to the poor innocent *Lad*, few People take much notice, and the *Officers* who put him out, the least of any Body."[282] The point of sending poor children out of the parish was to ensure that they became entitled to a settlement elsewhere, thereby relieving the originating parish of responsibility for the child under the Poor Law.

The *Poor Act 1766*[283] sought to address the harshness of the parish system by providing that pauper children under the age of six were to "be sent into the Country ... there to be nursed and maintained at the Charge of their respective Parishes."[284] At the age of six, such children were either "put out Apprentice, or return to the Workhouse."[285] Apprentices were to be bound "for the Term of seven years, or Till they shall attain their respective Ages of twenty-one Years, and no longer."[286] To "excite Masters and Mistresses" to take on apprentices and discharge their duties properly, it was provided that "no such Parish Child shall be bound out an Apprentice with a Sum less than four Pounds two Shillings as an Apprentice Fee."[287] In legal terms, then, the model of parish apprenticeship in the mid-eighteenth century remained household-based, combining work and family life – at least to the extent that masters and mistresses fulfilled their care obligations.

The decades following the *Poor Act 1766* saw the beginnings of the sort of factory-based manufacturing that became synonymous with industrialization. Changes to agricultural production methods and the decline of household-based subsistence[288] contributed to growing numbers of poor children requiring external assistance. Accordingly, at this time, "the scale of parish apprenticeship increased as traditional forms of binding – to domestic service and farm work as well as local trades – were augmented by factory apprenticeship."[289] This development was

---

282 Thomas Andrews, *An enquiry into the causes of the encrease and miseries of the poor of England* (1738) at 43. See, to similar effect, Charles Dickens, "Little Pauper Boarders" 39:2 *All the Year Round* (28 August 1869) at 301, 302.

283 *An Act for the better Regulation of the Parish Poor Children, of the several Parishes therein mentioned, within the Bills of Mortality 1766*, 7 Geo III c 39.

284 7 Geo III, c 39, s 2. The minimum distance a child could be sent from London or Westminster depended on the age of the child: those under two "not suckled by the Mother" were to be sent more than five miles, while those above two and under six were to be sent at least three miles from those cities: ss 2 and 3.

285 7 Geo III, c 39, s 4.

286 7 Geo III, c 39, s 14.

287 7 Geo III, c 39, s 15.

288 See chapter 3, part I(A).

289 Honeyman, *Child Workers, supra* note 234 at 33. See also Beckert, *supra* note 57 at 62.

a product of factory demand as well as parish supply. According to the Webbs's study of the Poor Law: "The progress of the industrial revolution led to a demand for child labour in one manufacture after another ... The necessary operatives had to be brought from somewhere and the cheapest source was the workhouse of the south of England. Parish officers accordingly found themselves importuned by the agents sent by manufacturers to recruit their staffs, who, without asking any premium, carried off the children literally by cartloads, taking even infants of three or four years old."[290] Honeyman's more recent work suggests that premiums were in fact usually paid, the carting-off of children under the age of six was unusual, and in general the process of parish factory apprenticeship was "rigorous, well co-ordinated and formally recorded."[291] Nevertheless, the point remains that pauper children were, under the guise of apprenticeships, used as a source of cheap labour in the early phase of the Industrial Revolution.[292] "[H]ardly a county in the country was excluded from the practice ... Large provincial cities, such as Bristol, Birmingham and Liverpool were important providers of factory apprentices; but so too were smaller towns and even rural parishes."[293] Parishes and factories were active partners: newspapers throughout the latter part of the eighteenth century frequently contained advertisements offering or requiring apprentices.[294] The records suggest

---

290 Honeyman, *Child Workers*, *supra* note 234 at 34 citing Sidney and Beatrice Webb, *English Local Government, from the Revolution to the Municipal Corporations Act*, 7 vols (London: Longmans, Green, 1906–27) vol 7, *English Poor Law History: Part I. The Old Poor Law* (1927) at 201.

291 Katrina Honeyman, "Compulsion, Compassion and Consent: Parish Apprenticeship in Early-Nineteenth-Century England" in Nigel Goose and Katrina Honeyman, eds., *Childhood and Labour in Industrial England: Diversity and Agency, 1750–1914* (Farnham: Ashgate, 2013) 71 at 72 [Honeyman, "Compulsion"]. Execution of indentures was part of this process, just as it was in traditional, trade-based apprenticeship: Honeyman, *Child Workers*, *supra* note 234 at 40.

292 The practice continued into the nineteenth century. According to the 1815 Report from the Select Committee on Number and State of Parish Apprentices bound in England, between 1802 and 1811, 5815 children were bound as apprentices by parishes within and surrounding London; it also found that a high proportion of parish apprentices were involved in the production of cotton. Select Committee on Number and State of Parish Apprentices bound in England, *Report from the Committee on Parish Apprentices* (House of Commons, 1815) at 3, 5.

293 Honeyman, "Compulsion," *supra* note 291 at 72.

294 Honeyman, *Child Workers*, *supra* note 234 at 35, citing 21 October 1783, Minutes of Governors and Directors of the Poor, Parish of St James, Piccadilly, D1870, WAC: "In 1783, Poor Law officers of St James, Piccadilly, one of the wealthier London parishes, agreed the wording of an advertisement: '100 boys and 100 girls orderly in behaviour ... any manufacturer or tradesman willing to employ such children ... may come and look [on a date to be specified].'"

that certain London parishes, presumably overwhelmed with poor children, "sent groups of children, at peak times accounting for 90 per cent of their bindings, to the new textile factories."[295] The system, according to Mary Rose, was "a method of transmitting child labour into the low skilled trades, rather than an investment in the human capital of poor children."[296]

The most immediate legal ramification of the shift towards factory apprenticeship was new legislation to protect the "health and morals" of apprentices. The *Health and Morals of Apprentices Act 1802*[297] prescribed standards of cleanliness and ventilation in factories, restricted hours of work and prohibited night work, and required adequate changes of clothing and access to medical care when necessary. Basic instruction in "reading, writing and arithmetick" was also required.[298] The deeper change, however, was the move away from the household system – something that is not apparent from the law on the books at that time. Of course, the labour value of children had long been recognized,[299] and the older system of parish apprenticeship does not merit romanticizing. But large-scale factory apprenticeship severed whatever familial or household elements had previously existed. It seemed, at this point, that parish apprenticeship, like its traditional counterpart, was becoming little more than a form of state-directed (and partially protected) but privately administered wage labour.[300]

A rather different approach emerged, however, in the 1830s. The *Poor Law Amendment Act 1834*[301] emphasized apprenticeship as a primary

---

295 Honeyman, *Child Workers, supra* note 234 at 60.

296 Mary B. Rose, "Social Policy and Business; Parish Apprenticeship and the Early Factory System 1750–1834" (1989) 31:4 *Business Hist* 5 at 9 [Rose, "Parish Apprenticeship"].

297 *An Act for the Preservation of the Health and Morals of Apprentices and Others, Employed in Cotton and Other Mills, and Cotton and other Factories*, 42 Geo III, c 123.

298 42 Geo III, c 73, s 6. Another Act of the same year required overseers and guardians of the poor to keep a register of all children bound by them as apprentices: 42 Geo III, c 46.

299 Dunlop and Denman, *supra* note 210 at 27.

300 Honeyman, *Child Workers, supra* note 234 at 125.

301 4 & 5 Will IV, c 76. Like the *Apprentices Act 1814* (which repealed the apprenticeship provisions of the *Statute of Artificers*), the *Poor Law Amendment Act 1834* sought to implement the *laissez-faire* ideology of Adam Smith and his followers; it "stressed the aim of forcing the able-bodied poor onto the labour market ... [and] aimed to put in work all persons who were unable to maintain themselves." Bob Hepple, "Welfare Legislation and Wage-Labour" in Bob Hepple, ed., *The Making of Labour Law in Europe: A Comparative Study of Nine Countries up to 1945* (London: Mansell, 1986) 114 at 118.

means of dealing with pauper children, and also provided for care in the expanding workhouse system where apprenticeship was not possible.[302] Factory-based apprenticeship had ceased to be a viable option for workhouse children because feeding and housing scores of young apprentices had become cost-inefficient for factory owners.[303] Similarly, householders were by this time generally reluctant to house apprentices. In this context, the 1834 Act effectively directed large numbers of children into institutional state care – a distinct change from the early nineteenth century trend towards treating parish apprenticeship as a state-directed private work scheme.[304]

In 1844 the law compelling householders to accept pauper children as apprentices was repealed.[305] Nevertheless, the system was not entirely defunct. An 1847 General Consolidated Order of the Commissioners set out detailed rules for the binding of pauper children as apprentices,[306] and obliged masters to teach, feed, house and otherwise care for such

---

302 4 & 5 Will IV, c 76, s 15. Pursuant to the *Poor Law Amendment Act*, an 1842 General Order of the Poor Law Commissioners stipulated that children under the age of seven, if orphaned or lacking parental supervision, were to be sent to the country in accordance with the *Poor Act 1766*, 7 Geo III, c 39. Children over the age of seven and under the age of fifteen were to be housed in the workhouses, in separate areas according to their classification. These children, "for three of the working hours at least, every day," were to "be respectively instructed in reading, writing, arithmetic, and the principles of the Christian religion; and such other instruction shall be imparted to them as shall fit them for service, and train them to habits of usefulness, industry, and virtue." Otherwise, though, the children were liable to be put to work, alongside other persons "relieved in any workhouse, in return for the food and lodging afforded." Orders published 6 February 1842 in John Frederick Archbold, *The Poor Law, Comprising all the Authorities, to October, 1843, with Forms*, 3rd ed. (London: Shaw & Sons, 1844) at 231–7, arts 9, 22.

303 Rose, "Parish Apprenticeship," *supra* note 296 at 19.

304 Pushing children into workhouses was (presumably by necessity) somewhat at odds with the tenor of other parts of the *Poor Law Amendment Act 1834* that sought to privatize responsibility for family members; it was, however, consistent with the general emphasis on indoor relief in the Act (albeit as a last resort and subject to the principle of less eligibility). See further chapter 3, part II(B).

305 *Poor Law Amendment Act 1844*, 7 & 8 Vict c 101, s 13.

306 It declared that no child under the age of nine years, and no child who could not read and write his own name, could be bound as an apprentice by the guardians; nor could a child be bound "to a person who is not a housekeeper, or assessed to the poor rate in his own name," or to journeymen, persons working for others, persons under 21, or married women: General Consolidated Order of 24 July 1847, arts 52, 53 in John Frederick Archbold, *The Poor Law, Comprising the Whole of the Law of Settlement, and All the Authorities upon the subject of The Poor Law Generally, brought down to Hilary Term, 1856, with Forms*, 8th ed. (London: Shaw & Sons, 1856) at 534 [Archbold, *The Poor Law* 1856].

children. However, in line with the more general emphasis at this time on families of origin and concerns over maintaining "respectable" homes,[307] there were simply not enough householders willing to take on pauper children,[308] with the result that in this period some 40,000 children were cared for in workhouses.[309] The New Poor Law Board recognized that the workhouse system simply perpetuated the cycle of poverty, in no small part because of the absence of proper education.[310] The remedy, according to the Central Authority, was the establishment of schools specifically for the care and education of pauper children.[311] Some success was had in this endeavour, notably in Manchester,[312] but disagreements over funding and expenditure hampered development. In 1857, the *Industrial Schools Act*[313] empowered the Poor Law Guardians to "contract with the Managers of any Certified Industrial School for the Maintenance and Education of any Pauper Child," thereby providing another alternative to the workhouse.[314] In 1862 the *Poor Law (Certified Schools) Act*[315] conferred power on the guardian of any parish or union[316] to "send any poor Child to any School certified" under the Act.[317] Attendance, however, was not compulsory if it was against the wishes

---

307 See *supra* notes 251–4.

308 See Sidney and Beatrice Webb, *English Poor Law Policy* (London: Longmans, Green, 1910) at 110, referring to the statement of the Norwich Board of Guardians that "Masters will not consent to take into their houses pauper apprentices" [Webb and Webb, *English Poor Law Policy*].

309 *Ibid* at 104. They specifically give the figure 44,989 for 1858: *ibid* note 1.

310 Article 114 of the General Order of 1847 required a minimum of three hours' instruction in reading, writing and arithmetic, every working day: see Archbold, *The Poor Law* 1856, *supra* note 306 at 316. However, according to the Webbs, "No Order required the guardians to appoint a qualified schoolmaster, or, indeed, any teacher at all, or to buy any school-books. Year after year the returns from many unions continue to state 'No teachers workhouse,' without evoking from the Central Authority any compulsory Order." Webb and Webb, *English Poor Law Policy, supra* note 308 at 107.

311 The schools were either formed at a district level, following the *Poor Law (Schools) Act 1848*, 11 & 12 Vict, c 82, or within individual unions: Webb and Webb, *English Poor Law Policy, supra* note 308 at 108.

312 *Ibid* at 108 note 3.

313 20 & 21 Vict, c 48.

314 20 & 21 Vict, c 48, s 21. For analysis of the industrial schooling system in England see Gillian Carol Gear, *Industrial Schools in England 1857–1933: "Moral Hospitals" or "Oppressive Institutions"?* (PhD Dissertation, University of London, 1999) [unpublished].

315 25 & 26 Vict, c 43.

316 Unions were groups of parishes constituted under the 1834 Act.

317 25 & 26 Vict, c 43, s 1.

of the child's parents (or the child if over the age of 14);[318] moreover, the sending of a child to a certified school remained a matter of discretion for the guardians. Thus, while it was the case that during "the period 1847–1871, in the Metropolis and various large towns, the greater number of the boys and girls between five and fourteen were removed from the workhouses to these 'barrack schools' and similar institutions ... in hundreds of unions they remained unaffected by the new policy of the Central Authority, which apparently felt unable to require the boards of guardians to adopt it."[319]

The institutional nature of these barracks schools and particularly the workhouses generated its own counter-movement: boarding-out, which emphasized the importance of family-based, as opposed to institutionalized, care. As early as 1837, the Poor Law Commission "authorized the Clifton guardians to alter their rule requiring orphans to be relieved in the workhouse by adding the proviso, 'unless under special circumstances.'"[320] It was not until the 1860s, though, that "the question of boarding-out as a total principle of child care began to be presented regularly to the Poor Law Board."[321] In 1869, Charles Dickens, in a piece entitled "Little Pauper Boarders," observed that "[a]ccording to the practice generally adopted at the present time, these unfortunates receive the whole of their education within the walls of the workhouse ... the results are not satisfactory."[322] In his view, the "only alternative system appears to be that under which the children are boarded-out with such persons as may be willing to take charge of them and to look after their education."[323] The nature of this alternative was made abundantly clear by the campaigner Florence Hill, who, the following year, penned a lengthy piece in the *Contemporary Review* entitled "The Family System for Workhouse Children."[324] In it, she noted the 56,000 children "living

---

318 25 & 26 Vict, c 43, s 7.

319 Webb and Webb, *English Poor Law Policy, supra* note 308 at 112–13.

320 Michael Horsburgh, "'No Sufficient Security': The Reaction of the Poor Law Authorities to Boarding-Out" (1983) 12:1 *Int Soc Pol* 51 at 60 citing Public Record Office, Letter 7288/37, 5 September 1837; MH 12/4000; PRO, Letter 7599/37, 14 September 1837; MH 12/4000. However, an application by Speilsby Union to permit two orphan children to be boarded out in 1839 was quickly rejected: *ibid* citing PRO, Letter 3483/39, 29 April 1839; MH 12/6797.

321 *Ibid* at 62.

322 Dickens, *supra* note 282 at 301.

323 *Ibid* at 302.

324 Florence Hill, "The Family System for Workhouse Children" (1870) 15 *Contemporary Review* 240.

within the walls of the workhouse or the school,"[325] and observed that the "very uniformity" produced by these institutions "is precisely the opposite condition to that essential to the complete development of the human being."[326] In her view, despite the "best motives" of those advocates of industrial schools, "the training of children demands the thought, experience, and intuitions of a mother, at least, as much as of a father."[327]

In 1870, the year in which compulsory education became part of English law,[328] the Poor Law Board commissioned a report on the Scottish boarding-out system; it was "generally favourable ... [and] observed that the criteria for its success were: the careful selection of foster parents; liberal boarding-out allowances; and supervision by paid officers."[329] A report in the same year on English practices found that 21 unions were using the system. Thus, on 25 November 1870, the Board issued an order "directed to specific urban unions, authorizing boarding-out beyond the bounds of the union, and prescribing the manner of its administration." While this outcome was hardly an official adoption of boarding-out as a national policy, it was the beginning of an official move (in some respects back) to the familialization of child welfare in England.[330] A foster parent was required to sign an undertaking to "bring up the child *as one of his own children*, and provide the child with proper food, lodging, and washing, and endeavor to train the child in habits of truthfulness, obedience, personal cleanliness and industry, as well as in suitable domestic and outdoor work."[331]

Echoing the emphasis on families of origin in the context of traditional apprenticeship, the late nineteenth century also saw a shift away from compulsory removal of children from parents, and a diminution

---

325 *Ibid* at 243, though she also observed that only some 20,000 were orphaned and deserted.

326 *Ibid* at 245.

327 *Ibid* at 246.

328 *Elementary Education Act 1870*, 33 & 34 Vict c 75.

329 Horsburgh, *supra* note 320 at 67–8.

330 See "The Boarding-Out System," *The Examiner and London Review*, 3 December 1870 at 769: "The subject has been under the careful consideration of the Poor-Law Department for some months past, and the result of their labours is contained in an order by which the Boards of Guardians in one hundred and ten Unions and twenty-four populous parishes and townships throughout England, are empowered to place out, beyond their own limits, the pauper children under their charge between the ages of two and ten years."

331 *Ibid* at 770 (emphasis added).

in the perceived role of the state with respect to the private family.[332] According to Marianne Moore, "[t]his trend was reflected in the child protection movement, which began to see the solution to child protection as the promotion of family life, rather than the promotion of industrial schools."[333] Attention therefore shifted to the reformation of troubled family units, rather than their dissolution. Where that objective was impossible, however, and children were removed from their parents (or placed in state care), the focus was similarly family-based. The Poor Law Board, for instance, issued Orders in 1889 which repeated the obligation on a foster parent to "bring up the child as one of his own children."[334] State supervision of families with boarded-out children was also made as minimally invasive as possible to encourage "filial relations" between foster parents and children.[335] Within the schooling system for children in state care, there were also efforts to provide at least some of the benefits of a family-based upbringing by way of "cottage"[336] and "scattered"[337] homes.[338] What is notably absent from these principles and directives is any mention of work: the relation between foster parent and child is quite clearly *not* conceptualized in terms of service or the master-servant relation; it had become, instead, a welfare-based relation based more on the model of parent and child.

By the early twentieth century, "[t]here had been a great increase in the number of children boarded out, both relatively in relation to

---

332 Moore links this shift in state practice to the extension of the franchise and the state's greater awareness "of the effects of its policies and their popularity … [which] led to a more appeasing type of social policy": Marianne Moore, "Social Control or Protection of the Child? The Debates on the Industrial Schools Acts 1857–1894" (2008) 33:4 *J Fam Hist* 359 at 380.

333 *Ibid*.

334 General Boarding of Children in Unions Order, 28 May 1889, in Archbold, *The Poor Law* 1856, *supra* note 306 at 347.

335 Moore, *supra* note 332 at 382.

336 Children were "grouped in bodies of not more than twenty-five or thirty in separate houses on a common ground of considerable acreage … under the supervision, not only of 'house-mothers,' but also of a superintendent of the whole": Webb and Webb, *English Poor Law Policy*, *supra* note 308 at 186.

337 *Ibid* at 186–7: "cottages taken here and there throughout the union, not adjacent to each other, wherein the children live under the care of matrons or foster parents, and whence they attend the public elementary schools."

338 According to the Webbs, by 1906, "the total number of children in 'district or separate schools' was no more than 12,393, whilst in 'cottage and other homes' there were 14,590": *ibid* at 187. For a realistic account of the difficulties for both children and carers in cottage homes see Jean Heywood, *Children in Care: The Development of the Service for the Deprived Child* (London: Routledge & Paul, 1959) at 120–1.

children in care, and absolutely, the figures having risen from 2,799 on the 1st July 1885 to 11,596 on the 1st January, 1914";[339] parish apprenticeship, on the other hand, was a largely moribund institution, though it had not disappeared entirely.[340] Most notably, the *Poor Law Act 1930* made it "the duty of the council of every county and county borough … (c) to set to work or put out as apprentices all children whose parents are not, in the opinion of the council, able to keep and maintain their children …."[341] The final nail in the coffin came with the 1946 *Report of the Care of Children Committee*.[342] Based on empirical investigation into the operation of the boarding-out system, it recommended:

> 21. Boarding out is to be preferred to institutional care for children who are suitable for boarding out wherever entirely satisfactory homes can be found; and a vigorous effort should be made by local authorities to extend the system.
>
> 22. A fresh attempt to secure the necessary foster homes should be made with the aid of appropriate national and local organisations.

Heeding this advice, the *Children Act 1948*[343] stipulated that local authorities were to "discharge their duty to provide accommodation and maintenance for a child in their care" in one of two ways:[344]

---

339 Heywood, *supra* note 338 at 119 citing *Forty-Third Annual Report of the Local Government Board, 1913–14*. Part I – Administration of the Poor Law, the Unemployed Workmen Act, and the Old Age Pensions Acts (1914) App at 78 ff.

340 In the Webbs' *English Poor Law Policy*, *supra* note 308, within a chapter devoted to the powers of local government boards, one finds a brief discussion of parish apprenticeship alongside a more comprehensive treatment of boarding out and poor law schools. John Clarke's *Social Administration Including the Poor Laws* (London, Pitman, 1922) included a chapter on "Children under the Poor Law," in which apprenticeship was given last place in a consideration of workhouses, schools, emigration, and boarding out.

341 *Poor Law Act 1930*, 20 & 21 Geo V, c 17, s 15.

342 Care of Children Committee, *Report of the Care of Children Committee* (London: HM Stationary Office, 1946). The 1946 report followed on the heels of the 1945 *Report on the Circumstances which led to the Boarding-out of Dennis and Terence O'Neill at Bank Farm, Minsterly, and the Steps Taken to Supervise their Welfare*, which investigated the death of a foster child and "called not for less but for better fostering": Robert Holman, "The Place of Fostering in Social Work" (1975) 5:1 *Brit J Soc Work* 3 at 3.

343 11 & 12 Geo VI, c 43.

344 From that time, then, all boarding was to be pursuant to the *Children Act 1948*: UK, HL Deb, 16 March 1848, vol 154, col 846 (Lord Chancellor). For discussion of the Act's passage, and its clear preference for boarding out over institutional care, see Stephen Cretney, *Family Law in the Twentieth Century: A History* (Oxford: Oxford University Press, 2003) at 682.

1. by boarding him out on such terms as to payment by the authority and otherwise as the authority may, subject to the provisions of this Act and regulations thereunder, determine; or
2. where it is not practicable or desirable for the time being to make arrangements for boarding-out, by maintaining the child in a home provided under this Part of this Act or by placing him in a voluntary home the managers of which are willing to receive him.

Boarding-out had thus become the default position for children in need of care; failing that, a child was to be placed in state care facilities run along family lines.[345]

The process of change described here suggests a genealogical connection between early modern parish apprenticeship and the more recent system of boarding-out or foster care (which may in turn be connected to aspects of statutory adoption, which emerged in the early twentieth-century[346]). In a broader context, this transition formed part of the breakdown of the household along family/work lines. Parish apprenticeship in the eighteenth century was ultimately a service relation operating within the ambit of master-servant law, but an indispensable aspect of this relation was, perhaps in theory more than in practice, the provision of familial care. Under the weight of nineteenth century concerns with families of origin and respectability, the related repeal of laws obliging masters to take on poor children as apprentices, and the growth in industrial manufacturing, the method for dealing with these children was itself reconceived in distinctly industrial terms: factory "apprenticeship" and, when the costs of feeding and housing such children became clear to factory owners, institutionalized state care. Later, under the influence of Victorian family ideology, the growing emphasis on the child as a legal figure requiring protection,[347] and the early twentieth

---

345 According to Holman, the decade following the *Children Act 1948* saw widespread acceptance of boarding-out owing in part to "the popularization of Bowlby's thesis that children required above all else a close relationship with a parent figure along with the realization that fostering was cheaper than institutional care": Holman, *supra* note 342 at 4. The 1960s saw something of a reassessment of fostering in light of "what was considered a high breakdown rate amongst fosterings," though "it was still accepted as a humane and desirable form of child care" and by the mid-1970s it was "a major means of caring for children": *ibid* at 4–5.
346 *Adoption of Children Act 1926*, 16 & 17 Geo V, c 29. See further Heywood, *supra* note 338 at 116–17.
347 See Moore, *supra* note 332. See generally Philippe Ariès, *Centuries of Childhood: A Social History of Family Life*, translated by Robert Baldick (New York: Vintage Books, 1962).

century's emphasis on "the social,"[348] boarding out came to be seen as the preferable mode of caring for needy children. It was a reversion of sorts to the earlier family-based model of care seen in apprenticeship,[349] but in an intensified form, shorn of its roots in service and based instead on an idea of the private family, not the productive household.

IV. Conclusion

This chapter has shown how the extension of the domestic service model to waged workers (traced in chapter 3) was matched by an equivalent retreat in the regulation of domestic workers. The logic underpinning these different moves was, however, consistent, amounting to an extension of the master's formerly household-based authority over his family (in the older sense of the word) via increased legal control over workers who were less physically tethered to the household/home, and a complementary absence of control over the actions of masters with respect to those who remained within the household/home. In other words, patriarchal control over workers lived on in new, and possibly more complete, ways. This measure of control applied not only to paid domestic workers but also, through a series of legal and ideological factors, to wives, whose former productive contributions to the household were compromised and subsequently reimagined as unproductive forms of domesticity, and whose opportunities for paid employment outside of the home were progressively narrowed over the course of the nineteenth century. In this respect, the chapter sheds light on some of the legal moves that helped to reconstitute the household (and patriarchy) along gender-based family/market lines.

From another angle, the chapter's consideration of apprenticeship illustrates one of the ways that the integration of youth within the productive household also shifted under the weight of the move towards non-family-based forms of work, and a corresponding emphasis on families as sites of emotional nurturing rather than economic production. Reflecting the broad lines of disarticulation traced in this work as

---

348 Duncan Kennedy, "Three Globalizations of Law and Legal Thought" in David M. Trubek & Alvaro Santos, eds., *The New Law and Economic Development: A Critical Appraisal* (New York: Cambridge University Press, 2006) 27.

349 Unfortunately, as with parish apprenticeship, not all foster children experienced desired standards of care. For a relatively recent analysis of abuse in foster and children's homes in one area of England see Georgina F. Hobbs, Christopher J. Hobbs, and Jane M. Wynne, "Abuse of Children in Foster and Residential Care" (1999) 23:12 *Child Abuse & Neglect* 1239.

a whole, it showed how traditional apprenticeship transformed from a paradigmatically familial work relation into an unusual but nonetheless clearly employment-based relation exterior to the private family. It then demonstrated how, in a parallel process, parish apprenticeship eventually shed its connection to the world of work, becoming instead the precursor to modern forms of fostering – a mode of state-administered care conceptualized within legal thought as firmly within the sphere of welfare and family law.

Chapter Five

Legislating Marriage

When one wants to obtain something from the population concerning sexual behavior, demography, the birth rate, or consumption, then one has to utilize the family. The Family will change from being a model to being an instrument; it will become a privileged instrument for the government of the population.[1]

I. Introduction

The eighteenth century saw the beginning of the end of the productive household and the appearance, instead, of the family in its modern (now traditional) form. As the master-servant relation was progressively disarticulated from the household, the relation of husband and wife became, in Carole Pateman's words, "constitutive of domestic relations."[2] Indeed, the wellbeing of England herself came to be seen as intimately connected to "the conjugal state of the population" because, in the words of the Registrar-General for the 1851 Census, "[m]arriage is generally the origin of the elementary community of which larger communities … and ultimately the nation are constituted."[3] Chapter 2 traced this process on a taxonomical level within scholarly legal thought. In particular, it showed how the creation of the field of Family

---

1 Michel Foucault, *Security, Territory, Population. Lectures at the Collège de France, 1977–1978*, edited by Michel Senellart, translated by Graham Burchell (New York: Vintage, 2007) at 105.

2 Carole Pateman, *The Sexual Contract* (Palo Alto: Stanford University Press, 1988) at 116.

3 Registrar General, "Introduction to the Census" (1851) in Leonore Davidoff and Catherine Hall, *Family Fortunes: Men and Women of the English Middle Class 1780–1850*, revised ed. (London: Routledge, 2002) at 321. See also C.J. Bunyon, *A Profitable Book Upon Domestic Law* (London: Longmans, Green, and Co, 1875) at 47.

Law occurred through a legal-conceptual distinction between the family and the market (work), and an elevation of the status-infused marital relation to the core of the domestic relations. Chapters 3 and 4 traced some of the key shifts in the staged process by which work came to occupy an autonomous legal space largely premised on wage labour conducted outside of the home (and women's unpaid labour conducted within the home). This chapter considers how, from a legislative perspective, the family appeared "as an element within the population and as a fundamental relay in its government."[4] No longer a model for political obligation, the family was instead constituted by the English state in the eighteenth- and nineteenth-centuries as an instrumental legal-social unit, partly through legislation that positioned marriage at the core of the private (non-productive) family, and treated the marital relation as a site of national importance and legitimate public concern warranting legal intervention.[5] As Philomila Tsoukala has observed in the European context, "[t]he institutional stakes of consolidating family regulation at the national level were very high since they were related to consolidating the nation-state ... debates for and against the nationalization of family life were aimed at shaping and producing a certain form of homogeneous identity."[6] This legislative emphasis on marriage and the family also involved the extension of patriarchal norms and affirmation of male dominance (in the figure of the husband) within the non-productive, private sphere of the family,[7] along lines paralleling the subordination involved in the extension of the service model to most forms of work.

Part II examines the legislative assertion of state (as opposed to Church) control over marital validity in *Lord Hardwicke's Act 1753*,[8]

---

4 Foucault, *supra* note 1 at 104–5. See further chapter 1, part II(B).

5 This oscillation between public and private created a tension between abstention and intervention on the part of the state. For example, in *Balfour v Balfour* [1919] 2 KB 571, the Court of Appeal impliedly rejected a contractual approach to the marriage relation, finding that an agreement between the spouses concerning payment of money was unenforceable because marriage gave rise to a presumption that there was no common intention to create legal relations. While denying that marriage was, in this respect, a private relation, the Court simultaneously justified its conclusion by constructing the family and the home as "a domain into which the King's writ does not seek to run, and to which his officers do not seek to be admitted."

6 Philomila Tsoukala, "Marrying Family Law to the Nation" (2010) 58:4 *Am J Comp L* 873 at 876.

7 See Christopher L. Tomlins, *Freedom Bound: Law, Labor, and Civic Identity in Colonizing English America, 1580–1865* (New York: Cambridge University Press 2010) at 375.

8 *An Act for the Better Preventing of Clandestine Marriage, 1753*, 26 Geo II, c 33 [*Lord Hardwicke's Act*].

showing how the Act amounted to an assertion of both the public importance of marriage, and its status as a conduit for the dispensation of state benefits. This usurpation of ecclesiastical authority over marriage continued in the nineteenth century with *Lord Lyndhurst's Act 1835*,[9] which rendered the hitherto canonical prohibited degrees of affinity and consanguinity matters of public regulation, and the *Civil Marriage Act 1836*,[10] which dispensed with the requirement that marriages be conducted in Anglican churches.

Part III addresses two specific ways in which nineteenth-century English statute law emphasized the centrality of the marital relation to both state and family by constituting marriage as the fulcrum upon which certain financial rights and obligations were awarded or imposed.[11] In a manner consonant with the idea, central to FLE, that laws cutting across different areas, or which are not conventionally considered as forming part of the law of the family (in its household or nuclear form) have influenced social practices and legal understandings of family in important ways,[12] Part III focusses on provisions in laws dealing with poverty and accident compensation. It begins with the bastardy provisions in the *Poor Law Amendment Act 1834*,[13] which imposed sole financial responsibility for illegitimate children on mothers. Building on the discussion of English Poor Laws in chapter 3, it shows that the illegitimacy provisions in the *Poor Act 1834* were part of a broader effort to channel the population into acceptable forms of private support based on marriage and the family. It also shows, however, that not all marriages were equal in the eyes of the law – part of the motivation for the reform was also to avoid improvident, post-birth marriages based on (male) fear and (female) coercion; marriages that, in the eyes of the Poor Law Commissioners and parliamentarians, undermined the family and weakened the state. The analysis then shifts to legal provisions enabling fatal accident compensation claims on behalf

---

9 *An Act to render certain Marriages valid, and to alter the Law with respect to certain voidable Marriages, 1835*, 5 & 6 Will IV, c 104 [*Lord Lyndhurst's Act*].

10 *An Act for Marriages in England, 1836*, 6 & 7 Will IV, c 135 [*Civil Marriage Act*].

11 As Katherine O'Donovan has noted, "[t]he roles of wife and husband are defined in legislation in which the state is concerned with economic redistribution": Katherine O'Donovan, "Family Law and Legal Theory" in William Twining, ed., *Legal Theory and Common Law* (Oxford: Basil Blackwell, 1986) 184 at 192.

12 See Janet Halley and Kerry Rittich, "Critical Directions in Comparative Family Law: Genealogies and Contemporary Studies of Family Law Exceptionalism" (2010) 58:4 *Am J Comp L* 753.

13 *An Act for the Amendment and better Administration of the Laws relating to the Poor in England and Wales 1834*, 4 & 5 Will IV, c 76 [*Poor Act 1834*].

of family dependents. It shows how the *Fatal Accidents Act 1846*,[14] and subsequent employee-specific legislation, confined recovery to spouses and legitimate children,[15] thereby solidifying the legal understanding of marriage as the core relation within the family, and its status as an integral component in state efforts to manage the population.

Part IV addresses the English state's most significant nineteenth century interventions in marriage law: the introduction of judicial divorce via the *Matrimonial Causes Act 1857*,[16] and the conferral of (some) legislative protection over married women's property via the *Married Women's Property Acts* of 1870 and 1882.[17] Until relatively recently, divorce reform tended to be read as "part of the judicial reform movement which culminated in the Judicature Act of 1873,"[18] and analysis of the debates in Parliament focussed heavily on the religious questions that so vexed many in both the Houses of Commons and Lords;[19] while reform of the law concerning married women's property tended to be analysed in terms of its technical inadequacies.[20] More recent feminist readings of the *Matrimonial Causes Act* and the *Married Women's Property Acts* have highlighted both the crucial role that women played in advocating

---

14 *An Act for compensating the Families of Persons killed by Accidents*, 1846, 9 & 10 Vict c 93 [*Fatal Accidents Act*].

15 Though illegitimate dependent children were brought within the scope of workmen's compensation laws passed in the early twentieth century: see *infra* part III(B).

16 *An Act to amend the Law relating to Divorce and Matrimonial Causes in England*, 1857, 20 & 21 Vict c 85 [*Matrimonial Causes Act*].

17 *Married Women's Property Act, 1870*, 33 & 34 Vict, c 93; *Married Women's Property Act, 1882*, 45 & 46 Vict, c 75.

18 Mary Lyndon Shanley, "'One Must Ride Behind': Married Women's Rights and the Divorce Act of 1857" (1982) 25:3 *Vict Stud* 355 at 355, noting that "most scholars have discussed the Divorce Act as part of the judicial reform movement which culminated in the Judicature Act of 1873" [Shanley, "One Must Ride Behind"]. See also Mary Lyndon Shanley, *Feminism, Marriage, and the Law in Victorian England, 1850–1895* (Princeton NJ: Princeton University Press, 1989) at 47, noting that the *Matrimonial Causes Act* is "[u]sually hailed in histories of English jurisprudence as a watershed statute that created both the action for civil divorce and the new Court of Divorce" [Shanley, *Feminism, Marriage and the Law*].

19 Margaret K. Woodhouse, "The Marriage and Divorce Bill of 1857" (1959) 3:3 *Am J Leg Hist* 260.

20 See A.V. Dicey, *Lectures on the Relation Between Law & Public Opinion in England During the Nineteenth Century* (London: Macmillan, 1905) at 369–93; Otto Kahn-Freund, "Inconsistencies and Injustices in the Law of Husband and Wife" (1952) 15:2 *Mod L Rev* 183; Otto Kahn-Freund, "Matrimonial Property – Some Recent Developments" (1959) 22:3 *Mod L Rev* 241 [Kahn-Freund, "Matrimonial Property"]; Otto Kahn-Freund, "Recent Legislation on Matrimonial Property" (1970) 33:6 *Mod L Rev* 601.

for reform, and the deeply patriarchal terms upon which those reforms were granted.[21] Alongside these orthodox and feminist interpretations, part III shows that the *Matrimonial Causes Act* and the *Married Women's Property Acts* also advanced a deeply conservative and regulatory understanding of marriage:[22] part of the rationale for the enactment of these laws was the perceived national interest in weeding out "bad" marriages and stabilizing family life by conferring a limited measure of financial autonomy on poorer women; while the models chosen for each reform effectively extended state control over family life by constituting entirely new regimes of family regulation that required parties to seek judicial permission to dissolve their unions, and treated married women's entitlement to personal interests in property as a form of statutory largesse.

II. Civilizing Marriage

A. *Lord Hardwicke's Act*

Beginning in the twelfth century, and for around 600 years thereafter, the Church exercised exclusive legal jurisdiction over marriage in England.[23] That position changed in the mid-eighteenth century with the

21 Shanley, *Feminism, Marriage and the Law*, *supra* note 18; Shanley, "One Must Ride Behind," *supra* note 18; Mary Lyndon Shanley, "Suffrage, Protective Labor Legislation, and Married Women's Property Laws in England" (1986) 12:1 *Signs* 62 [Shanley, "Married Women's Property"]; Rebecca Probert, "The Double Standard of Morality in the Divorce and Matrimonial Causes Act 1857" (1999) 28 *Anglo-Am L Rev* 73 [Probert, "Double Standard"]; Lee Holcombe, *Wives & Property: Reform of the Married Women's Property Law in Nineteenth-Century England* (Toronto: University of Toronto Press, 1983).

22 Stephen Cretney has observed that the objective of the *Matrimonial Causes Act* was "to promote reverence for the nuptial tie": Stephen Cretney, *Family Law in the Twentieth Century: A History* (Oxford: Oxford University Press, 2003) at 166. However, Cretney's analysis of this aspect focusses more heavily on the ways that courts interpreted the new law in the years following its passage; my concern in this section is to show how parliamentary discourse advanced this idea.

23 Frederick Pollock and Frederic William Maitland, *The History of English Law Before the Time of Edward I* (Cambridge: Cambridge University Press, 1895) vol 2 at 367. See also George Elliott Howard, *A History of Matrimonial Institutions Chiefly in England and the United States with an Introductory Analysis of the Literature and the Theories of Primitive Marriage and the Family* (Chicago: University of Chicago Press, 1904) at 333 (noting that "[i]n England between the seventh and the twelfth centuries the ecclesiastical authority in matrimonial questions was slowly established"). There was a brief period of civil marriage during the Interregnum, but jurisdiction reverted back to the Church after the Restoration: *ibid* at 418–35.

passage of *Lord Hardwicke's Act*, which asserted civil jurisdiction over questions of marital validity. While *Lord Hardwicke's Act* was, at least according to its own terms, passed to counter "Mischiefs and Inconveniencies [that] have arisen from Clandestine Marriages,"[24] it marked the beginning of a much broader trend in English law and policy towards situating marriage as a relation of public and indeed national significance[25] warranting state oversight, and amounting to a critical lever for the exercise of governmental power.[26]

Under canon law, the consent of both spouses was the essence of and fundamental criterion for marriage.[27] Accordingly, a binding marriage could be created by a verbal exchange of vows between a man and a woman, expressed in the present tense (*sponsalia per verba de praesenti*).[28] Promises to marry could also be made in the future tense (*sponsalia per verba de futuro, repromissio futurarum nuptiarum*), but such promises were only treated as binding if consummated. Private marriages of this sort

---

24 26 Geo II, c 33, s 1. Commentators have proposed a variety of reasons for why the Act was passed, including the expansion of bourgeois notions of respectable behaviour, self-interest on the part of elites concerned to protect their children and their property, judicial displeasure at the haphazard state of affairs arising out of clandestine marriage practices, the sheer determination of Lord Hardwicke to bring about reform, and the 1753 case of *Cochrane v Campbell* (Paton's *Reports of Cases decided in the House of Lords on Appeal from Scotland*, I (1726–57) at 519–32), which concerned the validity of a Scottish marriage of some 30 years duration in the face of an alleged prior contract (on this latter point see Howard, *supra* note 23 at 448). As Rebecca Probert has pointed out, these explanations are capable of coexisting, and support for each position can be found in the parliamentary debates that resulted in the bill's passage into law. Rebecca Probert, *Marriage Law and Practice in the Long Eighteenth Century* (Cambridge: Cambridge University Press, 2009) at 211–12 [Probert, *Marriage Law*]. In any event, I am much less concerned with the reasons for why the Act was passed than with its effect in constituting marriage as a legal relation governed by state law.

25 This is not to suggest that it was the first time that the English state had used the law to influence marriage practices. In 1556, for example, the age of 24 was fixed as the earliest possible point for termination of apprenticeships in London. This was extended to all cities and corporate towns by the *Statute of Artificers, 1562*, 5 Eliz c 4, as part of a deliberate strategy to check "ouer hastie maryages and over sone setting upp of householdes of an by the youthe": Ralph A. Houlbrooke, *The English Family, 1450–1700* (Harlow: Longman Group, 1984) at 67.

26 Foucault, *supra* note 1 at 103–5; discussed in chapter 1, part II(B).

27 This position appears to have been "almost universally accepted by canonists after the late 1180s as the critical test of whether a marriage existed or not": Probert, *Marriage Law, supra* note 24 at 23 quoting James A. Brundage, *Law, Sex, and Christian Society in Medieval Europe* (Chicago: University of Chicago Press, 1987) at 268–9. See also Howard, *supra* note 23 at 336–9.

28 Probert, *Marriage Law, supra* note 24 at 26.

were considered immediately *binding* in the eyes of God, but in the temporal realm (including the Spiritual Courts), the difficulties associated with proof quickly led to the enactment of canon laws "stressing that marriages should be celebrated with a due formality which allowed the public expression of that consent, precisely to avoid the problems that might ensue from a private exchange of consent."[29] The ecclesiastical and common law courts also made it clear that an alleged private exchange of words was unlikely to be considered satisfactory in cases concerning, respectively, matrimonial causes and property interests.[30] According to Rebecca Probert: "[T]he need to operate a workable legal system meant that the canonists' theory that a marriage was made by consent was heavily modified in practice by the requirement that such consent be proved to the satisfaction of the court that a contract *per verba de praesenti* could be enforced. Hasty words breathed in a moment of private passion might create a marriage "in the eyes of God" but if either reneged on the contract it would be impossible to prove it as a matter of law."[31] Despite the canonical position on consent, then, the reality for anyone concerned about property or legal enforcement of

---

29 *Ibid* at 23–4. Until 1753 it was possible under canon law for a party who believed a promise of marriage to have been made to seek to have the marriage confirmed by a decree for specific performance in the ecclesiastical courts. For promises *per verba de praesenti*, the parties were required to celebrate the marriage *in facie ecclesiae* (i.e., before the parties' congregation in Church), default of which could lead to admonition, excommunication, or imprisonment. Breach of a promise *per verba futuro* did not give rise to an order for excommunication unless consummation had taken place, though the party in breach was still made to suffer penance: *ibid* at 35–36. See also Edward Manson, "Breach of Promise of Marriage" (1910) 11:1 *J Soc Comp Leg* 156 at 158 referring to Swinburne, Sponsals [*sic.*] 1, 17 (see Henry Swinburne, *A Treatise of Spousals, or Matrimonial Contracts: Wherein All the Questions relating to that Subject are ingeniously Debated and Resolved* (London, 1686)). For a study of early cases compelling performance see R.H. Helmholtz, *Marriage Litigation in Medieval England* (New York: Cambridge University Press, 1974), chapter 2. For discussion of cases post-1753 in which the remedy sought was damages not performance see chapter 6 herein.

30 Probert, *Marriage Law, supra* note 24 at 42. There was no issue if both parties agreed that there had been mutual promises to marry. Few cases, however, were so simple: *ibid* at 28. On medieval recognition of marriages performed *in facie ecclesiae* by common law courts, as opposed to a private contract without a ceremony, see Frederick Pollock and Frederic William Maitland, *The History of English Law Before the Time of Edward I* (Cambridge: Cambridge University Press, 1895), vol. II at 378.

31 *Ibid* at 34. See also *Lindo v Belisario* (1795) 1 Hag Con 216. On problems of proof see Lawrence Stone, *Road to Divorce: England 1530–1987* (New York: Oxford University Press, 1990) at 72–75. The idea that solemnization *in facie ecclesiae* was a requirement of English marriage law prior to *Lord Hardwicke's Act* was narrowly (and controversially) approved by the House of Lords in *R v Millis* (1844) 10 Cl &

marital rights was that solemnization in Church, following the reading of banns or the procuring of a marriage license from a church official, was strongly advisable.[32] As one commentator put it: "The common law does not esteem a Couple who are betroth'd or espous'd, even by Words of present Time, to be so far Man and Wife, as to give either Party any Interest or Property in the other's Lands or Goods, or to Legitimate their Issue, until the Marriage be solemniz'd according to the Rites of the Church of England."[33]

These canonical and common law requirements meant that most marriages prior to the passage of *Lord Hardwicke's Act* were conducted in accordance with the procedures preferred by both church and state.[34] A significant minority of people,[35] however, engaged in clandestine forms of marriage for reasons of privacy, expense, or a combination thereof.[36] Typically, a clandestine marriage was performed before witnesses by a clergyman using the prescribed language in the Book of Common Prayer, and the marriage was entered into some sort of marriage register; however, it took place outside of the parish church of one of the spouses, and without the calling of banns.[37] Instead, members of the clergy issued marriage licenses, obtained in blank form from bishops' registrars, to couples (at a profit);[38] or, as with the infamous Fleet

---

F 534. See further Rebecca Probert, "R v Millis Reconsidered: Binding Contracts and Bigamous Marriages" (2008) 28:3 *Legal Studies* 337.

32 See Helmholtz, *supra* note 29 at 29–31; Howard, *supra* note 23 at 380.

33 T. Salmon, *A Critical Essay concerning Marriage* (London, 1724) at 180, quoted in Probert, *Marriage Law, supra* note 24 at 41–2.

34 Probert, *Marriage Law, supra* note 24 at 46–59. See also her critique of previous efforts to paint a more disorderly image of English marriage practices prior to 1753: *ibid*, chapter 1.

35 *Ibid* at 206, noting "that although clandestine marriages were common, most differed little from regular marriages." See Stone, *supra* note 31 at 107 for figures on clandestine marriages in London.

36 According to John Gillis, "it was the privacy rather than the savings that made clandestine marriage so attractive. Widows and widowers making second marriages against the wishes of family preferred the secrecy. So too did couples disparate in age or social station … Sailors on short leave, persons marrying within the prohibited degrees, widows wanting to retain their jointures, and pregnant women near to their time all found clandestine wedding advantageous." John R. Gillis, *For Better, For Worse: British Marriages, 1600 to the Present* (New York: Oxford University Press, 1985) at 96.

37 R.B. Outhwaite, *Clandestine Marriage in England, 1500–1850* (London: Hambledon Press, 1995) at 22–3; Stone, *supra* note 31 at 97; Howard, *supra* note 23 at 349.

38 Stone, *supra* note 31 at 102, 106–7.

marriages, conducted the marriage without any license at all.[39] Despite these abnormalities, clandestine marriages were, at least in principle,[40] recognized as valid under canon and common law[41] – and it seems that "the scale of clandestineness from the late sixteenth century onwards was unprecedented."[42] According to Lawrence Stone, in the decade prior to the passage of *Lord Hardwicke's Act*, "as many as 6,600 marriages a year were being conducted within the Rules of the Fleet, out of a total in all England of about 47,000."[43]

According to certain historians, most notably John Gillis, R.B. Outhwaite and Stephen Parker, marriage was, for at least some communities in England and Wales in the sixteenth and seventeenth centuries, less "an individualized legal procedure, a matter between the couple and the constituted authorities of church or state" and more "a social drama involving family, peers, and neighbors in a collective process aimed at making things right economically, social, and psychologically, as well as legally."[44] Proof of marriage, or at least betrothal, did not therefore necessarily have to come in the form of church solemnization, or even involve a priest, but could be in the form of handfasting and trothplights[45] – essentially public forms of betrothal, witnessed perhaps by a couple's neighbours, peers and/or family members, but without the intervention or presence of the church and its representatives. The parties to these agreements did not necessarily consider them equivalent to regular forms of marriage performed according to

---

39 Outhwaite, *supra* note 37 at 26–9. See Stone, *supra* note 31 at 109 for a discussion of the regulatory shifts that occurred with respect to the Fleet in the late seventeenth and early eighteenth centuries.

40 The poor quality of the records kept by many clergy could lead to rejection of the validity of a clandestine marriage. For example, it seems that in the 1730s judges at the Old Bailey "began to reject Fleet registers as evidence for or against the frequent charges of bigamy in which they figured": Stone, *supra* note 31 at 115–16. In contrast, "the ecclesiastical courts were tending to accept the legality of clandestine marriages on the basis of evidence so flimsy that it would not have been accepted in any secular court": *ibid* at 117.

41 *Ibid* at 98. See also Katherine O'Donovan, *Sexual Divisions in Law* (London: Weidenfeld and Nicolson, 1985) at 45–6 [O'Donovan, *Sexual Divisions*].

42 Gillis, *supra* note 36 at 92.

43 Stone, *supra* note 31 at 115.

44 Gillis, *supra* note 36 at 17. See also Stephen Parker, *Informal Marriage, Cohabitation, and the Law, 1750–1989* (New York: St Martin's Press, 1990). For criticism of these and other authors on this point see Probert, *Marriage Law, supra* note 24, chapter 2. For an argument that Probert appears unwilling to recognize the possibility that social opprobrium, or indeed tolerance, might result in historical silence see Craig Lind, "The Truth of Unmarried Cohabitation and the Significance of History" (2014) 77:4 *Mod L Rev* 641.

45 Outhwaite, *supra* note 37 at 21–2.

the rites of the Church of England (which, along with the English state, certainly did *not* accord these rites an equivalent status to marriage *in facie ecclesiae*[46]), but they were also more than private declarations of love (or acceptance),[47] and functioned as important ceremonial rites at a community level.[48]

Lord Hardwicke's Act intervened in this state of affairs by imposing *civil* requirements for the making of a valid marriage. As Probert has noted, the new law did not differ dramatically from the requirements under canon law when account is made for the Church's clear preference for marriage *in facie ecclesiae*, and the higher legal status of solemnized marriages under both ecclesiastical and common law.[49] Still, it is important to understand what it actually said. Under the terms of the Act, a legally valid marriage was one preceded by banns published in a church "of or belonging to such Parish or Chapelry wherein the Persons to be married shall dwell," or where the parties had obtained a licence from the Church belonging to the Parish in which "one of the Persons to be married shall have been for the Space of four Weeks immediately before the granting of such Licence."[50] Deviation from this requirement rendered a marriage void.[51] Persons under the age of 21, if marrying by licence, had to obtain parental consent; if marrying by banns, the absence of parental objection was sufficient.[52] In addition, the ecclesiastical courts were stripped of their authority to compel solemnization based on promises of marriage.[53] In one important respect, though, the

---

46 Probert, *Marriage Law, supra* note 24, chapter 2.

47 Outhwaite, *supra* note 37 at 21–2.

48 O'Donovan, *Sexual Divisions, supra* note 41 at 49.

49 Probert, *Marriage Law, supra* note 24 at 220.

50 26 Geo II, c 33, ss 1, 4. These formalities were not new: banns had been required since the twelfth century and licenses were introduced in the sixteenth century: *ibid* at 222.

51 26 Geo II, c 33, s 8 stated that "all Marriages solemnized ... without Publication of Banns, or Licence of Marriage from a Person or Persons having Authority to grant the same first had and obtained shall be null and void to all Intents and Purposes whatsoever." Failure to comply with formalities prior to 1753 did not render a marriage void or voidable, though a marriage conducted after the making of an earlier marriage contract (which did not itself infringe the prohibited degrees set out in the Succession Acts passed during the reign of Henry VIII) did render the marriage voidable: *ibid* at 39. The force of section 8 of *Lord Hardwicke's Act* was diminished by section 10, which provided that a marriage could not be rendered invalid on the basis that the parties had not truthfully resided in the place where banns had been called or where the marriage was solemnized: *ibid* at 224.

52 26 Geo II, c 33, ss 3 and 11.

53 26 Geo II, c 33, s 13. As chapter 6 shows, this feature of the Act contributed to the nineteenth century popularity of the money-based action for breach of promise to marry.

Act limited its own effectiveness by confining its operation to England and Wales[54] – it remained entirely possible, therefore, for parties to cross the border into Scotland and marry according to the law in force there, which continued to recognize marriage by private consent alone.[55]

It is debatable just how important these changes were in their effect on the incidence and conduct of marriages in England.[56] However, it is suggested here that the real significance of *Lord Hardwicke's Act* was as much to do with the shift in authority from the (Anglican) Church to the state as it was with the question of void versus inchoate or imperfectly solemnized marriages.[57] In this respect, one may agree with Probert's exacting analysis of the situation prior to and in after the passage of *Lord Hardwicke's Act*, and her claim that "there was general continuity between the canon law and the new statutory requirements," without also following her in downplaying "the bureaucratic elements" of the Act.[58] The law in its details had not changed dramatically, and the Church certainly remained involved in marriage solemnization, but the Act asserted the primacy of the British state in questions concerning marital validity,[59] and marriage was rendered a "religious rite capable of being deployed by the British state for the extension of its administrative power."[60] In this respect, *Lord Hardwicke's Act* both constituted and paved the way for future development of the legal idea of marriage as a private relation of significant public importance. It would remain "civil," as William Blackstone had declared in his *Commentaries*

---

54 26 Geo II, c 33, s 18.

55 See chapter 6.

56 Probert, *Marriage Law, supra* note 24 at 220–4.

57 As Christopher Flint has argued, the Act "appears to mark a change in conception … from regarding matrimony (and therefore family) as a private spiritual sacrament to a public event inseparable from secular political activities": Christopher Flint, *Family Fictions: Narrative and Domestic Relations in Britain, 1866–1798* (Palo Alto: Stanford University Press, 1998) at 54. See also Janet Halley, "What Is Family Law? A Genealogy. Part I" (2011) 23:1 *Yale JL & Human* 1 at 10.

58 Probert, *Marriage Law, supra* note 24 at 220.

59 The ecclesiastical courts did, however, retain jurisdiction over disputes concerning the validity of marriage and applications for dissolution, though questions concerning custody (and breaches of promise to marry) were the province of the common law courts, and occasionally the Court of Chancery. It was only with the passage of the *Matrimonial Causes Act* that ecclesiastical jurisdiction over marriage was shifted into the newly created Court of Divorce and Matrimonial Causes. See Stephen Waddams, "English Matrimonial Law on the Eve of Reform (1828–57)" (2000) 21:2 *J Leg Hist* 59.

60 Lisa O'Connell, "'By Ordinance of Nature': Marriage, Religion and the Modern English State" (2011) 28:2 *Parergon* 149 at 154.

on the Laws of England[61] (and became increasingly so through further legislative interventions in the nineteenth century[62]), but marriage also became imbued with a degree of national importance and state oversight that would, in the nineteenth century, lead judges and scholars to complicate Blackstone's further description of marriage as a contract which "the law treats as it does all other contracts."[63]

B. Lord Lyndhurst's Act

In 1835, *Lord Lyndhurst's Act*[64] was passed (apparently[65]) to correct what was perceived to be an "unreasonable" measure of uncertainty occasioned by the canonical position that marriages within the prohibited degrees of affinity were "voidable only by Sentence of the Ecclesiastical Court pronounced during the Lifetime of both the Parties thereto."[66] That position was derived from the *Succession to the Crown Act 1533*,[67] which fixed the degrees of affinity and consanguinity, and provided that a separation "from the Bonds of such unlawful Marriage … shall be good, lawful, firm and permanent for ever."[68] Due to Henry VIII's ongoing nuptial difficulties, however, the Act ultimately "set in motion a bewildering sequence of statutory changes in prohibited relationships," culminating in Archbishop Parker's Admonition to All Such as Intend to Marry, "which included a table of prohibited relationships that was

---

61 William Blackstone, *Commentaries on the Laws of England*, 4 vols (Oxford: Clarendon Press, 1765–9), book 1 at 421.

62 See *infra* parts II(B) and (C).

63 Blackstone, *supra* note 61, book I at 421. See chapters 2 and 6 herein on, respectively, the scholarly and judicial dimensions of this process.

64 5 & 6 Will VI, c 54.

65 According to Nancy F. Anderson, "The 'Marriage with a Deceased Wife's Sister Bill' Controversy: Incest Anxiety and the Defense of Family Purity in Victorian England" (1982) 21:2 *J Brit Stud* 67 at 67, the impetus for Lyndhurst's action on the matter was his concern to ensure the legitimacy and inheritance of the son of the seventh Duke of Beaufort, who had married his deceased wife's half-sister.

66 5 & 6 Will IV, c 54, Preamble.

67 25 Hen VIII, c 22, ss 3 and 4. See also *Succession to the Crown Act 1536*, 28 Hen VIII, c 7, ss 9 and 10.

68 25 Hen VIII, c 22, s 4. The *Marriage Act 1540*, 32 Hen VIII, c 38, built upon 25 Hen VIII, c 22 (1533) (and following laws) by invalidating any claim of voidability. In other words, only the degrees countenanced under the 1533 Act (and its subsequent iterations in the tumultuous 1530s, when Henry VIII's marriage were, to put it mildly, in flux) rendered a marriage voidable. The 1540 Act was repealed by the *Marriages (Pre-Contract) Act 1548*, 2 & 3 Edward VI, c 23. See Outhwaite, *supra* note 37 at 19. Perhaps out of abundant caution, the 1540 Act was also repealed some 400 years later by the *Marriage Act 1949*, c 76, Sch 5.

ordered to be displayed in 1563 in parish churches throughout the realm."[69] Settling the prohibited degrees was only part of the issue, though. The problem of the liminal nature of marriages that infringed the prohibited degrees remained: as long as nobody objected to the match in ecclesiastical court the union was valid and, perhaps most importantly, children born of the marriage were legitimate. This validity of marriage and birth could, however, be instantly stripped away by a decree from the church courts that a couple was within the prohibited degrees. Lord Lyndhurst therefore proposed to eradicate this legal uncertainty created by the merely voidable nature of marriages that infringed the prohibited degrees, and Parliament readily agreed, passing an Act that simultaneously declared valid all marriages made in contravention of the prohibited degrees prior to 31 August 1835; and rendering absolutely *void* all future marriages that transgressed the prohibited degrees.

While *Lord Lyndhurst's Act* is most often associated with the ensuing 70-year debate in England over the desirability of preventing marriage between a man and his deceased wife's sister,[70] it should also be seen as a more general continuation of the project begun via *Lord Hardwicke's Act*. In operational terms the two Acts were in fact quite similar; each took an existing body of canon law and practice (albeit in the case of prohibited degrees an area subject to much state meddling under Henry VIII), transformed it into municipal law, and extended the consequences for contravention of those provisions. But the real significance of *Lord Lyndhurst's Act*, like *Lord Hardwicke's Act*, was its further assertion of state control over the validity of English marriages. For roughly 300 years the affinity issue had operated along the lines eventually established under Henry VIII. By the eighteenth and nineteenth centuries, though, relations between husbands and wives were being legislatively transformed into matters of public concern, and one important dimension of this state control was the moral (and financial) dimensions of marriage. This is made particularly clear in the mid-nineteenth century case of *Brook v*

---

69 Outhwaite, *supra* note 37 at 6.

70 See Anderson, *supra* note 65; Bramwell, "Marriage with a Deceased Wife's Sister," *The Nineteenth Century: A Monthly Review* (September 1886) 403; David G. Barrie, *Sin, Sanctity and the Sister-in-Law: Marriage with a Deceased Wife's Sister in the Nineteenth Century* (Abingdon: Routledge, 2018); Angela Fernandez, "An Important Debate in Nineteenth-Century America: May a Man Marry his Deceased Wife's Sister?" (unpublished, on file with author).

Brook,[71] which arose out of *Lord Lyndhurst's Act's* prohibition on marrying one's sister-in-law. The case is discussed in detail in chapter 6, but in essence the House of Lords held that a marriage between English subjects that transgressed the prohibited degrees was void even if the marriage was conducted in a jurisdiction that permitted such marriages (in this case Denmark), and in accordance with the formal requirements of that place. In other words, England's national interest in the marriages of persons domiciled within its borders justified the extra-territorial application of the legislative strictures contained in *Lord Lyndhurst's Act*.

C. Civil Marriage Act

The year after *Lord Lyndhurst's Act* was passed saw another important legislative intervention in English marriage law: the *Civil Marriage Act*.[72] While *Lord Hardwicke's Act* had asserted the English state's control over the requirements for a valid marriage, it did so in a manner that otherwise upheld the authority of the Anglican Church by requiring that solemnization take place within the Church of England. That remained the law until 1836, when the *Civil Marriage Act* decreed that marriages could henceforth be solemnized in registered places (churches) or "in the Presence of the Superintendent Registrar and some Registrar of the District, and in the Presence of Two Witnesses";[73] that is, a marriage could be conducted without the involvement of the Church.[74] This option required the giving of notice to the Superintendent Registrar of the district in which each party had resided for the preceding seven days,[75] and the reading of a marriage notice on three separate occasions by the Poor Law Guardians.[76] The Act also made provision for religious minorities, though along different lines. Jews and Quakers had to comply with the civil preliminaries required in cases of purely civil marriage, but aside from that solemnization was a question for their own religious

---

71 (1861) 9 *HLC* 193.

72 6 & 7 Will IV, c 85.

73 6 & 7 Will IV, c 85, s 21.

74 According to George Howard, it was not until the passage of this Act – "the full triumph of civil marriage" – that "the logical results of the new doctrines" promulgated by Martin Luther in the sixteenth century were "at last attained": Howard, *supra* note 23 at 399.

75 6 & 7 Will IV, c 85, s 4.

76 6 & 7 Will IV, c 85, s 6.

authorities.[77] Protestant dissenters and Catholics also had to comply with the civil preliminaries, but solemnization in a religious setting could only take place if the building was registered for that purpose, and a civil registrar had to be present.[78]

The *Civil Marriage Act* was a classically liberal move: in its secularism and pluralism it upheld the primacy of individual conscience and choice; yet it also extended state control over marriage,[79] not only through its stipulations as to validity but also by requiring that records be kept of all marriages conducted in England and Wales.[80] That feature of the Act was part of a sweeping effort to quantify the population. As Lord John Russell explained in debate over the Civil Marriage Bill, it was "important to enable the Government to acquire a general knowledge of the state of the population of the country ... there should be a general registration of births, marriages and deaths."[81] Accordingly, section 23 introduced a requirement that "the Registrar shall forthwith register every Marriage solemnized ... in his Presence in a Marriage Register Book" in accordance with *An Act for registering Births, Deaths, and Marriages in England*,[82] which was passed at the same time as the *Civil Marriage Act*. Section 24 of the *Births, Deaths and Marriages Act* required registrars to provide copies of their Marriage Register Books to the Superintendent Registrar on a quarterly basis. This introduction of statistical measurements of marriage (or at least the raw data upon which such measurements could be conducted) points to an understanding within English law and politics that marriage was a crucial means for regulating the population and implementing state policy – an idea explored further in the next Part.

---

77 6 & 7 Will IV, c 85, s 2.

78 6 & 7 Will IV, c 85, ss 18 and 20.

79 Leonard Shelford expressed a similar sentiment in his *A Practical Treatise of The Law of Marriage and Divorce, and Registration; as altered by the recent statutes; containing also the mode of proceedings on divorces in the Ecclesiastical Courts and in Parliament; the right to the custody of children; voluntary separation between husband and wife; the husband's liability to wife's debts; and the conflict between the laws of England and Scotland respecting divorce and legitimacy* (London: S Sweet, 1841) at 4: "[N]otwithstanding the origin and divine institution of marriage," he declared, "human legislatures have very properly assumed the power of regulating the exercise of the right of marriage, on account of its leading to relations, duties, and consequences, materially affecting the welfare and peace of society."

80 Cretney, *supra* note 22 at 9.

81 UK, HC Deb, 12 February 1836, vol 31, col 368 (Lord Russell) quoted in Probert, *Marriage Law, supra* note 24 at 336.

82 6 & 7 Will IV, c 86 [*Births, Deaths and Marriages Act*].

III. Incentivizing Marriage

A. Poor Laws

In chapter 3 it was shown how the early nineteenth century English state sought to lessen its financial responsibility for the poor by emphasizing personal and familial responsibility, and reducing dependence on parish relief. One crucial feature of the *Poor Act 1834*[83] was the eradication of wage-relief and the extension of the workhouse system of indoor relief – moves that were ultimately designed to channel the working population into wage labour or, in the absence thereof, private forms of support. This section discusses another dimension of this legislative process of privatizing financial responsibility for personal life: the bastardy provisions in the *Poor Act 1834*, which removed unwed mothers' abilities to claim financial support from putative fathers, and capped claims against the parish at the level of support provided to widows. The object of this reform was, obviously, to reduce the number of illegitimate births; at a deeper level, though, this disincentive was designed to encourage women to marry before engaging in sexual activity, thereby increasing the chances that parish support would be unnecessary because, within the prevailing family/market ideology of the time, wives were expected to tend to the family while husbands footed the bill. In this respect, the *Poor Act 1834* was an intended stimulus to social practice and also points towards a legal notion of family centred on the marital relation.[84]

Laws dealing with financial responsibility for illegitimate children had been around for almost 250 years by the time of the *Poor Act 1834*. "Concerning Bastards begotten and born out of lawful Matrimony, (an Offence against God's Law and Man's Law)," the *Poor Act 1575*[85] decried the system under which "the said Bastards being now left to be kept at the Charges of the Parish where they be born, to the great Burden of the same Parish, and in defrauding of the Relief of the impotent and aged true Poor of the same Parish, and to the evil Example of Encouragement of lewd Life."[86] It therefore provided for "the Punishment of

---

83 4 & 5 Will IV, c 76.

84 See further Ariela R. Dubler, "In the Shadow of Marriage: Single Women and the Legal Construction of the Family and the State" (2003) 112:7 *Yale LJ* 1641 (discussing the legal construction of marriage through the treatment of unmarried women, specifically, American widows' rights to dower).

85 18 Eliz, c 3.

86 18 Eliz, c 3, s 2.

the Mother and reputed Father of such Bastard Child ... for the better Relief of every such Parish," and conferred upon Justices of the Peace the discretion to "take Order for the Keeping of every such Bastard Child, by charging such Mother or reputed Father, with the payment of Money weekly or other Sustentation for the Relief of such Child." Persons "making Default in not performing of the said Order" were "to be committed to ward to the common Gaol."[87] The object of the *Poor Act 1575*, to force parents to support their children,[88] seems not to have been realized, judging by the stricter provisions of the *Vagabonds Act 1609*,[89] which provided that any lewd woman whose illegitimate child became chargeable to the parish was to be committed to the house of correction for one year. This fusion of criminal and poor law was eventually dispensed with during the reign of George II, in favour of the system that so concerned the Commissioners in 1834.

In essence, the law prior to the *Poor Act 1834* enabled a Justice to charge a man with financial responsibility for a child based on the mother's declaration that he was the child's father. In his *Treatise of the Laws for the Relief and Settlement of the Poor*, Michael Nolan set out some of the problems with this system:

> It seems that proceedings under this statute may be altogether *ex parte*. No summons need issue to bring the person accused before the justice; and it appears unnecessary that he should be present at the woman's examination. When the reputed father is brought by warrant before the justice, the magistrate has no power to examine into the merits of the case, but is bound by the express terms of the statute to commit him to the common gaol or house of correction, unless he gives security, or enters into a recognizance with sufficient surety.[90]

Procedural injustice against young *men* was part of the problems associated with the old law,[91] but the deeper issue identified by the

---

87 18 Eliz, c 3, s 2.

88 *Poor Law Commissioners' Report of 1834. Copy of the Report Made in 1834 by the Commissioners for Inquiring into the Administration and Practical Operation of the Poor Laws* (London: HM Stationary Office, 1905) at 165 [1834 Poor Law Report].

89 7 Ja I, c 4, s 7.

90 Michael Nolan, *Treatise of the Laws for the Relief and Settlement of the Poor*, 4th ed. (London, 1825) at 288–9, cited in 1834 Poor Law Report, *supra* note 88 at 166.

91 The Commissioners' concern for young men (see especially 1834 Poor Law Report, *supra* note 88 at 167) did not extend to the mothers of illegitimate children, who were constructed as morally derelict schemers. Mr. Simeon, for instance, whose evidence before the House of Lords in 1831 was extracted in the Report, spoke of how "a

Commissioners was how the imposition of financial responsibility on alleged fathers often led to one of two undesirable outcomes: (a) an improvident marriage based on a calculation by a man that it was better to marry a woman than be subject to an order for support; or (b) parish responsibility for the support of an illegitimate child in the event that a man failed to pay the amount ordered (which was generally greater than the amount provided under the Old Poor Law to women with legitimate children) or when no man was able to be fixed with responsibility.

The problem with the first outcome was that it created the wrong sort of families. Reflecting prevailing family ideology,[92] which by this point – at least among the class of men who authored the 1834 Poor Law Report and implemented its recommendations in statutory form – tended to view the family "as a discrete and private social unit" centred on the couple of husband and wife, with an emphasis "on emotion as the prime basis of family relationships,"[93] the 1834 Poor Law Report waxed lyrically on the virtue of marriages based on "affection" and "esteem."[94] Unsurprisingly, then, a marriage based on financial calculation and possible coercion was seen as not being conducive to proper family life. According to the Commissioners: "[A]s soon as he finds that the evil of becoming the father of a bastard is otherwise inevitable, he avoids it by marrying the woman during her pregnancy – a marriage of which we may estimate the consequences, when we consider that it is founded, not on affection, not on esteem, not on the prospect of providing for a family, but on fear on one side, and vice on both."[95] This "prospect of all being cured by a forced marriage" was, in the view of the witness Charles Sawyer, "the most active inducement to incontinence in the female." Women, he said, were induced by the law to act as "corruptor[s]; and boys, much under the age of twenty, are continually converted by this process into husbands."[96] Another witness declared that the law promised to women "if not a pecuniary reward, in many instances, the powerful aid of parish officers in obtaining a husband: they effect, and often by the most shameful practices, *marriages which*

---

woman of dissolute character may pitch upon any unfortunate young man whom she has inveigled into her net": *ibid* at 176.

92 See chapter 1, part II(A).

93 Michael Anderson, *Approaches to the History of the Western Family 1500–1914* (Cambridge: Cambridge University Press, 1995) at 30 [Anderson, *Approaches*].

94 1834 Poor Law Report, *supra* note 88 at 168.

95 *Ibid*.

96 *Ibid* at 173.

ought to have been discountenanced."[97] The Commissioners declared that the existing Bastardy Laws "offer[ed] temptations to the crime which they were intended to punish," and contributed to "domestic misery and vice which are the necessary consequence of premature and ill-assorted marriage."[98] Clearly, not every marriage was a good marriage.

If no marriage took place, either the putative father or the parish was fixed with financial responsibility for mother and child. In the first instance, and setting aside the possible injustice of imposing responsibility on a man who was not a child's father, such an order theoretically met the need of impoverished mothers for financial assistance. However, as one witness put it, "the custom prevails of overseers paying over to the mother of a bastard the sum directed by the order of maintenance, *whether it be recovered from the father or not*, and this comes under the denomination of 'Pay' in pauper language."[99] These sums were also payable if no order had been made against a man. Thus, it was said that "[t]he allowance made to the mother for the support of her child, *and secured to her by the parish in case of the putative father failing to pay the amount awarded*, is an encouragement to the offence."[100] Moreover, "[t]he sum allowed to the mother of a bastard is generally greater than that given to the mother of a legitimate child."[101] One witness estimated that "[a] bastard child is ... about 25 per cent more valuable to a parent than a legitimate one."[102]

At a deeper level, these factors were seen as contributing to population increase, which, following Thomas Malthus,[103] clearly alarmed the Commissioners.[104] Towards the end of their discussion of the bastardy issue, the Commissioners expressed anxiety over "the number of illegitimate births, and the still greater number of legitimate births which are the consequence"[105] – the logic being that illegitimacy led to forced marriage which led to more legitimate, though not necessarily

---

97 *Ibid* at 174 (emphasis added).

98 *Ibid* at 346. See also Anna Clark, "The New Poor Law and the Breadwinner Wage: Contrasting Assumptions" (2000) 34:2 *J Soc Hist* 261 at 264.

99 1834 Poor Law Report, *supra* note 88 at 170 (emphasis added).

100 *Ibid* (emphasis in original).

101 *Ibid*.

102 *Ibid* at 171. See also at 172.

103 See chapter 1, part II(B).

104 Thomas Malthus is not mentioned in the Report but his influence is apparent: U.R.Q. Henriques, "Bastardy and the New Poor Law" (1967) 37 *Past & Present* 103; Simon Deakin and Frank Wilkinson, *The Law of the Labour Market: Industrialization, Employment and Legal Evolution* (Oxford: Oxford University Press, 2005) at 145.

105 1834 Poor Law Report, *supra* note 88 at 178.

desirable, births. This was precisely the point made by Mr. Simeon in evidence given to the House of Lords in 1831, and extracted in the 1834 Poor Law Report, to the effect that "the rapid increase of the population" was "[a]lmost entirely" caused by "the effect of the Bastardy Laws in forcing early marriages."[106]

The Commissioners' proposed remedy for the issues caused by the existing state of the law with respect to illegitimate children was the imposition of complete financial responsibility on unwed mothers[107] (that is, the removal of financial recourse against putative fathers), and a reduction in the support provided by the parish to the same level as that given to widows.[108] These moves would, they argued, discourage "vice"[109] and instead encourage women to procure "the assistance of a husband and a father" *before* engaging in sexual activity. In the Commissioners' words: "Marriage will always be preferred by the woman if she can attain it, and she ought not to be placed in circumstances in which marriage shall be most easily attained by previous concession."[110]

---

106 *Ibid* at 177.

107 Enacted in s 71 of the *Poor Law Amendment Act, 1834*, 4 & 5 Will IV, c 76, which also provided that an illegitimate child followed its mother's settlement. This section of the Act chimed with Malthus's claim that illegitimacy could be reduced by placing the onus of self-control on women: Henriques, *supra* note 104 at 110. It can also be read as reflecting a broader trend in the 1834 Poor Law Report and the *Poor Act 1834* towards what Sandra Fredman has called "the strident laissez faire individualism of the time": Sandra Fredman, *Women and the Law* (Oxford: Clarendon Press, 1997) at 85. Equally, though, the bastardy provisions were a product of family ideology and strict ideas about appropriate gender roles, in particular, that child-rearing should occur in the context of marriage – and that marriage should have occurred as a result of mutual affection rather than financial calculation.

108 This equalization was part of a broader trend towards privatizing financial responsibility for the poor. As the Commissioners put it: "One great advantage which will follow from giving an unmarried mother no advantage over a widow with a legitimate child, will be, that her parents will be forced, if it is necessary, to contribute to her support to that of her infant." 1834 Poor Law Report, *supra* note 88 at 349.

109 This view was expressed again by the Select Committee in its sixth report in 1840. It declared that "every law which directly or indirectly enables an unmarried woman to impose on an unmarried man the obligation of paternity, contravenes the principle on which the institution of marriage is founded, and tends inevitably to encourage concubinage and forced marriages": *Sixth Annual Report of the Poor Law Commissioners* (London: HM Stationary Office, 1840) at 37, quoted in Henriques, *supra* note 104 at 118.

110 1834 Poor Law Report, *supra* note 88 at 350. See also *Sixth Annual Report, supra* note 108 at 21–2 (reaffirming the view expressed in the 1834 Poor Law Report that paternal financial responsibility outside marriage encouraged illegitimacy).

That is, the removal of public enforcement of private financial assistance from men, enacted in s 69 of the *Poor Act 1834*, would encourage women to enter into marriages grounded in mutual affection, rather than lust, avarice, and resignation. Those women would then be able to assume their proper domestic responsibilities and, in turn, rely on the financial support of their husbands.[111] Ideally, then, "women were to be treated not as autonomous individuals but as dependent upon their men";[112] it was only in the event of moral failure that autonomy was imposed as a form of financial punishment.[113] In this respect, the *Poor Act 1834* can be seen as part of a broader legal mosaic that effectively constituted marriage as the only thinkable form of coupling for women in nineteenth-century England – a form that also relied upon gender-based distinctions between work and family.

When a marriage occurred *after* the birth of an illegitimate child, the Commissioners recommended that the husband be fixed with financial liability for the child. The basis for this proposal was said to be the general liability of husbands for the debts of their wives, "and there seems no reason why this peculiar liability, a liability which must almost always be notorious to him, should be excepted."[114] Enacted in section 52 of the *Poor Act 1834*, this move presumably compromised the marriage prospects of at least some unwed mothers, but that was partly the point: improvident marriages were to be avoided, so if a man *voluntarily* shouldered responsibility for a woman and her child, it could be assumed that the marriage was based on the requisite values of affection and esteem. The underlying logic involved replacing one form of private financial assistance with another form based not only on marriage, but a legal conception of marriage as the sentimental core of the domestic family, and a primary element in a broader gender-based pact distributing responsibility over the discrete zones of family and economy.

In the end, the bastardy provisions as enacted in the *Poor Act 1834* were short-lived. Evidence given to the Select Committee on the Administration of the Relief of the Poor in 1838 suggested that the imposition of sole financial responsibility on mothers had had no discernible effect

---

111 See chapter 1, part II(A) and chapter 4, part II(B).

112 Pat Thane, "Women and the Poor Law in Victorian and Edwardian England" (1978) 6 *Hist Workshop J* 29 at 32.

113 In this respect, Clark's argument that the amendments asserted women's independence is correct, but the deeper logic relied on dependence in the manner identified by Thane: see *ibid* and Clark, *supra* note 98 at 267.

114 1834 Poor Law Report, *supra* note 88 at 349.

on illegitimacy rates (more recent analysis suggests that this impression was broadly correct, with illegitimate births increasing throughout the 1830s and 1840s[115]); and had instead "produced irritation and complaints."[116] Indeed, it appeared that the unintended effect of the law had been to inculcate in at least some groups of men the idea that extra-marital sex could be enjoyed without responsibility; whereas custom had previously dictated that marriage would follow if pregnancy occurred (at least if the parties were of the same class), the *Poor Act 1834* removed the legal incentive to marry, leaving only a moral duty to support mother and child. Accordingly, in 1839 an Act was passed that provided "Means for obtaining Orders upon the putative Fathers of Bastard Children for their Support and Maintenance."[117] A further Act passed in 1844 gave single mothers an independent right to apply for affiliation orders and seek financial support from alleged fathers, who in turn were made liable to civil recovery orders in the event of a failure to pay, and imprisonment if recovered property was insufficient to meet the liability.[118]

This shift back to the system that prevailed prior to the *Poor Act 1834* shows that top-down legal approaches to population management were not always successful when it came to orienting social practices. Nevertheless, it remains the case that the bastardy provisions in the *Poor Act 1834*, and their replacement measures, point to a nineteenth-century legal conception of marriage as the central relation within the private family, and the family as a central relay point in the governance of the English state.

B. Compensation Statutes

Legal prioritization of marriage continued in the first statutory intervention into the emerging field of accident compensation and modern tort

---

115　Michael Mason, *The Making of Victorian Sexuality* (Oxford: Oxford University Press, 1994) at 66.

116　*A Copy of the Report of the Poor Law Commissioners to Sir James Graham, on the Law concerning the Maintenance of Bastards, dated the 31st day of January 1844* (London: HM Stationary Office, 1844) at 4.

117　*An Act to enable Justices of the Peace in Petty Sessions to make Orders for the Support of Bastard Children, 1839*, 2 & 3 Vict, c 85.

118　*Poor Law Amendment Act 1844*, 7 & 8 Vict c 101, s 2. See Thane, *supra* note 112 at 32; Henriques, *supra* note 104 at 119; Thomas Nutt, "Illegitimacy, Paternal Financial Responsibility, and the 1834 Poor Law Commission Report: The Myth of the Old Poor Law and the Making of the New" (2010) 63:2 *Econ Hist Rev* 335 at 342–3.

law: the *Fatal Accidents Act 1846*.[119] The Act defined "Family" in distinctly narrow terms, providing that "every such Action shall be for the Benefit of the Wife, Husband, Parent, and Child of the Person whose Death shall have been so caused."[120] Non-marital relations (aside from parent-child relations) were excluded. So too were relations between masters and servants. In this latter respect, the Act amounted to a distinct shift away from the household model of family relations. Hitherto, family-based financial claims were based on a "loss of services," wherein a master or husband claimed for the loss of his servant's or wife's services – and claims in cases of death were not permitted. The *Fatal Accidents Act* flipped this approach on its head, dispensing with masters and servants altogether,[121] and providing a remedy for wives and children (as well as husbands) in cases of death. In these ways, the Act contributed to a narrowing of the legal construction of the family, and helped to further constitute a legal consciousness in which marriage – itself a relation constituted by municipal law[122] – formed the core of family life.

At common law, "the death of a human being could not be complained of as an injury."[123] Death also extinguished any rights to compensation for injury on the part of a victim or the victim's family.[124] In *Baker v Bolton*,[125] the plaintiff brought suit against the proprietors of a stagecoach that had overturned between London and Portsmouth. Baker himself was hurt, but his wife eventually succumbed to her injuries and died about a month after the accident. At trial, Lord Ellenborough instructed the jury that for the purposes of quantifying damages, they could only consider Baker's own injuries, and the loss of his wife's society and his attendant distress in the period between the accident and her death. Loss occasioned by Mrs. Baker's death was not compensable.[126]

---

119 9 & 10 Vict, c 93. As John Fabian Witt has argued, "the histories of torts and the modern family are interwoven in generally unappreciated ways": John Fabian Witt, "From Loss of Services to Loss of Support: The Wrongful Death Statutes, the Origins of Modern Tort Law, and the Making of the Nineteenth-Century Family" (2000) 25:3 *Law & Soc Inq* 717 at 721.

120 9 & 10 Vict c 93, s 2.

121 The action for loss of services remained part of the common law, such that masters could sue for injuries sustained by their servants where such injury occasioned a loss of services. See William Holdsworth, *The Law of Master and Servant: Including that of Trades Unions and Combinations* (London: Routledge, 1876) at 82.

122 See *supra* part II.

123 *Baker v Bolton* (1808) 1 Camp 493.

124 Peter Handford, "Lord Campbell and the Fatal Accidents Act" (2013) 129 *Law Q Rev* at 420.

125 (1808) 1 Camp 493.

126 See Handford, *supra* note 124 at 428 for discussion of the controversy occasioned by Lord Ellenborough's reading of the law.

As travel by road became increasingly common in the nineteenth century, accidents increased, and generated calls for reform to provide a measure of compensation for the families of deceased persons.[127] But "it was the revolution in transport, particularly passenger transport, brought by the railways that presented the most compelling case for reform of the law relating to fatal accidents."[128] In 1845, Lord Lyttelton introduced the Death by Accidents Compensation Bill, which differed little from the version, sponsored by Lord Campbell, passed in 1846.[129] Section 1 of the *Fatal Accidents Act* provided:

> Whereas no Action at Law is now maintainable against a Person who by his wrongful Act, Neglect, or Default may have caused the Death of another Person, and it is oftentimes right and expedient that the Wrongdoer in such Case should be answerable in Damages for the Injury so caused by him: … whensoever the Death of a Person shall be caused by wrongful Act, Neglect, or Default, and the Act, Neglect, or Default is such as would (if Death had not ensued) have entitled the Party injured to maintain an Action and recover Damages in respect thereof, then and in every such Case the Person who would have been liable if Death had not ensued shall be liable to an Action for Damages, notwithstanding the Death of the Person injured, and although the Death shall have been caused under such Circumstances as amount in Law to Felony.[130]

The Act therefore conferred a right of action on the personal *representative* of the deceased person; *dependents* were not given their own personal right of action (as was provided by the law in Scotland). Rather, as section 2 stated, "every such Action shall be for the benefit of the Wife, Husband, Parent, and Child of the Person whose Death shall have been so caused, and shall be brought by and in the Name of the Executor or Administrator of the Person deceased."[131] The "family" was thus constructed in terms of relations between husbands and wives, and parents and children; cohabiting partners were expressly excluded, as were illegitimate children because at common law "child" meant a legitimate

---

127 *Ibid* at 420, 432–3.

128 *Ibid* at 433.

129 Lord Lyttelton's bill was defeated in the Commons in 1835. It was reintroduced by Lord Campbell in April 1846: *ibid* at 439–40.

130 9 & 10 Vict c 93, s 1.

131 As Handford has noted, the Act was in this sense a curious hybrid in that it operated as a claim on behalf of the deceased, yet measured loss by reference to the dependents: Handford, *supra* note 124 at 441.

child.[132] Marriage – either one's own or one's parents' – thus became the baseline condition for compensation in fatal accident cases. Unlike many American statutes on the subject,[133] the English law did not exclude husbands from potential compensation, but debates over the passage of the *Fatal Accidents Act* in Parliament reveal distinctly gendered assumptions about (husbands') financial responsibilities within families.[134]

Conferring the right of action on the deceased's personal representative also limited the types of claims that could be brought because it meant that defences which could have been raised against the deceased (had he survived the accident and brought a claim in his own right) could also be raised against the representative. Cases involving injured employees were therefore generally outside the scope of the Act because of the common employment rule laid down in *Priestley v Fowler*,[135] which provided an employer with a defence against the imposition of vicarious liability based on the employee's implied assumption of risk. As Handford notes, "[t]he defence of common employment, once established, ruled out practically all employee claims: many railways were large organisations and their employees performed many different functions, but the courts assumed without question that they were all in common employment."[136] The courts also limited the damages that could be claimed on behalf of dependents by holding that only pecuniary loss was compensable; damages for emotional harm were outside the scope of the *Fatal Accidents Act*.[137]

Providing an (indirect) avenue for dependent family members to claim for loss of *support* also amounted to a distinct shift away from a household-based model of compensation predicated on loss of *services*.[138] In the eighteenth century, actions for personal injury centred on the loss occasioned to a master by reason of injury to a member of his household. As Blackstone put it in his discussion of master and servant:

A master also may bring an action against any man for beating or maiming his servant; but in such case he must assign, as a special reason for so

---

132 Ginger S. Frost, *Living in Sin: Cohabiting as Husband and Wife in Nineteenth-Century England* (Manchester: Manchester University Press, 2008) at 23–4.

133 Witt, *supra* note 119.

134 See, e.g., UK, HC Deb, 22 July 1846, vol 87, col 1374 (Sir G. Grey), in which reference is repeatedly made to support for widows and the consequences for families of losing "perhaps their most important member."

135 (1837) 3 M&W 1.

136 Handford, *supra* note 124 at 441.

137 *Blake v Midland Railway Co* (1852) 18 QB 93.

138 Witt, *supra* note 119.

doing, his own damage by the loss of his service; and this loss must be proved upon the trial.… Also if any person do hire or retain my servant, being in my service, for which the servant departeth from me and goeth to serve the other, I may have an action for damages against both the new master and the servant, or either of them … The reason and foundation upon which all this doctrine is built, seem to be the property that every man has in the service of his domestics; acquired by the contract of hiring, and purchased by giving them wages.[139]

A husband possessed a similar right in respect of his wife. Alongside actions in trespass based on abduction and adultery was the "third injury … of *beating* a man's wife or otherwise ill using her." In cases of "common assault, battery, or imprisonment, the law gives the usual remedy to recover damages, by action of trespass *vi et armis*." However, "if the beating or other maltreatment be very enormous so that thereby the husband is deprived for any time of the company and assistance of his wife, the law then gives him a *separate* remedy by action upon the case for this ill-usage, *per quod consortium amisit*, in which he shall recover a satisfaction in damages."[140]

As Blackstone pointed out, "in these relative injuries, notice is only taken of the wrong done to the superior of the parties related, by the breach and dissolution of either the relation itself, or at least the advantages accruing therefrom; while the loss of the inferior by such injuries is totally unregarded."[141] In stark contrast, the *Fatal Accidents Act* "noticed" the situation of the "inferiors" by enabling executors to claim, on behalf of dependents, financial redress for loss of support. The action for loss of services remained part of the common law,[142] so masters and husbands could still claim in respect of harms committed against their servants and wives, but the *Fatal Accidents Act* foregrounded the private family in ways that were hitherto unknown to the law of personal injury, and situated the marital relation at the heart of this legal conception of the family and its financial wellbeing.

Towards the end of the nineteenth century a statutory exception to the common employment rule was enacted with respect to certain classes of

---

139 Blackstone, *supra* note 61, book I at 416–17. See also book III at 142.
140 *Ibid*, book III at 140.
141 *Ibid*, book III at 142. The reason for this, he suggested, was "that the inferior hath no kind of property in the company, care, or assistance of the superior, as the superior is held to have in those of the inferior; and therefore the inferior can suffer no loss or injury": *ibid*, book III at 142–3.
142 Holdsworth, *supra* note 121 at 82.

workers. Under the *Employers' Liability Act 1880*,[143] "personal injury ... caused to a workman" was made compensable in enumerated situations covering defective machinery and equipment, negligence on the part of superintendents or other persons whose orders the worker was bound to and did conform, acts or omissions of persons in the service of the employer done in conformity with the employer's rules, or by reason of negligence in relation to the operation of railways.[144] The class of employees able to take advantage of the Act was limited to railway servants and persons to whom the *Employers and Workmen Act 1875*[145] applied.[146] Thus, domestic servants were excluded from the *Employers' Liability Act*,[147] as were, for instance, "an omnibus conductor, the driver of a tramcar, a shop assistant, a clerk, a seaman."[148]

Crucially, the *Employers' Liability Act* enabled personal representatives of deceased workmen to bring claims against employers by providing "the same right of compensation and remedies against the employer as if the workman had not been a workman of nor in the service of the employer, nor engaged in his work,"[149] thereby avoiding both the common employment rule and the rule that the death of a person was not itself a cause of action (which had already been limited under the *Fatal Accidents Act*).[150] According to John Salmond, "the claim in such a case ... must conform to the requirements of both of these Acts."[151] Thus, claims by the personal representatives of deceased workers on behalf of dependents were again made contingent on marriage – only the surviving spouse or legitimate child of a deceased worker was able to have a claim brought on his or her behalf. The same approach was adopted in the *Workmen's Compensation Act 1897*,[152] but the *Workmen's Compensation Act 1906* expanded the meaning of "family" to include grandparents, grandchildren, step-parents and step-children, siblings and

---

143 43 & 44 Vict c 42 [*Employers' Liability Act*].

144 43 & 44 Vict. c 42, s 1.

145 38 & 39 Vict, c 90.

146 43 & 44 Vict, c 42, s 8.

147 See further chapter 4, part II(A).

148 John Salmond, *The Law of Torts: A Treatise on the English Law of Liability for Civil Injuries*, 2nd ed. (London: Stevens & Haynes, 1910) at 100.

149 43 & 44 Vict, c 42, s 1.

150 Salmond, *supra* note 148 at 100.

151 *Ibid*.

152 60 & 61 Vict c 37, s 7, "Dependents." The 1897 Act removed the need to demonstrate wrongdoing on the part of a particular person within an organization, providing instead for compensation based on the fact of injury during the course of employment (subject to certain limiting criteria).

half-siblings, alongside spouses, parents and children.[153] Illegitimate children and their carers (whether parents or grandparents) were also brought within the scope of "dependents,"[154] alongside (but not forming part of) "[m]ember[s] of a family."[155] In this respect, the *Workmen's Compensation Act 1906* constituted a more expansive legal approach to the family and its financial security, but it still largely hinged on the existence of marriage.

Read together, the *Fatal Accidents Act* and the *Workmen's Compensation Acts* provide insight into the interlinked development of modern tort law and legal conceptions of family and work. The *Fatal Accidents Act* involved a shift away from a household-based approach to injury compensation by recognizing the right of a group of family members, narrowly defined by reference to marriage and not including masters, to recover damages. The *Workmen's Compensation Acts* built on this platform – and in the process helped to solidify the distinction between work and family – by recognizing the right of *family* to claim against *employers* for injuries occasioned during work conducted outside of the home.

IV. Stabilizing Marriage

A. Divorce

The introduction of judicial divorce via the *Matrimonial Causes Act 1857*[156] constituted a partial liberalization of English marriage law when considered against the restrictive ecclesiastical position concerning divorce *a vincula matrimonii*. However, in a manner that intersected with the debates over, and the eventual forms of, the *Married Women's Property Acts*,[157] the introduction of judicial divorce relied upon and was designed to extend deeply conservative and patriarchal conceptions of marriage. In this respect, the *Matrimonial Causes Act* – and the terms upon which it was introduced – point to a legal conception of marriage as a relation central to both the private family and, by extension, to the English nation.

Before 1857, divorce and marital separation in England fell under ecclesiastical jurisdiction. True divorce (divorce *a vincula matrimonii*),

---

153 *Workmen's Compensation Act, 1906*, 6 Edward VII, c 58, s 13, "Member of a family."
154 6 Edward VII, c 58, s 13, "Dependants" [*sic*].
155 6 Edward VII, c 58, s 13, "Member of a family."
156 20 & 21 Vict, c 85.
157 See *infra* part IV(B).

in which the parties were free to re-marry, operated to void (annul) the marriage altogether based on contravention of a canonical prohibition, for instance, marriage within the prohibited degrees or the existence of a pre-contract with another person.[158] Divorce *a mensa et thoro* (from bed and board), on the other hand, was an order for separation based on, for example, adultery; but it did not dissolve the marriage.[159] Divorce was also possible by private Act of Parliament, but it was a tedious and expensive process open in practice only to the wealthy and the well connected.[160] Within the lower classes, among whom customary forms of marriage were comparatively more common, and for whom parliamentary divorce was virtually impossible, there is evidence of less formal modes of marriage termination than the options offered by church and state. Desertion was one option, but a more ritualized practice that gained in popularity in the eighteenth century in cases where property was not in issue was wife sale,[161] which on a customary level carried considerable social weight if practiced in the requisite form.[162] Other options available to more impecunious members of society included

---

158 See *supra* note 68.

159 Shanley, "One Must Ride Behind," *supra* note 18 at 357.

160 It was first necessary to obtain a divorce *a mensa et thoro* in the ecclesiastical courts. For a husband, it was then necessary to pursue an action in the civil courts for criminal conversation against his wife's paramour. Only then could a petition be brought before Parliament to divorce the parties. Women were not required (or indeed able) to bring an action for criminal conversation, but the grounds upon which they could seek a divorce were limited to aggravated forms of adultery involving bigamy or incest, whereas men were only required to show simple adultery. See *First Report of the Commissioners Appointed by Her Majesty to Enquire into the Law of Divorce, and More Particularly into the Mode of Obtaining Divorces A Vinculo Matrimonii* (1853), British Parliamentary Papers, vol 40 at 11 [First Divorce Report]. The double standard was not laid down as a rule so much as it was a practice that developed over time; the only four instances in which a woman obtained a divorce by Act of Parliament involved aggravated adultery by the husband: *ibid*. For a study of private petitions brought between 1700 and 1857 see Sybil Wolfram, "Divorce in England 1700–1857" (1985) 5:2 *Oxford J Leg Stud* 155.

161 See Samuel Pyeatt Menefee, *Wives for Sale: An Ethnographic Study of British Popular Divorce* (New York: St. Martin's Press, 1981). According to John Gillis, "[a]ccounts of wife sale suggest a plebeian constituency of people below the rank of respectable artisans but above that of wholly pauperized workers ... the rite itself was not meant to deal with marriages in which property was involved": Gillis, *supra* note 36 at 218.

162 For details see Gillis, *supra* note 36 at 214–15. Newspaper reports suggest that wife sale reached peak popularity in the 1820s and 1830s, followed by a sudden drop in the 1840s – a result, it would seem, of magistrates' efforts to stamp out the practice and, presumably, the general shift towards broad social acceptance of middle class marital ideals. See Stone, *supra* note 31 at 146–7.

forms of community-based mediation and counselling administered through religious and workers' organisations.[163]

In 1853, "the Commissioners appointed by Her Majesty to Enquire into the Law of Divorce" under the leadership of Lord Campbell (the Campbell Commission), delivered their First Divorce Report.[164] Reflecting the fact that it was procedural difficulties related to parliamentary divorce that generated calls for broader reform, rather than concern over hardships experienced by women and the poor,[165] the Campbell Commission recommended the establishment of a new tribunal to hear divorce applications, comprised of a Vice-Chancellor, a common law judge, and a judge of the ecclesiastical court. It recommended no change, however, to the practice of limiting divorce *a vinculo* to men, except "in cases of aggravated enormity, such as incest or bigamy."[166] It was only after the publication of the First Divorce Report and a failed bill in 1854[167] that public and parliamentary debate began to focus on the harshness for women of the existing and proposed laws. Under the influence of Caroline Norton and her representative in the House of Lords, Lord Lyndhurst, as well as the group of women led by Barbara Leigh Smith, and the Law Amendment Society (a group of Whig lawyers led by Lord Brougham), Parliament was forced to consider not only the institutional question of transferring power over matrimonial causes from the ecclesiastical courts to the temporal courts, but also the possibility of equalizing women's access to the new regime.[168] Throughout 1856 and 1857, the Houses of Commons and Lords debated various divorce bills, finally passing the *Matrimonial Causes Act* in August 1857.

The *Matrimonial Causes Act* stripped the ecclesiastical courts of power over matrimonial causes and vested such powers in a newly constituted Court for Divorce and Matrimonial Causes.[169] Henceforth, it provided, "[a]ll Petitions, either for the Dissolution or for a Sentence of Nullity of Marriage ... shall be heard and determined by Three or more

---

163 Tim Stretton, "Marriage, Separation and the Common Law in England, 1540–1660" in Helen Berry and Elizabeth Foyster, eds., *The Family in Early Modern England* (Cambridge: Cambridge University Press, 2007) 18.

164 First Divorce Report, *supra* note 160.

165 See Stone, *supra* note 31 at 369; Henry Kha and Warren Swain, "The Enactment of the Matrimonial Causes Act 1857: The Campbell Commission and the Parliamentary Debates" (2016) 37:3 *J Leg Hist* 303 at 322.

166 First Divorce Report, *supra* note 160 at 22.

167 Matrimonial Causes Bill 1854. See UK, HL Deb, 13 June 1854, vol 134, cols 1–28.

168 See Shanley, "One Must Ride Behind," *supra* note 18; Shanley, *Feminism, Marriage and the Law, supra* note 18 at 35–44; Stone, *supra* note 31 at 368–2.

169 20 & 21 Vict, c 85, ss 2, 6.

Judges of the said Court, of whom the Judge of the Court of Probate shall be One."[170] As commentators have noted, this institutional change set the stage for the modern system of family courts,[171] but it can also be understood as part of a process of constituting the family as a distinct juristic category, with its own body of laws *and* its own system of civil administration. Far from inaugurating a regime of private ordering or minimal state intervention, the *Matrimonial Causes Act* constituted an entirely new court to administer divorce, and imposed a rigid set of rules (based on existing practices) governing the circumstances in which orders for separation and divorce could be made, based on the belief that marriage "is so manifestly essential to the best interests of society, that before it can be dissolved it must be clearly established by the strictest proof that [an] offence has been committed."[172] In this sense, while the Act certainly liberalized marriage by permitting exit in *some* circumstances, it did so in a manner that made divorce contingent upon permission from the judicial arm of the English state. As noted in chapter 2, this feature of the Act seems to have formed part of the reason that legal scholars writing in the wake of the Act's passage did not treat the advent of divorce as indicating any sort of contractualization of the marital relation; in fact, quite the contrary seems to have been the case.[173] As John Salmond wrote in the early twentieth century, marriage "creates a status ... for although it is entered into by way of consent, *it cannot be dissolved in that way*, and the legal condition created by it is determined by the law, and cannot be modified by the agreement of the parties."[174]

The grounds upon which divorce could be sought from the new Court reflected the gender-based distinction that had existed in applications for divorce by private Act; the new law provided that a husband could seek dissolution on the ground of his wife's adultery, but a wife could only seek such an order on the ground that "her Husband has been guilty of

---

170 20 & 21 Vict, c 85, s 10.

171 See, e.g., Kha and Swain, *supra* note 165 at 322; Cretney, *supra* note 22 at 161–3; R.H. Graveson, "The Background of the Century" in R.H. Graveson and F.R. Crane, eds., *A Century of Family Law* (London: Sweet & Maxwell, 1957) 1.

172 First Divorce Report, *supra* note 160 at 1. It took until 1969 for divorce in England to be made possible without proof of fault, though separation for two years was still required even if both parties consented, and five years if one party did not: *Divorce Reform Act 1969*, c 55, subs 2(d), (e).

173 See chapter 2, part V.

174 John Salmond, *Jurisprudence*, 4th ed. (London: Stevens & Haynes, 1913) at 211 (emphasis added). See also J.E.G. de Montmorency, "Divorce Law in England" (1926) 75:1 *U Penn L Rev* 36 at 46: "a decree for dissolution of marriage ... involves a change of status."

incestuous Adultery, or of Bigamy with Adultery, or of Rape, or of Sodomy or Bestiality, or of Adultery coupled with such Cruelty as without Adultery would have entitled her to a Divorce a Mensa et Thoro, or of Adultery coupled with Desertion, without reasonable Excuse, for Two Years or upwards."[175] This provision is the clearest indication that the reforms were by design an extremely limited liberalization of the marital relation – one that was not intended in any way to challenge the superior position of men within marriage, the family, or English society.

Debates over the Bill support this reading of the *Matrimonial Causes Act* as a deeply conservative and openly patriarchal amendment to English law. The basic ideological commitment to marriage as a central pillar within English society was one shared by pro- and anti- divorce parliamentarians; the difference was whether divorce would help or hinder social wellbeing. Detractors drew a connection between the indissolubility of marriage and social cohesion. Spencer Walpole (who was in favour of judicial divorce) characterized their position thus:

> [T]he sacred relations of marriage were about to broken; that we were going to introduce the most lax insecurity into our English homes; that the position of women, which has been raised so high by the influence of Christianity, was about to be lowered, and that the whole state of the morals of the country was to be degraded by the passing of a measure which would facilitate divorces to an undue extent and in a manner unsanctioned either by reason or by Scripture.[176]

A survey of debates in both Houses supports Walpole's reading. Lord Redesdale, for instance, declared (with no evidence): "From the earliest period no such remedy had ever been open to the nation at large, and the consequence was that in no country in the world was there more domestic happiness or greater regard for the marriage tie than in England."[177] In the Commons, Loftus Wigram declared that divorce was "intimately connected with the moral well-being of the community,"[178] while Fred-

---

175 20 & 21 Vict, c 85, s 17. Divorce *a mensa et thoro* was re-christened "Judicial Separation," with husbands and wives equally able to approach the Court for such an order "on the Ground of Adultery, or Cruelty, or Desertion without Cause for Two Years and upwards."

176 UK, HC Deb, 31 July 1857, vol 147, col 874.

177 UK, HL Deb, 3 March 1857, vol 144, col 1718. Much the same claim was made by the Bishop of Oxford: "there was no nation in Europe in which the whole family purity was so much prized as among the mass of the people of these islands": UK, HL Deb, 19 May 1857, vol 145, col 528.

178 UK, HC Deb, 30 July 1857, vol 147, col 754.

erick Lygon stated that "[e]xperience had taught that increased facilities of divorce only increased the tendency to divorce, and the House would not do well to break hastily, in a few weeks, the most precious link in the chain of social order that bound society together."[179]

Proponents of reform shared their counterparts' veneration of the family, but (in a manner that foreshadowed divorce reform in the second half of the twentieth century[180]) argued that introducing limited access to divorce would protect marriage (and by extension the nation) by weeding out failed couplings. Walpole argued that the Bill would, "tend to uphold the sacredness of the marriage tie, to discourage the inducements to that sin, which of all other is the worst for the moral purity of society, and to preserve to us that blessed security and peace which now constitute – as God grant they may ever constitute – the charm, the happiness, and the unspeakable blessing which now surrounds an English home."[181] Lord Lyndhurst claimed that permitting divorce in cases of adultery would encourage public morality. "What," he asked, "will follow if all hope of legal redress is refused in this case to that portion of the people?" Naturally, in his view, "acts of brutal violence."[182]

Sitting beneath the threshold question of whether divorce should be permitted at all was the equally contentious issue of the grounds upon which divorce ought to be allowed. As noted above, the double-standard camp prevailed in this part of the debate; the arguments that were advanced on both sides, though, shed light on legal (and social) conceptions of marriage in the mid-nineteenth century. Lord Lyndhurst based his argument for equalizing access to divorce on the contractual nature of the relation: "The man promises during their joint lives to support, protect, and cherish the woman, and that he will never forsake her for another. There can be no more sacred promise, no more forcible engagement, no contract more binding. But if he disregards that promise, and abandons his wife, why was the contract still to be binding upon her? In

---

179 UK, HC Deb, 30 July 1857, vol 147, col 749.
180 See John Dewar and Stephen Parker, "English Family Law since World War II: From Status to Chaos" in Sanford N. Katz, John Eekelaar and Mavis Maclean, eds., *Cross Currents: Family Law and Policy in the United States and England* (Oxford: Oxford University Press, 2010) 123 at 128, noting that the "primary objective of the reformed divorce law [Divorce Reform Act 1969 and Matrimonial Proceedings and Property Act 1970] was to 'buttress the stability of marriage'" (citing Law Commission, *Reform of the Ground of Divorce – The Field of Choice* (London: HM Stationary Office, 1966) at 15).
181 UK, HC Deb, 31 July 1857, vol 147, col 885.
182 UK, HL Deb, 3 March 1857, vol 144, col 1693.

commercial contracts if one party violated the agreement the other was released from it. Why should not the same principles be extended to cases such as he had mentioned?"[183] The analogy with commercial contracts essentially updated Blackstone's claim that English law treated marriage "as it does all other contracts"[184] with an equality-based gloss that foreshadowed the feminist liberalism of John Stuart Mill.[185] In this sense, while there was undoubtedly something radical about Lyndhurst's proposal, it also drew on a much older tradition of treating marriage as a private agreement.[186] Blackstone did not go this far because the canonical grip on conceptions of marriage was simply too strong in the mid-eighteenth century, despite the passage of *Lord Hardwicke's Act*, but it was an obvious corollary of a contractual approach to marriage. As Sir William Heathcote, opposing Lyndhurst's approach, correctly perceived, to permit grounds for divorce beyond adultery logically led to a point at which "the mutual consent of the parties was sufficient to dissolve a marriage."[187] Even Lyndhurst, however, would not go this far, expressing his disapproval of a proposed clause that would have permitted private separation (not dissolution) agreements. Quoting Lord Stowell, he characterized "a private separation as an illegal contract, implying a dereliction of stipulated duties, which the parties are not at liberty to desert."[188] The Bishop of Oxford agreed, and argued that to permit parties such freedom suggested that "in dealing with the law of marriage Parliament was dealing with some trifling rules affecting the transfer of property," rather than "a great institution ... upon which the purity and happiness of this Christian land" depended.[189] In the House of Commons, English purity was compared to the "deplorable position in which the Prussians stood at this moment – a position from which the best men were now recoiling with horror." What, precisely, was the

---

183 UK, HL Deb, 19 May 1857, vol 145, col 505.

184 Blackstone, *supra* note 61, book I at 421.

185 John Stuart Mill, *The Subjection of Women*, 3rd ed. (London: Longman, Green, Reader, and Dyer, 1870).

186 Of course, the Act also challenged the religious nature of marriage, a point at which many MPs took umbrage. Sir William Heathcote, for instance, observed "that marriage, which was in almost all countries a civil contract, was a ceremonial which in this country received in addition, in almost every case, a religious sanction": UK, HC Deb, 21 August 1857, vol 147, col 1987. See generally Woodhouse, *supra* note 19.

187 UK, HC Deb, 30 July 1857, vol 147, col 737.

188 UK, HL Deb, 3 March 1857, vol 144, col 1696.

189 UK, HL Deb, 3 March 1857, vol 144, col 1707. See also the statement of Mr. Bowyer: "It was not a Bill for establishing partnerships with limited liability. It was not a Bill for rendering more speedy and easy the dissolution of partnerships." UK, HC Deb, 30 July 1857, vol 147, col 757.

nature of this position? "[A] law that reduced marriage to the level of the most ordinary contract, capable of being put an end to without difficulty by the consent of the parties."[190]

Lyndhurst's plea for equal divorce rights was rejected – as was his contractual approach to marriage. This is hardly surprising in the broader context of nineteenth century English legal thought and culture.[191] On a legal level, scholars and judges were, by this point, beginning to think of marriage in terms of status, and as an exceptional species of contract, due to the suite of non-modifiable rights and obligations that attached to marriage irrespective of consent.[192] On a social level, it was simply unthinkable to adopt a consent-based approach to the relation that would have effectively dissolved one core element of patriarchy by imposing on men and women equal responsibility for marital transgressions. As Walter Houghton observed in his analysis of the Victorian mindset, "after marriage, quite as much as before, the Victorian ethic made fidelity the supreme virtue and sexual irregularity the blackest of sins…. Adultery, especially in the case of a wife, and no matter what the extenuating circumstances, was spoken of with horror."[193] Thus, Earl Grey opined that, "Parliament ought to provide some means by which all ranks of society should be relieved from *wives* who had committed adultery,"[194] and the Lord Chancellor, in a much-quoted passage, declared:

> It had even been the feeling of that house – indeed, it was a feeling common to mankind in general – that, although the sin in both cases was the same, the effect of adultery on the part of the husband was very different from that of adultery on the part of the wife. It was possible for a wife to pardon a husband who had committed adultery; but it was hardly possible for a husband ever really to pardon the adultery of a wife, and therefore it was that in their practice in that House their Lordships had always made a great distinction between the two cases.[195]

---

190 UK, HC Deb, 30 July 1857, vol 147, col 741 (Sir William Heathcote). A similar comparison was made to the situation in post-revolutionary France, leading to the re-imposition of restrictions on divorce in 1803 and the affirmation in 1816 of the indissolubility of marriage: UK, HC Deb, 30 July 1857, vol 147, col 749 (Mr. Puller).

191 Probert notes that there was no "sustained denunciation of the double standard in the literature of the period": Probert, "Double Standard," *supra* note 21 at 83.

192 See chapters 2 and 6.

193 Walter E. Houghton, *The Victorian Frame of Mind, 1830–1870* (New Haven: Yale University Press, 1985) at 356.

194 UK, HL Deb, 3 March 1857, vol 144, col 1717 (emphasis added).

195 UK, HL Deb, 19 May 1857, vol 145, col 490.

In essence, allowing men to divorce women for their adultery was permissible because a wife's transgression threatened the very core of the family – and by extension posed a threat to the nation. In Walpole's words, "the adultery of the wife necessarily breaks asunder all family ties."[196] As guardians of "the blessedness of the family home,"[197] Victorian wives were shouldered with a moral responsibility that could not brook unfaithfulness. Thus, on the broader question of whether divorce should be permitted at all, some MPs argued in favour based on the idea that divorce would promote social harmony by permitting men to divorce unfaithful wives. Lord Lyndhurst reasoned in this manner: "A man finds his wife committing adultery; he has no remedy; he cannot apply to a court of justice to dissolve his marriage; he therefore continues to live on with her, committing acts of brutal and degrading violence on her – or he turns her out, and she goes to live with the adulterer. What, he asked, was the effect of such a scene upon the lower orders of the people?"[198] In a similar vein, the Marquess of Lansdowne spoke of "the vice and misery of every kind that ensue from the want of this power of separation," leading (among the poorer classes) not only "to actual vice that is tolerated by the absence of divorce – the wife living in a state of adultery and incontinency – but to that other vice which is the greatest bane of the lower orders of this country – the vice of drunkenness."[199] In contrast, bringing the law to bear against men who were, in Cranworth's phrase, "a little profligate," was seen as excessive and perhaps itself likely to threaten family harmony.[200] In this way, the *Matrimonial Causes Act* reinforced the primacy of the husband within the family by setting wives on a moral pedestal – at the will of her husband a wife could be cast aside for infidelity, but a wife held no such complementary prerogative except in cases of aggravation.[201] This

---

196 UK, HC Deb, 31 July 1857, vol 147, col 880.

197 UK, HC Deb, 31 July 1857, vol 147, col 881 (Mr. Walpole).

198 UK, HL Deb, 19 May 1857, vol 145, col 499. See also UK, HL Deb, 3 March 1857, vol 144, col 1693 (Lord Lyndhurst).

199 UK, HL Deb, 3 March 1857, vol 144, col 1715.

200 Shanley, "One Must Ride Behind," *supra* note 18 at 364. See also Stone, *supra* note 31 at 384.

201 While rape (of another woman, not a wife) was eventually included as an aggravating circumstance, it says something about attitudes to women at the time that one of the objections to this move was "that rape was an offence against the woman ravished, by which, as committed generally under the impulse of sudden passion, the wife was far less insulted and injured than by habitual adultery with a mistress or other women": UK, HL Deb, 24 August 1857, vol 147, col 2016 (Lord Redesdale).

gendered approach to "the greatest wrong which a man can suffer"[202] is also evident in the Act's provision permitting a cuckolded husband to claim damages from his wife's lover – a continuation of the older action for criminal conversation in a revamped statutory form.[203]

The nexus between female respectability and marriage also led to the inclusion of a provision in the Act permitting adulterers to remarry.[204] This was a point of considerable controversy in debates. The Bishop of Oxford sought to have included a provision preventing an adulterer from remarrying, but the Lord Chancellor declined to take such a path "because it involves a most cruel punishment on the woman … in ordinary cases a man who has committed adultery, which has resulted in a divorce, would feel himself bound in honour to make all the reparation he can by marrying the woman whom he has excluded from society."[205] Lord Brougham also opposed the Bishop on this point, arguing that the burden of such a restriction would fall with disproportionate weight on women, dooming them "to the alternative of prostitution or want – of sinning or starving – of the streets or the workhouse."[206] The point, of course, was not to express forgiveness towards "fallen" women, but rather to prevent social decay by transferring responsibility for such a woman from the state to another man through the device of marriage.

The double-standard incorporated in the *Matrimonial Causes Act* remained part of English law until the early twentieth century, when the *Matrimonial Causes Act 1923*[207] equalized the grounds of divorce for men and women, and introduced divorce based on cruelty and desertion.[208] Wives were thus placed on an equal footing with husbands, and both parties were provided with additional grounds upon which they could approach the courts to extricate themselves from marital hardship. Yet it was the same basic concern with strengthening marriage, families, and the nation that animated support for reform in Parliament. Cecil Wilson argued that the Bill "would tend rather to the strengthening of those ties than to their loosening" by holding men and women to equal standards of propriety.[209] Duncan Millar concurred with Wilson, claiming that in Scotland "the fact that this cause of action [adultery] was

---

202 UK, HC Deb, 31 July 1857, vol 147, col 864 (Sir George Grey).
203 20 & 21 Vict, c 85, s 33. Section 59 abolished the action of criminal conversation.
204 20 & 21 Vict, c 85, s 52.
205 UK, HL Deb, 3 March 1857, vol 144, col 1687. See also UK, HL Deb, 19 May 1857, vol 145, col 491 (Lord Chancellor).
206 UK, HL Deb, 4 June 1857, vol 145, col 1098.
207 13 & 14 Geo V, c 19.
208 See further Montmorency, *supra* note 174 at 44.
209 UK, HC Deb, 2 March 1923, vol 160, cols 2387–8.

given to the wife has ... proved to be a strong deterrent" to infidelity on the part of men.[210] "Instead of injuring society and weakening family ties," he claimed, "it has all been the opposite way."[211] Equality was thus presented and endorsed as a means of strengthening family bonds and enhancing national wellbeing. The ongoing fault-based structure was an integral feature of the post-1923 divorce regime because it operated as a means for the more effective weeding out of "bad" marriages that threatened to undermine the institution, while denying exit based on such factors as loss of affection. Men and women were (formally) equal in their ability to attribute fault for marital breakdown, but dissolution was still possible only where there was proof of some kind of marital offence that went to the core of the relation – a legislative recognition of the national importance in sorting the marital wheat from the dissolute chaff that continued to underscore the centrality of marriage within the English legal family.[212] Of course, for many women in the second half of the nineteenth-century divorce was a virtual economic impossibility, irrespective of formal legal capacity, given the constraints that fettered their ability to generate income, or at least sufficient income upon which to live.[213]

B. Married Women's Property

According to Blackstone, English law in the mid-eighteenth century treated marriage "in no other light than as a civil contract."[214] The results of this contract were, however, unusual: "By marriage, the husband and wife are one person in law; that is, the very being or legal existence of the woman is suspended during the marriage, or at least incorporated and consolidated into that of the husband: under whose wing, protection, and *cover*, she performs every thing; and is therefore called in our law-french a *feme-covert*; is said to be *covert-baron*, or lord; and her condition during her marriage is called her *coverture*."[215] Nineteenth-century

---

210 UK, HC Deb, 2 March 1923, vol 160, col 2397.

211 UK, HC Deb, 2 March 1923, vol 160, col 2399.

212 This approach continued well into the second half of the twentieth century. As Dewar and Parker note apropos the *Divorce Reform Act 1969*, c 55, "the preservation of marriage as an institution was thought to require the decent burial of individual marriages that were dead, so that the parties to it could then remarry": Dewar and Parker, *supra* note 180 at 128.

213 See chapter 4, part II(B).

214 Blackstone, *supra* note 61, book I at 421.

215 *Ibid*, book I at 430. As Lee Holcombe has noted, "[i]t was not the fact of being female but the status of wife that entailed severe legal disabilities": Holcombe,

reform of the law governing married women's property challenged this conception of the effects of marriage by chipping away at the fused legal identity of husband and wife. The *Married Women's Property Acts* of 1870 and 1882[216] provided some (less wealthy) women with a measure of financial protection within marriage through the extension of older equitable principles concerning separate property.[217] However, the reforms expressly drew back from treating wives as independent legal actors and emphasized a distinctly hierarchical and patriarchal conception of the marital relation. The primary concern among parliamentarians was in fact the solidity of home and family,[218] which translated into efforts to reform the law in such a way that marital relations (and hence families) were actually strengthened by giving women *limited* property rights in a form that did not fundamentally challenge male dominance. The process played out in distinctly class-based terms. The perceived brutishness of lower class men meant that protecting their wives through property law was in the public interest; that, in turn, would (it was thought) ensure the wellbeing of such families. Conversely, nothing more than the extant arrangement of settlement[219] was deemed necessary for the upper classes because of the (apparently) upstanding nature of its men and the unthinkable prospect of allowing women to independently control significant wealth. While recent analysis of the Acts has justifiably tended to focus on their limitations from the perspective of women's equality,[220] this section shows that the

---

supra note 21 at 4. Carole Pateman argues that "[u]ntil late into the nineteenth century the legal and civil position of a wife resembled that of a slave": Pateman, *supra* note 2 at 119.

216 *Married Women's Property Act 1870*, 33 & 34 Vict, c 93; *Married Women's Property Act 1882*, 45 & 46 Vict, c 75.

217 By the nineteenth century, marriage settlements had rendered the old custom of dower, by which a wife who survived her husband acquired a one-third life interest in his lands, largely redundant. The *Dower Act 1833*, 3 & 4 Will IV, c 105, also effectively ended dower right by permitting a husband to expressly bar his wife's right to dower by deed during his lifetime, or in his will. While the Act in its terms certainly restricted wives' interests in property, it had little practical effect and was passed with a view to simplifying transfers in land, more than to restrict widows' interests in property: UK, HC Deb, 14 February 1833, vol 15, col 657 (Solicitor General). See generally Holcombe, *supra* note 21 at 21–2.

218 See Ben Griffin, "Class, Gender, and Liberalism in Parliament, 1868–1882: The Case of the Married Women's Property Acts" (2003) 46:1 *Hist J* 59 at 62.

219 See J.H. Baker, *An Introduction to English Legal History*, 3rd ed. (London: Butterworths, 1990) at 553–4.

220 Shanley, *Feminism, Marriage, and the Law*, *supra* note 18; Shanley, "Married Women's Property," *supra* note 21; Holcombe, *supra* note 21. As Griffin has argued,

Married Women's Property Acts' deliberately limited incursion into coverture was part of a broader legal effort to consolidate the constitutive function of marriage within the family, and the family's central position within English society.

The implications of coverture for property interests between husbands and wives were complicated, but ultimately reducible to a single general principle: "a husband on marriage became for most purposes the almost absolute master of his wife's property."[221] This common law position was unacceptably risky for wealthy families; in particular, there was concern to ensure that if children were not born, a daughter's property would not remain with the husband's family but revert to her own bloodline.[222] Accordingly, in the sixteenth and seventeenth centuries, the practice developed of settling property on married women through "uses" – the progenitors of modern trusts.[223] Through these devices, fathers were able to confer interests in property on their daughters by conveying the legal title to a third party for the use or benefit of the daughter. Given that the daughter did not hold legal title, her husband had no corresponding legal claim to the property; and the Courts of Chancery upheld the trustee's obligations towards the daughter on the basis of conscience.

Generally speaking, then, women from wealthier families enjoyed partial relief from the strictness of the common law. Other women, however, remained legally fused with their husbands, and devoid of equitable protection over any income they might earn or any property conveyed to them. The first major challenge to this state of affairs came from women in the 1850s.[224] Lee Holcombe suggests that a period of economic prosperity in the wake of the "hungry forties" "fuelled feminist discontent with the legal position of women."[225] While family/market ideology stressed the impropriety of married women engaging in paid labour outside of the home, economic reality meant that "by

---

    understanding the gender dimensions of the Acts also requires paying attention to the class and gender identities of by male politicians: Griffin, *supra* note 218.

221 Dicey, *supra* note 20 at 371. See also at 370 note 2 for analysis of the complexities of a husband's control over different forms of property.

222 Holcombe, *supra* note 21 at 38.

223 *Ibid* at 38–9.

224 This is not to suggest that calls for reform only emerged at this time. The infamous separation of Caroline and George Norton in the 1830s highlighted how, in the absence of judicial divorce, women who no longer resided with their husbands nevertheless remained subject to the strictures of coverture; such women were entitled to maintenance but not to the fruits of their own labour. *Ibid* at 50–7.

225 *Ibid* at 48.

1851 there were in the country well over three-quarters of a million married women at work."[226] Under the rules of coverture, the income earned by working wives was automatically treated in law as the property of their husbands – a situation that many women found not only demeaning but also detrimental to the wellbeing and economic survival of their families. Recognizing this situation, in 1854 Barbara Leigh Smith published a brief work that summarized "the Most Important Laws Concerning Women," and soon after formed the first English women's committee to advocate for reform of the laws concerning married women's property. [227] Through a series of public meetings held around the country, a mass of evidence was gathered that attested to the suffering experienced by women as a result of the property laws.[228] Frances Cornwallis distilled this evidence, and the case for reform, in a series of articles published in the *Westminster Review* in 1856. Foreshadowing one of the key arguments that eventually led to reform, Cornwallis argued that "the true ends of marriage were actually subverted by the existing laws" because male dominance undercut the idea of *mutual* affection and support that formed the basis of (nineteenth-century conceptions of) marriage.[229] Anna Mary Howitt augmented this literary effort by heading a petition campaign that garnered more than 26,000 signatures in over 70 petitions, including that of Elizabeth Barrett Browning.[230]

In March 1856, Lord Brougham presented a formal petition from the married women's property committee to the House of Lords by Lord Brougham, and Sir Erskine Perry did the same in the Commons. It declared, "it is time that legal protection be thrown over the produce of their [married women's] labour, and that in entering the state of marriage, they no longer pass from freedom into the condition of a slave, all whose earnings belong to his master and not to himself."[231] In May of that year, the Law Amendment Society carried a resolution which declared that the common law rules relating to married women's property were "unjust in principle and injurious in their operation," the principles of equity were "in accordance with the requirements of the age," and conflict between the two streams of law "ought to be terminated

---

226 *Ibid* at 49, noting also that "[t]hese working wives were mostly women of the lower classes, but there were among them a relatively small but growing number of middle-class women."
227 *Ibid* at 58.
228 *Ibid* at 65.
229 *Ibid* at 68.
230 *Ibid* at 70–1.
231 *Ibid* at 86.

by a general law based on the principles of equity which should apply to all classes."[232] Ten days later, Erskine Perry presented the same resolution to the House of Commons, but withdrew it on the advice of Sir Alexander Cockburn, who cautioned against abstract resolutions and suggested instead the introduction of legislation to cure what was part of the broader recognized problem of general disconformity between law and equity.[233] Heeding this advice, Perry introduced a Married Women's Property Bill following the Whigs' return to power in 1857. It was approved in the Commons but then "dropped from sight" as the divorce question consumed whatever appetite Parliament had for marriage-related law reform.[234]

As debate over the divorce bill proceeded, Lord St Leonards successfully inserted a provision that protected the property of wives deserted by their husbands, but which gave no protection to married women in general. According to Holcombe, St Leonards "hoped by his amendment to prevent what he considered 'a greater evil' – that is, passage of Perry's Married Women's Property Bill, which be believed to be 'a most mischievous one,' certain to 'place the whole marriage law of this country on a different footing and give a wife all the distinct rights of citizenship.'"[235] Perry's efforts at further reform of the divorce bill failed, and the *Matrimonial Causes Act* provided: "In every Case of a Judicial Separation the Wife shall, whilst so separated be considered as a Feme Sole for the Purposes of Contract, and Wrongs and Injuries, and suing and being sued in any Civil Proceeding."[236]

This basic concession effectively stymied efforts at further reform until the mid-1860s, when extension of the parliamentary franchise and reform of the country's arcane court system, with its separately administered streams of law and equity, occupied much social and political debate.[237] This climate was conducive to women's equality claims,[238]

---

232 *Ibid* at 87.

233 *Ibid* at 89–90. Earlier in 1856 the Personal Laws Committee of the Law Amendment Society had issued a report which condemned the division between law and equity, in particular, the class-based dimensions of the split insofar as protection for married women was concerned. *Ibid* at 65.

234 *Ibid* at 93.

235 *Ibid* at 102.

236 20 & 21 Vict, c 85, s 16.

237 Holcombe, *supra* note 21 at 209.

238 Rosemary Auchmuty makes the important point that while women campaigners sought "equal treatment for married women, in the sense that they wanted them to receive *the same* treatment as men and single women," they did *not* consider the sexes to be equal in the modern sense. "Few believed, and no one seriously argued,

and a second Married Women's Property Committee was formed, this time centred in Manchester.[239] Eventually, through its efforts[240] and with the assistance of prominent Londoners,[241] most notably John Stuart Mill, a bill was introduced in 1869 by Russell Gurney, which declared that the "Law of Property and Contract with respect to married women is unjust in principle."[242] Opponents in the Commons objected strenuously to this clause on the basis that it challenged the primacy of the husband as the head of the family;[243] following debate in Committee the Bill was amended to simply state, "it is desirable to amend the law of property and contract with respect to married women."[244] That Bill was eventually dropped after passing through second reading in the House of Lords.

In 1870, two rival bills were introduced in the Commons: one by Gurney, which was essentially the same as the 1869 Bill; and a new Bill introduced by Henry Cecil Raikes. Raikes' measure would have made a husband trustee for his wife's property, with a power on the wife's part to apply to a County Court to have the property vested in another trustee in cases of mismanagement – an indication of "how tenaciously Raikes held to the idea that, except under extraordinary circumstances of demonstrable male incompetence, wives should not be independent

---

that women were or could be the equals of men in intellectual capacity, artistic creativity or physical strength. On the contrary, it was precisely *because* they were already unequal that the additional legal and educational restrictions imposed on them were so unfair." Rosemary Auchmuty, "The Married Women's Property Acts: Equality Was Not the Issue" in Rosemary Hunter, ed., *Rethinking Equality Projects in Law: Feminist Challenges* (Oxford: Hart, 2008) 13 at 17 (emphasis in original).

239 Holcombe, *supra* note 21 at 117–32.

240 "All together the Married Women's Property Committee presented 29 petitions with some 33,000 signatures to parliament in 1868. The following year the committee presented to the House of Commons 113 petitions with more than 42,000 signatures, including one petition signed by John Stuart Mill and nearly 1,400 others and one presented for Susannah Palmer by Russell Gurney, while 70 petitions with some 30,000 signatures were presented to the House of Lords." *Ibid* at 145.

241 *Ibid* at 132–41.

242 George Shaw-Lefevre introduced a Married Women's Property Bill into the Commons in 1868 but owing to the late stage at which it was introduced the Bill was eventually withdrawn.

243 According to Griffin, "[t]he most striking feature of the debates on the Married Women's Property Bills is how little time was spent discussing the principle of sexual equality, and how much time was spent discussing the idea that giving married women property rights would cause discord in the home": Griffin, *supra* note 218 at 62.

244 Shanley, "Married Women's Property," *supra* note 21 at 70–1.

of their husbands."[245] That Bill was voted down in the Commons by a vote of 208 to 46.[246] Gurney's Bill passed through the Commons (with predictable criticism from Raikes of its "novel principle of civil equality between the sexes"[247]) but encountered significant resistance from the Lords, primarily on the basis that extending property rights to married women would challenge the status of husbands as the heads of families, and introduce discord into what was supposed to be a haven of harmony – the family home.

Lord Penzance argued that the Bill "would subvert the principle on which the marriage relation had hitherto stood, and its tendency would be to cause increased discord and separation."[248] That principle seemed to be a strict separation of zones along family/work lines, and the superiority of husbands in household disputes: Penzance worried about the possibility of wives entering into the marketplace and setting up businesses to rival those of their husbands; indeed, a woman might even enter "into partnership with her cousin, who need not be a woman"! Thus, a "husband who expected his wife to keep his home and attend to the children might find her opening a Berlin wool shop with her cousin John as a partner." He continued by arguing that fiscal equality would end in "violence and cruelty on the part of the husband leading to a separation."[249] Lord Westbury agreed that the Bill was "an entire subversion of the system of domestic rule which had prevailed in this country for more than 1,000 years," and suggested that conferring power on women with respect to property would lead to capricious waste, "enabl[ing] her to contract, so that she might take a fancy to buying any number of bracelets." Like Eve, a married woman in control of her property would "certainly yield" to temptation.[250] Even the Earl of Shaftesbury thought that "somebody must regulate the affairs of the family … [and] the head of the family must be the husband."[251] He also made clear the class-interests that were at stake:[252] "As regarded the upper classes, the provisions of the Bill went far beyond what was necessary, and struck at the root of domestic happiness, introducing insubordination, equality, and something more. They would allow a

---

245 *Ibid* at 72.

246 *Ibid* at 73.

247 UK, HC Deb, 18 May 1870, vol 201, col 888.

248 UK, HL Deb, 21 June 1870, vol 202, col 603.

249 UK, HL Deb, 21 June 1870, vol 202, col 604.

250 UK, HL Deb, 21 June 1870, vol 202, cols 606–7.

251 UK, HL Deb, 21 June 1870, vol 202, col 617.

252 UK, HL Deb, 21 June 1870, vol 202, col 610. See further Griffin, *supra* note 218 at 66–83.

married woman to hold and deal with property like a *feme sole*." On the other hand, the Lords generally thought it necessary to introduce some form of protection for "the wife of a working man [who] was the moving principle of the whole family."[253] That is, conferring a measure of financial protection on lower class women would, it was thought, have the effect of insulating those women from their husbands' potentially dissolute habits (such habits being confined, the Lords told themselves, to the lower orders[254]), thereby alleviating some financially based marital stress and helping to protect the family unit.

In its amended form,[255] then, the Bill (which became the *Married Women's Property Act 1870*) simply provided that certain types of property were to be treated as a married woman's "separate estate"; that is, married women were *not* to be treated as *femes sole*. "Only some of a wife's property was removed from her husband's control, and that by creating a fictional trust rather than by giving a married woman the same ability to control her property as her single sisters enjoyed."[256] This extension of the equitable settlement to women of lesser means reflected the fact that while settlements "were certainly intended in part to protect daughters against unwise marriages, they were not intended to do so at the expense of what was seen as the divinely ordained and necessary relationship between husband and wife."[257]

The situation thus remained essentially the same for women with any substantial interests in property because those women were, in

---

253 UK, HL Deb, 21 June 1870, vol 202, col 613 (Earl of Shaftesbury). See also Holcombe, *supra* note 21 at 175.

254 Griffin, *supra* note 218 at 66–7, 71.

255 "Led by Lord Cairns, the select committee of the Lords tore the Commons' bill to shreds, striking out fourteen of its seventeen substantive clauses and replacing them with new provisions, and amending the other three." Holcombe, *supra* note 21 at 177.

256 Shanley, "Married Women's Property," *supra* note 21 at 68. This limited property encompassed a wife's earnings; investments in certain instruments; and property coming to her as beneficiary of an intestate estate, and legacies of less than £200. Money earned before marriage or before the Act came into effect was not covered, while investments could only be treated as separate property if the account was so registered. The limitation on legacies was intended to facilitate receipt by poorer women; wealthier women receiving larger bequests were still required to obtain a settlement from the courts of equity, which had jurisdiction over legacies in excess of £200. Despite these various restrictions, clauses that imposed financial responsibilities on wives remained in place after the Lords had finished with the Bill. As Shanley has pointed out, this superficial nod to gender equality masked women's unequal access to economic and social resources: *ibid* at 75–6.

257 Griffin, *supra* note 218 at 74.

all likelihood, already protected by equitable marriage settlements –
and there was little appetite in Parliament for any change that would
enable those women to challenge their husbands, whose character
was, in any event, thought to be unimpeachable.[258] Poorer women,
however, were granted *some* rights to their earnings, but only in the
form of separate estates; and unless a couple was separated, it was
questionable whether a woman would actually see the income held in
trust for her benefit. The property-based changes enacted in the 1870
law thus amounted to an attempt by Parliament to extend upper- and
middle class family ideology to the lower orders. There was absolutely no question that marriage was, and ought to remain, the core
relation within the private family; on the contrary, reform of married women's property laws targeted lower class families in order
to stabilize marriages believed to be suffering from the taint of male
dissolution.[259]

In the following decade it became clear that the 1870 Act was rid-
dled with problems that went beyond its basic conservatism,[260] and
further attempts were made to establish the right of married women
to be treated as *femes sole*.[261] Eventually, the *Married Women's Property
Act 1882*[262] extended equitable protection to all of a married woman's
property,[263] but it fell far short of conferring equal rights upon wives.[264]

---

258 *Ibid* at 78.

259 As Shanley has noted, "feminists won (albeit partially) the legal measures they
sought without their ideology making much headway even among liberal MPs":
Shanley, "Married Women's Property," *supra* note 21 at 75.

260 For example, it was decided in one case that a wife was not able to sue her husband
for stealing her property, even after a judicial separation. Griffin, *supra* note 218
at 80 referring to *Manchester Evening News*, 13 November 1878. The passage of the
Supreme Court of Judicature Act 1873, 36 & 37 Vict c 66, also made it clear that further
resolution was needed with respect to the common law's treatment of married
women's property: *ibid* at 81.

261 Coleridge introduced a bill in 1875 that used the language of *feme sole* rights, while
John Hinde Palmer's 1880 bill spoke of a woman's ability to deal with her property
"as if she were unmarried": Shanley, *Feminism, Marriage and the Law, supra* note 18
at 125.

262 45 & 46 Vict, c 75.

263 As Dicey put it, "the Act, as it were, provides every woman on her marriage with a
settlement": Dicey, *supra* note 20 at 389.

264 Confusingly, the Act speaks of a married woman's ability to deal with "separate
property, in the same manner as if she were a feme sole": s 1(1). This blend of
common law and equitable principles points to the concern at the time with
removing the difficulties caused by the coexistence of law and equity. The *Supreme
Court of Judicature Act 1873*, 36 & 37 Vict c 66, had brought procedural fusion to

Mary Lyndon Shanley has described the effect of the 1882 Act as follows:

> The language that gave married women control of their property and enabled them to make contracts and wills by proclaiming that a married woman's property was to be her "separate property" or "separate estate" circumscribed a married woman's ability to use and be responsible for her property in particular and significant ways. A married woman did not acquire full contractual capacity; her contract did not bind her personally but only her separate property. Even property a married woman acquired after incurring a debt was not liable to satisfy the debt, since it was not her "separate property" at the time she made the contract.[265]

In the broader context of the dissolution of the legal household and the ideological shift towards confining women's work to the domestic realm, and casting that work as unproductive, it is both pertinent and unsurprising to find that the protection afforded women by the *Married Women's Property Acts* also ignored women's domestic contributions as sources of enforceable interests in property. Under the Acts, a married woman was entitled to retain earnings derived from employment separate from her husband (i.e., wage labour),[266] but the idea that a wife's domestic labour alone gave rise to any kind of enforceable interest in matrimonial property was not recognized until the second half of the twentieth century (though maintenance orders were of course possible in the event of divorce).[267] As Otto Kahn-Freund observed: "Equality of treatment of husband and wife was restricted to those cases in which they exercised equal economic functions: work for wages, professional activities, etc. It did not extend to the contribution the wife made to

---

English law, but the 1882 Act was part of further efforts to align the separate streams in a more substantive way. See further Holcombe, *supra* note 21 at 210.

265 Shanley, *Feminism, Marriage and the Law, supra* note 18 at 126–7. See also Holcombe, *supra* note 21 at 201–5; Dicey, *supra* note 20 at 389–90.

266 45 & 46 Vict, c 75, s 2.

267 Moreover, as Cretney has noted, the separate property regime established by the 1882 Act meant that in cases where title to the matrimonial home was in the husband's name only (standard practice in the first half of the twentieth century), he "was, therefore, legally entitled to the lot": Stephen Cretney, "The Family and the Law – Status or Contract?" (2003) 15:4 *CFLQ* 403 at 408. It was only with the *Matrimonial Causes Act 1973* that a court was required to have regard to "the contributions made by each of the parties to the welfare of the family, including any contribution made by looking after the home or caring for the family," for the purpose of exercising its powers with respect to financial provision orders and property adjustment orders: s 25(f).

the family's well-being as a housewife and a mother ... It ignored the diversity of normal economic functions of husband and wife, and was, in a sense, as mechanical as the crude idea of "freedom of contract" which insists on treating as "equals" landlord and tenant, employer and employee."[268] The courts also tended towards strictness when ascertaining just how "separate" a woman's employment was from her husband – it seems that an almost complete lack of involvement by a husband in a wife's endeavours needed to be shown in order for a wife to retain her interest in moneys earned; that is, a husband's property interest in his wife's labour remained in the absence of clear evidence to the contrary.[269]

The 1882 Act also did nothing to preclude the continued use of marriage settlements by wealthier families; in particular, restraints upon anticipation, by which women were prevented from pledging anything but the income from their property in order to raise capital, remained in force.[270] Separate legal regimes thus continued to govern the property interests of women from different classes: equitable settlements under the law of trusts for the wealthy, and statutory protection for everyone else. In essence, Parliament had decided that women who were married to dissolute husbands – the lower classes, in the self-serving world view of many MPs and Lords – should enjoy an expanded set of property rights but only in the mediated form of settlements; while for wealthier women, nothing more than the extant trust-based settlement system was necessary. The underlying logic of this class-based approach and the extension of property rights to women of lesser means was less about gender (or class) equality and more about constructing a legal regime that protected the marriage-based family unit – across all classes – in terms that accorded with the gendered ideology of the times. In this respect, the *Married Women's Property Acts* can be seen to have formed part of a congeries of laws that spoke the language of liberalism but which in actuality extended patriarchy in a range of ways.[271] As William

---

268 Kahn-Freund, "Matrimonial Property," *supra* note 20 at 248.

269 For example, in a Scottish case, *Dryden v M'Gibbon; M'Gibbon v Dryden* [1907] SC 1131, the Court of Session held that the *Married Women's Property Act 1877*, 40 & 41 Vict c 29, did not apply in a situation where a wife managed a business run by the couple; her employment had to be under some other person unless the business was entirely removed from her husband's control. In *Lovell v Newton* (1878) 4 CPD 7, a wife was held to have been operating a business outside of her husband's control when his alcohol-related illness prevented him from any involvement with the business. See also *Morrison v Tawse's Executrix* (1888) 16 R 247.

270 Shanley, "Married Women's Property," *supra* note 18 at 75.

271 See chapters 3 and 4.

Pinder Eversley put it in his discussion of the effects of the 1882 Act, "a married woman's ... matrimonial status is not affected – the common law right of the husband to her society and comfort remains; he is still the head of the family."[272]

V. Conclusion

Alexis de Tocqueville once observed that "industrial nations have a particularly serious idea of marriage."[273] This chapter points to the veracity of de Tocqueville's insight in the English legislative context. Over the course of the eighteenth and nineteenth centuries, the English Parliament advanced a conception of marriage as a relation of significant public importance because of its centrality to the private family, and the corresponding national interest in its regulation. In the mid-eighteenth century, the English state clearly signalled its interest in the marital relations of its citizens with *Lord Hardwicke's Act's* usurpation of ecclesiastical authority over marital validity and remedies for breach of promises to marry. Further Acts in the 1830s consolidated civil control over the validity of English marriages. Throughout the nineteenth century, Parliament also emphasized that marriage was the English state's preferred relational model for its citizens through legislation that incentivized marriage by way of financial punishment and inducement; and sought to stabilize existing marriages via a partial incursion into coverture, and the provision of limited access to judicial divorce. In these respects, marriage and the private family were constituted in law as publicly important means for, and ends to, the proper functioning of the English nation. In accordance with prevailing ideology, this process played out in distinctly patriarchal terms that affirmed the dominance of husbands, rather than masters, within the newly confined sphere of the family. The following chapter shows that these legislative moves formed part of a broader legal process, involving judicial (and, as chapter 2 demonstrated, scholarly) interventions, through which marriage was positioned at the centre of the legal (and social) family.

---

272 William Pinder Eversley, *The Law of the Domestic Relations: Including Husband and Wife, Parent and Child, Guardian and Ward, Infants, and Master and Servant* (London: Stevens and Haynes, 1885) at 403. See also Shanley, *Feminism, Marriage and the Law, supra* note 18 at 127–8; Tomlins, *supra* note 7 at 377.

273 Alexis de Tocqueville, *Democracy in America,* translated by Arthur Goldhammer (New York: Library of America, 2004) at 695.

Chapter Six

The Public Importance of Marriage in English Common Law

The contract of marriage is the most important of all human transactions. It is the very basis of the whole fabric of civilized society. The *status* of marriage is *juris gentium*, and the foundation of it, like that of all other contracts, rests on the consent of the parties. But it differs from other contracts in this, that the rights, obligations, or duties, arising from it, are not left entirely to be regulated by the agreements of the parties, but are, to a certain extent, matters of municipal regulation, over which the parties have no control, by any declaration of their will.[1]

I. Introduction

Previous chapters have traced some of the ways that scholars and legislators in the eighteenth and nineteenth centuries helped to construct a legal conception of marriage as the primary relation within the private family[2] – a relation which, for that very reason, came to be defined in large

---

1 *Duntze (or Levett) v Levett* (1816) (Lord Robertson) [*Duntze*] in James Fergusson, *Reports of Some Recent Decisions by the Consistorial Court of Scotland in Actions of Divorce, Concluding for the Dissolution of Marriages Celebrated Under the English Law* (Edinburgh, 1817) at 70 ff, extracted in Joseph Story, *Commentaries on the Conflict of Laws, Foreign and Domestic, in Regard to Contracts, Rights, and Remedies, and Especially in Regard to Marriages, Divorces, Wills, Successions and Judgments* (Boston: Hilliard, Gray, 1834) at 101 §109 (emphasis in Story).

2 I think it is unquestionable that law and legal thought in this domain helped to shape the contours of broader cultural attitudes and practices; as O'Donovan has noted, "legal structures constitute the family and roles within it": Katherine O'Donovan, "Family Law and Legal Theory" in William Twining, ed., *Legal Theory and Common Law* (Oxford: Basil Blackwell, 1986) 184 at 192. However, my point in this chapter is not so much to trace the mutually constitutive nature of legal and social thought (and

measure by its public importance and the degree of state involvement in its formation, subsistence, and dissolution.[3] This chapter addresses the role played by the English judiciary in this process through the lens of two distinct (and distinctly periodized) spheres of legal activity: the action for breach of promise to marry; and the validity and dissolubility of marriages within the (then) developing field of private international law. At a macro level, it shows how, in each of these domains, judicial conceptions of marriage gradually shifted away from the canonical understanding of marriage as a private exchange of promises (albeit preferably solemnized *in facie ecclesiae*[4]), moving instead towards a view of marriage as an exceptional species of contract: one whose formation was regulated by the state; to which ordinary contractual principles did not always apply; and which in its essence was, at least in certain contexts, a form of status owing to the degree of state control over its existence. In this respect, the chapter shows how judges used contract (the archetypal device for *private* legal ordering[5]) as a tool for the construction of *public* norms in the area of domestic relations;[6] and also how contract itself became exceptionalized in its application to the family – a development contiguous with the intellectual process of constructing the family and its Family Law as oppositional to the market and its Law

---

practice) vis-à-vis the family and marriage (to the extent that law and society can even be considered as separate domains), but rather to show how the specifically legal understanding of marriage as a relation of public importance developed in English common law and legal thought. On the constitutive nature of law, the difficulties associated with the law/society distinction, and the merits of doctrinally focussed legal history see Robert W. Gordon, "Critical Legal Histories" (1984) 36 Stan L Rev 57 at 100–125.

3 See chapters 2 and 5 for discussion of, respectively, the scholarly and legislative dimensions of this transition.

4 Rebecca Probert, *Marriage Law and Practice in the Long Eighteenth Century* (Cambridge: Cambridge University Press, 2009), chapter 2 [Probert, *Marriage Law*].

5 Hugh Collins, "Contract and Legal Theory" in Twining, *supra* note 2 at 136.

6 The press was crucial to the dissemination of these ideas through the frequent reports of law cases in newspapers and periodicals, particularly those of a salacious or scandalous type. It will be seen below that many of the reports of the cases referred to in this chapter are from London newspapers. This is not, however, to suggest that the press simply functioned as a mouthpiece for the judiciary. Rather, David Lemmings' argument that "the theatre and counter-theatre that had been a function of courtroom proceedings before the mid-eighteenth century were not stifled by 'lawyerisation' but rather partly relocated to the 'public sphere' of the press," suggests that both the judiciary and the press were important shapers of public opinion and standards in matters of law. See David Lemmings, "Introduction: Criminal Courts, Lawyers and the Public Sphere" in David Lemmings, ed., *Crime, Courtrooms and the Public Sphere in Britain, 1700–1850* (London: Routledge, 2012) 1 at 4.

of Contract.[7] At a micro level, the chapter shows that these movements were subject to contestation as judges oscillated between adherence to the essentially medieval conception of marriage as a private contract, and a more modern understanding of the relation as infused with public importance and subject to non-modifiable forms of state regulation.

Part II addresses the initiating exchange of promises to marry, and the action for breach of promise to marry, which came to prominence in the wake of *Lord Hardwicke's Act's* prohibition on ecclesiastical orders for specific performance of such promises.[8] It shows that while the very nature of the action framed the promise to marry in terms of contract, in practice judges (as well as lawyers and litigants) departed from the approach taken in early cases in which plaintiffs sought to enforce promises to marry, and deviated from the consolidating body of principles comprising the Law of Contract,[9] by effectively restricting the action to women, lowering the standard of proof in questions over offer and acceptance, and permitting damages awards based on emotional harm. By remaining within the bounds of contract these cases upheld the traditional emphasis on individual consent in marriage formation. At the same time, by stretching the application of contractual doctrine almost to breaking point, the cases helped to consolidate a legal understanding of marriage as a relation of utter centrality to the private family and its Law of Domestic Relations,[10] and underscored the particular social and economic importance of marriage for women in ways that extended male conjugal rights and the prevailing ideology of gender-based separate spheres.[11]

---

7 See chapter 2; also Janet Halley and Kerry Rittich, "Critical Directions in Comparative Family Law: Genealogies and Contemporary Studies of Family Law Exceptionalism" (2010) 58:4 *Am J Comp L* 753.

8 *An Act for the Better Preventing of Clandestine Marriage, 1753*, 26 Geo II, c 33 [*Lord Hardwicke's Act*].

9 In speaking of contract and the Law of Contract I do not mean to suggest that the understanding of these concepts and categories remained static throughout the eighteenth and nineteenth centuries; the details of bargaining theory were undoubtedly in a state of flux. That, however, does not diminish the claim that marriage was treated as an exceptional species of contract. For a comprehensive analysis of the development of modern English contract law see David J. Ibbetson, *A Historical Introduction to the Law of Obligations* (Oxford: Oxford University Press, 2001).

10 See, e.g., William Pinder Eversley, *The Law of the Domestic Relations: Including Husband and Wife, Parent and Child, Guardian and Ward, Infants, and Master and Servant* (London: Stevens and Haynes, 1885).

11 Carole Pateman, *The Sexual Contract* (Palo Alto: Stanford University Press, 1988), chapters 5 and 6. See also Christopher L. Tomlins, *Freedom Bound: Law, Labor, and Civic*

Part III considers the approach taken to marriage within eighteenth and nineteenth-century English (and Scottish) private international law. It shows that English courts in the eighteenth and early nineteenth centuries approached the issue of cross-jurisdictional marital validity in terms that drew little or no distinction between marriage and commercial contracts; in other words, a marriage solemnized outside of England was, like a contract made outside of England, valid within England so long as it comported with the requirements of the place of celebration. However, in the second half of the nineteenth century, under the influence of Scottish legal thought, English courts and scholars shifted away from this approach and emphasized instead England's deep interest in regulating certain aspects of the marriages of its subjects. In doctrinal terms, this emphasis on the national interest in marriage involved a shift away from the language and ideology of contract, in favour of a re-characterization of marriage as a form of status – not in the traditional sense of hereditary subordination to patriarchy,[12] but rather the modern legal sense of a relation "which concerns the public generally" and involves the imposition of non-modifiable rights and obligations.[13] This dimension of the story also intersects in interesting and important ways with the evolution of legal thought described in chapter 2, and the contribution made by a number of the scholars and judges discussed there to the development of the field of private international law.

Identity in Colonizing English America, 1580–1865 (New York: Cambridge University Press 2010) at 375.

12 See especially Henry Sumner Maine, *Ancient Law* (New York: Dorset Press, 1986) at 141.

13 *Salvesen or Von Lorang v Administrator of Austrian Property* [1927] AC 641. See also R.H. Graveson, *Status in the Common Law* (London: Athlone, 1953) at 2. English law and legal thought thus extended the broader trend within nineteenth-century Classical Legal Thought (CLT) towards distinguishing between contractual and status relations, into the consolidating field of private international law. According to Duncan Kennedy, CLT distinguished the emerging Law of Contract from putatively non-will based relations such as those within the domestic/familial sphere. The classical legal field was constructed by a process of abstracting hitherto scattered principles of contract into a coherent legal core, and subtracting from this contractual core quasi-contract, status, and tort. Within this framing, family relations were treated as forms of status because of their regulation by the state, thereby creating a conceptual and taxonomic distinction between the Law of Contract and the Law of Domestic Relations. See Duncan Kennedy, *The Rise & Fall of Classical Legal Thought* (Washington, DC: Beard Books, 2006) at 184–209.

II. Stretching the Bounds of Contract: The Action for Breach of Promise to Marry

The previous chapter discussed the ways in which *Lord Hardwicke's Act* fundamentally marked marriage as a relation of state interest. Intervening in the Church's longstanding authority over marital validity, the Act created civil conditions for the creation of a valid marriage, and thus constituted marriage as a *"civil* contract."[14] This assertion of civil jurisdiction over the law of marital validity extended to remedies for the breach of promises to marry. Whereas canon law was willing to compel parties to solemnize their promises *in facie ecclesiae,*[15] *Lord Hardwicke's Act* dispensed with this option altogether.[16] Consequently, jilted parties were left to fall back on the option offered by English common law: the action for breach of promise to marry, in which the remedy sought was not performance but monetary solatium.

The action for breach of promise developed in the seventeenth century. The first case appears to have been *Stretch v Parker,* heard during the reign of Charles I (1625–1649), in which it was said: "if A in consideration that B promised him to take to be her husband, promises to take B to be his wife *infra breve tempus* after, and after A marries another woman, B may have an action upon the case against A upon this promise, for this is a good consideration."[17] In 1672, in the case of *Holcroft v Dickenson,*[18] the plaintiff alleged that the defendant, by his breach of promise, had "hindered her preferment to her damage of 100 pounds." By majority, the Court of Common Pleas held that the action was maintainable at common law, rejecting the argument that the

---

14 Janet Halley, "What Is Family Law? A Genealogy. Part I" (2011) 23:1 *Yale JL & Human* 1 at 10.

15 Henry Swinburne, *A Treatise of Spousals, or Matrimonial Contracts: Wherein All the Questions relating to that Subject are ingeniously Debated and Resolved* (London, 1686) at 231–3. Such orders were backed by the threat of penance or excommunication. According to Helmholtz, "[b]y far the most common matrimonial cause in the medieval Church courts was the suit brought to enforce a marriage contract": R.H. Helmholtz, *Marriage Litigation in Medieval England* (New York: Cambridge University Press, 1974) at 25. This medieval approach differed from earlier English law, which treated a promise to marry as a betrothal, giving rise to a monetary claim in the event of a failure to complete. See Edward Manson, "Breach of Promise of Marriage" (1910) 11:1 *J Soc Comp Leg* 156 at 157.

16 26 Geo II, c 33, s 13.

17 *Stretch v Parker,* Mich 12 Car Rot 21; Ro Abr 22, cited in J. Dundas White, "Breach of Promise of Marriage" (1894) 10:2 *Law Q Rev* 135 at 135.

18 3 Keble 148 cited in White, *supra* note 17 at 135. See also *Harrison v Cage & Uxor* (1741) Carth 467.

only consideration in such matters was spiritual. Moreover, the Court affirmed the contractual nature of the agreement: "a promise that if the plaintiff would marry the defendant within a fortnight, the defendant would marry the plaintiff."[19] While "suit on such promise to execute the marriage must be in the Spiritual Courts," the same could not be said for "loss which is grounded on the agreement which is a temporal act."

Viewed in the broader context of seventeenth-century English attitudes towards marriage, it is not especially surprising that common law courts applied an early form of contractual analysis to breaches of promise to marry.[20] In his study of English family life in the period 1450–1700, Ralph Houlbrooke observed that while "the character of the proposed partner, and personal affection or love" were relevant factors in partner choice, "advancement of the individual or the family" and "[m]aterial substance" were often primary concerns because marriage at this point "was one of the chief means of securing that 'livelihood' upon whose possession individual and family security and independence chiefly rested."[21] Nevertheless, the action remained relatively marginal until the mid-eighteenth century, despite the success of plaintiffs such as Sarah Holt, who in 1730 was awarded £2000 damages for breach of a promise of marriage made by Knox Ward.[22] That changed with the passage of *Lord Hardwicke's Act*. From that point, and under the weight of increasing legal (and social) emphasis on marriage as the central relation within the private family, and the tightening connection between femininity and domesticity,[23] the action for breach of promise to marry took off.

---

19 The Court also referred to "one mutual promise of marriage" and declared, "nor is there a more valuable consideration in our law than marriage": 3 Keble 148.

20 Indeed, even in 1879, when the action displayed notable variations from ordinary contractual principles, MacColla declared: "In strictness, then, what is generally known as an action for breach of *promise* of marriage, is in reality an action for breach of a *contract* of marriage." Charles MacColla, *Breach of Promise: Its History and Social Considerations* (London: Pickering & Co., 1879) at 17.

21 Ralph A. Houlbrooke, *The English Family, 1450–1700* (Harlow: Longman Group, 1984) at 73–4. Among the upper classes "marriages were the occasion for the making of carefully worded treaties or settlements, which grew more and more elaborate as time went by": *ibid* at 83.

22 *A Collection of Remarkable Cases, for the Instruction of both Sexes, In the Business of Love and Gallantry. Being a modest and clear View of the three following Tryals. Viz. I. Of Richard Lyddel, Esq; for a Criminal Conversation with Lady Abergavenny. II. Of Knox Ward, Esq; for a Promise of Marriage to Miss Sarah Holt. III. Of Coll. Francies Chartres, for a Rape committed on the Body of Anne Bond, his Servant* (London, 1730) at 14.

23 In the words of Lord Lyndhurst: "The first thing to which a woman looks in early life is a matrimonial union, on which she may build all her prospects of future

These cases played an important role in consolidating the nineteenth-century legal understanding of marriage as a relation of significant public importance owing to its constitutive role within domestic relations, and its corresponding centrality to the gender-based separate spheres of family and work. In particular, courts contributed to the legal construction of the proper female subject as married, domestically oriented, and in a relationship of subservience to (and dependence upon) her husband, by departing from earlier case law and stretching the contractual foundations of the action in (at least[24]) three ways:

1. Feminizing the action through a de facto prohibition on men bringing claims, which emphasized and extended the expectation that women were, and ought to be, economically dependent upon men (preferably husbands, but in the event of a reputation-sullying breach of promise, the man who had compromised a woman's present and future prospects of marriage).
2. Lowering the standards of evidence with respect to offer and acceptance of marriage proposals, which extended the scope for a finding that a binding promise had been made, thereby enabling more men to be held to account for their words and actions. This approach in turn delineated the seriousness with which courts viewed women's (perceived and often also very real) need to be married, and the central position of marriage within the family.
3. By enlarging the scope of compensable heads of damage to include emotional distress – a move that underscored and extended the idea that women *ought* to be (or at least ought to *appear* to be) emotionally distraught over a broken marriage promise, and that men

---

happiness." UK, HL Deb, 3 March 1857, vol 144, col 1694. See generally Frances Olsen, "The Family and the Market: A Study of Ideology and Legal Reform" (1983) 96:7 *Harv L Rev* 1497; Pateman, *supra* note 11.

24 See Saskia Lettmaier, *Broken Engagements: The Action for Breach of Promise to Marry and the Feminine Ideal, 1800–1940* (New York: Oxford University Press, 2010) 34, 54, for further (arguable) deviations from contractual principles. Referring to the case of *Chamberlain v Williamson* (1814) 2 M & S 408, Lettmaier argues that the refusal of courts to permit an executor to bring a claim against a promisor deviated from the ordinary principle that contract claims survive the death of a party: at 54. That is true, but it must also be noted that in general contracts involving personal skill or service do not survive the death of the obligor. So, for instance, "an apprenticeship contract is terminated by the death of the master, and no claim to the services of the apprentice survives to the executor": William Anson, *Principles of the Law of Contract* (Oxford: Clarendon Press, 1879) at 298. So, it is correct to say that promises to marry were treated as somewhat exceptional vis-à-vis executors, but only to the extent of placing them within another category of contracts concerning personal services.

were responsible for women's economic support, whether or not a marriage took place.

Specific performance of marriage promises had been legislatively removed from the remedial menu, but the common law responded by emphasizing the danger for men of attempting to avoid their promises to women. In this respect, by awarding particular female litigants monetary damages (and the success rate was spectacularly high[25]), the courts constructed a general legal framework that operated as a strong encouragement to men to uphold their promises, based on the idea that marriage was the central, publicly important relation within the private family.[26]

A. Heart Balm for Women (Only)

Prior to *Lord Hardwicke's Act*, and for a number of decades thereafter, men brought actions for breach of promise just as much as women.[27] In 1741, for instance, an action of *assumpsit* was brought by a man against a woman for her refusal to honour her promise to marry him. According to the report of the case, "the cause was tried at the assises in Norfolk, and there was a verdict for the plaintiff, and 400l. damages, the woman being worth 3000l. when the plaintiff courted her, and afterwards by the death of her brother worth double that sum."[28] In another case heard in 1780, a merchant sued a widow for reneging on her promise to marry him; a decision she said was based simply on her growing dislike of the

---

25 Lettmaier, *supra* note 24 at 92.

26 This construction of marriage and women's role therein led many (upper- and middle class) women in the later nineteenth century to reject the action as a hindrance to women's equality. As Ginger Frost has observed, "[t]he nascent English women's movement of the late nineteenth century particularly faced a dilemma when confronted by the contradictions of an action that violated the very notion of women's equality and yet also offered valuable protection to many poorer women." Broadly speaking, abolitionists emphasized the action's gendered operation and its tendency to reinforce the nexus between women, marriage, and the domestic realm. Women who were in favour of retaining the action recognized this connection but argued that for many women, particularly women without economic resources of their own, marriage remained a crucial form of economic support – one that could be placed out of reach by the opprobrium of a broken engagement. Ginger S. Frost, "'I Shall Not Sit Down and Crie': Women, Class and Breach of Promise of Marriage Plaintiffs in England, 1850–1900" (1994) 6:2 *Gender & History* 224 at 225–6 [Frost, "Crie"].

27 Lettmaier, *supra* note 24 at 27–8. This being said, such claims were, for much of the eighteenth century, relatively uncommon: *ibid*.

28 *Harrison v Cage & Uxor* (1741) Carth 467.

plaintiff. The Court upheld the man's claim on the basis of expenses he incurred in preparation for the marriage, awarding him £600.[29] By the nineteenth century, though, courts and broader society came to view breach of promise claims by men as a form of gender deviance. Under the weight of separate spheres ideology, claims by men were viewed as emasculating because they amounted either to an assertion of a (feminine) desire for domesticity, or for the economic support of a woman.[30] Such claims therefore inverted accepted gender roles and their corresponding associations with increasingly distinct realms of work and family. While the law did not specifically exclude men from bringing breach of promise claims, courts made it abundantly clear that such actions would be given short shrift. In this manner, courts gave de facto approval to a distinct departure from the principle of mutuality that applied to commercial contracts.[31] As a contributor to *London Society* wrote in 1870:

> Our law possesses many beautiful principles, and one of them in regard to all contracts is that there must be *mutuality*; that is, that there shall be a common obligation on both sides to do or perform something, the obligation entailing a corresponding one to make compensation in case of breach. In theory there is mutuality in a marriage contract: in practice there is none. A man is made to pay damages if he runs off his bargain. How many men, however, have the courage to bring an action when they are jilted?[32]

The contributor's reading of the situation is supported by recent analysis of breach of promise cases, which found that women instigated over 95 per cent of claims in nineteenth-century England.[33] Specific cases from

---

29 *Schreiber v Frazer* (1780) referred to in Ginger S. Frost, *Promises Broken: Courtship, Class, and Gender in Victorian England* (Charlottesville: University Press of Virginia, 1995) at 16 [Frost, *Promises Broken*].

30 *The Times* noted in 1878: "As a tolerated custom the action for breach of promise of marriage has long been extinct on the male side of the question. No well-advised man would venture to call a woman into court for not fulfilling her promise to marry him." 12 February 1878 at 9.

31 As Lettmaier has suggested, "[i]n its practical restriction of the right of action to female plaintiffs, the nineteenth-century breach-of-promise suit then was .... no longer 'pure contract'": Lettmaier, *supra* note 24 at 30.

32 G.W.H., "Breach of Promise of Marriage," *London Society* (August 1870) 161 at 163.

33 Lettmaier, *supra* note 24 at 27; Frost, "Crie," *supra* note 26 at 225. Research into conviction rates in late eighteenth- and early nineteenth-century trials for property offences in London also reveals a distinctly gendered dimension: men were forty per cent more likely to be convicted, and "were also subjected to a harsher range of punishments than females": Peter King, *Crime and Law in England, 1750–1849* (Cambridge: Cambridge University Press, 2006) at 167–9.

the period give a sense of the opprobrium attached to actions brought by men. For example, in 1849 a man did "have the courage to bring an action" for a woman's breach of her promise to marry him. In response, counsel for the defendant ridiculed the claim as one "in which it was difficult to refrain from laughing," and asked the Court (and the jury), "Was there a man among them who did not despise the man who came into court with such a case as this?" The jury apparently shared this sentiment, finding in favour of the plaintiff on the evidence before the Court, but awarding him the nominal sum of one farthing.[34]

The following year, counsel for a female defendant informed the jury that, "[f]ortunately such ridiculous actions were not often brought on the part of a man," and proceeded to deride the idea that the plaintiff's heart was broken, characterizing him instead as a gold-digger seeking "the young lady's fortune." The jury agreed, awarding this plaintiff, too, just one farthing in damages. The judge in the case also declared, "that such actions should not be brought, and that he should, if requested, certify to deprive the plaintiff of costs."[35] This latter step was taken by the court in a case brought in 1875, despite the plaintiff succeeding in his claim and being awarded five guineas by the jury. As the plaintiff's counsel observed, "the refusal to certify [for costs] was ... virtually an absolute condemnation of the action.... The decision seemed to amount to this – that a gentleman should never come into court in such a case."[36]

That breach of promise to marry "was peculiarly a woman's action"[37] by this point is also apparent in the House of Commons debate that accompanied the introduction in 1879 of a motion to abolish the action at common law.[38] Mr. Herschell, the sponsor of the motion, noted the "scandalous" case of a man who had brought a claim against a woman out of "sheer avarice," being aware of her aversion to having her letters to the plaintiff read in court, and paying him £1000 to settle the claim.[39] In a more measured register, though, Herschell then observed that even in legitimate circumstances, "it was impossible for a man to obtain justice, for it was always difficult to get the facts fairly weighted by a jury. If he attempted, in the course of the case, to suggest that the woman was anything but an angel in temper – a very embodiment of all the female virtues – so that there would be some reason to justify a man

---

34 *Kershaw v Cass*, *The Times*, 21 March 1849 at 7.

35 *Nicholson v Turnbull*, *The Times*, 4 March 1850 at 7.

36 *Townsend v Bennett*, *The Times*, 20 April 1875 at 11.

37 UK, HC Deb, 6 May 1879, vol 245, col 1880 (Mr. Forsyth).

38 See further MacColla, *supra* note 20 at 52–4.

39 UK, HC Deb, 6 May 1879, vol 245, col 1869 (Mr. Herschell).

in not marrying her, the mere suggestion was enough to bring down upon him a whole torrent of invective from Judge, counsel, and jury."[40] He then noted that the action was essentially premised on the idea that "had the promise not been broken the *woman* would have had a home, a husband, and a maintenance."[41]

This gendered departure from older approaches to the action, and specifically from the contractual principle of mutuality, lent the exchange of promises to marry an exceptional character, based, it seems, on the fact that the relation concerned the family, and touched on mutually reinforcing legal and social ideas around the position of women as *wives* in the private domestic realm, functioning in turn as counterparts and supporting pillars for men's work in the public sphere of the market.[42]

---

40 UK, HC Deb, 6 May 1879, vol 245, col 1869 (Mr. Herschell).

41 UK, HC Deb, 6 May 1879, vol 245, col 1870 (Mr. Herschell). Herschell actually railed against this association of women with the domestic realm, declaring it "was not true that a woman earned her livelihood by performing her conjugal, social, and domestic duties." UK, HC Deb, 6 May 1879, vol 245, col 1872. In stark contrast, Sir Eardley Wilmot "maintained that marriage and a settlement in life were the one object of a woman's life, whereas men had numerous engagements to occupy their time and attention": UK, HC Deb, 6 May 1879, vol 245, cols 1876–7. In other words, men had their work, whereas a woman's lot was in the home – marriage and domestic labour were her work. The extent to which this view prevailed amongst the Commons more generally is unclear; the motion to abolish the action was carried 106 to 65, but this may have been directed by self-interest more than any ideological commitment to gender equality. In any event, no further action was taken on the matter, and subsequent attempts in the 1880s also faltered. See The Law Commission, *Breach of Promise of Marriage*, Report No 26 (London: HM Stationary Office, 1969) at 6 [15]. The action was not repealed until 1970: *Law Reform (Miscellaneous Provisions) Act 1970*, c 33.

42 Statutory amendments to the law of evidence in breach of promise cases eventually contributed to a counter-movement in social attitudes towards women who brought breach of promise claims. Prior to 1869, English law prohibited a party from giving evidence in her own cause. (The general rule had been amended in respect of most actions in 1851 in England: *An Act to amend the Law of Evidence, 1851*, 14 & 15 Vict, c 99. Section 4 expressly made an exception for breach of promise cases.) Female claimants in breach of promise suits were thus effectively shielded from public view, since male relatives and lawyers could bring claims on their behalf. In the absence of cross-examination revealing the contrary, it was simply assumed by courts that breach of promise resulted in emotional distress, meaning that the only real question was whether a promise had been made, and broken. The *Evidence Further Amendment Act 1869*, 32 & 33 Vict c, 68, s 1, abolished this rule, and in conjunction with high-Victorian decorum, made it effectively unthinkable for upper- and middle class women, who until that time had brought the majority of claims, to submit to the public spectacle of a breach of promise claim. (Some women presumably also refused to bring claims on ideological grounds: see *supra* note 25.) As *The Times* put it in 1878, a "lady of delicate feeling would rather die than make it, whether in private

B. "It Would Be Indelicate to Expect that She Should Consent in Words"

Cases to enforce a promise of marriage prior to *Lord Hardwicke's Act* "required an actual exchange of promises and words which clearly related to marriage."[43] In his analysis of medieval marriage litigation, R.H. Helmholtz noted that in a case in which "a man and a woman 'clasped hands in the manner of contracting marriage, but no words were spoken,' the court held that no marriage had been contracted."[44] Canon law "also refused to admit the existence of a valid marriage from conduct alone."[45] There was much uncertainty about the necessary content of the words that had to be spoken to create a binding promise, but "words were necessary … as long as the parties could talk at all.… What created the indissoluble bond was the *exchange of words* of present consent."[46] In the nineteenth century, however, the approach to evidence concerning the exchange of promises departed from this hitherto clear principle in ways that stretched the contractual foundations of the action and suggested that marriage contracts were increasingly viewed as exceptional forms of contract. Specifically, courts adopted an extremely strict approach to male conduct concerning offers of marriage, and an equivalently permissive approach to female conduct with respect to acceptance of marriage proposals. The logic underpinning these doctrinal moves seems to have been the idea that marriage was a woman's true calling in life; courts therefore bent over backwards to ensure recompense for women whose marital prospects had been so cruelly sullied – and to send a more general message to men that it was perhaps in their own interest to perform according to their promises and avoid a damages award.

---

or, still more, with all the glaring publicity of an Assize Court, amid the scowls and the sneers of an assembled county": *The Times*, 12 February 1878 at 9. While women from the lower classes picked up the reins and continued to bring claims in the later parts of the century, by the early twentieth century they too had decided that the public dimensions of the action (and perhaps its patriarchal overtones) outweighed potential private benefits, and the action for breach of promise to marry effectively died a social death. See further Lettmaier, *supra* note 24 at 95–100, 132–37, 172; Frost, "Crie," *supra* note 26 at 225.

43 Helmholtz, *supra* note 15 at 45.

44 *Ibid* citing Canterbury YII, fols 28r, 31r (1373).

45 *Ibid* at 46.

46 *Ibid* at 34. See also Lettmaier, *supra* note 24 at 24–5. In the early case of *Holcroft v Dickenson* (1674) 3 Keble 148, "one mutual promise of marriage" is referred to as the basis for the action, but there is no discussion of what constituted acceptable evidence of mutual promises.

The exceptional nature of promises to marry within contractual doctrine is apparent in Joseph Chitty's 1841 *Practical Treatise on The Law of Contracts*, in which it was said of contracts in general: "In order to constitute a binding contract, there must be a definitive promise by the party charged, accepted by the person claiming the benefit of such promise. There must be a request on one side and an assent on the other. No contract is raised by a mere *ex parte* affirmation in discourse; a mere overture or offer to enter into an agreement not expressly and absolutely assented to by both parties."[47] Of cases concerning a contract to marry, however, Chitty said, "[i]t is not … necessary to prove an express promise to marry *in totidem verbis*. The contract may be evidenced by the unequivocal conduct of the parties, and by a general yet definite and reciprocal understanding between them, their friends and relations, evinced and corroborated by their actions, that a marriage was to take place."[48] That is, in cases concerning promises to marry, courts were content to hold parties to a different standard of proof with respect to offer and acceptance than that which applied in ordinary circumstances. The determination of what amounted to behaviour indicating an intimacy from which an intention to make or accept a marriage proposal might reasonably be inferred was thus constituted as a judicial vehicle for the reflection and extension of social norms. For men, the approach adopted by the courts to offers of marriage may have seemed particularly harsh, holding them to standards of almost impossible propriety. In contrast, the courts took an exceptionally accommodating approach to evidence of women's acceptance of proposals, though in its own way this approach also affirmed strict nineteenth-century ideas around feminine decorum and (lack of) agency. The message was clear: marriage was central to the private family, to women, and to the English nation; and courts were willing to assist in the construction of these norms by adjusting general principles of contract to fit the specifics of promises to marry.

As a matter of legal doctrine, implication was by no means foreign to general contract law concerning offer and acceptance.[49] The standard in

---

47 Joseph Chitty, *A Practical Treatise on the Law of Contracts, Not Under Seal: And the Usual Defences to Actions Thereon*, 3rd ed. by Tompson Chitty (London: S Sweet, 1841) at 9 [Chitty, *Practical Treatise*] citing *Jackson v Galloway* (1838) 5 Bing (NC). See further Lettmaier, *supra* note 24 at 36.

48 Chitty, *Practical Treatise*, *supra* note 47 at 536.

49 As Chitty put it, "[t]he assent of a party to an agreement, in other words, his promise, is either *express* or *implied.… Implied* are such as reason and justice dictate; and which, therefore, the law presumes that every man undertakes to perform." As examples, he referred only to instances in which some form of work was completed

cases concerning marriage, however, was markedly different. Concerning offers, the case of *Billing v Smith* (1861) is particularly instructive. According to Lettmaier:

> [N]one of the witnesses for the plaintiff could testify to an express promise of marriage. All their evidence amounted to was that the defendant had been frequently seen in the plaintiff's shop, that his deportment towards her had been "gallant," and that they had once been "very deeply in conversation." Despite the fact that there was a perfectly innocent explanation for the defendant's visits – he was the plaintiff's landlord and therefore obliged to call for his rent from time to time – and although one witness admitted under cross-examination that the defendant's conduct was only "such as a gentleman would pay to every other female," the jury arrived at the conclusion that Mr Smith had made Mrs Billing an offer of marriage and awarded her £50.[50]

Another case, *Morris v Maddox*,[51] concerned an alleged promise to marry arising out of conduct in a public house called the Unicorn Inn. The plaintiff, Ann Morris, met John Maddox when she began to work at the Inn, which was run by her brother-in-law. There was no evidence of any particular proposal of marriage, but Ann's relatives claimed that John's visits to the Inn increased after Ann's arrival and, it seems, "he no longer paid for what he drank at the Unicorn, but was entertained by the landlord gratis." On this basis, the jury found that John had impliedly promised to marry Ann.[52]

An equally permissive attitude is evident in cases where acceptance of an offer was in issue. In *Hutton v Mansell*,[53] for instance, Chief Justice Holt upheld a claim for breach of promise in spite of there being "no actual promise on the woman's side." In his view, "there was sufficient evidence to prove that the woman likewise promised, because she carried herself as one consenting and approving the promise of the man."[54]

Indeed, it seems that a woman's family could consent on her behalf (without any kind of agency relationship). The 1826 case of *Daniel v Bowles*[55] is perhaps the clearest illustration of this principle. On 20

---

for another person (which would now be classified as claims for restitution based on unjust enrichment, rather than claims based on an implied contract). *Ibid* at 19–20.

50 Lettmaier, *supra* note 24 at 35.

51 *Morning Chronicle*, 25 March 1856, in Lettmaier, *supra* note 24 at 35.

52 Lettmaier, *supra* note 24 at 35–6.

53 (1795) 3 Salk 16.

54 (1795) 3 Salk 16.

55 (1826) 2 Car & P 553.

February of that year, Captain Bowles was introduced to the plaintiff and her mother in Pisa. Six days later, he declared his love for Miss Daniel to her mother. An interview thereafter took place between Captain Bowles, Miss Daniel, and her mother. The report of the case then says the following: "The defendant introduced the subject, and said, that he hoped that there was no objection on the part of the young lady's parents. The witness [Miss Daniel's mother] replied, that there was none, upon which he took her hand, and said to her, "from this time consider me as your son." *It did not appear that the plaintiff made any observation.*"[56] It was subsequently discovered that Captain Bowles was already married and a claim was brought on behalf of Miss Daniel for breach of promise. Counsel for Captain Bowles claimed, "that there was not sufficient evidence of a promise to support the action, there ought to be mutual promises, and there was no proof of any promise by the plaintiff." However, the Court rejected this approach to the issue. In the words of Chief Justice Best: "I think that her being present, and not making any objection, coupled with what happened afterwards, shews that she consented, and would be sufficient to enable the defendant to maintain an action against her. It would be indelicate to expect that she should consent in words. No doubt that the Jury must be satisfied that there were mutual promises; but I think there is evidence from which they may be inferred."[57] Treatise writers later in the century reiterated this principle.[58] Charles MacColla in his 1879 work, *Breach of Promise*, wrote that "[a]n express promise to marry ... cannot always be shown.... In such cases the jury consider the conduct of the parties during the alleged engagement, and evidence may be given showing whether their friends and relatives regarded and received them as persons engaged to be married."[59] Similarly, Nevill Geary, in *The Law of Marriage and Family Relations: A Manual of Practical Law*, declared: "The promise need not be in express words, but may be evidenced by the unequivocal conduct of their friends and relations, that a marriage is to take place."[60]

---

56 (1826) 2 Car & P 553 at 553–4 (emphasis added).

57 (1826) 2 Car & P 553 at 534. See also *Gough v Farr* (1827) 2 Car & P 631.

58 The same principle appears to have applied in the United States: see BJF, "Actions for Breach of Promise of Marriage" (1872) 20:2 *Am Law Reg* 65 at 68.

59 MacColla, *supra* note 20 at 20. This approach to acceptance may have been informed by older approaches to marriage agreements, in which the wishes (or lack thereof) of the parties to be married were subsidiary to the benefits accruing to their respective families. See Houlbrooke, *supra* note 21 at 68–73.

60 Nevill Geary, *The Law of Marriage and Family Relations: A Manual of Practical Law* (London: A&C Black, 1892) at 411. See also A Solicitor, *A Familiar Compendium of the Law of Husband and Wife; in Two Parts* (London, 1831) at 176.

These examples show that courts in the nineteenth century developed the modern legal emphasis on marriage as the central relation within the private family partly by drawing upon and stretching the boundaries of contractual doctrine. Offer and acceptance of marriage remained necessary in order to ground a claim for breach of promise to marry, but the courts developed an approach that dramatically increased the chances that a legally actionable exchange of promises would be found, and they did so in ways that drew upon and extended social and legal norms concerning female passivity, the nexus between femininity and domesticity, and the duty of men to support women – preferably within marriage, but in lieu thereof through damages awards.

C. *Expectations of Emotional Harm*

Courts also emphasized the (public) importance of marriage to women and the legal family by stretching contractual doctrine concerning compensable heads of damage. In contrast with the approach to damages for breach of commercial contracts, courts in breach of promise cases took account of the emotional harm experienced by the female victim of a broken engagement (and the nefarious behaviour of the male defendant), as well as her economic loss. This development – a move away from both the "conventional economics of contract"[61] and the practice established in early breach of promise cases, which conceptualized the action in distinctly mercantile terms[62] – reinforced a number of ideas: that marriage was a relation of such unique importance that it was to be *expected* that a woman would feel socially humiliated by a breach of promise to marry; that the loss occasioned by a breach of promise went far beyond (though still included) the financial advancement of a good match (or, for lower class women, the support provided by a husband's wages); and that the law would provide a remedy for women that reflected the private and public significance of marriage.

Nineteenth century law was generally strict about which types of loss were compensable.[63] According to John Mayne's *Treatise on Damages*,

---

61 Lettmaier, *supra* note 24 at 48.

62 In *Holcroft*, it was alleged that the defendant by his breach of promise had "hindered her preferment to her damage of 100 pounds": *Holcroft v Dickenson* (1674) 3 Keble 148. Soon after, in *Harrison v Cage & Uxor* (1741) Carth 467, a man was awarded £400 after his betrothed married another man – the basis of the award was clearly loss of advancement, "the woman being worth £3000 when the plaintiff courted her, and after the death of her brother worth double that sum." See White, *supra* note 17 at 135–36.

63 As was tort law, which generally prohibited recovery for mental anxiety that did not fall within the category of "nervous shock" occasioned by witnessing an accident. In

"as a general rule, the primary and immediate result of the breach of contract alone can be looked to"; thus, the party in breach was to be held liable "in proportion to the benefit he is to receive from its performance."[64] Under the second limb of *Hadley v Baxendale*,[65] damages arising from circumstances peculiar to the case (that is, not in the usual course of things) were held to be recoverable only if the person in breach knew of the special circumstances (and, it was later held, specifically agreed to the additional liability[66]). Injured feelings and the motive of a party in breach were not relevant factors.[67] And yet they *were* relevant in breach of promise cases.[68]

In Mayne's view, while actions for breach of promise to marry "ought strictly to have been considered under the head of Contracts," they were "of so exceptional a nature" that it was preferable to consider such claims outside of contract. In part, this was because these actions were the only class of case in which "the motives or conduct of a party breaking a contract, or any injurious circumstances not flowing from the breach itself, could be considered in damages where the action is on the contract."[69] The relevance of the defendant's conduct is apparent from extant forms of pleading. In the 1809 edition of his *Treatise on Pleading*, Chitty's template for a claim "For not marrying" included a description of the putative defendant as "not regarding his said promise and undertaking, but contriving and fraudulently intending craftily and subtly to deceive and injure the said [plaintiff]."[70] In 1885, William Pinder Eversley summarized this approach to damages in breach of

---

Lynch v Knight (1864) 9 HLC 398, Lord Wensleydale declared that, "[m]ental pain or anxiety the law cannot value and does not pretend to redress." See John Salmond, *The Law of Torts*, 2nd ed. (London: Stevens & Haynes, 1910) at 349.

64 John D. Mayne, *Mayne's Treatise on Damages*, 3rd ed. by John D. Mayne and Lumley Smith (London: Stevens & Haynes, 1877) at 35.

65 [1854] EWHC 70.

66 *British Columbia Saw Mill Co v Nettleship* [1868] LR 3 CP 499. See further Mayne, *supra* note 64 at 32–33.

67 On injured feelings see *Addis v Gramophone Company Limited* [1909] AC 488. On motive see Mayne, *supra* note 64 at 35.

68 In the American context, the principles upon which damages for breach of promise were awarded was the subject of a strenuous attack by George Lawyer: "Indeed so generously favored have been actions of this kind, that the amount of recovery is not dependent upon the real loss occasioned by the breach, while in all other actions for breaches of contract the actual damage alone is the full measure of the award." George Lawyer, "Are Actions For Breach of the Marriage Contract Immoral?" (1884) 38 *Central LJ* 272 at 272.

69 Mayne, *supra* note 64 at 35.

70 Joseph Chitty, *A Treatise on Pleading: With a Collection of Practical Precedents, and Notes Thereon* (London, 1809) vol 2 at 90–1.

promise cases: "What are known as "sentimental damages," such as for injured feelings and the like, on the breach of *this contract alone* are allowed to be reckoned in the assessment of the fine;[71] and the strict pecuniary loss caused by the breach of the defendant, e.g., loss of an establishment in life, or a share of the affluence of the defendant,[72] is not the only item taken into consideration."[73] It was not always thus. Damages in the foundational cases of *Holcroft v Dickenson* and *Harrison v Cage & Uxor* were clearly based upon pecuniary concerns; and in cases where plaintiffs could not quantify the loss of expected financial gain, damages were calculated according to expenses actually incurred, not affective harm.[74] *Chamberlain v Williamson*[75] is an early example of the nineteenth-century shift in approach to damages for breach of promise. The case is typically considered in relation to its finding that an executor cannot bring a breach of promise claim because of the personal nature of the promise.[76] In the course of explaining this principle, Lord Ellenborough described the damage occasioned by breach of promise of marriage as a "personal suffering of the testator" and analogized the harm to claims arising in tort; indeed, he said that such a claim was not based on "an increase in the individual transmissible personal estate" but was rather in the nature of a claim for "personal injury" – and hence could not survive to an executor.[77]

Perhaps the clearest judicial statement of the principle to be applied concerning aggravated damages in breach of promise cases is that of the Court of Common Pleas in *Berry v Da Costa*,[78] an appeal against an award of damages in a case brought by the daughter of a dressmaker against the defendant, "a gentleman of some position."[79] The

---

71 *Frost v Knight* (1865) LR 7 Ex 111.

72 *Jones v James*, 18 LT 243. *Berry v Da Costa* (1866) LR 1 CP 331.

73 Eversley, *supra* note 10 at 127 (emphasis added). See also Manson, *supra* note 15 at 158. As a consequence of the focus on the particular injury to a particular plaintiff, an unfortunate practice became evident in which women of what might euphemistically be described as "greater charm" tended to receive higher damages awards than their plainer sisters. Thus, as White wrote in 1894, "If the girl be pretty, the jury generally give her heavy damages; if she be unattractive, they often have a sneaking sympathy with the man." White, *supra* note 15 at 141.

74 Lettmaier, *supra* note 24 at 25–6 referring to *Schreiber v Frazer* (1780).

75 (1814) 2 M & S 408.

76 See, e.g., Joseph Chitty, *A Practical Treatise on the Law of Contracts Not Under Seal; and Upon the Usual Defences to Actions Thereon*, 4th ed. by John A Russell (London: S Sweet, 1850) at 471.

77 (1814) 2 M & S 408 at 415–16.

78 *Berry v Da Costa* (1866) LR 1 CP 331.

79 *The Times*, 15 January 1866 at 11.

Court rejected the contention that the trial judge had misdirected the jury on the principles to be applied in assessing damages. According to *The Times*, "Their Lordships were of opinion that there was no misdirection, as in an action for breach of promise the jury were not limited to giving damages for the pecuniary loss involved in the loss of position only, but were bound to give compensation for the injured feelings of the plaintiff."[80]

Thus, in debates accompanying the aforementioned parliamentary motion to abolish the action for breach of promise, Mr. Herschell noted that, "[i]n cases of this kind the law departed altogether from the ordinary rules in assessing damages for breach of contract. Wounded feelings were taken into account, while no regard was paid to other circumstances of the case."[81] Sir Henry James expressed a similar view, declaring that it "was an exceptional action ... the only action in which damages could be recovered for wounded feelings."[82] Indeed, by the early twentieth century, treatise writers went so far as to claim that "punitive or vindictive damages may be awarded in this species of action."[83] Whereas early editions of Mayne's *Treatise on Damages* had avoided characterizing damages for breach of promise as exemplary, the 1909 edition under the stewardship of Lumley Smith classified damages for breach of promises to marry as the *single exception* to the general rule in English law prohibiting exemplary damages for breach of contract.[84] Indeed, as late as 1957, Peter Bromley's *Family Law* declared: "It is on the subject of damages that contracts to marry differ most radically from other contracts; for whereas the general rule is that the plaintiff may recover compensation only for material loss, in the case of breach of promise to marry he may also claim exemplary damages."[85]

---

80 *Ibid*. The article also cites the case of *Smith v Woodbine* as authority for the same proposition. Both *Berry v Da Costa* and *Smith v Woodbine* were subsequently cited in parliamentary comment on the 1890 Bill to abolish actions for breach of promise to marry. G.R. Dodd (London) claimed, relying on those cases, "The rule that damages should be limited to pecuniary loss resulting not too remotely from the breach of contract is not applicable to these actions." See *The Law Times*, vol 89, 11 October 1890 at 387.

81 UK, HC Deb, 6 May 1879, vol 245, col 1870.

82 UK, HC Deb, 6 May 1879, vol 245, col 1886.

83 Frederick Octavius Arnold, *The Law of Damages and Compensation,* 2nd ed. (London: Butterworth, 1919) at 221.

84 John D. Mayne, *Mayne's Treatise on Damages,* 8th ed. by Lumley Smith (London: Stevens & Haynes, 1909) at 49, 575.

85 Peter M. Bromley, *Family Law* (London: Butterworths, 1957) at 23; see also 24–5 referring in particular to *Berry v Da Costa* (1866) LR 1 CP 331.

By placing a woman's injured feelings and loss of future (social and legal) status at the centre of the action, and imposing orders for damages that transcended standard contractual principles, nineteenth century courts cast promises to marry as distinctive exceptions to ordinary contractual principles. This judicial process of exceptionalizing promises to marry reinforced the legal (and social) nexus between women and marriage by constructing a doctrinal approach to damages for broken promises that rested on the expectation of women's emotional harm. That this departure from ordinary contractual principles was premised on the familial basis of the contract shows how contract itself became exceptionalized when it touched the family, and points to the public importance of marriage within the nineteenth-century legal conception of the private family.

III. The Status of Marriage in the Conflict of Laws

Despite the apparent strictness of its prohibition on clandestine marriages, *Lord Hardwicke's Act* undercut itself by providing that a marriage could not be invalidated on the ground that the parties had not been residents of the place in which the banns were published or where the marriage was celebrated.[86] "As long as banns were called *somewhere*, or a licence obtained, the requirements of the Act would be satisfied."[87] Moreover, the Act only applied to England and Wales,[88] meaning that couples wishing to evade the requirements of the Act could simply cross the border to Scotland (or another jurisdiction) and wed one another in accordance with the rather more lenient Scots law of marriage, which recognized as valid any vow made before witnesses.[89] According to John Gillis, "[t]he principal clients of Gretna Green and other border

---

86 26 Geo II, c 33, s 10. This carve-out may have reflected a consensus that it was simply beyond the power of English law to operate in such an extra-territorial manner.

87 Probert, *Marriage Law, supra* note 4 at 224.

88 26 Geo II, c 33, s 18. See also *Compton v Bearcroft* (1769) 2 Hag Con 444.

89 John R. Gillis, *For Better, For Worse: British Marriages, 1600 to the Present* (New York: Oxford University Press, 1985) at 195. This difference between the marriage laws of England and Scotland gestures towards a much broader point concerning the diffusion of English law throughout the Union and the British Empire. Pursuant to the *Acts of Union 1707*, "all law governing commerce and all law structuring government were to be converted to English law." Certain other domains of law were "excepted from union and allocated to Scottish courts," including the law of marriage and divorce. This deliberate difference between English and Scottish marriage law "turned the law of marriage into a pivotal spot for Scottish resistance to English law": Halley, *supra* note 13 at 27–30 citing John W. Cairns, "Scottish Law, Scottish Lawyers and the Status of the Union" in John Robertson, ed., *A Union for

marriage shops were not the few rich runaways enshrined in legend, but thousands of quite ordinary folk who, for a variety of reasons, wished a cheap, quick, and private union."[90] Nevertheless, it was the cases involving rich runaways and those of some social prominence that generally came before the courts.

These cases raised difficult questions concerning the validity of foreign marriages, and the jurisdiction of courts in one state to regulate and dissolve marriages conducted in another state. In the course of resolving these issues, English courts in the mid-nineteenth century moved away from the older legal emphasis on mutual consent and deference to the law of the place of celebration (*lex loci celebrationis*) in matters of both form and substance, and towards a view (contested but ultimately accepted) that the country with the most significant connection to the marriage should govern issues of capacity, with domicile as the determining factor,[91] leaving only matters of form to the law of the place of celebration (if different to the place of domicile). In this way, courts advanced a new conception of marriage as an exceptional species of contract on the basis that marriage was a relation of such public importance that states were entitled to set conditions for the creation of legally valid marriages that domiciliaries could not simply avoid by marrying abroad.[92] The flipside of this recognition of the national dimensions of marriage was acknowledgment by the English courts that in cases concerning dissolution, English law did not necessarily continue to govern marriages conducted in England when a married couple was domiciled elsewhere. This recognition of the national interest in marriage, and the non-modifiable terms and conditions that automatically affected capacity to marry and which attached to solemnized marriages by virtue of the law of the place of domicile, led to a general movement towards distinguishing marriage from contracts of a commercial nature (governed by *lex loci contractus*), resulting in a new legal concept of marriage

---

Empire: Political Thought and the Union of 1707* (Cambridge: Cambridge University Press, 1995) 243 at 266–7.

90 Gillis, *supra* note 89 at 195.

91 *Le Mesurier v Le Mesurier* [1895] AC 517 (PC).

92 As Niedhardt has observed, "[c]onflict rules applicable to the family cemented links between individuals, territories and nations." In contrast, "the law governing international economic relations dissolved jurisdictional borders": Alberto-Horst Niedhardt, *The Transformation of European Private International Law: A Genealogy* (PhD Dissertation, European University Institute, 2018) at 191 [unpublished].

as a form of status (though one that still arose through a contractual or contract-like exchange of promises).[93]

A. *Marriage, Contract, and Deference to* Lex Loci Celebrationis

In the mid-eighteenth century, English law determined the validity of a marriage celebrated outside England by asking whether the marriage was solemnized according to *lex loci celebrationis*. The same approach was taken in cases concerning commercial contracts.[94] In this particular respect, English law remained wedded to a largely medieval conception of marital validity, and aligned with seventeenth-century continental ideas concerning the treatment of marriage and other contracts in cross-jurisdictional contexts.[95]

A clear example of English law's adherence to *lex loci celebrationis* in questions of cross-border marital validity, and of the legal-conceptual equivalency between marriage and contract in the mid-eighteenth century, is the case of *Scrimshire v Scrimshire*.[96] It was a suit for restitution of conjugal rights brought by "a lady of good character" called Miss Jones. She and Mr. Scrimshire were English subjects, and were domiciled in England. Scrimshire sought a declaration that the marriage, which was celebrated in France, was null and void on the basis of formal improprieties under French law, most notably that at the time of solemnization both he and Miss Jones were under the age of 25 and had not obtained parental consent to the union. In determining the matter, Sir Edward Simpson asserted that "all nations have consented, or must be presumed to consent, for the common benefit and advantage, that such marriages should be good or not, *according to the laws of the*

---

93   The general emphasis on domicile in these cases also had the effect of reinforcing the sexual hierarchy within marriage because, following the unity of person idea that underpinned the doctrine of coverture, a woman's domicile was *ipso facto* taken to be that of her husband. See William Burge, *Commentaries on Colonial and Foreign Laws Generally, and In Their Conflict With Each Other, and With the Law of England* (London: Saunders & Benning, 1838) Vol I at 35.

94   See *Robinson v Bland* (1760) 2 Burr 1077, in which Lord Mansfield declared that "the place where the contract is made, and not where the action is brought, is to be considered in expounding and enforcing the contract": at [142]. In reaching this conclusion, Lord Mansfield expressly endorsed the position taken by Huber that contracts were governed either by *lex loci contractus* or the law intended by the parties. See Niedhardt, *supra* note 92 at 120–1, referring to Huber, Bk 1, title 3, s 10.

95   For example, Grotius' view that the law of the place of contracting governed ongoing conduct under the agreement, regardless of whether the parties had a merely temporary link with that jurisdiction: Niedhardt, *supra* note 92 at 118.

96   (1752) 2 Hag Con 395 [*Scrimshire*].

country where they are made."[97] That is, the distinction between formal and essential validity did not exist in mid-eighteenth century English law; fundamental prohibitions (for instance, the taboo against marriage between parents and children) could invalidate a foreign marriage, but as a general principle the question of capacity was a matter for the law of the place of celebration.[98] Sir Edward also observed that the same position held with respect to commercial contracts: "the law of England takes notice of the law of nations in commercial and maritime affairs."[99] In other words, while English canon law provided that failure by persons under the age of 21 to obtain parental consent did *not* affect the validity of the marriage,[100] the fact that French law, being the law of the place of celebration, deemed all marriages involving persons under 25 void if solemnized without parental consent, meant that this marriage between English subjects was also void. Respect for the laws of *other* nations, regardless of domicile,[101] therefore meant that Miss Jones lost her suit, though she was awarded £400 *nomine expensarum.*[102]

Restitution of conjugal rights also formed the basis of the claim in perhaps the most famous case from the nineteenth century on the question of cross-border marital validity: *Dalrymple v Dalrymple.*[103] The issue in *Dalrymple* was the validity in England of a marriage celebrated in Scotland and, if it were valid, the extent to which Scots law continued to govern the marriage. In essence, John Dalrymple, "the son of a Scotch noble family," and Johanna Gordon, "the daughter of a gentleman in a respectable condition of life," exchanged mutual promises of marriage, which, under Scots law, constituted a valid marriage. Sir William Scott confirmed that, "the law of Scotland binds Mr. Dalrymple though a minor, a soldier, and a foreigner, as effectively as it would do if he had been an adult living in a civil capacity, and with an established domicil

---

97 (1752) 2 Hag Con 395 at [417] (emphasis added).

98 Burge, *supra* note 93 at 188–89. The question of whether deliberately evasive marriages ought to be recognized by the law of England was first raised in *Butler v Dolben* (1756) 2 Lee 312. The case was brought by the father of the husband; however, as the couple went through a further, valid ceremony once the young man came of age, the issue as to the validity of the first marriage was left undetermined. See Probert, *Marriage Law, supra* note 4 at 265, note 120.

99 (1752) 2 Hag Con 395 at [420].

100 Probert, *Marriage Law, supra* note 4 at 225, referring to Canon 100 of the 1604 code. In England, failure to obtain consent made the marriage irregular: *Scrimshire* (1752) 2 Hag Con 395 at [395]–[6].

101 See, e.g., *Ryan v Ryan* (1816) 2 Phill 332, discussed in Burge, *supra* note 93 at 187.

102 (1752) 2 Hag Con at [422].

103 (1811) 2 Hag Con 54 at [54] [*Dalrymple*]. See also *Montague v Montague* (1824) 2 Add 375.

in that country."[104] Thus, despite its clandestine and irregular nature, it was held that "Miss Gordon's marriage rights must be tried by reference to the law of the country, where, if they exist at all, they had their origin."[105] In other words, the validity of the marriage and the law governing its ongoing existence were questions for Scottish, not English, law: "[T]he only principle applicable to such a case by the law of England is, that the validity of the marriage rights must be tried by reference to the law of the country, where, if they exist at all, they had their origin. Having furnished this principle, the law of England withdraws altogether, and leaves the legal question to the exclusive judgment of the law of Scotland."[106] The rationale for this approach was the medieval (and canonical) emphasis on consent as the basis of marriage – an emphasis that led judges to treat marriage as a species of, or analogue to, contract.[107] As Sir William declared, "having been led by the manner in which these qualifications are sometimes described, to suppose at first that they were of a peculiar and characteristic nature, I really cannot, upon consideration, discover in them any thing more than the ordinary qualifications requisite in all contracts."[108] In other words, the idea that marriage was a relation of sufficient public importance that the English law of marriage, or at least aspects thereof, travelled with persons domiciled in England, was itself foreign to English legal thought in the early nineteenth century.

---

104 (1811) 2 Hag Con 54 at [61].

105 (1811) 2 Hag Con 54 at [59].

106 (1811) 2 Hag Con 54 at [59].

107 At the time *Dalrymple* was heard, and indeed well into the nineteenth century, the main authority concerning conflicts issues in commercial contracts was a short case involving a dispute between performers at the Royal Circus: *Male v Roberts* (1800) 3 Esp 163, discussed in Clive M. Schmitthoff, *A Textbook of the English Conflict of Laws (Private International Law)* (London: Pitman, 1945) at 111. While performing in Edinburgh, the defendant, Roberts, a minor under English law, contracted with one Cockburn for the supply of liquor. Roberts failed to pay his debt in a timely manner and Cockburn arrested him to prevent him from absconding. The plaintiff, Male, paid Cockburn and Roberts was released. Back in England, Male then sued Roberts to recover his expenses. The defendant relied on his minority. Consistent with the approach taken by Lord Mansfield in *Robinson v Bland* (1760) 2 Burr 1077, Lord Eldon found that "the cause of action arose in Scotland; the contract must be therefore governed by the laws of that country." In other words, Roberts's incapacity under English law did not make the contract invalid. However, Male then failed to present evidence as to whether a contract with a minor was valid under Scots law; accordingly, he was non-suited and the claim was dismissed.

108 (1811) 2 Hag Con 54 at [104].

Consistently with this approach, the first major English work on private international law, William Burge's *Commentaries on Colonial and Foreign Law Generally, and In Their Conflict With Each Other, and With the Law of England* (1838), firmly declared that a marriage valid in the place of celebration should be treated as valid in the place of domicile, even if the place of domicile would have prevented its celebration:[109]

> The law of England has adopted this principle in its fullest extent.[110] It admits the validity of a marriage contracted in Scotland by English subjects according to the law of that kingdom, although the marriage would be invalid according to the law of England, and notwithstanding the parties had acquired no *bona fide* domicile in Scotland, but had resorted thither for the purpose of making a contract, which if they had remained in England they were prohibited from making.[111]

B. Dissolution, Domicile, and State Control

The validity of marriage was one important angle in this jurisdictional debate; its counterpart was the extent to which the courts of a country in which a marriage was *not* solemnized could entertain suits for divorce, and the enforceability of foreign divorce decrees. This section is concerned with the approach of English courts to the question of when foreign courts could dissolve marriages connected to England (and the influence of Scottish law on English attitudes to this issue).[112] Predictably, given England's prohibition on judicial divorce until 1857,[113] the question that generally arose in the first half of the nineteenth century was whether Scottish courts could dissolve English marriages. The English answer, set forth in *R v Lolley*,[114] was an emphatic "No." In contrast, the Scottish answer to the

---

109 Burge, *supra* note 93 at 187.

110 *Ryan v Ryan*, 2 Phill Rep 332; *Ilderton v Ilderton*, 2 H Bl 145, *Scrimshire v Scrimshire*, 2 Hag Con 395; *Middleton v Janverin*, Ib 437; *Herbert v Herbert*, 2 Phill Rep 430; *Montague v Montague*, 2 Add 375.

111 *Compton v Bearcroft*, Arches, 16 Feb 1767; Delegates, 4 Feb 1769; *Grierson v Grierson*, Lib Reg A 1780, F 552; *Bedford v Varney*, 1762; *Brook v Oliver*, 2 Hag Con Rep 59.

112 Section D, on the other hand, looks at the English courts' views on their own jurisdiction to dissolve marriages with a foreign connection.

113 *Matrimonial Causes Act 1857*, 20 & 21 Vict c 85.

114 (1812) 2 Cl & F 567 [*Lolley*]. This infamous bigamy case concerned the validity of a divorce granted by the Scottish courts. The marriage in question took place in England, between English subjects, who were domiciled in England. Mr. Lolley committed adultery in both England and Scotland, and upon this basis Mrs. Lolley sought and obtained a decree of divorce from the Scottish courts. Mr. Lolley then married another woman while his first wife was still alive, which resulted in him

question of whether its courts could dissolve an English marriage was "Yes," so long as there was some physical nexus between the parties and Scotland. The case of *Duntze (or Levett) v Levett*, heard some four years after *Lolley*, is instructive – and crucially important to the development of English private international law concerning marriage.[115]

Duntze involved two English subjects who married in England and whose legal residence was England. The husband subsequently took up temporary lodgings in Scotland, which he shared with a lover. Mrs. Levett then applied for a divorce in Scotland based on Mr. Levett's adultery. The Court of Sessions held that his *temporary* presence in Scotland was sufficient to confer jurisdiction on the Scottish courts; otherwise, restrictive English marriage laws would govern the conduct of persons living in Scotland.[116] While this finding did not amount to a rejection of the older legal conception of marriage as a relation constituted by the private exchange of promises (given that Scots law specifically recognized private marriages), the finding asserted the absolutely crucial idea that marriage is a relation of national (and public) importance,[117] meaning that the state in which parties resided could legitimately apply its own law to aspects of the relation, rather than simply deferring to the law of the place of celebration. In this respect, the judgment amounted to a repudiation of the position concerning ongoing marriage rights taken by most civilian jurists up to that point;[118] that is to say, the consent of the parties and conformity with the rules of *lex loci celebrationis* did *not* exclusively govern ongoing marriages.

Pursuant to this conception, Lord Robertson distinguished marriage from other species of contracts because, as Janet Halley has written, "[i]f marriage were contract, … *lex loci contractus* would be the rule; English law would apply; and benighted, feudal English marriage rules could easily be imposed on Scottish courts."[119] That is, *Lolley* – at least as it was then understood – would apply in Scotland, meaning that the Scottish courts could never dissolve an English marriage. Against this position, Lord Robertson set forth the idea that "marriage is fundamental to social order, and therefore completely public and under the exclusive control

---

being charged with bigamy in England. The Court hearing the case denied the validity of the Scottish divorce and upheld the conviction for bigamy.

115 *Duntze, supra* note 1. In what follows I draw upon Janet Halley's discussion of the case: Halley, *supra* note 14 at 22–4.

116 Halley, *supra* note 14 at 23.

117 *Ibid* at 23–5.

118 Huber, for instance, was of the view that marriages continued to be governed by the law of the place of celebration: Niedhardt, *supra* note 92.

119 Halley, *supra* note 14 at 23.

of the territorial state. This fundamental and foundational posture of marriage explains why it cannot be left to the 'discretion or caprice' or the 'will' of the parties."[120] Ordinary contracts, he seemed to imply, "*can* be left to the caprice, discretion, and will of the parties"[121] – which is precisely how English law approached cross-border commercial contracts.[122]

Some 20 years after *Levett* was heard, the English House of Lords in *Warrender v Warrender*[123] backed away from the position in *Lolley*, and reached a similar, though somewhat more restrictive, conclusion to that of Lord Robertson in *Duntze* on the question of "whether the Scotch Courts have jurisdiction to entertain suits for dissolving marriages contracted and solemnized in England, according to the law of England."[124] Whereas Lord Robertson was content to confer jurisdiction based on temporary residence, Lord Brougham in *Warrender* based Scottish jurisdiction on the fact that the husband (and therefore his wife) was *domiciled* there.[125] (Consistently with this view, Lord Brougham held that the true basis for the decision in *Lolley* was, or ought to be treated as, absence of domicile, and to the extent that it stood for a more encompassing position it was wrongly decided.[126]) Thus, he declared, "the contract and all its incidents, and the rights of the parties to it, and the wrongs committed by them respecting it, must be dealt with by the Courts of the country where the parties reside, and where the contract is to be carried into execution."[127] In other words, states could legitimately regulate the marriages of persons residing within their borders, even if those marriages were solemnized under foreign law. In this respect, the

---

120 *Ibid* at 25.

121 *Ibid*.

122 See *Male v Roberts* (1800) 3 Esp 163 (discussed *supra* note 107).

123 (1835) 2 Cl & F 488 [*Warrender*]. The marriage at issue in *Warrender* involved a Scotsman and an Englishwoman. After the marriage they resided in Scotland for a brief period before returning to England, where they soon separated. The husband returned to Scotland while the wife lived abroad, where it was subsequently alleged she engaged in an affair. Upon that basis, the husband sought – and was granted – dissolution of the English marriage by the Scottish courts. The House of Lords affirmed the decision.

124 (1835) 2 Cl & F 488 at 488–9.

125 According to Story, *supra* note 1 at 39, §41, "In a strict and legal sense, that is properly the domicil of a person, where he has his true, fixed, permanent home, and principal establishment, and to which, whenever he is absent, he has the intention of returning, (*animus revertendi.*)." See further *Udny v Udny* (1869) LR 1 HL 441 at 457, finding that civil status "is governed universally by one single principle, namely that of domicil."

126 (1835) 2 Cl & F 488 at 540–51; *Niboyet v Niboyet* (1878) 4 PD 1 [*16].

127 (1835) 2 Cl & F 488 at 533–4 (emphasis added).

case may also be read as supporting the idea that Scottish courts can only undo Scottish marriages, but adopting an expansive approach to what exactly constitutes a Scottish marriage; in other words, domicile "made" the marriage Scottish. To achieve this result, Lord Brougham equated residence for the purposes of dissolution with domicile, referring to "the home where they are to fulfil their mutual promises, and perform those duties which were the objects of the union; in a word, their domicile."[128]

While Lord Brougham did not go so far as to suggest that states of domicile could regulate the formation of a marriage solemnized abroad ("[t]he general principle is denied by no one that the *lex loci* is to be the governing rule in deciding upon the validity or invalidity of all personal contracts"[129]), he clearly envisioned a role for domiciliary states in the ongoing regulation of foreign marriages, extending to but not only encompassing dissolution. Thus, in a manner that foreshadowed subsequent developments concerning marriage formation,[130] Lord Brougham declared that the ongoing application of *lex loci celebrationis* to a marriage "confounds incidents with essence," meaning that "an Englishman marrying in Prussia ... [who] marries with a view to English domicile, his contract will be judged by English law."[131] Thus, it did not follow that "a marriage indissoluble by the *lex loci* is to be held indissoluble everywhere"; such reasoning would mean that "a marriage dissoluble by the *lex loci* must be held everywhere dissoluble."[132] That is, if English courts took the view that English marriages were indissoluble in Scotland *in toto*, they would have to accept the reverse proposition – that Scottish couples could seek a judicial divorce in England. As Lord Brougham declared, though, "so absurd

---

128 (1835) 2 Cl & F 488 at 536. This emphasis on party intention also foreshadowed subsequent debates over whether present domicile, or future intended matrimonial domicile, should govern the making of a valid marriage. See further see P.D. Maddaugh, "Validity of Marriage and the Conflict of Laws: A Critique of the Present Anglo-American Position" (1973) 23:2 *U Toronto LJ* 117.

129 (1835) 2 Cl & F 488 at 529.

130 See *Brook v Brook* (1861) 9 HLC 193 at 207.

131 (1835) 2 Cl & F 488 at 535. This dimension of Lord Brougham's judgment was referred to by Savigny in his *Private International Law* in support of the contention that "the territorial law of every marriage must be fixed according to it; and the place away from the domicile where the marriage may be celebrated is quite immaterial": Friedrich Carl von Savigny, *Private International Law, and the Retrospective Operation of Statutes: A Treatise on the Conflict of Laws, and the Limits of Their Operation in Respect of Place and Time*, translated by William Guthrie, 2nd ed. (Edinburgh: T. & T. Clark, 1880) at 291 §379.

132 (1835) 2 Cl & F 488 at 534.

a proposition never could for a moment be entertained"[133] because of England's ongoing prohibition on divorce (except by private Act of Parliament), which was not open to challenge on the basis that parties resident or domiciled in England had married under the laws of a place that permitted divorce.

Questions over the dissolution of foreign marriages were thus the vehicle by which English (and Scottish) courts began to recognize the national and extra-contractual dimensions of marriage. Subsequent cases would extend this recognition to the formation and validity of foreign marriages.

C. Domicile and Marital Validity

In 1856 the English Parliament attempted to circumvent the common law's ongoing deference to *lex loci* in questions of marital validity by enacting a legislative prohibition on the recognition of irregular marriages solemnized in Scotland, unless one of the parties had his or her usual place of residence there, or had lived in Scotland for 21 days immediately prior to the marriage.[134] The Act said nothing, however, about the validity of other foreign marriages, and appeared to assume the validity of Scots marriages that complied with the new residency requirements.

So, in the next major case that dealt with the issue, *Simonin v Mallac*,[135] it was determined that "the personal status arising from such [marriage] contract is to be ascertained by the law of this country in which the contract was made, and not any special law of the country of the domicil of the parties to the contract."[136] In language recalling the judgment in *Scrimshire*, Sir Cresswell Cresswell stated that, "[i]n general, the personal competency or incompetency of individuals to contract has been held to depend upon the law of the place where the contract was made."[137] Accordingly, "the fact that the parties were forbidden by their domiciliary law to marry without the consent of certain other

---

133 (1835) 2 Cl & F 488 at 534–5.

134 *Act for Amending the Law of Marriage in Scotland 1856*, 19 & 20 Vict, c 96.

135 (1860) 2 SW & TR 67 [*Simonin*]. The marriage in question was between French subjects and took place in England without the parties having obtained the consents required by French matrimonial law. Soon after, the couple returned to Paris, where Valérie sought and obtained a declaration of nullity from the Civil Tribunal in Paris. She then sought an equivalent English declaration.

136 2 SW & TR 67. The quote is from the headnote to the case.

137 (1860) 2 SW & TR 67 at 77.

persons afforded no ground for a decree of nullity."[138] This emphasis on the law of the place of celebration cast doubt over the approach taken in *Warrender*, and the idea that states have legally recognized interests in regulating the foreign marriages of their domiciliaries.

The following year, however, in *Brook v Brook*,[139] the House of Lords introduced a fundamental limit to the general deference to *lex loci celebrationis* displayed in *Scrimshire*, *Dalrymple*, and *Simonin*. Instead, the Lords emphasized the extra-territorial interests of states in the formation of marriages involving persons domiciled within their borders – an approach that treated marriage as a relation of public interest along the lines adumbrated in *Duntze* and *Warrender* (though hewing more closely to the latter in doctrinal terms by making domicile the relevant threshold for jurisdiction).

Brook dealt with an issue that particularly vexed nineteenth century moralists and legislators: marriage between a man and his deceased wife's sister.[140] In 1835, it had been declared by the legislature, as a matter of civil and not simply ecclesiastical law, that these marriages were null and void in England.[141] William Brook, however, married his deceased wife's sister, Emily Armitage, in Denmark, where such marriages were permitted. The couple was domiciled in England at the time of the marriage. Some five years after the marriage, both William and Emily died of cholera within two days of each other. In a will executed on the day he died, William made provision for his five children – three of whom were born to Emily and two to his first wife. (One child died soon after the parents.) During the administration of the will, the question arose as to whether the second marriage was valid. The answer was "No." Lord Campbell stated: "There can be no doubt of the general rule, that "a foreign marriage, valid according to the law of a country where it is celebrated is good everywhere." But while the forms of

---

138 John Alderson Foote, *Foreign and Domestic Law: A Concise Treatise on Private International Jurisprudence, Based on the Decision in the English Courts*, 3rd ed. (London: Stevens & Haynes, 1904) at 365.

139 (1861) 9 HLC 193 [*Brook*].

140 See, e.g., Bramwell, "Marriage With a Deceased Wife's Sister," *The Nineteenth Century: A Monthly Review* (September 1886) 403; Nancy F. Anderson, "The 'Marriage with a Deceased Wife's Sister Bill' Controversy: Incest Anxiety and the Defense of Family Purity in Victorian England" (1982) 21:2 *J Brit Stud* 67.

141 Strictly, *An Act to render certain Marriages valid and, to alter the Law with respect to certain voidable Marriages*, 5 & 6 Will IV, c 54 (Lord Lyndhurst's Act), declared marriages void that were contrary to the prohibited degrees as set out in 28 Hen VIII, c 7, s 11 – marriage to a deceased wife's sister was included in that Act. See further chapter 5, Pt II(B).

entering into the contract of marriage are to be regulated by the *lex loci contractus*, the law of the country in which it is celebrated, the essentials of the contract depend upon the *lex loci domicilii*, the law of the country in which the parties are domiciled at the time of the marriage, and in which the matrimonial residence is contemplated."[142] The crucial element in this passage is the emphasis it places on states' continuing interests in the foreign marriages of their domiciliaries, and the consequent formulation of a legal test that distinguished between formal and essential validity. While the law up to this point[143] had certainly recognized that there were limits to the general principle concerning recognition of foreign marriages, those limits had been cast as exceptions to the general rule.[144] Recall that in Burge's 1838 *Commentaries* it was declared, in reference to "the validity of a marriage contracted in conformity, not with its own law, but with that of the country in which it was celebrated," that "[t]he law of England has adopted this principle in its fullest extent."[145] By 1910, though, Renton and Phillimore, in *The Comparative Law of Marriage and Divorce* (reprinted from Burge's *Commentaries*) stated that "[t]he *former* law of England adopted this principle in its fullest extent."[146] In later times, they wrote, the courts in England "made an important qualification of the rule by recognizing prohibitions imposed on the parties by their personal law as incapacities which followed them everywhere."[147] *Brook* was cited in support of this claim.[148]

---

142 (1861) 9 HLC 193 at 207. This passage can support an approach that considers the actual domicile of the parties at the time of the marriage (the dual domicile test), as well as one that treats the parties' intended matrimonial domicile as dispositive. The latter approach would bring the judgment into greater congruity with the test applied in commercial contracts cases, but the overall tenor of the judgment suggests that greater weight is to be placed on the actual, as opposed to intended, place of domicile. See Richard Fentiman, "The Validity of Marriage and the Proper Law" (1985) 44:2 *Cambridge LJ* 256 at 263.

143 The shift in approach may be related to the establishment in 1857 of the Divorce Court pursuant to the *Matrimonial Causes Act 1857*: Maddaugh, *supra* note 128 at 119.

144 Burge, *supra* note 93 at 188.

145 *Ibid* at 187.

146 William Burge, *The Comparative Law of Marriage and Divorce*, edited by Alexander Wood Renton and George Grenville Phillimore (London: Sweet & Maxwell, 1910) at 242 (emphasis added).

147 *Ibid* at 244.

148 See also A.V. Dicey, *A Digest of the Law of England With Reference to the Conflict of Laws* (London: Stevens, 1896) at 629 note 2; W.N. Hibbert, *International Private Law or The Conflict of Laws* (London: Stevens & Haynes, 1927) at 212; Maddaugh, *supra* note 128 at 119.

The recognition in *Brook* of the national dimensions of marriage also suggested the existence of a critical distinction between marriage and contract because essential validity "involves problems relating to the creation of the status of husband and wife."[149] As Schmitthoff later put it, "English law ... does not accept the strictly logical conclusions of the doctrine of the Christian marriage, but, since 1861,[150] attaches more weight to the status character of the marriage."[151] In other words, the public importance of marriage meant that treating the relation as akin to commercial contracts had become, within English private international law, inappropriate. This dimension of *Brook* is consonant with the view laid out by Lord Robertson in *Duntze*, though the influence of the Scottish judgment is only indirectly apparent. Tracing that influence tells us something about the role of scholarly thought in the development of the field of English private international law.

It was observed above that Lord Robertson differentiated marriage "from other contracts" because "the rights, obligations, or duties, arising from it, are not left entirely to be regulated by the agreements of the parties, but are, to a certain extent, matters of municipal regulation, over which the parties have no control, by any declaration of their will." The application of this idea in the context of the marriage in *Brook* involved discussion of the American conflicts scholar Joseph Story, whose treatment of marriage was profoundly influenced by none other than Lord Robertson.[152] In the first edition of his *Conflict of Laws*, Story extracted a large portion of Lord Robertson's judgment in *Duntze*, including the passage above concerning "municipal regulation" (and the epigraph to this chapter). In *Brook*, Lord Campbell paid particular attention to Story's treatment of marriage, particularly his discussion of the circumstances in which a marriage performed according to the laws of a foreign state might nevertheless be held invalid (sections that immediately followed the extracted portions of Lord Robertson's judgment). According to Story, incestuous marriage was one such ground, but it should be limited to those instances agreed upon by Christian nations. On this approach, marriage to a deceased wife's sister might not offend against local law because it was not universally condemned.[153] Lord Campbell, however, pointed to Story's parallel contention that a state might refuse to recognize a marriage based on "the public law of a country, from

---

149 Maddaugh, *supra* note 128 at 118.
150 Since *Brook* (1861) 9 HLC 193.
151 Schmitthoff, *supra* note 107 at 296.
152 Halley, *supra* note 14 at 22–5.
153 *Brook* (1861) 9 HLC 193 at [209].

motives of policy."[154] He then declared that Story "could hardly mean his qualification [concerning incest] to apply to a country like England, in which the limits of marriages to be considered incestuous are exactly defined by public law."[155] Municipal regulation of the type described by Lord Robertson was thus taken by Lord Campbell to constitute a sufficient basis for the denial of marital validity, despite compliance with the formalities of *lex loci celebrationis*.

This framing of the relation was also congruent with the approach to inter-jurisdictional questions over marriage advanced by the Prussian jurist Friedrich Carl von Savigny in his *Treatise on the Conflict of Laws*,[156] which formed part of his nine-volume *System of the Modern Roman Law*, published in German between 1840 and 1849. In that work, Savigny advocated a "universalist" approach that sought to locate the legal system with which a particular issue was most closely connected. In the case of marriage, that was clearly the place of (the husband's) domicile, not the place of celebration.[157] This approach rested on a deeper distinction between family relations and obligations[158] – as Savigny put it, "marriage has nothing in common with the obligatory contracts"[159] because of the "peculiar, completely distinctive, nature of the family" and its critical role in the constitution of "the completely formed state."[160]

Savigny's universalist approach to conflicts (like his distinction between family relations and obligations[161]) was profoundly influential on English judges and treatise writers in the later nineteenth century:

---

154 *Brook* (1861) 9 HLC 193 at [210]. The case that until very recently provided the basic definition of marriage under English law, *Hyde v Hyde and Woodmansee*, 1 P&D 130 (1866), is an example of this refusal to recognize a foreign marriage based on public policy.

155 *Brook* (1861) 9 HLC 193 at [210].

156 Savigny, *supra* note 131 at 291–2 §379.

157 "There is no doubt as to the true seat of the marriage relation; it must be presumed to be at the domicile of the husband, who, according to the laws of all nations and of all times, must be recognised as the head of the family": *ibid* at 291 §379.

158 See further chapter 2, part IV(B). For discussion of the influence of this aspect of Savigny's thought on English treatise writers see chapter 2, part VI.

159 Savigny, *supra* note 131 at 291 §379.

160 *Ibid*.

161 Which in turn reflected Savigny's "combination, in the single idea of legal science as the elaboration of 'the system,' of a universalizing legal formalist will theory with the idea that particular regimes of state law reflect diverse underlying nonlegal societal normative order." Duncan Kennedy, "Three Globalizations of Law and Legal Thought" in David M. Trubek & Alvaro Santos, eds., *The New Law and Economic Development: A Critical Appraisal* (New York: Cambridge University Press, 2006) 19 at 27.

"It led to a conscious attempt to assimilate the English conflictual rules to those prevailing on the Continent. This resulted in some radical changes, especially in the field of status and capacity, where the courts, despite local precedents to the contrary, sought to establish the universality of status and resulting capacity on the basis of the law of the domicil."[162] This dimension of Savigny's work, especially his treatment of marriage, was influenced by Story;[163] and, as we have seen, Story in turn drew heavily on Lord Robertson's decision in *Duntze*. Now, it is not clear that Savigny directly influenced the Lords' speeches in *Brook*, particularly given that Guthrie's English translation of Savigny's *Treatise on the Conflict of Laws* was not published until 1869. However, in light of Savigny's influence on the broader development of English private international law, and the role played by Story (and thus indirectly) Lord Robertson in the formulation of Savigny's own views on the topic,[164] it is worth pausing to mark this early synchronicity.

Brook suggested that marriage was coming to be conceptualized within English judicial thought as an exceptional species of contract that, owing to the non-modifiable terms and conditions imposed by states of domicile, had the legal character of status. Not all English judges agreed with this approach, though, and the next major case to grapple with these issues, *Sottomayor v De Barros (No 1)*,[165] muddied the waters. In essence, Lord Justice Cotton applied the distinction drawn in *Brook* between form and essence, but cast a measure of doubt on the extent to which the approach taken in *Brook* differed from other contracts.[166] That is, he suggested the rather curious possibility that

---

162 P.E. Nygh, *Conflict of Laws in Australia*, 2nd ed. (Sydney: Butterworths, 1971) at 80 citing Savigny, *supra* note 131 at 148 §362.

163 Savigny, *supra* note 131 at 291–2 §379, notes (c) and (d).

164 Niedhardt, *supra* note 92 at 183–4.

165 (1877) 3 PD 1 [*Sottomayor (No 1)*].

166 The case concerned the validity of an English marriage. Portuguese subjects domiciled in Portugal, where marriage between first cousins was prohibited, established residence in England in 1858. In 1866 they married before a registrar in London, and in 1873 returned to Portugal. Questions of law and fact were tried separately, and so the first round of cases assumed Portuguese domicile and dealt with the implications of this assumption at law (see *infra* note 168 on the factual question of domicile). At first instance Sir Robert Phillimore found that the marriage was valid. On appeal, however, it was declared null and void. This in itself was sound under the test established in *Brook*, but Lord Justice Cotton also asserted a measure of correspondence between commercial contracts and marriage that did not accord with the judgments in *Brook* and *Male v Roberts*. In his estimation, "*it is a well-recognised principle of law that the question of personal capacity to enter into any contract is to be decided by the law of domicile.... The law of a country*

commercial contracts, like marriage, carried status-like elements in the sense that *lex domicilii* travelled with contracting parties.[167] However, in *Sottomayor v De Barros (No 2)*,[168] which dealt with the factual question of domicile,[169] Hannen P cast doubt over Cotton LJ's posited equivalency between commercial contracts and marriage in *Sottomayor (No 1)*, and suggested instead that "very many and serious difficulties arise if marriage be regarded only in the light of a contract. It is indeed based upon the contract of the parties, but it is a status arising out of a contract to which each country is entitled to attach its own conditions, both as to its creation and duration."[170] In other words, commercial relations and marital relations were conceptually, and increasingly legally, distinct from one another.[171]

The conflicts scholar John Alderson Foote expressed a similar view of the reasoning in *Sottomayor (No 1)*[172] and suggested that the principles set forth in the case "should not be extended, as some passages of the judgment in that case seem to imply they might be, to the question of the capacity of the parties to a commercial contract."[173] In his estimation, the essentials of ordinary contracts "are governed by that

---

where a marriage is solemnised must alone decide all questions relating to the validity of the ceremony by which the marriage is alleged to have been constituted; but, *as in other contracts*, so in that of marriage, personal capacity must depend on the law of domicile." (1877) 3 PD 1 at 5 (emphasis added).

167 This was quite extraordinary in the 1870s, given the emphasis then being placed on the ideology of freedom of contract. See *Printing and Numerical Supply Co v Sampson* (1875) LR 19 Eq 465.

168 (1879) 5 PD 94 [*Sottomayor (No 2)*].

169 In *Sottomayor (No 1)*, at first instance and in the Court of Appeal, it had been assumed that both parties were domiciled in Portugal despite residing in England. In *Sottomayor (No 2)*, however, Hannen P held that the husband was in fact domiciled in England by reason of his father's domicile in that country. The wife remained domiciled in Portugal despite her English residence because her father was domiciled in Portugal at the time of the marriage. Accordingly, in contrast to the Court of Appeal, Hannen P held that the marriage was valid under English law.

170 *Sottomayor (No 2)* [1879] 5 PD 94.

171 In this respect, the judgment in *Sottomayor (No 2)* was consonant with Savigny's general distinction between family relations and obligations, and his more specific emphasis on domicile in cases concerning the former, and party intention in the latter. See Ernest G. Lorenzen, "Validity and Effects of Contracts in the Conflict of Laws" (1921) 30:6 *Yale LJ* 565 at 567–8.

172 Foote, *supra* note 138 at 360. Foote also distinguished marriage from contract by referring to the 'crowning anomaly' at the heart of such a conflation, being that marriage "is a contract, if a contract at all, for the breach of which no action can lie, and no damages be recovered": *ibid* at 362.

173 *Ibid* at 362. See also C.K. Allen, *Legal Duties and Other Essays in Jurisprudence* (Oxford: Clarendon Press, 1931) at 63.

law which the parties intended by their agreement to adopt," which, "*prima facie*, is the law of the place where the contract was made (*lex loci celebrationis*); but may be any other which the parties have sufficiently indicated their intention of adopting."[174] The validity of *marriage*, however, is not a matter only of party intention and *lex loci celebrationis*, but also the law of the parties' domicile. Why treat marriage in this distinctive manner? According to Foote, because, "it is of the greatest moral and social importance to the public interests of every country, for reasons which need not be specified, that those persons who live together within its limits in what they call matrimony, should be married in fact. It cannot be said that the breach or repudiation of a contract within a town is a social or public evil in at all the same sense that the illegitimate connection of the sexes is so."[175] In other words, marriage was a relation of significant public, and indeed national, importance carrying a host of state-imposed rights and obligations – a status, in the modern legal sense, and distinct from the (ideologically) private realm of commercial contracts. This dimension of the development of English private international law is thus broadly consistent with the more general nineteenth-century globalization of Classical Legal Thought, which relied in part on a "distinction, within private law, between the law of obligations and family law."[176] Within this framework, the will theory (the idea that private law rules constituted "a set of rational derivations from the notion that government should protect the rights of legal persons, which meant helping them to realize their will"[177]) "came to an end at the family."[178] State-imposed conditions or incapacities were thus held to impede the realization of individual wills in the service of national ends.[179] (Conversely, economic liberalism was the governing ideology in matters of commerce and trade.) In the context of private international law, this approach resulted in the extension of states' own municipal rules concerning essential aspects of marriage to issues of validity and ongoing incidents (and maintenance of the older idea

---

174 Foote, *supra* note 138 at 465. See also John Westlake, *A Treatise on Private International Law: With Principal Reference to Its Practice in England*, edited by Norman Bentwich (London: Stevens & Haynes, 1925) at 294. In 1937 the House of Lords confirmed English law's deference to party intention in ordinary contracts in *R v International Trustee* [1937] AC 500.

175 Foote, *supra* note 138 at 361–2.

176 Kennedy, *supra* note 161 at 32.

177 *Ibid* at 26.

178 *Ibid* at 32.

179 *Ibid* at 34–5.

that commercial contracts should be regulated according to the parties' intended law or *lex loci contractus*).

D. *Dissolving the Status of Marriage*

We saw above (section B) that in the 1830s the English courts' approach to the ability of foreign courts to dissolve marriages with an English connection relaxed under the influence of Scottish legal thought. The counterpart to this question, and the focus of this section, was the extent to which English courts could dissolve marriages with a foreign connection. The 1878 case of *Niboyet v Niboyet* is instructive.[180] It concerned a marriage celebrated in the British territory of Gibraltar in 1856 between an Englishwoman and a Frenchman. The husband was a French diplomat who served in England. The wife sought dissolution of the marriage based on the husband's alleged adultery. Lord Justice Brett neatly summed up the issue: "The adultery was committed in England. The wife was resident in England. The petition was served in England. The husband was residing in England. But the husband had never been domiciled in England."[181] The latter point was clear from the husband's diplomatic status, which meant that he never lost his French domicile. Lord Justice Brett therefore posed the relevant question as follows: "Whether, it being admitted by the petitioner that the respondent has a French domicil, this Court has any jurisdiction as a matter of general law?"[182] The majority answered this question in the affirmative, and held that English jurisdiction existed "while the matrimonial home is English."[183] Lord Justice Brett dissented on the basis of domicile; in his view, "[t]he status of marriage is the legal position of the married person as such in the community or in relation to the community. Which community is it which is interested in such relation? None other than the community of which he is a member."[184] Consequently, "the only law which should assume to alter his status as a married man is the law of the country of his domicil."[185] On this point, history vindicated Lord Justice Brett; in *Le Mesurier v Le Mesurier*,[186] the Privy Council expressly overruled the majority's emphasis in *Niboyet* on matrimonial home and

---

180 (1878) 4 PD 1 [*Niboyet*]. See also *Deck v Deck* (1860) 163 ER 926.
181 (1878) 4 PD 1 at [*10].
182 (1878) 4 PD 1 at [*10].
183 (1878) 4 PD 1 at [*9] per James LJ.
184 (1878) 4 PD 1 at [*13].
185 (1878) 4 PD 1 at [*13].
186 [1895] AC 517 (PC) [*Le Mesurier*].

confirmed that it is domicile that confers jurisdiction over matrimonial causes. Nevertheless, *Niboyet* stands as a further example of English courts emphasizing England's national interest in marriage regulation, even if the majority somewhat overreached in the process.

Nearly 50 years later, in *Salvesen or Von Lorang v Administrator of Austrian Property*,[187] the House of Lords affirmed the national interest in marriage regulation along the lines adumbrated by Lord Justice Brett in *Niboyet*. The details of the case are complex, but for present purposes the relevant question before the Lords was whether a German dissolution decree concerning a marriage conducted in France involving British and Austrian subjects domiciled in Germany was to be treated as binding in England (and Scotland).[188] Referring to Lord Justice Brett's observation in *Niboyet* "that the court of the domicile was the only Court that was entitled to alter the status of married people,"[189] Viscount Haldane affirmed the binding nature of the German judgment and made the following pertinent remarks on the nature of marriage and its consequences for the law of conflicts:

> For what does status mean in this connection? *Something more than a mere contractual relation between the parties to the contract of marriage.* Status may result from such a contractual relationship, but only when the contract has passed into something which private international law recognises as having been superadded to it by the authority of the State, something which the jurisprudence of that State under its law imposes when within its

---

187 [1927] AC 641; 137 LTR 571 [*Salvesen*].

188 The case concerned a dispute over entitlement to certain funds. The Administrator claimed the fund was payable to him under a charge created by the Treaty of Peace (Austria) Order 1920, on the basis that the appellant was an Austrian national by reason of her marriage to one Herr von Lorang. The appellant contended that the marriage to von Lorang was null and void and hence that her interest in the fund could not be challenged by the Administrator. The marriage took place in Paris in June 1897, at which time the appellant was a British subject domiciled in Scotland. The appellant claimed that she and von Lorang did not observe the necessary formalities of residence and publication required by French law, and because the Registrar in Paris had been induced to perform the marriage ceremony upon the faith of a misleading certificate attesting to von Lorang's domicile in France. In 1898, the couple settled in Wiesbaden, Germany, where they remained until 1923, interrupted only by the First World War. By the time of the Scottish proceedings, the appellant had sought and obtained a declaration of nullity from the Court at Wiesbaden, on the basis of evidence presented by a qualified French jurist that the marriage was defective under French law. The question, therefore, was whether the courts of Scotland were bound to recognize the Wiesbaden judgment.

189 [1927] AC 641; 137 LTR 571 at 573.

boundaries the ceremony has taken place. This juridical outcome is more than any mere outcome of the agreement *inter se* to marry of the parties. It is due to a result which concerns the public generally, and which the State where the ceremony took place superadds something which may or may not be capable of being got rid of subsequently by proceedings before a competent public authority, but which meantime carries with it rights and obligations as regards the general community until so got rid of.[190]

Salvesen thus affirmed the idea, first aired in the Scottish case of *Duntze* over a century prior, that marriage is a relation of public importance into which states can legitimately intervene to further national interests; though in line with subsequent English authorities, it confined this idea to marriages involving persons domiciled in England. *Salvesen* also confirmed the corresponding idea that the suite of rights and obligations superadded to marriage irrespective of the parties' will creates a distinction between marriage and ordinary commercial contracts, and that marriage was, in law, a form of status.

IV. Conclusion

This chapter has traced some of the ways in which English courts in the nineteenth century constructed an idea of marriage as the central relation within the private family, and hence a relation of public and national importance, by construing it as an exceptional species of contract. In cases concerning breach of promise to marry, courts departed from earlier authority and stretched the contractual foundations of the action in ways that stressed the centrality of marriage to the family, its place within the gender-based separate spheres of work and domestic life, and the correlative social and economic importance of marriage for women. In the law of conflicts, courts gradually moved away from a view of marriage as defined by mutual consent and governed (formally and substantively) by reference to the place in which the marriage was celebrated/contracted. Instead, English courts, partly under the influence of Scottish legal thought, and in ways that intersected with both American and civilian legal thought concerning conflicts of law (and the disaggregation of family and market, and marriage and contract) began to recognize the national interest in marriage. The result was a (contested) move towards conceptualizing marriage as a relation over which states of domicile could legitimately exercise jurisdiction (and

---

190 [1927] AC 641; 137 LTR 571 at 573 (first emphasis added).

a recognition of the limitations of *lex loci celebrationis* in circumstances of changed domicile); and a corresponding shift towards treating the relation as a form of status because of the non-modifiable terms and conditions imposed by the state on the basis of the public importance of, and national interest in, marriage.

Marriage, Family, and Work: Past and Present

[T]he power exerted by a legal regime consists less in the force that it can bring to bear against violators of its rules than in its capacity to persuade people that the world described in its images and categories is the only attainable world in which a sane person would want to live.[1]

This book has traced some of the ways that English law and legal thought in the long nineteenth century constructed the family and Family Law through a process of disaggregating the "private œconomical relations" of the medieval/early modern legal household along family/work (and corresponding private/public, status/contract, and female/male) lines. In this concluding chapter, I want to revisit the principal intellectual and institutional shifts surveyed in the preceding chapters, and also consider how this historical lens provides a platform for critical analysis of the contemporary moment.[2]

At the broadest level, the story told in the preceding chapters involved two mutually reinforcing narratives: the gradual extrusion of productive work from the household, and its re-characterization as a market-based (and wage-based) activity performed outside of the home pursuant to a legal regime that spoke the languages of both contract and subordination; and a new emphasis on marriage as the core relation within the private, non-productive family, which resulted in

---

1 Robert W. Gordon, "Critical Legal Histories" (1984) 36 *Stan L Rev* 57 at 109.
2 On "the mental and political constraints of false necessity" see Karl Klare, "Labor Law as Ideology: Toward a New Historiography of Collective Bargaining Law" (1981) 4 *Indus Rel LJ* 450 at 482. See also Roberto Mangabeira Unger, *False Necessity: Anti-Necessitarian Social Theory in the Service of Radical Democracy. Part I of Politics: A Work in Constructive Social Theory* (Cambridge, MA: Cambridge University Press, 1987).

the conceptualization and treatment of marriage as a site of legitimate public concern and intervention.

Chapter 1 introduced the household as the legal-conceptual launching pad for the analysis in subsequent chapters. Noting the generally more capacious approach to "family" that prevailed in England until around the mid-eighteenth century, it drew attention to the paradigmatic legal reflection of the productive household: William Blackstone's "private œconomical relations" in his *Commentaries on the Laws of England*.[3] The "three great relations in private life are," Blackstone said, "1. That of *master and servant*; ... 2. That of *husband and wife*; ... 3. That of *parent and child* ...."[4] In other words, the household (for all of its differing historical configurations[5]) amounted to an integrated domain of work *and* family life; the intersecting legal forces that contributed to the disaggregation of this (actually existing and conceptual) model, and its re-constitution as the (actually and mythically) distinct domains of work (law) and family (law), was thus established as the principal focus of the ensuing analysis.

Methodologically, the chapter situated this subsequent analysis within a broadly critical tradition of legal history, and the slightly more targeted and contemporary framework of Family Law Exceptionalism, which emphasizes the artificiality and historicity of the modern legal (and social, political and economic) segregation of the family from the domain of work and the market.[6] Drawing on these theoretical frames, it marked out a zone of analysis principally oriented towards intellectual and institutional forms of legal change, focussing in particular on "mandarin materials": treatises, cases, statutes and parliamentary debates. In particular, it drew attention to the importance of legal consciousness in historical analysis as a way of understanding "when our categories for organizing how we speak about law solidified into something like their present shape."[7]

Building on this concern with the intellectual dimensions of legal change, the second part of the chapter proposed two further analytical frameworks for investigating the moves and processes involved in

---

3 William Blackstone, *Commentaries on the Laws of England*, 4 vols (Oxford: Clarendon Press, 1765–9) book I at 410.

4 *Ibid.*

5 Bridget Hill, *Women, Work, and Sexual Politics in Eighteenth-Century England* (Oxford: Basil Blackwell, 1989) at 26.

6 Janet Halley and Kerry Rittich, "Critical Directions in Comparative Family Law: Genealogies and Contemporary Studies of Family Law Exceptionalism" (2010) 58:4 *Am J Comp L* 753.

7 Gordon, *supra* note 1 at 99.

the disaggregation of the productive household: (law as[8]) ideology and population management. The point was to highlight a range of ideas and motivations that appear to have been pertinent to contemporaneous practices and intellectual moves, and which also, with the benefit of contemporary hindsight, might help us to think through and connect seemingly isolated legal-historical developments. The section on ideology (broadly defined as the legitimating function of ideas in social and legal life) considered a set of binaries that shaped the legal processes through which the household was disassembled and reconstituted as the separate domains of family and work: the overarching family/market distinction; the related division of the world into public and private domains; the more legalistic distinction between status and contract (or paternalism and individual freedom); and, cutting across each of these distinctions, the traditional male/female binary. The relevance of these ideological binaries to the overarching narrative is perhaps best recalled by way of example. In chapter 3, for instance, we saw how commitments to market ideology influenced the enclosure of land in the eighteenth and nineteenth centuries, with significant flow-on effects for poorer families; broadly speaking, husbands were channelled into market-based wage labour, while wives were increasingly confined to the family sphere to perform the work necessary to its functioning. Under the sway of ideas around public and private, and the proper scope of family life, wives' domestic labour was, as chapter 4 showed, increasingly treated as unproductive, while their participation in paid work was complicated through legal moves that reflected and deepened the gendered basis of the family/market, private/public divide.

The section on population management suggested the utility of Michel Foucault's genealogy of modern governance practices for understanding some of the legal moves that helped to disarticulate work and family and constitute them as separate legal (and social) domains. Crucially, Foucault suggested that from roughly the eighteenth century onwards, "the problem of population" resulted in a shift away from governance practices based upon the model of the patriarchal family, towards a focus on the economy (or market) in its modern (i.e., non-household-based) meaning. Within this new model of governance, the family as a distinct entity "appears as an element within the population

---

8 See Christopher Tomlins, "Foreword: 'Law As ...' III – *Glossolalia*: Toward a Minor (Historical) Jurisprudence" (2015) 5 *UC Irvine L Rev* 239; Christopher Tomlins and John Comaroff, "'Law As ...': Theory and Practice in Legal History" (2011) 1:3 *UC Irvine L Rev* 1039; Catherine L. Fisk and Robert W. Gordon, "'Law As ...': Theory and Method in Legal History" (2011) 1:3 *UC Irvine L Rev* 519.

and as a fundamental relay in its government."[9] The idea of population management as it was used in this book thus attempted to show how specific efforts by the English state to organize its population fitted within and contributed to a division of the world along family/work lines – partly through moves that relied upon the types of ideological commitments surveyed in the preceding section. The analysis then connected Foucault's work to aspects of English Utilitarianism, specifically, the population-centred approaches to governance evident in the works of Jeremy Bentham and Thomas Malthus. Again, the utility of these analytical frameworks is best demonstrated by example. In both chapters 3 and 5, we saw how reform of the Old Poor Law via the *Poor Law Amendment Act 1834*[10] sought to manage the population in quite specific ways: the curtailing of outdoor relief and the institution of the principle of less eligibility were distinctly Benthamite and Malthusian efforts to channel the poor out of reliance on the state and into wage labour (or reliance on the private family); the provisions concerning bastardy, meanwhile, penalized single mothers by imposing upon them sole financial responsibility for their children, thereby underscoring the importance of marriage and its centrality to English family life.

Chapter 2 showed that part of the nineteenth-century legal construction of the family involved a distinctly intellectual and scholarly effort to mark out a specialized, autonomous zone of law governing domestic relations, culminating in the modern category of Family Law. Beginning with Blackstone's legal model of the household, the chapter provided a genealogy of conceptual and taxonomic change spanning a nearly 200-year period, concluding with the publication in 1957 of Peter Bromley's text, *Family Law*.[11] Functioning as a microcosm of the broader narrative of legal change undergirding the book as a whole, the chapter traced two principal movements in scholarly legal thought. The first was the extrusion of productive work relations (in the narrow sense of work for pay) from the household, and their relocation within an increasingly freestanding Law of Master and Servant. It was shown that this process occurred in a staged manner, with more traditionally familial work relations (domestic service and apprenticeship) remaining housed within the Law of Domestic Relations until the early twentieth century when they, too, were shifted into the successor category to the Law of Master

---

9 Michel Foucault, *Security, Territory, Population. Lectures at the Collège de France, 1977–1978*, edited by Michel Senellart, translated by Graham Burchell (New York: Vintage, 2007) at 104.

10 4 & 5 Will IV, c 76 [*Poor Act 1834*].

11 Peter M. Bromley, *Family Law* (London: Butterworths, 1957).

and Servant: Employment Law.[12] The second movement involved an increasing emphasis on the public importance of marriage, and the degree of state involvement in its formation, subsistence and eventually dissolution; and a corresponding elevation of the husband-wife relation to the head of the Domestic Relations (as masters and servants gradually moved out into the distinct, non-domestic sphere of work relations). By way of example, William Pinder Eversley's 1885 text, *The Law of the Domestic Relations*,[13] re-ordered Blackstone's "private œconomical relations" and placed husband and wife at the head of the list; Eversley also excised all work relations except those intimately connected to the home (domestic service and apprenticeship). Some 70 years later, Bromley classified the family "as a basic social unit which consists normally of a husband and wife and their children," and excluded *all* work relations due to their "essentially contractual" nature.[14] Marriage was thus constructed as the basis of this new legal family, and (at this point[15]) constituted the core of Family Law.

Ideas around contract and status played a crucial role in these twin movements. With respect to marriage, scholars increasingly identified the husband-wife relation as a form of (achieved) status (rather than a purely civil contract, as Blackstone had described it[16]) owing to the suite of non-modifiable rights and obligations that attached to the relation irrespective of party consent; this feature of the relation distinguished marriage, so it was said, from the emerging Law of Contract, which was

---

12 See R.W. Lee, "Obligations" in Edward Jenks, ed., *A Digest of English Civil Law*, 5 vols (London: Butterworth & Co, 1905–17), vol 2 (1906) at 161.

13 William Pinder Eversley, *The Law of the Domestic Relations: Including Husband and Wife, Parent and Child, Guardian and Ward, Infants, and Master and Servant* (London: Stevens and Haynes, 1885).

14 Bromley, *supra* note 11 at 1.

15 On the dramatic increase in the importance of parent-child relations in the second half of the twentieth century see, e.g., Sonia Harris-Short, Joanna Miles and Rob George, *Family Law: Text, Cases, and Materials*, 3rd ed. (Oxford: Oxford University Press, 2015) at 2; Alison Diduck and Katherine O'Donovan, "Feminism and Families: *Plus Ca Change?*" in Alison Diduck and Katherine O'Donovan, eds., *Feminist Perspectives on Family Law* (Abingdon: Routledge-Cavendish, 2006) 1 at 6; Gillian Douglas, "Marriage, Cohabitation, and Parenthood – from Contract to Status?" in Sanford N. Katz, John Eekelaar and Mavis Maclean, eds., *Cross Currents: Family Law and Policy in the United States and England* (Oxford: Oxford University Press, 2010) 211 at 211–12; Leanne Smith, "The Development of Parent-Child Relationships in Family Law: The Cascade of Change" in Gillian Douglas, Mervyn Murch and Victoria Stephens, eds., *International and National Perspectives on Child and Family Law; Essays in Honour of Nigel Lowe* (Cambridge: Intersentia, 2018) 23.

16 Blackstone, *supra* note 3, book I at 421.

coming to be seen as an abstract body of principles based on commercial relations and an ideological commitment to the market-based realization of individual wills. Correspondingly, some scholars sought to characterize work relations as a specialized branch of the Law of Contract – a move most clearly apparent in the multi-volume *Digest of English Civil Law* (1905–17).[17] The chapter also showed how these attempts to systematize (and drive a wedge between) the English law of family and work relations formed part of a much broader scholarly effort to establish English law as a science – a system of principles amenable to taxonomy in the manner of the natural sciences. Blackstone's *Commentaries* were the major opening move, and subsequent works by John Austin, Frederick Pollock, Thomas Holland and John Salmond (among others) refined the mass (or mess) of pre-eighteenth century English law into a more coherent body of principles and demarcated fields – of which Family Law was one part. In a complementary manner, the chapter also showed how these (and other) English scholars were influenced by civilian legal thought, most notably Friedrich Carl von Savigny's *System of the Modern Roman Law*.[18] In this respect, the chapter interwove a minor story of legal transplantation within the broader tapestry of the scholarly development of English law along scientific lines.

From a contemporary perspective, the analysis in chapter 2 reveals the modernity and mutability of Family Law as a legal category. Just as scholars in the nineteenth and twentieth centuries laboured to separate the household into the domains of work and family, current and future scholarship has the potential to undo this fissure, and create conceptual space for new ways of dealing with relationship plurality. To an extent, this process has already begun. Unlike Bromley's archetypically 1950s definition of family and the scope of Family Law, the trend in recent scholarly texts is to question the boundaries of who and what constitutes family, often through engagement with sociological work that analyses shifting patterns and modes of relationship formation.[19] Scholars also

---

17 Jenks, *supra* note 12.

18 Friedrich Carl von Savigny, *System of the Modern Roman Law*, translated by William Holloway (Madras: J. Higginbotham, 1867).

19 Jonathan Herring, for instance, commences his text, *Family Law* (Harlow: Pearson Longman, 2011) by questioning (rather than declaring, *à la* Bromley) the nature and scope of the field. In chapter 1, entitled "What Is family Law?," Herring says: "The notion of a 'family' is notoriously difficult to define. Many people have a stereotypical image of what the 'ideal family' is like – a mother, a father and two children. Yet this family composition is not the family form that most people will have experienced. Only 24 per cent of households in 2009 consisted of a couple with dependent children. So the image of two parents and two children as the ideal

recognize the deep connections between family life and areas outside of the "traditional" (that is, modern) scope of Family Law.[20] Perhaps the most useful contribution on this front is Halley and Rittich's suggestion that the "foreground" rules of Family Law such as those concerning adult personal relationships and parent-child relationships ("Family Law 1") need to be viewed alongside "other rules, lying in the background," that play an important distributive and structural role: "the explicit family-targeted provisions peppered throughout substantive legal regimes that seem to have no primary commitment to maintaining the distinctiveness of the family – regimes ranging from tax law to immigration law to bankruptcy law" ("Family Law 2"); various rules "that contribute structurally but silently to the ways in which family life is lived, such as rules concerning employment dismissal" ("Family

---

family is just that, an ideal; a powerful ideal, but not the most common family form." See also Alison Diduck and Felicity Kaganas, *Family Law, Gender and the State: Text, Cases and Materials*, 3rd ed. (Oxford: Hart, 2012) ch 1; Rebecca Probert and Maebh Harding, *Cretney and Probert's Family Law*, 10th ed. (London: Sweet & Maxwell, 2018) at 1–7; Frances Burton, *Family Law*, 2nd ed. (London: Taylor & Francis, 2015) at 1–10; Harris-Short, Miles and George, *supra* note 15 at 1–3. Given its history, it is perhaps unsurprising that recent editions of Bromley's *Family Law* do not engage in extensive consideration of sociological work on family structures, or the possibilities for a more expansive legal approach to different family forms. Nevertheless, in marked contrast to the original edition of the work, the current editors, Nigel Lowe and Gillian Douglas, note that "it is difficult, if not impossible to define" the word "family," and refer to the advent of same-sex marriage and jurisprudence from the European Court of Human Rights interpreting the scope of article 8, which refers to "family life." Updating Bromley's original definition, they "regard the family as a basic social unit constituted by at least two people, whose relationship may fall into one of three categories": first, "two persons in a marital relationship (including civil partners), or who are living together in a manner similar to spouses"; second, "a parent living with one or more children"; and third, "brothers and sisters or other person related by blood or marriage": Nigel Lowe and Gillian Douglas, *Bromley's Family Law*, 11th ed. (Oxford: Oxford University Press, 2015) at 1–2.

20 Modern writers frequently refer to the field's interaction with other areas of law such as taxation, immigration, employment, and social security: see Herring, *supra* note 19 at 15; Probert and Harding, *supra* note 19 at 5; Diduck and Kaganas, *supra* note 19 at 21; Rebecca Probert, "Under One Roof: Law's Interactions with Family Life" in Rebecca Probert, ed., *Family Life and the Law: Under One Roof* (Aldershot: Ashgate, 2007) 1 at 1–2; Alison Diduck, "What Is Family Law For?" (2011) 64:1 *Current Leg Probs* 287 at 289. However, these areas tend not to be covered because, as Jonathan Herring has noted, "any book that attempts to state all the laws which might affect family life would be enormous": Herring, *supra* note 18 at 15. For American perspectives on this issue see Janet Halley, "What Is Family Law? A Genealogy. Part I" (2011) 23:1 *Yale JL & Human* 1 at 5–6; Jill Elaine Hasday, *Family Law Reimagined* (Cambridge, MA: Harvard University Press, 2014), chapter 2.

Law 3"); and informal norms ("Family Law 4"). As discussed in greater detail at the end of this chapter, these and other scholars are all contributing to an important re-examination of the goals, functions and boundaries of the legal family and Family Law. In this respect, chapter 2 underscores the importance of intellectual efforts to effect change in legal forms and structures, and the potential for future scholarly initiatives to develop the field along new and perhaps more desirable lines.[21]

Chapters 3 through 6 expanded the scope of the analysis to consider some of the institutional (as well as intellectual) dimensions of legal change – statutory, judicial, and parliamentary – that contributed to the legal construction of the family as a private, non-productive sphere anchored by the relation between husband and wife. Chapters 3 and 4 focussed on particular aspects of the extrusion of work from the household, while chapters 5 and 6 considered the legislative and judicial elevation and exceptionalization of the marriage relation within English law and legal thought.

Chapter 3 commenced with an examination of how eighteenth and nineteenth-century parliamentary enclosures consolidated agricultural interests among wealthy landowners, resulting in a loss of common rights to land among the rural poor. It showed that the commons were a crucial component of subsistence-based production for many poor families, providing pasture for the grazing of animals, and sources of food and fuel for people; and that in those parts of England that were hardest hit by parliamentary enclosure (most notably the Midlands), the loss of common rights was an important contributing factor in the broader move towards a system of work predicated on wage labour conducted outside of the family home. It further suggested that this result was at least in part the product of market

---

21 To a less detailed extent, chapter 2 also reveals some of the moves that helped to create the field of Employment Law. In this respect, it also points to the possibilities for further development in that field, particularly in respect of the current centrality of the contract of employment and the residues of master-servant law secreted therein. See further Simon Deakin and Frank Wilkinson, *The Law of the Labour Market: Industrialization, Employment and Legal Evolution* (Oxford: Oxford University Press, 2005) at 303–13; Hugh Collins, "Contractual Autonomy" in Alan Bogg *et al*, eds., *The Autonomy of Labour Law* (Oxford: Hart, 2015) 45; Hugh Collins, "The Productive Disintegration of Labour Law" (1997) 26:4 *Industrial LJ* 295; Mark Freedland, "General Introduction – Aims, Rationale, and Methodology" in Mark Freedland *et al*, eds., *The Contract of Employment* (Oxford: Oxford University Press, 2016) 1 [Freedland *et al, The Contract of Employment*]; Mark Freedland and Nicola Kountouris, *The Legal Construction of Personal Work Relations* (Oxford: Oxford University Press, 2011); Alain Supiot, *Beyond Employment: Changes in Work and the Future of Labour Law in Europe* (Oxford: Oxford University Press, 2001).

ideology, veneration of private property, and a perceived need to manage the population into waged work. The section also highlighted the distinctly gendered implications of enclosure, which compromised women's abilities to engage in home-based production because of care and domestic responsibilities. Families were thus rendered increasingly reliant upon cash wages earned by men outside of the home, which in turn presumed the existence of a wife to perform unpaid domestic work within the home. In this respect, the disaggregation of family and work caused (in part) by enclosures helped to instantiate new models of patriarchy based on the subservience of workers to their masters (a point explored in greater depth in the second part of the chapter), and the (even more complete) economic dependence of women upon their husbands (a move that was augmented by further legal interventions discussed in chapter 4).

The next section of the chapter considered how the *Poor Act 1834* functioned as an institutional push in the direction of wage labour performed outside of the home by curtailing outdoor relief and casting state assistance as a distinctly (and designedly) unpleasant last resort. In essence, it showed that the *Poor Act 1834* helped to construct a legal understanding of work as essentially synonymous with wage labour performed outside of the family sphere (unless one was engaged in domestic service); and thus underscored the idea of the family as a private unit constituted by marriage and (legitimate) birth only. As noted above, these modes of population management were directly influenced by the utilitarianism of Bentham, and Malthusian concerns over population increase and inadequate resources. The result was a market-oriented liberalization of the labour market designed to free the parish and community from responsibility towards the labouring population and render that same population "totally dependent on wages."[22] Coercion was built into the system via the principle of less eligibility, which held that state assistance (in the form of workhouses) was to be pitched at such a low level that only the truly desperate would submit to its indignities – others would "choose" to enter the labour force or, it was hoped, seek assistance from their families. In this latter sense, the *Poor Act 1834* also sought to privatize responsibility for family members – family in this context referring to the narrow, marriage- and birth-based model that was becoming dominant within legal and social discourse and practice.

---

22 Antonella Picchio, *Social Reproduction: The Political Economy of the Labour Market* (Cambridge: Cambridge University Press, 1992) at 62.

Cumulatively, these sections on property law and poor laws demonstrated that the legal construction of the family as a private entity distinct from the world of work was partly constituted through reforms in areas well outside the parameters of modern fields of work and family law. Recognizing the historical diversity of the legal interventions that helped to construct the modern understanding of family, and the scope of its field of regulation, underscores one of the central points of FLE: the inadequacy of analysis (contemporary and historical) that ignores the economic dimensions of family life, and the myriad ways in which laws across the entire spectrum of regulation influence, and are influenced by, prevailing conceptions of the family.[23]

In the present context, one can discern parallels between the effects (and ideological underpinnings) of enclosure and poor laws on work and family practices, and privatizing moves since the 1980s (and particularly since 2008) that have wound back provisions for public infrastructure, resulting in even greater reliance on wages and private family support; and the compounding of this dimension of austerity governance by workfare schemes that oblige people "to perform state-chosen labour as a condition for receiving state benefits."[24] If history is our guide, questioning these sorts of moves is important not only because of their basic unfairness but also to counter what seems to be a new (neoliberal) form of a much older (classically liberal) set of ideas that entrenched the family/work divide in the nineteenth century.

The second part of chapter 3 showed that the disaggregation of the household model of the family into the discrete domains of work and family, and specifically the move towards an economy based on wage labour, was partially constituted by a series of statutory and judicial moves that transposed the patriarchal dominance of household masters over their families (servants, wife, and children) into the realm of paid work. While classical liberalism characterized the wage relationship as one based in consent and contract, the analysis in chapter 3 showed that

---

23 Halley and Rittich, *supra* note 6; Halley, *supra* note 20; Kerry Rittich, "Black Sites: Locating the Family and Family Law in Development" (2010) 58:4 *Am J Comp L* 102; Kerry Rittich, "Families on the Edge: Governing Home and Work in a Globalized Economy" (2010) 88:5 *NC L Rev* 1527 [Rittich, "Families on the Edge"]; Hila Shamir, "The State of Care: Rethinking the Distributive Effects of Familial Care Policies in Liberal Welfare States" (2010) 58:4 *Am J Comp L* 953; Ann Shalleck, "Introduction: Comparative Family Law: What Is the Global Family? Family Law in Decolonization, Modernization and Globalization" (2011) 19:2 *Am U J Gender, Soc Pol & L* 449.

24 Guy Standing, *A Precariat Charter: From Denizens to Citizens* (London: Bloomsbury Academic, 2014) at 262–8, 357–8.

this consent-based framework was entirely consistent, theoretically and practically, with worker subordination and a structural prioritization of the interests of masters. Beginning in the early eighteenth century, a series of statutes built upon the regime established by the *Statute of Artificers 1562*,[25] and imposed increasingly punitive sanctions on workers for breach of employment agreements. In essence, these laws expanded the class of workers against whom imprisonment orders could be made, added misbehaviour to the list of possible grounds for imprisonment (hitherto confined to refusals to enter into service, absconding from service, and failure to complete work), and increased potential prison sentences. Masters, of course, were immune from this regime, being subject only to civil wage recovery claims. The *Master and Servant Act 1823*[26] consolidated these various targeted laws into one punitive statute that made absconding from work and refusing to enter into work under a contract of hiring punishable by up to three months' imprisonment. The courts augmented this legislative process by expanding the legal meaning of "service" to encompass not only domestic and menial servants but also a large swathe of waged workers. In essence, the deeply hierarchical model of master and *domestic* servant relations was expanded into a general Law of Master and Servant that applied to a shifting but generally increasing class of workers. (Ironically, as chapter 4 noted, domestic servants were eventually excluded from this regime altogether owing to the familial nature of their work.) The point of this legally imposed subordination was to secure performance; indeed, the *Master and Servant Act 1867*[27] specifically permitted orders for specific performance. At its core, then, this second part of chapter 3 showed that the extrusion of work relations from the household occurred in a manner that spoke the language of contract but which in reality involved a state-directed extension of the pre-eighteenth century master's power over his servants; in this respect, the patriarchalism of the classical and medieval household lived on in new forms via the subordination of workers labouring outside of their masters' (and their own) homes.

The legacy of eighteenth- and nineteenth-century master and servant law remains woven into the folds of modern employment law.[28] Criminalization of workers may be in the past, but hierarchy and outright subordination remain characteristic of many employment relationships –

---

25 5 Eliz, c 4.
26 *An Act to enlarge the Powers of Justices in determining Complaints between Masters and Servants, and between Masters, Apprentices, Artificers and others 1823*, 4 Geo IV, c 34.
27 30 & 31 Vict, c 141.
28 See *supra* note 21.

precisely because of the statutory and judicial expansion of employees'/ servants' duties and obligations towards their masters/employers in previous centuries. As Joanne Conaghan has observed, this structural prioritization of employer interests eventually led to an understanding of determinations over working time "as falling squarely within an employer's 'entitlement,'" setting the stage for modern forms of subordination rooted in the employer's contractual entitlement (unless restrained by statute or collective bargaining) to dictate working hours.[29] Perhaps the most obvious manifestation of this normative framework is the rise of flexible working arrangements involving no fixed or guaranteed hours of remunerated work.[30] These forms of work tend to reinforce the distinction between work and family by rendering workers even more reliant on wages (since flexible arrangements generally do not include paid vacations and medical leave), and "negative[ly] impact[ing] on family life, caring responsibilities and personal relationships."[31]

While the legal moves traced in chapter 3 affected women and children in both direct and indirect ways, the gendered nature of the family/work split meant that a greater proportion of men were channelled into forms of wage labour conducted outside of the home, and subject to the coercive rules of the master-servant regime. Accordingly, chapter 4 focussed on some of the ways that legal change in the eighteenth and nineteenth-centuries affected women's work and youth apprenticeship. In accordance with the nineteenth-century ideological association of women and domesticity, the first part of the chapter addressed women's paid and unpaid labour in the home. On the paid front, it showed that the legislative and judicial extension of the master and *domestic* servant model to most forms of paid work in the eighteenth and nineteenth centuries was accompanied by the excision and

---

29 Joanne Conaghan, "Time to Dream? Flexibility, Families, and the Regulation of Working Time" in Judy Fudge and Rosemary Owens, eds., *Precarious Work, Women, and the New Economy: The Challenge to Legal Norms* (Oxford: Hart, 2006) 101 at 102–4, referring to *Johnson v Nottinghamshire Combined Police Authority* [1974] ICR 170.

30 *Ibid.* See further Abi Adams and Jeremias Prassl, *Zero-Hours Work in the United Kingdom*, International Labour Office, Conditions of Work and Employment Series No 101 (2018) at 23, noting that "[t]he power that schedule flexibility places in the hands of managers is an emerging theme from the academic and media coverage" concerning zero hours contracts.

31 A. Wood, B. Burchell, A. Coutts, *From Zero Joy to Zero Stress: Making Flexible Scheduling Work* (Cambridge, 2016) at 6 quoted in Adams and Prassl, *supra* note 30 at 31. For a global perspective on this issue see Rittich, "Families on the Edge," *supra* note 23.

exceptionalization of domestic service from this general legal template governing English work relations. Subordination of domestic workers (always a feature of English law) continued, but more through a legally created lacuna derived – like the general master-servant regime – from the perceived need to maintain the authority of household heads, but in this case over people still working within their homes. Thus, the series of statutes that extended masters' control over workers (and which provided those workers with a limited measure of recourse against masters) did not apply to domestics; and in the late eighteenth century the Court of King's Bench held that the *Statute of Artificers* did not apply to domestic servants.[32] Despite calls for greater regulation of domestics in the nineteenth century, the familial nature of their work stymied reform. Masters wanted the ability to punish recalcitrant domestics, but their existence within the increasingly private realm of the home meant there was a limit as to what those same masters would accept in terms of oversight. Women bore the brunt of this exceptional treatment of domestic service. The feminization of domestic service in the nineteenth century appears to have been the product of "diminishing facilities for earning money at home"[33] – a result partly brought about by enclosure and the loss of common rights, as well as the move towards factory-based production, which decimated home-based forms of textile production. The exclusion of domestic service from significant parts of the law applying to "ordinary" (male) workers thus continued the patriarchal dominance of (male) household heads over their (female) subordinates within the private realm of the family home.

This pattern continued into twentieth century – a 1945 report on domestic service noted its "purely personal" nature, and one of its correlative and defining features: a lack of control over time, i.e., the master's ability to exercise near total control over his domestic servant. What this suggests is that the disarticulation of work and family was a messy and in certain respects incomplete process. As a matter of legal classification and taxonomy, scholars eventually shifted domestic service out of the domestic and familial sphere,[34] but on an institutional legal level it is clear that domestics retained a connection to the families for whom they worked (but no longer formed part of) that was thought to justify their ongoing exceptional treatment in law. While modern English law

---

32 *The King v Inhabitants of Hulcott* (1796) 6 Term 583, 101 ER 716.

33 Clara E. Collet, "The Collection and Utilisation of Official Statistics bearing on the Extent and Effects of the Industrial Employment of Women" (1898) 61:2 *J Royal Stat Soc* 219 at 224.

34 Lee, *supra* note 12; Bromley, *supra* note 11.

does treat paid domestic work as a form of contract-based employment, it remains an exceptional species of work through its exclusion from numerous legal provisions[35] – a direct result of the ongoing application of the idea that domestic work is somehow different to work performed outside of the home,[36] with results that continue to disproportionately affect women.[37]

Chapter 4 then addressed women's *unpaid* domestic work. It focussed in particular on some of the ways that nineteenth-century legislation and employer practices combined to complicate married women's participation in wage labour outside of the home, thereby tightening the association between housework and housewifery; the augmentation of this process through male breadwinner ideology, and the background role played by the relaxation of anti-combination laws in strengthening trade union claims for family wages; and the devaluation of women's work in the home, demonstrated through changes to the English census. Protective labour laws, it was suggested, gave legal form to a distinct ideology that treated married women's paid labour outside of the home as productive of domestic and national discord. The *Factory Acts* and their ilk may not have directly resulted in women eschewing paid work, but they helped (and were designed) to constitute a legal and social world view that rendered less thinkable women's participation in work outside of the home, and strengthened the idea that a wife's principal occupation was (or ought to be) unpaid maintenance of the family. Building on this idea, employers in the late nineteenth century began to institute marriage bars that directly excluded married women from particular occupations and "induced, if not compelled, such women to invest deeply in their roles as housewives and mothers."[38] In this respect, the channelling of wives into the private sphere of the home functioned as a critical precondition for men's paid work outside of the home, thereby reinforcing the gendered basis of the family/work

---

35 Einat Albin and Jeremias Prassl, "Fragmenting Work, Fragmented Regulation" in Freedland *et al, The Contract of Employment, supra* note 20, 209 at 226.

36 See Einat Albin, "From 'Domestic Servant' to 'Domestic Worker'" in Judy Fudge, Shae McCrystal and Kamala Sankaran, eds., *Challenging the Legal Boundaries of Work Regulation* (Oxford: Hart, 2012) 231.

37 On the disproportionate impact of precarious work on women see Judy Fudge and Rosemary Owens, "Precarious Work, Women, and the New Economy: The Challenge to Legal Norms" in Fudge and Owens, *supra* note 29, 8 at 12–15.

38 Kerry Rittich, "Feminization and Contingency: Regulating the Stakes of Work for Women" in Joanne Conaghan, Richard Michael Fischl and Karl Klare, *Labour Law in an Era of Globalization: Transformative Practices and Possibilities* (Oxford: Oxford University Press, 2002) 117 at 131 [Rittich, "Feminization and Contingency"].

divide. By the late nineteenth century, this attitude towards work and family life was broadly accepted among workers (and many of their wives), resulting in agitation for male wages that would support a family and enable a wife to remain within her proper sphere: the home. In contrast to other parts of the world,[39] the law in England did not directly instantiate a family wage; what it did, do, however, was remove some of the barriers to large-scale agitation by workers for changes to working conditions. In this sense, laws passed in the 1870s that modified existing restrictions on worker combinations functioned as background conditions for the extension of family wage ideology and the demarcation of family and work as discrete, gendered zones. This distinction was further entrenched by the casting of women's work within the home as unproductive. Evidence of this devaluation was presented in the form of nineteenth-century census data, which showed a clear move towards characterizing unpaid work within the home as an economically unproductive activity, albeit simultaneously casting such work as "the most important of all female occupations."[40]

As with paid domestic work, the historical (or at least nineteenth and twentieth century) treatment of unpaid domestic work continues to cast a long shadow. In Conaghan's pithy terms, modern labour law "is not primarily or even predominantly about the world of work. It is about *paid* work."[41] Unpaid domestic work, still disproportionately performed by women, remains largely invisible in law, despite the obvious reliance of paid workers on forms of unpaid work.[42] As Kerry Rittich has observed, this continuation of longstanding historical trends is partly a product of the continuing currency of classical economic "beliefs that value resides unproblematically in market prices" and hence that "the nature of productive work is uncontroversial and self-evident."[43] Historical legal

---

39 Notably Australia – see the judgment of the Commonwealth Court of Conciliation and Arbitration in *Ex parte HV McKay* (1907) 2 CAR 1 (the Harvester case).

40 Census of England and Wales, 1881, 43 & 44 Vict c 37, *Vol IV. General Report* (London, 1883) at 29.

41 Joanne Conaghan, "Work, Family, and the Discipline of Labour Law" in Joanne Conaghan and Kerry Rittich, eds., *Labour Law, Work, and Family: Critical and Comparative Perspectives* (Oxford: Oxford University Press, 2005) 19 at 34 [Conaghan, "Discipline of Labour Law"]. See also Karl Klare, "The Horizons of Transformative Labour and Employment Law" in Conaghan, Fischl and Klare, *supra* note 37, 3 at 10.

42 Conaghan, "Discipline of Labour Law," *supra* note 41 at 28. See also Joanne Conaghan, "Women, Work, and Family: A British Revolution?" in Conaghan, Fischl and Klare, *supra* note 38, 53 at 69, noting labour law's "schematic and conceptual dependence on women's unpaid labour." See further Carole Pateman, *The Sexual Contract* (Palo Alto: Stanford University Press, 1988) chapter 5.

43 Rittich, "Feminization and Contingency," *supra* note 38 at 134.

(and social) moves to channel women into unpaid work also continue to influence women's employment.[44] Marriage bars and protective laws no longer target women, but "the legacy of sex-based job discrimination and pay scales" remains, with women continuing to be "crowded into a limited range of occupations, … and over-represented in low-paid and atypical caring jobs."[45] One of the results of this devaluation of women's paid (and unpaid) work is a reliance on family law[46] (either through a wife's entitlement to economic support within a marriage,[47] or by recognizing a wife's stake in matrimonial property and possible entitlement to spousal support, based on her contributions to the family[48]) instead of, or alongside, the law of work to compensate women for unpaid contributions to the family (and possibly for taking on low paid work outside of the home, instead of high-paying careers, to enable the fulfilment of domestic duties). In this respect, it is apparent that family and work remained artificially segregated from one another, with unpaid work still having to *prove* its legal and economic value.

The second part of chapter 4 focussed on youth and apprenticeship – historically the most familial of work relations. Commencing with the early modern roots of apprenticeship law in the *Statute of Artificers* and *Poor Relief Act 1601*,[49] it traced the differing legal paths of traditional and parish apprenticeship over the nineteenth century. Concerning traditional apprenticeship, the chapter showed how legal and social changes combined to transform the relation between master and apprentice from a hybrid of work, instruction, and family care, to a relation premised on the contractual obligation of apprentices to *work*, and the much more limited reciprocal obligation of masters to teach. The element of family-based care was gradually whittled away as apprentices increasingly remained within their own families of origin (or lodged outside of their and their masters' homes), shifting the nature of the relation sharply in

---

44 Sandra Fredman and Judy Fudge, "The Contract of Employment and Gendered Work" in Freedland *et al, supra* note 20, 231 at 236.

45 *Ibid.*

46 Judy Fudge, "Labour as a 'Fictive Commodity': Radically Reconceptualizing Labour Law" in Guy Davidov and Brian Langille, eds., *The Idea of Labour Law* (Oxford: Oxford University Press, 2011) 121 at 136.

47 A husband's common law duty to support his wife through the provision of necessities remains extant, though the means by which maintenance can now be claimed by separated spouses are now governed by the *Domestic Proceedings and Magistrates' Courts Act 1978*, c 22 and the *Matrimonial Causes Act 1973*, c 18, s 27: Lowe and Douglas, *supra* note 19 at 915–16.

48 Burton, *supra* note 19, chapter 7.

49 *An Act for the Relief of the Poor 1601*, 43 Eliz I, c 2.

the direction of paid labour (wages increasingly replaced the provision of accommodation, food, and medical assistance). Like domestic service, though, this process was protracted and less than entirely clear; unlike other workers, apprentices remained subject to imprisonment under the *Employers and Workmen Act 1875*,[50] and the particular provisions of an apprenticeship contract might retain residues of older forms of obligation.[51] Within scholarly legal thought, this ambiguity was reflected in Eversley's inclusion of apprentices alongside domestic servants in the master-servant relations that still comprised part of the Law of Domestic Relations.[52] By the early twentieth century, however, apprenticeship had shifted into the realm of Employment within the *Digest of English Civil Law*, and Frank Tillyard in *Industrial Law* characterized apprenticeship as simply "a special form of the contract of service," differing "from the ordinary contract of service in that the master undertakes to teach the apprentice."[53] For traditional apprentices, the imbrication of work and family life was essentially over – and remains so to this day.[54] Indeed, apprenticeship as a form of training is now a relatively unusual path for youth in England. Reflecting this practical reality, modern texts on employment and labour law pay scant attention to apprenticeship, in marked contrast to the importance accorded to the relation of master and apprentice in historical works. Legal attention has instead shifted to the relationship between children and their parents (and carers and guardians).[55]

The analysis of apprenticeship in chapter 4 then proceeded to trace a markedly different path for parish apprenticeship. Since the precondition for parish apprenticeship was the inability (or non-existence) of a family of origin to care for a child, the state remained involved in the lives of indigent children at the same time as the institution of apprenticeship was undergoing dramatic change. At first, the rise of industrial manufacturing in the late eighteenth century led to so-called "factory apprenticeship," which largely dispensed with the element of care and treated children as little workers in the low-skilled trades. It seemed, at

---

50 38 & 39 Vict, c 90.

51 William Holdsworth, *The Law of Master and Servant: Including that of Trades Unions and Combinations* (London: Routledge, 1876) at 176–7.

52 Eversley, *supra* note 13, part V, chapter V.

53 Frank Tillyard, *Industrial Law* (London: A&C Black, 1916) at 30.

54 Legally, apprenticeship remains a somewhat exceptional species of employment, though it falls within the broad definition of the contract of employment in the *Employment Rights Act 1996*, c 18, s 230(2). See Simon Deakin and Gillian Morris, *Labour Law*, 6th ed. (Oxford: Hart, 2012) at 172–4.

55 See *supra* note 15.

this point, that parish apprenticeship was following traditional apprenticeship down the path of work, rather than family. Eventually, though, the cost of housing and feeding factory apprentices generated a shift away from the practice, and pauper children were channelled into institutional care, the conditions of which resulted in a further move (back) to family-based forms of care through the boarding out system. Beginning in the latter part of the nineteenth century, persons taking pauper children into their homes were required to sign an undertaking to "bring up the child as one of his own"; by the mid-twentieth century, the Care of Children Committee declared its preference for family-based over institutional care, and this prioritization was enacted into law in the *Children Act 1948*.[56] In essence, parish apprenticeship shifted from a hybrid relation based on work and family care, to a system of state-enforced child welfare premised on a preference for family-based care and the absence of work. It was a reversion of sorts to the earlier family-based model of care seen in apprenticeship, but in an intensified form, shorn of its roots in service and based instead on an idea of the private family, not the productive household.

Family-based care outside of employment remains the preferred model for care of needy children in England and Wales. In an interesting historical reversal of sorts, however, there have recently been calls to recognize foster carers as employees of the state.[57] While claims of this nature have thus far not been well received by the courts, they suggest the future possibility of a return to an older recognition of the integration of work and family life (and an important recognition that at least some care work is productive work), albeit in a radically new manner that would cast persons once deemed masters as employees.

Chapter 5 shifted the focus of the book to the second main process underpinning the shift from the legal household to the legal family: the elevation of marriage to the position once occupied by master-servant relations, and the refashioning of husband-wife relations as "constitutive of domestic relations."[58] It focussed in particular on the legislative dimensions of this process, notably the manner in which the English state signalled the national interest in and importance of marriage, the

---

56 11 & 12 Geo VI, c 43.

57 See Alan Bogg, "Foster Parents and Fundamental Labour Rights," UK Labour Law Blog, 25th July 2018, https://uklabourlawblog.com/2018/07/25/foster-parents -and-fundamental-labour-rights-alan-bogg/ (accessed 11 April 2019); Clive Coleman, "Foster Carer Fights for Workers' Rights," *BBC News*, 9 October 2017, https://www .bbc.com/news/uk-41543651 (accessed 11 April 2019).

58 Pateman, *supra* note 42 at 116.

idea of the marital relation as a conduit for the dispensation of benefits, and the centrality of marriage to family life. The chapter began with the English state's assertion of civil (rather than ecclesiastical) control over marital validity in *Lord Hardwicke's Act*,[59] and suggested that the Act constituted and paved the way for future development of the legal idea of marriage as a private relation of significant public importance warranting additional state intervention. It then suggested that legislation passed in the 1830s that rendered void future marriages that contravened the canonical prohibited degrees (*Lord Lyndhurst's Act*[60]), and which permitted civil marriage outside of the Church (*Civil Marriage Act*[61]), ought to be viewed as continuing the project of "civilizing" marriage that began with *Lord Hardwicke's Act*. The next part of the chapter looked at a series of legislative moves that "incentivized" marriage. Beginning with the bastardy provisions of the *Poor Act 1834*, it argued that the imposition of full financial responsibility for illegitimate children on mothers was designed not only to lower the number of illegitimate births but also to channel women into marriages based on affection and esteem, rather than an alleged father's calculation that it was better to marry a woman than be subject to an order for support, thereby ensuring a measure of financial security for mothers and their children, and the creation of strong (marriage-based) families.

The chapter then addressed some of the ways that nineteenth-century compensation statutes rendered entitlement to claim and recover damages for the death of (male) breadwinners by accident, and later in the context of work, contingent upon the existence of marriage (one's own or one's parents'). In particular, it showed how the *Fatal Accidents Act 1846*[62] tipped the older common law action for loss of services on its head by conferring upon wives the ability to claim for the loss of their husbands' earnings – a distinct change from the common law ability of a master (which also remained in existence) to claim for the loss of his servant's services. This move, it was argued, formed part of a legal narrowing of the family, and helped to constitute a world view (and legal consciousness) in which marriage formed the core of family life. The last part of the chapter built upon this idea by showing that the introduction of judicial divorce and the conferral of (limited) legislative protection over married women's property amounted to a deeply

---

59 *An Act for the Better Preventing of Clandestine Marriage 1753*, 26 Geo II, c 33.
60 *An Act to render certain Marriages valid and, to alter the Law with respect to certain voidable Marriages 1835*, 5 & 6 Will VI, c 54.
61 *An Act for Marriages in England 1836*, 6 & 7 Will IV, c 85.
62 *An Act for compensating the Families of Persons killed by Accidents 1846*, 9 & 10 Vict, c 93.

regulatory and conservative effort to "stabilize" marriage. Alongside their liberalizing elements, these laws sought to entrench marriage as the state's preferred relational form, and the core of family life, by providing a means for the weeding out of bad marriages, and providing poorer women with a measure of financial autonomy to (somewhat) insulate them and their children from intemperate husbands. Evidence for this claim was drawn from close analysis of parliamentary debates concerning the bills that resulted in the *Matrimonial Causes Act 1857*,[63] the *Married Women's Property Acts* of 1870 and 1882.[64]

From a contemporary perspective, the legislative introduction of civil partnerships for same-sex couples in 2004, and the extension of marriage rights to same-sex couples in 2013, would seem to build upon this broad historical narrative of English legislation designed to entrench the marital relation. Of course, the *Civil Partnership Act 2004*, c 33 (CPA) instituted a parallel form of relationship recognition that left marriage in its traditional opposite-sex form, but this very move, despite (or perhaps because of) of its "separate but equal" ideology, re-emphasized the normative superiority of marriage.[65] As Barker and Monk have noted, the CPA took "marriage as its template and replicate[d] most of its legal rights and responsibilities."[66] Exclusion from marriage was thus cast as

---

63 *An Act to amend the Law relating to Divorce and Matrimonial Causes in England 1857*, 20 & 21 Vict, c 85.

64 *Married Women's Property Act 1870*, 33 & 34 Vict c 93; *Married Women's Property Act 1882*, 45 & 46 Vict, c 75.

65 One of the ways it achieved this was by excluding opposite-sex couples from the scheme – a deliberate move that was designed to underscore the centrality of marriage and avoid the criticism that same sex unions undermine that institution. See, for instance, the comments of Baroness Scotland in the House of Lords debate over the Civil Partnership Bill: UK, HL Deb, 22 April 2004, vol 660, col 388.

66 Nicola Barker and Daniel Monk, "From Civil Partnership to Same-Sex Marriage: A Decade in British Legal History" in Nicola Barker and Daniel Monk, eds., *From Civil Partnership to Same-Sex Marriage: Interdisciplinary Reflections* (Abingdon: Routledge, 2015) 1 at 3. The few differences that did exist have largely been removed following the passage of the *Equality Act 2010*, c 15 (notably, the prohibition on conducting civil partnership ceremonies in religious premises), and the *Human Fertilisation and Embryology Act 2008*, c 22 (introducing a presumption of parentage on the part of civil partners concerning children born through assisted reproduction). *Ibid* at 3–4. Until recently the one outstanding area of difference was provision for pension entitlements, which were limited to the date upon which the Act came into force – a restriction that was also carried over into the *Marriage (Same Sex Couples) Act 2013*, c 30. However, in *Walker v Innospec Ltd & Ors* [2017] UKSC 24, the Supreme Court held that this differential treatment violated European Union law. Accordingly, civil partners and same-sex spouses are now entitled to be treated equally to heterosexual spouses for the purposes of pension entitlements.

inherently disadvantageous.[67] In this respect, just as nineteenth-century laws sought to embed marriage as the primary relational model within English society, the CPA can be viewed as an attempt to bring a newly acceptable class of (former?[68]) sexual outlaws within the scope of state recognition,[69] but in a manner that also reinforced the primacy of marriage. This exclusionary stance was remedied by the *Marriage (Same Sex Couples) Act 2013*, c 30 (MSSCA),[70] but in taking this step the law (and lawmakers) once again affirmed the public importance of marriage – and of stabilizing same-sex relationships through extension of marital rights. Arguments on both sides of the political spectrum portrayed same-sex marriage as a move that would strengthen the institution of marriage generally, and by extension, the English state[71] – a discursive framing that bears more than a passing resemblance to the family stabilization arguments mobilized by proponents of judicial divorce in debates over the Matrimonial Causes Bill 1857. In this respect, while the CPA and MSSCA certainly expanded the relationship recognition menu for same-sex couples, they can also be seen as part of a much

---

67 Nicola Barker, "Sex and the Civil Partnership Act: The Future of (Non) Conjugality?" (2006) 14:2 *Fem Leg Stud* 241 at 243 [Barker, "Sex and the CPA"].

68 The *Civil Partnership Act 2004*, c 33 arguably presents a de-sexualized vision of lesbian and gay relationships by excluding non-consummation as a ground for voidability (since consummation is defined at common law in heterosexual terms), and by not inherently requiring monogamy because adultery (also defined in heterosexual terms) is not a ground for dissolution (though non-monogamy might constitute a basis for dissolution on the grounds of unreasonable behaviour). See Barker, "Sex and the CPA," *supra* note 67.

69 This posture was evident on both sides of the political spectrum. For discussion see Carl Stychin, "Family Friendly? Rights, Responsibilities and Relationship Recognition" in Diduck and O'Donovan, *supra* note 15, 21 at 21–23.

70 Remedied in the sense of removing an obvious measure of formal legal inequality. I do not mean to suggest that extending the ability to marry to same-sex couples by any means atoned for centuries of marginalization and persecution, or that marriage meets the social, economic, and relational needs of all non-heterosexual people.

71 See, e.g., Andrew Gilber, "An Unnatural Union? – British Conservatism and the Marriage (Same Sex Couples) Act 2013" in Alison Diduck, Noam Peleg and Helen Reece, *Law in Society: Reflections on Children, Family, Culture and Philosophy: Essays in Honour of Michael Freeman* (Leiden: Brill Nijhoff, 2015) 489 at 490, quoting David Cameron, Speech to Conservative Party Conference, Manchester, 5 October 2011; Nicola Barker, "After the Wedding, What Next? Conservatism and Conjugality" in Barker and Monk, *supra* note 65 220 at 221, quoting Peter Tatchell, "How the Tories Were Won to Marriage Equality" (13 October 2011), http://www.petertatchell.net /lgbt_rights/partnerships/how-the-tories-were-won-to-marriage-equality/ (accessed 11 April 2019).

longer effort on the part of the English state to reinforce the centrality of marriage in family life.[72]

Chapter 6 built upon the analysis in chapters 2 and 5 by addressing some of the ways in which nineteenth-century English judges constructed marriage as a relation of public importance partly by distinguishing it from ordinary commercial contracts. It began with the action for breach of promise to marry. Prior to *Lord Hardwicke's Act*, these promises were specifically enforceable in the ecclesiastical courts. With the Act's eradication of this remedy, however, the money-based action for breach of promise (which developed in the seventeenth century) rose to prominence. The analysis showed that in its early phase, the action was treated in distinctly contractual terms that appeared to draw little distinction between contracts to marry and commercial contracts. In the nineteenth century, however, courts departed from orthodox contractual principles in ways that contributed to the legal construction of marriage as a publicly important relation, and (hence) an exceptional species of contract. In particular, analysis of the cases demonstrated a feminization of the action through a de facto prohibition on claims by men (thus reinforcing the expectation that women were, and ought to be, economically dependent upon men); a lowering of the standards of evidence with respect to offer and acceptance of marriage proposals (thereby enabling more men to be held accountable for their words, and signalling the judiciary's belief in the importance of marriage to women and society); and an expansion of the compensable heads of damage to include emotional distress (underscoring women's perceived (or socially/judicially desired) emotional investment in marriage). Specific performance of marriage promises had been legislatively removed from the remedial menu, but the common law responded by emphasizing

---

72 A similar argument can be made concerning the limited extension of rights to same-sex and opposite-sex cohabitants. While there has unquestionably been a move away from outright hostility, English law has maintained a relatively hands-off approach to cohabitants that arguably continues to prioritize the status of marriage. See generally Rebecca Probert, *The Changing Legal Regulation of Cohabitation: From Fornicators to Family, 1600–2010* (Cambridge: Cambridge University Press, 2012) at 201–14; Jens Martin Scherpe and Brian Sloan, "Contractualisation of Family Law in England & Wales: Autonomy vs Judicial Discretion" in Frederick Swennen, ed., *Contractualisation of Family Law – Global Perspectives* (Cham: Springer, 2015) 165; Gillian Douglas, Julia Pearce and Hilary Woodward, "Cohabitants, Property and the Law: A Study of Injustice" (2009) 72:1 *Mod L Rev* 24. In a corresponding manner, married couples remain more constrained than cohabitants in their ability to contract out of relationship-generated rights and obligations. See Scherpe and Sloan, *supra* note 72; *Radmacher v Granatino* [2010] UKSC 42 (affirming the principle in *Hyman v Hyman* [1929] AC 601 that married parties cannot oust the jurisdiction of the courts).

the danger for men of attempting to avoid their promises to women. In essence, by awarding the vast majority of female litigants damages for broken promises of marriage, the courts constructed a general legal framework that exceptionalized the contract to marry, and which operated as a strong encouragement to men to uphold their promises based on the idea that marriage was the central, publicly important relation within the private family.

The second part of chapter 6 traced a similar process of marriage exceptionalism within nineteenth-century English private international law. It showed how, in a series of cases involving questions over the validity of foreign marriages and the jurisdiction of courts in one state to regulate and dissolve marriages conducted in another state, English courts moved away from an older legal emphasis on mutual consent and deference to the law of the place of celebration (*lex loci celebrationis*) in matters of both form and substance. In its place, courts developed a view (contested but ultimately accepted) that the country with the most significant connection to the marriage should govern issues of capacity, with domicile as the determining factor, leaving only matters of form to the law of the place of celebration (if different to the place of domicile). In this way, English courts advanced a new conception of marriage as an exceptional species of contract on the basis that marriage was a relation of such public importance that states were entitled to set conditions for the creation of legally valid marriages that domiciliaries could not simply avoid by marrying abroad. The flipside of this recognition of the national dimensions of marriage was acknowledgment by the English courts that in cases concerning dissolution, English law did not necessarily continue to govern marriages conducted in England when a married couple was domiciled elsewhere. This recognition of the national interest in marriage, and the non-modifiable terms and conditions that automatically affected capacity to marry and which attached to solemnized marriages by virtue of the law of the place of domicile, led to a general movement towards distinguishing marriage from contracts of a commercial nature (governed by *lex loci contractus*), resulting in a new legal concept of marriage as a form of status (though one that still arose through a contractual or contract-like exchange of promises). In this respect, the analysis showed how judicial perceptions of marriage aligned in important ways with the shift, traced in chapter 2, in scholarly understandings of marriage as a form of status, distinct from the realm of ordinary commercial contracts. In a further parallel, the analysis in chapter 6 demonstrated the profound influence of Scottish legal thought on English judicial attitudes towards the national dimensions of marriage, complementing and reinforcing the importance of civilian legal thought on the English legal construction of the family and its Family Law.

The emphasis on domicile in cross-border marital validity and dissolution cases remains extant in English law.[73] The advent of civil partnerships and same-sex marriage did, however, introduce an interesting statutory exception to this common law position. Under both the CPA and MSSCA, English courts are permitted to assume jurisdiction over a divorce application brought by a same-sex couple (only) not domiciled in England or Wales if the couple married or registered in either of those places and "it appears to the court to be in the interests of justice to assume jurisdiction."[74] While in practical terms this carve-out is limited to people who were residents of England or Wales at the time of marriage or registration,[75] it also shares elements of the early nineteenth-century common law emphasis on the law of the place of celebration (recognizing, of course, that judicial divorce was not possible in England until 1857). What is new, it seems, is thus in some respects quite old, with England once again asserting its jurisdiction over persons married, but no longer domiciled, within its borders.

Stepping back from the detail in these chapters, and contemporary parallels, it is apparent that a number of general points can be made about the legal construction of the family and Family Law in English law and legal thought in the long nineteenth century. At perhaps the broadest level, what is apparent is the sheer breadth of the combined intellectual and institutional effort it took to disaggregate the legal household into the separate domains of work (law) and family (law). In other words, the emergence of the family and Family Law in the forms characterized by Bromley as archetypical and functionally accurate was far from

---

73 *Domicile and Matrimonial Proceedings Act 1973*, c 45, s 5(2); EC Reg No 2201/2003 of 27 November 2003, Art 3(1).

74 *Domicile and Matrimonial Proceedings Act 1973*, c 45, Sch A1, cl 2(1)(c)(iii), inserted by *Marriage (Same Sex Couples) Act 2013*, c 30, Sch 4, Pt 4; *Civil Partnership Act 2004*, c 33, s 221. To the extent that a foreign jurisdiction's marriage and/or civil partnership law comports with the laws in England and Wales concerning same-sex couples, the ordinary rules will apply. It is only in cases of disconformity that could result in "limping marriages" that the exception is enlivened and English courts are empowered to assume jurisdiction in the manner described below.

75 The residency requirements for marriage and civil partnership in England and Wales provide that notice may only be given if both parties have lived in England and Wales for at least seven days, and in the case of foreign nationals, the notice period may be extended from the usual 28 days to up to 70 days: see Catherine Fairbairn, *Marriage: Residence Requirements*, House of Commons Briefing Paper No 00644 (2017).

inevitable; rather, it was the product of a series of intersecting and contingent processes. While many of these moves were institutional efforts to manage the English population along productive and reproductive lines, ideas and ideology also played a crucial role in the legal construction of the family and Family Law. On this intellectual front, it is also clear that cross-pollination of legal ideas played a formative role in the distinction between family and contract, with English scholars and judges adopting and adapting civilian (most notably German and Scottish) legal ideas into their own legal consciousness and practice. On both substantive and methodological levels, the analysis further demonstrated that the legal construction of the family involved and traversed a range of domains that are now generally considered outside the scope of Family Law – most obviously the law of work in its various guises, but also property law, welfare law, tort law and criminal law.

On a more doctrinal level, and sitting beneath the broad process of extruding work relations from the household and reframing them as synonymous with wage labour, and the parallel process of elevating marriage to the core of the family, a particular set of legal ideas and principles also developed. The legal exceptionalism of marriage, and its framing as a form of status distinct from ordinary contractual relations, is a theme that cuts across the scholarly development of Family Law, as well as the legislative and judicial treatment of marriage as an institution of public importance, crucial to the wellbeing of the English state.[76] Legal exceptionalism is also apparent in the treatment of domestic service as distinct from the general law of work. Read together, these parts of the story suggest that in this particular historical context, contract itself was rendered exceptional when it touched upon the domain of the family. Extending the contractual analysis, it is clear that the coexistence of contract and subordination in the world of work is another dimension of this story. In the sphere of paid work outside the home this was apparent in the development of the coercive master-servant regime governing most work relations; and subordination of paid workers within the home continued through the exceptional treatment of domestic service. Allied to this hierarchical conception of (paid) work relations was a long process of complicating and devaluing women's work. This dimension of the story commenced with the problems created for women by enclosure, continued with an exploration of various ways that the law was deployed to exclude women from paid work and

---

76 In a corresponding manner, we saw how marriage was transformed into an instrument for the governance and management of the population in ways that comport with Foucault's theory of governmentality.

foster an ideology of female dependence, and concluded by noting the late nineteenth-century move towards treating housework as unproductive. This association between women, wifedom, and housewifery is also apparent in judicial attitudes towards (men's) breaches of promises to marry. Cutting across virtually all of these dimensions was the extension and consolidation of patriarchy along new lines. While the dominance of the classical household master diminished in certain respects in the nineteenth century (for example, the reduction of masters'/husbands' rights to physically chastise servants/wives), it also lived on in new configurations: masters/employers were granted sweeping new powers to seek criminal punishment of servants/workers, domestic servants remained subject to complete control by masters over their time, and wives were rendered ever more economically dependent on their husbands as avenues for paid work were closed and women's place in the home solidified.

These doctrinal developments were in no small part influenced by an intersecting set of ideological commitments. Aspects of the contract/status binary have already been addressed. Market ideology (in its classical liberal form) is evident in the general prioritization of contract and consent-based legal relations seen in scholarly texts and judicial decisions; and in legislative efforts to deal with issues such as land reform and poverty through market- and work-based solutions. Family ideology (in the classically Victorian sense) is also clearly on display in these same legal domains, with scholars, judges and legislators emphasizing in different ways the centrality of marriage to family life. Judges and legislators also helped to construct the corresponding idea that a wife's place was in the home, caring for her family. In the area of apprenticeship, market and family ideology combined to disarticulate the work dimensions of apprenticeship from the master's household, resulting in the movement of traditional apprenticeship towards the domain of work, with apprentices remaining with their own families, and the eventual (re)characterization of parish apprenticeship in terms of family-based care. And, as noted throughout this book, family/market (and contract/status) ideology was intimately connected to conceptions of public and private, and played out in distinctly gendered terms.

In the contemporary moment, I suspect that as a matter of experience and intuition, many people would broadly agree that the notion of the family as a private unit insulated from market forces (and other influences) does not accurately reflect the myriad ways in which family life is shaped by (and shapes) relations with employers, state agencies administering areas such as tax, welfare and immigration (to name but a few), and the legal rules that apply in each of these domains.[77] Similarly, though perhaps more controversially, it is apparent that many people do not consider existing models of adult relationship recognition adequate in the face of increasing recognition of the diversity and plurality of adult personal relationships,[78] and the arguably irrelevant nature of conjugality to legal recognition of adult relationships.[79] The analysis presented in this book suggests that the distinction between family and work (and myriad other areas of regulation), and the still powerful legal emphasis on marriage, are the results of distinct historical processes of disaggregation and reconstruction. Put differently, the structures and allegiances that govern our affective and economic lives are not as natural or immutable as they sometimes appear:[80] if the productive household of the eighteenth century was unmade, perhaps it can also be remade along lines that better reflect the imbrication of family and market, and differing relational models.[81] As Halley and Rittich note, "[t]o deconstruct FLE in this context is to put the family and the market, family law and contract, back into contiguity."[82] And, as Diduck and Kaganas ask, "[w]hat if the idea of the family … were based solely on the giving of mutual affection or support?" or, alternatively, "[w]hat if it were an economic dependence between two or more people that distinguished families from other groups of people?"[83]

One possibility suggested by the historical analysis in this book is that a return to the idea of the household may offer a legal and conceptual path forward to addressing the legal exceptionalism of the family. This is precisely the move advocated by Halley and Rittich, who suggest the concept of the *"economic family* … to put the husband, the wife, and the child back into the context of the economically functioning household in which they live."[84] Crucially, they define a household for

---

77 See *supra* note 20.

78 See *supra* note 19.

79 The best discussion of this issue is the Law Commission of Canada's 2001 report, *Beyond Conjugality: Recognizing and Supporting Close Personal Adult Relationships* (Ottawa: Law Commission of Canada, 2001). See also Brenda Cossman and Bruce Ryder, "Beyond *Beyond Conjugality*" (2017) 30:2 *Can J Fam L* 227; Barker, "Sex and the CPA," *supra* note 66.

80 See Gordon, *supra* note 1; Klare, *supra* note 2; Unger, *supra* note 2.

81 As noted in chapter 1 at note 29, I reject the argument that exposing historical contingency is hopelessly vague in the absence of concrete suggestions for reform.

82 Halley and Rittich, *supra* note 6 at 758.

83 Diduck and Kaganas, *supra* note 19 at 3.

84 Halley and Rittich, *supra* note 6 at 758 (emphasis in original). See also Halley, *supra* note 20 at 5 (expressing a desire "to reconstruct family law so that it becomes possible to teach the family and its law as *distributive*" (emphasis in original)).

this purpose not in terms of the old patriarchal authority of the master, but instead as "a human association bounded through social negotiation and aimed at securing human reproduction, including reproduction from day to day of its members as well as the production of new human beings." This refocussing of attention on economic *and* affective connections means that a household "may be either larger or smaller than the legally recognized family, may include non-family members, and may be made up by people with no recognized family relationship to each other."[85] Domestic workers, for instance, would thus retake their position within the legal household.[86] Space might also be created for thinking about ways of more appropriately dealing with non-dyadic adult relationships, and relationships (dyadic or multi-party) without any actual or presumed sexual component, without needing to cabin such relations within the framework of family and Family Law.

Family law scholars in England have advanced related suggestions, albeit in ways that speak more to the question of relationship recognition than the links between markets and families. Anne Bottomley and Simone Wong, for instance, advocate "the notion of a 'shared household,' which is not defined either by sexual partners of familial relationships, but rather by a shared emotional economy." They contend "that we should begin by envisaging such a household and then consider the kinds of patterns within such a household which might give rise to an argument for legal recognition."[87] Bottomley and Wong's focus on emotion and care is shared by Jonathan Herring, who advocates "[m]aking family less sexy … and more careful" by "focusing the interventions of family law on caring relationships, rather than sexual ones."[88] In his view, the major goals of family law – "the support and promotion of forms of intimate life; the protection of individuals from abuse within the course of family life; and the remedying of disadvantages and advantages caused by a relationship" – are not served by a focus on the existence of a sexual relationship between parties.[89] Rather, a caring

---

85 Halley and Rittich, *supra* note 6 at 759.

86 *Ibid* at 769.

87 Anne Bottomley and Simone Wong, "Shared Households: A New Paradigm for Thinking about the Reform of Domestic Property Relations" in Diduck and O'Donovan, *supra* note 15, 39 at 43. While Bottomley and Wong focus their analysis on intervention in property issues, their approach seems applicable in the broader context of relationship recognition.

88 Jonathan Herring, "Making Family Law Less Sexy … and More Careful" in Robert Leckey, ed., *After Legal Equality: Family, Sex, Kinship* (Abingdon: Routledge, 2015) 25 at 25.

89 *Ibid* at 28.

relationship, marked by the meeting of needs, respect, responsibility, and relationality (i.e., caring "should never be seen as unidirectional") should be key.[90] To this end, Herring suggests that, "if we are to centre care, we should abandon the terminology 'family law.'"[91]

Herring is not alone in this view. Reflecting the analysis in this book, Alison Diduck has noted that "the entrenching of a particular family form at a particular historic time as the subject of family" led to the "creation of a coherent notion of 'family law.'" However, she also proposes that, "contemporary social changes may signal a time now for a challenge to that coherent notion."[92] In this vein, John Eekelaar has recently reiterated his suggestion that it is unnecessary to bring non-sexual adult relationships within the scope of Family Law because, "[i]n truth, we are dealing with the role of the law in relation to what is usually referred to as people's 'personal,' or 'private,' lives.... It would therefore seem appropriate, and could perhaps be liberating, to abandon the label 'family' law, and replace it with the expression 'personal law.'"[93]

While these various suggestions may seem far-fetched in view of what can sometimes appear to be a natural distinction between the family and the market, and the widespread acceptance and use of the Family Law umbrella within legal pedagogy and practice, the history presented in this book shows us that the legal regulation of family and work relationships is far from immutable – and that further change, if desired, is possible.

---

90 *Ibid* at 26–8.

91 *Ibid* at 38.

92 Alison Diduck, "Family Law and Family Responsibility" in Jo Bridgeman, Heather Keating and Craig Lind, eds., *Responsibility, Law and the Family* (Aldershot: Ashgate, 2008) 251 at 266.

93 John Eekelaar, *Family Law and Personal Life*, 2nd ed. (Oxford: Oxford University Press, 2017) at 28. See also John Eekelaar, *Family Law and Personal Life* (Oxford: Oxford University Press, 2006) at 31.

Bibliography

Cases

Addis v Gramophone Company Limited [1909] AC 488.
Aldridge v Merry [1913] IR 308.
Baker v Bolton (1808) 1 Camp 493.
Balfour v Balfour [1919] 2 KB 571.
Bazeley v Forder (1868) LR 3 QB 559.
Berry v Da Costa (1866) LR 1 CP 331.
Best v Fox [1952] AC 716.
Blake v Midland Railway Co (1852) 18 QB 93.
British Columbia Saw Mill Co v Nettleship [1868] LR 3 CP 499.
Brockbank v The Whitehaven Junction Railway Company (1862) 7 H&N 834.
Brook v Brook (1861) 9 HLC 193.
Butler v Dolben (1756) 2 Lee 312.
Callwell v Callwell (1860) 164 ER 1274.
Chamberlain v Williamson (1814) 2 M&S 329.
Compton v Bearcroft (1769) 2 Hag Con 444.
Coventry Corp v Surrey CC [1935] AC 199.
Dalrymple v Dalrymple (1811) 2 Hag Con 54.
Daniel v Bowles (1826) 2 Car & P 553.
Deck v Deck (1860) 163 ER 926.
Dryden v M'Gibbon; M'Gibbon v Dryden [1907] SC 1131.
Duntze v Levett (1816) in James Fergusson, *Reports of Some Recent Decisions by the Consistorial Court of Scotland in Actions of Divorce, Concluding for the Dissolution of Marriages Celebrated Under the English Law* (Edinburgh, 1817) at 70 ff.
Ex parte Baker (1857) 7 El & Bl 687.
Ex parte HV McKay (1907) 2 CAR 1.
Frost v Knight (1865) LR 7 Ex 111.
George v Davis [1911] 2 KB 445.

Gough v Farr (1827) 2 Car & P 631.

Hadley v Baxendale [1854] EWHC 70.

Harrison v Cage & Uxor (1741) Carth 467.

Hart v Aldridge (1774) 1 Cowp 55.

Holcroft v Dickenson (1674) 3 Keble 148.

Hutton v Mansell (1795) 3 Salk 16.

Hyde v Hyde and Woodmansee (1866) 1 P&D 130.

Hyman v Hyman [1929] AC 601.

In re William Baker (1857) 2 H&N 219.

Jackson v Galloway (1838) 5 Bing (NC).

Johnson v Nottinghamshire Combined Police Authority [1974] ICR 170.

Le Mesurier v Le Mesurier [1895] AC 517 (PC).

Lindo v Belisario (1795) 1 Hag Con 216.

Lovell v Newton (1878) 4 CPD 7.

Lowther v The Earl of Radnor & Anor (1806) 8 East 113.

Lynch v Knight (1864) 9 HLC 398.

Male v Roberts (1800) 3 Esp 163.

Montague v Montague (1824) 2 Add 375.

Morrison v Tawse's Executrix (1888) 16 R 247.

Niboyet v Niboyet (1878) 4 PD 1.

Price v Rhondda UDC [1923] 1 Ch 372.

Printing and Numerical Supply Co v Sampson (1875) LR 19 Eq.

R v International Trustee [1937] AC 500.

R v Lolley (1812) 2 Cl & F 567.

R v Millis (1844) 10 Cl & F 534.

R v R [1991] UKHL 12.

Radmacher v Granatino [2010] UKSC 42; [2011] 1 AC 534.

Raynard v Chase (1756) 1 Burr 2.

Robinson v Bland (1760) 2 Burr 1077.

Ryan v Ryan (1816) 2 Phill 332.

Salvesen (or Von Lorang) v Administrator of Austrian Property [1927] AC 641.

Scrimshire v Scrimshire (1752) 2 Hag Con 395.

Simonin v Mallac (1860) 2 SW & TR 67.

Sottomayor v De Barros (1877) 3 PD 1.

Sottomayor v De Barros (1879) 5 PD 94.

Spain v Arnott (1816–19) 2 Stark 256.

Steel v Houghton (1788) 1 HBL 52.

Stretch v Parker, Mich 12 Car Rot 21; Ro Abr 22.

The King v Inhabitants of Barton-upon-Irwell (1814) 2 M&S 329.

The King v Inhabitants of Brampton (1777) Cald 11.

The King v Inhabitants of Hulcott (1796) 6 Term 583.

Turner v Mason [1845] 153 ER 411.

Udny v Udny (1869) LR 1 HL 441.

Walker v Innospec Ltd & Ors [2017] UKSC 24.

Warrender v Warrender (1835) 2 Cl & F 488.

Yewens v Noakes (1832) 1 Mood CC 370.

Statutes

Adoption of Children Act 1926, 16 & 17 Geo V, c 29.

An Act concerning the King's Succession 1533, 25 Hen VIII, c 22.

An Act containing divers Orders for Artificers Labourers, Servants of Husbandry and Apprentices 1562, 5 Eliz I, c 4.

An Act for amending and rendering more effectual the several Laws now in being, for the more effectual preventing of Frauds and Abuses by Persons employed in the Manufacture of Hats, and in the Woollen, Linen, Fustian, Cotton, Iron, Leather, Fur, Hemp, Flax, Mohair, and Silk Manufactures; and also for making Provisions to prevent Frauds by Journeymen Dyers 1777, 17 Geo III, c 56.

An Act for Amending the Law of Marriage in Scotland 1856, 19 & 20 Vict, c 96.

An Act for better regulating Apprentices, and Persons working under Contract 1766, 6 Geo III, c 25.

An Act for compensating the Families of Persons killed by Accidents 1846, 9 & 10 Vict c 93.

An Act for consolidating in one Act certain Provisions usually inserted in Acts of Inclosure; and for facilitating the Mode of proving the several Facts usually required on the passing of such Acts 1801, 41 Geo III, c 109.

An Act for dividing, allotting and inclosing the Open Common Field, Meadows, Pastures, Commons, and Waste Lands in the Parish of Walton-upon-Thames and the Manor of Walton Leigh in the County of Surrey 1800, 39 & 40 Geo III, c 86.

An Act for further Amendment of the Laws relating to the Poor in England 1844, 7 & 8 Vict, c 101.

An Act for Marriages in England 1836, 6 & 7 Will IV, c 135.

An Act for Regulating the Journeymen Taylors within the Weekly Bills of Mortality 1720, 7 Geo I, c 13.

An Act for supplying some Defects in the Laws for the Relief of the Poor in this Kingdom 1696, 8 & 9 Will III, c 30.

An Act for the Amendment and better Administration of the Laws relating to the Poor in England and Wales 1834, 4 & 5 Will IV, c 76.

An Act for the Amendment of the Law relating to Dower 1833, 3 & 4 Will IV, c 105.

An Act for the better adjusting and more easy Recovery of the Wages of certain Servants; and for the better Regulation of such Servants, and of certain Apprentices 1747, 20 Geo III, c 19.

An Act for the better Cultivation, Improvement, and Regulation of the Common Arable Fields, Wades, and Commons of Pasture, in this Kingdom 1773, 13 Geo III, c 81.

An Act for the Better Preventing of Clandestine Marriage 1753, 26 Geo II, c 33.

An Act for the better Protection of Persons under the Care and Control of others as Apprentices or Servants; and to enable the Guardians and Overseers of the Poor to institute and conduct Prosecutions in certain Cases 1851, 14 & 15 Vict, c 11.

An Act for the better Regulation of the Parish Poor Children, of the several Parishes therein mentioned, within the Bills of Mortality 1766, 7 Geo III, c 39.

An Act for the better Relief of the Poor in this Kingdom 1662, 14 Cha II, c 12.

An Act for the establishment of the imperiall Crowne of this Realme 1536, 28 Hen VIII, c 7.

An Act for the further Regulation of Parish Apprentices 1792, 32 Geo III, c 57.

An Act for the Preservation of the Health and Morals of Apprentices and Others, Employed in Cotton and Other Mills, and Cotton and other Factories 1802, 42 Geo III, c 123.

An Act for the Punishment of idle and disorderly Persons, and Rogues and Vagabonds, in that Part of Great Britain called England 1824, 5 Geo IV, c 83.

An Act for the Relief of the Poor 1601, 43 Eliz I, c 2.

An Act to amend an Act, passed in the Fifth Year of Queen Elizabeth, intituled An Act containing divers Orders for Artificers Labourers, Servants of Husbandry and Apprentices 1814, 54 Geo III, c 96.

An Act to amend the Law for the Formation of Districts for the Education of Infant Poor 1848, 11 & 12 Vict, c 82.

An Act to amend the Law of Evidence 1851, 14 & 15 Vict, c 99.

An Act to amend the Law relating to Divorce and Matrimonial Causes in England 1857, 20 & 21 Vict, c 85.

An Act to amend the Laws for the Prevention of Frauds and Abuses by Persons employed in the Woollen, Worsted, Linen, Cotton, Flax, Mohair, and Silk Hosiery Manufactures; and for the further securing the Property of the Manufacturers and the Wages of the Workmen engaged therein 1843, 6 & 7 Vict, c 40.

An Act to amend the Laws relating to Labour in Factories 1844, 7 & 8 Vict, c 15.

An Act to consolidate and amend the Statute Law of England and Ireland relating to Offences against the Person 1861, 24 & 25 Vict, c 100.

An Act to enable Justices of the Peace in Petty Sessions to make Orders for the Support of Bastard Children 1839, 2 & 3 Vict, c 85

An Act to enlarge the Powers of Justices in determining Complaints between Masters and Servants, and between Masters, Apprentices, Artificers and others 1823, 30 & 31 Vict, c 141.

An Act to limit the Hours of Labour of young Persons and Females in Factories 1847, 10 & 11 Vict, c 29.

An Act to make better Provision for the Care and Education of vagrant, destitute, and disorderly Children, and for the Extension of Industrial Schools 1857, 20 & 21 Vict, c 48.

An Act to prohibit the Employment of Women and Girls in Mines and Collieries, to regulate the Employment of Boys, and to make other Provisions relating to Persons working therein 1842, 5 & 6 Vict, c 99.

An Act to provide for the Education and Maintenance of Pauper Children in certain Schools and Institutions 1862, 25 & 26 Vict, c 43.

An Act to regulate the Labour of Children and young Persons in the Mills and Factories of the United Kingdom 1833, 3 & 4 Will IV, c 103.

An Act to render certain Marriages valid, and to alter the Law with respect to certain voidable Marriages 1835, 5 & 6 Will IV, c 104.

An Act to repeal so much of several Act passed in England and Scotland respectively, as empowers Justices of the Peace to rate Wages, or set Prices of Work, for Artificers, Labourers or Craftsmen 1813, 53 Geo III, c 40.

Children Act 1948, 11 & 12 Geo VI, c 43.

Civil Partnership Act 2004, c 33.

Conspiracy and Protection of Property Act 1875, 38 & 39 Vict, c 86.

Custody of Infants Act 1873, 36 & 37 Vict, c 12.

Custody of Infants Act 1891, 55 Vict, c 13.

Divorce Reform Act 1969, c 55.

Domestic Proceedings and Magistrates' Courts Act 1978, c 22.

Domicile and Matrimonial Proceedings Act 1973, c 45.

Elementary Education Act 1870, 33 & 34 Vict, c 75.

Employers and Workmen Act 1875, 38 & 39 Vict, c 90.

Employers' Liability Act 1880, 43 & 44 Vict, c 42.

Employment Rights Act 1996, c 18.

Equality Act 2010, c 15.

Evidence Further Amendment Act 1869, 32 & 33 Vict, c 68.

Factory Acts Extension Act, 1867, 30 & 31 Vict, c 103.

For Marriages to stand notwithstanding Pre-Contracts 1540, 32 Hen VIII, c 38.

Guardianship of Infants Act 1886, 49 & 50 Vict, c 27.

Human Fertilisation and Embryology Act 2008, c 22.

Law Reform (Miscellaneous Provisions) Act 1970, c 33.

Marriage Act 1949, 12, 13 & 14 Geo VI, c 76.

Marriage (Same Sex Couples) Act 2013, c 30.

Married Women's Property Act 1870, 33 & 34 Vict, c 93.

Married Women's Property Act 1882, 45 & 46 Vict, c 75.

Married Women's Property (Scotland) Act 1877, 40 & 41 Vict, c 29.

Master and Servant Act 1867, 30 & 31 Vict, c 141.

Matrimonial Causes Act 1923, 13 & 14 Geo V, c 19.

Matrimonial Causes Act 1973, c 18.

National Insurance Act 1911, 1 & 2 Geo V, c 55.

Ordinance of Labourers 1349, 23 Edw III, c 1–8.

Poor Act 1575, 18 Eliz I, c 3.

Poor Law Act 1930, 20 & 21 Geo V, c 17.
Sex Disqualification (Removal) Act 1919, 9 & 10 Geo 5, c 71.
Statute of Labourers 1351, 25 Edw III, Stat I, c I.
Supreme Court of Judicature Act 1873, 36 & 37 Vict, c 56.
The Repeal of an Act made in the xxij Year of King Henry the Eighth, which was made, That Marriage contracted in the Face of the Church, and consummate with bodily Knowledge, to be deemed lawful, any former Contract notwithstanding 1548, 2 & 3 Edw VI, c 23.
Trade Union Act 1871, 34 & 35 Vict, c 31.
Unemployment Insurance Act 1920, 10 & 11 Geo V, c 30.
Unemployment Insurance Act 1935, 25 & 26 Geo V, c 8.
Workmen's Compensation Act 1897, 60 & 61 Vict, c 37.
Workmen's Compensation Act 1906, 6 Edw VII, c 58.

Orders

Poor Law Commissioners, *General Boarding of Children in Unions Order*, 28 May 1889.
Poor Law Commissioners, *General Consolidated Order*, 24 July 1847.
Poor Law Commissioners, *Outdoor Relief Prohibitory Order*, 21 December 1844.

Books, Chapters, and Articles

A Collection of Remarkable Cases, for the Instruction of both Sexes, In the Business of Love and Gallantry. Being a modest and clear View of the three following Tryals. Viz. I. Of Richard Lyddel, Esq; for a Criminal Conversation with Lady Abergavenny. II. Of Knox Ward, Esq; for a Promise of Marriage to Miss Sarah Holt. III. Of Coll. Francies Chartres, for a Rape committed on the Body of Anne Bond, his Servant (London, 1730).
A Solicitor, *A Familiar Compendium of the Law of Husband and Wife; in Two Parts* (London, 1831).
Albin, Einat, "From 'Domestic Servant' to 'Domestic Worker'" in Judy Fudge, Shae McCrystal and Kamala Sankaran, eds., *Challenging the Legal Boundaries of Work Regulation* (Oxford: Hart, 2012).
Albin, Einat, and Jeremias Prassl, "Fragmenting Work, Fragmented Regulation: The Contract of Employment as a Driver of Social Exclusion" in Mark Freedland *et al*, eds., *The Contract of Employment* (Oxford: Oxford University Press, 2016).
Allen, C.K., *Legal Duties and Other Essays in Jurisprudence* (Oxford: Clarendon Press, 1931).
– "Status and Capacity" (1930) *46 Law Q Rev* 277.
Anderson, Michael, *Approaches to the History of the Western Family 1500–1914* (Cambridge: Cambridge University Press, 1995).

Anderson, Nancy F., "The 'Marriage with a Deceased Wife's Sister Bill' Controversy: Incest Anxiety and the Defense of Family Purity in Victorian England" (1982) 21:2 *J Brit Stud* 67.

Andrews, Thomas, *An enquiry into the causes of the encrease and miseries of the poor of England* (1738).

Anonymous, *Reflections on the relative situations of master and servant, historically and politically considered; the irregularities of servants; the employment of foreigners; and the general inconveniences resulting from the want of proper regulations* (London: W. Miller, 1800).

Anson, William, *Principles of the Law of Contract* (Oxford: Clarendon Press, 1879).

Archbold, John Frederick, *The Poor Law, Comprising all the Authorities, to October, 1843, with Forms*, 3rd ed. (London: Shaw & Sons, 1844).

– *The Poor Law, Comprising the Whole of the Law of Settlement, and All the Authorities upon the subject of The Poor Law Generally, brought down to Hilary Term, 1856, with Forms*, 8th ed. (London: Shaw & Sons, 1856).

– *A Summary of the Law Relative to Pleading and Evidence in Criminal Cases; with Precedents of Indictment, &c. and the Evidence Necessary to Support Them* (London, 1822).

Ariès, Philippe, *Centuries of Childhood: A Social History of Family Life*, translated by Robert Baldick (New York: Vintage Books, 1962).

Arnold, Frederick Octavius, *The Law of Damages and Compensation*, 2nd ed. (London: Butterworth, 1919).

Arnot, R. Page, *The Miners: A History of the Miners' Federation of Great Britain 1889–1910* (London: Allen & Unwin, 1949).

Atiyah, Patrick S., *The Rise and Fall of Freedom of Contract* (Oxford: Clarendon Press, 1985).

Auchmuty, Rosemary, "The Married Women's Property Acts: Equality Was Not the Issue" in Rosemary Hunter, ed., *Rethinking Equality Projects in Law: Feminist Challenges* (Oxford: Hart, 2008).

Austin, John, *Lectures on Jurisprudence or The Philosophy of Positive Law*, 4th ed., edited by Robert Campbell (London: John Murray, 1873).

– *The Province of Jurisprudence Determined* and *The Uses of the Study of Jurisprudence* (Indianapolis: Hackett, 1998).

Baker, Charles E., *The Law of Master and Servant* (London: F. Warne, 1881).

Baker, J.H., *An Introduction to English Legal History*, 3rd ed. (London: Butterworths, 1990).

– "Review of The Rise and Fall of Freedom of Contract. By P.S. Atiyah" (1980) 43:4 *Mod L Rev* 467.

Barker, Nicola, "After the Wedding, What Next? Conservatism and Conjugality" in Nicola Barker and Daniel Monk, eds., *From Civil Partnership to Same-Sex Marriage: Interdisciplinary Reflections* (Abingdon: Routledge, 2015).

– "Sex and the Civil Partnership Act: The Future of (Non) Conjugality?" (2006) 14:2 *Fem Leg Stud* 241.

Barker, Nicola, and Daniel Monk, "From Civil Partnership to Same-Sex Marriage: A Decade in British Legal History" in Nicola Barker and Daniel Monk, eds., *From Civil Partnership to Same-Sex Marriage: Interdisciplinary Reflections* (Abingdon: Routledge, 2015).

Barrett, Michèle, and Mary McIntosh, "The 'Family Wage': Some Problems for Socialists and Feminists" (1980) 4:2 *Capital & Class* 51.

Barrie, David G., *Sin, Sanctity and the Sister-in-Law: Marriage with a Deceased Wife's Sister in the Nineteenth Century* (Abingdon: Routledge, 2018).

Batchelor, T., *General View of the Agriculture of the County of Bedfordshire* (1808).

Beauvoir, Simone de, *The Second Sex*, translated by Constance Borde and Sheila Malovany-Chevallier (New York: Vintage Books, 2011).

Beckert, Sven, *Empire of Cotton: A Global History* (New York: Vintage Books, 2015).

Belsey, Catherine, *Critical Practice* (London: Methuen, 1980).

Benenson, Harold, "The 'Family Wage' and Working Women's Consciousness in Britain, 1880–1914" (1991) 19:1 *Politics & Society* 71.

Bentham, Jeremy, *The Collected Works of Jeremy Bentham: A Comment on the Commentaries and A Fragment on Government*, edited by J.H. Burns and H.L.A. Hart (Oxford: Oxford University Press, 1977).

– "Essay II. Fundamental Positions in Regard to the Making Provision for the Indigent Poor" (1796), in M. Quinn, ed., *The Collected Works of Jeremy Bentham: Writings on the Poor Laws, Volume I* (Oxford: Oxford University Press, 2001)

– "Indirect Legislation," Bentham Papers in the Library of University College, London, lxxxvii.

– *An Introduction to the Principles of Morals and Legislation* (Oxford: Clarendon Press, 1876).

– *Theory of Legislation*, translated from the French of Etienne Dumont by R. Hildreth, vol 1 (Boston: Weeks, Jordan, & Company, 1840).

Berry, Helen, and Elizabeth Foyster, "Introduction" in Helen Berry and Elizabeth Foyster, eds., *The Family in Early Modern England* (Cambridge: Cambridge University Press, 2007).

Bird, James Barry, *The Laws Respecting Masters and Servants, Articled Clerks, Apprentices, Manufacturers, Labourers, and Journeymen*, 3rd ed. (London, 1799).

– *The Laws Respecting Masters and Servants, Articled Clerks, Apprentices, Manufacturers, Labourers, and Journeymen* (London, 1795).

Bix, Brian H., *Jurisprudence: Theory and Context*, 7th ed. (London: Sweet & Maxwell, 2015).

– "Private Ordering and Family Law" (2010) 23:2 *J Am Academy Mat L* 249.

B.J.F., "Actions for Breach of Promise of Marriage" (1872) 20:2 *Am Law Reg* 65.

Blackburn, Sheila C., "Curse or Cure? Why Was the Enactment of Britain's 1909 Trade Boards Act So Controversial?" (2009) 47:2 *Brit J Indust Rel* 214.

Blackstone, William, *An Analysis of the Laws of England*, 3rd ed. (Oxford, 1758).

– *Commentaries on the Laws of England*, 4 vols (Oxford: Clarendon Press, 1765–9).

Blumenthal, Susanna L., "Of Mandarins, Legal Consciousness, and the Cultural Turn in US Legal History: Robert W. Gordon. 1984. Critical Legal Histories. *Stanford Law Review* 36: 57–125" (2012) 37:1 *Law & Soc Inquiry* 167.

Boorstin, Daniel J., *The Mysterious Science of the Law* (Cambridge, MA: Harvard University Press 1941).

Booth, William James, *Households: On the Moral Architecture of the Economy* (Ithaca: Cornell University Press, 1993).

Bottomley, Anne, and Simone Wong, "Shared Households: A New Paradigm for Thinking about the Reform of Domestic Property Relations" in Alison Diduck and Katherine O'Donovan, eds., *Feminist Perspectives on Family Law* (Abingdon: Routledge-Cavendish, 2006).

Bourne [Sturt], George, *Change in the Village* (New York: G.H. Doran, 1912).

Brandt, William, *A Treatise on the Law, Practice and Procedure of Divorce and Matrimonial Causes under the Act 20 & 21 Vict. c. 85; containing The Act, also the rules, orders and forms issued thereunder; together with precedents* (London: Butterworths, 1858).

Brewer, Holly, "The Transformation of Domestic Law" in Michael Grossberg and Christopher Tomlins, eds., *The Cambridge History of Law in America: Volume I, Early America (1580–1815)* (New York: Cambridge University Press, 2008).

Brierly, J.L., "Sir Thomas Erskine Holland" (1926) 42 *Law Q Rev* 475.

Bromley, Peter M., *Family Law* (London: Butterworths, 1957).

Brooks, Christopher W., *Lawyers, Litigation and English Society since 1450* (London: Hambledon Press, 1998).

– *Pettyfoggers and Vipers of the Commonwealth: The "Lower Branch" of the Legal Profession in Early Modern England* (Cambridge: Cambridge University Press, 1986).

Brown, Wendy, *Undoing the Demos* (New York: Zone Books, 2015).

Browne, Arthur, *A Compendious View of the Civil Law, and of The Law of the Admiralty, Being the Substance of a Course of Lectures Read in the University of Dublin, Vol I* (Butterworth, 1798).

Browne, George, *A Treatise on the Principles and Practices of the Court for Divorce and Matrimonial Causes: With The Statutes, Rules, Fees and Forms Relating Thereto*, 2nd ed. (London: H. Sweet, 1868).

Browning, William Ernst, *An Exposition of the Laws of Marriage and Divorce, as administered in the Court for Divorce and Matrimonial Causes, with the method of procedure in each kind of suit; illustrated by copious notes of cases* (London: W. Ridgway, 1872).

Brundage, James A., *Law, Sex, and Christian Society in Medieval Europe* (Chicago: University of Chicago Press, 1987).

Bunyon, C.J., *A Profitable Book Upon Domestic Law* (London: Longmans, Green, and Co, 1875).

Burchell, Graham, "Peculiar Interests: Civil Society and Governing 'The System of Natural Liberty'" in Graham Burchell, Colin Gordon and Peter Miller, *The Foucault Effect: Studies in Governmentality* (Chicago: University of Chicago Press, 1991).

Burge, William, *Commentaries on Colonial and Foreign Laws: Generally, and in their Conflict with Each Other, and with the Law of England* (London: Saunders and Benning 1838).

– *The Comparative Law of Marriage and Divorce*, edited by Alexander Wood Renton and George Grenville Phillimore (London: Sweet & Maxwell, 1910).

Burn, Richard, *The Justice of the Peace, and Parish Officer* (1755 and 1793 editions).

Burton, Frances, *Family Law*, 2nd ed. (London: Taylor & Francis, 2015).

Cairns, John W., "Blackstone, an English Institutist: Legal Literature and the Rise of the Nation State" (1984) 4:3 *Oxford J Leg Stud* 318.

– "Scottish Law, Scottish Lawyers and the Status of the Union" in John Robertson, ed., *A Union for Empire: Political Thought and the Union of 1707* (Cambridge: Cambridge University Press, 1995).

Carrington, Paul D., "Of Law and the River" (1984) 34:2 *J Legal Educ* 222.

Casswell, J.D., *The Law of Domestic Servants*, 2nd ed. (London: Jordan & Sons, 1914).

Chambers, J.D., "Enclosure and Labour Supply in the Industrial Revolution" (1953) 5:3 *Econ Hist Rev* 319.

Chambers, J.D., and G.E. Mingay, *The Agricultural Revolution, 1750–1880* (London: Batsford, 1966).

Chapman, John, "The Chronology of English Enclosure" (1984) 37:4 *Econ Hist Rev* 557.

– "The Extent and Nature of Parliamentary Enclosure" (1987) 35:1 *Agr Hist Rev* 25.

Chitty, Joseph, *Commentaries on the Laws of England: By the Late Sir W. Blackstone* (London: W. Walker, 1826).

– *A Practical Treatise on the Law of Contracts Not Under Seal; and Upon the Usual Defences to Actions Thereon*, 4th ed. by John A. Russell (London: S. Sweet, 1850).

– *A Practical Treatise on the Law of Contracts, Not Under Seal: And the Usual Defences to Actions Thereon*, 3rd ed. by Tompson Chitty (London: S. Sweet, 1841).

– *A Practical Treatise on the Law Relative to Apprentices and Journeymen, and Exercising Trades* (London, 1812).

– *A Treatise on Pleading: With a Collection of Practical Precedents, and Notes Thereon* (London, 1809).

Clare, John, *Selected Poems*, edited by J.W. & A. Tibble (London: Dent, 1979).

Clark, Anna, "The New Poor Law and the Breadwinner Wage: Contrasting Assumptions" (2000) 34:2 *J Soc Hist* 261.

Clark, John D., *General View of the Agriculture of the County of Hereford* (London: Colin Macrae, 1794).

– "On commons in Brecknock" (1794) XXII *Ann Ag* 633.

Clarke, John, *Social Administration Including the Poor Laws* (London, Pitman, 1922).

Cohen, Morris R., "Property and Sovereignty" (1927) 13 *Cornell L Rev* 8.

Collet, Clara E., "The Collection and Utilisation of Official Statistics bearing on the Extent and Effects of the Industrial Employment of Women" (1898) 61:2 *J Royal Stat Soc* 219.

Collier, Jane, Michelle Z. Rosaldo and Sylvia Yanagisako, "Is There a Family? New Anthropological Views" in Barrie Thorne with Marilyn Yalom, eds., *Rethinking the Family: Some Feminist Questions* (New York: Longman Press, 1982).

Collingwood, R.G., *The Idea of History* (Connecticut: Martino Publishing, 2014).

Collins, Hugh, "Contract and Legal Theory" in William Twining, ed., *Legal Theory and Common Law* (Oxford: Basil Blackwell, 1986).

– "Contractual Autonomy" in Alan Bogg *et al*, eds., *The Autonomy of Labour Law* (Oxford: Hart, 2015).

– *Marxism and Law* (Oxford: Clarendon Press, 1982).

– "The Productive Disintegration of Labour Law" (1997) 26:4 *Industrial LJ* 295.

Collyer, J., *The Parents' and Guardians' Directory* (1761).

Conaghan, Joanne, "Time to Dream? Flexibility, Families, and the Regulation of Working Time" in Judy Fudge and Rosemary Owens, eds., *Precarious Work, Women, and the New Economy* (Oxford: Hart Publishing, 2006).

– "Women, Work, and Family: A British Revolution?" in Joanne Conaghan, Richard Michael Fischl and Karl Klare, *Labour Law in an Era of Globalization: Transformative Practices and Possibilities* (Oxford: Oxford University Press, 2002).

– "Work, Family, and the Discipline of Labour Law" in Joanne Conaghan and Kerry Rittich, eds., *Labour Law, Work, and Family: Critical and Comparative Perspectives* (Oxford: Oxford University Press, 2005).

Conaghan, Joanne, and Kerry Rittich, "Introduction: Interrogating the Work/ Family Divide" in Joanne Conaghan and Kerry Rittich, eds., *Labour Law, Work, and Family: Critical and Comparative Perspectives* (Oxford: Oxford University Press, 2005).

Cossman, Brenda, and Bruce Ryder, "Beyond *Beyond Conjugality*" (2017) 30:2 *Can J Fam L* 227.

Cott, Nancy F., *The Bonds of Womanhood: "Woman's Sphere" in New England, 1780–1835* (New Haven: Yale University Press, 1977).

Crenshaw, Kimberlé, "Race, Reform and Retrenchment: Transformation and Legitimation in Antidiscrimination Law" (1988) 101 *Harv L Rev* 1331.

Cretney, Stephen, "The Family and the Law – Status or Contract?" (2005) 15:4 *CFLQ* 403.

– *Family Law in the Twentieth Century: A History* (Oxford: Oxford University Press, 2003).

– "From Status to Contract" in Francis Rose, ed., *Consensus Ad Idem: Essays in the Law of Contract in Honour of Guenter Treitel* (London: Sweet & Maxwell, 1996).

Dalton, Michael, *The Countrey Justice, Containing the Practice of the Justices of the Peace out of their Sessions: Gathered for the better help of such Justices of Peace as have not been much conversant in the studie of the Lawes of this Realme*, 5th ed. (printed by the assignes of John Mori, 1635).

Davidoff, Leonore, "Domestic Service and the Working-Class Life Cycle" (1973) 26 *Soc Stud Lab Hist* 10.

– "Mastered for Life: Servant and Wife in Victorian and Edwardian England" (1974) 7:4 *J Soc Hist* 406.

Davidoff, Leonore, and Catherine Hall, *Family Fortunes: Men and Women of the English Middle Class 1780–1850*, revised ed. (London: Routledge, 2002).

Davies, David, *The Case of Labourers in Husbandry States and Considered, in Three Parts* (London, 1795).

Davis, Dennis, and Karl Klare, "Transformative Constitutionalism and the Common and Customary Law" (2010) 26:3 *SAJHR* 403.

Davis, James Edward, *Labour and Labour Laws*, 9th ed. (private reprint from *Encyclopaedia Britannica*, 1883).

– *The Labour Laws* (London: Butterworths, 1875).

Deakin, Simon, and Gillian Morris, *Labour Law*, 6th ed. (Oxford: Hart, 2012).

– and Frank Wilkinson, *The Law of the Labour Market: Industrialization, Employment and Legal Evolution* (Oxford: Oxford University Press, 2005).

Defoe, Daniel, *A Plan of the English Commerce Being a Compleat Prospect of the Trade of this Nation, as well the Home Trade as the Foreign* (London, 1728).

– *The Great Law of Subordination Consider'd; or, the Insolence and Unsufferable Behaviour of Servants in England duly enquir'd into* (London, 1724).

Dewar, John, and Stephen Parker, "English Family Law since World War II: From Status to Chaos" in Sanford N. Katz, John Eekelaar and Mavis Maclean, eds., *Cross Currents: Family Law and Policy in the United States and England* (Oxford: Oxford University Press, 2010).

Diamond, Stephen, "Not-So-Critical Legal Studies" (1985) 6 *Cardozo L Rev* 693.

Dicey, A.V., *Can English Law Be Taught At The Universities?* (London, 1883).

– *A Digest of the Law of England With Reference to the Conflict of Laws* (London: Stevens, 1896).

– *Lectures on the Relation Between Law and Public Opinion in England During the Nineteenth Century* (London: Macmillan, 1905).

Diduck, Alison, and Felicity Kaganas, "Family Law and Family Responsibility" in Jo Bridgeman, Heather Keating and Craig Lind, eds., *Responsibility, Law and the Family* (Aldershot: Ashgate, 2008).

– *Family Law, Gender and the State: Text, Cases and Materials*, 3rd ed. (Oxford: Hart, 2012).

– "What Is Family Law For?" (2011) 64:1 *Current Leg Probs* 287.

Diduck, Alison, and Katherine O'Donovan, "Feminism and Families: *Plus Ca Change?*" in Alison Diduck and Katherine O'Donovan, eds., *Feminist Perspectives on Family Law* (Abingdon: Routledge-Cavendish, 2006).

Dixon, William John, *Law, Practice and Procedure in Divorce and other Matrimonial Causes* (London: Reeves and Turner, 1883).

Douglas, Gillian, "Marriage, Cohabitation, and Parenthood – from Contract to Status?" in Sanford N. Katz, John Eekelaar and Mavis Maclean, eds., *Cross Currents: Family Law and Policy in the United States and England* (Oxford: Oxford University Press, 2010).

Douglas, Gillian, Julia Pearce and Hilary Woodward, "Cohabitants, Property and the Law: A Study of Injustice" (2009) 72:1 *Mod L Rev* 24.

Dowell, Stephen, *A History of Taxation and Taxes in England From the Earliest Times to the Year 1885*, 2nd ed. (London: Longmans, 1888).

Dubber, Markus D., "Legal History as Legal Scholarship: Doctrinalism, Interdisciplinarity, and Critical Analysis of Law" in Markus D. Dubber and Christopher Tomlins, eds., *The Oxford Handbook of Legal History* (Oxford: Oxford University Press, 2018).

– "New Historical Jurisprudence: Legal History as Critical Analysis of Law" (2015) 2:1 *Crit Analysis L* 1.

Dubler, Ariela R., "In the Shadow of Marriage: Single Women and the Legal Construction of the Family and the State" (2003) 112:7 *Yale LJ* 1641.

Dud, John, and Robert Cleaver, *A Godly Forme of Household Government, for the Ordering of Private Families* (1598).

Dunlop, O. Jocelyn, and Richard D. Denman, *English Apprenticeship & Child Labour: A History* (London: T. Fisher Unwin, 1912).

Duxbury, Neil, *Frederick Pollock and the English Juristic Tradition* (Oxford: Oxford University Press, 2004).

– *Patterns of American Jurisprudence* (Oxford: Oxford University Press, 1995).

Eagleton, Terry, *Ideology: An Introduction* (London: Verso, 1991).

Ebery, M., and B. Preston, *Domestic Service in Late Victorian and Edwardian England, 1871–1914* (Reading: University of Reading, 1976).

Edwards, Laura F., *The People and Their Peace: Legal Culture and the Transformation of Inequality in the Post-Revolutionary South* (Chapel Hill: University of North Carolina Press, 2009).

Eekelaar, John, *Family Law and Personal Life* (Oxford: Oxford University Press, 2006).
– *Family Law and Personal Life*, 2nd ed. (Oxford: Oxford University Press, 2017).
– "The End of an Era?" (2003) 28:1 *J Fam Hist* 28.
Everitt, Alan, "Farm Labourers" in Joan Thirsk, ed., *The Agrarian History of England and Wales* (Cambridge: Cambridge University Press, 1967–85).
Eversley, William Pinder, *The Law of the Domestic Relations: Including Husband and Wife, Parent and Child, Guardian and Ward, Infants, and Master and Servant* (London: Stevens and Haynes, 1885).
Farmer, Lindsay, *Making the Modern Criminal Law: Criminalization and Civil Order* (Oxford: Oxford University Press, 2016).
Fentiman, Richard, "The Validity of Marriage and the Proper Law" (1985) 44:2 *Cambridge LJ* 256.
Fergusson, James, *Reports of Some Recent Decisions by the Consistorial Court of Scotland in Actions of Divorce, Concluding for the Dissolution of Marriages Celebrated Under the English Law* (Edinburgh: Archibald Constable and Company, 1817).
Fernandez, Angela, "An Important Debate in Nineteenth-Century America: May a Man Marry his Deceased Wife's Sister?" (unpublished, on file with author).
– "Tapping Reeve, Coverture and America's First Legal Treatise" in Angela Fernandez and Markus D. Dubber, eds., *Law Books in Action: Essays on the Anglo-American Legal Treatise* (Oxford: Hart, 2012).
– and Markus D. Dubber, "Introduction: Putting the Legal Treatise in Its Place" in Angela Fernandez and Markus D. Dubber, eds., *Law Books in Action: Essays on the Anglo-American Legal Treatise* (Oxford: Hart, 2012).
Filmer, Robert, *Patriarcha* (1680).
Fischl, Richard Michael, "The Question That Killed Critical Legal Studies" (1992) 17:4 *Law & Soc Inquiry* 779.
Fish, Stanley, "Anti-Professionalism" (1986) 7 *Cardozo L Rev* 645.
Fisk, Catherine L., and Robert W. Gordon, "'Law As …': Theory and Method in Legal History" (2011) 1:3 *UC Irvine L Rev* 519.
Flint, Christopher, *Family Fictions: Narrative and Domestic Relations in Britain, 1866–1798* (Palo Alto: Stanford University Press, 1998).
Foladare, Irving S., "A Clarification of 'Ascribed Status' and 'Achieved Status'" (1969) 10:1 *Soc Quart* 53.
Folbre, Nancy, "The Unproductive Housewife: Her Evolution in Nineteenth-Century Economic Thought" (1991) 16:3 *Signs* 463.
Foote, John Alderson, *Foreign and Domestic Law: A Concise Treatise on Private International Jurisprudence, Based on the Decision in the English Courts*, 3rd ed. (London: Stevens & Haynes, 1904).
Fox, Alan, *Beyond Contract: Work, Power and Trust Relations* (London: Faber, 1974).

Foucault, Michel, *The Birth of Biopolitics. Lectures at the Collège de France, 1978–1979*, edited by Michel Senellart, translated by Graham Burchell (New York: Palgrave Macmillan, 2008).
– *The History of Sexuality. Volume I, The Will to Knowledge*, translated by Robert Hurley (London: Penguin Books, 2008).
– "Nietzche, Genealogy, History" in Paul Rabinow, ed., *The Foucault Reader* (New York: Pantheon Books, 1983) 77.
– *The Politics of Truth*, edited by Sylvère Lotringer, translated by Lysa Hochroth and Catherine Porter (Los Angeles: Semiotext(e), 2007).
– *Power/Knowledge. Selected Interviews and Other Writings 1972–1977*, edited by Colin Gordon, translated by Colin Gordon *et al* (New York: Vintage, 1980).
– *Security, Territory, Population. Lectures at the Collège de France, 1977–1978*, edited by Michel Senellart, translated by Graham Burchell (New York: Vintage, 2007).
– *Society Must Be Defended. Lectures at the Collège de France, 1975–1976*, edited by Mauro Bertani and Alessandro Fontana, translated by David Macey (New York: Picador, 2003).
Fraser, Patrick, *A Treatise on the Law of Scotland, as Applicable to the Personal and Domestic Relations, Comprising Husband and Wife, Parent and Child, Guardian and Ward, Master and Servant, and Master and Apprentice* (Edinburgh: T. & T. Clark, 1846).
Fredman, Sandra, *Women and the Law* (Oxford: Clarendon Press, 1997).
Fredman, Sandra, and Judy Fudge, "The Contract of Employment and Gendered Work" in Mark Freedland *et al*, *The Contract of Employment* (Oxford: Oxford University Press, 2016).
Freedland, Mark, "General Introduction – Aims, Rationale, and Methodology" in Mark Freedland *et al*, eds., *The Contract of Employment* (Oxford: Oxford University Press, 2016).
Freedland, Mark, and Nicola Kountouris, *The Legal Construction of Personal Work Relations* (Oxford: Oxford University Press, 2011).
Freeman, Michael, "Family Values and Family Justice" (1997) 50 *Current Leg Probs* 315.
Friedmann, Wolfgang, "Some Reflections on Status and Freedom" in Ralph A. Newman, ed., *Essays in Jurisprudence in Honor of Roscoe Pound* (Indianapolis: Bobbs-Merrill, 1962).
Frost, Ginger S., "'I Shall Not Sit Down and Crie': Women, Class and Breach of Promise of Marriage Plaintiffs in England, 1850–1900" (1994) 6:2 *Gender & History* 224.
– *Living in Sin: Cohabiting as Husband and Wife in Nineteenth-Century England* (Manchester: Manchester University Press, 2008).
– *Promises Broken: Courtship, Class, and Gender in Victorian England* (Charlottesville: University Press of Virginia, 1995).

Fudge, Judy, "Labour as a 'Fictive Commodity': Radically Reconceptualizing Labour Law" in Guy Davidov and Brian Langille, eds., *The Idea of Labour Law* (Oxford: Oxford University Press, 2011).

Fudge, Judy, and Rosemary Owens, "Precarious Work, Women, and the New Economy: The Challenge to Legal Norms" in Judy Fudge and Rosemary Owens, eds., *Precarious Work, Women, and the New Economy: The Challenge to Legal Norms* (Oxford: Hart, 2006).

Gabel, Peter, and Duncan Kennedy, "Roll Over Beethoven" (1984) 36 *Stan L Rev* 1.

Gavison, Ruth, "Feminism and the Public/Private Distinction" (1992) 45:1 *Stan L Rev* 1.

Geary, Nevill, *The Law of Marriage and Family Relations: A Manual of Practical Law* (London: A. & C. Black, 1892).

Geldart, W.M., "Family Law" in Edward Jenks, ed., *A Digest of English Civil Law*, 5 vols (London: Butterworth & Co, 1905–17), vol 4 (1916).

George, M. Dorothy, *England in Transition: Life and Work in the Eighteenth Century* (Harmondsworth: Penguin Books, 1953).

Gilber, Andrew, "An Unnatural Union? – British Conservatism and the Marriage (Same Sex Couples) Act 2013" in Alison Diduck, Noam Peleg and Helen Reece, *Law in Society: Reflections on Children, Family, Culture and Philosophy: Essays in Honour of Michael Freeman* (Leiden: Brill Nijhoff, 2015).

Giles, Judy, "Help for Housewives: Domestic Service and the Reconstruction of Domesticity in Britain, 1940–50" (2001) 10:2 *Women Hist Rev* 299.

Gillis, John R., *For Better, For Worse: British Marriages, 1600 to the Present* (New York: Oxford University Press, 1985).

– *A World of Their Own Making: Myth, Ritual, and the Quest for Family Values* (Cambridge, MA: Harvard University Press, 1996).

Glendon, Mary Ann, *The Transformation of Family Law: State, Law, and Family in the United States and Western Europe* (Chicago: University of Chicago Press, 1989).

Gordley, James, *The Philosophical Origins of Modern Contract Doctrine* (Oxford: Clarendon Press, 2011).

Gordon, Robert W., "Critical Legal Histories" (1984) 36 *Stan L Rev* 57.

– "'Critical Legal Histories Revisited': A Response" (2012) 37:1 *Law & Soc Inquiry* 200.

– "Unfreezing Legal Reality: Critical Approaches to Law" (1987) 15 *Fla St U L Rev* 195.

Gordon, Robert W., and William Nelson, "An Exchange on Critical Legal Studies between Robert W. Gordon and William Nelson" (1988) 6:1 *Law & Hist Rev* 139.

Graveson, R.H., "The Background of the Century" in R.H. Graveson and F.R. Crane, eds., *A Century of Family Law* (London: Sweet & Maxwell, 1957).

– *Status in the Common Law* (London: Athlone, 1953).

Graveson, R.H., and F.R. Crane, *A Century of Family Law, 1857–1957* (London: Sweet & Maxwell, 1957).

Green, Bernard, "*Family Law*. By P.M. Bromley. London. Butterworths. Second edition. 1962. Pp. xxv, 516." (1963) 15:1 *U Toronto LJ* 249.

Griffin, Ben, "Class, Gender, and Liberalism in Parliament, 1868–1882: The Case of the Married Women's Property Acts" (2003) 46:1 *Hist J* 59.

Hakim, Catherine, "Census Reports as Documentary Evidence: The Census Commentaries 1801–1951" (1980) 28:3 *Soc Rev* 551.

Hale, Matthew, *The Analysis of the Law: Being a Scheme, or Abstract, of the Several Titles and Partitions of the Law of England, Digested into Method* (1713).

Hale, Robert, "Coercion and Distribution in a Supposedly Noncoercive State" (1923) 38 *Pol Science Quart* 470.

Halley, Janet, "Behind the Law of Marriage (I): From Status/Contract to the Marriage System" (2010) 6 *Unbound* 1.

– "What Is Family Law? A Genealogy. Part I" (2011) 23:1 *Yale JL & Human* 1.

– "What Is Family Law? A Genealogy. Part II" (2011) 23:2 *Yale JL & Human* 189.

Halley, Janet, and Kerry Rittich, "Critical Directions in Comparative Family Law: Genealogies and Contemporary Studies of Family Law Exceptionalism" (2010) 58(4) *Am J Comp L* 753.

Hamawi, Jack, *Family Law* (London: Stevens, 1953).

Hamilton, Cicely, *Marriage as a Trade* (London: Chapman and Hall, 1910).

Hammond, J.L., and Barbara Hammond, *The Village Labourer, 1760–1832: A Study of the Government of England Before the Reform Bill* (London: Longman, 1995).

Handford, Peter, "Lord Campbell and the Fatal Accidents Act" (2013) 129 *Law Q Rev* 420.

Harris-Short, Sonia, Joanna Miles and Rob George, *Family Law: Text, Cases, and Materials*, 3rd ed. (Oxford: Oxford University Press, 2015).

Hart, H.L.A., "Introduction" in John Austin, *The Province of Jurisprudence Determined* and *The Uses of the Study of Jurisprudence* (Indianapolis: Hackett, 1998).

Hartmann, Heidi, "Capitalism, Patriarchy, and Job Segregation by Sex" (1976) 1:3 *Signs* 137.

Hartog, Hendrik, "Pigs and Positivism" (1985) 7:4 *Wis L Rev* 899.

Hasday, Jill Elaine, "The Canon of Family Law" (2004) 57:3 *Stan L Rev* 825.

Hay, Douglas, "England, 1562–1875: The Law and Its Uses" in Douglas Hay and Paul Craven, eds., *Masters, Servants, and Magistrates: Britain & the Empire, 1562–1955* (Chapel Hill: University of North Carolina Press, 2004).

Hegel, G.W.F., *Philosophy of Right*, translated by T.M. Knox (Oxford: Oxford University Press, 1969).

Heise, Arnold, *Outline of a System of the General Civil Law for Pandectist Lectures* (*Grundriss eines Systems des Gemeinen Civilrechts zum Behuf von Pandekten-Corlensungen* (1807).

Helmholtz, R.H., *Marriage Litigation in Medieval England* (Cambridge: Cambridge University Press, 1974).

Henriques, U.R.Q., "Bastardy and the New Poor Law" (1967) 37 *Past & Present* 103.

Hepple, Bob, "Welfare Legislation and Wage-Labour" in Bob Hepple, ed., *The Making of Labour Law in Europe: A Comparative Study of Nine Countries up to 1945* (London: Mansell, 1986).

Herring, Jonathan, *Family Law* (Harlow: Pearson Longman, 2011).

– "Introduction" in Jonathan Herring, ed., *Family Law: Issues, Debates*, Policy (Milton Park: Willan, 2001).

– "Making Family Law Less Sexy … and More Careful" in Robert Leckey, ed., *After Legal Equality: Family, Sex, Kinship* (Abingdon: Routledge, 2015).

Heywood, Jean, *Children in Care: The Development of the Service for the Deprived Child* (London: Routledge & Paul, 1959).

Hibbert, W.N., *International Private Law or The Conflict of Laws* (London: Stevens & Haynes, 1927).

Hickel, Jason, *The Divide: Global Inequality from Conquest to Free Markets* (New York: W.W. Norton & Co, 2018).

Higgs, Edward, "Domestic Servants and Households in Victorian England" (1983) 8:2 *Soc Hist* 201.

– "The Tabulation of Occupations in the Nineteenth-Century Census, with Special Reference to Domestic Servants" (1982) 28 *Loc Pop Stud* 58.

– "Women, Occupations and Work in the Nineteenth Century Censuses" (1987) 23 *Hist Workshop J* 59.

Higgs, Edward, and Amanda Wilkinson, "Women, Occupations and Work in the Victorian Censuses Revisited" (2016) 81 *Hist Workshop J* 17.

Hill, Bridget, *Women, Work, and Sexual Politics in Eighteenth-Century England* (Oxford: Basil Blackwell, 1989).

Hill, Christopher, *Reformation to Industrial Revolution* (Harmondsworth: Pelican Books, 1969).

Hobbs, Georgina F., Christopher J. Hobbs, and Jane M. Wynne, "Abuse of Children in Foster and Residential Care" (1999) 23:12 *Child Abuse & Neglect* 1239.

Hobsbawm, Eric J., *The Age of Revolution: Europe 1789–1848* (London: Weidenfeld and Nicolson, 1962).

– *Industry and Empire: From 1750 to the Present Day*, revised ed. (London: Penguin Books, 1999).

Hobsbawm, Eric J., and George Rudé, *Captain Swing* (London: Lawrence and Wishart, 1969).

Hoeflich, Michael H., "John Austin and Joseph Story: Two Nineteenth Century Perspectives on the Utility of the Civil Law for the Common Lawyer" (1985) 29:1 *Am J Leg Hist* 37.

- "Law & Geometry: Legal Science from Leibniz to Langdell" (1986) 30 *Am J Leg Hist* 95.
- "Savigny and His Anglo-American Disciples" (1989) 37 *Am J Comp L* 17.
Hohfeld, Wesley Newcomb, *Fundamental Legal Conceptions as Applied in Judicial Reasoning and Other Legal Essays*, edited by Walter Wheeler Cook (New Haven: Yale University Press, 1923).
Holcombe, Lee, *Wives and Property: Reform of the Married Women's Property Law in Nineteenth-Century England* (Toronto: University of Toronto Press, 1983).
Holdsworth, William, *The Law of Master and Servant: Including that of Trades Unions and Combinations* (London: Routledge, 1876).
- *Some Makers of English Law: The Tagore Lectures. 1857–56* (Cambridge: Cambridge University Press, 1938).
Holland, Thomas Erskine, "The Classification of the Statutes" (1869) in Thomas Erskine Holland, *Essays Upon the Form of the Law* (London: Butterworths, 1870).
- *The Elements of Jurisprudence* (Oxford: Clarendon Press, 1880).
Holman, Robert, "The Place of Fostering in Social Work" (1975) 5:1 *Brit J Soc Work* 3.
Honeyman, Katrina, *Child Workers in England, 1780–1820: Parish Apprentices and the Making of the Early Industrial Labour Force* (Aldershot: Ashgate, 2007).
- "Compulsion, Compassion and Consent: Parish Apprenticeship in Early-Nineteenth-Century England" in Nigel Goose and Katrina Honeyman, eds., *Childhood and Labour in Industrial England: Diversity and Agency, 1750–1914* (Farnham: Ashgate, 2013).
- *Women, Gender and Industrialisation in England, 1700–1870* (Basingstoke: Macmillan, 2000).
Horn, Pamela, *Labouring Life in the Victorian Countryside* (Dublin: Gill and Macmillan, 1976).
Horrell, Sara, and Jane Humphries, "Women's Labour Force Participation and the Transition to the Male-Breadwinner Family, 1790–1865" (1995) 48:1 *J Econ Hist* 89.
Horsburgh, Michael, "'No Sufficient Security': The Reaction of the Poor Law Authorities to Boarding-Out" (1983) 12:1 *Int Soc Pol* 51.
Horwitz, Morton, "The History of the Public/Private Distinction" (1982) 130:6 *U Penn L Rev* 1423.
Houghton, Walter E., *The Victorian Frame of Mind, 1830–1870* (New Haven: Yale University Press, 1985).
Houlbrooke, Ralph A., *The English Family, 1450–1700* (Harlow: Longman Group, 1984).
Hugo, Gustav, *Manual of Today's Roman Law* (1798), first published as *Institutionen des heutigen Romishchen Rechts* (1789).

380   Bibliography

Humphries, Jane, "Class Struggle and the Persistence of the Working-Class Family" (1977) 1:3 *Cambridge J Econ* 241.
– "Enclosures, Common Rights, and Women: The Proletarianization of Families in the Late Eighteenth and Early Nineteenth Centuries" (1990) 50:1 *J Econ Hist* 17.
– "'… The Most Free from Objection' … The Sexual Division of Labor and Women's Work in Nineteenth-Century England" (1987) 47:4 *J Econ Hist* 929.
– "Protective Legislation, the Capitalist State, and Working Class Men: The Case of the 1842 Mines Regulation Act" (1981) 7 *Feminist Rev* 1.
– "The Sexual Division of Labor and Social Control: An Interpretation" (1991) 23:3–4 *Rev Rad Pol Econ* 269.
Hunt, Alan, and Gary Wickham, *Foucault and Law: Towards a Sociology of Law as Governance* (London: Pluto Press, 1994).
Hurst, James Willard, *Law and the Conditions of Freedom in the Nineteenth-Century United States* (Madison: University of Wisconsin Press, 1956).
Hutchins, B.L., and A. Harrison, *A History of Factory Legislation* (London: P.S. King, 1903).
Ibbetson, David J., *A Historical Introduction to the Law of Obligations* (Oxford: Oxford University Press, 2001).
Jenks, Edward, ed., *A Digest of English Civil Law*, 5 vols (London: Butterworth & Co, 1905–17).
– *Husband & Wife in the Law* (London: J.M. Dent & Co, 1909).
Johnson, Phillip E., "Do You Sincerely Want to Be Radical?" (1984) 36 *Stan L Rev* 247.
Johnson, Samuel, *Dictionary of the English Language* (1755).
Kahn-Freund, Otto, "Blackstone's Neglected Child: The Contract of Employment" (1977) 93 *Law Q Rev* 508.
– "Inconsistencies and Injustices in the Law of Husband and Wife" (1952) 15:2 *Mod L Rev* 183.
– "Matrimonial Property – Some Recent Developments" (1959) 22:3 *Mod L Rev* 241.
– "Recent Legislation on Matrimonial Property" (1970) 33:6 *Mod L Rev* 601.
Kamen, Henry, *European Society, 1500–1700* (London: Hutchinson, 1984).
Kant, Immanuel, *The Philosophy Of Law: An Exposition of the Fundamental Principles of Jurisprudence as The Science of Right*, translated by W. Hastie (Edinburgh: T. & T. Clark, 1887).
Kelman, Mark, *A Guide to Critical Legal Studies* (Cambridge, MA: Harvard University Press, 1987).
Kennedy, David, and William W. Fisher III, "Introduction" in David Kennedy and William W. Fisher III, eds., *The Canon of American Legal Thought* (Princeton: Princeton University Press, 2006).
Kennedy, Duncan, "From the Will Theory to the Principle of Private Autonomy: Lon Fuller's Consideration and Form" (2000) 100:1 *Colum L Rev* 94.

– *The Rise & Fall of Classical Legal Thought* (Washington, DC: Beard Books, 2006).

– "Savigny's Family/Patrimony Distinction and Its Place in the Global Genealogy of Classical Legal Thought" (2010) 58:4 *Am J Comp L* 811.

– "The Structure of Blackstone's Commentaries" (1979) 28:2 *Buff L Rev* 205.

– "Three Globalizations of Law and Legal Thought" in David M. Trubek & Alvaro Santos, eds., *The New Law and Economic Development: A Critical Appraisal* (New York: Cambridge University Press, 2006).

Kenny, Courtney, *Outlines of Criminal Law* (Cambridge: Cambridge University Press, 1902).

Kha, Henry, and Warren Swain, "The Enactment of the Matrimonial Causes Act 1857: The Campbell Commission and the Parliamentary Debates" (2016) 37:3 *J Leg Hist* 303.

King, Peter, *Crime and Law in England, 1750–1849* (Cambridge: Cambridge University Press, 2006).

Klare, Karl E., "The Horizons of Transformative Labour and Employment Law" in Joanne Conaghan, Richard Michael Fischl and Karl Klare, *Labour Law in an Era of Globalization: Transformative Practices and Possibilities* (Oxford: Oxford University Press, 2002).

– "Labor Law as Ideology: Toward a New Historiography of Collective Bargaining Law" (1981) 4 *Indus Rel LJ* 450.

– "The Public/Private Distinction in Labor Law" (1982) 130:6 *U Penn L Rev* 1358.

Kletzer, Christoph, "Custom and Positivity: An Examination of the Philosophic Ground of the Hegel-Savigny Controversy" in Amanda Perreau-Saussine and James B Murphy, eds., *The Nature of Customary Law* (Cambridge: Cambridge University Press, 2007).

Knox, William Walker, *British Apprenticeship, 1800–1914* (PhD Dissertation, University of Edinburgh, 1980) [unpublished].

Kornhauser, Lewis A., "The Great Image of Authority" (1984) 36 *Stan L Rev* 349.

Kussmaul, Ann, *Servants in Husbandry in Early Modern England* (Cambridge: Cambridge University Press, 1981).

Lane, Joan, *Apprenticeship in England, 1600–1914* (London: UCL Press, 1996).

Lasch, Christopher, *Haven in a Heartless World: The Family Besieged* (New York: Basic Books, 1979).

Laslett, Peter, "Mean Household Size in England Since the Sixteenth Century" in Peter Laslett and Richard Wall, eds., *Household and Family in Past Time* (Cambridge: Cambridge University Press, 1972).

Lawyer, George, "Are Actions For Breach of the Marriage Contract Immoral?" (1884) 38 *Central LJ* 272.

Leake, Martin, *The Elements of the Law of Contracts* (London: Stevens, 1867).

Leckey, Robert, "Shifting Scrutiny: Private Ordering in Family Matters in Common-Law Canada" in Frederik Swennen, *Contractualisation of Family Law – Global Perspectives* (Cham: Springer, 2015).

Lee, R.W., "Obligations" in Edward Jenks, ed., *A Digest of English Civil Law*, 5 vols (London: Butterworth & Co, 1905–17), vol 2 (1906).

Lemmings, David, "Introduction: Criminal Courts, Lawyers and the Public Sphere" in David Lemmings, ed., *Crime, Courtrooms and the Public Sphere in Britain, 1700–1850* (London: Routledge, 2012) 1.

– *Law and Government in England during the Long Eighteenth Century: From Consent to Command* (Basingstoke: Palgrave Macmillan, 2015).

– *Professors of the Law: Barristers and English Legal Culture in the Eighteenth Century* (New York: Oxford University Press, 2000).

Leslie, Stephen, *The English Utilitarians* (London: Duckworth & Co, 1900).

Lettmaier, Saskia, *Broken Engagements: The Action for Breach of Promise of Marriage and the Feminine Ideal, 1800–1940* (Oxford: Oxford University Press, 2010).

Levine, David, "Production, Reproduction, and the Proletarian Family in England, 1500–1851" in David Levine, ed., *Proletarianization and Family History* (Orlando: Academic Press, 1984).

Levine, Philippa, "Consistent Contradictions: Prostitution and Protective Labour Legislation in Nineteenth-Century England" (1994) 19:1 *Soc Hist* 17.

Levine-Clark, M., "Engendering Relief: Women, Ablebodiedness and the New Poor Law in Victorian England" (2000) 11 *J Women's Hist* 107.

Lewis, Jane, *Women in England 1870–1950* (Bloomington: Indiana University Press, 1984).

Lind, Craig, "The Truth of Unmarried Cohabitation and the Significance of History" (2014) 77:4 *Mod L Rev* 641.

Linton, Ralph, *The Study of Man: An Introduction* (New York: Appleton-Century-Crofts, 1936).

Lobban, Michael, "Blackstone and the Science of Law" (1987) 30:2 *Hist J* 311.

– "Mapping the Common Law: Some Lessons from History" (2014) 1 *NZLR* 21.

Locke, John, *Second Treatise of Government*, edited by C.B. Macpherson (Indianapolis: Hackett, 1980).

Long, George, *Two Discourses Delivered in the Middle Temple Hall, with an Outline of the Course* (London: T. & J.W. Johnson, 1848).

Lorenzen, Ernest G., "Validity and Effects of Contracts in the Conflict of Laws" (1921) 30:6 *Yale LJ* 565.

Lowe, Nigel, "Obituary: Professor Peter Mann Bromley," *Family Law*, 3 April 2013.

Lowe, Nigel, and Gillian Douglas, *Bromley's Family Law*, 11th ed. (Oxford: Oxford University Press, 2015).

MacColla, Charles, *Breach of Promise: Its History and Social Considerations* (London: Pickering & Co, 1879).

MacDonagh, Oliver, "The Nineteenth-Century Revolution in Government: A Reappraisal" (1958) 1 *Hist J* 52.

Macdonald, Alexander, *Handybook of the Law Relative to Masters, Workmen, Servants, and Apprentices, in All Trades and Occupations* (London: W. Mackenzie, 1868).

Macdonnell, John, *The Law of Master and Servant* (London: Stevens and Sons, 1883).

Macpherson, C.B., *The Political Theory of Possessive Individualism: Hobbes to Locke* (Toronto: Oxford University Press, 2011).

Macqueen, John Fraser, *A Practical Treatise on Divorce and Matrimonial Jurisdiction under the Act of 1857 and new orders* (London: W. Maxwell, 1858).

Maddaugh, P.D., "Validity of Marriage and the Conflict of Laws: A Critique of the Present Anglo-American Position" (1973) 23:2 *U Toronto LJ* 117.

Maine, Henry Sumner, *Ancient Law* (New York: Dorset Press, 1986).

Malthus, Thomas R., *An Essay on the Principle of Population, as It Affects the Future Improvement of Society. With Remarks on the Speculation of Mr. Godwin, M. Condorcet, and Other Writers* (London, 1798).

– *An Essay on the Principle of Population; or, A View of its Past and Present Effects on Human Happiness; with an inquiry into our prospects respecting the future removal or mitigation of the evils which its occasions*, 6th ed. (London: John Murray, 1826).

Mannheim, Karl, *Ideology and Utopia. Collected Works of Karl Mannheim: Volume 1* (Oxford: Routledge, 1997).

Manson, Edward, "Breach of Promise of Marriage" 11:1 *J Soc Comp Leg* (1910) 156.

Marciniak, Angela, "'Prevention of Evil, Production of Good': Jeremy Bentham's Indirect Legislation and Its Contribution to a New Theory of Prevention" (2017) 43:1 *Hist Eur Ideas* 83.

Martin, Peter W. et al., "'Of Law and the River,' and of Nihilism and Academic Freedom" (1985) 35:1 *J Legal Educ* 1.

Mason, Michael, *The Making of Victorian Sexuality* (Oxford: Oxford University Press, 1994).

Mayne, John D., *Mayne's Treatise on Damages*, 8th ed. by Lumley Smith (London: Stevens & Haynes, 1909).

– *Mayne's Treatise on Damages*, 3rd ed. by John D. Mayne and Lumley Smith (London: Stevens & Haynes, 1877).

McGregor, Oliver, *Divorce in England: A Centenary Study* (London: Heinemann, 1957).

Menefee, Samuel Pyeatt, *Wives for Sale: An Ethnographic Study of British Popular Divorce* (New York: St Martin's Press, 1981).

Menkel-Meadow, Carrie, "Feminist Legal Theory, Critical Legal Studies, and Legal Education or 'The Fem-Crits Go to Law School'" (1988) 38 *J Legal Educ* 61.

Merritt, Adrian, "The Historical Role of the Law in the Regulation of Employment – Abstentionist or Interventionist?" (1982) 1 *Aust JL Soc* 56.

Miles, Joanna, "Marriage and Divorce in the Supreme Court and the Law Commission: For Love or Money?" (2011) 74:3 *Mod L Rev* 430.

Mill, John Stuart, *On Liberty*, edited by Gertrude Himmelfarb (London: Penguin Books, 1974).

– *Principles of Political Economy With Some of Their Applications to Social Philosophy* (London: W. Parker, 1848).

– *The Subjection of Women*, 3rd ed. (London: Longman, Green, Reader, and Dyer, 1870).

Milsom, S.F.C., *The Nature of Blackstone's Achievement* (London, 1981).

Mingay, G.E., *Parliamentary Enclosure in England: An Introduction to Its Causes, Incidence, and Impact, 1750–1850* (London: Longman, 1997).

Moore, Marianne, "Social Control or Protection of the Child? The Debates on the Industrial Schools Acts 1857–1894" (2008) 33:4 *J Fam Hist* 359.

Morley, Edith Julia, *Women Workers in Seven Professions: A Survey of Their Economic Conditions and Prospects* (London: Routledge, 1914).

Müller-Freienfels, Wolfram, "Book Reviews: Graveson, R.H. – Crane, F.R. (eds.) *A Century of Family Law 1857–1957*. London: Sweet & Maxwell Ltd., 1957. P. xviii, 459" (1959) 8:1 *Am J Comp L* 92.

– "The Emergence of *Droit de Famille* and *Familienrecht* in Continental Europe and the Introduction of Family Law in England" (2003) 28:1 *J Fam Hist* 31.

Murphy, Kate, "A Marriage Bar of Convenience? The BBC and Married Women's Work 1923–39" (2014) 25:4 *Twentieth Cent Brit Hist* 533.

Neeson, J.M., *Commoners: Common Right, Enclosure and Social Change in England, 1700–1820* (Cambridge: Cambridge University Press, 1993).

Niedhardt, Alberto-Horst, *The Transformation of European Private International Law: A Genealogy* (PhD Dissertation, European University Institute, 2018) [unpublished].

Nolan, Michael, *Treatise of the Laws for the Relief and Settlement of the Poor*, 4th ed. (London, 1825).

Norrie, Alan, *Crime, Reason and History: A Critical Introduction to Criminal Law*, 2nd ed. (London: Butterworths, 2001).

Nutt, Thomas, "Illegitimacy, Paternal Financial Responsibility, and the 1834 Poor Law Commission Report: The Myth of the Old Poor Law and the Making of the New" (2010) 63:2 *Econ Hist Rev* 335.

Nygh, P.E., *Conflict of Laws in Australia*, 2nd ed. (Sydney: Butterworths, 1971).

O'Connell, Lisa, "'By Ordinance of Nature': Marriage, Religion and the Modern English State" (2011) 28:2 *Parergon* 149.

O'Donovan, Katherine, "Family Law and Legal Theory" in William Twining, ed., *Legal Theory and Common Law* (Oxford: Basil Blackwell, 1986) 184.

– *Sexual Divisions in Law* (London: Weidenfeld and Nicolson, 1985).

Ogilvie, William, *An Essay on the Right of Property in Land, With Respect to its Foundation in the Law of Nature, and the Rights of the People!* (1780).

Okin, Susan Moller, *Justice, Gender, and the Family* (New York: Basic Books, 1989).

Olsen, Frances, "The Family and the Market: A Study of Ideology and Legal Reform" (1983) 96:7 *Harv L Rev* 1497.

Outhwaite, R.B., *Clandestine Marriage in England, 1500–1850* (London: Hambledon Press, 1995).

Parker, Stephen, *Informal Marriage, Cohabitation and the Law, 1750–1989* (Houndmills, Basingstoke: Macmillan, 1990).

Pateman, Carole, *The Sexual Contract* (Palo Alto: Stanford University Press, 1988).

Pedersen, Susan, *Family, Dependence, and the Origins of the Welfare State: Britain and France, 1914–1945* (Cambridge: Cambridge University Press, 1993).

Picchio, Antonella, *Social Reproduction: The Political Economy of the Labour Market* (Cambridge: Cambridge University Press, 1992).

Pinchbeck, Ivy, *Women Workers in the Industrial Revolution, 1750–1850*, 3rd ed. (London: Virago, 1981).

Plucknett, T.F.T., *Early English Legal Literature* (Cambridge: Cambridge University Press, 1958).

Polanyi, Karl, *The Great Transformation: The Political and Economic Origins of Our Time* (Boston: Beacon Press, 2001).

Pollock, Frederick, *Principles of Contract at Law and in Equity: Being a Treatise of the General Principles Concerning the Validity of Agreements, With a Special View to the Comparison of Law and Equity, and With References to the Indian Contract Act, and Occasionally to Roman, American, and Continental Law* (London: Stevens, 1876).

– "The Science of Case Law" in Frederick Pollock, *Essays in Jurisprudence and Ethics* (London: Macmillan, 1882) ch IX.

– *A Treatise on the Principles of Obligations Arising from Civil Wrongs in the Common Law* (London: Blackstone, 1887).

Pollock, Frederick, and Frederic William Maitland, *The History of English Law Before the Time of Edward I* (Cambridge: Cambridge University Press, 1895).

Posner, Richard A., "Blackstone and Bentham" (1976) 19:3 *JL & Econ* 569.

Pothier, Robert Joseph, *Treatise on Obligations, Considered in a Moral and Legal View, Translated from the French of Pothier*, 2 vols (Newbern, NC: Martin & Ogden, 1802).

Pound, Roscoe, *Interpretations of Legal History* (New York: Macmillan, 1923).

Powell, John Joseph, *Essay Upon the Law of Contracts and Agreements* (1790).

Pritchard, Robert A. and W.T. Pritchard, *A Hand-Book on the Law of Marriage and Divorce* (London: V. & R. Stevens and G.S. Norton, 1859).

Probert, Rebecca, *The Changing Legal Regulation of Cohabitation: From Fornicators to Family, 1600–2010* (Cambridge: Cambridge University Press, 2012).
– "Chinese Whispers and Welsh Weddings" (2005) 20 *Cont Change* 211.
– "The Double Standard of Morality in the Divorce and Matrimonial Causes Act 1857" (1999) 28 *Anglo-Am L Rev* 73.
– "Family Law – A Modern Concept?" [2004] *Family Law* 901.
– *Marriage Law and Practice in the Long Eighteenth Century* (Cambridge: Cambridge University Press, 2009).
– "R v Millis Reconsidered: Binding Contracts and Bigamous Marriages" (2008) 28:3 *Legal Studies* 337.
– "Under One Roof: Law's Interactions with Family Life" in Rebecca Probert, ed., *Family Life and the Law: Under One Roof* (Aldershot: Ashgate, 2007).
Probert, Rebecca, and Maebh Harding, *Cretney and Probert's Family Law*, 10th ed. (London: Sweet & Maxwell, 2018).
Quinn, Michael, "Jeremy Bentham, Choice Architect: Law, Indirect Legislation, and the Context of Choice" (2017) 43:1 *Hist Eur Ideas* 11.
Rawlins, William Donaldson, *The Specific Performance of Contracts: An Expansion of an Article in the Encyclopaedia of the Laws of England* (London: Sweet & Maxwell, 1899).
Rehbinder, Manfred, "Status, Contract, and the Welfare State" (1971) 23:5 *Stan L Rev* 941.
Reeve, Tapping, *The Law of Baron and Femme; of Parent and Child; of Guardian and Ward; of Master and Servant; and of the Powers of Courts of Chancery, with an Essay on the Terms, Heir, Heirs, and Heirs of the Body* (New Haven: Oliver Steele, 1816).
Ricardo, David, *On the Principles of Political Economy and Taxation* (London: Murray, 1817).
Rittich, Kerry, "Black Sites: Locating the Family and Family Law in Development" (2010) 58:4 *Am J Comp L* 102.
– "Families on the Edge: Governing Home and Work in a Globalized Economy" (2010) 88:5 *NC L Rev* 1527.
– "Feminization and Contingency: Regulating the Stakes for Work for Women" in Joanne Conaghan, Richard Michael Fischl and Karl Klare, eds., *Labour Law in an Era of Globalization: Transformative Practices and Possibilities* (Oxford: Oxford University Press, 2002).
– "Making Natural Markets: Flexibility as Labour Market Truth" (2014) 65:3 *N Ir Leg Q* 323.
Rose, Mary B., "Social Policy and Business; Parish Apprenticeship and the Early Factory System 1750–1834" (1989) 31:4 *Business Hist* 5.
Rose, Sonya O., *Limited Livelihoods: Gender and Class in Nineteenth-Century England* (New York: Routledge, 1992).
Routh, Guy, *Occupations of the People of Great Britain, 1801–1981; with a Compendium of a Paper "Occupations of the People of the United Kingdom, 1801–81 by Charles Booth"* (Basingstoke: Macmillan, 1987).

Rule, John, *The Experience of Labour in Eighteenth-Century Industry* (London: Croom Helm, 1981).

Ruskin, John, "Of Queen's Gardens" in John Ruskin, *Sesame and Lilies and The Political Economy of Art* (London: Collins, 1890).

Salmon, T., *A Critical Essay concerning Marriage* (London, 1724).

Salmond, John, "The History of Contract" (1887) 3 *Law Q Rev* 166.

– *Jurisprudence* (London: Stevens and Haynes, 1902).

– *Jurisprudence*, 4th ed. (London: Stevens and Haynes, 1913).

– *The Law of Torts: A Treatise on the English Law of Liability for Civil Injuries*, 2nd ed. (London: Stevens & Haynes, 1910).

Santos, Boaventura de Sousa, *Toward a New Common Sense: Law, Science and Politics in Paradigmatic Transition* (London: Routledge, 1995).

Savigny, Friedrich Carl von, *Of the Vocation of Our Age for Legislation and Jurisprudence*, translated by Abraham Hayward (London: Littlewood and Company, 1831).

– *Private International Law, and the Retrospective Operation of Statutes: A Treatise on the Conflict of Laws, and the Limits of Their Operation in Respect of Place and Time*, translated by William Guthrie, 2nd ed. (Edinburgh: T. & T. Clark, 1880).

– *System of the Modern Roman Law*, translated by William Holloway (Madras: J. Higginbotham, 1867).

– *Vom Beruf unserer Zeit fur Rechtsgeschichte und Getzgebung* (1814).

Scherpe, Jens Martin, and Brian Sloan, "Contractualisation of Family Law in England & Wales: Autonomy vs Judicial Discretion" in Frederik Swennen, *Contractualisation of Family Law – Global Perspectives* (Cham: Springer, 2015).

Schmidt, Katharina Isabel, "Henry Maine's 'Modern Law': From Status to Contract and Back Again?" (2017) 65:1 *Am J Comp L* 145.

Schmitthoff, Clive M., *A Textbook of the English Conflict of Laws (Private International Law)* (London: Pitman, 1945).

Schochet, Gordon J., *Patriarchalism in Political Thought: The Authoritarian Family and Political Speculation and Attitudes Especially in Seventeenth-Century England* (Oxford: Blackwell, 1975).

Schouler, James, *A Treatise on the Law of the Domestic Relations Embracing Husband and Wife, Parent and Child, Guardian and Ward, Infancy, and Master and Servant* (Boston: Little, Brown & Co, 1870).

Schwarz, L.D., "Custom, Wages and Workload in England during Industrialization" (2007) 197 *Past & Present* 143.

Schwarz, Leonard, "English Servants and Their Employers during the Eighteenth and Nineteenth Centuries" (1999) 52:2 *Econ Hist Rev* 236.

Scott, Elizabeth S., and Robert E. Scott, "From Contract to Status: Collaboration and the Evolution of Novel Family Relationships" (2015) 115:2 *Colum L Rev* 293.

Seccombe, Wally, *A Millennium of Family Change: Feudalism to Capitalism in Northwestern Europe* (London: Verso, 1992).

– "Patriarchy Stabilized: The Construction of the Male Breadwinner Wage Norm in Nineteenth-Century England" (1986) 11:1 *Soc Hist* 53.

Seliger, Martin, *Ideology and Politics* (London: Allen & Unwin, 1976).

Shalleck, Ann, "Introduction: Comparative Family Law: What Is the Global Family? Family Law in Decolonization, Modernization and Globalization" (2011) 19:2 *Am U J Gender, Soc Pol & L* 449.

Shamir, Hila, "The State of Care: Rethinking the Distributive Effects of Familial Care Policies in Liberal Welfare States" (2010) 58:4 *Am J Comp L* 953.

Shanley, Mary Lyndon, *Feminism, Marriage, and the Law in Victorian England, 1850–1895* (Princeton, NJ: Princeton University Press, 1989).

– "'One Must Ride Behind': Married Women's Rights and the Divorce Act of 1857" (1982) 25:3 *Vict Stud* 355.

– "Suffrage, Protective Labor Legislation, and Married Women's Property Laws in England" (1986) 12:1 *Signs* 62.

Shelford, Leonard, *Practical Treatise of The Law of Marriage and Divorce, and Registration; as altered by the recent statutes; containing also the mode of proceedings on divorces in the Ecclesiastical Courts and in Parliament; the right to the custody of children; voluntary separation between husband and wife; the husband's liability to wife's debts; and the conflict between the laws of England and Scotland respecting divorce and legitimacy* (London: S. Sweet, 1841).

Shorter, Edward, *The Making of the Modern Family* (New York: Fontana Books, 1977).

Siegel, Reva B., "'The Rule of Love': Wife Beating as Prerogative and Privacy" (1996) 105:8 *Yale LJ* 2117.

Silbey, Susan, "After Legal Consciousness" (2005) 1 *Ann Rev Law Soc Sci* 323.

Simpson, A.W.B., *A History of the Common Law of Contract: The Rise of the Action of Assumpsit* (Oxford: Clarendon Press, 1987).

– "Innovation in Nineteenth Century Contract Law" (1975) 91 *Law Q Rev* 247.

– "The Rise and Fall of the Legal Treatise: Legal Principles and the Forms of Legal Literature" (1981) 48:3 *U Chicago L Rev* 632.

– "The Salmond Lecture" (2007) 38 *VUWLR* 669.

Smith, Adam, *An Inquiry into the Nature and Causes of the Wealth of Nations*, vol 1 (London, 1776).

Smith, Leanne, "The Development of Parent-Child Relationships in Family Law: The Cascade of Change" in Gillian Douglas, Mervyn Murch and Victoria Stephens, eds., *International and National Perspectives on Child and Family Law; Essays in Honour of Nigel Lowe* (Cambridge: Intersentia, 2018).

Snell, K.D.M., *Annals of the Labouring Poor: Social Change and Agrarian England, 1660–1900* (Cambridge: Cambridge University Press, 1985).

– "The Apprenticeship System in British History: The Fragmentation of a Cultural Institution" (1996) 25:4 *Hist Educ* 303.

Somers, Margaret A., "Citizenship and the Place of the Public Sphere: Law, Community, and Political Culture in the Transition to Democracy" (1993) 58:5 *Am Soc Rev* 587.

Standing, Guy, *A Precariat Charter: From Denizens to Citizens* (London: Bloomsbury Academic, 2014).

Stanley, Amy Dru, "Beggars Can't Be Choosers: Compulsion and Contract in Postbellum America" (1992) 78: 4 *J Am Hist* 1274.

Steedman, Carolyn, *Labours Lost: Domestic Service and the Making of Modern England* (New York: Cambridge University Press, 2009).

– *Master and Servant: Love and Labour in the English Industrial Age* (Cambridge: Cambridge University Press, 2007).

Steinfeld, Robert, *Coercion, Contract, and Free Labor in the Nineteenth Century* (Cambridge: Cambridge University Press, 2001).

– *The Invention of Free Labor: The Employment Relation in English and American Law and Culture, 1350–1870* (Chapel Hill: University of North Carolina Press, 1991).

Stolzenberg, Emily, "The New Family Freedom" (2018) 59:6 *Boston College L Rev* 1984.

Stone, Lawrence, *The Family, Sex and Marriage in England, 1500–1800*, abridged ed. (Harmondsworth: Penguin Books, 1979).

– *Road to Divorce: England 1530–1987* (Oxford: Oxford University Press, 1990).

Stone, Olive M., *Family Law: An Account of the Law of Domestic Relations in England and Wales in the Last Quarter of the Twentieth Century, with Some Comparisons* (London: Macmillan, 1977).

Story, Joseph, *Commentaries on the Conflict of Laws, Foreign and Domestic, in Regard to Contracts, Rights, and Remedies, and Especially in Regard to Marriages, Divorces, Wills, Successions and Judgments* (Boston: Hilliard, Gray and Company, 1834).

Stretton, Tim, "Marriage, Separation and the Common Law in England, 1540–1660" in Helen Berry and Elizabeth Foyster, eds., *The Family in Early Modern England* (Cambridge: Cambridge University Press, 2007).

Stychin, Carl, "Family Friendly? Rights, Responsibilities and Relationship Recognition" in Alison Diduck and Katherine O'Donovan, eds., *Feminist Perspectives on Family Law* (Abingdon: Routledge-Cavendish, 2006).

Sugarman, David, "Bourgeois Collectivism, Professional Power and the Boundaries of the State: The Private and Public Life of the Law Society, 1825 to 1914" (1996) 3 *Int'l J Legal Prof* 81.

– "Law, Economy and the State in England, 1750–1914: Some Major Issues" in David Sugarman, ed., *Legality, Ideology and The State* (London: Academic Press, 1983).

- "Legal Theory, the Common Law Mind and the Making of the Textbook Tradition" in William Twining, ed., *Legal Theory and Common Law* (Oxford: Basil Blackwell, 1986).
- "Promoting Dialogue between History and Socio-Legal Studies: The Contribution of Christopher W. Brooks and the 'Legal Turn' in Early Modern English History" (2017) 44:S1 *J Law & Soc* S37.
- "Robert W. Gordon in Conversation with David Sugarman," *Law & History Review*, https://lawandhistoryreview.org/article/robert-w-gordon-in-conversation-with-david-sugarman/ (accessed 25 March 2021).

Supiot, Alain, *Beyond Employment: Transformations in Work and the Future of Labour Law in Europe* (Oxford: Oxford University Press, 2001).

Swabey, M.C. Merttins, *The Act to Amend the Law Relating to Divorce and Matrimonial Causes in England, the Divorce Act Amendment Act (1858), and the Legitimacy Declaration Act, 1858* (London: Shaw, 1859).

Swain, Warren, *The Law of Contract, 1670–1870* (Cambridge: Cambridge University Press, 2015).

Swennen, Frederik, "Private Ordering in Family Law: A Global Perspective," in Frederik Swennen, *Contractualisation of Family Law – Global Perspectives* (Cham: Springer, 2015).

Swinburne, Henry, *A Treatise of Spousals, or Matrimonial Contracts: Wherein All the Questions relating to that Subject are ingeniously Debated and Resolved* (London, 1686).

Tadmor, Naomi, *Family and Friends in Eighteenth-Century England: Household, Kinship, and Patronage* (Cambridge: Cambridge University Press, 2001).

Tadros, Victor, "Between Governance and Discipline: The Law and Michel Foucault" (1998) 8:1 *Oxford J Leg Stud* 75.

Tennyson, Alfred Lord, *The Works of Alfred Lord Tennyson* (London: Macmillan & Co., 1895).

Tennyson, Robert, "From Unanimity to Proportionality: Assent Standards and the Parliamentary Enclosure Movement" (2013) 31:1 *L & Hist Rev* 199.

Thane, Pat, "Women and the Poor Law in Victorian and Edwardian England" (1978) 6 *Hist Workshop J* 29.

Thompson, E.P., *The Making of the English Working Class* (London: Penguin, 2013).

- *The Poverty of Theory and Other Essays* (New York: Merlin Press, 1978).
- "Time, Work-Discipline, and Industrial Capitalism" (1967) 38 *Past & Present* 56.

Thompson, John B., *Ideology and Modern Culture: Critical Social Theory in the Era of Mass Communication* (Cambridge: Polity, 1990).

Thomson, David, *England in the Nineteenth Century, 1815–1914* (Harmondsworth, Middlesex: Penguin Books, 1950).

Thornton, Margaret, "The Cartography of Public and Private" in Margaret Thornton, ed., *Public and Private: Feminist Legal Debates* (New York: Oxford University Press, 1995).

– "Loss of Consortium: Inequality Before the Law" (1984) 10:2 *Syd L Rev* 260.

Tidswell, Richard Thomas, and Ralph Daniel Makinson Littler, *The Practice and Evidence in Cases of Divorce and other Matrimonial Causes: Together with the Acts, Rules, Forms, &c.* (London: W. Benning, 1860).

Tilly, Louise A., and Joan W. Scott, *Women, Work & Family* (New York: Routledge, 1989).

Tillyard, Frank, *Industrial Law* (London: A. & C. Black, 1916).

Tocqueville, Alexis de, *Democracy in America,* translated by Arthur Goldhammer (New York: Library of America, 2004).

Todd, Selina, "Domestic Service and Class Relations in Britain 1900–1950" (2009) 203 *Past & Present* 181.

Tomlins, Christopher, "Foreword: 'Law As …' III – *Glossolalia*: Toward a Minor (Historical) Jurisprudence" (2015) 5 *UC Irvine L Rev* 239.

– *Freedom Bound: Law, Labor, and Civic Identity in Colonizing English America, 1580–1865* (New York: Cambridge University Press 2010).

– "Law 'And,' Law 'In,' Law 'As': The Definition, Rejection and Recuperation of the Socio-legal Enterprise" (2013) 29:2 *Law in Context* 137.

Tomlins, Christopher, and John Comaroff, "'Law As …': Theory and Practice in Legal History" (2011) 1:3 UC Irvine L Rev 1039.

Tosh, John, *A Man's Place? Masculinity and the Middle Class Home in Victorian England* (New Haven: Yale University Press, 1999).

Trumbach, Randolph, *The Rise of the Egalitarian Family: Aristocratic Kinship and Domestic Relations in Eighteenth-Century England* (New York: Academic Press, 1978).

Tsoukala, Philomila, "Marrying Family Law to the Nation" (2010) 58:4 *Am J Comp L* 873.

Turner, Michael, *English Parliamentary Enclosure: Its Historical Geography and Economic History* (Folkestone: Archon Books, 1980).

Unger, Roberto Mangabeira, *False Necessity: Anti-Necessitarian Social Theory in the Service of Radical Democracy. Part I of Politics: A Work in Constructive Social Theory* (Cambridge MA: Cambridge University Press, 1987).

Valenze, Deborah, *The First Industrial Woman* (New York: Oxford University Press, 1995).

Valverde, Mariana, "'Giving the Female a Domestic Turn': The Social, Legal and Moral Regulation of Women's Work in British Cotton Mills, 1820–1850" (1988) 21:4 *J Soc Hist* 619.

Veblen, Thorstein, *The Theory of the Leisure Class: An Economic Study of Institutions* (New York: Modern Library, 1934).

Waddams, Stephen, "English Matrimonial Law on the Eve of Reform (1828–57)" (2000) 21:2 *J Leg Hist* 59.

Wall, Richard, "Mean Household Size in England from Printed Sources" in Peter Laslett and Richard Wall, eds., *Household and Family in Past Time* (Cambridge: Cambridge University Press, 1972).

Watson, Alan, "The Structure of Blackstone's Commentaries" (1988) 97:5 *Yale LJ* 795.

Webb, Beatrice, *The Case for the Factory Acts*, 2nd ed. (London: G. Richards, 1902).

Webb, Sidney, and Beatrice Webb, *English Local Government, from the Revolution to the Municipal Corporations Act*, 7 vols (London: Longmans, Green, 1906–27) vol 7, *English Poor Law History: Part I. The Old Poor Law* (1927).

– *English Poor Law Policy* (London: Longmans, Green, 1910).

– *Industrial Democracy* (London, 1898).

Weber, Max, *The Protestant Ethic and the Spirit of Capitalism*, translated by Talcott Parsons (New York: Dover Publications, 2003).

Welstead, Mary, and Susan Edwards, *Family Law*, 4th ed. (Oxford: Oxford University Press, 2013).

West, Robin, "Jurisprudence and Gender" (1988) 55:1 *U Chicago L Rev* 1.

Westlake, John, *A Treatise on Private International Law: With Principal Reference to Its Practice in England*, edited by Norman Bentwich (London: Stevens & Haynes, 1925).

Wharton, J.J.S., *An Exposition of the Laws Relating to the Women of England; showing their Rights, Remedies, and Responsibilities, in every position of life* (London: Longman, Brown and Green, 1853).

White, George, *A Few Remarks on the State of the Laws, at Present in Existence, for Regulating Masters and Work-People, Intended as A Guide for the Consideration of the House, in Their Discussions on the Bill for Repealing Several Acts Relating to Combinations of Workmen, and for More Effectually Protecting Trade, and for Settling Disputes Between Masters and Servants* (London, 1823).

White, J. Dundas, "Breach of Promise of Marriage" (1894) 10:2 *Law Q Rev* 135.

Williams, Joan C., "Culture and Certainty: Legal History and the Reconstructive Project" (1990) 76 *Va L Rev* 713.

Williams, Karel, *From Pauperism to Poverty* (Abingdon: Routledge, 2017).

Williams, Thomas Walter, *The Whole Law Relative to the Duty and Office of a Justice of the Peace* (1812).

Winfield, P.H., *Text-Book of the Law of Tort* (London: Sweet & Maxwell, 1937).

Witt, John Fabian, "From Loss of Services to Loss of Support: The Wrongful Death Statutes, the Origins of Modern Tort Law, and the Making of the Nineteenth-Century Family" (2000) 25:3 *Law & Soc Inq* 717.

Witte Jr., John, *From Sacrament to Contract: Marriage, Religion, and Law in the Western Tradition*, 2nd ed. (Louisville, KY: Westminster John Knox Press, 2012).

Wohl, Anthony, "Introduction" in Anthony Wohl, ed., *The Victorian Family: Structure and Stresses* (New York: St. Martin's Press, 1978).

Wolfram, Sybil, "Divorce in England 1700–1857" (1985) 5:2 *Oxford J Leg Stud* 155.

Wood, A., B. Burchell, and A. Coutts, *From Zero Joy to Zero Stress: Making Flexible Scheduling Work* (Cambridge, 2016).

Wood, Thomas, *An Institute of the Laws of England; or, The Laws of England in their Natural Order, according to Common Use* (London, 1720).

Woodhouse, Margaret K., "The Marriage and Divorce Bill of 1857" (1959) 3:3 *Am J Leg Hist* 260.

Wordie, J.R., "The Chronology of English Enclosure, 1500–1914" (1983) 36:2 *Econ Hist Rev* 483.

Wright, Danaya C., "The Crisis of Child Custody: A History of the Birth of Family Law in England" (2002) 11:2 *Colum J Gender & L* 175.

– "'Well Behaved Women Don't Make History': Rethinking English Family, Law, and History" (2004) 19:2 *Wis Women's LJ* 211.

Young, Arthur, "Inquiry into the Propriety of Applying Wastes to the Better Maintenance and Support of the Poor" (1801) XXXVI *Ann Ag*.

Zaretsky, Eli, *Capitalism, the Family, and Personal Life*, revised ed. (New York: Harper & Row, 1986).

Government Reports and Documents

A Copy of the Report of the Poor Law Commissioners to Sir James Graham, on the Law concerning the Maintenance of Bastards, dated the 31st day of January 1844 (London: HM Stationery Office, 1844).

Adams, Abi and Jeremias Prassl, *Zero-Hours Work in the United Kingdom*, International Labour Office, Conditions of Work and Employment Series No 101 (2018).

Care of Children Committee, *Report of the Care of Children Committee* (London: HM Stationery Office, 1946).

Census of England and Wales, 1881, 43 & 44 Vict c 37, *Vol IV, General Report* (London: HM Stationery Office, 1883).

Children's Employment Commission, *First Report of the Commissioners. Mines* (London: HM Stationery Office, 1842).

Children's Employment Commission, *Second Report of the Commissioners. Trades and Manufactures* (London: HM Stationery Office, 1843).

Fairbairn, Catherine, *Marriage: Residence Requirements*, House of Commons Briefing Paper No 00644 (2017).

First Report of the Commissioners Appointed by Her Majesty to Enquire into the Law of Divorce, and More Particularly into the Mode of Obtaining Divorces A Vinculo Matrimonii (London: HM Stationery Office, 1853).

Forty-Third Annual Report of the Local Government Board, 1913–14. Part I – Administration of the Poor Law, the Unemployed Workmen Act, and the Old Age Pensions Acts (1914).

Home Office, *Report by Sir Walter Monckton on the circumstances which led to the boarding-out of Dennis and Terence O'Neill at Bank Farm, Minsterly, and the steps taken to supervise their welfare* (London: HM Stationery Office, 1945).

Law Commission of Canada, *Beyond Conjugality: Recognizing and Supporting Close Personal Adult Relationships* (Ottawa: Law Commission of Canada, 2001).

Memorandum Relating to the Administration of Out-relief, February 1878, in *Seventh Report of the Local Government Board, 1877–78* (1878).

Ministry of Labour, *Report of the Committee Appointed to Enquire into the Present Conditions as to the Supply of Female Domestic Servants* (London: HM Stationery Office, 1923).

Ministry of Labour and National Service, *Report on Post-War Organisation of Private Domestic Employment* (London: HM Stationery Office, 1945).

Ministry of Reconstruction, Women's Advisory Committee, *Report of the Women's Advisory Committee on the Domestic Service Problem together with Reports by Sub-Committees on Training, Machinery of Distribution, Organisation and Conditions* (London: HM Stationery Office, 1919).

Minute of the Poor Law Commissioners respecting the means of enforcing an out-door labour test, 31 October 1842, in *Ninth Annual Report of the Poor Law Commissioners* (1843).

Poor Law Commissioners' Report of 1834. Copy of the Report Made in 1834 by the Commissioners for Inquiring into the Administration and Practical Operation of the Poor Laws (London: HM Stationery Office, 1905).

Report from the Committee on Parish Apprentices (House of Commons, 1815).

Report from the Committee on the Woollen Manufacture of England; &c. (1806).

Report of the Poor Law Commissioners to the Most Noble the Marquis of Normanby, Her Majesty's Principal Secretary of State for the Home Department, on the Continuance of the Poor Law Commission on the Continuance of the Poor Law Commission, and on Some Further Amendment of the Laws Relating to the Relief of the Poor (London: HM Stationery Office, 1840).

Report of the Select Committee on the Expense and Mode of Obtaining Enclosure (1800).

Royal Commission on Marriage and Divorce, *Report 1951–1955* (London: HM Stationery Office, 1956).

Sixth Annual Report of the Poor Law Commissioners (London: HM Stationery Office, 1840).

The Law Commission, *Breach of Promise of Marriage* (London: HM Stationery Office, 1969).

The Law Commission, *Reform of the Ground of Divorce – The Field of Choice* (London: HM Stationery Office, 1966).

Newspapers, Non-Legal Periodicals, and Blogs

"Berry v Da Costa," *The Times*, 15 January 1866 at 11.

Bogg, Alan, "Foster Parents and Fundamental Labour Rights," UK Labour Law Blog, 25th July 2018, https://uklabourlawblog.com/2018/07/25/foster-parents-and-fundamental-labour-rights-alan-bogg/ (accessed 11 April 2019).

Bramwell, "Marriage With a Deceased Wife's Sister," *The Nineteenth Century: A Monthly Review*, September 1886 at 403.

Coleman, Clive, "Foster Carer Fights for Workers' Rights," *BBC News*, 9 October 2017, https://www.bbc.com/news/uk-41543651 (accessed 11 April 2019).

Dickens, Charles, "Little Pauper Children," 39:2 *All the Year Round*, 28 August 1869 at 301.

G.W.H., "Breach of Promise of Marriage," *London Society*, August 1870 at 161.

Hill, Florence, "The Family System for Workhouse Children" (1870) 15 Contemporary Review 240.

Howell, George, "Trades Unions, Apprentices, and Technical Education" (1877) 30 Contemporary Review 833.

"Kershaw v Cass," *The Times*, 21 March 1849 at 7.

"Morris v Maddox," *Morning Chronicle*, 25 March 1856.

"Nicholson v Turnbull," *The Times*, 4 March 1850 at 7.

"Professor Peter Bromley," *The Times*, 28 March 2013 at 66.

Tatchell, Peter, "How the Tories Were Won to Marriage Equality" (13 October 2011), http://www.petertatchell.net/lgbt_rights/partnerships/how-the-tories-were-won-to-marriage-equality/ (accessed 11 April 2019).

Ten Hours' Advocate, 24 October 1846.

"The Boarding-Out System," *The Examiner and London Review*, 3 December 1870.

"The Workmen's Compensation Act, 1906," *The Lancet*, 12 January 1907.

"To the Many Grotesque or Ridiculous Objects," *The Times,* 12 February 1878 at 9.

"Townsend v Bennett," *The Times*, 20 April 1875 at 11

Parliamentary Debates

Children Bill

- HL Deb, 16 March 1848, vol 154, cols 794–851

Death by Accident Compensation Bill

- HC Deb, 22 July 1846, vol 87, cols 1365–75

Divorce and Matrimonial Causes Bill

- HL Deb, 3 March 1857, vol 144, cols 1685–1722
- HL Deb, 4 June 1857, vol 145, cols 1096–1100
- HL Deb, 19 May 1857, vol 145, cols 483–538
- HC Deb, 30 July 1857, vol 147, cols 718–75
- HC Deb, 31 July 1857, vol 147, cols 825–95
- HL Deb, 24 August 1857, vol 147, cols 2014–68

Factories Bill

- HC Deb, 15 March 1844, vol 73, cols 1073–155

Marriage With a Deceased Wife's Sister Bill

- HC Deb, 6 May 1879, vol 245, cols 1789–1806 1880

Married Women (Employment) Bill

- HC Deb, 11 February 1927, vol 202, col 440

Married Women's Property Bill

- HC Deb, 18 May 1870, vol 201, cols 878–92
- HL Deb, 21 June 1870, vol 202, cols 600–22

Matrimonial Causes Bill

- HL Deb, 13 June 1854, vol 134, cols 1–28

Matrimonial Causes (England & Wales) Bill

- HC Deb, 2 March 1923, vol 160, cols 2344–413

Registration of Births, &c, – Dissenters' Marriages Bill

- HC Deb, 12 February 1836, vol 31, cols 367–85

Index